MACROECONOMICS ESSENTIALS

Growth

Countries with a high GDP per capita have a lot of physical and human capital per worker and that capital is organized using the best technological knowledge to be highly productive. (page 97)

Good **institutions** such as property rights, honest government, political stability, a dependable legal system, and competitive and open markets create **incentives** to invest in physical and human capital, create new technological knowledge, and organize the factors of production to be highly productive. (page 99)

GDP can be written in terms of a production function as $Y = F(A, K, e \times L)$ where Y is output or GDP, A is ideas, K is physical capital, e is human capital per worker (education), and L is the number of workers. (page 116)

Holding e and L constant, and choosing a particular function, we simplify as: $Y = \sqrt{K}$

The **iron logic of diminishing returns** says that increases in K increase Y but at a diminishing rate. (page 117)

Investment is output that is not consumed. (page 119)

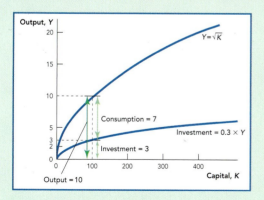

Capital depreciates. It wears out, rusts, and falls apart. Depreciation is a linear function of the capital stock: for example,

$Depreciation = 0.02 \times K$. (page 120)

If investment > depreciation, the capital stock and output grow. If investment < depreciation, the capital stock and output fall. (page 121)

The iron logic of diminishing returns and a linear depreciation rate imply that at some point all of investment must be just enough to balance capital depreciation. When investment = depreciation, neither the capital stock nor output grows. This is known as the **steady state**. (page 121)

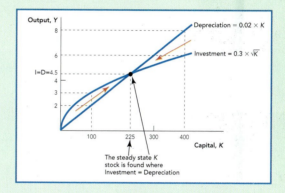

An increase in A, better ideas, means the same capital stock, K, can produce more output. (page 123)

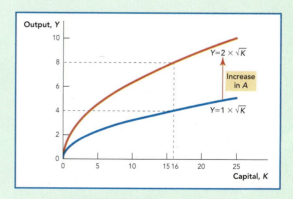

Better ideas are necessary for sustained economic growth.

MODERN PRINCIPLES:
MACROECONOMICS

Tyler Cowen
George Mason University

Alex Tabarrok
George Mason University

Worth Publishers

Economics is the study of how to get the most out of life.

Tyler and Alex

Senior Publisher: Craig Bleyer
Senior Acquisitions Editor: Sarah Dorger
Senior Marketing Manager: Scott Guile
Consulting Editor: Paul Shensa
Development Editor: Bruce Kaplan
Associate Media and Supplements Editor: Lorraine Klimowich
Assistant Supplements Editor: Tom Acox
Director of Market Research and Development: Steven Rigolosi
Associate Managing Editor: Tracey Kuehn
Project Editors: Dana Kasowitz
                Timothy Rodes, Pre-PressPMG
Art Director: Babs Reingold
Cover Designer: Kevin Kall
Text Designer: Lissi Sigillo
Photo Editor: Christine Buese
Photo Researcher: Julie Tesser
Production Manager: Barbara Anne Seixas
Composition: Pre-PressPMG
Printing and Binding: RR Donnelley
Cover Photo: Ralph Mercer/Getty Images

Library of Congress Cataloging-in-Publication Number: 2009925111

ISBN-13: 978-1-4292-0249-7
ISBN-10: 1-4292-0249-1

Printed in the United States of America

Second Printing

Worth Publishers
41 Madison Avenue
New York, NY 10010
www.worthpublishers.com

ABOUT THE AUTHORS

Tyler Cowen (left) is Holbert C. Harris Professor of Economics at George Mason University. His latest book is *Discover Your Inner Economist: Use Incentives to Fall in Love, Survive Your Next Meeting, and Motivate Your Dentist*. With Alex Tabarrok, he writes an economics blog at www.marginalrevolution.com. He also writes regularly for the popular press, including the *New York Times, the Washington Post, Forbes, the Wilson Quarterly, Money Magazine*, and many other outlets.

Alex Tabarrok (right) is Bartley J. Madden Chair in Economics at the Mercatus Center at George Mason University and director of research for *The Independent Institute*. His recent research looks at bounty hunters, judicial incentives and elections, crime control, patent reform, methods to increase the supply of human organs for transplant, and the regulation of pharmaceuticals. He is the editor of the books *Entrepreneurial Economics: Bright Ideas from the Dismal Science* and *The Voluntary City: Choice, Community, and Civil Society* among others. His papers have appeared in the *Journal of Law and Economics, Public Choice, Economic Inquiry, the Journal of Health Economics, the Journal of Theoretical Politics, the American Law and Economics Review,* and many other journals. Popular articles have appeared in the *New York Times, the Wall Street Journal, Forbes,* and many other magazines and newspapers.

BRIEF CONTENTS

CONTENTS

PREFACE: TO THE INSTRUCTOR

About This Book

Macroeconomics has never seemed more important, so welcome to the first edition of *Modern Principles: Macroeconomics*.

Modern. Simpler. These were our goals. We knew that to reflect modern macroeconomics we had to cover the Solow model and the economics of ideas, real business cycles, and New Keynesian economics. While most textbooks now cover the rudiments of economic growth, the importance of ideas as a driving factor is rarely even mentioned. Other textbooks do not offer a balanced treatment of real business cycle theory and New Keynesian theory, instead favoring one theory and relegating the other to a few pages that are poorly integrated with the overall macro model. In contrast, we believe that adequately explaining business fluctuations, unemployment, and both the potential and limits of monetary and fiscal policy requires a balanced treatment of both models.

We also knew that financial crises and bubbles are very real, and that short-run fluctuations are a social and economic issue around the world. In fact, we included substantial material on banking panics, bubbles, wealth shocks, and the importance of financial intermediation in the very first draft of *Modern Principles*. Our book incorporates these topics from the ground floor rather than attempting to squeeze such material into hastily added boxes or appended paragraphs.

We also knew that our efforts to reflect modern macroeconomics would be wasted if we reached only a small percentage of the students. We had to make the material simpler, more compelling, and more intuitive. By boiling the Solow model down to its essence and by providing multiple paths through the material, we have made it accessible to all principles students.

Our modern approach to business fluctuations is also more advanced yet simpler at the same time. It is more advanced because we recognize that all recessions are not alike. The economy is buffeted by shocks stemming from different sources, amplified and spread by different transmission mechanisms. As a result, a balanced approach to real business cycles and New Keynesian economics, with both models rooted in microeconomic intuition, is necessary if students are to understand their world. By discussing both the real business cycle and New Keynesian approaches to business fluctuations, we can better explain the different types of recessions from the Great Depression to the recessions of the 1970s and the current recession.

Our approach to business fluctuations is simpler because we model business fluctuations as fluctuations in the growth rate of output, rather than in the level of output. That creates a natural progression from growth theory to business fluctuations. Moreover, by embedding real business cycles and the New Keynesian models within a single, unified dynamic AD-AS model we simplify presentation and make a sophisticated account of business fluctuations accessible to principles students of all levels. Our modern approach also means that we can offer a more realistic analysis of monetary and fiscal policy in responding to the different types of shocks.

Modern Principles is designed to be accessible to college and university students, whether they are economics majors or not, whether they know advanced mathematics or not. *Modern Principles* aims to make the world intelligible to all readers and users. From this desire stems our tagline *See the Invisible Hand. Understand Your World.*

In short, we believe that no other textbook offers a more modern or more accessible treatment of economic growth and business fluctuations.

Guiding Principles and Innovations: In a Nutshell

Modern Principles offers the following features and benefits:

1. Why are some nations rich and other nations poor? *Modern Principles* has more material on development and growth than any other principles textbook.

2. *Modern Principles* has the most intuitive development of the Solow model of growth in any textbook.

3. The real business cycle model is developed as a natural extension of the Solow model.

4. *Modern Principles* is the only principles book with a balanced treatment of real business cycle theory and New Keynesian macroeconomics.

5. Financial panics and asset bubbles are covered—a topic of great interest in today's environment! There are separate and comprehensive chapters on financial intermediation and on the stock market. We also cover the financial crisis that began in 2007.

6. *Modern Principles* explains how fiscal and monetary policy work differently, depending on whether the shock hitting the economy is a real shock or a nominal shock.

7. Today's students live in a globalized economy. Events in China, India, Europe, and the Middle East affect their lives. *Modern Principles* features international examples and applications. We cover the world from Algeria to Zimbabwe.

8. Less is more. This is a textbook of *principles*, not a survey or encyclopedia. A textbook that focuses on what is important helps the student to focus on what is important. There are fewer yet more consistent and more comprehensive models.

9. No tools without applications. Real-world applications are used to develop theory. Applications are not pushed aside into distracting boxes that students do not read.

10. Excel is used as a tool in appendices to help students develop insight, hands-on experience, and modeling ability.

Tools for Learning

Macroeconomics should come across as elegant, intuitive, and unified, not as a mess. Thus, we cover more content with fewer distinct models than ever before, thereby focusing on what is truly essential. That is why the book has a text length of only 431 pages, making it shorter than its major competitors, while actually covering more material.

Economics should be a practical discipline, so we embraced the principle of "No tools without applications." We also teach students the essential real-world facts about macroeconomics, including the global economy. The book has chapters on international economics, but the global coverage turns up in most of the book's chapters; international economics is no longer marginalized.

We strive for clarity and simplicity in the methods of presentation, not just the content.

1. Vivid applications

Nothing sticks with a student like a good example. *Modern Principles* is full of vivid illustrations of core economic principles. For example, in the opening to our chapter on inflation we write:

> Robert Mugabe had a problem. The dictatorial president of Zimbabwe needed money. Unfortunately, Mugabe's policy of seizing commercial farms had driven productive farmers and entrepreneurs out of the country, frightened off foreign investors, and pushed Zimbabwe, once called the breadbasket of Africa, to the verge of mass starvation. Zimbabwe had almost nothing left to tax, but Mugabe still needed money to bribe his enemies and reward his supporters, especially the still loyal Zimbabwean Army. Mugabe thus turned to the last refuge of needy governments, the printing press.

Our opening example suggests (a) the proximate cause of inflation (an increase in the supply of money), (b) why a government might print money at breakneck speed (when alternative taxes become unavailable), and (c) how economics is a practical science that can help students to understand their world.

2. Simpler graphs

Modern Principles presents macroeconomics with fewer curves than you will find in other macroeconomics books, yet without skimping on substantive results. This follows from our presentation of integrated and consistent macroeconomic models, especially for aggregate demand and aggregate supply. We don't need to shift to a new analytical apparatus for each macroeconomic topic. To the student it will feel that macroeconomics *makes sense* and that macroeconomics involves learning one integrated approach, covering both growth and business cycles. Some textbooks serve up a bewildering array of shifting curves, multiple and possibly conflicting graphs, or even overlaid transparencies to capture all of the curves and shifts. We say if the idea is intuitive—as good economics should be—the graph should be intuitive too.

Economics students *do* need to learn how to think in terms of graphs. But that's best done by making graphs manageable, not by making graphs forbidding.

3. No set-off boxes that interrupt the flow of the text

We know that students usually skip these boxes. So we've skipped them too. If the material is important enough for the student to learn, we've put it in the text. If it's not important, we've left it out. We want our pages to look attractive and easy to read. That will get students to read more of the material that really matters.

4. Extensive questions and problems sections

At the end of each chapter, we typically start with "Facts and Tools," questions designed to test knowledge of basic concepts. The next section "Thinking and Problem Solving" tests whether the student can apply those concepts to examples and also to problems that require a definite solution. The final section

"Challenges" tests whether the students understand key concepts in a deep fashion and can apply them to non-trivial examples and problems. If students can do well in the challenges, they have not just memorized some material but are truly thinking like economists. The multiple tiers for the end-of-chapter material help us teach both different skills and different levels of understanding.

5. Excel appendices

Modern Principles gives the instructor the option of running simulations with the students, using the common software package Excel. For instance, how does "catch-up" growth work in the Solow model and how quickly does it operate? Try a hands-on approach, using numbers taken from the model. Or how do bond prices vary inversely with interest rates? We all know that quantitative magnitudes matter, so why not give the student a good sense of this? We walk the student through this material in a step-by-step manner. But notice: if you don't wish to cover or present this material, no other part of the text depends on it.

6. Nuggets

The margins of the chapter offer captioned photos, cartoons, and short informational bits, all designed to extend the basic material. The examples are chosen for being memorable and sometimes for being humorous. Reading a principles textbook is not always sugar but every now and then it should be fun. The students should look forward to at least some part of the reading and some part of the lesson. We have written *Modern Principles* with this philosophy.

7. Notation

The book has a minimum of notational requirements. Students need to be familiar with simple one-line equations, with basic algebra, and with reading graphs. For help with reading graphs we offer a useful 14-page appendix.

The treatment of aggregate demand and aggregate supply is done in terms of inflation and growth space. Changes in prices drive macroeconomic decisions, not the absolute level of prices, so inflation is on the vertical axis. Putting growth on the horizontal axis unifies growth and business fluctuations and makes it easy to derive a simple but serviceable aggregate demand curve. In the chapters on aggregate demand and supply, our framework enables us to place the New Keynesian model and the real business cycle model in a single consistent model that is built up from the Solow model and the quantity theory of money. To express changes in economic variables economists often write growth rates, such as the growth rate in the money supply, with a dot on top such as $\dot{M}$. We have made growth notation easier for students to remember by writing growth rates with arrows so the growth rate of the money supply is written $\vec{M}$ and so on. Other notation is minimal and standard.

What's in the Chapters?

The book is divided into key parts, namely Supply and Demand, Economic Growth, Business Fluctuations, Macroeconomic Policy and Institutions, and International Economics.

Part 1: Supply and Demand

We review the key aspects of supply and demand and the price system, done in four chapters. We present microeconomics in terms of the idea of incentives, first and foremost. Microeconomics should be intuitive, should teach the skill of thinking like an economist, and should be drawn from examples from everyday life. These chapters run as follows.

Chapter 1: The Big Ideas

What is economics all about? We present the core ideas of incentives, opportunity cost, the importance of economic growth, and the inevitability of some business fluctuations. The point is to make economics intuitive and compelling and to hook the student with examples from everyday life.

Chapter 2: Supply and Demand

This chapter focuses on demand curves, supply curves, how and why they slope, and how they shift. The chapter focuses on some basic fundamentals of economic theory, using the central example of the market for oil. We also take special care to illustrate how demand and supply curves can be read "horizontally" or "vertically." That is, a demand curve tells you the quantity demanded at every price and the maximum willingness to pay (per unit) for any quantity. It takes a bit more work to explain these concepts early on, but students who learn to read demand curves in both ways get a deeper understanding of the curves and they find consumer and producer surplus, taxes, and the analysis of price controls much easier to understand.

Chapter 3: Equilibrium: How Supply and Demand Determine Prices

Market clearing is an essential idea for both microeconomics and macroeconomics. In this chapter, students learn how a well-functioning market will operate, how prices clear markets, the meaning of maximizing gains from trade, and how to shift supply and demand curves. The chapter concludes with a section on understanding the price of oil, a topic that recurs in the discussion of macroeconomics proper.

Chapter 4: Price Ceilings and Price Floors

This chapter is concerned with shortages, surpluses, how markets malfunction when prices are controlled, and the results of those malfunctions. Other textbooks focus on the partial equilibrium responses to a price control that can be illustrated in a diagram. We explain many of the subtler responses to a price ceiling, for example, reductions in product quality. And we move beyond explaining the effects of controls in one market to explain how controls misallocate resources across markets and distort the price system. In addition to giving students a better grasp of the price system, this prepares students for later results in macroeconomics concerning sticky prices.

Part 2: Economic Growth

Why are some nations rich while others are mired in terrible poverty? How can growth be extended to all parts of our world? Students are eager to understand the key issues of growth and development and economics has much of importance to teach on this vital topic. Thus, we begin the macroeconomics part of the book with economic growth.

Chapter 5: GDP and the Measurement of Progress

A visitor to India can see squalor in the streets but also cell phones, new stores, rising literacy, and better fed people. In the United States, the economy moves from a boom in which jobs are easy to find to a bust when people tighten their belts and hope for better times. How do we measure these changes? We focus on the definition, limitations, and meaning of GDP *and* the motivation for studying GDP as a measure of economic change. GDP chapters can be dry so we enliven our treatment through real-world examples and comparisons.

Chapter 6: The Wealth of Nations and Economic Growth

We present the basic facts of economic growth: (1) GDP per capita varies enormously between nations, (2) everyone used to be poor, and (3) there are growth miracles and growth disasters. The key factors behind economic growth include capital, labor, and technology, but we also offer the student a deeper understanding of the importance of incentives and institutions. It is important to connect the physical factors of production with an understanding of how they got there. That means combining Solow and Romer-like models with institutional economics and an analysis of property rights.

A quick tour of the world shows why the student needs to learn different approaches to understanding economic growth.

Let's say we wish to understand why South Korea is wealthy while North Korea starves. The best approach is to consider the roles of property rights and incentives in the two countries, a topic we cover in Chapter 6. Let's say we want to understand why China had been growing at 10 percent a year for almost 30 years. Then, the students need to learn the Solow model and the idea of "catch-up," which we cover in the first half of Chapter 7. Finally, let's say we want to understand why growth rates today are higher than in the nineteenth century, or why the future might bring a very high standard of living. We then need to turn to the Romer model and the idea of increasing returns to scale, which we cover in the second half of Chapter 7. Our approach to economic growth presents all these ideas in an integrated fashion.

Chapter 7: Growth, Capital Accumulation, and the Economics of Ideas: Catching Up vs. The Cutting Edge

Yes, the Solow model finally has come to a principles book. Maybe that sounds daunting, but we offer a super simple version of Solow, intuitive every step along the way. One reviewer for the chapter wrote:

> This chapter is by itself one of the greatest selling points of the book. The chapter is superbly written and presents a difficult concept in a way that an intro-level student would not have trouble understanding. The authors . . . have done a great service to both instructors and students.

Another wrote:

> My first reaction was "No way the Solow model belongs in macro principles." However, after reading both the growth chapters, I changed my mind. These are excellent.

The Solow model stands at the foundation of modern approaches to economic growth. We cover some math but focus on the intuition behind the model, for instance how diminishing returns to capital explains why China can grow faster than the United States. We cover capital growth, investment, and depreciation as concepts relevant for economic growth. As optional material, we explain how an increase in the investment rate increases GDP per capita but in the long run does not increase the growth rate. We also cover why ever more capital cannot be the reason for long-run economic growth and the importance of ideas for economic growth. The appendix offers the quantitative relations of the Solow model in a simple spreadsheet.

The Solow model also leads into a discussion of how ideas are generated and why incentives and spillovers matter for idea generation. *Modern Principles* introduces the notion of increasing returns, as can arise from the production of ideas, and explains its economic importance. Larger economies might grow faster than smaller economies, and growth rates might increase over time, for reasons explained by the work of Paul Romer and other economists.

Chapter 8: Savings, Investment, and the Financial System

Financial intermediation doesn't always receive a lot of attention from macro textbooks, but recent events have shown that the topic is critical. *Modern Principles* presents basic concepts behind intermediation, including consumption smoothing, the demand and supply of savings, equilibrium in the market for loanable funds, and the role of banks, bonds, and stock markets. We explain bank failures, panics, illiquidity, insolvency, and what happens when financial intermediation fails. Students should understand why it is bad if a country has a broken banking system and how it got that way. All of this analysis will later be integrated with aggregate demand and supply. At the end of the chapter, an appendix presents bond pricing in terms of a spreadsheet and shows economically why bond prices and interest rates vary inversely. Modern macro-economics is very much about banking and this chapter reflects the importance of the topic.

Chapter 9: Stock Markets and Personal Finance

The stock market is the one topic that just about every student of economics cares about, and yet it is neglected in many macroeconomics textbooks. We view the stock market as a good "teaching moment" as well as an important topic in its own right. What else in macroeconomics commands so much attention from the popular press? Yet not every macro course gives the student the tools to understand media discussions or dissect fallacies. We remedy that state of affairs. This chapter covers passive versus active investing, the trade-off between risk and return, "how to really pick stocks," diversification, why high fees should be avoided, compound returns (note the link to growth theory), and asset price bubbles. The operation of asset markets is something students need to know if they are to understand today's economy and also the financial crisis.

And, yes, in this chapter we do offer students some very direct and practical investment advice. Most people should diversify and "buy and hold," and we explain why. In terms of direct, practical value, we try to make this book worth its price!

Part 3: Business Fluctuations

Chapter 10: Unemployment and Labor Force Participation

We define the different kinds of unemployment: frictional, structural, and cyclical. We consider how unemployment is linked to economic growth and how so much unemployment can arise from business cycles. We cover structural unemployment in both Europe and the United States, and we also cover labor-force participation rates to a greater extent than in other textbooks. Why is it, for example, that in Belgium only one-third of men ages 55–64 are working, while in the United States only one-third of men this age are retired! The chapter helps students to understand employment protection laws, labor-force participation, lifecycle effects, minimum wages, taxes, pensions, and even how the pill increased female labor-force participation. All of these points also will provide foundations for the later discussion of unemployment, wage stickiness, and aggregate demand.

Chapter 11: Inflation and the Quantity Theory of Money

We start with a vivid example, namely hyperinflation in Zimbabwe, and explain how the rate of inflation rose into the quadrillions. We then introduce the quantity of money as a central concept in macroeconomics that will be used to explain inflation and, in future chapters, aggregate demand. We define inflation and present various price indices, including CPI, PPI, and the GDP deflator. As Milton Friedman explained, "inflation is always and everywhere a monetary phenomenon." The chapter covers the costs of inflation in detail: price confusion and money illusion, the redistribution of wealth, the breakdown of financial intermediation, and the interaction of inflation with the tax system. We explain why inflation happens and why inflation can be so difficult to end. An appendix creates a real price series for homes using Excel and the Internet.

Chapter 12: Business Fluctuations and the Dynamic Aggregate Demand–Aggregate Supply Model

We start by introducing a skeleton model of business fluctuations, on which the next chapter will build. We present the simplest real business cycle model and relate it to real-world concepts and examples. Supply-side fluctuations show up as shifts in the Solow growth curve, while a dynamic aggregate demand curve is based on the quantity theory. Using the quantity theory to derive an AD curve reduces the number of models the students must learn and allows us to proceed quickly to sophisticated analyses of monetary and fiscal policy. Shifts in aggregate demand do not influence the real growth rate in the real business cycle model. We then introduce the New Keynesian model with sticky prices and a short-run aggregate supply curve, responsive to both real and nominal shocks. The chapter ends by considering how the model can be used to explain the Great Depression of the 1930s. An instructor's appendix available online (www.SeeTheInvisibleHand.com) discusses transition dynamics for both real and aggregate demand shocks.

Chapter 13: The Real Business Cycle Model: Shocks and Transmission Mechanisms

Real business cycle models can be forbiddingly complex, but they are built on the simple underlying ideas of shocks and how transmission mechanisms amplify and spread shocks. We illustrate real-world shocks and we give intuitive explanations of transmission mechanisms such as intertemporal substitution, uncertainty and irreversible investments, labor adjustment costs, time bunching, and sticky wages and prices. An appendix ties together the real business cycle analysis of business fluctuations and the Solow model.

Part 4: Macroeconomic Policy and Institutions

Chapter 14: The Federal Reserve System and Open Market Operations

To understand the Federal Reserve system, we introduce key concepts such as the U.S. money supplies, fractional reserve banking, the reserve ratio, the money multiplier, open market operations, and Fed influence over interest rates. With these tools in hand, we revisit concepts of aggregate demand, in particular through monetary policy. We cover all the core tools of monetary policy, including the recent innovations of Ben Bernanke, such as the term auction facility, in response to the financial crisis. We treat the Federal Reserve as a major manager of systematic risk and analyze when the Fed is likely to succeed in this task and why the task is a difficult one, with attention to the concepts of moral hazard and also confidence building. The appendix covers the money multiplier process in detail.

Chapter 15: Monetary Policy

Building on the analysis of the Fed, we consider the dilemmas of monetary policy in detail. The relevant cases include, among others: negative shocks to aggregate demand, rules vs. discretion, analyzing a decline in the rate of monetary growth, and responding to negative real shocks. We devote special attention to the Fed as a manager of market confidence and to how the Fed should respond to positive shocks and possible asset price bubbles, including to the housing market.

Chapter 16: The Federal Budget: Taxes and Spending

Students need to understand the institutional details of government receipts and spending. That includes tax revenues (their size and nature), the individual income tax, taxes on capital gains and interest and dividends, the alternative minimum tax, Social Security and Medicare taxes, the corporate income tax, and the question of who really pays federal taxes. In addition, we cover state and local taxes and the components of spending, including Medicare, defense, discretionary spending, and other areas. Students should have a good sense of where the money comes from and what it is spent on. We also analyze the national debt, interest on the debt, and deficits. We consider the speculative question of whether the U.S. government will someday go bankrupt and what the answer to such a question depends on.

Chapter 17: Fiscal Policy

What forms does fiscal policy take and when does it work best to improve macroeconomic performance? What are the limits of fiscal policy and when will a fiscal stimulus work best? We cover crowding out, bond vs. tax finance of expansionary fiscal policy, tax rebates and tax cuts, automatic stabilizers, and Ricardian equivalence. Students also learn when fiscal policy is potent enough, when timing issues get in the way of effective fiscal policy, and whether fiscal policy can address the macroeconomic problems from negative real shocks. When is government debt a problem and how can debt crises bring an economy to its knees? The overall purpose of this chapter is to teach students when fiscal policy is a good or bad idea.

Part 5: International Economics
Chapter 18: International Trade and Globalization

The basics of international trade start with the division of knowledge and economies of scale and comparative advantage as foundations for trade. We consider the costs of protectionism, international trade and market power, trade and wages, and trade and jobs. Is protectionism ever a good idea? The chapter also offers a brief history of globalization as it relates to trade.

Chapter 19: International Finance

The multiplicity of currencies sometimes makes international finance a daunting topic, but we keep it simple and show how it applies core economic principles that students already understand. The topics include the U.S. trade deficit, the balance of payments, the current account, the capital account (the financial account), the Official Reserves account, and the two sides of accounting identity behind the balance of payments. All of these topics are explained in terms of consistent economic intuitions. We also consider what a trade deficit really means, and we relate that to the trading behavior of individuals. The chapter analyzes exchange rates and their determinants in terms of supply and demand analysis, as stems from goods markets and asset markets. Long-run exchange rates have an (imperfect) connection to purchasing power parity, due to trade and economic arbitrage. Building on aggregate demand analysis, we consider how monetary and fiscal policy affect exchange rates and so influence output and employment. In this framework we consider the relative merits of fixed vs. floating exchange rates. The chapter closes with a presentation of the nature and functions of the IMF and World Bank.

Alternative Paths through the Book

Modern Principles has been written with trade-offs in mind. We offer four primary options. First, we expect that many students will have covered microeconomics in a previous class so Chapters 2–4 can be skipped or assigned for review. (Of course, we recommend *Modern Principles: Microeconomics* for these previous classes!) One possible exception is that our discussion of price ceilings in the first half of Chapter 4 focuses on Richard Nixon's imposition of price and wage controls on the entire U.S. economy in 1971. Our example and discussion is thus much more amenable to a macroeconomic interpretation than is the typical discussion of price ceilings. As an option, an instructor could cover this material in a half class after covering Chapter 11 on inflation.

The second option is to cover only a portion of the Solow model in Chapter 7. We sometimes do this in our larger classes so this will be a good choice for many. The chapter has been written so the most intuitive and important aspects of the model are covered in the beginning, more difficult and detailed material in the middle may be skipped, and then important material on growth and ideas is covered toward the end of the chapter. The material in the middle may be skipped without loss of continuity. Instructors with smaller and more advanced classes can easily cover the full chapter. The instructor's guide written by John Dawson offers many excellent tips for covering this material.

One important point: it is not at all necessary to teach the Solow model to cover our chapters on business fluctuations. We offer a "Solow growth curve" in these chapters, but without delving into the details of the Solow model, the curve is readily explained as a potential growth curve analogous to a potential GDP curve.

Our chapter on stock markets is optional, but students truly enjoy learning this material so we encourage everyone to cover it, time allowing.

The third major option is that we have divided the chapters in macroeconomic policy and institutions so that an instructor can cover monetary policy without covering the details of the Federal Reserve system and open market operations, and one can cover fiscal policy without covering the details of the federal budget: taxes and spending. The details are important and these chapters place monetary and fiscal policy within an institutional context so we do not necessarily recommend this approach but when time binds, more options are better than fewer.

The fourth major option is to leave international trade and globalization to a microeconomics class and to skip international finance. To us, international economics means primarily that economics can help us to understand the world, not just one country and not just one time. As a result, we have included many international examples throughout *Modern Principles: Macroeconomics* and *Modern Principles: Microeconomics*. If time constrains, the details of tariffs, exchange rates, and trade deficits may be left to another course. Alas, we live in a finite world.

Supplements and Media
Innovative Resources for Teaching *Modern Principles: Macroeconomics*

Cowen and Tabarrok take a modern approach to macroeconomics. Worth Publishers takes an equally modern approach to instructor resources and supplementary material. In addition to providing traditional resources, which we list below, the economics team at Worth will be working constantly throughout this first edition to develop new resources that will help keep your course current, exciting to the students, and most of all, relevant to today's economic environment. Check www.worthpublishers.com/cowentabarrok for the latest developments in supplements and media.

Instructor Supplements
Instructor's Resource Manual with Solutions Manual

Prepared by John Dawson (Appalachian State University). For each chapter in the textbook, the Instructor's Resource Manual provides:

> *Learning Objectives:* bulleted list of the key "takeaways" of the chapter.

> *Chapter Outline:* listing chapter heads and subheadings for quick reference.

> *Chapter Narrative:* detailed coverage of chapter material, including breakdowns of graphs, Teaching Tips, Strategies, Key Learning Points, and Potential Pitfalls.

> *Inside-* and *Outside-the-Classroom Activities:* problems and exercises relating to chapter material designed to engage students in lecture material.

> Detailed solutions to all of the end-of-chapter questions and problems from the textbook prepared by Garett Jones (George Mason University).

Printed Test Bank

The test bank provides creative and versatile questions ranging in levels of difficulty and format to assess students' comprehension, interpretation, analysis, and synthesis skills. Containing roughly 135 questions per chapter, the test bank offers a variety of multiple-choice, true/false, and short-answer questions. The test bank is being coordinated by David Gillette (Truman State University). Authors of test questions are Lillian Kamal (University of Hartford), Mark Wheeler (University of Western Michigan), Jim Self (Indiana University), Jim Lee (Texas A&M—Corpus Christi), and J. J. Arias (Georgia College and State University).

Computerized Test Bank

The printed test bank will be available in CD-ROM format for both Windows and Macintosh users. With Diploma software, instructors can easily create and print tests as well as write and edit questions.

Instructor's Resource CD-ROM

Using the Instructor's Resource CD-ROM, instructors can easily build classroom presentations or enhance online courses. This CD-ROM contains all text figures (in JPEG and PPT formats), PowerPoint Lecture Presentations with animated figures and tables, and detailed solutions to all end-of-chapter questions in the textbook.

Student Supplements

Study Guide

Prepared by David Mitchell (University of South Alabama). For each key section of each chapter, the study guide provides:

> *Brief Chapter Summary.*

> *Key Terms:* listed, with space for students to write in the definitions themselves.

> *Detailed Section Summaries with Student Tips and Concept-Related Questions:* including coverage of all applications, tips to help students with difficult concepts, and 3–5 questions per section to reinforce learning of key concepts.

> *Self-Test End-of-Chapter Questions:* 15–20 application-oriented, multiple-choice questions.

> *Worked-Out solutions:* including solutions to all study guide review questions.

Online Offerings

Companion Web Site for Students and Instructors

www.SeeTheInvisibleHand.com

The companion site is a virtual study guide for students and an excellent resource for instructors. For each chapter in the textbook, the tools on the site include:

Instructor Resources:

> **Quiz Gradebook:** The site gives instructors the ability to track students' interactions with the practice quizzes via an online gradebook. Instructors may choose to have students' results emailed directly to them.

> **PowerPoint Lecture Presentations:** These customizable PowerPoint slides, prepared by Michael Applegate (Oklahoma State University), are designed to assist instructors with lecture preparation and presentation by providing learning objectives, animated figures and tables, equations from the textbook, key concepts, and bulleted lecture outlines.

> **Illustration PowerPoint Slides:** A complete set of figures and tables from the textbook in JPEG and PowerPoint formats.

> **Images from the Textbook:** Instructors have access to a complete set of figures and tables from the textbook in high-res and low-res JPEG formats.

Student Resources:

> **Self-Test Quizzes:** This quizzing engine provides 20 multiple-choice questions per chapter with immediate and appropriate feedback along with topic references for students to refer back to in the textbook for further review.

The questions as well as the answer choices are randomized to give students a different quiz with every refresh of the screen.

> **Key Term Flashcards:** Students can test themselves on the key terms with these pop-up electronic flashcards.

eBook

Students who purchase the *Modern Principles* eBook have access to the interactive textbook featuring:

> Quick, intuitive navigation

> Customizable note-taking

> Highlighting

> Searchable glossary

> Self-testing

With the *Modern Principles* eBook, instructors can:

> Focus on only the chapters they want. You can assign the entire text or a custom version with only the chapters that correspond to your syllabus. Students see your customized version, with your selected chapters only.

> Annotate any page of the text. Your notes can include text, Web links, and even photos and images from the book's media or other sources. Your students can get an eBook annotated just for them, customized for your course.

> Access online quizzing. The eBook integrates the online quizzing from the book's companion Web site.

WebCT E-pack and Blackboard Cartridge

Cowen/Tabarrok *Modern Principles: Macroeconomics* text-specific, rich Web content, including preprogrammed quizzes, tests pulled from the computerized test bank, activities, and an array of other materials, is available for users of WebCT or Blackboard in the appropriate format.

EconPortal—*AVAILABLE FOR SPRING 2011*

EconPortal is the digital gateway to *Modern Principles*, designed to enrich your course and improve your students' understanding of economics. EconPortal provides a powerful, easy-to-use, completely customizable teaching and learning management system complete with the following:

> *An Interactive eBook with Embedded Learning Resources:* The eBook's functionality will provide for highlighting, note-taking, graph and example enlargements, and a full text and glossary search. Embedded icons will link students directly to resources available to enhance their understanding of the key concepts.

> *A Personalized Study Plan for Students, Featuring Diagnostic Quizzing:* Students will be asked to take the PSP: Self-Assessment Quiz after they have read the chapter and before they come to the lecture that discusses that chapter. Once they've taken the quiz, a personalized study plan (PSP) based on the quiz results is created for them. This PSP will provide a path to the appropriate eBook materials and resources for further study and exploration, helping students learn and retain the course material.

> *A Fully Integrated Learning Management System:* EconPortal is meant to be a fully customizable and highly interactive one-stop shop for all the resources tied to the book. The system will carefully integrate the teaching and learning resources for the book into an easy-to-use system. EconPortal will enable you to create assignments from a variety of question types to prepare self-graded homework, quizzes, or tests, saving many hours of preparation time.

> Instructors can assign and track any aspect of their students' EconPortal activities. The Gradebook will capture students' results and allow for easily exporting reports as well as importing grades from offline assignments.

Additional Offerings

i>clicker

Developed by a team of University of Illinois physicists, i>clicker is the most flexible and most reliable classroom response system available. It is the only solution created *for* educators, *by* educators—with continuous product improvements made through direct classroom testing and faculty feedback. You'll love i>clicker no matter your level of technical expertise, because the focus is on *your* teaching, *not the technology.* To learn more about packaging i>clicker with this textbook, please contact your local sales rep or visit www.iclicker.com.

Wall Street Journal **Edition:** For adopters of the Cowen/Tabarrok textbook, Worth Publishers and the *Wall Street Journal* are offering a 15-week subscription to students at a tremendous savings. Instructors also receive their own free *Wall Street Journal* subscription plus additional instructor supplements created exclusively by the *Wall Street Journal*. Please contact your local sales rep for more information or go to the *Wall Street Journal* online at www.wsj.com.

Financial Times **Edition:** For adopters of the Cowen/Tabarrok textbook, Worth Publishers and the *Financial Times* are offering a 15-week subscription to students at a tremendous savings. Instructors also receive their own free *Financial Times* subscription for one year. Students and instructors may access research and archived information at www.ft.com.

Dismal Scientist: A high-powered business database and analysis service comes to the classroom! Dismal Scientist offers real-time monitoring of the global economy, produced locally by economists and professionals at Economy.com's London, Sydney, and West Chester offices. Dismal Scientist is *free* when packaged with the Cowen/Tabarrok textbook. Please contact your local sales rep for more information or go to www.economy.com.

The Economist has partnered with Worth Publishers to create an exclusive offer that will enhance the classroom experience. Faculty receive a complimentary 15-week subscription when 10 or more students purchase a subscription. Students get 15 issues of *The Economist* at a huge savings.

Inside and outside the classroom, *The Economist* provides a global perspective that helps students keep abreast of what's going on in the world, and gives insight into how the world views the United States. *The Economist* ignites dialogue, encourages debate, and enables readers to form well-reasoned opinions—while providing a deeper understanding of key political, social, and business issues. Supplement your textbook with the knowledge and insight that only *The Economist* can provide.

To get 15 issues of *The Economist*, go to www.economistacademic.com/worth.

Acknowledgments

We are most indebted and grateful to the following focus group participants, reviewers, and class testers for their comments and suggestions. Every one of them has contributed to the final product, *Modern Principles.*

Rashid Al-Hmoud
Texas Tech University

Michael Applegate
Oklahoma State University

J. J. Arias
Georgia College and State University

Jim Barbour
Elon University

Robert Beekman
University of Tampa

Ryan Bosworth
North Carolina State University

Jennifer Brown
Eastern Connecticut State University

Shawn Carter
Jacksonville State University

Philip Coelho
Ball State University

Jim Couch
North Alabama University

Scott Cunningham
University of Georgia

Amlan Datta
Texas Tech University

John Dawson
Appalachian State University

Timothy M. Diette
Washington and Lee University

Ann Eike
University of Kentucky

Tisha Emerson
Baylor University

Molly Espey
Clemson University

William Feipel
Illinois Central University

Gary Galles
Pepperdine University

Neil Garston
California State University, Los Angeles

David Gillette
Truman State University

Stephan F. Gohmann
University of Louisville

Michael Gootzeit
University of Memphis

Carole Green
University of South Florida

Paul Grimes
Mississippi State University

Philip J. Grossman
St. Cloud State University

Darrin Gulla
University of Kentucky

Kyle Hampton
The Ohio State University

Joe Haslag
University of Missouri—Columbia

Sarah Helms
University of Alabama—Birmingham

Matthew Henry
University of Georgia

John Hsu
Contra Costa College

Jeffrey Hummel
Golden Gate University

Dennis Jansen
Texas A&M University

Bruce Johnson
Centre College

Veronica Kalich
Baldwin Wallace College

Lillian Kamal
University of Hartford

John Keating
University of Kansas

Logan Kelly
Bryant University

Brian Kench
University of Tampa

David Kreutzer
James Madison University

Gary Lape
Liberty University

Rodolfo Ledesma
Marian College

Jim Lee
Texas A&M University—Corpus Christi

Edward Lopez
San Jose State University

Hari Luitel
St. Cloud State University

Douglas Mackenzie
State University of New York—Plattsburgh

Michael Makowsky
Towson University

John Marcis
Coastal Carolina University

Meghan Millea
Mississippi State University

Stephen Miller
University of Nevada, Las Vegas

Ida Mirzaie
The Ohio State University

David (Mitch) Mitchell
South Alabama University

Ranganath Murthy
Bucknell University

Todd Myers
Grossmont College

Andre Neveu
Skidmore College

Lydia Ortega
San Jose State University

Alexandre Padilla
Metropolitan State College of Denver

Biru Paksha Paul
State University of New York—Cortland

John Perry
Centre College

Dennis Placone
Clemson University

Jennifer M. Platania
Elon University

Brennan Platt
Brigham Young University

Benjamin Powell
Suffolk University

Margaret Ray
University of Mary Washington

Dan Rickman
Oklahoma State University

Fred Ruppel
Eastern Kentucky University

Mikael Sandberg
University of Florida

Michael Scott
University of Oklahoma

James Self
Indiana University

David Shideler
Murray State University

Mark Showalter
Brigham Young University

Martin Spechler
Indiana University–Purdue University, Indianapolis

David Spencer
Brigham Young University

Richard Stahl
Louisiana State University

Dean Stansel
Florida Gulf Coast University

Kay Strong
Bowling Green State University—Firelands

Jim Swofford
University of South Alabama

Sandra Trejos
Clarion University of Pennsylvania

Marie Truesdell
Marian College

Norman T. Van Cott
Ball State University

Kristin A. Van Gaasbeck
California State University—Sacramento

Michael Visser
Sonoma State University

Christopher Waller
Notre Dame University

Yoav Wachsman
Coastal Carolina University

Robert Whaples
Wake Forest University

Doug Walker
Georgia College and State University

Mark Wheeler
Western Michigan University

Additional suggestions for improving the manuscript were given by our talented supplement authors. John Dawson, Appalachian State University, taught our Solow growth chapter in a summer class and provided invaluable comments on how to make the presentation even better. David Gillette, Truman State University, contributed useful perspectives on the introductory macro chapters. David Mitchell, University of South Alabama, gave numerous suggestions on making the material clearer. We are grateful to all of them.

We were fortunate to have several eagle-eyed readers of the proofs of the book during the production process. James L. Lapp and Lillian Kamal, University of Hartford, were careful readers of the page proofs. Eric P. Chiang, Florida Atlantic University, did a great job examining the revised page proofs. All three of these reviewers had a remarkable focus on detail.

Our colleague Garett Jones and his expertise have been a lifesaver for the problems and questions. We were fortunate to have research assistance from Amanda Agan, Robert Warren Anderson, Eli Dourado, Yan Li, Ross Williams, and David Youngberg. The Mercatus Center supplied an essential work environment. Jane Perry helped us to proof many of the chapters and with Lisa Hill-Corley provided important daily assistance. Teresa Hartnett has done a great job as our agent.

Most of all we are grateful to the team at Worth. The idea for this book was conceived by Paul Shensa, who has seen it through with wise advice from day one until the end. Craig Bleyer has been a wonderful publisher and Sarah Dorger has led the editing work and been a joy to work with. Becca Hicks was a delight to work with and introduced us to the key elements of a textbook. Bruce Kaplan, our primary development editor, is the George Martin of book production; he has done a tremendous amount of nitty-gritty work on the manuscript to make every note just right and he has offered excellent counsel throughout.

We are fortunate to have had such a talented production and design group for our book. Dana Kasowitz coordinated the entire production process with the help of Timothy Rodes and Tracey Kuehn. Kevin Kall created the beautiful interior design and the cover. Christine Buese went beyond the call of duty in tracking down sometimes obscure photos. Barbara Seixas showed a deft hand with the manufacturing aspects of the book. It has been a delight to work with all of them.

The supplements were put together by several people. Matt Driskill put together the supplements team. Tom Acox ably brought the supplements package to market. Marie McHale and Lorraine Klimowich provided essential effort on the electronic Portal. And, the work of Stacey Alexander and Laura McGinn helped bring the content to print.

Two people stand out in the marketing of this book. Steven Rigolosi ran the extensive market development program that introduced this book to the market. Scott Guile has been energetic and relentless in marketing this book.

Most of all, we want to thank our families for their support and understanding. Tyler wishes to offer his personal thanks to Natasha and Yana. It is Alex's great fortune to be able to thank Monique, Connor, and Maxwell and his parents for years of support and encouragement.

Tyler Cowen
Alex Tabarrok

1

The Big Ideas

The prisoners were dying of scurvy, typhoid fever, and small-pox, but nothing was killing them more than bad incentives. In 1787, the British government had hired sea captains to ship convicted felons to Australia. Conditions on board the ships were monstrous; some even said the conditions were worse than on slave ships. On one voyage, more than a third of the males died and the rest arrived beaten, starved, and sick. A first mate remarked cruelly of the convicts "let them die and be damned the owners have [already] been paid for their passage."[1]

The British public had no love for the convicts, but it wasn't pre-pared to give them a death sentence either. Newspapers editorial-ized in favor of better conditions, clergy appealed to the captains' sense of humanity, and legislators passed regulations requiring better food and water, light and air, and proper medical care. Yet the death rate remained shockingly high. Nothing appeared to be working until an economist suggested something new. Can you guess what the economist suggested?

Instead of paying the captains for each prisoner placed on board ship in Great Britain, the economist suggesting paying for each prisoner that walked off the ship in Australia. In 1793, the new system was implemented and imme-diately the survival rate shot up to 99 percent. One astute observer explained what had happened, "economy beat sentiment and benevolence."[2]

The story of the convict ships illustrates the first big lesson that runs throughout this book and throughout economics, *incentives matter.*

By **incentives,** we mean rewards and penalties that motivate behavior. Let's take a closer look at incentives and some of the other big ideas in economics. On first reading, some of these ideas may seem surprising or difficult to under-stand. Don't worry: we will be explaining everything in more detail.

Incentives are rewards and penalties that motivate behavior.

1

We see the following list as the most important and fundamental contributions of economics to human understanding; we call these contributions **Big Ideas**. Some economists might arrange this list in a different manner or order, but these are generally accepted principles among good economists everywhere.

Big Idea One: Incentives Matter

When the captains were paid for every prisoner that they took on board, they had little incentive to treat the prisoners well. In fact, the incentives were to treat the prisoners badly. Instead of feeding the prisoners, for example, some of the captains hoarded the prisoners' food, selling it in Australia for a tidy profit.

When the captains were paid for prisoners who survived the journey, however, their incentives changed. Whereas before, the captains had benefited from a prisoner's death, now the incentive system "secured to every poor man who died at least one sincere mourner."[3] The sincere mourner? The captain, who at least was sincere about mourning the money he would have earned had the poor man survived.

Incentives are everywhere. In the United States, we take it for granted that when we go to the supermarket the shelves will be stocked with kiwi fruit from New Zealand, rice from India, and wine from Chile. Every day we rely on the work of millions of other people to provide us with food, clothing, and shelter. Why do so many people work for our benefit? In his 1776 classic, *The Wealth of Nations*, Adam Smith explained:

> It is not from the benevolence of the butcher, the brewer, or the baker, that we expect our dinner, but from their regard to their own interest.

Do economists think that everyone is self-interested all the time? Of course not. We love our spouses and children just like everyone else! But economists do think that people respond in predictable ways to incentives of all kinds. Fame, power, reputation, sex, and love are all important incentives. Economists even think that benevolence responds to incentives. It's not surprising to an economist, for example, that charities publicize the names of their donors. Some people do give anonymously, but how many buildings on your campus are named Anonymous Hall?

Big Idea Two: Good Institutions Align Self-Interest with the Social Interest

The story of the convict ships hints at a second lesson that runs throughout this book: When self-interest aligns with the broader public interest, we get good outcomes, but when self-interest and the social interest are at odds, we get bad outcomes, sometimes even cruel and inhumane outcomes. Paying the ship captains for every prisoner who walked off the ship was a good payment system because it created incentives for the ship captains to do the right thing, not just for themselves but also for the prisoners and for the government that was paying them.

It's a remarkable finding of economics that under the right conditions markets align self-interest with the social interest. You can see what we mean by thinking back to the supermarket we mentioned earlier. The supermarket is stocked with

products from around the world because markets channel and coordinate the self-interest of millions of people to achieve a social good. The farmer who awoke at 5 AM to tend his crops, the trucker who delivered the goods to the market, the entrepreneur who risked his or her capital to build the supermarket—each of these people acted in their own interest, but in so doing they also acted in your interest.

In a striking metaphor, Adam Smith said that when markets work well, those who pursue their own interest end up promoting the social interest, as if led to do so by an "invisible hand." The idea that the pursuit of self-interest can be in the social interest—that at least sometimes, "greed is good"—was one of the most surprising discoveries of economic science, and after several hundred years this insight is still not always appreciated. Throughout this book, we emphasize ways in which individuals acting in their self-interest produce outcomes that were not part of their intention nor design, but which nevertheless have desirable properties. The invisible hand icon, seen in the margin, will be a symbol of these ideas.

see the invisible hand

Markets, however, do not always align self-interest with the social interest. Sometimes the invisible hand is absent, not just invisible. Market incentives, for example, can be too strong. A firm that doesn't pay for the pollution that it emits into the air has too great an incentive to emit pollution. Fishermen sometimes have too strong an incentive to catch fish, thereby driving the stock of fish into collapse. In other cases, market incentives are too weak. Did you get your flu shot this year? The flu shot prevents you from getting the flu (usually) but it also reduces the chances that other people will get the flu. When deciding whether to get a flu shot, did you take into account the social interest or just your self-interest?

When markets don't properly align self-interest with the social interest, another important lesson of economics is that government can sometime improve the situation by changing incentives with taxes, subsidies, or other regulations.

Big Idea Three: Trade-offs Are Everywhere

Vioxx users were outraged when in September 2004 Merck withdrew the arthritis drug from the market; at the time a new study showed that Vioxx could cause strokes and heart attacks. Vioxx had been on the market for 5 years and had been used by millions of people. Patients were angry at Merck and at the Food and Drug Administration (FDA). How could the FDA, which is charged with ensuring that new pharmaceuticals are safe and effective, have let Vioxx onto the market? Many people demanded more testing and safer pharmaceuticals. Economists worried that approved pharmaceuticals could become too safe.

Too safe! Is it possible to be too safe?! Yes, because trade-offs are everywhere. Researching, developing, and testing a new drug costs time and resources. On average, it takes about 12 years and $900 million dollars to bring a new drug to market. More testing means that approved drugs will have fewer side effects, but there are two important trade-offs: *drug lag* and *drug loss*.

Testing takes time so more testing means that good drugs are delayed, just like bad drugs. On average, new drugs work better than old drugs. So the longer it takes to bring new drugs to market, the more people are harmed who could have benefited if the new drugs had been approved earlier.[4] You can die because an unsafe drug is approved—you can also die because a safe drug has *not yet* been approved. This is *drug lag*.

Testing not only takes time, it is costly. The greater the costs of testing, the fewer new drugs there will be. The costs of testing are a hurdle that each potential drug must leap if it is to be developed. Higher costs mean a higher hurdle, fewer new drugs and fewer lives saved. You can die because an unsafe drug is approved—you can also die because a safe drug is *never* developed. This is *drug loss*.

Thus, society faces a trade-off. More testing means the drugs that are (eventually) approved will be safer but it also means more drug lag and drug loss. When thinking about FDA policy, we need to look at both sides of the trade-off if we are to choose wisely.

Trade-offs are closely related to another important idea in economics, opportunity cost.

Opportunity Cost

The **opportunity cost** of a choice is the value of the opportunities lost.

Every choice involves something gained and something lost. The **opportunity cost** of a choice is the value of the opportunities lost. Consider the choice to attend college. What is the cost of attending college? At first, you might calculate the cost by adding together the price of tuition, books, and room and board—that might be $15,000 a year. But that's not the opportunity cost of attending college. What opportunities are you losing when you attend college?

The main opportunity that is lost when you attend college is (probably) the opportunity to have a full-time job. Most of you reading this book could easily get a job earning $25,000 a year or maybe quite a bit more (Bill Gates was a college dropout). If you spend four years in college, that's $100,000 that you are giving up to get an education. The opportunity cost of college is probably higher than you thought. Perhaps you ought to ask more questions in class in order to get your money's worth! (But go back to the list of items we totaled earlier—tuition, books, and room and board—one of these items should *not* count as part of the opportunity cost of college. Which one? Answer: Room and board is not a cost of college if you would have to pay for it whether you go to college or not.)

The concept of opportunity cost is important for two reasons. First, if you don't understand the opportunities that you are losing when you make a choice, you won't recognize the real trade-offs that you face. Recognizing trade-offs is the first step to making wise choices. Second, most of the time people do respond to changes in opportunity costs—*even when money costs have not changed*—so if you want to understand behavior, you need to understand opportunity cost.

What would you predict, for example, would happen to college enrollment during a recession? The price of tuition, books, and room and board doesn't fall during a recession but the opportunity cost of attending college does fall. Why? During a recession, the unemployment rate increases so it's harder to get a high-paying job. That means you lose less by attending college when the unemployment rate is high. We, therefore, predict that college enrollments increase when the unemployment rate increases; in opportunity costs terms, it is cheaper to go to college. Figure 1.1 shows that this is correct—when the unemployment rate is unusually high (above trend), the college enrollment rate tends to be unusually high as well. The reverse is also true: When the economy is booming and the unemployment rate is unusually low, the college enrollment rate tends to be low as well. Of course, many other factors other than the unemployment rate influence college enrollment rates so the relationship is not

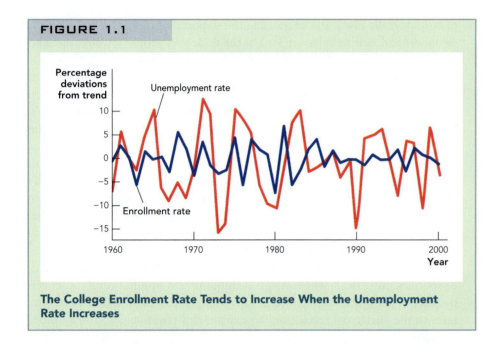

FIGURE 1.1

Percentage deviations from trend

Unemployment rate

Enrollment rate

Year

The College Enrollment Rate Tends to Increase When the Unemployment Rate Increases

exact, but Figure 1.1 shows that as a general tendency the enrollment rate tends to be unusually high when the unemployment rate is unusually high.

Big Idea Four: Thinking on the Margin

People cheered when, in the 1990s, Speaker of the House Newt Gingrich advocated mandatory executions for drug dealers. But economists wondered why Gingrich wanted to *decrease* the penalty for murder. How does the death penalty for drug dealers decrease the penalty for murder? Think about it this way: Suppose that Gingrich's bill becomes law and the police bust into an apartment where three drug dealers have hidden their stash. What happens? The drug dealers know that if they give up, they will be put to death. So why not try to kill the police? If the dealers are lucky, they get away. If the dealers are unlucky, they are no worse off than if they didn't fight because when drug dealing is a capital offense, drug dealers face no *additional* penalty for murder.

Imposing the death penalty on drug dealers may decrease the number of drug dealers but increase the number of murders. Similarly, if we increase the penalties for robbery we are reducing the additional or *marginal* penalty for armed robbery. Thus, tougher penalties for robbery can increase the number of armed robberies. Is this a good trade-off?

The surprising effects of policies to "get tough on crime" illustrate the importance of what economists call *thinking on the margin*. When a drug dealer decides whether to commit the crime of murder, he or she doesn't think about the penalty for murder—the drug dealer thinks about the marginal or additional penalty for murder given what he or she is doing already. More generally, most choices are usually marginal choices—should we do a little bit more or a little bit less of some activity?

In this book, you will find lots of talk about marginal choices, which includes marginal cost (the addition to cost from producing one more unit), marginal revenue (the addition to revenue from producing one more unit), and the marginal tax rate (the tax rate on an additional dollar of income). This point about

margins is really just a way of restating the importance of trade-offs. If you wish to understand human behavior, look at the trade-offs people actually face. Those trade-offs usually involve choices about a little bit more or a little bit less.

Let's give a personal example that illustrates the importance of thinking on the margin. Say you have graduated from your university and are earning a healthy salary of $64,000 a year. You are offered another job with a higher salary, but it's in a different town and you really don't want to move. Should you take the new job? A lot will depend on how much of the higher income you get to keep and how much the government will take in taxes. To figure this out, don't ask how much of your current income is taken in taxes. Ask how much tax there will be on your additional income if you take the new job. The average tax rate on income of $64,000 is about 13 percent, but the government will take 25 percent of every dollar you earn above $64,000. The new job may not look so good when you look at the relevant tax rate for your choice, namely the marginal tax rate.

The importance of thinking at the margin did not become commonplace in economics until 1871, when marginal thinking was simultaneously discovered by three economists: Stanley Jevons, Carl Menger, and Leon Walras. Economists refer to the "marginal revolution" to explain this transformation in economic thought.

Big Idea Five: Tampering with the Laws of Supply and Demand Has Consequences

Nearly two thousand years ago the Roman Emperor Diocletian made it illegal to sell beef, grain, eggs, clothing, and a thousand other goods at prices greater than he decreed. Merchants who disobeyed were sentenced to death. The historian Lactantius reported the results: "the people brought provisions no more to markets, since they could not get a reasonable price for them and this increased the dearth [shortage] so much, that at last after many had died by it, the law itself was set aside."

Markets respond in predictable ways to price controls. When President Richard Nixon imposed price controls on the U.S. economy in 1971, the results were very similar to those in Diocletian's time: shortages, long lines, lower quality goods, and waste. And, just as in Diocletian's time, the policy was eventually abandoned as a failure.

Price controls are hardly a thing of the past. Even today when the price of gasoline rises, consumers become angry and politicians will sometimes try to appease this anger by promising to make high prices illegal. But economics explains why price controls rarely work. Rather than solving the problem of low purchasing power, price controls tend to make the situation worse by reducing the incentive to supply goods.

We think that many of the most important issues in the world today cannot be understood without understanding economics. Throughout this textbook we will use the icon seen in the margin to emphasize some of the most important ways in which economics helps you to Understand Your World.

Big Idea Six: The Importance of Wealth and Economic Growth

In 2007, more than half a billion people in the world contracted malaria and about a million of them—mostly children—died from it. Today, we think of

malaria as a "tropical" disease but malaria was once common in the United States. George Washington caught malaria, as did James Monroe, Andrew Jackson, Abraham Lincoln, Ulysses S. Grant, and James A. Garfield. Malaria was present in America until the late 1940s, when the last cases were wiped out by better drainage, removal of mosquito breeding sites, and the spraying of insecticides. The lesson? Wealth—the ability to pay for the prevention of malaria—ended malaria in the United States and wealth comes from economic growth, so the incidence of malaria is not just about geography—it's also about economics.

Malaria is far from the only problem that diminishes with wealth and economic growth. In the United States, one of the world's richest countries, 993 out of every 1,000 children born survive to the age of 5. In Liberia, one of the world's poorest countries, only about 765 children survive to age 5 (i.e., 235 of every 1,000 children die before seeing their fifth birthday). Overall, it's the wealthiest countries that have the highest rates of infant survival.

Indeed, if you look at most of the things that people care about, they are much easier to come by in the wealthier economies. Wealth brings us flush toilets, antibiotics, higher education, the ability to choose the career we want, fun vacations, and of course a greater ability to protect our families against catastrophes. Wealth also brings women's rights and political liberty, at least in most (but not all) countries. Wealthier economies lead to richer and more fulfilled human lives. In short, *wealth matters and understanding economic growth is one of the most important tasks of economics*.

Big Idea Seven: Institutions Matter

If wealth is so important, what makes a country rich? The most proximate cause is that wealthy countries have lots of physical and human capital per worker and they produce things in a relatively efficient manner, using the latest technological knowledge. But why do some countries have more physical and human capital and why is it organized well using the latest technological knowledge? In a word, incentives, which of course relates back to Big Idea One.

Entrepreneurs, investors, and savers need incentives to save and invest in physical capital, human capital, innovation, and efficient organization. Among the most powerful institutions for supporting good incentives are property rights, political stability, honest government, a dependable legal system, and competitive and open markets.

Consider South and North Korea. South Korea has a per capita income more than 10 times greater than its immediate neighbor, North Korea. South Korea is a modern, developed economy but in North Korea people still starve or can go for months without eating meat. And yet both countries were equally poor in 1950 and of course the two countries share the same language and cultural and historical background. What differs is their economic systems and the incentives at work.

Macroeconomists are especially interested in the incentives to produce new ideas. If the world never had any new ideas the standard of living eventually would stagnate. But in fact entrepreneurs innovate with iPhones, soil fertilizer, the Prius, and many other discoveries. Just about any device you use in daily life is based on a multitude of ideas and innovations, the lifeblood of economic growth. New ideas, of course, require incentives and that means an active scientific community and the freedom and incentive to put new ideas into action. Ideas also have peculiar properties. One apple feeds one man but one idea can

feed the world. Ideas, in other words, aren't used up when they are used and that has tremendous implications for understanding the benefits of trade, the future of economic growth, and many other topics.

Big Idea Eight: Economic Booms and Busts Cannot Be Avoided but Can Be Moderated

We have seen that growth matters and that the right institutions foster growth. But no economy grows at a constant pace. It advances and recedes, rises and falls, booms and busts. In a recession, wages fall and many people are thrown into miserable unemployment. Unfortunately, we cannot avoid all recessions. Booms and busts are part of the normal response of an economy to changing economic conditions. When the weather is bad in India, for example, crops fail and the economy grows more slowly or perhaps it grows not at all. The weather doesn't much affect the economy in the United States, but the U.S. economy is buffeted by other unavoidable shocks.

Although some booms and busts are part of the normal response of an economy to changing economic conditions, not all booms and busts are normal. The Great Depression (1929–1940) was not normal, but rather it was the most catastrophic economic event in the history of the United States. National output plummeted by 30 percent, unemployment rates exceeded 20 percent, and the stock market fell to less than a third of its original value. Almost overnight the United States went from confidence to desperation. The Great Depression, however, didn't have to happen. Most economists today believe that if the government, especially the U.S. Federal Reserve, had acted more quickly and more appropriately, the Great Depression would have been shorter and less deep. At the time, however, the tools at the government's disposal—monetary and fiscal policy—were not well understood.

Today, the tools of monetary and fiscal policy are much better understood. When used appropriately, these tools can reduce swings in unemployment and GDP. Unemployment insurance can also reduce some of the misery that accompanies a recession. The tools of monetary and fiscal policy, however, are not all powerful. At one time it was thought that these tools could end all recessions, but we know now that this is not the case. Furthermore, when used poorly, monetary and fiscal policy can make recessions worse and the economy more volatile.

A significant task of macroeconomic theory is to understand both the promise and the limits of monetary and fiscal policy in smoothing out the normal booms and busts of the macroeconomy.

Big Idea Nine: Prices Rise When the Government Prints Too Much Money

Yes, economic policy can be useful but sometimes policy goes awry, for instance when **inflation** gets out of hand. Inflation, one of the most common problems in macroeconomics, refers to an increase in the general level of prices. Inflation makes people feel poorer but, perhaps more important, rising and especially volatile prices make it harder for people to figure out the real values of goods, services, and investments. For these and other reasons, most people (and economists) dislike inflation.

Inflation is an increase in the general level of prices.

But where does inflation come from? The answer is simple: Inflation comes about when there is a sustained increase in the supply of money. When people have more money, they spend it, and without an increase in the supply of goods, prices must rise. As Economics Nobel Laureate Milton Friedman once wrote: "Inflation is always and everywhere a monetary phenomenon."

The United States, like other advanced economies, has a central bank called the Federal Reserve Bank. The Federal Reserve Bank has the power and the responsibility to regulate the supply of money in the American economy. This power can be used for good, such as when the Federal Reserve holds off or minimizes a recession. But the power also can be used for great harm if the Federal Reserve encourages too much growth in the supply of money. The result will be inflation and economic disruption.

In Zimbabwe, the government has been running the printing presses at full tilt for many years and by the end of 2007 prices were rising at an astonishing rate of 150,000 percent a year. The United States has never had a problem of this scope or anything close to it but inflation remains a perennial concern.

Amazingly, the inflation rate in Zimbabwe kept rising in 2008 and is now close to the highest inflation rate ever recorded with prices rising by *billions* of percent per month!

Inflation rates of 150,000 percent a year mean that this Zimbabwean $10 million note isn't enough to buy a hamburger and fries.

Big Idea Ten: Central Banking Is a Hard Job

The U.S. central bank, the Federal Reserve Bank ("the Fed"), is often called on to combat recessions. But this is not always easy to do. Typically, there is a lag—often of many months—between when the Fed makes a decision and when the effects of that decision on the economy are known. In the meantime, economic conditions have changed so you should think of the Fed as shooting at a moving target. No one can foresee the future perfectly and so the Fed's decisions are not always the right ones.

As mentioned above, too much money in the economy means that inflation will result. But not enough money in the economy is bad as well and can lead to a recession or a slowing of economic growth. These ideas are an important and extensive topic in macroeconomics, but the key problem is that a low or falling money supply forces people to cut their prices and wages and this adjustment doesn't always go smoothly.

The Fed is always trying to get it "just right," but some of the time it fails. Sometimes the failure is a mistake the Fed could have avoided, but other times it simply isn't possible to always make the right guess about where the world is headed. Thus, in some situations the Fed must accept a certain amount of either inflation or unemployment. Central banking relies on economic tools, but in the final analysis it is as much an art as a science.

Most economists think that the Fed does more good than harm. But if you are going to understand the Fed, you have to think of it as a highly fallible institution that faces a very difficult job.

The Biggest Idea of All: Economics Is Fun

When you put all these ideas and others together, we think that economics is both exciting and important. Economics teaches us how to make the world a better place. It's about the difference between wealth and poverty, work and

unemployment, happiness and squalor. Economics increases your understanding of the distant past, present events, and future possibilities.

As you will see, the basic principles of economics hold everywhere, whether it is in a rice paddy in Vietnam or a stock market in Sao Paulo, Brazil. No matter what the topic, the principles of economics apply to all countries, not just to your own. Moreover, in today's globalized world, events in China and India influence the economy in the United States, and vice versa. For this reason, you will find that our book is truly international and full of examples and applications from Algeria to Zimbabwe.

But economics is also linked to everyday life. Economics can help you think about your quest for a job, how to manage your personal finances and how to deal with debt, inflation, a recession, or a bursting stock market bubble. In short, economics is about understanding your world.

We are excited about economics and we hope that you will be too. Perhaps some of you will even become economics majors. If you are thinking about majoring, you might want to know that economics is the fastest-growing major over the last 10 years. That reflects the value of an economics degree and the world's recognition of that value. But if your passion lies elsewhere, that's okay too, a course in the principles of economics will take you a long way toward understanding your world. With a good course, a good professor, and a good textbook, you'll never look at the world the same way again. So just remember: *See the Invisible Hand. Understand Your World.*

□ CHAPTER REVIEW

KEY CONCEPTS

Incentives, p. 1

Opportunity cost, p. 4

Inflation, p. 8

FACTS AND TOOLS

1. A headline[5] in the *New York Times* read: "Study Finds Enrollment Is Up at Colleges Despite Recession." How would you rewrite this headline now that you understand the idea of opportunity cost?

2. When bad weather in India destroys the crop harvest, does this sound like a fall in the total "supply" of crops or a fall in people's "demand" for crops? Keep your answer in mind as you learn about economic booms and busts later on.

3. How much did national output fall during the Great Depression? According to the chapter, which government agency might have helped to avoid much of the Great Depression had it acted more quickly and appropriately?

4. The chapter lists four things that entrepreneurs save and invest in. Which of the four are actual objects, and which are more intangible, like concepts or ideas or plans? Feel free to use Wikipedia or some other reference source to get definitions of unfamiliar terms.

5. Who has a better incentive to work long hours in a laboratory researching new cures for diseases: a scientist who earns a percentage of the profits from any new medicine she might invent, or a scientist who will get a handshake and a thank you note from her boss if she invents a new medicine?

THINKING AND PROBLEM SOLVING

1. In recent years, Zimbabwe has had hyperinflation, with prices tripling (or more!) every month. According to what you learned in this chapter, what do you think the government can do to end this hyperinflation?

2. Some people worry that machines will take jobs away from people, making people permanently

unemployed. In the United States, only 150 years ago most people were farmers. Now, machines do almost all of the farm work and fewer than 2 percent of Americans are farmers, yet that 2 percent produces enough food to feed the entire country while still exporting food overseas.

a. What happened to all of those people who used to work on farms? Do you think most adult males in the U.S. are unemployed nowadays, now that the farm work is gone?

b. Some people say that it's okay for machines to take jobs, since we'll get jobs fixing the machines. Just from looking around, do you think that most working Americans are earning a living by fixing farm equipment? If not, what do you think most working people are doing instead? (We'll give a full answer later in this book.)

3. Let's connect Big Ideas Six and Nine: Do you think that people in poor countries are poor because they don't have enough money? In other words, could a country get richer by printing more pieces of paper called "money" and handing those out to its citizens?

4. Nobel Prize–winner Milton Friedman said that a bad central banker is like a "fool in the shower." In a shower, of course, when you turn the faucet right now, it won't show up in the showerhead for a few seconds. So if a "fool in the shower" is always making big changes in the temperature based on how the water feels *right now*, the water is likely to swing back and forth between too hot and too cold. How does this apply to central banking?

5. According to the United Nations, there were roughly 300 million humans on the planet a thousand years ago. Essentially all of them were poor by modern standards: They lacked antibiotics, almost all lacked indoor plumbing, and none traveled faster than a horse or a river could carry them. Today, between 1 and 3 billion humans are poor out of about 7 billion total humans. So, over the last thousand years, what has happened to the *fraction* of humans who are poor: Did it rise, fall, or stay about the same? What happened to the total *number* of people living in deep poverty: Rise, fall, or no change?

CHALLENGES

1. We claim that part of the reason the Great Depression was so destructive is because economists didn't understand how to use government policy very well in the 1930s. In your opinion, do you think that economists during the Great Depression would have agreed? In other words, if you had asked them why the Depression was so bad, would they have said, "Because the government ignored our wise advice," or would they have said, "Because we don't have any good ideas about how to fix this?" What does your answer tell you about the confidence of economists and other experts?

2. Some problems that economists try to solve are easy *as economic problems* but hard *as political problems*. Medical doctors face similar kinds of situations: Preventing most deaths from obesity or lung cancer is easy *as a medical problem* (eat less, exercise more, don't smoke) but hard *as a self-control problem*. With this in mind, how is ending hyperinflation like losing 100 pounds?

3. As Nobel prize winner and *New York Times* columnist Paul Krugman has noted, the field of economics is a lot like the field of medicine: They are fields where knowledge is limited (both are new as real scientific disciplines), and where many cures are quite painful ("opportunity cost"), but where regular people care deeply about the issues. What are some other ways that economics and medicine are alike?

4. Economics is sometimes called "the dismal science." Of the big ideas in this chapter, which sound "dismal"—like bad news?

2

Supply and Demand

The world runs on oil. Every day about 82 *million* barrels of "black gold" flow from the earth and the sea to fuel the world's demand. Changes in the demand for and supply of oil can plunge one economy into recession while igniting a boom in another. In capitals from Washington to Riyadh, politicians carefully monitor the price of oil and so do ordinary consumers. Gasoline is made from oil so when world events like war in the Middle East disrupt the oil supply, prices at the corner gas station rise. The oil market is arguably the single most important market in the world.

The most important tools in economics are supply, demand, and the idea of equilibrium. Even if you understand little else, you may rightly claim yourself economically literate if you understand these tools. Fail to understand these tools and you will understand little else. In this chapter, we use the supply and demand for oil to explain the concepts of supply and demand. In the next chapter, we use supply, demand, and the idea of equilibrium to explain how prices are determined. So pay attention: this chapter and the next one are important. Really important.

The Demand Curve for Oil

How much oil would be demanded if the price of oil were $5 per barrel? What quantity would be demanded if the price were $20? What quantity would be demanded if the price were $55? A demand curve answers these questions. A **demand curve** is a function that shows the quantity demanded at different prices.

In Figure 2.1 on the next page we show a hypothetical demand curve for oil and a table illustrating how a demand curve can be constructed from information on prices and quantities demanded. The demand curve tells us, for example, that at a price of $55 per barrel buyers are willing and able to buy

A **demand curve** is a function that shows the quantity demanded at different prices.

13

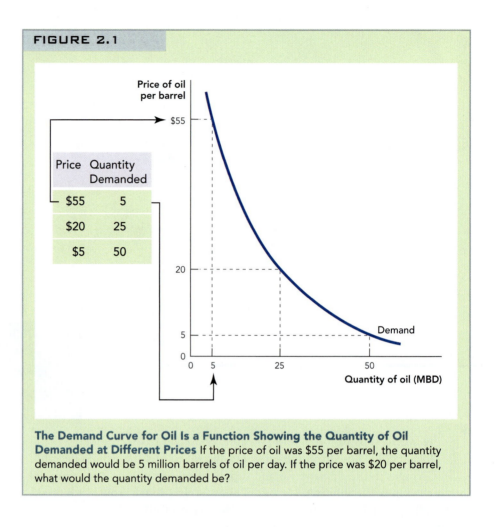

FIGURE 2.1

Price	Quantity Demanded
$55	5
$20	25
$5	50

The Demand Curve for Oil Is a Function Showing the Quantity of Oil Demanded at Different Prices If the price of oil was $55 per barrel, the quantity demanded would be 5 million barrels of oil per day. If the price was $20 per barrel, what would the quantity demanded be?

The **quantity demanded** is the quantity that buyers are willing and able to buy at a particular price.

5 million barrels of oil a day or, more simply, at a price of $55 the **quantity demanded** is 5 million barrels a day (MBD).

Demand curves can be read in two ways. Read "horizontally" we can see from Figure 2.2 that at a price of $20 per barrel demanders are willing and able to buy 25 million barrels of oil per day. Read "vertically" we can see that the maximum price that demanders are willing to pay for 25 million barrels of oil a day is $20 per barrel. Thus, demand curves tell us the quantity demanded at any price or the maximum willingness to pay (per unit) for any quantity. Some applications are easier to understand with one reading than with the other so you should be familiar with both.

Okay, a demand curve is a function that shows the quantity that demanders are willing to buy at different prices. But what does the demand curve *mean*? And why is the demand curve negatively sloped; that is, why is a greater quantity of oil demanded when the price is low?

Oil has many uses. A barrel of oil contains 42 gallons, and a little over half of that is used to produce gasoline (19.5 gallons) and jet fuel (4 gallons). The remaining 18.5 gallons are used for heating and energy generation and to make products such as lubricants, kerosene, asphalt, plastics, tires, and even rubber duckies (which are actually made not from rubber but from vinyl plastic).

Oil, however, is not equally valuable in all of its uses. Oil is more valuable for producing gasoline and jet fuel than it is for producing heating or rubber duckies. Oil is very valuable for transportation because in that use oil has few substitutes. There is

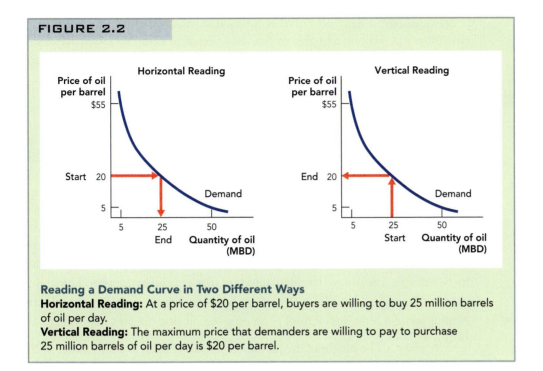

FIGURE 2.2

Reading a Demand Curve in Two Different Ways
Horizontal Reading: At a price of $20 per barrel, buyers are willing to buy 25 million barrels of oil per day.
Vertical Reading: The maximum price that demanders are willing to pay to purchase 25 million barrels of oil per day is $20 per barrel.

no reasonable substitute for oil as jet fuel, for example, and while some hybrids like the Prius are moderately successful, pure electric cars remain costly and inconvenient. There are more substitutes for oil in heating and energy generation. In these fields, oil competes directly or indirectly against natural gas, coal, and electricity. Within each of these fields are also more and less valuable uses. It's more valuable, for example, to raise the temperature in your house on a winter's day from 40 degrees to 65 degrees than it is to raise the temperature from 65 degrees to 70 degrees. Vinyl has high value as wire wrapping because it is fire retardant, but we can probably substitute wooden toy boats for rubber duckies.

The fact that oil is not equally valuable in all of its uses explains why the demand curve for oil has a negative slope. When the price of oil is high, consumers will choose to use oil *only* in its most valuable uses (e.g., gasoline and jet fuel). As the price of oil falls, consumers will choose to also use oil in its less and less valued uses (heating and rubber duckies). Thus, a demand curve summarizes how millions of consumers choose to use oil given their preferences and the possibilities for substitution. Figure 2.3 illustrates these ideas with a demand curve for oil.

FIGURE 2.3

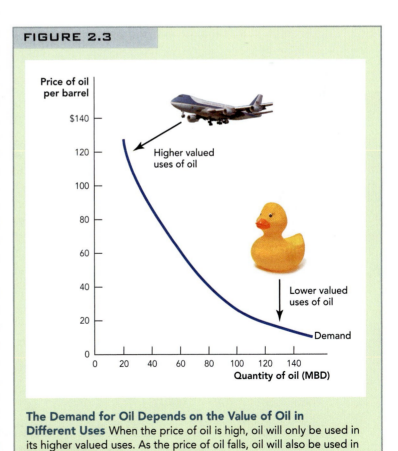

The Demand for Oil Depends on the Value of Oil in Different Uses When the price of oil is high, oil will only be used in its higher valued uses. As the price of oil falls, oil will also be used in lower valued uses.

(Top photo: EuroStyle Graphics/Alamy)

(Bottom: Lew Robertson/Corbis)

In summary, a demand curve is a function that shows the quantity that demanders are willing and able to buy at different prices. The lower the price the greater the quantity demanded—this is often called the "law of demand."

Consumer Surplus

Consumer surplus is the consumer's gain from exchange, or the difference between the maximum price a consumer is willing to pay for a certain quantity and the market price.

Total consumer surplus is measured by the area beneath the demand curve and above the price.

If a consumer, say the President of the United States, is willing to pay $80 per barrel to fuel his jet plane but the price of oil is only $20 per barrel then the President earns a consumer surplus of $60 per barrel. If Joe is willing to pay $25 and the price of oil is $20 per barrel, then Joe earns a consumer surplus of $5 per barrel. **Consumer surplus** is the consumer's gain from exchange. Adding up consumer surplus for each consumer and for each unit, we can find **total consumer surplus.** On a graph, *total consumer surplus is the shaded area beneath the demand curve and above the price* (see Figure 2.4).

It's often convenient to approximate demand and supply curves with straight lines—this makes it easy to calculate areas like consumer surplus. The right panel of Figure 2.4 simplifies the left panel. Now we can calculate consumer surplus using a little high school geometry. Recall that the area of a triangle is $\frac{\text{height} \times \text{base}}{2}$. The height of the consumer surplus triangle is $60 = $80 - 20 and the base is 90 million barrels so consumer surplus equals $2,700 million ($60 \times 90 \text{ million}/2$).

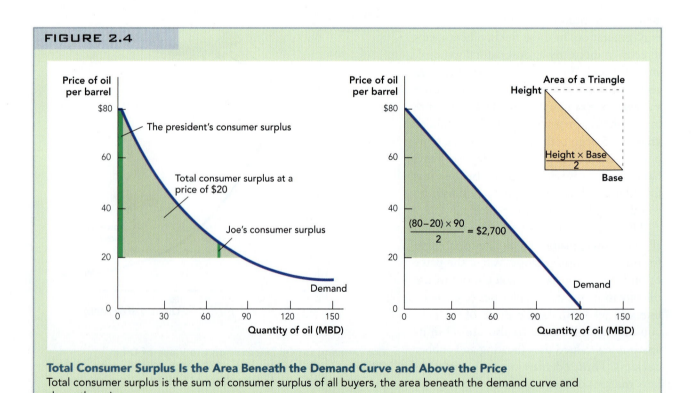

FIGURE 2.4

Total Consumer Surplus Is the Area Beneath the Demand Curve and Above the Price
Total consumer surplus is the sum of consumer surplus of all buyers, the area beneath the demand curve and above the price.
In the right panel we show that consumer surplus is easy to calculate with a linear demand curve.

What Shifts the Demand Curve?

The demand curve for oil tells us the quantity of oil that people are willing to buy at a given price. Assume for example that at a price of $25 per barrel, the world demand for oil is 70 million barrels per day. An increase in demand means that at a price of $25, the quantity demanded increases to say 80 million barrels per day. Or, equivalently, it means that the maximum willingness to pay for 70 million barrels increases to say $50 per barrel. The left panel of Figure 2.5 shows an increase in demand. *An increase in demand shifts the demand curve outward, up and to the right.*

The right panel of Figure 2.5 shows a decrease in demand. *A decrease in demand shifts the demand curve inward, down, and to the left.*

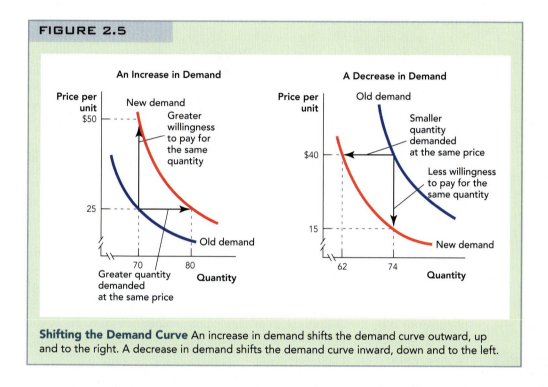

FIGURE 2.5

Shifting the Demand Curve An increase in demand shifts the demand curve outward, up and to the right. A decrease in demand shifts the demand curve inward, down and to the left.

What kinds of things will increase or decrease demand? Unfortunately for economics students, a lot of things! Here is a list of some important demand shifters:

Important Demand Shifters

> Income
> Population
> Price of substitutes
> Price of complements
> Expectations
> Tastes

If you must, memorize the list. But keep in mind the question, "What would make people willing to buy a greater quantity at the same price?" Or equivalently, "What would make people willing to pay more for the same quantity?" With these questions in mind, you should always be able to come up with a pretty good list on your own.

Here are some examples of demand shifters in action.

Income When people get richer, they buy more stuff. In the United States, people buy bigger cars when their income increases and big cars increase the demand for oil. When income increases in China or India, many people buy their first car and that too increases the demand for oil. Thus, an increase in income will increase the demand for oil exactly as shown in the left panel of Figure 2.5.

When an *increase* in income *increases* the demand for a good, we say the good is a **normal good**. Most goods are normal; for example, cars, electronics, and restaurant meals are normal goods. Can you think of some goods for which an increase in income will *decrease* the demand? When we were young economics students, we didn't have a lot of money to go to expensive restaurants. For 50 cents and some boiling water, however, we could get a nice bowl of instant ramen noodles. Ah, good times. When our income increased, however, our demand for ramen noodles decreased—we don't buy ramen noodles anymore! A good like ramen noodles for which an *increase* in income *decreases* the demand is called an **inferior good**. What goods are you consuming now that you probably wouldn't consume if you were rich? Economic growth is rapidly increasing the incomes of millions of poor people in China and India. What goods do poor people consume in these countries today that they will consume less of 20 years from now?

Population More people, more demand. That's simple enough. Things get more interesting when some subpopulations increase more than others. The United States, for example, is aging. Today the 65-year-old and older crowd makes up about 13 percent of the population. By 2030, 19.4 percent of the population will be 65 years or older. In fact, demographers estimate that by 2030 18.2 million people in the United States will be over 85 years of age![1] What sorts of goods and services will increase in demand with this increase in population? Which will decrease in demand? Entrepreneurs want to know the answers to these questions because big profits will flow to those who can anticipate new and expanded markets.

Price of Substitutes Natural gas is a substitute for oil in some uses such as heating. Suppose that the price of natural gas goes down. What will happen to the quantity of oil demanded? When the price of natural gas goes down, some people will switch from oil furnaces to natural gas, so the quantity of oil demanded will decrease—the demand curve shifts down and to the left. Figure 2.6 illustrates.

More generally, a decrease in the price of a **substitute** will decrease demand for the other good. A decrease in the price of Pepsi, for example, will decrease the demand for Coca-Cola. A decrease in the price of rental apartments will reduce the demand for condominiums. Naturally, an increase in the price of a substitute will increase demand for the other substituted good.

Price of Complements **Complements** are things that go well together: French fries and ketchup, sugar and tea, DVD movies and DVD players. More technically, good A is a complement to good B if greater consumption of A encourages greater consumption of B. Ground beef and hamburger buns are complements. Suppose the price of beef goes down. What happens to the demand for hamburger buns? If the price of beef goes down, people buy more ground beef and they also increase their demand for hamburger buns, that is, the demand curve

---

A **normal good** is a good for which demand increases when income increases.

An **inferior good** is a good for which demand decreases when income increases.

Demographics and Demand
The number of old people in the United States is increasing. How will this increase in the elderly population shift the demand curve for different goods?

If two goods are **substitutes** a decrease in the price of one good leads to a decrease in demand for the other good.

If two goods are **complements** a decrease in the price of one good leads to an increase in the demand for the other good.

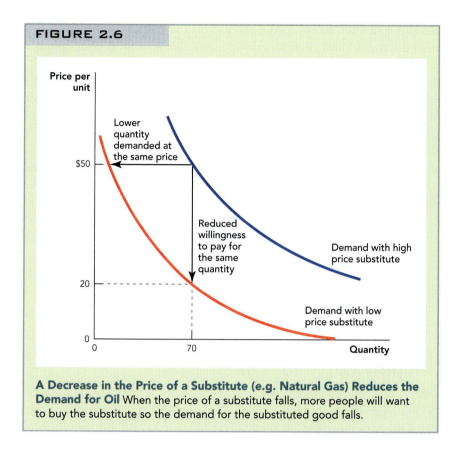

FIGURE 2.6

A Decrease in the Price of a Substitute (e.g. Natural Gas) Reduces the Demand for Oil When the price of a substitute falls, more people will want to buy the substitute so the demand for the substituted good falls.

for hamburger buns shifts up and to the right. A supermarket having a sale on ground beef, for example, will also want to stock up on hamburger buns.

A decrease in the price of a complement increases the demand for the complementary good. An increase in the price of a complement decreases the demand for the complementary good. It sounds complicated, so just remember that ground beef and hamburger buns are complements and you should be able to work out the relationship.

Expectations In July 2007, a construction worker in the oil fields of Southern Nigeria was kidnapped. On hearing the news, oil prices around the world jumped to record high levels.[2] Was a single construction worker so critical to the world supply of oil? No. What spooked the world's oil markets was the fear that the kidnapping was the beginning of large-scale disruption in the Niger Delta, Nigeria's main oil producing region and the base for many anti-government rebels. Fear of future disruptions increased the demand for oil as businesses and governments worked to increase their emergency stockpiles. In other words, *the expectation of a reduction in the future oil supply increased the demand for oil today.*

You have probably responded to expectations about future events in a similar way. When the weather forecaster predicts a big storm, many people rush to the stores to stock up on storm supplies. In the week before Hurricane Katrina hit New Orleans, for example, sales of flashlights increased by 700 percent and battery sales increased by 250 percent compared to the week before.[3]

Expectations are powerful—they can be as powerful in affecting demand (and supply) as events themselves.

Tastes In the 1990s, doctors warned that too much fat could lead to heart attacks and demand for beef decreased. The 2001 publication of *Dr. Atkins' New*

Diet Revolution, a book promising weight loss on a high-protein, low-carb diet, increased the demand for beef. Steakhouses like Outback Steakhouse and the Brazilian-inspired Fogo De Chao started to appear everywhere.

Michael Jordan's popularity and his six NBA championships with the Chicago Bulls created a huge increase in demand for Nike's innovative Air Jordans. Demand for the shoes was so high that some young boys became victims of "shoe jackings." Changes in tastes caused by fads, fashions, and advertising can all increase or decrease demand.

Can tastes change something like the demand for oil? Sure. The environmental movement has made people more aware of global climate change and how the consumption of oil adds carbon dioxide to the atmosphere. As a result, the demand for hybrid cars has increased, more people are recycling things like plastic bags, and nuclear power is once again being discussed as an alternative source of energy. All of these changes can be understood as a change in tastes or preferences.

The bottom line is that while many different factors can shape market demand, most of these factors should make intuitive sense. After all, you are, on a daily basis, part of market demand.

The Supply Curve for Oil

How much oil would oil producers supply to the world market if the price of oil were $5 per barrel? What quantity would be supplied if the price were $20? What quantity if the price were $55? A supply curve for oil answers these questions.

The **supply curve** for oil is a function showing the quantity of oil that suppliers would be willing and able to sell at different prices or more simply the supply curve shows the **quantity supplied** at different prices. Figure 2.7 shows a hypothetical supply curve for oil. The price is on the vertical axis and the quantity of oil is on the horizontal axis. The table beside the graph shows how a supply curve can be constructed from a table of prices and quantities supplied.

The supply curve tells us, for example, that at a price of $20 the quantity supplied is 30 million barrels of oil a day.

As with demand curves, supply curves can be read in two ways. Read "horizontally" Figure 2.8 shows that at a price of $20 per barrel suppliers are willing to sell 30 million barrels of oil per day. Read "vertically" the supply curve tells us that to produce 30 million barrels of oil a day suppliers must be paid at least $20 per barrel. Thus, the supply curve tells us the maximum quantity that suppliers will supply at different prices or the minimum price at which suppliers will sell different quantities. The two ways of reading a supply curve are equivalent, but some applications are easier to understand with one reading than with the other so you should be familiar with both.

Our hypothetical supply curve is not realistic because we just made up the numbers. But now that we know the technical meaning of a supply curve—*a function that shows the quantity that suppliers would be willing to sell at different prices*—we can easily explain its economic meaning.

Saudi Arabia, the world's largest oil producer, produces about 10 million barrels of oil per day. Surprisingly, the United States is not far behind, producing nearly 9 million barrels per day. But there is one big difference between Saudi oil and U.S. oil: U.S. oil costs much more to produce. The United States has been producing major quantities of oil since early 1901 when, after drilling to

The **supply curve** is a function that shows the quantity supplied at different prices.

The **quantity supplied** is the amount of a good that sellers are willing and able to sell at a particular price.

FIGURE 2.7

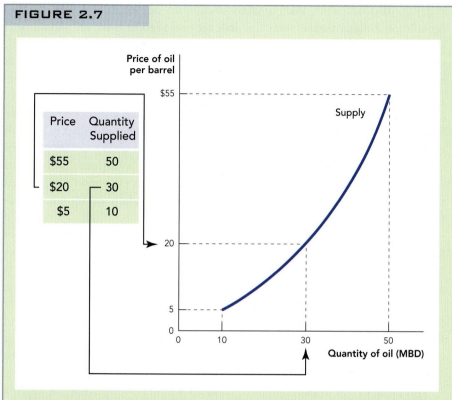

Price	Quantity Supplied
$55	50
$20	30
$5	10

The Supply Curve for Oil Is a Function Showing the Quantity of Oil Supplied at Different Prices If the price of oil was $20 per barrel, the quantity of oil supplied would be 30 million barrels of oil per day. How much oil would suppliers be willing and able to sell at $55?

FIGURE 2.8

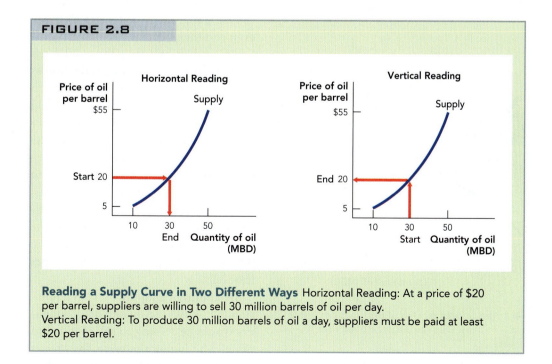

Reading a Supply Curve in Two Different Ways Horizontal Reading: At a price of $20 per barrel, suppliers are willing to sell 30 million barrels of oil per day.
Vertical Reading: To produce 30 million barrels of oil a day, suppliers must be paid at least $20 per barrel.

a depth of 1,020 feet, mud started to bubble out of an oil well dug in Spindletop, Texas. Minutes later the drill bit exploded into the air and a fountain of oil leapt 150 feet into the sky. It took nine days to cap the well, and in the process a million barrels of oil were spilt. No one had ever seen so much oil. Within months the price of oil dropped from $2 per barrel to just 3 cents per barrel.[4]

It's safe to say that the United States will never see another gusher like Spindletop. Today the typical new well in the United States is drilled to a depth of more than two miles. Instead of gushing, most of the wells must be pumped or flooded with water in order to push the oil to the surface.[5] All of this makes oil production in the United States much more expensive than it used to be and much more expensive than in Saudi Arabia, where oil is more plentiful than anywhere else in the world.

In Saudi Arabia, lifting a barrel of oil to the surface costs about $2. Costs in Iran and Iraq are only slightly higher. Nigerian and Russian oil can be extracted at a cost of around $5 and $7 per barrel, respectively. Alaskan oil costs around $10 to extract. Oil from Britain's North Sea costs about $12 to extract. There is more oil in Canada's tar sands than in all of Iran, but it costs about $22.50 per barrel to get the oil out of the sand.[6] In the continental United States, one of the oldest and most developed oil regions in the world, lifting costs are about $27.50. At a price of $40 per barrel, it becomes profitable to "sweat" oil out of Oklahoma oil shale.

Putting all of this together, we can construct a simple supply curve for oil. At a price of $2 per barrel, the only oil that would be profitable to produce would be oil from the lowest cost wells in places like Saudi Arabia. As the price of oil rises, oil from Iran and Iraq become profitable. When the price reaches $5, Nigerian and then Russian producers begin to just break even. As the price rises yet further toward $10, Alaskan oil starts to break even and then become profitable. North Sea, Canadian, and then Texan oil fields come online and increase production as the price rises further. At higher prices, it becomes profitable to extract oil using even more exotic technologies or deeper wells in more inhospitable parts of the world. Figure 2.9 illustrates.

What's important to understand about Figure 2.9 is that as the price of oil rises, it becomes profitable to produce oil using methods and from regions of the world with higher costs of production. The higher the price of oil, the deeper the wells.

In summary, a supply curve is a function that shows the quantity that suppliers would be willing to sell at different prices. The higher the price, the greater the quantity supplied—this is often called the "law of supply."

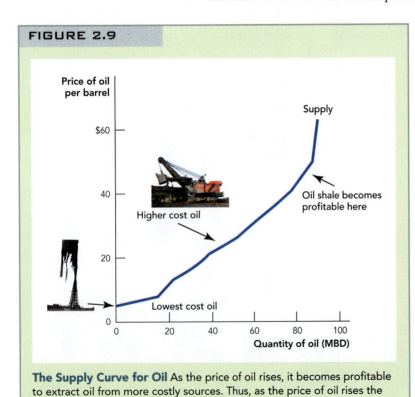

FIGURE 2.9

Price of oil per barrel

Supply

$60

40

Oil shale becomes profitable here

Higher cost oil

20

0

Lowest cost oil

0   20   40   60   80   100

Quantity of oil (MBD)

The Supply Curve for Oil As the price of oil rises, it becomes profitable to extract oil from more costly sources. Thus, as the price of oil rises the quantity of oil supplied increases.

(Top photo: Dan Lamont/Corbis)

(Bottom: Bettmann/Corbis)

Producer Surplus

Figure 2.9 suggests two other concepts of importance. If the price of oil is $40 per barrel and Saudi Arabia can produce oil at $2 per barrel, then we say that Saudi Arabia earns a **producer surplus** of $38 per barrel. Similarly, if the price of oil is $40 per barrel and Nigeria can produce at $5 a barrel, Nigeria earns a producer surplus of $35 per barrel. Adding the producer surplus for each producer for each unit, we can find total producer surplus. Fortunately, this is easy to do on a diagram. *Total producer surplus is the shaded area above the supply curve and below the price* (see Figure 2.10).

Producer surplus is the producer's gain from exchange, or the difference between the market price and the minimum price at which a producer would be willing to sell a particular quantity.

Total producer surplus is measured by the area above the supply curve and below the price.

What Shifts the Supply Curve?

The second important concept suggested by Figure 2.9 is the connection between the supply curve and costs. What happens to the supply curve when the cost of producing oil falls? Suppose, for example, that a technological innovation in oil drilling such as sidewise drilling allows more oil to be produced at the same cost. What happens to the supply curve? The supply curve tells us how much suppliers are willing to sell at a particular price. The new technology makes some oil fields profitable that were previously unprofitable, so *at any price* suppliers are now willing to supply a greater quantity. Equivalently, the new technology lowers costs, so suppliers will be willing to sell any given quantity at a lower price. Either way economists say that a decrease in costs increases supply. In terms of the diagram, *a decrease in costs mean that the supply curve shifts down and to the right.* The left panel of Figure 2.11 on the next page illustrates. Of course, *higher costs mean that the supply curve shifts in the opposite direction, up and to the left* as illustrated in the right panel of Figure 2.11.

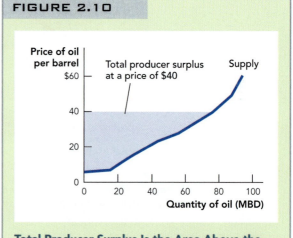

FIGURE 2.10

Total Producer Surplus Is the Area Above the Supply Curve and Below the Price Total producer surplus is the sum of the producer surplus of each seller, the area above the supply curve and below the price.

Once you know that a decrease in costs shifts the supply curve down and to the right and an increase in costs shifts the supply curve up and to the left, then you really know everything there is to know about supply shifts. It can take a little practice, however, to identify the many factors that can change costs. Here are some important supply shifters:

Important Supply Shifters

> Technological innovations and changes in the price of inputs

> Taxes and subsidies

> Expectations

> Entry or exit of producers

> Changes in opportunity costs

It can also help in analyzing supply shifters to know that sometimes it's easier to think of cost changes as shifting the supply curve right or left, and sometimes it's a little easier to think of cost changes as shifting the supply curve up or down. These two methods of thinking about supply shifts are equivalent and correspond to the two methods of reading a supply curve, the horizontal and

FIGURE 2.11

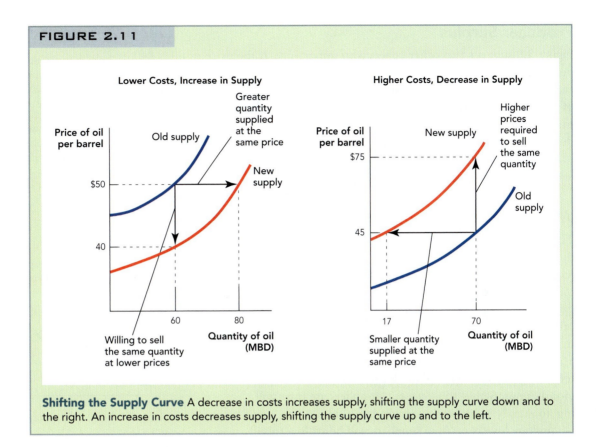

Shifting the Supply Curve A decrease in costs increases supply, shifting the supply curve down and to the right. An increase in costs decreases supply, shifting the supply curve up and to the left.

vertical readings respectively. We will give examples of each method as we examine some cost shifters in action.

Technological Innovations and Changes in the Price of Inputs We have already given an example of how improvements in technology can reduce costs, thus increasing supply. A reduction in input prices also reduces costs and thus has a similar effect. A fall in the wages of oil rig workers, for example, will reduce the cost of producing oil, shifting the supply curve down and to the right as in the left panel of Figure 2.11. Alternatively, an increase in the wages of oil rig workers will increase the cost of producing oil, shifting the supply curve up and to the left as in the right panel of Figure 2.11.

Taxes and Subsidies We can get some practice using up or down shifts to analyze a cost change by examining the effect of a $10 oil tax on the supply curve for oil. As far as firms are concerned, a tax on output is the same as an increase in costs. If the government taxes oil producers $10 per barrel, this is exactly the same to producers as an increase in their costs of production of $10 per barrel.

In Figure 2.12, notice that before the tax, firms require $40 per barrel to sell 60 million barrels of oil per day (point *a*). How much will firms require to sell the same quantity of oil when there is a tax of $10 per barrel? Correct, $50. What firms care about is the take-home price. If firms require $40 per barrel to sell 60 million barrels of oil, that's what they require regardless of the tax. When the government takes $10 per barrel, firms must charge $50 to keep their take-home price at $40. Thus, in Figure 2.12, notice that the $10 tax shifts the supply curve up by exactly $10 at *every point* along the curve.

FIGURE 2.12

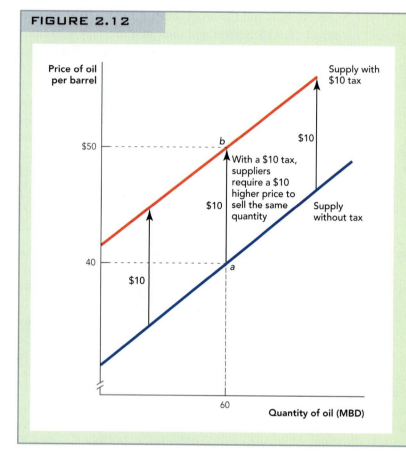

A Tax on Industry Output Shifts the Supply Curve Up by the Amount of the Tax When suppliers pay no tax, they are willing to supply 60 MBD of oil for a price of $40 per barrel. If they must pay a tax of $10 per barrel, they will be willing to supply 60 MBD for $10 more, or $50 a barrel. Thus a tax shifts the supply curve up by the amount of the tax.

It's important to avoid one possible confusion. All we have said so far is that a $10 tax shifts the supply curve for oil up by $10. We haven't said anything about the effect of a tax on the *price* of oil—that's because we have not yet analyzed how market prices are formed. We are saving that topic for Chapter 3.

How does a subsidy, a tax-benefit, or write-off shift the supply curve? We will save that analysis for the end of chapter problems but here's a hint: a subsidy is the same as a negative or "reverse" tax.

Expectations Suppliers who expect that prices will increase in the future have an incentive to sell less today so that they can store goods for future sale. Thus, the expectation of a future price increase shifts today's supply curve to the left as illustrated in Figure 2.13. The shifting of supply in response to price expectations is the essence of *speculation*, the attempt to profit from future price changes.

Entry or Exit of Producers When the United States signed the North American Free Trade Agreement (NAFTA), reducing barriers to trade among the United

FIGURE 2.13

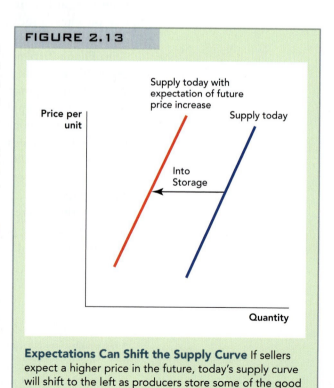

Expectations Can Shift the Supply Curve If sellers expect a higher price in the future, today's supply curve will shift to the left as producers store some of the good for future sale.

FIGURE 2.14

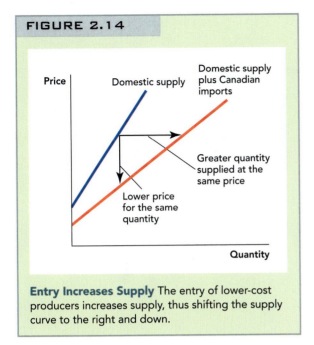

Entry Increases Supply The entry of lower-cost producers increases supply, thus shifting the supply curve to the right and down.

States, Mexico, and Canada, Canadian producers of lumber entered the U.S. market and increased the supply of lumber. We can most easily think about this as a shift to the right of the supply curve.

In Figure 2.14 the domestic supply curve is the supply curve for lumber before NAFTA. The curve labeled domestic supply plus Canadian imports is the supply curve for lumber after NAFTA allowed Canadian firms to sell in the United States with fewer restrictions. The entry of more firms meant that at any price a greater quantity of lumber was available, that is, the supply curve shifted to the right.*

In a later chapter, we discuss the effects of foreign trade at greater length.

Changes in Opportunity Costs The last important supply shifter, changes in opportunity costs, is the trickiest to understand. Recall from Chapter 1 that when the unemployment rates increase more people tend to go to college. If you can't get a job, you aren't giving up many good opportunities by going to college. Thus, when the unemployment rate increases, the (opportunity) cost of college falls and so more people attend college. Notice that to understand how people behave, you must understand their opportunity costs.

Now suppose that a farmer is currently growing soybeans but that he could also use his land to grow wheat. If the price of *wheat* increases, then the farmer's opportunity cost of growing soybeans increases and the farmer will want to shift land from soybean production into the more profitable alternative of wheat production. As land is taken out of soybean production, the supply curve for soybeans shifts up and to the left.

In Figure 2.15, notice that before the increase in the price of wheat, farmers would be willing to supply 2,800 million bushels of soybeans at a price of $5 per bushel (point *a*). But when the price of wheat increases, farmers are only willing to supply 2,000 million bushels of soybeans at a price of $5 per bushel because an alternative use of the land (growing wheat) is now more valuable. Equivalently, before the increase in the price of wheat, farmers were willing to sell 2,800 million bushels of soybeans for $5 per bushel but after their opportunity costs increase farmers require $7 per bushel to sell the same quantity (point *c*).

Similarly, a decrease in opportunity costs shifts the supply curve down and to the right. If the price of wheat falls, for example, the opportunity cost of growing soybeans falls and the supply curve for soybeans will shift down and

---

* It is equally correct to think of new entrants as shifting the supply curve down. Remember, it's ultimately costs that shift supply and what increases supply is entry of *lower-cost* producers. Industry costs fell when Canadian producers entered the market because many Canadian producers had lower costs than some U.S. producers. As lower-cost Canadian producers entered the industry, higher-cost U.S. producers exited the industry and industry costs decreased, thus shifting the supply curve down.

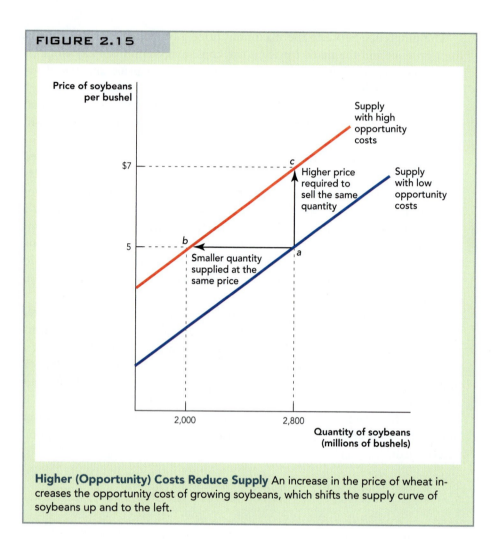

FIGURE 2.15

Higher (Opportunity) Costs Reduce Supply An increase in the price of wheat increases the opportunity cost of growing soybeans, which shifts the supply curve of soybeans up and to the left.

to the right. It's just another example of a running theme throughout this chapter, namely that both supply and demand respond to incentives.

□ Takeaway

In this chapter we have presented the fundamentals of the demand curve and the supply curve. The next chapter and much of the rest of this book build on these fundamentals. We thus give you fair warning. If you do not understand this chapter and the next, you will be lost!

Key points to know are that a demand curve is a function that shows the quantity demanded at different prices. In other words, a demand curve shows how customers respond to higher prices by buying less and to lower prices by buying more. Similarly, a supply curve is a function that shows the quantity supplied at different prices. In other words, a supply curve shows how producers respond to higher prices by producing more and to lower prices by producing less.

CHECK YOURSELF

> Technological innovations in chip making have driven down the costs of producing computers. What happens to the supply curve for computers? Why?

> The U.S. government subsidizes making ethanol as a fuel made from corn. What effect does the subsidy have on the supply curve for ethanol?

The difference between the maximum price a consumer is willing to pay for a product and the market price is the consumer's gain from exchange or consumer surplus. The difference between the market price and the minimum price at which a producer is willing to sell a product is the producer's gain from exchange or producer surplus. You should be able to identify total consumer and producer surplus on a diagram, again as we have outlined in the chapter.

When it comes to what shifts the supply and demand curves, we have listed some factors in this chapter. Yes, you should know these lists but more fundamentally you should know that an increase in demand *means* that buyers want a greater quantity at the same price or, equivalently, they are willing to pay a higher price for the same quantity. Thus, anything that causes buyers to want more at the same price or be willing to pay more for the same quantity increases demand. In a pinch, just think about some of the factors that would cause you to want more of a good at the same price or that would make you willing to pay more for the same quantity.

Similarly, an increase in supply *means* that sellers are willing to sell a greater quantity at the same price or, equivalently, they are willing to sell a given quantity at a lower price. Again, what would make you willing to sell more of a good for the same price or sell the same quantity for a lower price? (Here's a hint—you might be willing to do this if your costs had fallen.) Supply and demand curves are not just abstract constructs, they also shape your life.

In the next chapter, we will use supply curves and demand curves to answer one of the most crucial questions in economics: How is the price of a good determined?

▫ CHAPTER REVIEW

KEY CONCEPTS

Demand curve, p. 13

Quantity demanded, p. 14

Consumer surplus, p. 16

Total consumer surplus, p. 16

Normal good, p. 18

Inferior good, p. 18

Substitutes, p. 18

Complements, p. 18

Supply curve, p. 20

Quantity supplied, p. 20

Producer surplus, p. 23

Total producer surplus, p. 23

FACTS AND TOOLS

1. When the price of a good increases the quantity demanded _____. When the price of a good decreases the quantity demanded _____.

2. When will people search harder for substitutes for oil: When the price of oil is high or when the price of oil is low?

3. Your roommate just bought an iPod for $200. She would have been willing to pay $500 for a machine that could store and replay that much music. How much consumer surplus does your roommate enjoy from the iPod?

4. What are three things that you'll buy less of once you graduate from college and get a good job? What kinds of goods are these called?

5. When the price of Apple computers goes down, what probably happens to the demand for Windows-based computers?

6. **a.** When the price of olive oil goes up, what probably happens to the demand for corn oil?

   b. When the price of petroleum goes up, what probably happens to the demand for natural gas? To the demand for coal? To the demand for solar power?

7. **a.** If everyone thinks that the price of tomatoes will go up next week, what is likely to happen to demand for tomatoes today?

   b. If everyone thinks that the price of gasoline will go up next week, what is likely to happen to the demand for gasoline today? (Note: Is this change in demand caused by consumers or by gas station owners?)

8. Along a supply curve, if the price of oil falls, what will happen to the quantity of oil supplied? Why?

9. If the price of cars falls, are carmakers likely to make more cars or fewer cars, according to the supply curve? (Notice that the "person on the street" often thinks the opposite is true!)

10. When is a pharmaceutical business more likely to hire highly educated, cutting-edge workers and use new, experimental research methods: When the business expects the price of its new drug to be low or when it expects the price to be high?

11. Imagine that a technological innovation reduces the costs of producing high-quality steel. What happens to the supply curve for steel?

12. When oil companies expect the price of oil to be higher next year, what happens to the supply of oil today?

13. Do taxes usually increase the supply of a good or reduce the supply?

THINKING AND PROBLEM SOLVING

1. Consider the following supply curve for oil. Note that MBD stands for "millions of barrels per day," the usual way people talk about the supply of oil:

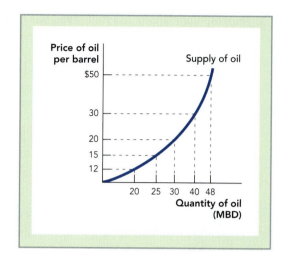

a. Based on the above supply curve, fill in the table below:

Price	Quantity Supplied
$12	
	40

b. If the price for a barrel of oil was $15, how much oil would oil suppliers be willing to supply?

c. What is the lowest price at which suppliers of oil would be willing to supply 20 MBD?

2. From the following table of prices per 100 pencils and quantities supplied (in hundreds of pencils), draw the supply curve for pencils:

Price	Quantity Supplied
$5	20
$15	40
$25	50
$35	55

3. Suppose LightBright and Bulbs4You were the only two suppliers of 60-watt lightbulbs in Springfield. Draw the supply curve for the 60-watt lightbulb industry in Springfield from the following tables for the two companies. To create this "light bulb industry supply curve," note that you'll add up the *total* number of bulbs that the industry will supply at a price of $1 (15 bulbs), and then do the same for the prices of $5, $7, and $10:

Price	Bulbs Supplied by LightBright	Bulbs Supplied by Bulbs4You
$1	10	5
$5	15	7
$7	25	15
$10	35	20

4. Using the following diagram, identify and calculate total producer surplus if the price of oil is $50 per barrel. Recall that for a triangle, Area = (1/2) × Base × Height. (You never thought you'd use that equation unless you became an engineer, did you?)

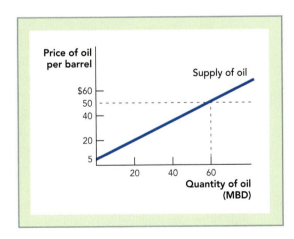

5. In Sucrosia, the supply curve for sugar is as follows:

Price (per 100 pound bag)	Quantity
$30	10,000
$50	15,000
$70	20,000

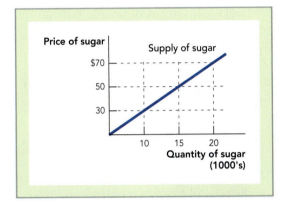

Under pressure from nutrition activists, the government decides to tax sugar producers with a $5 tax per 100 pound bag. Using the figure above, draw the new supply curve. After the tax is enacted, what price will bring forth quantities of 10,000? 15,000? 20,000? Give your answers in the table below.

Price (per 100 pound bag)	Quantity
	10,000
	15,000
	20,000

6. Consider the farmers talked about in the chapter who have land that is suitable for growing both wheat and soybeans. Suppose all farmers are currently farming wheat but the price of soybeans rises dramatically.

   a. Does the opportunity cost of producing wheat rise or fall?

b. Does this shift the supply curve for wheat (as in one of the panels of Figure 2.11), or is it a movement along a fixed supply curve?

What direction is this shift or movement? Illustrate your answer on the figure below:

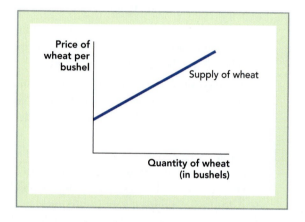

7. Consider the following demand curve for oil:

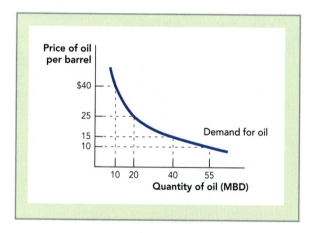

a. Using the above demand curve, fill in the following table:

Price	Quantity Demanded
	55
$25	

b. If the price was $10, how much oil would be demanded?

c. What is the maximum price (per barrel) demanders will pay for 20 million barrels of oil?

8. From the following chart, draw the demand curve for pencils (in hundreds):

Price	Quantity Demanded (in hundreds)
$5	60
$15	45
$25	35
$35	20

9. If the price of glass dramatically increases, what are we likely to see a lot less of: Glass windows or glass bottles? Why?

10. Let's think about the demand for plasma TVs.

a. If the price for a 50" plasma TV is $2,010, and Newhart would be willing to pay $3,000, what is Newhart's consumer surplus?

b. Consider the figure below for the total demand for plasma TVs. At $2,010 per TV, 1,200 TVs were demanded, what would be the total consumer surplus? Calculate the total and identify it on the diagram.

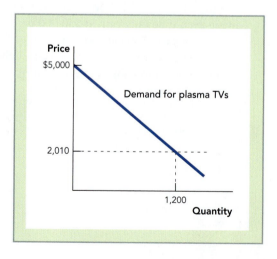

c. Where is Newhart in the figure above?

11. If income increases and the demand for good X shifts as shown below, then is good X a normal or inferior good? Give an example of a good like good X.

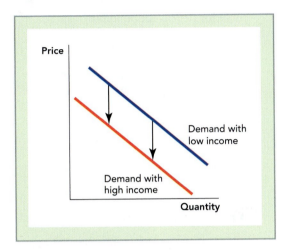

12. Assume that butter and margarine are substitutes. What will happen to the demand curve for butter if the price of margarine increases? Why?

13. Cars and gasoline are complements. What will happen to the demand curve for gasoline if the price of cars decreases? Why? (Hint: What happens to the quantity demanded of cars?)

CHALLENGES

1. Michael is an economist. He loves being an economist so much that he would do it for a living even if he only earned $30,000 per year. Instead, he earns $80,000 per year. (Note: This is the average salary of new economists with a Ph.D. degree.) How much producer surplus does Michael enjoy?

2. The economist Bryan Caplan recently found a pair of $10 arch supports that saved him from the pain of major foot surgery. As he stated on his blog (econlog.econlib.org), he would have been willing to pay $100,000 to fix his foot problem, but instead he only paid a few dollars.

    a. How much consumer surplus did Bryan enjoy from this purchase?

    b. If the sales tax was 5 percent on this product, how much revenue did the government raise when Bryan bought his arch supports?

    c. If the government could have taxed Bryan based on his *willingness to pay* rather than on how much he *actually* paid, how much sales tax would Bryan have had to pay?

3. For most young people, working full time and going to school are substitutes: You tend to do one or the other. When it's tough to find a job, does that raise the opportunity cost of going to college or does it lower it? When it's tough to find a job, does the demand for college rise or fall?

4. What should happen to the "demand for speed" (measured by the average speed on highways) once airbags are included on cars?

5. The industrial areas in Northeast Washington, D.C., were relatively dangerous in the 1980s. Over the last two decades, the area has become a safer place to work (although there are still seven times more violent crimes per person in these areas compared to another D.C. neighborhood, Georgetown). When an area becomes a safer place to work, what probably happens to the "supply of labor" in that area?

3

Equilibrium: How Supply and Demand Determine Prices

I n Chapter 2, we introduced the supply curve and the demand curve. In that chapter, we wrote things like "if the price is $20 per barrel, the quantity supplied will be 50 million barrels per day (MBD)" and "if the price is $50, the quantity demanded will be 120 MBD." But how is price determined?

We are now ready for the big event: Equilibrium. Figure 3.1 puts the supply curve and demand curve for oil together in one diagram. Notice the one point where the curves meet. The price at the meeting point is called the equilibrium price and the quantity at the meeting point is called the equilibrium quantity.

The equilibrium price is $30 and the equilibrium quantity is 65 MBD. What do we mean by equilibrium? We say that $30 and 65 are the equilibrium price and quantity because at any other price and quantity, economic forces are put in play that push prices and quantities toward these values. The equilibrium price and quantity are the only price and quantity that in a free market are stable. The sketch at right gives an intuitive feel for what we mean by equilibrium—the force of gravity pulls the ball down the side of the bowl until it comes to a state of rest. We will now explain the economic forces that push and pull prices toward their equilibrium values.

Equilibrium and the Adjustment Process

Imagine that demand and supply were as in Figure 3.1, but the price was $50, above the equilibrium price of $30—we would then have the situation depicted in the left panel of Figure 3.2.

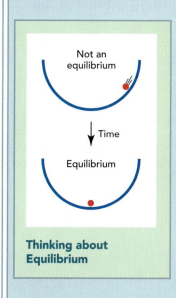

Thinking about Equilibrium

33

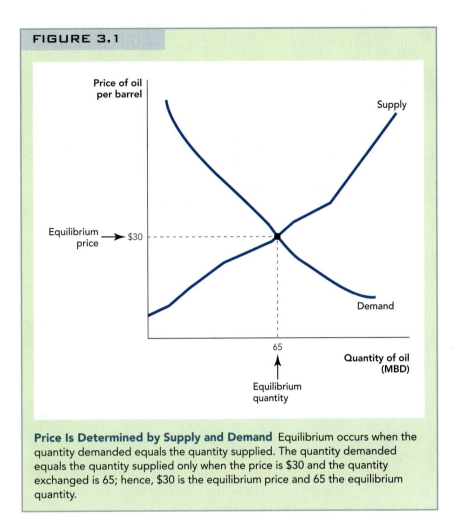

FIGURE 3.1

Price Is Determined by Supply and Demand Equilibrium occurs when the quantity demanded equals the quantity supplied. The quantity demanded equals the quantity supplied only when the price is $30 and the quantity exchanged is 65; hence, $30 is the equilibrium price and 65 the equilibrium quantity.

A **surplus** is a situation in which the quantity supplied is greater than the quantity demanded.

At a price of $50, suppliers want to supply 100, but at that price the quantity demanded by buyers is just 32, which creates an excess supply or **surplus** of 68. What will suppliers do if they cannot sell all of their output at a price of $50? Hold a sale! Each seller will reason that by pricing just a little bit below his or her competitors, he or she will be able to sell much more. *Competition will push prices down whenever there is a surplus.* As competition pushes prices down, the quantity demanded will increase and the quantity supplied will decrease. Only at a price of $30 will equilibrium be restored because only at that price does the quantity demanded (65) equal the quantity supplied (65).

What if price is below the equilibrium price? The right panel of Figure 3.2 shows that at a price of $15 demanders want 95 but suppliers are only willing to sell 24, which creates an excess demand or **shortage** of 71. What will sellers do if they discover that at a price of $15 they can easily sell all of their output and still have buyers asking for more? Raise prices! Buyers also have an incentive to offer higher prices when there is a shortage because when they can't buy as much as they want at the going price, they will try to outbid other buyers by offering sellers a higher price. *Competition will push prices up whenever there is a shortage.* As prices are pushed up, the quantity supplied increases and the quantity demanded decreases until at a price of $30 there is no longer an incentive for prices to rise and equilibrium is restored.

A **shortage** is a situation in which the quantity demanded is greater than the quantity supplied.

The **equilibrium price** is the price at which the quantity demanded is equal to the quantity supplied.

If competition pushes the price down whenever it is above the **equilibrium price** and it pushes the price up whenever it is below the equilibrium price, what happens at the equilibrium price? *The equilibrium price is stable because at the equilibrium*

FIGURE 3.2

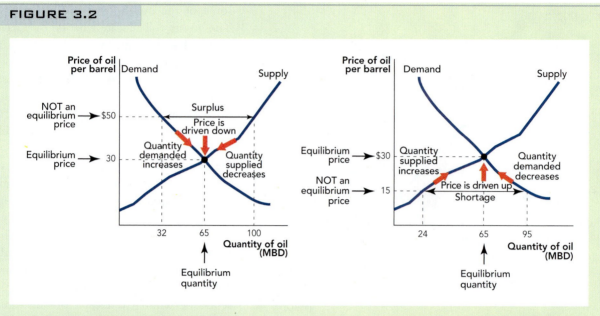

A Surplus Drives Prices Down At a price of $50 there is a surplus of oil. When there is a surplus, sellers have an incentive to decrease their price and buyers have an incentive to offer lower prices. The price decreases until at $30 the quantity demanded equals the quantity supplied and there is no longer an incentive for price to fall.

A Shortage Drives Prices Up At a price of $15 there is a shortage of oil. When there is a shortage, sellers have an incentive to increase the price and buyers have an incentive to offer higher prices. The price increases until at a price of $30 the quantity supplied equals the quantity demanded and there is no longer an incentive for the price to rise.

price *the quantity demanded is exactly equal to the quantity supplied.* Because every buyer can buy as much as he or she wants at the equilibrium price, buyers don't have an incentive to push prices up. Since every seller can sell as much as he or she wants at the equilibrium price, sellers don't have an incentive to push prices down. Of course, buyers would like lower prices, but any buyer who offers sellers a lower price will be scorned. Similarly, sellers would like higher prices, but any seller who tries to raise his or her asking price will quickly lose customers.

Who Competes with Whom?

Sellers want higher prices and buyers want lower prices so the person in the street often thinks that sellers compete *against* buyers.

But economists understand that regardless of what sellers want, what they do when they compete is lower prices. *Sellers compete with other sellers.* Similarly, buyers may want lower prices but what they do when they compete is raise prices. *Buyers compete with other buyers.*

If the price of a good that you want is high, should you blame the seller? Not if the market is competitive. Instead, you should "blame" other buyers for outbidding you.

Gains from Trade Are Maximized at the Equilibrium Price and Quantity

Figure 3.3 on the next page provides another perspective on the market equilibrium. Consider Panel A. At a price of $15 suppliers will voluntarily produce 24 million barrels of oil per day. But notice that this is only enough oil to satisfy

CHECK YOURSELF

> If high gasoline prices lead to a decrease in the demand for large trucks and SUVs, what will automobile companies do to sell the trucks and SUVs already manufactured?

> Consider clothes sold at outlet malls. Have sellers produced too few or too many of the particular items based on demand? What actions are sellers taking to move their goods out the door?

FIGURE 3.3

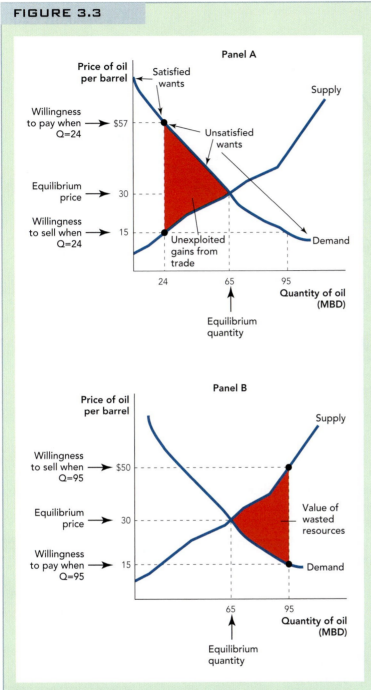

Panel A

Price of oil per barrel

Satisfied wants

Willingness to pay when → $57
Q=24

Unsatisfied wants

Supply

Equilibrium price → 30

Willingness to sell when → 15
Q=24

Unexploited gains from trade

Demand

24   65   95

↑
Equilibrium quantity

Quantity of oil (MBD)

Panel B

Price of oil per barrel

Supply

Willingness to sell when → $50
Q=95

Equilibrium price → 30

Value of wasted resources

Willingness to pay when → 15
Q=95

Demand

65   95

↑
Equilibrium quantity

Quantity of oil (MBD)

At the Equilibrium Quantity There Are No Unexploited Gains from Trade nor Any Wasteful Trades **Panel A:** Unexploited gains from trade exist when quantity is below the equilibrium quantity. Buyers are willing to pay $57 for the 24th unit and sellers are willing to sell the 24th unit for $15, so not trading the 24th unit leaves $42 in unexploited gain from trade. Only at the equilibrium quantity are there no unexploited gains from trade.
Panel B: Resources are wasted at quantities greater than the equilibrium quantity. Sellers are willing to sell the 95th unit for $50, but buyers are willing to pay only $15 so selling the 95th unit wastes $35 in resources. Only at the equilibrium quantity are there no wasted resources.

some of the buyers' wants. Which ones? The buyers will allocate what oil they have to their highest-valued wants. In Panel A of Figure 3.3, the 24 MBD of oil will be used to satisfy the wants labeled "Satisfied Wants." All other wants will remain unsatisfied. Now suppose that suppliers could be induced to sell just one more barrel of oil. How much would buyers be willing to pay for this barrel of oil? We can read the value of this additional barrel of oil by the height of the demand curve at 24 MBD. Buyers would be willing to pay up to $57 (or $56.99 if you want to be very precise), the value of the first unsatisfied want for an additional barrel of oil when 24 MBD are currently being bought. How much would sellers be willing to accept for one additional barrel of oil? We can read the lowest price at which sellers are willing to sell an additional barrel of oil by the height of the supply curve at 24 MBD. (Since sellers will be just willing to sell an additional barrel of oil when it covers their additional costs we can also read this as the cost of producing an additional barrel of oil when 24 MBD are currently being produced.) Sellers would be willing to sell an additional barrel of oil for as little as $15.

Buyers are willing to pay $57 for an additional barrel of oil, and sellers are willing to sell an additional barrel for as little as $15. Trade at any price between $57 and $15 can make both buyers and sellers better off. There are potential gains from trade so long as buyers are willing to pay more than sellers are willing to accept. Now notice that *there are unexploited gains from trade at any quantity less than the* **equilibrium quantity.** Economists believe that in a free market unexploited gains from trade won't last for long. We expect, therefore, that in a free market the quantity bought and sold will increase until the equilibrium quantity of 65 is reached.

We have shown that gains from trade push the quantity toward the equilibrium quantity. What about a push for trade coming from the other direction? In a free market, why won't the quantity bought and sold *exceed* the equilibrium quantity?

Now consider Panel B of Figure 3.3. Suppose that for some reason suppliers produce a quantity of 95 MBD. At a quantity of 95, it costs suppliers $50 to produce the last barrel of oil (say by squeezing it out of the Athabasca tar sands). How much is that barrel of oil worth to buyers? Again we can read this from the height of the demand curve at 95 MBD. It's only $15 (they get a few extra rubber duckies). So if quantity supplied exceeds the equilibrium quantity, it costs the sellers more to produce a barrel of oil than that barrel of oil is worth to buyers.

In a free market, suppliers won't spend $50 to produce something they can sell for at most $15—that's a recipe for bankruptcy.* We expect, therefore, in a free market, the quantity bought and sold will decrease until the equilibrium quantity of 65 MBD is reached.

Suppliers won't try to drive themselves into bankruptcy, but if they did would this be a good thing? Even at the equilibrium quantity, buyers have unsatisfied wants. Wouldn't it be a good idea to satisfy even more wants? No. The reason is that resources are wasted if the quantity exceeds the equilibrium quantity.

Imagine once again that suppliers were producing 95 units, and thus were producing many barrels of oil whose cost exceeded their worth. This would be a loss not just to the suppliers but also to society. Producing oil takes resources—labor, trucks, pipes, and so forth. Those resources, or the value of those resources, could be used to produce something people really are willing to pay for—economics textbooks, for example, or iPods. If we waste resources producing barrels of oil for $50 that are only worth $15, we have less resources to produce goods that cost only $32 but that people value at $75. We have only a limited number of resources and getting the most out of those resources means neither producing too little of a good (as in Panel A of Figure 3.3) or too much of a good (as in Panel B). Markets can help us to achieve this goal.

Figure 3.3 shows why in a free market there tends not to be unexploited gains from trade—at least not for long—nor wasteful trades. Put these two things together and we have a remarkable result. *A free market maximizes the gains from trade.* The gains from trade can be broken down into producer surplus and consumer surplus, so we can also say that *a free market maximizes producer plus consumer surplus.*

Figure 3.4 on the next page illustrates how the gains from trade—producer plus consumer surplus—are maximized at the equilibrium price and quantity. Maximizing the gains from trade, however, requires more than just producing at the equilibrium price and quantity. In addition, goods must be produced at the lowest possible cost and they must be used to satisfy the highest value demands. In Figure 3.4, for example, notice that every seller has lower costs than every non-seller. Also, every buyer has a higher willingness to pay for the good than every non-buyer.

Imagine if this claim were not true; suppose, for example, that Joe is willing to pay $50 for the good and there are two sellers, Alice with costs of $40 and Barbara with costs of $20. It's possible that Joe and Alice could make a deal, splitting the gains from trade of $10. At a price of $44, for example, Joe could earn $6 in consumer surplus ($50–$44) and Alice could earn $4 in producer surplus ($44–$40). But this trade would not maximize the gains from trade because if Joe and Barbara trade, the gains from trade are much higher, $30.

The **equilibrium quantity** is the quantity at which the quantity demanded is equal to the quantity supplied.

---

* Can you think of when suppliers might do this? What about if they were being subsidized by the government? In that case, the buyers might value the good less than the cost to sellers, but so long as the government makes up the difference the sellers will be happy to sell a large quantity.

FIGURE 3.4

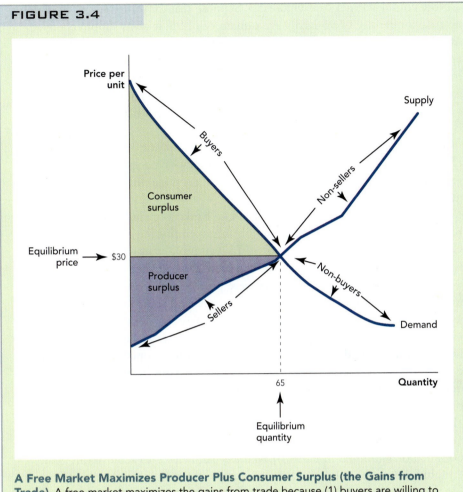

A Free Market Maximizes Producer Plus Consumer Surplus (the Gains from Trade) A free market maximizes the gains from trade because (1) buyers are willing to pay more for the good than non-buyers, (2) sellers are willing to sell the good at a lower price than non-sellers, and (3) there are no mutual profitable deals between non-sellers and non-buyers.

Thus, when we say that a free market maximizes the gains from trade, we mean three closely related things:

1. The supply of goods is bought by the buyers with the highest willingness to pay.

2. The supply of goods is sold by the sellers with the lowest costs.

3. Between buyers and sellers there are no unexploited gains from trade nor any wasteful trades.

Together these three conditions imply that the gains from trade are maximized.

One of the remarkable lessons of economics is that under the right conditions, the pursuit of self-interest leads not to chaos but to a beneficial order. The maximization of the gains from trade in markets populated solely by self-interested individuals is one application of this central idea.

Does the Model Work? Evidence from the Laboratory

It's easy to see the equilibrium price and quantity when we draw textbook supply and demand curves, but in a real market the demanders and sellers do not know the true curves. Moreover, the conditions required to maximize the

see the invisible hand

CHECK YOURSELF

> As the price of cars goes up, which marketplace wants will be the first to stop being satisfied? Give an example.

> In the late 1990s, telecommunication firms laid a greater quantity of fiber-optic cable than the market equilibrium quantity (as proven by later events). Describe the nature of the losses from too much investment in fiber-optic cable. What market incentives exist to avoid these losses?

gains from trade are quite sophisticated. So how do we know whether the model really works?

In 1956, Vernon Smith launched a revolution in economics by testing the supply and demand model in the lab. Smith's early experiments were simple. He took a group of undergraduate students and broke them into two groups, buyers and sellers. Buyers were given a card, which indicated their maximum willingness to pay. Sellers were given a card, which indicated their cost, the minimum price at which they would be willing to sell. The buyers and sellers were then instructed to call out bids and offers ("I will sell for $3.00" or "I will pay $1.50"). Each student could earn a profit by the difference between their willingness to pay or sell and the contract price. For example, if you were a buyer and your card said $3.00 and you were able to make a deal with a seller to buy for $2.00, then you would have made a $1.00 profit.

The students knew only their own willingness to pay or to sell, but Vernon Smith knew the actual shape of the supply and demand curves. Smith knew the curves because he knew exactly what cards he had handed out. Data from one of Smith's first experiments is shown in Figure 3.5. Smith handed out 11 cards to sellers and 11 to buyers. The lowest cost seller had costs of 75 cents, the next lowest cost seller had costs of $1.00. Thus, at any price below 75 cents the quantity supplied on the market supply curve was zero, between 75 cents and $1 the quantity supplied was 1 unit, between $1.00 and $1.25, the next highest cost, 2 units, and so forth. Looking at the figure can you see how many units were demanders willing to buy at a price of $2.65? At a price of $2.65, the quantity demanded is 3 units. (To test yourself, identify, by their willingness to pay, exactly which three buyers are willing to buy at a price of $2.65.)

FIGURE 3.5

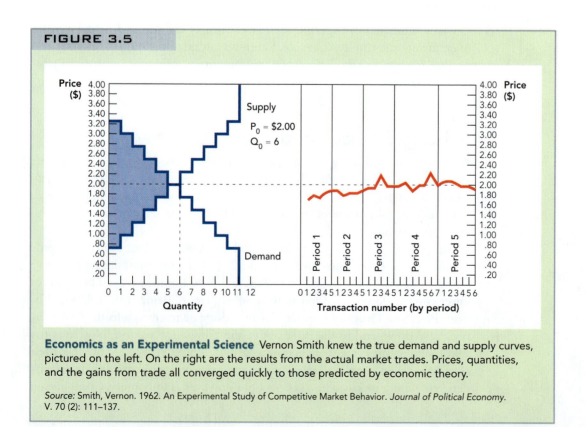

Economics as an Experimental Science Vernon Smith knew the true demand and supply curves, pictured on the left. On the right are the results from the actual market trades. Prices, quantities, and the gains from trade all converged quickly to those predicted by economic theory.

Source: Smith, Vernon. 1962. An Experimental Study of Competitive Market Behavior. *Journal of Political Economy.* V. 70 (2): 111–137.

The idea of economics as an experimental science came to Vernon Smith in a fit of insomnia in 1956. Nearly 50 years later, Smith was awarded the 2002 Nobel Laureate in Economics.

Smith knew from the graph that the equilibrium price and quantity as predicted by the supply and demand model was $2.00 and 6 units. But what would happen in the real world? Smith ran his experiment for 5 periods, each period about 5 minutes long. The right side of the figure shows the price for each completed trade in each period. The prices quickly converged toward the expected equilibrium price and quantity so that in the last period the average price was $2.03 and the quantity exchanged was 6 units.

Smith's market converged rapidly to the equilibrium price and quantity exactly as predicted by the supply and demand model. But recall that the model also predicts that a free market will maximize the gains from trade. Remember our conditions for efficiency, which in this context are that the supply of goods must be bought by the demanders with the highest willingness to pay, the supply of goods must be sold by the suppliers with the lowest costs, and the quantity traded should be equal to 6 units, neither more nor less.

So what happened in Smith's test of the market model? In the final period, 6 units were bought and sold and the buyers had the six highest valuations and the sellers the six lowest costs—exactly as predicted by the supply and demand model. Producer plus consumer surplus or total surplus was maximized. In fact, in the entire experiment only once was a seller with a cost greater than equilibrium price able to sell and only once was a buyer with a willingness to pay less than the equilibrium price able to buy—so total surplus was very close to being maximized throughout the experiment.

Vernon Smith began his experiments thinking that they would prove the supply and demand model was wrong. Decades later he wrote:

> I am still recovering from the shock of the experimental results. The outcome was unbelievably consistent with competitive price theory. . . . But the results *can't* be believed, I thought. It must be an accident, so I must take another class and do a new experiment with different supply and demand schedules.[1]

Many thousands of experiments later, the supply and demand model remains of enduring value. In 2002, Vernon Smith was awarded the Nobel Prize in Economics for establishing laboratory experiments as an important tool in economic science.

Shifting Demand and Supply Curves

Another way of testing the supply and demand model is to examine the model's predictions about what happens to equilibrium price and quantity when the supply or demand curves shift. Even if the model doesn't give us precise predictions (outside of the lab), we can still ask whether the model helps us to understand the world.

Imagine, for example, that technological innovations reduce the costs of producing a good. As we know from Chapter 2, a fall in costs shifts the supply curve down and to the right as shown in Figure 3.6 on the next page. The result of lower costs is a lower price and an increase in quantity. Begin at the Old Equilibrium Price and Quantity at point *a*. Now a decrease in costs shifts the Old Supply curve down and to the right out to the New Supply curve. Notice at the Old Equilibrium Price there is now a surplus—in other words, now that their costs have fallen, suppliers are willing to sell more at the old price than demanders are willing to buy. The excess supply, however, is temporary. Competition

FIGURE 3.6

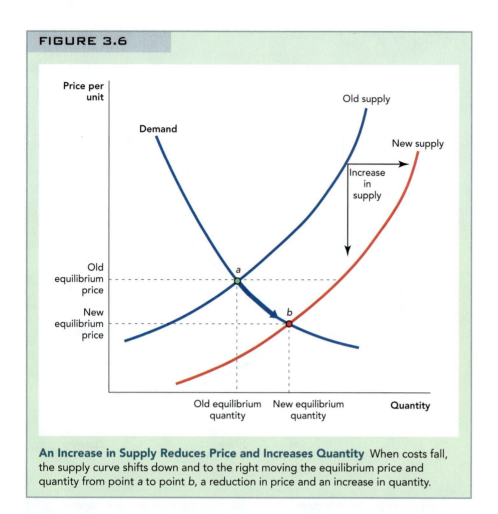

An Increase in Supply Reduces Price and Increases Quantity When costs fall, the supply curve shifts down and to the right moving the equilibrium price and quantity from point *a* to point *b*, a reduction in price and an increase in quantity.

between sellers pushes prices down and as prices fall the quantity demanded increases. Prices fall and quantity demanded increases until the New Equilibrium Price and Quantity are established at point *b*. At the new equilibrium, the quantity demanded equals the quantity supplied.

We can see this process at work throughout the economy. As technological innovations reduce the price of computer chips, for example, prices fall and the quantity of chips—used in everything from computers to cell phones to toys—increases.

What about a decrease in supply? A decrease in supply will raise the market price and reduce the market quantity, exactly the opposite effects to an increase in supply. But don't take our word for it. Draw the diagram. The key to learning demand and supply is not to try to memorize everything that can happen. Instead focus on learning how to use the tools. If you know how to use the tools, you can deduce what happens to price and quantity for any configuration of demand and supply and for any set of shifts simply by drawing a few pictures.

Figure 3.7 on the next page shows the same process for an increase in demand. Begin with the Old Equilibrium Price and Quantity at point *a*. Now suppose that demand increases to New Demand. As a result, the price and quantity are driven up to the New Equilibrium Price and Quantity at point *b*. Notice this time we omitted discussion of the temporary transition. So here's a good test of your knowledge. Can you explain *why* the price and quantity demanded increased with an increase in demand? Hint: What happens at the Old Equilibrium Price after demand has increased to New Demand?

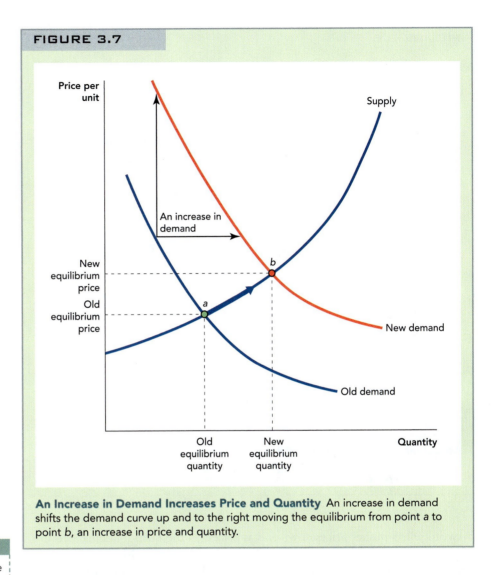

FIGURE 3.7

An Increase in Demand Increases Price and Quantity An increase in demand shifts the demand curve up and to the right moving the equilibrium from point *a* to point *b*, an increase in price and quantity.

CHECK YOURSELF

> Flooding in Iowa destroys some of the corn and soybean crop. What will happen to the price and quantity for each of these crops?

> Resveratrol, which is found in the plant Japanese knotweed (and is also a component of red wine), has recently been shown to increase life expectancy in worms and fish. What are your predictions about the price and quantity grown of Japanese knotweed?

> With the increase in gasoline prices, demand has shifted away from large cars and SUVs, and toward hybrid cars such as the Prius. Draw a graph showing the supply and demand for hybrid cars before and after an increase in the price of gasoline. What do you predict will happen to the price of hybrids as the price of gasoline rises?

Of course, if we can analyze an increase in demand, then a decrease in demand is just the opposite: a decrease in demand will tend to decrease price and quantity. Once again, draw the diagram!

Do you recall the list of demand and supply shifters that we presented in Chapter 2? We can now put all that knowledge to good use. With demand, supply, and the idea of equilibrium, we have powerful tools for analyzing how changes in income, population, expectations, technologies, input prices, taxes and subsidies, alternative uses of industry inputs, and other factors will change market prices and quantities. In fact, with our tools of demand, supply, and equilibrium, we can analyze and understand *any* change in *any* competitive market.

Terminology: Demand Compared to Quantity Demanded and Supply Compared to Quantity Supplied

Sometimes economists use very similar words for quite different things. (We're sorry but unfortunately it's too late to change terms.) In particular, there is a big difference between demand and quantity demanded. For example, an

increase in the quantity demanded is a movement *along* a fixed demand curve. An increase in demand is a *shift* of the entire demand curve (up and to the right).

Don't worry: you are *already* familiar with these differences, we just need to point them out to you and explain the associated differences in terminology. Panel A of Figure 3.8 is a repeat of Figure 3.6, showing that an increase in supply reduces the equilibrium price and increases the equilibrium quantity. But now we emphasize something a little different—the increase in supply pushes the

FIGURE 3.8

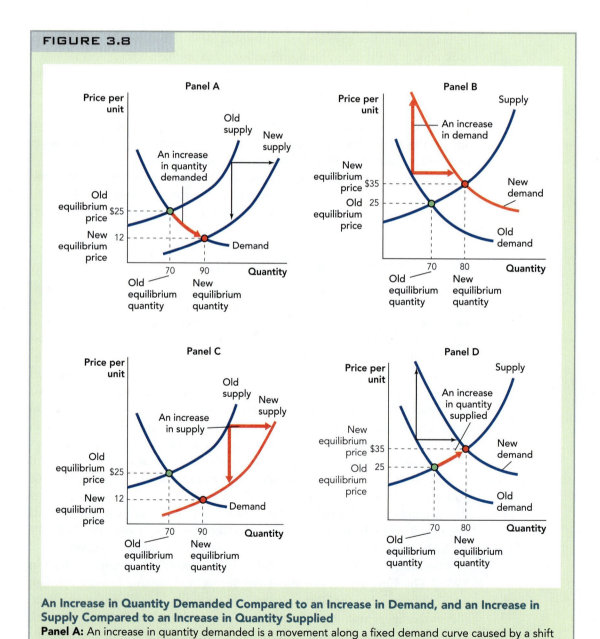

An Increase in Quantity Demanded Compared to an Increase in Demand, and an Increase in Supply Compared to an Increase in Quantity Supplied

Panel A: An increase in quantity demanded is a movement along a fixed demand curve caused by a shift in the supply curve.

Panel B: An increase in demand is a shift in the demand curve up and to the right.

Panel C: An increase in supply is a shift in the supply curve down and to the right.

Panel D: An increase in quantity supplied is a movement along a fixed supply curve caused by a shift in the demand curve.

price down, thereby causing an increase in the *quantity demanded* from 70 units to 90 units. Notice that the increase in the quantity demanded is a movement along the demand curve. In Panel A, the demand has not changed, only the quantity demanded. Notice also that changes in the quantity demanded are always caused by changes in supply. In other words, *shifts* in the supply curve cause movements *along* the demand curve.

Panel B is a repeat of Figure 3.7 and it shows an *increase in demand*. Notice that an increase in demand is a shift in the entire demand curve up and to the right. Indeed, we can also think about an increase in demand as the creation of a new demand curve, appropriately labeled New Demand.

Similarly, an increase in supply is a *shift* of the entire supply curve while an increase in quantity supplied is a movement *along* a fixed supply curve. If you look closely at Panels A and B, you will see that we have already shown you a shift in supply and a change in quantity supplied! But to make things clear, we repeat the analysis for supply in Panels C and D: the graphs are the same but now we emphasize different things.

Panel C shows an increase in supply, a shift in the entire supply curve down and to the right. Panel D shows an increase in quantity supplied, namely a movement from 70 to 80 units along a fixed supply curve.

By comparing Panels A and C we can see that shifts in the supply curve create changes in quantity demanded. And by comparing Panels B and D we can see that shifts in the demand curve create changes in the quantity supplied.

Understanding the Price of Oil

We can use the supply and demand model to understand some of the major events that have determined the price of oil over the past half century. Figure 3.9 on the next page shows the *real price* of oil in 2005 dollars between 1960 and 2005. (The real price corrects prices for inflation—we will cover this process and what it means in Chapter 11).

From the early twentieth century to the 1970s, the demand for oil increased steadily, but major discoveries and improved production techniques meant that the supply of oil increased at an even faster pace leading to modest declines in price. Contrary to popular belief, slightly declining prices over time are common for minerals and other natural resources supplied under competitive conditions.

Although the streets of Baghdad were paved with tar as early as the eighth century, the discovery and development of the modern oil industry in the Middle East was made primarily by U.S., Dutch, and British firms much later. For many decades, these firms controlled oil in the Middle East, giving local governments just a small cut of their proceeds. It's hard to take your oil well and leave the country, however, so the major firms were vulnerable to taxes and nationalization.

The Iranian government nationalized the British oil industry in Iran in 1951.* The Egyptians nationalized the Suez Canal, the main route through which oil flowed to the West, in 1956, leading to the Suez Crisis—a brief war that pitted Egypt against an alliance of the United Kingdom, France, and Israel. Further nationalizations and increased government control of the oil industry occurred throughout the 1960s and early 1970s.

---

*The nationalization was reversed in 1953 when the government of Mohammad Mosaddeq was toppled by a CIA-backed coup that brought the king, Mohammad Reza Pahlavi, back to power. The coup would have repercussions a quarter century later with the coming of the Iranian revolution, when the American-backed government was overthrown by Islamic radicals.

FIGURE 3.9

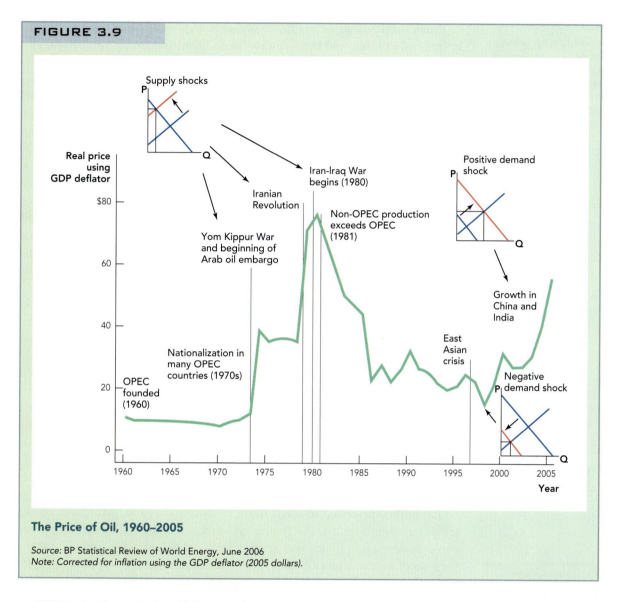

The Price of Oil, 1960–2005

Source: BP Statistical Review of World Energy, June 2006
Note: Corrected for inflation using the GDP deflator (2005 dollars).

OPEC, the Organization of the Petroleum Exporting Countries, was formed in 1960.* Initially OPEC restricted itself to bargaining with the foreign nationals for a larger share of their oil revenues. By the early 1970s, however, further nationalizations in the OPEC countries made it possible for OPEC countries to act together in order to reduce supply and raise prices.

A triggering event for OPEC was the Yom Kippur War. Egypt and Syria attacked Israel in 1973 in an effort to regain the Sinai Peninsula and the Golan Heights, which Israel had captured in 1967. In an effort to punish Western countries that had supported Israel, a number of Arab exporting nations cut oil production. Supply had been increasing by about 7.5 percent per year in the previous decade, but between 1973 and 1974 production was dead flat. Prices shot up, increasing in real dollars from $14.50 to $46 per barrel in just one year. The large increase in price from a small decline in supply (relative to what it would have been without the cut in production) demonstrated how much the world depended on oil.

* OPEC was founded by Iran, Iraq, Kuwait, Saudi Arabia, and Venezuela, later joined by Qatar (1961), Indonesia (1962), Libya (1962), United Arab Emirates (1967), Algeria (1969), Nigeria (1971), Ecuador (1973–1992), and Gabon (1975–1994). More recently, Ecuador rejoined OPEC in 2007, Angola joined in 2007, and Indonesia left in 2008.

▶▶ SEARCH ENGINE

Statistics on world energy prices, consumption, production, reserves and other areas can be found at the **BP Statistical Review of World Energy.** The **Energy Information Administration** focuses on the United States.

Prices stabilized, albeit at a much higher level, after 1974, but political unrest in Iran in 1978 followed by revolution in 1979 cut Iranian oil production. This time the reduction in supply was accidental rather than deliberate, but the result was the same—sharply higher prices. When Iraq attacked Iran in 1980, production in both countries diminished yet again, pushing prices to their highest level in the twentieth century—$75.31 in 2005 dollars. Prices might have been driven even higher if demand had not been reduced by a recession in the United States.

Higher prices attract entry. In 1972, the United Kingdom produced 2,000 barrels of oil per day. By 1978, with the opening of the North Sea wells, the UK was producing one million barrels per day. In the same period, Norway increased production from 33,000 to 287,000 barrels per day and Mexico doubled its production from 506,000 barrels per day to just over one million barrels per day. By 1982, non-OPEC production exceeded OPEC production for the first time since OPEC was founded. Iranian production also began to recover, increasing by one million barrels per day in 1982. Prices began to fall during the 1980s and 1990s.

Prices can also fluctuate with shifts in demand. A sharp fall in prices came in 1997 when the economy of South Korea (the tenth largest economy in the world) and that of Indonesia, Thailand, and other East Asian countries went into a severe recession. Income fell, reducing the demand for oil and reducing oil prices. As these countries recovered, however, the demand for oil increased along with prices.

The economies of China and India have surged in the early twenty-first century to the point where millions of people are for the first time in the history of their country able to afford an automobile. In 1949, the communists confiscated all the private cars in China. As late as 2000, there were just 6 million cars in all of China, but by 2005 there were 20 million. Total highway miles more than doubled in the same five years.[2] This increased demand for oil has pushed prices up to levels not seen since the 1970s.[*] Moreover, unlike temporary events such as the Iranian revolution and the Iran-Iraq war, the increase in demand in China and in other newly developing nations will not reverse soon. In the United States, there's nearly one car for every two people. China has a population of 1.3 billion people, so there is plenty of room for growth in the number of cars and thus the demand for oil. What is your prediction for future oil prices?

CHECK YOURSELF

> In Figure 3.9, you will notice a jump in oil prices around 1991. What happened in this year to increase price? Was it a supply shock or a demand shock?

> In Figure 3.9, during what period would you include a small figure for positive supply shocks (increases in supply?) Explain the causes behind the positive supply shocks and the effect of these shocks on the price of oil.

☐ Takeaway

Now that you have finished reading this chapter you should read it again. Really. Understanding supply and demand is critical to understanding economics, and in this chapter we have covered the most important aspects of the supply and demand model, namely how supply and demand together determine equilibrium price and quantity. You should understand, among other ideas, the following:

1. Market competition brings about an equilibrium in which the quantity supplied is equal to the quantity demanded.

---

[*] Improved technology is continually lowering the cost of discovering and producing oil (shifting the supply curve down and to the right), so what has happened in recent years is not simply an increase in demand but an increase in demand that has outstripped the increase in supply.

2. Only one price/quantity combination is a market equilibrium and you should be able to identify this equilibrium in a diagram.

3. You should understand and be able to explain the incentives that enforce the market equilibrium. What happens when the price is above the equilibrium price? Why? What happens when the price is below the equilibrium price? Why?

4. Gains from trade are maximized at the equilibrium price and quantity and no other price/quantity combination maximizes the gains from trade.

5. You should know from Chapter 2 the major factors that shift demand and supply curves and from this chapter be able to explain and predict the effect of any such shift on the equilibrium price and quantity.

6. A "change in demand [the demand curve]" is not the same thing as "a change in quantity demanded"; a "change in supply [the supply curve]" is not the same thing as "a change in quantity supplied."

Most important, you should be able to work with supply and demand to answer questions about the world.

□ CHAPTER REVIEW

KEY CONCEPTS

Surplus, p. 34

Shortage, p. 34

Equilibrium price, p. 34

Equilibrium quantity, p. 37

FACTS AND TOOLS

1. If the price in a market is above the equilibrium price, does this create a surplus or a shortage?

2. When the price is above the equilibrium price, does greed (in other words, self-interest) tend to push the price down or does it push it up?

3. Jon is on eBay, bidding for a first edition of the influential Frank Miller graphic novel *Batman: The Dark Knight Returns.* In this market, who is Jon competing with: the seller of the graphic novel or the other bidders?

4. Now, Jon is in Japan, trying to get a job as a full-time translator; he wants to translate English TV shows into Japanese and vice versa. He notices that the wage for translators is very low. Who is the "competition" that is pushing the wage down: Does the competition come from businesses who hire the translators or from the other translators?

5. Jules wants to purchase a Royale with cheese from Vincent. Vincent is willing to offer this tasty burger for $3. The most Jules is willing to pay for the tasty burger is $8 (after all, his girlfriend is a vegetarian, so he doesn't get many opportunities for tasty burgers).

    a. How large are the potential gains from trade if Jules and Vincent agree to make this trade? In other words, what is the sum of producer and consumer surplus if the trade happens?

    b. If the trade takes place at $4, how much producer surplus goes to Vincent? How much consumer surplus goes to Jules?

    c. If the trade takes place at $7, how much producer surplus goes to Vincent? How much consumer surplus goes to Jules?

6. What happened in Vernon Smith's lab? Choose the right answer:

    a. The price and quantity were close to equilibrium but gains from trade were far from the maximum.

    b. The price and quantity were far from equilibrium and gains from trade were far from the maximum.

    c. The price and quantity were far from equilibrium but gains from trade were close to the maximum.

    d. The price and quantity were close to equilibrium and gains from trade were close to the maximum.

7. When supply falls, what happens to quantity demanded in equilibrium? (This should get you

to notice that both suppliers *and* demanders change their behavior when one curve shifts.)

8. **a.** When demand increases what happens to price and quantity in equilibrium?

    b. When supply increases what happens to price and quantity in equilibrium?

    c. When supply decreases what happens to price and quantity in equilibrium?

    d. When demand decreases what happens to price and quantity in equilibrium?

9. **a.** When demand increases what happens to price and quantity in equilibrium?

    b. When supply increases what happens to price and quantity in equilibrium?

    c. When supply decreases what happens to price and quantity in equilibrium?

    d. When demand decreases what happens to price and quantity in equilibrium?

    No, this is not a mistake. Yes, it is that important.

10. What's the best way to think about the rise in oil prices in the 1970s, when wars and oil embargoes wracked the Middle East? Was it a rise in demand, a fall in demand, a rise in supply, or a fall in supply?

11. What's the best way to think about the rise in oil prices in the last 10 years, as China and India have become richer: Was it a rise in demand, a fall in demand, a rise in supply, or a fall in supply?

THINKING AND PROBLEM SOLVING

1. Suppose the market for batteries looks as follows:

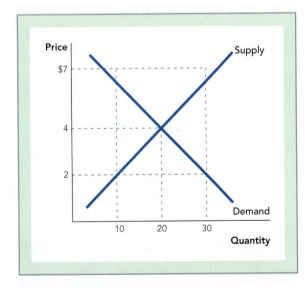

What is the equilibrium price and quantity?

2. Consider the following supply and demand tables for bread. Draw the supply and demand curves for this market. What is the equilibrium price and quantity?

Price of One Loaf	Quantity Supplied	Quantity Demanded
$0.50	10	75
$1	20	55
$2	35	35
$3	50	25
$5	60	10

3. If the price of a one-bedroom apartment in Washington, D.C., is currently $1,000 per month, but the supply and demand curves look as follows, then is there a shortage or surplus of apartments? What would we expect to happen to prices? Why?

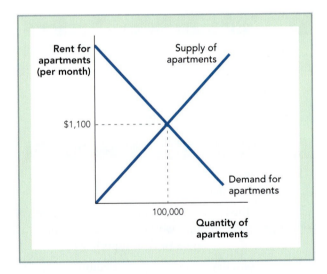

4. Determine the equilibrium quantity and price without drawing a graph.

Price of Good X	Quantity Supplied	Quantity Demanded
$22	100	225
$25	115	200
$30	130	175
$32	150	150
$40	170	110

5. In the figure below how many pounds of sugar are sellers willing to sell at a price of $20? How much is demanded at this price? What is the buyer's willingness to pay when the quantity is 20 lbs? Is this combination of $20 per pound and a quantity of 20 pounds an equilibrium? If not, identify the unexploited gains from trade.

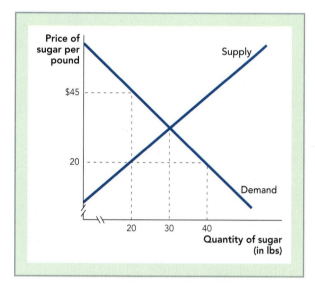

6. The market for marbles is represented in the graph below. What is the total producer surplus? The total consumer surplus? What are the total gains from trade?

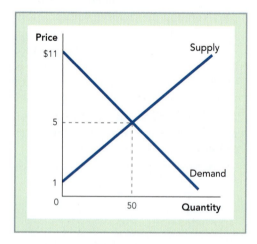

7. Suppose you decided to follow in Vernon Smith's footsteps and conducted your own experiment with your friends. You give out 10 cards, 5 cards to buyers with the figures for willingness to pay of $1, $2, $3, $4, and $5, and 5 cards to sellers with the amounts for costs of $1, $2, $3, $4, and $5. The rules are the same as Vernon Smith implemented.

   a. Draw the supply and demand curves for this market. At a price of $3.50 how many units are demanded? And supplied?

b. Assuming the market works as predicted, and the market moves to equilibrium, will the buyer who values the good at $1 be able to purchase? Why or why not?

8. If the price of margarine decreases, what happens to the demand for butter? What happens to the equilibrium quantity and price for butter? What would happen if butter and margarine were not substitutes? Use a supply and demand diagram to support your answer.

9. The market for sugar is diagramed below:

   a. What would happen to the equilibrium quantity and price if the wages of sugar cane harvesters increased?

   b. What if a new study was published that emphasized negative health effects of consuming sugar?

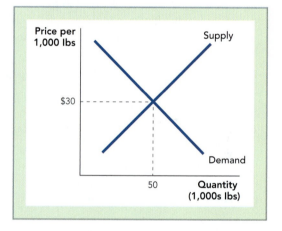

10. If a snowstorm was forecast for the next day, what would happen to the demand for snow shovels? Is this a change in quantity demanded or a change in demand? This shift in the demand curve would affect the price; would this cause a change in quantity supplied or a change in supply?

11. In the 1990s, the Atkins diet, which emphasized eating more meat and fewer grains, became very popular. What do you suppose that did to the price and quantity of bread? Use supply and demand analysis to support your answer.

12. In recent years, there have been news reports that toys made in China are unsafe. When those news reports show up on CNN and Fox News, what probably happens to the demand for toys made in China? What probably happens to the equilibrium price and quantity of toys made in China? Are Chinese toymakers probably better or worse off when such news comes out?

CHALLENGES

1. For many years it was illegal to color margarine yellow (margarine is naturally white). In some states, margarine manufacturers were even required to color margarine pink! Who do you think supported these laws? Why? Hint: Your analysis in question 8 from the previous section is relevant!

2. Think about two products, "safe cars" (a heavy car such as a BMW 530xi with infrared night vision, four-wheel antilock brakes, and electronic stability control), and "dangerous cars" (a lightweight car such as _____ (name removed for legal reasons, but you can fill in as you wish)).

   a. Are these two products substitutes or complements?

   b. If new research makes it easier to produce safe cars, what happens to the supply of safe cars? What will happen to the equilibrium price of safe cars?

   c. Now that the price of safe cars has changed, how does this impact the demand for dangerous cars?

   d. Now let's tie all of these links into one simple sentence:

   "In a free market, as engineers and scientists discover new ways to makes cars safer, the number of dangerous cars sold will tend to _____."

3. Many clothing stores often have clearance sales at the end of each season. Using the tools you learned in this chapter can you think of an explanation why?

4. a. If oil executives read in the newspaper that massive new oil supplies have been discovered under the Pacific Ocean but will likely only be useful in 10 years, what is likely to happen to the supply of oil *today*? What is the likely equilibrium impact on the price and quantity of oil *today*?

   b. If oil executives read in the newspaper that new solar-power technologies have been discovered but will likely only become useful in 10 years, what is likely to happen to the supply of oil *today*? What is the likely equilibrium impact on the price and quantity of oil *today*?

   c. What's the short version of the above scenarios? Fill in the blank: If we learn *today* about promising *future* energy sources, today's price of energy will _____ and today's quantity of energy will _____.

5. Economists often say that prices are a "rationing mechanism." If the supply of a good falls, how do prices "ration" these now-scarce goods in a competitive market?

6. When the crime rate falls in the area around a factory, what probably happens to wages at that factory?

7. Let's take the idea from the previous question and use it to explain why businesses sometimes try to make their employees happy. If a business can make the job seem fun (by having inexpensive pizza parties) or at least safe (by nagging the city government to put police patrols around the factory), what probably happens to the supply of labor? What happens to the equilibrium wage if a factory or office or laboratory becomes a great place where people "really want to work?" How does this explain why the hourly wage for the typical radio or television announcer is only $13 per hour, lower than almost any other job in the entertainment or broadcasting industry?

   (*Source:* Bureau of Labor Statistics, *National Occupational Employment and Wage Estimates,* available online.)

4

Price Ceilings and Price Floors

On a quiet Sunday in August 1971, President Richard Nixon shocked the nation by freezing all prices and wages in the United States. It was now illegal to raise prices—even if both buyers and sellers voluntarily agreed to the change. Nixon's order, one of the most significant peacetime interventions into the U.S. economy ever to occur, applied to almost all goods, and even though it was supposed to be in effect for only 90 days, it would have lasting effects for over a decade.

Market prices signal information and create incentives to economize and seek out substitutes. Markets are linked geographically, across different products, and through time. In this chapter, we show how price controls—laws making it illegal for prices to move above a maximum price (price ceilings) or below a minimum price (price floors)—interfere with all of these processes. We begin by explaining how a price control affects a single market, and then we turn to how price controls delink some markets and link others in ways that are counterproductive.

Price Ceilings

Nixon imposed price controls in an effort to control inflation, a sustained increase in the general level of prices. In Chapter 11, we examine the causes of inflation at greater length. You can understand this chapter as looking at how one attempt to solve the problem of inflation did not work. Fortunately, Chapter 11 also examines some better solutions.

At the time of Nixon's freeze, market prices were increasing because of inflation so the typical situation quickly came to resemble that in Figure 4.1 on the next page. The controlled or frozen price, the highest price at which people were legally allowed to buy and sell, was below the uncontrolled or market equilibrium price.

51

FIGURE 4.1

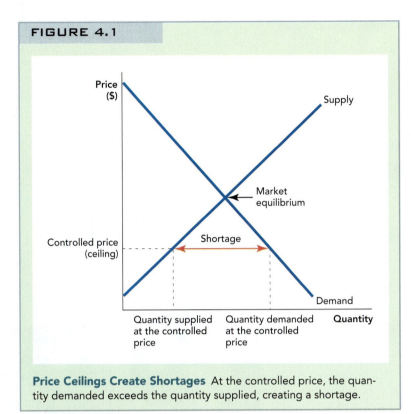

Price Ceilings Create Shortages At the controlled price, the quantity demanded exceeds the quantity supplied, creating a shortage.

A **price ceiling** is a maximum price allowed by law.

A shortage of vinyl in 1973 forced Capitol Records to melt down slow sellers so they could keep pressing Beatles' albums.

When the maximum price that can be legally charged is below the market price we say that there is a **price ceiling**. Economists call it a price ceiling because prices cannot legally go higher than the ceiling. Price ceilings create five important effects:

1. Shortages
2. Reductions in quality
3. Wasteful lines and other search costs
4. Lost gains from trade
5. Misallocation of resources

Shortages

When prices are held below the market price, the quantity demanded exceeds the quantity supplied. Economists call this a shortage. Figure 4.1 shows that the shortage is measured by the difference between the quantity demanded at the controlled price and the quantity supplied at the controlled price. Notice also that the lower the controlled price is relative to the market equilibrium price, the larger the shortage.

In some sectors of the economy, shortages appeared soon after prices were controlled in 1971. Increased demand in the construction industry, for example, meant that price controls hit that sector especially hard. Ordinarily, increased demand for steel bars, for example, would increase the price of steel bars, encouraging more production. But with a price ceiling in place, demanders could not signal their need to suppliers nor could they provide suppliers with an incentive to produce more. As a result, shortages of steel bars, lumber, toilets (for new homes), and other construction inputs were common. By 1973, there were shortages of wool, copper, aluminum, vinyl, denim jeans, paper, plastic bottles, and more.

Reductions in Quality

At the controlled price, demanders find that there is a shortage of goods—they cannot buy as much of the good as they would like. Equivalently, at the controlled price, sellers find that there is an excess of demand or, in other words, *sellers have more customers than they have goods*. Ordinarily, this would be an opportunity to profit by raising prices, but when prices are controlled, sellers can't raise prices without violating the law. Is there another way that sellers can increase profits? Yes. It's much easier to evade the law by cutting quality than by raising price, so when prices are held below market levels, quality declines.

Thus, even when shortages were not apparent, quality was reduced. Books were printed on lower-quality paper, 2" × 4" lumber shrank to $1\frac{5}{8}$" × $3\frac{5}{8}$", and new automobiles were painted with fewer coats of paint. To help deal with the shortage of paper some newspapers even switched to a smaller font size.

Another way quality can fall is with reductions in service. Ordinarily sellers have an incentive to please their customers, but when prices are held below market levels, sellers have more customers than they need *or want*. Customers without potential for profit are just a pain so when prices cannot rise we can expect

service quality to fall. The full service gasoline station, for example, disappeared with price controls in 1973 and instead of staying open for 24 hours, gasoline stations would close whenever the owner wanted a lunch break.

Wasteful Lines and Other Search Costs

The most serious shortage during the 1970s was for oil. The OPEC embargo in 1973 and the reduction in supply caused by the Iranian revolution in 1979 increased the world price of oil, as we saw in Chapter 3. In the United States, however, price controls on domestically produced oil had not been lifted and thus the United States faced intense shortages of oil and the classic sign of a shortage, lines.

Figure 4.2 focuses on the third consequence of controlling prices below market prices: wasteful lines.

The Great Matzo Ball Debate

In 1972, AFL-CIO boss George Meany complained that the number of matzo balls in his favorite soup had sunk from four to three, in effect raising the price.

C. Jackson Grayson, chairman of the U.S. Price Commission, was worried about the bad publicity, so on *Face the Nation* he triumphantly held aloft a can of Mrs. Adler's soup claiming that his staff had opened many cans and concluded there were still four balls per can.

Whoever was right about the soup, Meany was certainly the better economist: price ceilings reduce quality.

FIGURE 4.2

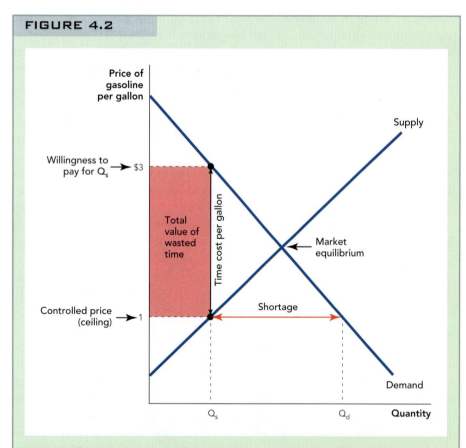

Prices Ceilings Create Wasteful Lines At the controlled price, the quantity of gasoline supplied is Q$_s$ and buyers are willing to pay as much as $3 for a gallon of gasoline. But the maximum price that sellers can charge is $1. The difference between what buyers are willing to pay and what sellers can charge encourages buyers to line up to buy gasoline. Buyers will line up until the total price of gasoline, the out-of-pocket price plus the time cost, increases to $3. Time spent waiting in line is wasted time. The total value of wasted time is given by the time cost per gallon multiplied by the quantity of gallons bought.

At the controlled price of $1, sellers supply Q$_s$ units of the good. How much are demanders willing to pay (per unit) for these Q$_s$ units? Recall that the demand curve shows the willingness to pay, so follow a line from Q$_s$ up to the demand curve to find that demanders are willing to pay $3 per unit for

Q_s units. The price controls, however, make it illegal for demanders to offer sellers a price of $3, but there are other ways of paying for gas.

Knowing that there is a shortage, some buyers might bribe station owners (or attendants) to fill up their tanks. Suppose that the average tank holds 20 gallons. Buyers would then be willing to pay $60 for a fill-up, the legal price of $20 plus a $40 under-the-table bribe. Thus, if bribes are common the total price of gasoline—the legal price plus the bribe price—will rise to $3 per gallon ($60/20 gallons).

Corruption and bribes can be common, especially when price controls are long lasting, but they were not a major problem during the gasoline shortages of the 1970s. Nevertheless, the total price of gasoline did rise well above the controlled price. Instead of competing by paying bribes, buyers competed by their willingness to wait in line. Remember that at the controlled price the quantity of gasoline demanded is greater than the quantity supplied, so some buyers are going to be disappointed—they are going to get less gasoline than they want and some buyers may get no gasoline at all. Buyers will compete to avoid being left with nothing. Let's assume that all gasoline station owners refuse bribes. Unfortunately, honesty does not eliminate the shortage. A "first-come, first served" system is honest, but buyers who get to the gasoline station early will get the gas, leaving the latecomers with nothing. Under this situation, how long will the lineups get?

Suppose that buyers value their time at $10 an hour and, as before, the average fuel tank holds 20 gallons. Eager to obtain gas during the shortage, a buyer arrives at the station early, perhaps even before it opens, and must wait in line for an hour before he is served. His total price of gas is $30, $1 per gallon for 20 gallons in out-of-pocket cost plus $10 in time cost. Since the total value of the gas is $60, that's still a good deal. But if it's a good deal for him, it's probably a good deal for other buyers too, so the next time he wants to fill up he is likely to discover that others have preceded him and now he has to wait longer. How much longer? Following the logic to its conclusion we can see that the line will lengthen until the total cost for 20 gallons of gasoline is $60, $20 in dollars paid to the station owner plus $40 in time costs. The price per gallon, therefore, rises to $3 ($60/20 gallons)—exactly as occurred with bribes!

Price controls do not eliminate competition. They merely change the form of competition. Is there a difference between paying in bribes and paying in time? Yes. Paying in time is much more wasteful. When a buyer bribes a gasoline station owner $40, at least the gasoline station owner gets the bribe. But when a buyer spends $40 worth of time or four hours waiting in line, the gasoline station owner doesn't get to add four hours to his life. The bribe is transferred from the buyer to the seller, but the time spent waiting in line is simply lost. Figure 4.2 shows that when the quantity supplied is Q_s, the total price of gasoline will tend to rise to $3, a $1 money price plus a time-price of $2 per gallon. The total amount of waste from waiting in line is given by the shaded area, the per gallon time price ($2) multiplied by the number of gallons bought (Q_s).*

When the quantity demanded exceeds the quantity supplied, someone is going to be disappointed.

---

*We need to qualify this slightly. If *every* buyer has a time value of $10 per hour, then the total time wasted will be the area as shaded in the diagram. If some buyers have a time value lower than $10, say $5 per hour, they will wait in line for 4 hours, paying $20 in out-of-pocket costs but only $20 in time costs. If these buyers value the gasoline as high as does the marginal buyer, at $60 for 20 gallons, they will earn what economists call a "rent" of $20; thus, not all of the rectangle would be wasted. Regardless of whether all the rectangle or just some of the rectangle is wasted, it's important to see that (1) price ceilings generate shortages and lineups, (2) the lineups mean that the total price of the controlled good is higher than the controlled price (and perhaps even higher than the uncontrolled price), and (3) the time spent waiting in line is wasted.

Lost Gains from Trade

Price controls also reduce the gains from trade. In Figure 4.3, at the quantity supplied, Q_s, how much would demanders pay for one *additional* gallon of gasoline? The willingness to pay for a gallon of gas at Q_s is $3, so demanders would be willing to pay just a little bit less, say $2.95, for an additional gallon. How much would suppliers require to sell an additional gallon? Supplier cost is read off the supply curve, so reading up from the quantity Q_s to the supply curve we find that the willingness to sell at Q_s is $1; suppliers would be willing to supply an additional unit for just a little bit more, say $1.05.

FIGURE 4.3

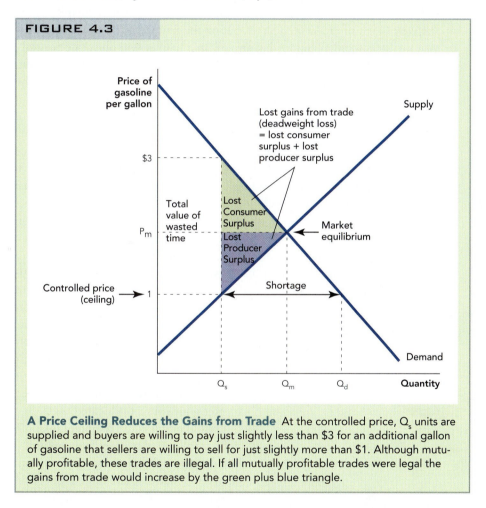

A Price Ceiling Reduces the Gains from Trade At the controlled price, Q_s units are supplied and buyers are willing to pay just slightly less than $3 for an additional gallon of gasoline that sellers are willing to sell for just slightly more than $1. Although mutually profitable, these trades are illegal. If all mutually profitable trades were legal the gains from trade would increase by the green plus blue triangle.

Demanders are willing to pay $2.95 for an additional gallon of gas, suppliers are willing to sell an additional gallon for $1.05, and so there is $1.90 of potential gains from trade to split between them. But it's illegal for suppliers to sell gasoline at anything more than $1. Buyers and sellers want to trade, but they are prevented from doing so by the threat of jail. If the price ceiling were lifted and trade were allowed, the quantity traded would expand from Q_s to Q_m and buyers would be better off by the green triangle labeled "Lost consumer surplus," while sellers would be better off by the blue triangle labeled "Lost producer surplus." But with a price ceiling in place, the quantity supplied is Q_s and together the lost consumer and producer surplus are lost gains from trade (economists also call this a **deadweight loss**).

Recall from Chapter 3 that we said that in a free market the quantity of goods sold maximizes the sum of consumer and producer surplus. We can now

A **deadweight loss** is the total of lost consumer and producer surplus when not all mutually profitable gains from trade are exploited. Price ceilings (and price floors) create a deadweight loss.

see that in a market with a price ceiling, the sum of consumer and producer surplus is not maximized because the price control prevents mutually profitable gains from trade from being exploited.

In addition to these losses, price controls cause a misallocation of scarce resources; let's see how that works in more detail.

Misallocation of Resources

Prices send signals to entrepreneurs about demand and supply, and they give entrepreneurs incentives to move resources from low valued uses to high valued uses. Price controls distort signals and eliminate incentives. Imagine that it's sunny on the West Coast of the United States, but on the East Coast there is a cold winter that increases the demand for heating oil. In a market without price controls, the increase in demand in the East pushes up prices in the East. Eager for profit, entrepreneurs buy oil in the West, where the oil is not much needed and the price is low, and they move it to the East, where people are cold and the price of oil is high. In this way, the price increase in the East is moderated and supplies of oil move to where they are needed most.

Now consider what happens when it is illegal to buy or sell oil at a price above a price ceiling. No matter how cold it gets in the East, the demanders of heating oil are prevented from bidding up the price of oil, so there's *no signal* and *no incentive* to ship oil to where it is needed most. Price controls mean that oil is misallocated. Swimming pools in California are heated while homes in New Jersey are cold. In fact, this was exactly what occurred in the United States, especially in the harsh winter of 1972–1973.

Once again recall from Chapter 3 that we said that in a free market the supply of goods is bought by the demanders who have the highest willingness to pay. We can now see that in a market with a price ceiling demanders with the highest willingness to pay have no easy way to signal their demands nor do suppliers have an incentive to supply their demands. As a result, in a controlled market goods are misallocated.

Price controls cause resources (like oil) to be misallocated not just geographically, but also across different uses. Recall from Chapter 2 that the demand curve for oil shows the uses of oil from the highest valued uses to the lowest valued uses. In case you forgot, Figure 4.4 shows the key idea: high valued uses are at the top of the curve and low valued uses at the bottom. Without market prices, however, we have no guarantee that oil will flow to its highest valued uses. As we have just seen, in a situation with price controls, it's possible to have plenty of oil to heat swimming pools in California (hello, rubber ducky!) and not enough oil for heating cold homes in New Jersey. Similarly, in 1974 *Business Week* reported, "While drivers

Distorted signals cause resources to be misallocated.

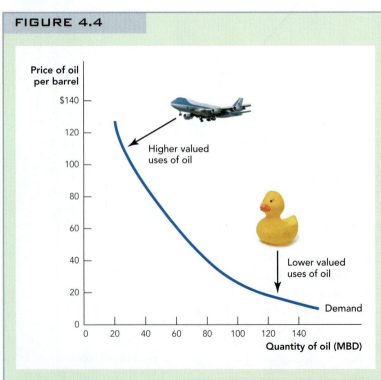

FIGURE 4.4

Price of oil per barrel

$140

120

100 — Higher valued uses of oil

80

60

40 — Lower valued uses of oil

20

0

Demand

0   20   40   60   80   100   120   140

Quantity of oil (MBD)

The Demand for Oil Depends on the Value of Oil in Different Uses
When the price of oil is high, oil will only be used in the higher valued uses. As the price falls, oil will also be used in lower valued uses.

wait in three-hour lines in one state, consumers in other states are breezing in and out of gas stations."[1]

Figure 4.5 illustrates the problem more generally. As we know, at the controlled price, the quantity demanded (Q_d) exceeds the quantity supplied (Q_s) and there is a shortage. Ideally, we would like to allocate the quantity of oil supplied, Q_s, to its highest-valued uses; these are illustrated at the top of the demand curve by the thick line. But the potential consumers of the oil with the highest valued uses are legally prevented from signaling their high value by offering to pay oil suppliers more than the controlled price. Oil suppliers, therefore, have no incentive to supply oil to just the consumers with the highest valued uses. Instead, oil suppliers will give the oil to any user who is willing to pay the controlled price—but most of these users of oil have lower valued uses. Like the lines at the gas station, it's first come, first served. In fact, the only uses of oil that definitely will not be satisfied are the least valued uses. (Why not? The users with the least valued uses are not even willing to pay the controlled price.)

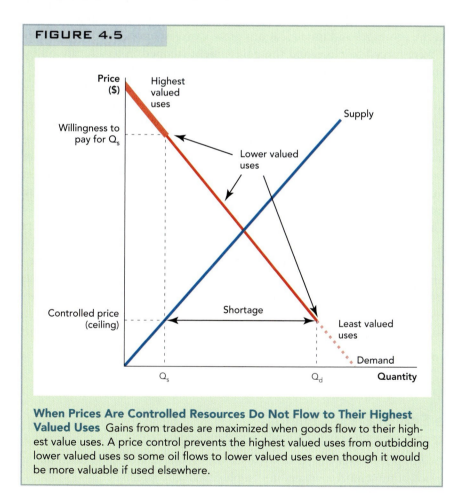

FIGURE 4.5

When Prices Are Controlled Resources Do Not Flow to Their Highest Valued Uses Gains from trades are maximized when goods flow to their highest value uses. A price control prevents the highest valued uses from outbidding lower valued uses so some oil flows to lower valued uses even though it would be more valuable if used elsewhere.

When a crisis in the Middle East reduces the supply of oil, the price system rationally responds by reallocating oil from lower valued uses to the highest value uses. In contrast, when the supply of oil is reduced and there are price ceilings, oil is allocated according to random and often trivial factors. The shortage of heating oil in 1971, for example, was exacerbated by the fact that President Nixon happened to impose price controls in *August* when

For want of a nail
the shoe was lost.
For want of a shoe
the horse was lost.
For want of a horse
the rider was lost.
For want of a rider
the battle was lost.
For want of a battle
the kingdom was lost.
And why was the nail wanting?
Price controls.

the price of heating oil was near its seasonal low.[2] Since the price of heating oil was controlled at a low price while gasoline was controlled at a slightly higher price, it was more profitable to turn crude oil into gasoline than into heating oil. As winter approached, the price of heating oil would normally have risen and refiners would have turned away from gasoline production to the production of heating oil, but price controls removed the incentive to respond rationally.

Misallocation and Production Chaos Shortages in one market create breakdowns and shortages in other markets, so the chaos of price controls expands even into markets without price controls. In ordinary times, we take it for granted that products will be available when we want them, but in an economy with many price controls, shortages of key inputs can appear at any time. In 1973, for example, million-dollar construction projects were delayed because a few thousand dollars worth of steel bars were unavailable.[3]

Perhaps the height of misallocation occurred when shortages of steel drilling equipment made it difficult to expand oil production; this mistake took place even as the United States was undergoing the worst energy crisis in its history.[4]

As the shortages and misallocations grew worse, schools, factories, and offices were forced to close, and the government stepped in to allocate oil by command. President Nixon ordered gasoline stations to close between 9 P.M. Saturday and 12:01 A.M. Monday.[5] The idea was to prevent "wasteful" Sunday driving, but the ban simply encouraged people to fill their tanks earlier. Daylight savings time and a national 55 mph speed limit were put into place (the latter not to be repealed until 1995). Some industries, such as agriculture, were given priority treatment for fuel allocation, while others were forced to endure cutbacks. Fuel for noncommercial aircraft, for example, was cut by 42.5 percent in November of 1973, sending the local economy of Wichita, Kansas, where aircraft producers Cessna, Beech, and Lear were located, into a tailspin.[6]

Some of these ideas for conserving fuel were probably sensible while others were not, but without market prices, it's hard to tell which is which. The subtlety of the market process in allocating oil and taking advantage of links between markets is difficult, even impossible, to duplicate. C. Jackson Grayson was chairman of President Nixon's Price Commission, but after seeing how controls worked in practice he said:

> Our economic understanding and models are simply not powerful enough to handle such a large and complex economic system better than the marketplace.[7]

The End of Price Ceilings

Price controls for most goods were lifted by April 1974, but controls on oil remained in place. Over the next 7 years, controls on oil would be eased but at the price of substantial increases in complexity and bureaucracy.

Price controls on oil ended as abruptly as they had begun when on the morning of January 20, 1981, Ronald Reagan was inaugurated as president, and before lunch with Congress, he performed his first act as president—eliminating all controls on oil and gasoline. As expected, the price of oil in the United States rose a little but the shortage ended overnight. Within a year, prices began to fall as supply increased and within a few years they were well below the levels of 1979.

see the invisible hand

President Nixon said no to commercial holiday lights during the Christmas of 1973.

UNDERSTAND YOUR **world**

Fluctuations in the price of oil have continued to occur, of course, but since the ending of controls, there has been no shortage of oil in the United States.

Price Floors

When governments control prices, it is usually with a price ceiling designed to keep prices below market levels, but occasionally the government intervenes to keep prices above market levels. Can you think of an example? Here's a hint. Buyers usually outnumber sellers, so it's probably no accident that governments intervene to keep prices below market levels more often than they intervene to keep prices above market levels. The most common example of a price being controlled above market levels is the exception that proves the rule because it involves a good for which sellers outnumber buyers. Here's another hint. You own this good.

The good is labor and the most common example of a price controlled above the market level is the minimum wage.

When the minimum price that can be legally charged is above the market price, we say that there is a **price floor.** Economists call it a price floor because prices cannot legally go below the floor. Price floors create four important effects:

1. Surpluses
2. Lost gains from trade (deadweight loss)
3. Wasteful increases in quality
4. Misallocation of resources

Surpluses

Figure 4.6 on the next page graphs the demand and supply of labor and shows how a price held above the market price creates a surplus, a situation where the quantity of labor supplied exceeds the quantity demanded. We have a special word for a surplus of labor: unemployment.

The idea that a minimum wage creates unemployment should not be surprising. If the minimum wage did not create unemployment, the solution to poverty would be easy—raise minimum wages to $10, $20, or even $100 an hour! But at a high enough wage, none of us would be worth employing.

Can a more moderate minimum wage also create unemployment? Yes. A minimum wage of $5.85 an hour, the federal minimum in 2007, won't affect most workers who, because of their productivity, already earn more than $5.85 an hour. In the United States, for example, about 97 percent of all workers paid by the hour already earn more than the minimum wage. A minimum wage, however, will decrease employment among low-skilled workers. The more employers have to pay for low-skilled workers, the fewer low-skilled workers they will hire.

Young people, for example, often lack substantial skills and are more likely to be made unemployed by the minimum wage. About a quarter of all workers earning the minimum wage are teenagers (ages 16–19) and more than half are less than 25 years of age.[8] Studies of the minimum wage verify that the unemployment effect is concentrated among teenagers.[9]

In addition to creating surpluses, a price floor, just like a price ceiling, reduces the gains from trade.

CHECK YOURSELF

> Since World War II, New York City has had rent control for many of its apartments, with ceilings placed on the rent that landlords can charge. You are moving to New York City. Will you find a surplus or shortage of apartments?

> Some landlords in New York City demand that new tenants pay $500 or $1,000 key money (landlords will not hand over a set of apartment keys until this nonrefundable payment is made). How does key money fit into our model of the effects of price ceilings?

> In rent-controlled New York City, over time, what do you think will happen to the upkeep of the rent-controlled buildings? What is the landlord's incentive structure?

A **price floor** is a minimum price allowed by law.

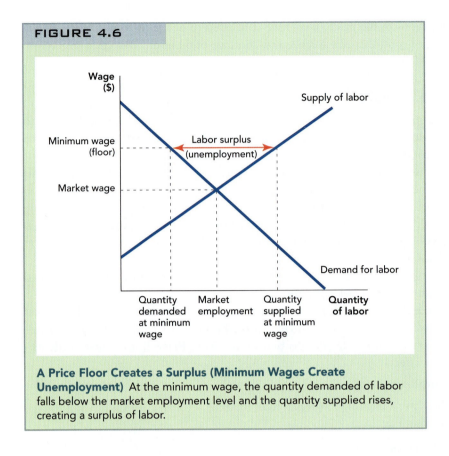

FIGURE 4.6

A Price Floor Creates a Surplus (Minimum Wages Create Unemployment) At the minimum wage, the quantity demanded of labor falls below the market employment level and the quantity supplied rises, creating a surplus of labor.

Lost Gains from Trade

Notice in Figure 4.7 that at the minimum wage employers are willing to hire Q_d workers. Employers would hire more workers if they could offer lower wages and, importantly, workers would be willing to work at lower wages if they were allowed to do so. If employers and workers could bargain freely, the wage would fall and the quantity of labor traded would increase to the level of market employment. Notice that at the market employment level, the gains from trade increase by the green and blue triangles. The green triangle is the increase in consumer surplus (remember that in this example it is the employers who are the consumers of labor) and the blue triangle is the increase in producer (worker) surplus.

Although the minimum wage creates some unemployment and reduces the gains from trade, the influence of the minimum wage in the American economy is very small. Even for the young, the minimum wage is not very important because although most workers earning the minimum wage are young, most young workers earn more than the minimum wage. As we noted above, a majority of workers earning the minimum wage are younger than 25 years old but 93.9 percent of workers younger than 25 earn more than the minimum wage.[10]

These facts may surprise you. The minimum wage is hotly debated in the United States. Democrats often argue that the minimum wage must be raised to help working families. Republicans respond that a higher minimum wage will create unemployment and raise prices as firms pass on higher costs to customers. Neither position is realistic. At best, the minimum wage will raise the wages of some teenagers and young workers whose wages would increase anyway as they improve their education and become more skilled. At worst, the minimum wage

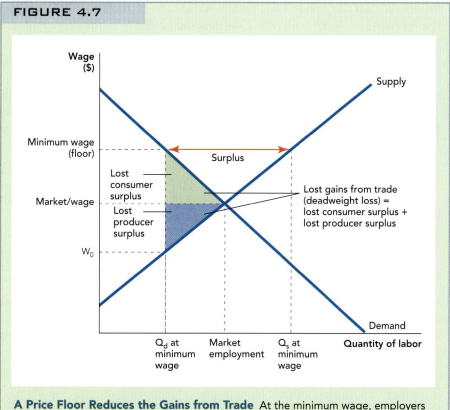

FIGURE 4.7

A Price Floor Reduces the Gains from Trade At the minimum wage, employers are willing to hire more workers at just less than the minimum wage and workers are willing to work additional hours for just more than W_0. Although mutually profitable, these trades are illegal. If all mutually profitable trades were legal, the gains from trade would increase by the green plus blue triangles.

will raise the price of a hamburger and create unemployment among teenagers, many of whom will simply choose to stay in school longer (not necessarily a bad thing). The minimum wage debate is more about rhetoric than reality.

Even though small increases in the U.S. minimum wage won't change much, large increases would cause serious unemployment. A large increase in the minimum wage is unlikely in the United States, but it has happened elsewhere. In 1938, Puerto Rico was surprised to discover that it was bound by a minimum wage set well above the Puerto Rican average wage for unskilled labor.

Puerto Rico has a peculiar political status; it's an unincorporated U.S. territory classified as a commonwealth. In 1938, Congress passed the Fair Labor Standards Act, which set the first U.S. minimum wage at 25 cents an hour. At the time, the average wage in the United States was 62.7 cents an hour, but in Puerto Rico many workers were earning just 3 to 4 cents an hour. Congress, however, had forgotten to create an exemption for Puerto Rico so what was a modest minimum wage in the United States was a huge increase in wages in Puerto Rico.

Puerto Rican workers, however, did not benefit from the minimum wage. Unable to pay the higher wage, Puerto Rican firms went bankrupt, creating devastating unemployment. In a panic, representatives of Puerto Rico pleaded with the U.S. Congress to create an exemption for Puerto Rico. "The medicine is too strong for the patient," said Puerto Rican Labor Commissioner Prudencio Rivera Martinez. Two years later Congress finally did establish lower rates for Puerto Rico.[11]

Minimum wages in other countries are also sometimes considerably higher than in the United States. France combines a high minimum wage—compared to the United States nearly twice as high relative to the French median wage—with labor regulations that make it difficult to fire workers. As a result, firms are reluctant to hire young workers both because they are less productive than older workers, and thus less employable at a high minimum wage, and because hiring someone that you can't fire is more risky when the person doesn't have a history of employment. In 2005, 23 percent of French workers under 25 years old were unemployed.

To explain the other important effects of price floors—wasteful increases in quality and a misallocation of resources—we turn from minimum wages to airline regulation.

Wasteful Increases in Quality

Many years ago, flying on an airplane was extremely pleasurable; seats were wide, service was attentive, flights weren't packed, and the food was good. So airplane travel in the United States must have gotten worse, right? No, it has gotten better. Let's explain.

The Civil Aeronautics Board (CAB) extensively regulated airlines in the United States from 1938 to 1978. No firm could enter or exit the market, change prices, or alter routes without permission from the CAB. The CAB kept prices well above market levels, sometimes even denying requests by firms to lower prices!

We know that prices were kept above market levels because the CAB only had the right to control airlines operating *between* states. In-state airlines were largely unregulated. Using data from large states like Texas and California, it was possible to compare prices on unregulated flights to prices on regulated flights of the same distance. Prices on flights between San Francisco and Los Angeles, for example, were half the price of similar length flights between Boston and Washington, D.C.

In Figure 4.8, firms are earning the CAB-regulated fare on flights that they would be willing to sell at the much lower price labeled "willingness to sell." Initially, therefore, regulation was a great deal for the airlines, who took home the red area as producer surplus.

A price floor means that prices are held *above* market levels, so firms want more customers. The price floor, however, makes it illegal to compete for more customers by lowering prices. So how do firms compete when they cannot lower prices? Price floors cause firms to compete by offering customers higher quality.

When airlines were regulated, for example, they competed by offering their customers bone china, fancy meals, wide seats, and frequent flights. Sounds good, right? Yes, but don't forget that the increase in quality came at a price. Would you rather have a fine meal on your flight to Paris or a modest meal and more money to spend at a real Parisian restaurant?

If consumers were willing to pay for fine meals on an airplane, airlines would offer that service. But if you have flown recently, you know that consumers would rather have a lower price. An increase in quality that consumers are not willing to pay for is a wasteful increase in quality. Thus, as firms competed by offering higher quality, the initial producer surplus was wasted away

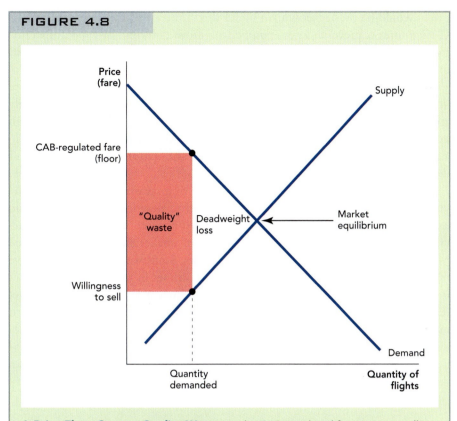

FIGURE 4.8

A Price Floor Creates Quality Waste At the CAB-regulated fare, price is well above a seller's willingness to sell. Sellers cannot compete by offering lower prices so they compete by offering higher quality. Higher quality raises costs and reduces seller profit. Buyers enjoy the higher quality but would prefer less quality at a lower price. Thus, the price floor encourages sellers to waste resources by producing more quality than buyers are willing to pay for.

in frills that consumers liked but would not be willing to pay for—hence, the red area is labeled "Quality" waste.

Airline costs increased over time for another reason. The producer surplus initially earned by the airlines was a tempting target for unions who threatened to strike unless they got their share of the proceeds. The airlines didn't put up too much of a fight because, when their costs rose, they could apply to the CAB for an increase in fares, thus passing along the higher costs to consumers. Many of the problems that older airlines have faced in recent times are due to generous pension and health benefits, which were granted when prices of flights were regulated above market levels.

By 1978, costs had increased so much that the airlines were no longer benefiting from regulation and were willing to accede to deregulation.[12] Deregulation lowered prices, increased quantity, and reduced wasteful quality competition.[13] Deregulation also reduced waste and increased efficiency in another way—by improving the allocation of resources.

Misallocation of Resources

Regulation of airline fares could not have been maintained for 40 years if the CAB had not also regulated entry. Firms wanted to enter the airline industry because the CAB kept prices high, but the CAB knew that if entry occurred,

Despite being more efficient than its rivals, airline regulation prevented Southwest from entering the national market until deregulation in 1978. Today, Southwest Airlines is one of the largest airlines in the world.

prices would be pushed down. So under the influence of the older airlines, the CAB routinely prevented new competitors from entering. In 1938, for example, there were 16 major airlines; by 1974 there were just 10 despite 79 requests to enter the industry.

Restrictions on entry misallocated resources because low-cost airlines were kept out of the industry. Southwest Airlines, for example, began as a Texas-only airline because it could not get a license from the CAB to operate between states. (Lawsuits from competitors also nearly prevented Southwest from operating in Texas.) Southwest was able to enter the national market only after deregulation in 1978.

The entry of Southwest was not just a case of increasing supply. One of the virtues of the market process is that it is open to new ideas, innovations, and experiments. Southwest, for example, pioneered consistent use of the same aircraft to lower maintenance costs, greater use of smaller airports like Chicago's Midway, and long-term hedging of fuel costs. Southwest's innovations have made it one of the most profitable and largest airlines in the world. Southwest's innovations have spread in turn to other firms such as JetBlue Airways, easyJet (Europe), and WestJet (Canada). Regulation of entry didn't just increase prices, it increased costs and reduced innovation. Deregulation improved the allocation of resources by allowing low-cost, innovative firms to expand nationally. Deregulation is the major reason why, today, flying is an ordinary event for most American families, rather than the province of the wealthy.

UNDERSTAND YOUR world

CHECK YOURSELF

> The European Union has a minimum legal price for butter, a price floor, that is often above the market equilibrium price. What do you think has been the result of this?

> The United States has set a price floor for milk above the equilibrium price. Has this led to shortages or surpluses? How do you think the U.S. government has dealt with this? (Hint: remember the cartons of milk you had in elementary school and high school? What was their price?)

☐ Takeaway

Price ceilings have several important effects: they create shortages, reductions in quality, wasteful lines and other search costs, lost gains from trade, and a misallocation of resources.

After reading this chapter, you should be able to explain all of these effects to your uncle. Also, to do well on the exam, you should be able to draw a diagram showing the price ceiling and correctly labeling the shortage. On the same diagram, can you locate the wasteful losses from waiting in line and the lost gains from trade? Review Figures 4.2 and 4.3 if you are having trouble with these questions. You should also understand why a price ceiling reduces product quality and how price ceilings misallocate resources, not just in the market with the price ceiling but potentially throughout the economy.

Price floors create surpluses, a loss of gains from trade, wasteful increases in quality, and a misallocation of resources.

After reading this chapter, you should be able to explain all of these effects to your aunt. Can you show, using the tools of supply and demand, why a price floor creates a surplus, a deadweight loss, and a wasteful increase in quality? You should be able to label these areas on a diagram. You should also be able to explain how price floors cause resources to be misallocated.

☐ CHAPTER REVIEW

Price ceiling, p. 52

Deadweight loss, p. 55

Price floor, p. 59

1. How does a free market eliminate a shortage?

2. When a price ceiling is in place keeping the price below the market price, what's larger: quantity demanded or quantity supplied? How does this explain the long lines and wasteful searches we see in price-controlled markets?

3. Is the minimum wage a "price ceiling" or a "price floor?" What about rent control?

4. How do U.S. business owners change their behavior when the minimum wage rises? How does this impact teenagers?

5. **a.** If the government forced all sellers of loaves of bread to sell at a price half the current price, what would happen to the quantity supplied of bread? To keep it simple, assume that people wait in line to get the bread they need. Would consumer surplus rise, fall, or are you unable to tell with the information given?

   b. With these price controls on bread, would you expect bread quality to rise or fall?

6. In the market depicted below there is either a price ceiling or a price floor—surprisingly, it doesn't matter which one it is: Whether it's an $80 price floor or a $30 price ceiling, the chart looks the same.

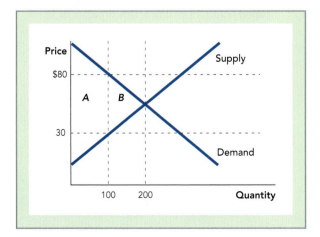

In the chart, there's a rectangle and a triangle. One represents the value lost from the "deals that don't get made" and one represents the value lost from "the deals that do get made." Which is which?

7. When the United States had price controls on oil and gasoline, some parts of the United States had a lot of gasoline while other states had long lines. As in the chapter, let's assume that winter oil demand is higher in New Jersey than in California. If there had been *no* price controls, what would have happened to the prices of gasoline in New Jersey and in California and how would "greedy businesspeople" have responded to these price differences?

8. **a.** If a government decides to make health insurance affordable by requiring all health insurance companies to cut their prices by 30 percent, what will probably happen to the number of people covered by health insurance?

   b. Here is a more subtle question. What will happen to the type of people (in particular their health status) that the insurance companies cover after the price control?

9. The Canadian government has wage controls for medical doctors. To keep things simple, let's assume that they set one wage for all doctors: $100,000 per year. It takes about 6 years to become a general practitioner or a pediatrician, but it takes about 8 or 9 years to become a specialist like a gynecologist, surgeon, or ophthalmologist. What kind of doctor would you want to become under this system? (Note: the actual Canadian system does allow specialists to earn a bit more than general practitioners, but the difference isn't big enough to matter.)

10. In rich countries, governments almost always set the fares for taxi rides. The prices for taxi rides are the same in safe neighborhoods and in dangerous neighborhoods. Where is it easier to find a cab? Why? If these taxi price controls were ended, what would probably happen to the price and quantity of cab rides in dangerous neighborhoods?

1. Business leaders often say that there is a "shortage" of skilled workers, and so they argue that immigrants need to be brought in to do

these jobs. For example, a recent AP article was entitled "New York farmers fear a shortage of skilled workers," and went on to point out that a special U.S. visa program, the H–2A program, "allows employers to hire foreign workers temporarily if they show that they were not able to find U.S. workers for the jobs."

(Source: Thompson, Carolyn. 2008. "N.Y. farmers fear a shortage of skilled workers" Associated Press, May 12.)

a. How do unregulated markets cure a "labor shortage" when there are no immigrants to boost the labor supply?

b. Why are businesses reluctant to cure the shortage this way?

2. On January 31, 1990, the first McDonald's opened in Moscow, capital of the then-Soviet Union. Economists often described the Soviet Union as a "permanent shortage economy," where the government kept prices permanently low in order to appear "fair."

"An American journalist on the scene reported the customers seemed most amazed at the 'simple sight of polite shop workers . . . in this nation of commercial boorishness.'"

(Source: http://www.history.com/this-day-in-history.do?action=Article&id=2563)

a. Why were most Soviet shop workers "boorish" while the McDonald's workers in Moscow were "polite"?

b. What does your answer to the previous question tell you about the power of economic incentives to change human behavior? In other words, how entrenched is "culture"?

McDonald's in Moscow: The First Day

3. Let's count the value of losses in a price-controlled market. The government decides it wants to make basic bicycles more affordable,

so it passes a law requiring that all one-speed bicycles sell for $30, well below the market price. Use the data below to calculate the losses, just as in Figure 4.3. Supply and demand are straight lines.

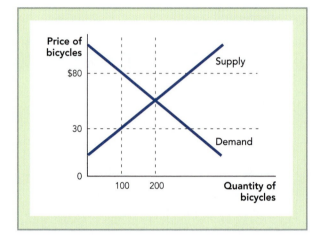

a. Assuming that people must wait in line to obtain a bicycle at the controlled price, what is the total value of wasted time?

b. What is the value of the lost gains from trade?

c. Note that we haven't given you the original market price of simple bicycles—why don't you need to know it? (Hint: The answer is a mix of geometry and economics.)

4. Between 2000 and 2008, the price of oil increased from $30 per barrel to $140 per barrel, and the price of gasoline in the United States rose from about $1.50 per gallon to over $4.00 per gallon. Unlike in the 1970s when oil prices spiked, there were no long lines outside gas stations. Why?

5. During a crisis such as Hurricane Katrina, governments often make it illegal to raise the price of emergency items like flashlights and bottled water. In practice, this means that these items get sold on a first-come, first-served basis.

a. If a person has a flashlight that she values at $5, but its price on the black market is $40, what gains from trade are lost if the government shuts down the black market?

b. Why might a person want to sell a flashlight for $40 during an emergency?

c. Why might a person be willing to pay $40 for a flashlight during an emergency?

d. When will entrepreneurs be more likely to fill up their pickup trucks with flashlights and drive into a disaster area: When they can sell their flashlights for $5 each or when they can sell them for $40 each?

6. We noted that in the 1970s price floors on airline tickets caused wasteful increases in the quality of airline trips. Does the minimum wage cause wasteful increases in the quality of workers? If so, how? In other words, how are minimum-wage workers like airplane trips?

7. In the 1970s AirCal and Pacific Southwest Airlines flew only within California. A major route for them was flying from San Francisco to Los Angeles, a distance of 350 miles. This is about the same distance as from Chicago to Cleveland. Do you think AirCal flights were cheaper or more expensive than flights from Chicago to Cleveland? Do you think AirCal flights had nicer meals than flights from Chicago to Cleveland?

8. A "black market" is a place where people make illegal trades in goods and services. For instance, during the Soviet era, it was common for American tourists to take a few extra pairs of Levi's jeans when visiting the Soviet Union: They would sell the extra pairs at high prices on the illegal black market.

   Consider the following claim: "Price-controlled markets tend to create black markets." Let's illustrate with the figure below. If there is a price ceiling in the market for cancer medication of $50 per pill, what is the *widest* price range within which you can *definitely* find both a buyer and a seller who would be willing to illegally exchange a pill for money? (There is only one correct answer.)

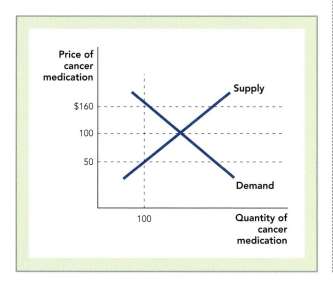

9. Notice that the argument of the previous question works for price floors as well. It's obvious why business owners would love to hire workers for less than the minimum wage; but if almost all companies obey the minimum wage law, why are some workers still willing to work for less than the minimum wage?

10. So, knowing what you know now about price controls, are you in favor of setting a $2 per gallon price ceiling on gasoline? Create a pro-price control and an anti-price control answer.

CHALLENGES

1. If a government decided to impose price controls on gasoline, what could it do to avoid the time wasted waiting in lines? There is surely more than one solution to this problem.

BETTMANN/CORBIS

2. President Jimmy Carter didn't just deregulate airline prices. He also deregulated much of the trucking industry as well. Trucks carry almost all of the consumer goods that you purchase, so almost every time you purchase something, you're paying money to a trucking company.

   a. Based on what happened in the airline industry after prices were deregulated, what do you think happened in the trucking industry after deregulation? You can find some answers here:

   http://www.econlib.org/Library/Enc/TruckingDeregulation.html

   For another look that is critical of trucking deregulation but comes to basically the same answers, see Michael Belzer, *Sweatshops on Wheels: Winners and Losers in Trucking Deregulation*, Thousand Oaks, CA: Sage, 2000.

b. Who do you think asked Congress and the president to keep price floors for trucking: consumer groups, retail shops like Wal-Mart, or the trucking companies?

3. In New York City, some apartments are under strict rent control, while others are not. This is a theme in many novels and movies about New York, including *Bonfire of the Vanities* and *When Harry Met Sally*. One predictable side effect of rent control is the creation of a black market. Let's think about whether it's a good idea to allow this black market to exist.

a. Harry is lucky enough to get a rent-controlled apartment for $300 per month. The market rent on such an apartment is $3,000 per month. Harry himself values the apartment at $2,000 per month, and he'd be quite happy with a regular, $2,000 per month New York apartment. If he stays in the apartment, how much consumer surplus does he enjoy?

b. If he illegally subleases his apartment to Sally on the black market for $2,500 per month and instead rents a $2,000 apartment, is he better off or worse off than if he obeyed the law?

4. Suppose you're doing some history research on shoe production in ancient Rome, during the reign of the famous Emperor Diocletian. Your records tell you how many shoes were produced each year in the Roman Empire, but it doesn't tell you the price of shoes. You find a document that says that in the year 301, Emperor Diocletian issued an "Edict on Prices," but you don't know whether he imposed price *ceilings* or price *floors*—your Latin is a little rusty. However, you can clearly tell from the documents that the number of shoes actually sold in markets fell dramatically, and that both potential shoe sellers and potential shoe buyers were unhappy with the edict. With the information given, can you tell whether Diocletian imposed a ceiling or a floor? If so, which is it? (Yes, there really was an Edict of Diocletian, and Wikipedia has excellent coverage of ancient Roman history.)

5. When are political connections and "who you know" more likely to be important: in a competitive market or in a price-controlled market?

5

GDP and the Measurement of Progress

A visitor to India is immediately struck by the contrast between extreme poverty and rapid economic growth. Squalor in India is obvious, 80 percent of India's population lives on less than $2 a day (as of 2005). Throughout India, you will see people living in the streets, children who have never been to school, fires burning on the sidewalk, and cripples begging for spare change.

But India's growing wealth is also obvious: cell phones are everywhere, new stores are opening, access to clean water is increasing, literacy is rising, and people are better fed. In the cities, there are more restaurants, more clothing shops, more factories, and more cars. India today has at least 100 million people at an American or European standard of living—a remarkable increase from just a few decades ago.

As a rough way of summarizing these changes in economic output and the standard of living, economists look to a country's Gross Domestic Product (GDP) and its gross domestic product per capita, two statistics designed to measure the value of economic production.

Figure 5.1 on the next page shows India's real GDP per capita—or GDP per person—for the 10-year period, 1993–2003. Over this period, India's real GDP per capita grew at an average rate of 4.5 percent a year. If this rate continues, India's GDP per capita will double in just less than 16 years. As we discuss below, real GDP per capita is a rough measure of a country's standard of living. Thus, in the 10 years preceding 2003, the standard of living in India increased by more than 50 percent. That is a notable improvement over India's previous growth performance and it represents the growing wealth of many people in India.

FIGURE 5.1

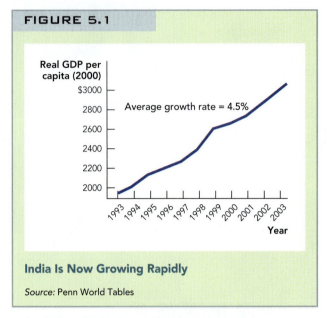

India Is Now Growing Rapidly

Source: Penn World Tables

TABLE 5.1 The 15 Largest Countries Ranked by GDP (2003)		
Rank	Country	GDP (Billions of U.S. Dollars)	GDP per Capita (in U.S. Dollars)
1	United States	$10,205	$34,875
2	China	6,396	4,970
3	India	3,139	2,990
4	Japan	3,070	24,036
5	Germany	2,080	25,188
6	Russia	1,703	11,788
7	United Kingdom	1,544	26,045
8	France	1,540	25,663
9	Italy	1,329	22,924
10	Brazil	1,312	7,204
11	Indonesia	968	4,122
12	Canada	881	27,844
13	Spain	870	20,644
14	South Korea	835	17,597
15	Mexico	828	7,938

Source: Penn World Tables

Table 5.1 lists GDP and GDP per capita for the 15 largest economies circa 2003 (converted into U.S. dollars). In the United States, where GDP was $10.205 trillion and the population was 292.6 million, GDP per capita was $34,875. Although China is the world's second largest economy with a 2003 GDP of $6.4 trillion, it has a population of 1.3 billion people, so per capita GDP is only $4,970, a little bit more than in El Salvador ($4,751) or Guatemala ($3,805). Similarly, India has the world's third largest economy but, after China, it has the world's second largest population, so GDP per capita in India is only $2,990.

Some poorer countries have grown considerably and have achieved a middle-income status between "rich" and "very poor." Examples would be Mexico, Brazil, and Chile; their per capita GDPs are around 9, 8, and 15 thousand dollars respectively. India and China are hoping to make similar gains.

Okay, we can see that GDP per capita gives us a rough guide to a country's standard of living, but what is GDP actually measuring? In this chapter, we will explain:

> What the GDP statistic means and how it is measured

> The difference between the level of GDP and the growth rate of GDP

> The difference between nominal GDP and real GDP

> How growth in per capita real GDP is a standard measure of economic progress

> The use of GDP in business cycle measurement

> Problems with GDP as a measure of output and welfare

What Is GDP?

Gross domestic product (GDP) is the market value of all final goods and services produced within a country in a year. **GDP per capita** is GDP divided by a country's population.

To repeat, GDP is the market value of all final goods and services produced within a country in a year. Let's take each part of this statement in turn.

GDP Is the Market Value . . .

GDP measures an economy's total output, which includes millions of different goods and services. But some goods are obviously more valuable than others: a Ford Mustang is worth more than an iPod. To measure total output, therefore, it doesn't make sense to simply add up quantities. Instead, GDP uses market values to determine how much each good or service is worth and then sums the total.

For example, in 2005 the U.S. economy produced approximately 12 million cars and light vehicles and 20 million personal computers.[1] If the average price of a car was $28,000 and the average price of a computer was $1,000, the market value of the production of cars was $336 billion ($28,000 × 12 million) and the market value of computer production was $20 billion ($1,000 × 20 million). Using prices in the calculations gives greater weight to goods and services that are more highly valued in the marketplace. Applying this procedure to all final goods and services yields a figure for GDP. In Table 5.2, we show the addition to GDP created by the production of cars and computers.

Gross domestic product (GDP) is the market value of all final goods and services produced within a country in a year.

GDP per capita is GDP divided by population.

. . . of All Final . . .

What is a *final* good or service? Some goods and services are sold to firms and then bundled or processed with other goods or services for sale at a later stage. These are called intermediate goods and services. We distinguish these from final goods and services, which are sold to final users and then consumed or held in personal inventories.

TABLE 5.2 GDP Is Calculated by Multiplying the Price of Final Goods and Services by Their Quantities and Adding the Market Values

Final Good	Price	×	Quantity	=	Market Value
Cars	$28,000	×	12 million	=	$336 billion
Computers	$1,000	×	20 million	=	$20 billion
					$356 billion ← Added to GDP

A computer chip is one example of an intermediate good. If an Intel chip were counted in GDP when it was sold to Dell, and then counted again when a consumer buys the Dell computer, the value of the computer chip would be counted twice. To avoid double counting, only the computer—the final good—is included in the calculation of GDP.

We do, however, count the production of machinery and equipment used to produce other goods as part of GDP. A tractor, for example, may help to produce soybeans, but the tractor is not part of the final product of soybeans. Thus, both tractor production and soybean production add to GDP, even though the computer chip does not.

. . . Goods and Services . . .

The output of an economy includes both goods and services. Services provide a benefit to individuals without the production of tangible output. For example, paying a consultant to fix a software problem on a computer is a service and its market value is included in GDP. Other services include haircuts, transportation, entertainment, and spending on medical care.

Entertainment is part of GDP

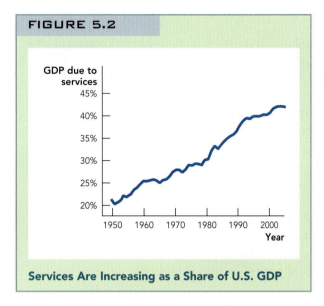

FIGURE 5.2

GDP due to services

Services Are Increasing as a Share of U.S. GDP

Since 1950, the portion of U.S. GDP created by the production of services has doubled from 21 to 42 percent (see Figure 5.2). Much of this increase is attributable to spending on medical services and recreational activities, which have both increased to more than 10 times their levels in 1950.[2]

Since U.S. GDP is about $14 trillion (2007), we can tell from the graph that the value of final services is about $5.88 trillion (0.42 × $14) and the value of final goods about $8.12 trillion (0.58 × $14).

. . . Produced . . .

GDP is meant to measure *production* so sales of used goods are not included in GDP. The sale of a used car, for example, is not included in GDP.

Similarly, sales of old houses and sales of financial securities like stocks and bonds are not included in the calculation of GDP. The sale of an old house does not add to GDP because the house was not produced in the year in which it sold. Sales of newly built houses, however, are counted in GDP. Stocks and bonds are claims to financial assets—they are not themselves produced goods or services—so sales of financial assets are not counted in GDP.

Even though the sale of old houses, used goods, and financial assets do not add to GDP the services of real estate agents, used-car salespeople, and brokers do add to GDP because the services provided by these agents are produced in the year in which they are sold.

. . . within a Country . . .

U.S. GDP is the market value of the goods and services produced by labor and property *located* in the United States, regardless of the nationality of the workers or the property owners. A citizen of Mexico who works temporarily in the United States adds to U.S. GDP. By the same reasoning, an American who works temporarily in Mexico contributes to Mexican GDP, not to U.S. GDP.

Gross national product (GNP) is very similar to GDP but GNP measures what is produced by the labor and property supplied by U.S. permanent residents wherever in the world that labor or property is located, rather than what is produced within the U.S. border. For a large nation like the United States, GDP and GNP are very similar but GDP has evolved into the more commonly used concept.

Gross national product (GNP) is the market value of all final goods and services produced by a country's permanent residents, wherever located, in a year.

. . . in a Year

GDP tells us how much the nation produced in a year, not how much the nation has accumulated in its entire history. You can think of GDP as being analogous to annual wages. Wages are not the same thing as wealth. Some retired people are wealthy even though their wages are low and some people with high wages have very little wealth (perhaps because they are at the beginning of their career or perhaps because they spend everything they earn and never save).

National wealth refers to the value of a nation's entire stock of assets. A tractor built in 1990 and still operating today is part of U.S. wealth but not part of today's GDP. One very crude estimate places U.S. national wealth at $53.3 trillion,[3] which is several times larger than its GDP of about $14 trillion.

Although we typically think of GDP on a yearly basis, it is also calculated every quarter of the year. The calculations are done by the Bureau of Economic Analysis (BEA) which is part of the Department of Commerce and based in Washington, D.C. If you want to see whether you understand what the bureau is up to, try testing yourself with the questions at right.

CHECK YOURSELF

> The Interstate Bakeries Corporation buys wheat flour to make into Wonder Bread. Does the purchase of wheat flour add to GDP?

> On eBay, you sell your collection of Pokémon cards. Does your sale add to GDP?

> An immigrant from Colombia works as a cook in a New York restaurant. Is the money he earns considered part of the GDP of the United States or Colombia?

Growth Rates

GDP tells us how much a country produced in a given year. The growth rate of GDP tells us how rapidly the country's production is rising or falling over time. To compute the growth rate of GDP from 2004 to 2005, for example, you need only two numbers: GDP at the end of both 2004 and 2005. Compute the percentage change as:

$$\frac{GDP_{2005} - GDP_{2004}}{GDP_{2004}} \times 100 = \text{GDP growth rate for 2005}$$

Using actual figures (in billions), we determine:

$$\frac{\$12,455 - \$11,712}{\$11,712} \times 100 = 6.34\%$$

Thus, the U.S. growth rate for 2005 was 6.34 percent.

CHECK YOURSELF

> If GDP in 1990 was $5,803 billion and GDP in 1991 was $5,995 billion, what was the growth rate of (nominal) GDP?

Nominal vs. Real GDP

The rate of growth expressed above did not adjust for price changes and is called the nominal growth rate. The alternative concept is the growth rate of real GDP and here is the background for understanding that distinction.

Nominal GDP is calculated using prices at the time of sale. Thus, GDP in 2005 is calculated using 2005 prices and GDP in 1995 is calculated using 1995 prices. If we want to compare GDP over substantial periods, using nominal GDP creates a problem. GDP in 2005, for example, was $12.4 trillion and GDP in 1995 was $7.4 trillion. Should we celebrate this roughly 70 percent increase in GDP $\left(\frac{12.4 - 7.4}{7.4} \times 100 = 67.6\%\right)$? Not so fast! Before we celebrate, we would like to know whether the increase was due mostly to greater production—more cars and computers—or to increases in prices between 1995 and 2005.

Economists usually are more interested in increases in production than increases in prices because only increases in production are true increases in the standard of living. But how can we measure increases in production while controlling for increases in prices? Here is what we know so far:

2005 Nominal GDP = 2005 Prices × 2005 Quantities = $12.4 trillion
1995 Nominal GDP = 1995 Prices × 1995 Quantities = $7.4 trillion

Nominal variables, such as nominal GDP, have not been adjusted for changes in prices.

Can you see how to compare the increase in production from 1995 to 2005? Suppose we calculate GDP in 1995 using 2005 prices instead of 1995 prices:

2005 GDP in 2005 Dollars = 2005 Prices × 2005 Quantities = $12.4 trillion

1995 GDP in 2005 Dollars = 2005 Prices × 1995 Quantities = $9.0 trillion

What this tells us is that if prices in 1995 were the same as in 2005, then GDP in 1995 would have been measured as $9.0 trillion. Economists also say that 1995 GDP in 2005 dollars is **real GDP** in 2005 dollars. Since 2005 GDP is already in 2005 dollars, it's also real GDP in 2005 dollars.

Now that we have real GDP in 1995 and real GDP in 2005, we can find the increase in real GDP. Between 1995 and 2005, the increase in real GDP was 37.8 percent $\left(\dfrac{12.4 - 9.0}{9.0} \times 100 = 37.8\% \right)$. Thus in 2005 the economy produced 37.8 percent more stuff, more goods and services, than in 1995. That's a good performance but it's less than the value we calculated earlier—67.6 percent—because prices also increased during this period.

When the media report that fourth quarter 2006 GDP growth was 2.2 percent, we are typically being told about the growth rate of nominal GDP. But if we want to compare GDP over time, we should always compare real GDP, that is, GDP calculated using the *same prices in all years*. Interestingly, it doesn't matter much what prices we use to calculate real GDP, so long as we use the same prices in all years.

Real GDP calculations become trickier, the longer the period we compare. In 1925, for example, what was the price of a computer? Economists and statisticians involved in computing real GDP must worry about the value of new goods and changes in the quality of old goods. The more years that pass, the harder it is to determine how to adjust for those quality changes.

Real variables, such as real GDP, have been adjusted for changes in prices by using the same set of prices in all time periods.

The real versus nominal distinction is an important one in economics and it will recur throughout this book. A **real variable** is one that corrects for inflation, namely a general increase in prices over time. In later chapters, we will discuss the real price of housing, real wages, and the real interest rate and we will show in more detail how to convert nominal data into real data.

Real GDP Growth

If pressed to choose a single indicator of *current* economic performance, most economists would probably choose real GDP growth. Figure 5.3 shows the annual percentage changes in real GDP for the United States from 1948 to 2007. U.S. real GDP growth was high during the 1960s, but rising inflation and the 1973 and 1979 oil price shocks lowered growth in the 1970s and early 1980s. Growth has been more solid since the mid-1980s, but is still somewhat lower than in the 1960s. Note that the long-term (since 1948) average growth of real U.S. GDP has been about 3.5 percent per year. You can use these figures as benchmarks to gauge current growth rates.

Real GDP Growth per Capita

Growth in real GDP per capita is usually the best reflection of changing living standards. Growth in GDP typically gives the same broad idea of how economic conditions are changing as growth in GDP per capita, but there can be

FIGURE 5.3

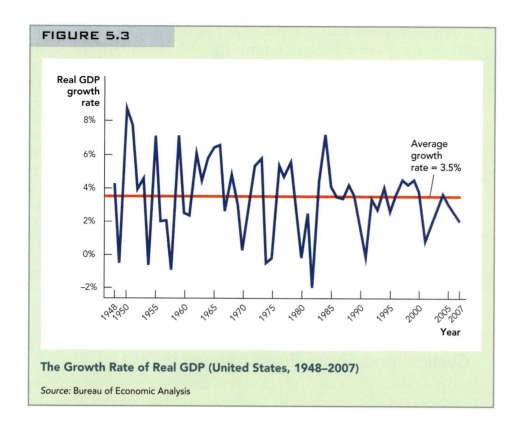

The Growth Rate of Real GDP (United States, 1948–2007)

Source: Bureau of Economic Analysis

big differences for countries with rapidly growing populations. For instance, between 1993 and 2003, Guatemala experienced real GDP growth of about 3.6 percent a year. That might sound good but over that same period population grew at 2.8 percent a year, so real GDP per capita in Guatemala grew at just 0.8 percent a year. In comparison, real GDP per capita in the United States typically grows by about 2.1 percent a year. Thus, not only is the United States richer than Guatemala, people in the United States are getting richer faster.

Figure 5.4 shows long-term growth rates of real GDP per capita across the globe over the 50-year period ending in 2003. The green-colored nations

FIGURE 5.4

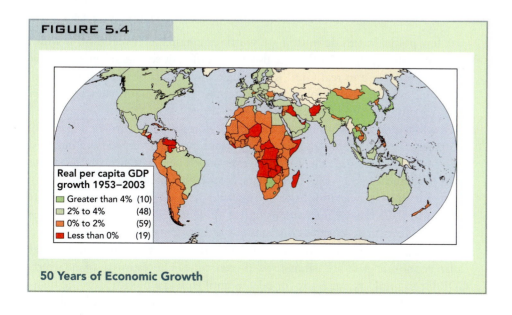

50 Years of Economic Growth

experienced growth rates of greater than 2 percent over the entire period. Taiwan, for example, averaged 6 percent growth of real GDP per capita per year. On the other end of the spectrum, the nations in dark red were growth disasters: they saw no growth or they even saw declines in GDP per capita over this period.

Nigeria is a tragic example of a growth disaster. In 1960, when Nigeria gained its independence from Great Britain, vast deposits of oil were discovered and the future looked bright. But a vicious civil war, dictatorship, and massive corruption meant that the oil wealth disappeared in arms purchases and secret Swiss bank accounts. Incredibly for an economy in the modern era, real GDP per capita in Nigeria was a little bit lower in 2000 than it had been in 1960.

Although it seems shocking that a country could be no richer in 2000 than in 1960, it's important to remember that throughout most of human history a failure to grow is *normal*. In the next chapter, we will begin to explain not just why some nations are poor but the truly mysterious question: Why are any nations rich?

Cyclical and Short-Run Changes in GDP

So far we have focused on GDP as a way to compare economic output across countries and over long periods. GDP is also used to measure short-run volatility in an economy, namely the ups and downs in economic growth that occur within the space of a few years. As we saw in Figure 5.3, U.S. growth rates varied considerably from 1948 to 2007. In some years, such as 1982, the growth rate was negative. **Recessions**—significant, widespread declines in real income and employment—are of special concern to policy makers and the public.

The National Bureau of Economic Research (NBER), a research organization based in Cambridge, Massachusetts, is considered the most authoritative source on identifying U.S. recessions. The official NBER definition of a recession is as follows:

> A recession is a significant decline in economic activity spread across the economy, lasting more than a few months, normally visible in real GDP, real income, employment, industrial production, and wholesale-retail sales.

A few points in this definition are worth emphasizing. A recession is widespread not only geographically but also across different sectors of the economy. Although a decline in real GDP is the single best indicator of a recession, declines will usually also be observed in income, employment, sales, and other measures of the health of an economy.

How often do recessions occur? Figure 5.5 plots real GDP growth and official U.S. recessions since 1948—this time using quarterly data (expressed as annualized rates) so we can better see the variability over time. There have been 11 recessions since 1948, indicated by the shaded bars. Notice that in addition to recessions, the figure illustrates expansions or booms when real GDP grows at a faster rate than normal. We call the fluctuations of real GDP around its long-term trend or "normal" growth rate **business fluctuations** or **business cycles**.

Defining when a recession begins and ends is not always obvious in part because economic data are often revised over time. The estimate of quarterly GDP, for example, is not ready for release until almost a month after the quarter is over. After that, additional rounds of updated estimates are published in

A **recession** is a significant, widespread decline in real income and employment.

Business fluctuations or **business cycles** are the short-run movements in real GDP around its long-term trend.

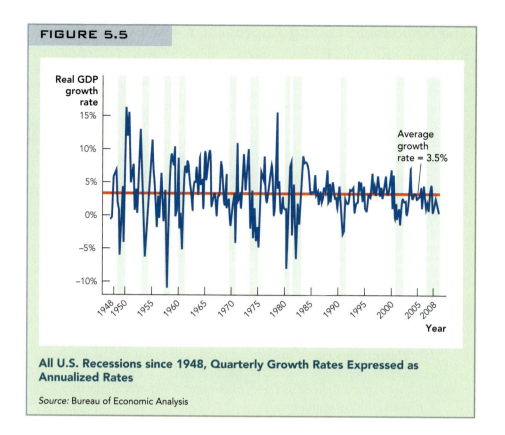

FIGURE 5.5

All U.S. Recessions since 1948, Quarterly Growth Rates Expressed as Annualized Rates

Source: Bureau of Economic Analysis

the following two months. The government often makes significant changes in GDP estimates between the original estimate and the final estimate. For example, the estimates of GDP for the fourth quarter of 2005 increased by $15 billion over the course of the three releases (from growth of $31.2 billion to growth of $46 billion). Updates can even occur years after the first estimates are released. This delay dampens the effectiveness of GDP as a timely indicator and means that understanding recessions and analysis of when they occurred can change over time.

There is debate, for example, about when the 2001 recession started. The official NBER starting date is March 2001, but data revisions have led many people to conclude that the recession actually started in late 2000. Why all the fuss about the timing? If you recall, the presidency changed at the beginning of 2001. Democrats would like to claim that the recession was caused by Republican economic policies, while Republicans want to show that the recession began during President Clinton's final term, before President Bush assumed office.

The Many Ways of Splitting GDP

Another way of understanding GDP is to study its components and how they fit together. Economists split the production of goods and services in many different ways depending on the questions they are asking. We present two common ways of splitting GDP:

1. National spending approach to GDP: $Y = C + I + G + NX$

2. Factor income approach to GDP: $Y = $ Wages + Rent + Interest + Profit

As we will see, both formulas prove useful for understanding business cycles and economic growth.

Economic data take time to collect and evaluate.

In April 1991, the NBER announced that a recession had started in July 1990. In 1992, the NBER announced that the recession had ended in March 1991, a few weeks before the recession was first recognized!

CHECK YOURSELF

> What are business fluctuations?
> Why is it sometimes difficult to determine if an economy is in a recession?

The National Spending Approach: $Y = C + I + G + NX$

Economists have found it useful, especially for the analysis of short-run economic fluctuations, to split GDP into consumption (C), investment (I), government purchases (G) and exports minus imports (NX). The latter two terms are often put together and written as net exports, NX. To understand why this is equivalent to thinking of GDP as the market value of all final goods and services produced within a country in a year, note that produced goods can be consumed, invested, or purchased by governments or foreigners. Finally, some consumed, invested, and government-purchased goods are imported. Imported goods are not part of U.S. GDP, so we subtract imports. Thus, GDP can also be written as:

$$\text{The national spending identity: } Y \equiv C + I + G + NX$$

Where:

Y = Nominal GDP (The market value all final goods and services)
C = The market value of consumption goods and services
I = The market value of investment goods also called capital goods
G = The market value of government purchases
NX = Net exports defined as the market value of exports minus the market value of imports

We explain each of these factors more in turn.

Consumption spending is private spending on final goods and services.

Consumption spending is private spending on final goods and services. Most consumption spending is made by households. Note that while economists think of education as an investment in "human capital," the Bureau of Economic Analysis includes education as a consumption spending alongside purchases of automobiles, MP3 players, and televisions. How would you classify your education spending? Are you here to consume (party!) or invest for the future (study hard!)?

Investment spending is private spending on tools, plant, and equipment used to produce future output.

Investment spending is private spending on tools, plant, and equipment that are used to produce future output. Most investment spending is made by businesses but an important exception is that consumer purchases of new homes are counted as investment. It's important to emphasize that by "investment," economists mean spending on tools, plant, and equipment (capital). When a farmer buys a tractor, that is investment. If your university builds new classrooms and labs, that is investment. Buying IBM stock, however, is not investment, as this is a mere change in ownership of some capital goods from one person to another.

Government purchases are spending by all levels of government on final goods and services. Transfers are not included in government purchases.

The third component of GDP is **government purchases**, or spending by all levels of government on final goods and services. Government purchases include spending on tanks, airplanes, office equipment, and roads, as well as spending on wages for government employees. This category includes both government consumption items (like toner cartridges for printers) and government investment items (like roads and levees) and is thus also called government consumption and investment purchases.

A large part of what government does is transfer money from one citizen to another citizen; about 21 percent of the spending of the federal government for example is for social security payments. Unemployment and disability insurance, various welfare programs, and Medicare are also large transfer programs. We do not include transfers in government purchases because if we did we would be double counting. When the senior citizen buys a television with his or her social security check, it is counted in the consumption portion of GDP. Thus, we do not also count the check as part of government purchases. Another way of thinking about this is that we count only government purchases of *final goods and services*. When the government sends a check to a senior citizen it is not purchasing a final good or service—it is transferring wealth.

Net exports is exports minus imports. If a nation sells more final goods and services abroad than it buys from other nations, net exports will be positive. A nation that imports more than it exports has negative net exports. The United States has had negative net exports for every quarter since the third quarter of 1980. Note that U.S. imports contribute to the GDP of other nations—the locations where that value was produced—and we don't want to count them twice, thus in GDP for the United States we include U.S. exports but subtract U.S. imports. Importing goods and services remains a valuable activity (French cheese is delicious!), but the purpose of the GDP measure is to evaluate production in the U.S. economy.

> **Net exports** are the value of exports minus the value of imports.

Figure 5.6 shows the four components of U.S. GDP in 2007. Consumption is by far the largest component, accounting for $9.7 trillion or 70.3 percent of U.S. GDP. Investment was $2.1 trillion or 15.2 percent of GDP, government purchases $2.7 trillion or 19.6 percent, and net exports −$0.7 trillion or −5.1 percent. If you look at the "long-term averages" part of Figure 5.6, you'll get an idea of the relative sizes of these numbers in recent times. Later on, in the chapters on aggregate demand and business cycles, you will see that changes in these categories represent one way of thinking about the causes or sources of short-run economic downturns and that is one reason why we have covered these particular categories.

The Factor Income Approach: The Other Side of the Spending Coin

When a consumer spends money, the money is received by workers (wages), landlords (rent), owners of capital (interest), and businesses (profit). Thus, we have yet another way of calculating GDP: we can add up all the spending or we can add up all the receiving. The first method is called the spending approach, while the second is called the factor income approach.

The factor income approach:
$$Y = \text{Wages} + \text{Rent} + \text{Interest} + \text{Profit}$$

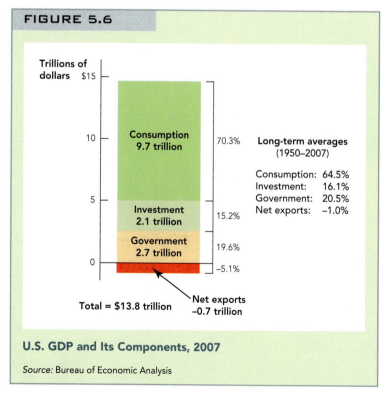

FIGURE 5.6

Trillions of dollars

Consumption 9.7 trillion — 70.3%

Investment 2.1 trillion — 15.2%

Government 2.7 trillion — 19.6%

Net exports −0.7 trillion — −5.1%

Total = $13.8 trillion

Long-term averages (1950–2007)

Consumption: 64.5%
Investment: 16.1%
Government: 20.5%
Net exports: −1.0%

U.S. GDP and Its Components, 2007

Source: Bureau of Economic Analysis

As usual, some corrections are necessary to get the accounting right. For example, not every dollar spent on goods and services is a dollar received in income. Sales taxes are one exception with which you can identify. Sales taxes create a difference between what consumers pay and what businesses and workers receive so if we calculate GDP using the income approach we need to add in sales taxes.[*]

For our purposes, the details are less important than the basic idea: every dollar spent is a dollar of income received so if we are careful in our accounting, we can measure GDP by summing up all the spending on final goods and services or by summing up everyone's income.

Why Split?

Each of the ways of splitting GDP throws a different light on the economy. Economists who study business fluctuations, for example, are often interested in splitting GDP according to the national spending identity because consumption, investment, government purchases, and net exports behave differently over time. Consumption spending, for example, tends to be much more stable than investment spending. Economists are interested in understanding why.

The factor income approach is useful if we are thinking about how economic growth is divided between wages, rent, interest, and profits. It turns out, for example, that the largest payment in GDP is to labor. Wages account for about 56 percent of GDP—more than most people expect and much larger than profits, which are less than 18 percent of GDP. The wage and profit shares of GDP are quite stable over time and even across countries. Economists are interested in understanding what drives the relative sizes of these shares.

It also helps to have more than one way of counting GDP because different methods are subject to different errors. Calculating GDP in more than one way lets us check our calculations.

No way of splitting GDP is better than another—it all depends on the questions being asked. Many other methods of splitting GDP are also possible and useful. We could look at the market value of food versus all other items, or durable versus nondurable goods, or we could break down GDP into finer geographic areas like regions or states (the latter is called gross state product). In principle, there are millions of ways of building a GDP measure by summing up its smaller parts. Economists continue to refine the idea of GDP, to improve the measurement of GDP, and to develop new ways of splitting GDP.

CHECK YOURSELF

> Which is the largest of the national spending components: C, I, G, or NX?

> Which is more stable, consumption spending or investment spending?

> Why does the income approach to GDP give the same answer (in theory!) as the spending approach? (In practice, the answers are close but differ due to accounting errors and data omissions.)

Problems with GDP as a Measure of Output and Welfare

GDP measures the market value of final goods and services. *But there are many goods and services for which we do not know the market value.* We don't know the market value, for example, of illegally produced goods and services because neither

---

[*] We also have to make some corrections for depreciation. Over time machines wear down, factories fall into disrepair, and homes age. Depreciated capital doesn't add to anyone's income but GDP measures production before depreciation so if we calculate GDP using the income approach we need to adjust for the depreciation of capital.

the buyers nor the sellers are willing to answer questions from government statisticians. An even more serious problem is that we don't know the market value of goods and service that are not bought and sold in markets. We don't know, for example, the market value of clean air because clean air is not bought and sold in a market.

Let's look in more detail at some examples of each of these problems.

GDP Does not Count the Underground Economy

Illegal or underground-market transactions are omitted from GDP. Sales of crack cocaine, for example, or sales of counterfeit DVDs are not reported and so do not show up in government statistics. Legal goods sold "under the table" to avoid taxes also do not show up in GDP.

Nations that have greater levels of corruption and higher tax rates usually have higher levels of underground transactions. In Haiti, the poorest country in the Western hemisphere, it takes an estimated 203 days of fighting the bureaucracy to start and register a legal business.[4] It is no wonder that so many Haitians keep their commercial activity outside the law. More generally, the size of the informal or "outside the law" sector in Latin America is estimated at 41 percent of officially measured GDP.[5]

Nations with a great deal of illegal and off-the-books activity are not as poor as they appear in the official GDP statistics. In the United States or Western Europe, the underground economy is likely between 10 and 20 percent of GDP; that percentage is small relative to the percentage in Haiti or most of Latin America but in absolute terms it is still quite large.

GDP Does not Count Nonmarket Production

Nonmarket production occurs when valuable goods and services are produced but no explicit payment is made. If a son mows his parent's lawn, the service will not be included in GDP. If a lawn care firm provided the identical work, it would be included in GDP. Yet either way the grass gets cut and economic output increases. Similarly, church workers deliver food to the elderly, volunteers pick up garbage in parks, and many blogs are written without pay as a hobby. Since there is no registered economic transaction, none of these activities are counted in GDP even though each adds to economic output.

The omission of nonmarket production introduces two biases into GDP statistics: biases over time and biases across nations.

In the United States, the portion of women who are in the official labor force has almost doubled since 1950, rising from 34 percent to about 60 percent today. As a result, mothers spend less time working at home than in 1950 but there are more nannies and house cleaners in the economy today. The mothers who worked at home in 1950 were not paid and their valuable services were not counted in GDP. Nannies and house cleaners today are paid and their services are counted in GDP (unless the nanny is hired "under the table" to avoid paying social security taxes, of course!). The result is that U.S. GDP in 1950 underestimates a little the real production of goods and services in 1950 relative to that of today.

Nonmarket production also affects GDP comparisons across countries. For example, many cultures discourage women from taking part in the official workforce.

Mr. Mom: Not increasing GDP

In India, women make up only 28 percent of the labor force, compared with 46 percent for the U.S.[6] The output of the other 72 percent of Indian women is not included in Indian GDP. Indian GDP statistics, therefore, underestimate the real production of goods and services in India.

Household production is especially important in poor countries and in rural areas. It is common to read of families, say in rural Mexico, which earn no more than $1,000 a year. Living off this sum sounds impossible to a contemporary American, but keep in mind that many of these families build their own homes (with help from relatives and friends), grow their own food, and sew their own clothes. Their lives are hard, but much of what they produce is not captured in GDP statistics.

GDP Does not Count Leisure

Leisure, or time spent not working, is also omitted from GDP statistics. People value leisure, just as they value food and transportation. But when people consume food and transportation, measured GDP increases. When people consume more leisure, however, measured GDP does not rise and in fact it will fall if we are not at work. Of course, for some forms of leisure we must make purchases like fishing rods and campers, which are counted in GDP, but it's difficult to measure the true value of leisure.

In the United States, the average workweek has fallen by 10 percent since 1964 (from 38 hours to about 34.5 hours per week). Moreover, work at home has also declined as washing machines, microwaves, and vacuum cleaners have made work at home easier and less time consuming. This growth in leisure time is an improvement in human well-being but is not reflected in GDP.

While the average workweek in the United States has fallen, it has dropped much farther in some other nations. Figure 5.7 shows the average number of hours worked per week in a selection of nations. While the workweek in the United States is down to about 34.5 hours, individuals in other developed nations such as France, Germany, and the United Kingdom work less. In the Netherlands, the average workweek is only 27 hours per week! Since leisure time is not added to GDP, the longer workweek will make the United States look better off compared to Europe than is actually the case. Note, however, that although the workweek in the United States is long compared to other developed countries the workweek is even longer in many poorer countries. In China, for example, the average workweek is about 42.5 hours.

GDP Does not Count Bads: Environmental Costs

GDP adds up the market value of final goods and services but does not subtract the value of bads. Pollution, for example, is a bad that is produced every year but this bad is not counted in the GDP statistics. GDP statistics also do not count the destruction of water aquifers, the accumulation of carbon dioxide in the atmosphere, or changing supplies of natural resources. Similarly, GDP statistics do not count the loss of animal or plant species as economic costs, unless those animals and plants had a direct commercial role in the economy. Other bads are also not counted in GDP. The bad of crime, for example, is not counted in the GDP statistics.

Since more pollution isn't counted as a bad, it's not surprising that less pollution is also not counted as a good. America has cleaner air and cleaner water than it did in 1960, but GDP statistics do not reflect this improvement.

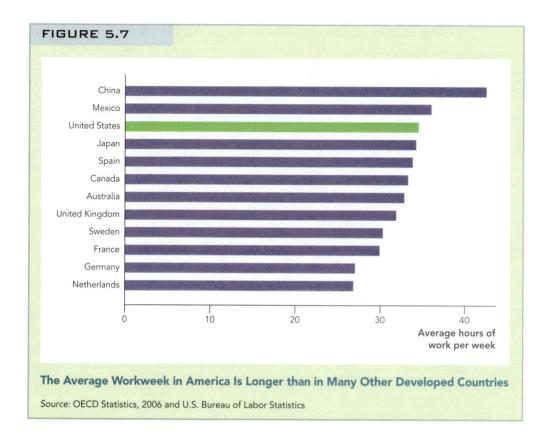

FIGURE 5.7

The Average Workweek in America Is Longer than in Many Other Developed Countries

Source: OECD Statistics, 2006 and U.S. Bureau of Labor Statistics

The movement for "green accounting" has tried to reform GDP statistics to cover the environment more explicitly. Most economists agree with the logic behind green accounting: GDP should measure the market value of all final goods and services even if those goods and services are not traded in markets. They also acknowledge other attempts to improve GDP statistics to take into account nonmarket production, leisure, crime, and so forth but most of these problems are very difficult to solve. Environmental amenities, for example, are difficult to value. How much, for instance, should be added to GDP because polar bears are present in Alaska? How much is a glacier worth? A coral reef? Estimates of the values of these resources may be computed for individual problems, but when it comes to the economy as a whole, the measurement task seems insurmountable. Rather than introduce so much uncertainty into the entire GDP concept, economists usually restrict green accounting (and other GDP modifications) to the analysis of particular problems.

GDP Does not Measure the Distribution of Income

GDP per capita is a rough measure of the standard of living in a country. But if GDP per capita grows by 10 percent this does not necessarily mean that *everyone's* income grows by 10 percent or even that the average person's income grows by 10 percent.

To see why, imagine that we have a country of four people, John, Paul, George, and Ringo, whose factor incomes in year 1 are 10, 20, 30, and 40. Using the factor income approach we know that GDP is 100 (10 + 20 + 30 + 40) and thus GDP per capita is 25 (100/4). GDP in year 1 and its distribution are shown in the first row of Table 5.3.

TABLE 5.3 Growth in GDP per Capita Can Be Distributed in Different Ways

	John	Paul	George	Ringo	GDP	GDP per Capita
Year 1	10	20	30	40	100	25
(a) Year 2	11	22	33	44	110	27.5
(b) Year 2	10	20	30	50	110	27.5
(c) Year 2	20	20	30	40	110	27.5

Now suppose that in year 2 GDP grows by 10 percent to 110 and thus GDP per capita grows to 27.5 (110/4). This growth in GDP, however, is consistent with any of the three outcomes shown in rows *a*, *b*, and *c* of Table 5.3. In row *a*, everyone's income grows by 10 percent—so John's income grows from 10 to 11, Paul's income grows from 20 to 22, and so forth. In row *b*, the growth in GDP is concentrated on Ringo, the richest person: his income grows by 25 percent (from 40 to 50) and everyone else's income stays the same. In row *c*, the growth in GDP is concentrated on John, the poorest person. His income grows by 100 percent (from 10 to 20) and everyone else's income stays the same.

GDP and GDP per capita grow by the same amount in each of these cases but in row *a* inequality stays the same, in row *b* inequality increases, and in row *c* inequality decreases.

In most countries most of the time, growth in GDP per capita is like row *a*: everyone's income grows by approximately the same amount.[7] Thus, growth in real GDP per capita usually does tell us roughly how the average person's standard of living is changing over time. In examining particular countries and periods, however, we might want to look more carefully at how growth in GDP is distributed. In other words, GDP figures are useful but they will always be imperfect.

CHECK YOURSELF

> Why does GDP not account for or try to measure certain things? What is the common thread throughout all of the uncounted variables?

> If two countries have the same GDP per capita, do they necessarily have the same level of inequality?

> If GDP does not account for everything, does that make the GDP statistic useless?

□ Takeaway

The primary topics of macroeconomics are economic growth and business fluctuations. But when we say that "the economy" is growing what do we mean? And what is it precisely that is fluctuating? If we want to understand growth and fluctuations, we need some concept that defines and measures growth and fluctuations.

The concept of gross domestic product was developed to quantify the ideas of economic growth and fluctuations. GDP, the market value of all final goods and services produced within a country in a year, is an estimate of the economic output of a nation over a year. When we say that an economy is growing we mean that GDP, or a closely related concept like GDP per capita, is growing. When we say that an economy is booming or contracting, we mean that growth in real GDP is above or below its long-run trend.

GDP can be measured and summed up in different ways, each of which casts a different light on the economy. The national spending identity, $Y = C + I + G +$

NX, splits GDP according to different classes of income spending. The factor income approach, $Y = $ Wages + Interest + Rent + Profit, splits GDP into different classes of income receiving.

GDP per capita is a rough estimate of the standard of living in a nation. Real GDP is GDP per capita corrected for inflation by calculating GDP using the same set of prices in every year. Growth in real GDP per capita tells us roughly how the average person's standard of living is changing over time.

GDP statistics are imperfect. GDP does not include the value of leisure, or goods bought and sold in the underground economy, nor does it include the value of goods that are difficult to price, such as the value of having polar bears in Alaska. GDP and GDP per capita also do not tell us anything about how equally GDP is distributed. Economists and statisticians try to refine and improve the measurement of GDP over time. GDP measures are imperfect but they have proven they are useful in estimating the standard of living and the scope of economic activity.

□ CHAPTER REVIEW

KEY CONCEPTS

Gross domestic product (GDP), p. 70

GDP per capita, p. 70

Gross national product (GNP), p. 72

Nominal variables, p. 73

Real variables, p. 74

Recession, p. 76

Business fluctuations (business cycles), p. 76

Consumption, p. 78

Investment, p. 78

Government purchases, p. 78

Net exports, p. 79

FACTS AND TOOLS

1. According to Table 5.1, what country has the highest GDP? What country on the list has the highest GDP per person? What countries on the list have the *second* highest GDP and the *second* highest GDP per person?

2. What is included in GDP: all goods, all services, or both?

3. What happened to spending on medical services and recreational activities since 1950?

4. Police officer: "I pulled you over for speeding. You were going 80 miles per hour."

   Driver: "But that's impossible, officer! I've only been driving for 15 minutes!"

The government reports GDP numbers every quarter. How does this story illustrate the meaning of "GDP per year" when the GDP number gets reported every three months?

5. Calculate the annual growth rate of nominal GDP in the following examples:

   Nominal GDP in 1930: $97 billion. Nominal GDP in 1931: $84 billion.

   Nominal GDP in 1931: $84 billion. Nominal GDP in 1932: $68 billion.

   Nominal GDP in 2000: $9,744 billion. Nominal GDP in 2001: $10,151 billion.

   (*Source:* Historical Tables, Budget of the United States Government, Congressional Budget Office)

6. Are the following included in U.S. GDP? Briefly explain why or why not:

   a. Used textbooks sold at your college bookstore.

   b. Used books sold at a garage sale.

   c. Cars made in the United States at a Toyota factory.

   d. Cars made in Germany at a General Motors factory.

   e. The price paid by a German tourist when staying at a New York hotel.

   f. The price paid by an American tourist staying at a Berlin hotel.

   g. A ticket for a Yankees game.

7. By definition, is nominal GDP higher than real GDP?

8. In the last 20 years, have recessions been getting more frequent or less frequent than they used to be?

9. According to the National Bureau of Economic Research, which of the following are "normally" part of the definition of a recession?

    A fall in nominal income

    A fall in employment

    A fall in real income

    A fall in the price level

10. Looking back over the last 10,000 years of human history, which is more "normal": For GDP per capita to grow or for GDP per capita to stay about the same?

11. Attach the appropriate fractions to the "long-term averages" in Figure 5.6. (Some fractions will be left over.) These fractions may turn out to be more memorable than the exact percentages in the figure.

Long-Run Averages	Fraction of GDP
Consumption	$\frac{1}{3}$
	$\frac{1}{8}$
Investment	$\frac{1}{5}$
	$-\frac{1}{14}$
Government purchases	$\frac{1}{4}$
	$\frac{2}{3}$
Net exports	$\frac{9}{10}$

12. What is the national spending identity? This identity is very important in macroeconomics. It is as important as basic anatomy in medical school: You won't be able to cure a person until you know what's inside a person.

THINKING AND PROBLEM SOLVING

1. Calculate GDP in this simple economy:

    Consumer purchases: $100 per year

    Investment purchases: $50 per year

    Government purchases: $20 per year

    Total exports: $50 per year

    Total imports: $70 per year

2. Since World War II, who were the only three recession-free U.S. presidents? (We'll revisit the question of how presidents matter for the economy in later chapters.)

3. We noted that "government purchases" don't include all government spending. A big part of what the U.S. government does is transfer money from one person to another. Social security (payments to retirees), and Medicare and Medicaid (paying for medical care for the elderly and the poor) make up most of these "government transfers." We'll look into this in more detail in Chapter 16, but right now, let's see how big "government transfers" are and how fast they've grown in the federal government's budget. The figures in this table are all in noninflation-adjusted dollars. Complete the table.

Year	Total Federal Transfers	Total Federal Spending	Transfers as Percent of Spending
1950	$13.6 Billion	$42.5 Billion	_____
2000	$1,057 Billion	$1,788 Billion	_____
Growth Rate in %:	_____	_____	

Source: Budget of the United States Government: Historical Tables, Fiscal Year 2003. Washington, D.C.: U.S. Government Printing Office.

4. Let's see what fraction of the economic pie goes to workers in the form of wages, and let's see if it has changed over the years. The "wage share" seems like it should be easy to calculate, but there's a problem. That problem brings us back to the big idea of opportunity cost. The problem itself is straightforward: When a small business owner makes money, should we count that as "wages" or as "profit?" Usually, a small business owner is working at the business most days, doing the kinds of tasks that you could easily pay someone else to do: In other words, from the looking-in-the-window perspective, a business owner looks like a worker, and workers earn wages. But since the owner gets to keep all the profits that are left over after paying off the other workers and the bank, it looks like the money that he or she earns should count as profit.

What to do? The *best* solution is to calculate the "opportunity cost" of the business owner's time: In other words, estimate roughly how much the business owner would get paid if he or she were working as an employee. It tells us how much of the business owner's income is truly wage income.

The *second* best solution, which we'll use in this question, is to just guess that one-third, one-half, or two-thirds of the business owner's income is really wages, and the rest is profit. As so often in economics, we make some assumptions; let's see if that changes our view of the economy. Using this measure, let's see what has happened to the slice of the pie going to workers:

Year	Wages (including salaries and bonuses)	Business Owner's Income
1959	62 percent of national income	11 percent of national income
2003	64 percent of national income	9 percent of national income

Source: *Survey of Current Business.* Bureau of Economic Analysis, March 2004.

Using the data above, complete the following table:

Year	Total Wages as percentage of national income		
	Including one-third of business income	Including one-half of business income	Including two-thirds of business income
1959			
2003			

So, now that you've calculated this, does it appear that "wage share" has risen by more than 5 percent, fallen by more than 5 percent, or stayed roughly the same over the decades? Does the one-third, one-half, or two-thirds business owner adjustment impact this conclusion?

5. Let's figure out GDP for Robinson Crusoe.

   a. Initially he is stuck on an island without the wisdom and local knowledge of Friday. Because Crusoe is a proper Englishman, he wants to keep his accounts. This year, he catches and eats 2,000 fish valued at one British pound (£) each, grows and eats 4,000 coconuts valued at 0.5 British pounds each, and makes 2 huts (housing) valued at 200 pounds each.

If government purchases are zero and there is no trade, what is C for Crusoe? What is I? What is Y? (We are going to start using those letters as if they mean something: See question 12 in the previous section.)

   b. One year, he learns of a tribe on a nearby island who are willing to trade with him: If he gives fish, they give clams. He produces just as much as before, but he trades 500 of the 2,000 fish and receives 10,000 clams valued at 5 clams per British pound. What is the British pound value of the exported fish? Of the imported clams? What are C, I, and X now? What is GDP now?

   c. The following year, Crusoe produces the same as in every other year, but a tribe on the other side of the island steals his two huts after he makes them, and gives him nothing in return. So he exports, but does not import at all. What are C, I, X, and Y now?

   d. In Crusoe's final year on the island, he produces the same as in every other year (he's a reliable worker), but a new shipwreck washes up on his island containing a clock worth £3, a new shirt worth £2, and a copy of Milton's *Paradise Lost* and Shakespeare's complete works, each worth £1. Treat these as imported consumer goods. What is GDP this year? (Note: Emphasize the "P" in GDP when considering your answer.) What are C, I, X, and Y this year? (Note: One of the four is bigger than usual, one is negative.)

   e. Is Crusoe probably happy about what happens in question 5c? Is he probably happy about what happens in question 5d? Keep these answers in mind for when we discuss the economics of trade later on.

6. Let's think about an economically sound way to measure the value of leisure. To keep this simple, we'll just think about the value of leisure to people who *could* work but who decide to stay home. Also, we won't think about how much *actual* workers value their free time, or how much children and retirees value their time.

   In a standard supply and demand labor model, firms "demand" labor while workers "supply" labor. Let's think about a labor market that is in equilibrium, with a wage of $20 per hour (close to the U.S. average) and with 150 million Americans working out of a total of 225 million working-age Americans.

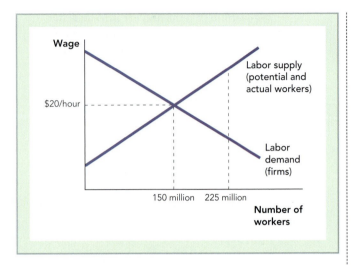

a. According to this simplified model of the U.S. economy, some workers *would* work if the wage were higher, but at the current wage, they'd rather stay home and watch re-runs of *Seinfeld* or (don't let this be you!) *Two and a Half Men*. For the workers who are right on the margin between working and not working, what would their wage be if wages rose ever so slightly and they went to work?

b. Let's use this wage as a shorthand for how much nonworkers value their time. After all, the "opportunity cost" of their free time must be at least this high, because otherwise they'd take a job. Now, let's calculate a GDP measure that adds in a rough estimate of the value enjoyed by these nonworkers. We'll use the following identity, and we'll round the value of nominal GDP to $14 trillion (close to the actual 2008 level).

Leisure-augmented GDP = Regular GDP + Total monetary value of leisure

If the average working person works 2,000 hours per year (that's a 40-hour week for 50 weeks a year), then what is the leisure-augmented value of U.S. GDP?

7. Consider the following two claims. The first would be a typical statement at the magazine *The Nation*, while the second would be a typical statement at the magazine *National Review*:

Europeans have strong labor unions, so their workers get a bigger share of the pie than American workers.

Since European businesses are highly regulated, they have little incentive to make big profits. Therefore, they get a much smaller share of national product than American workers.

It is true that Europeans have stronger labor unions than Americans, and it is true that European businesses face higher regulatory burdens than American businesses. But with that in mind, what is wrong with these two statements? What fact are they ignoring? And what does that fact tell us about what strong unions and high levels of government regulation *can't* do?

8. The underground economy and other nonmarket production make it hard to accurately measure the precise level of GDP. But GDP could still be very accurate for measuring changes in the economy. If Ben Bernanke, the Federal Reserve chairman, is trying to find out whether the U.S. economy has gone into a recession, are the difficulties of measuring nonmarket production likely to be important problems for his purposes? How is this like always wearing your shoes when you step on the bathroom scale?

9. a. U.S. GDP is approximately $14 trillion. If GDP were divided up equally among all 300 million Americans, what would each person get? If you and your nine best friends took almost all of the GDP for yourselves, but gave $1,000 per person for everyone else, how much would you get each year, just for yourself?

b. More seriously, currently 150,000 people in the United States earn over $1.5 million per year. If you could take their money and divide it up among the approximately 300 million other Americans, how much money could you give to each person every year? Note that $1.5 million is only the cutoff: On average, this group earns $3 million per year, so use that number in your calculations.

(*Source*: David Cay Johnston, "Richest Are Leaving Even the Rich Far Behind," *New York Times*, June 5, 2005, based on U.S. government data.)

10. Let's sum up some basic facts of U.S. economic history with numbers:

a. First, let's measure the size of the Great Depression:

| Real GDP in 1929 (peak): $323 billion | Real GDP in 1933 (trough): $206 billion |
| Price level in 1929: 33 | Price level in 1933: 24 |

Calculate the percent change in real GDP and the percent change in the price level from 1929 to 1933. First, calculate the total change, and then divide it by the number of years to get the more typical measure of "percent per year." (Note: this is four full years, not three or five.)

b. Second, let's measure how much the economy grew from the lowest depths of the Depression to the peak of World War II's economic boom:

Real GDP in 1933 (trough): $206 billion

Real GDP in 1945: $596 billion

Price level in 1933: 24

Price level in 1945: 38

Again, first calculate the total change, and then divide it by the number of years to get the more typical measure of "percent per year."

c. Finally, let's see if a growing economy must mean growing prices:

Real GDP in 1870: $36 billion

Real GDP in 1900: $124 billion

Price level in 1870: 22

Price level in 1900: 16

Calculate the total and annual growth rates as before. Note: The price level fell fairly smoothly across these three decades, a time when the economy grew rapidly and many great American novels were written about life in the growing cities.

(*Source:* Robert J. Gordon, ed., *The American Business Cycle: Continuity and Change.* Cambridge, MA, National Bureau of Economic Research, 1986.)

CHALLENGES

1. During World War II, the government did a good job measuring nominal GDP. But if the price level was calculated incorrectly, we might get a completely wrong idea about what happened with real GDP. During World War II, price ceilings were in place. That means that some things that would've been expensive were artificially cheap instead. Within a few years of the war's end, price controls finally ended, and the price level spiked up about 20 percent. If the true price level *during the war* was actually 20 percent higher than reported, would that mean that real GDP is higher than the official number in question 10b in the previous section, lower than that number, or is it still the same as that number?

2. If U.S. government statistics counted education spending as part of investment, which would rise, which would fall, and which would remain unchanged? (Note: You might use rise, fall, and unchanged more than once each or you might not.)

   Consumption   Investment   Gross Domestic Product

3. If U.S. government statistics counted people who are receiving unemployment benefits as people who are "government employees" hired to "search for work," which of the following would rise, which would fall, and which would remain unchanged? (Note: You might use rise, fall, and unchanged more than once each or you might not.)

   Consumption   Government Purchases   Gross Domestic Product

4. According to legend, some government employees do very little work. If this legend is true enough to be important, then we may be measuring GDP incorrectly. Officially, we say that these are "employed workers," but to a great extent these "employees" are really unemployed in any useful task; they are receiving transfer payments and watching YouTube for 40 hours per week. If instead government statistics counted these YouTube-watching government employees as simply retired or unemployed, which of the following would rise, which would fall, and which would remain unchanged? (Note: You might use rise, fall, and unchanged more than once each or you might not.)

   Consumption   Government Purchases   Gross Domestic Product

6

The Wealth of Nations and Economic Growth

In the United States, diarrhea is a pain, an annoyance, and of course an embarrassment. In much of the developing world, diarrhea is a killer, especially of children. Every year 1.8 million children die from diarrhea. To prevent the deaths of these children we do not need any scientific breakthroughs, nor do we need new drugs or fancy medical devices. What these children need most is one thing: economic growth.

Economic growth brings piped water and flush toilets, which together cut infant mortality from diarrhea by 70 percent or more. Malaria, measles, and infections also kill millions of children a year. Again, the lesson is clear, millions of children are dying who would live if there were more economic growth.

Figure 6.1 on the next page illustrates how health and wealth go together. The vertical axis shows GDP per capita and the horizontal axis shows how many children, out of every 1,000 births, survive to the age of 5. In the United States, one of the world's richest countries, 993 out of every 1,000 children born survive to the age of 5 (i.e., 7 out of every 1,000 die before the age of 5). In Liberia, one of the world's poorest countries, only about 765 children survive to age 5 (i.e., 235 of every 1,000 children die before seeing their fifth birthday). The graph illustrates a strong correlation between a country's GDP per capita and infant survival. The size of each country's data bubble is proportional to the population of that country; notice that India and China each have populations of over a billion people so economic growth in these countries has the potential to save millions of infants from an early death.

Infant health and wealth tend to move together; indeed, just about *any* standard indicator of societal well-being tends to increase with wealth. Infant survival rates, life expectancy, and nutrition (caloric intake levels), for example, all tend to be higher in wealthier nations. Educational opportunities, leisure, and

FIGURE 6.1

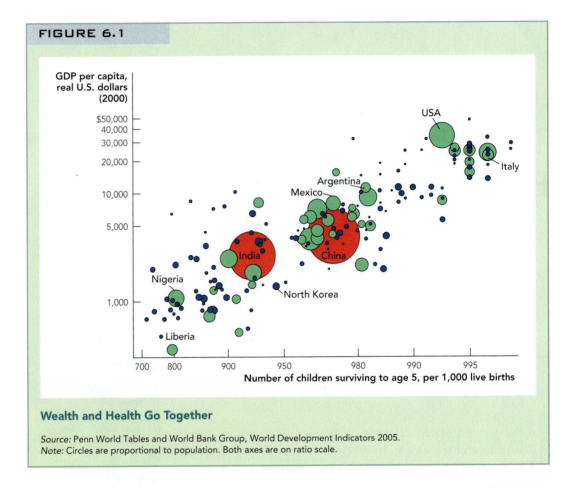

Wealth and Health Go Together

Source: Penn World Tables and World Bank Group, World Development Indicators 2005.
Note: Circles are proportional to population. Both axes are on ratio scale.

entertainment also tend to be higher in wealthier nations. Wealthier nations even have fewer conflicts such as civil wars and riots. And, of course, wealthier nations have more material goods such as televisions, iPods, and swimming pools.

Wealth is clearly important so we want answers to the following questions. Why are some nations wealthy while others are poor? Why are some nations getting wealthier faster than others? Can anything be done to help poor nations become wealthy? The answers to these questions are literally a matter of life and death. In this chapter and the next, we will try to answer these questions.

Key Facts about the Wealth of Nations and Economic Growth

Let's begin with some important facts about the wealth of nations and economic growth.

Fact One: GDP per Capita Today Varies Enormously among Nations

We already have some understanding of the enormous differences that exist in the wealth of nations and how these differences affect infant mortality and other measures of well-being. Figure 6.2 shows in more detail how GDP per capita differs around the world. To construct this figure we start on the left with the world's poorest country which happens to be the Democratic Republic of the Congo (DRC). The DRC (not labeled) accounts for just under 1% of the

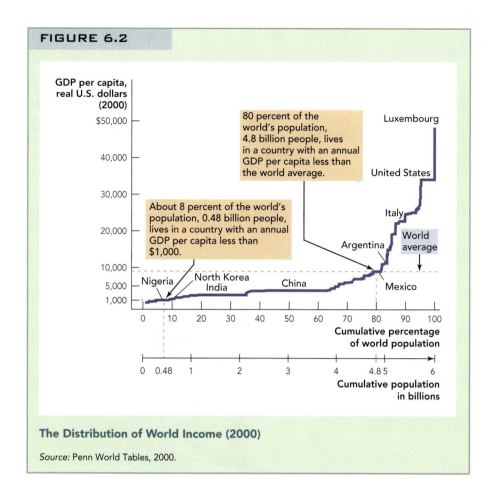

FIGURE 6.2

The Distribution of World Income (2000)

Source: Penn World Tables, 2000.

world's population. As we add successively richer countries and their populations we move further to the right in population and upwards in GDP per capita. The graph tells us, for example, that about 8 percent of the world's population—or 0.48 billion people in 2000—live in a country with a GDP per capita of less than $1,000—about the level in Nigeria. Moving further to the right we see that just over 60 percent of the world's population lives in a country with a GDP per capita equal to or less than $4,000, about the level in China. The red horizontal dashed line shows the world's average level of GDP per capita in 2000, $9,133, which is about the same as that of Mexico. Fully 80 percent of the world's population—or 4.8 billion people—live in a country with a GDP per capita less than average. In other words, most of the world's population is poor relative to the United States.

In thinking about poverty, remember that GDP per capita is simply an average, and there is a distribution of income within each country. In India, GDP per capita is around $3,000 but many Indians have yearly incomes that are less than $3,000 and some have yearly incomes that are higher than the average income in the United States. Around the world, about a billion people have incomes of less than $2 per day.

Fact Two: Everyone Used to Be Poor

The distribution of world income tells us that poverty is normal. It's wealth that is unusual. Poverty is even more normal when we think about human history. What was GDP per capita like in the year 1? No one knows for sure, but a good guesstimate is around \$400–\$600 per year in current dollars, not much different than for the very poorest people living in the world today. What's surprising is not that people in the past were poor but that *everyone* in the past was poor.

Figure 6.3 shows some estimates of GDP per capita in different regions of the world in different periods from the year 1 to 2000 AD. In the year 1, GDP per capita was about \$400–\$600 and this was approximately the same in all the major regions of the world. Today GDP per capita is more than 50 times as large in the richest countries as in the poorest countries.

FIGURE 6.3

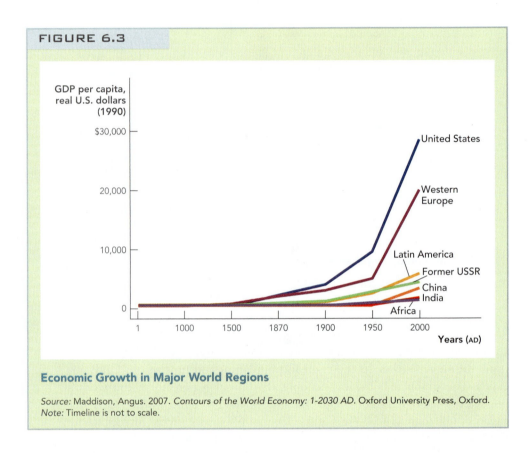

Economic Growth in Major World Regions

Source: Maddison, Angus. 2007. *Contours of the World Economy: 1-2030 AD.* Oxford University Press, Oxford.
Note: Timeline is not to scale.

Figure 6.3 illustrates something else of interest: GDP per capita was about the same in year 1 as it would be 1,000 years later and indeed about the same as it had been 1,000 years earlier. For most of recorded human history there was *no long-run growth in real per capita GDP*. Countries might grow in particular good years, but soon enough a disaster would ensue and the gains would be given back. Only beginning in the nineteenth century does it become clear that some parts of the world began to grow at a rate unprecedented in human history.

Figure 6.3 tells us that economic growth is unusual. But once economic growth begins, it can make some parts of the world rich while other parts languish at levels of per capita GDP similar to that in the Dark Ages. To see more clearly how small changes in economic growth can have enormous effects on GDP per capita, we pause for a primer on economic growth rates.

A Primer on Growth Rates Recall from Chapter 5 on GDP that a growth rate is the percentage change in a variable over a given time period such as a year. When we refer to **economic growth** we mean the growth rate of real per capita GDP.

Economic growth is the growth rate of real GDP per capita.

$$g_t = \frac{y_t - y_{t-1}}{y_{t-1}} \times 100$$

Where y_t is real per capita GDP in period t.

While computing growth rates is simple math, grasping the impact of growth rates on economic progress is critical. Keep in mind that even slow growth, if sustained over many years, produces large differences in real GDP per capita.

To appreciate the power of economic growth, let's consider a few cases. Suppose that the annual growth rate of real GDP per capita is 2 percent. How long will it take for real per capita GDP to double from $40,000 to $80,000? An average person on the street might answer "It will take 50 years to double your income at a 2 percent growth rate." But that is wrong because growth builds on top of growth. This is called "compounding" or "exponential growth."

We can better understand compounding by creating a simple table in a spreadsheet. In Table 6.1, per capita GDP is $40,000 at the beginning of year 1. Over the course of the year, we move across a row, and per capita GDP increases by 2 percent or $800 (note the formula for the increase in cell C2); thus at the end of one year per capita GDP is $40,800. In the second year, 2 percent growth yields $816 of new income (2 percent of $40,800), so at the end of two years, per capita GDP is $41,616. Two percent of this is $832.32. Each year (represented by moving down a row), the dollar increase in per capita GDP gets larger, as 2 percent of a growing number continues to grow.

TABLE 6.1 Excellent Growth

C2		f_x =B2*0.02	
A	**B**	**C**	**D**
Year	Beginning GDP	Increase in GDP	GDP at end of Year
1	(per capita)		
2	$40,000	$800	$40,800
3	$40,800	$816	$41,616
4	$41,616	$832	$42,448
36	35	$78,427	$1,569	$79,996

In fact, as Table 6.1 shows, at a 2 percent growth rate it takes only 35 years for GDP per capita to double.

There is a simple approximation, called the rule of 70, for determining the length of time necessary for a growing variable to double:

Rule of 70: If the annual growth rate of a variable is x percent, then the doubling time is $\frac{70}{x}$ years.

Table 6.2 illustrates the rule of 70 by showing how long it takes for GDP per capita to double given different growth rates. At a growth rate of 1 percent, GDP per capita will double approximately every 70 years (70/1 = 70). If growth increases to 2 percent, GDP per capita will double every 35 years (70/2 = 35). Consider the impact of a 4 percent growth rate. If this growth can be sustained, then GDP per capita doubles every 17.5 years (70/4 = 17.5). In 70 years, income doubles 4 times reaching a level 16 times its starting value!

TABLE 6.2 Years to Double Using the Rule of 70

Annual Growth Rate	Years to Double
0%	Never
1%	70
2%	35
3%	23.3
4%	17.5

The rule of 70 is just a mathematical approximation but it bears out the key concept that small differences in growth rates have large effects on economic progress.

Another way of seeing how small changes in the rate of economic growth can lead to big effects is to think about how rich people will be in the future. U.S. per capita GDP is about $46,000 (as of 2007). How many years will it take for real per capita GDP to increase to $1 million? If growth is 2 percent per year, which would be a little low by U.S. standards, average income will be $1 million per year in just 155 years. If GDP per capita grows at 3 percent per year, which is a little high by U.S. standards but certainly not impossible, then in just 105 years the average income will be approximately $1 million per year. You and I are unlikely to see this future, but if our grandchildren are lucky, they will see a world in which U.S. GDP per capita is a million dollars, more than 22 times higher than it is today.

Fact Three: There Are Growth Miracles and Growth Disasters

The United States is one of the wealthiest countries in the world because the United States has grown slowly but relatively consistently for over two hundred years. Can other countries catch up to the United States and if so will it take two hundred years? Fortunately other countries can catch up and amazingly quickly. Figure 6.4 shows two "growth miracles." Following World War II, Japan was one of the poorest countries in the world with a per capita GDP less than that of Mexico. From 1950 to 1970, however, Japan grew at an astonishing rate of 8.5 percent per year. Remember, at that rate, GDP per capita doubles in approximately 8 years (70/8.5 = 8.2)! Today, Japan is one of the richest countries in the world.

FIGURE 6.4

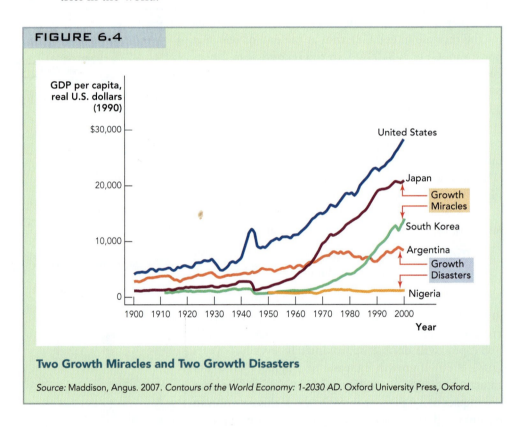

Two Growth Miracles and Two Growth Disasters

Source: Maddison, Angus. 2007. *Contours of the World Economy: 1-2030 AD.* Oxford University Press, Oxford.

In 1950, South Korea was even poorer than Japan with a GDP per capita about the same as that of Nigeria. South Korea's growth miracle began a little later than Japan's, but between 1970 and 1990, South Korea grew at a rate of 7.2 percent per year. Today, South Korea is a thriving, modern economy on par with many European economies.

Growth miracles are possible but so are growth disasters. Nigeria has barely grown since 1950 and was poorer in 2000 than in 1974 when high oil prices briefly bumped up its per capita GDP. More surprising is the case of Argentina. In 1900, Argentina was one of the richest countries in the world with a per capita GDP almost as large (75 percent) as that of the United States. By 1950, Argentina's per capita GDP had fallen to half that in the United States. In 1950, however, Argentina was still a relatively wealthy country with a per capita GDP more than twice as high as that of Japan and more than five times as high as that of South Korea. Argentina failed to grow much, however, and by 2000 Argentina's per capita GDP was less than a third of that of the United States; Japan and South Korea are now much wealthier than Argentina.

The gap between Argentina and many other countries is continuing to grow. China (not pictured) began its own growth miracle in the late 1970s. China is still a very poor nation with a per capita GDP that in 2007 is a little less than half that of Argentina. But China is growing rapidly—remember, if China continues to grow at 7 or 8 percent per year it will double its income in about 10 years. Even if Argentina grows modestly, China could pass Argentina in per capita GDP in less than 20 years.

Summarizing the Facts: Good and Bad News

The facts presented above imply both good and bad news. The bad news is that most of the world is poor and more than one billion people live on incomes of less than $2 per day. These people have greatly reduced prospects for health, happiness, and peace. The bad news, however, is old news. For most of human history, people were poor and there was no economic growth.

The good news is this: despite being a relatively recent phenomenon, economic growth has quickly transformed the world. It has raised the standard of living of most people in developed nations many times above the historical norm. Even though economic growth has yet to reach much of the world, there appears to be no reason why in principle economic growth cannot occur everywhere. Indeed, growth miracles tell us that it doesn't take 250 years to reach the level of wealth of the United States—South Korea was as poor as Nigeria in 1950 but today has a per capita GDP not that far behind Germany or the United Kingdom.

Progress, however, is not guaranteed. The growth disasters tell us that economic growth is not automatic. Some countries such as Nigeria show few signs that they have started along the growth path, while other countries such as Argentina seem to have fallen off the growth path. Understanding the wealth of nations and economic growth, therefore, is critical.

Understanding the Wealth of Nations

Let's begin with Figure 6.5 on the next page, a guide to the major factors behind the wealth of nations. At the bottom of the figure is what we would like to explain, GDP per capita. As we move up the figure we see some of the causes of the wealth of nations, beginning with the proximate or most direct causes and moving toward the ultimate or indirect causes.

The Factors of Production

The most proximate cause of the wealth of nations is this: countries with a high GDP per capita have a lot of physical and human capital per worker and that capital is organized using the best technological knowledge to be highly productive. Physical capital, human capital, and technological knowledge are called factors of production. Let's take a look at each factor of production.

By **physical capital** (or just "capital") economists mean tools in the broadest sense: pencils, desks, computers, hammers, shovels, tractors, cell phones, factories, roads, and bridges. More and better tools make workers more productive.

Farming is a good illustration of the role of capital. In much of the world, farmers are laborers pure and simple: they dig, seed, cut, and harvest using hard labor and a few simple tools like hoes and plows (often pulled by oxen). In the United States, farmers use a lot more capital—tractors, trucks, combines, and harvesters.

CHECK YOURSELF

> According to Figure 6.2, approximately what percentage of the world's population lived in China in 2000?

> If you make 5 percent on your savings in a bank account, how many years will it take for your savings to double? How about if you make 8 percent?

> In Figure 6.4, approximately when did Japan's real GDP per capita cross the $10,000 barrier? The $20,000 barrier? What was Japan's growth rate in that time span?

Physical capital is the stock of tools including machines, structures, and equipment.

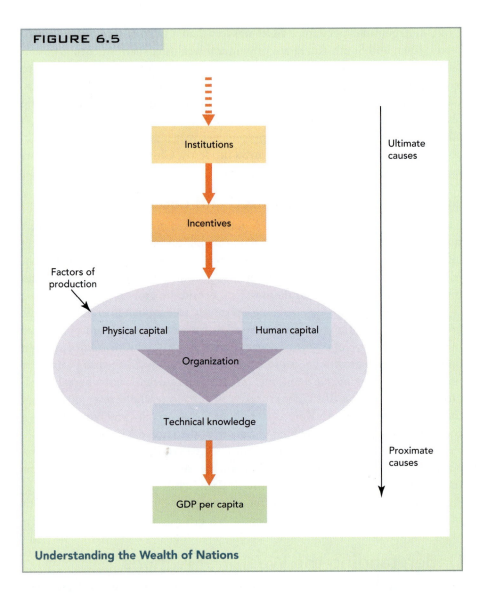

FIGURE 6.5

Understanding the Wealth of Nations

Farmers practicing capitalism

Human capital is the productive knowledge and skills that workers acquire through education, training, and experience.

It's not just farmers that use a lot of capital. The typical worker in the United States works with over $100,000 worth of capital. A typical worker in India works with less than one-tenth as much capital.

It's also not just physical capital that makes U.S. farmers productive. A farmer in the United States riding his tractor uses a GPS (global positioning system) receiver to triangulate his exact location using signals from a series of satellites orbiting the earth some 16,500 miles high. The tractor's location is combined with data from other satellites and land-based sensors to precisely adjust the amount of seed, fertilizer, and water to be applied to the land. The fertilizer has been carefully designed, and the seeds almost certainly have been genetically engineered.

The high-tech nature of farming in the United States draws our attention to the importance of human capital and technological knowledge. **Human capital** is *tools of the mind*, or the stuff in people's heads that makes them productive. Human capital is not something we are born with—it is produced by an investment of time and other resources in education, training, and experience. Farmers in the United States, for example, have more human capital than farmers in most of the world, and it's this human capital that enables them to take advantage of tools like GPS receivers. The same is true in the larger economy—the typical person in the United States, for example, has about 12 years of schooling while in Pakistan the typical person has less than 5 years of schooling.

The greater quantities of physical and human capital per worker used in U.S. farming make U.S. farmers more productive. U.S. farmers produce more than three times as much corn per acre than do farmers in Pakistan, for example.

The third factor of production is technological knowledge. This factor includes, for instance, the genetics, chemistry, and physics that form the basis of the techniques used in U.S. agriculture. (Did you know that the clocks on GPS satellites must be adjusted to account for the effects of Einstein's theory of relativity?)

Technological knowledge and human capital are related but different. Human capital is the knowledge and skills that a farmer needs to understand and to make productive use of technology. **Technological knowledge** is knowledge about how the world works—the kind of knowledge that makes technology possible. We increase human capital with education. We increase technological knowledge with research and development. Technological knowledge is potentially boundless. We can learn more and more about how the world works even if human capital remains relatively constant.

Improved technological knowledge has made U.S. farmers more productive over time. U.S. farms today produce more than two and half times as much output as they did in 1950 and they do so using *less* land! More physical and human capital has helped to drive this increase in output, but better technological knowledge has been the primary factor.[1]

The final factor, a factor often taken for granted, is organization. Human capital, physical capital, and technological knowledge must be organized to produce valuable goods and services. Who does this organizing and why? To answer this question, we turn to the issue of incentives and institutions.

Incentives and Institutions

South Korea has a per capita GDP more than 10 times higher than North Korea. Why? In one sense, we have just given an answer: South Korea has more physical and human capital per worker than North Korea.* But this answer is incomplete and partial. The answer is incomplete because we still want to know: *Why* does South Korea have more physical and human capital than North Korea? The answer is partial because poor countries like North Korea not only have less physical and human capital than rich countries, they also fail to organize the capital that they do have in the most productive ways. To understand the wealth of nations more deeply, we need to take a look at some of the indirect or more ultimate causes.

The example of South and North Korea is useful because we can rule out some explanations for the huge differences in wealth between these two countries. The explanation, for example, cannot be differences in the people, culture, or geography. Before South and North Korea were divided at the end of World War II, they shared the same people and culture, in other words, the same human

Technological knowledge is knowledge about how the world works that is used to produce goods and services.

CHECK YOURSELF

> Which country has more physical capital per worker: the United States or China? China or Nigeria?

> What are the three primary factors of production?

---

* What about technological knowledge? North Korea has access to most of the world's technological knowledge and is able, for example, to build sophisticated weapons—perhaps even a nuclear bomb—thus differences in technological knowledge probably only explain a small fraction of the differences in the wealth of nations.

Increases in technological knowledge, however, are clearly important for growth at the world level (as opposed to explaining differences in wealth across nations)—as we will discuss at greater length in the next chapter.

capital. South and North Korea also had similar levels of physical capital—natural resources were about the same in the South as the North, and if there were any advantages in man-made physical capital, they went to the North, which was at that time more industrialized than the South. When the two regions were split, therefore, South and North Korea were in all important respects the same, almost as if the split was designed as a giant social experiment.

South and North Korea differed in their economic institutions. Broadly speaking, South Korea had capitalism, and North Korea had communism. South Korea was never a pure capitalist economy, of course, but in South Korea the organizers of human capital, physical capital, and technological knowledge are private, profit-seeking firms and entrepreneurs to a much greater extent than in North Korea. In South Korea a worker earns more money if he provides goods and services of value to consumers or if he invents new ideas for more efficient production. Those same incentives do not exist in North Korea, where workers are rewarded for being loyal to the ruling communist party. In short, South Korea uses markets to organize its production much more than North Korea and so is able to take advantage of all the efficiency properties of markets that we discussed in Chapters 2 and 3.

Fifty years later the results of the "experiment" splitting North and South Korea are so clear they can be seen even from outer space, as seen in Figure 6.6.

FIGURE 6.6

Can You Tell Which Country Has Better Institutions?
South Korea and North Korea photographed at night from outer space.

Source: REUTERS/Jason Reed

The experiment splitting South and North Korea is especially dramatic. But wherever similar experiments have been tried, such as in East and West Germany, or Taiwan and China, the results have been similar.

We said earlier that countries with a high GDP per capita have a lot of physical and human capital that is organized using the best technological knowledge to be highly productive. But factors of production do not fall from the sky like manna from heaven. Factors of production must be produced. Similarly, factors of production do not organize themselves. Physical capital, human capital, and technology must be combined and organized purposively for it to be productive.

Do you remember Big Idea One and Big Idea Two from the introductory chapter? These ideas were that incentives matter and good institutions align self-interest with the social interest.

Thus, we can now deepen our understanding of the wealth of nations. Countries with a high GDP per capita have institutions that make it in people's self-interest to invest in physical capital, human capital, and technological knowledge and to efficiently organize these resources for production.

In short, the key to producing and organizing the factors of production are *institutions* that create appropriate *incentives*. Let's look at institutions and the incentives that they create in more detail.

Institutions

Institutions include laws and regulations but also customs, practices, organizations, and social mores—institutions are the "rules of the game" that shape human interaction and structure economic incentives within a society.

What kinds of institutions encourage investment and the efficient organization of the factors of production? Understanding institutions is an important area of research in economics, and there is considerable agreement that among the key institutions are property rights, honest government, political stability, a dependable legal system, and competitive and open markets.

Institutions are the "rules of the game" that structure economic incentives.

Institutions of Economic Growth

> Property rights

> Honest government

> Political stability

> A dependable legal system

> Competitive and open markets

Entire books have been written about each of these institutions and their role in economic growth. Indeed, much of this book is about property rights and the benefits of open markets and rivalrous economic competition. Thus, we will give only a few examples here of how each of these institutions create appropriate incentives, incentives that align self-interest with the social interest.

Property Rights   When the communist revolutionaries took control of China, they abolished private property in land. In the "Little Leap Forward," they put farmers to work in collectives of 100–300 families. Communal property meant that the incentives to invest in the land and work hard were low. Imagine that a day's work can produce an extra bushel of corn. Thus, an extra day's work on a commune with 100 families earned the worker 1/100th of a bushel of corn. Would you work an extra day for a few earfuls of corn? Under communal property, working an extra day doesn't add much to a worker's take-home pay and working a day less doesn't subtract much. Thus, *under communal property, effort is divorced from payment*

A **free rider** is someone who consumes a resource without working or contributing to the resource's upkeep.

so there is little incentive to work—in fact, there is an incentive not to work and to **free ride** on the work of others. In the "Great Leap Forward," the incentive to free ride was made even stronger when communes were increased to 5,000 families. But if everyone free rides, the commune will starve. Communal property in agricultural land did not align a farmer's self-interest with the social interest. And, as a result of this and many similar errors on the part of the Chinese leadership, some 20–40 million Chinese farmers and workers starved during this period.

The Great Leap Forward was actually a great leap backward—agricultural land was less productive in 1978 than it had been in 1949 when the communists took over. In 1978, however, farmers in the village of Xiaogang held a secret meeting. The farmers agreed to divide the communal land and assign it to individuals—each farmer had to produce a quota for the government but anything he or she produced in excess of the quota they would keep. The agreement violated government policy and as a result the farmers also pledged that if any of them were to be jailed the others would raise their children.

The change from collective property rights to something closer to private property rights had an immediate effect: investment, work effort, and productivity increased. "You can't be lazy when you work for your family and yourself," said one of the farmers.

Word of the secret agreement leaked out and local bureaucrats cut off Xiaogang from fertilizer, seeds, and pesticides. But amazingly, before Xiaogang could be stopped, farmers in other villages also began to abandon collective property. In Beijing, Mao Zedong was dead and a new set of rulers, seeing the productivity improvements, decided to let the experiment proceed.

In the five short years between 1978 and 1983, when China's central government endorsed individual farming, food production increased by nearly 50 percent and 170 million people were lifted above the World Bank's lowest poverty line. Simply put, increases in agricultural productivity brought about by the switch to individual farming were the greatest antipoverty program in the history of the world. By 1984, the collective farms were gone and soon after that China's leader Deng Xiaoping announced a new government policy: "it is glorious to be rich."

Property rights in land greatly increased China's agricultural productivity. With fewer workers producing more food, more workers were available to produce other goods. To take advantage of its millions of workers, China opened up to foreign investment, making the label "Made in China" common throughout the world. With their secret pact, the farmers of Xiaogang had begun a second and more successful Chinese revolution.[2]

Property rights are important institutions for encouraging investment in physical and human capital, not just in agriculture but throughout the economy. It can take decades, for example, for an investment in a new apartment building or a factory to pay off. As we will discuss further in Chapter 8 savings are necessary to generate investment and thus growth. But why do people save and invest? Savers won't save and investors won't invest if they don't expect that their property will be secure and they will receive a return for their savings and investment. Property rights are also important for encouraging technological innovation. For instance, investments in new pharmaceuticals take decades to pay off and they are risky—years of research and development sometimes have to be abandoned when the guinea pigs start to die unexpectedly. Just like farmers, investors and workers throughout the economy need to know that they will reap what they sow.

Honest Government   China under its former communist rulers was extreme in abolishing most forms of private property. In many other countries, private

property rights exist on paper—but only on paper. In a country like Zimbabwe, for example, an individual might have a legal right to land or a factory but everyone knows that the government can take these goods at any moment. Zimbabwe lacks the rule of law.

More generally, corruption is like a heavy tax that bleeds resources away from productive entrepreneurs. Resources "invested" in bribing politicians and bureaucrats cannot be invested in machinery and equipment, thus reducing productivity. Corrupt government officials will also harass entrepreneurs, creating excessive rules and regulations that force entrepreneurs to pay them to stop making trouble.

Not all taxes are bad of course. A tax that funds investment in roads, universities, or law and order can increase the productivity of private investments. Corruption, therefore, is a doubly bad tax because corruption makes it less profitable to be an entrepreneur at the same time as it makes it more profitable to be a corrupt politician or bureaucrat. At some point, corruption can feed on itself creating a poverty trap: few people want to be entrepreneurs because they know that their wealth will be stolen and thus there is no wealth to steal.

Figure 6.7 on the next page graphs corruption on the horizontal axis. The most corrupt countries like Somalia, Liberia, and North Korea are on the right, scoring about 2 on a 5-point scale running from −2.5 (least corrupt) to 2.5 (most corrupt). The least corrupt countries like Singapore, Iceland, the United States, and Norway are on the left. Real GDP per capita is on the vertical axis. Countries that are more corrupt have much lower per capita GDP.

Top Ten Least Corrupt Countries (2000)	Top Ten Most Corrupt Countries (2000)
Country	Country
Finland	North Korea
Singapore	Afghanistan
Sweden	Somalia
Iceland	Liberia
Netherlands	Equatorial Guinea
Denmark	Congo, Democratic Republic
New Zealand	Angola
Norway	Iraq
United Kingdom	Haiti
Switzerland	Myanmar
Source: World Bank, World Governance Indicators	Source: World Bank, World Governance Indicators

Political Stability Investors have more to fear than government expropriation—sometimes the threat of anarchy can be even worse. Liberia, for example, has had little but conflict for the past 40 years. Prior to the election in 2006 of President Ellen Johnson-Sirleaf, the first elected female head of state in Africa, it had been 35 years since a Liberian president assumed office by means other than bloodshed. Both the previous two national leaders (Charles Taylor and Samuel Doe) consistently used the force of government to eradicate their opposition. Who wants to invest in the future when civil war threatens to wash away all plans?

More generally, in many nations, civil war, military dictatorship, and anarchy have destroyed the institutions necessary for economic growth.

A Dependable Legal System The problem of poorly protected property rights is not always a problem of too much government—sometimes property rights are poorly protected because there is too little government. The legal system in many countries, for example, is of such low quality that no one knows for certain who owns what. In India, residents who purchase land often have to do so two or three times (from different parties), as there exists no reliable record of true ownership. A lawsuit, if you even bother to bring one, can take 20 years or more to resolve. In a major urban area, it's very difficult to build something as simple as a supermarket because developers cannot acquire good

Not a good place to grow

Bullet casings cover a street in Monrovia, the capital of Liberia, in the summer of 2003.

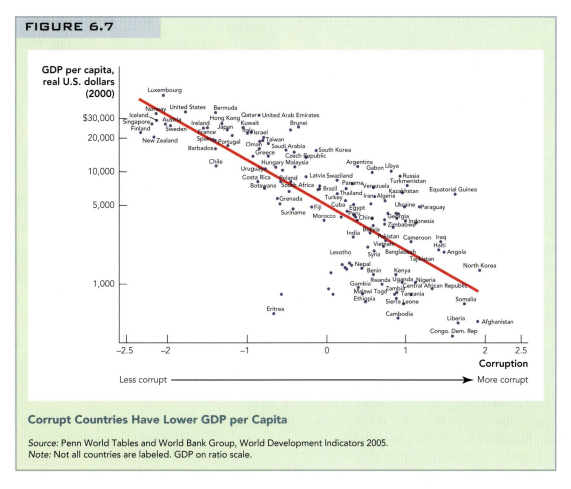

FIGURE 6.7

Corrupt Countries Have Lower GDP per Capita

Source: Penn World Tables and World Bank Group, World Development Indicators 2005.
Note: Not all countries are labeled. GDP on ratio scale.

title to a modestly sized piece of land. No one wants to build when they cannot protect their investment.

A good legal system facilitates contracts and protects private parties from expropriating one another. Few people think of the U.S. legal system as a paradigm of productivity but it is compared to the Indian legal system. In the United States, for example, it takes 17 procedures and 300 days to collect on a debt (say a bounced check). In India, it takes 56 procedures and 1,420 days to do the same thing. That's one reason why it is hard to borrow money in the first place: lenders know how hard it is to get their money back.

Competitive and Open Markets The factors of production must not only be produced—they must also be organized. Detailed studies from a large number of countries suggest that the failure to organize capital efficiently has a huge effect on the wealth of nations. Poor countries are poor, in other words, not just because they lack capital but also because they use the capital that they do have inefficiently. Overall, about half the differences in per capita income across countries are explained by differences in the amount of physical and human capital (some of those differences in capital spring from deeper differences in institutions) and about half the differences are explained by a failure to use capital efficiently. One study, for example, estimates that if India used the physical and human capital that it does have as efficiently as the United States uses its capital, India would be four times richer than it is today.[3]

Why does India use its capital inefficiently? The reasons are numerous, but competitive and open markets are one of the best ways to encourage the efficient

organization of resources. India, as well as other poor countries, has many inefficient and unnecessary regulations, which create monopolies or otherwise impede markets.

For instance, Indian shirts are usually made by hand in small shops of 3 or 4 tailors that design, measure, sew, and sell, all on the same premises. It sounds elegant but this is not Savile Row, the section of London where the finest tailors in the world create custom suits for the rich and powerful. Shirts would be cheaper and of higher quality if they were mass manufactured in small factories—the way shirts for Americans are produced. Why doesn't this happen in India? Shirts in India are produced inefficiently because, until recently, large-scale production was illegal.

India prohibited investment in shirt factories from exceeding about $200,000. This restriction meant that Indian shirt manufacturers could not take advantage of **economies of scale,** the decrease in the average cost of production that often occurs as the total quantity of production increases. India has been reforming its economy, which is one reason why economic growth in India has increased in recent years (as we discussed in Chapter 5). India recently lifted the ban on large garment factories, for example, but many, many regulations remain that reduce the productivity of the Indian economy.[4]

Poor countries also suffer from expensive red tape. Economists at the World Bank have estimated the time and cost to do simple tasks such as starting a business or enforcing a contract in a court of law. In the United States, for example, it takes about 5 days to start a business and the total costs of the procedures are minor, less than 1 percent of the average income per capita. In Peru, starting a business takes 72 days and 32.5 percent of income per capita. In Haiti, it takes 203 days and the costs are 127 percent of income per capita. Thus, even before a business is begun, a Peruvian or Haitian entrepreneur must invest extensively in dealing with bureaucracies—that same physical and human capital is not being used to produce goods and services.

> **Economies of scale** are the advantages of large-scale production that reduce average cost as quantity increases.

Institutions and Growth Miracles Revisited

When China changed its institutions from collective farming to individual farming, agricultural productivity increased dramatically and China began to grow. The example of China is enormously encouraging because it suggests that growth miracles could become common if more countries changed their institutions. But take a look again at Figure 6.5. Institutions have a large effect on increasing and organizing the factors of production and thus institutions have a large effect on economic growth. But where do institutions come from? Are institutions products of ideas? Culture? History? Geography? Luck? Try "all of the above" and then some.

If you consider the history of America, its constitution was written at a time when the ideas of John Locke and Adam Smith were popular and it inherited a tendency toward a market economy and democratic institutions from its colonizer, Great Britain. An open frontier meant cheap land and plenty of freedom to try new ideas and ways of living, perhaps influencing America's entrepreneurial culture even into modern times. And we are very lucky that George Washington had the virtue to stop at two Presidential terms, rather than trying to become the next king.

No one understands for certain all the influences that go into creating a nation's institutions which means that changing institutions isn't easy. When it comes to institutions, we know where we want to go but we don't always know how to get there. Understanding institutions, where they come from, and how they can be changed, is thus a key research question in economics.

□ Takeaway

It's hard to overstate the importance of economic growth. Once, everyone was poor. Today, GDP per capita is more than 50 times higher in the richest countries than in the poorest. Economic growth has raised billions of people out of near-starvation poverty but billions more remain in dire poverty with shocking consequences for their quality of life.

Fortunately, poor countries can catch up to rich countries and in a surprisingly short period of time. Growth "miracles" have brought Japan and South Korea up to European levels of wealth within the lifespan of a single generation. Since the agricultural reforms beginning in 1978, poverty in China has been reduced to an unprecedented degree and China continues to grow rapidly.

What makes a country rich? The most proximate cause is that countries with a high GDP per capita have lots of physical and human capital per worker and that capital is organized using the best technological knowledge to be highly productive.

How do countries get a lot of physical and human capital and how do they organize it using the best technological knowledge? Countries with a high GDP per capita have institutions that encourage investment in physical capital, human capital, technological innovation, and the efficient organization of resources. Among the most powerful institutions for increasing economic growth are property rights, honest government, political stability, a dependable legal system, and competitive and open markets.

□ CHAPTER REVIEW

KEY CONCEPTS

Economic growth, p. 94

Physical capital, p. 97

Human capital, p. 98

Technological knowledge, p. 99

Institutions, p. 101

Free rider, p. 102

Economies of scale, p. 105

FACTS AND TOOLS

1. Look at Figure 6.1. About how many babies die before the age of 5 in Nigeria versus Argentina? What is the difference in GDP per person in those two countries?

2. Look at Figure 6.2. About what fraction of the world's population lives in countries richer than Italy? What fraction lives in countries poorer than India?

3. The world's average (mean) GDP per capita is $9,133. There are roughly 6 billion people in the world.

   a. What is the world's total GDP?

   b. About 20 percent of the world's population produces 50 percent of the world's total GDP. (Notice the use of "produces," not "consumes." In popular discussion, you are more likely to hear about the people at the top "consuming" more than their share, not "producing" more than their share. But remember what the last letter of GDP stands for!) How much GDP does the top 20 percent produce?

c. What is the average GDP per capita of the most productive 20 percent of the world's population? (Hint: 20 percent of 6 billion people equals how many people?)

4. Now let's look at the productivity of the world's least productive 80 percent.

a. How much GDP do they produce? (Hint: You've already calculated this number in the previous question.)

b. What is the average GDP per capita of the least productive 80 percent of the world's population?

c. Now, the payoff: How productive is the average person in the top 20 percent compared to the average person in the bottom 80 percent of the planet? Answer this by dividing your answer to question 3c by your answer to question 4b. This chapter and the next are devoted to explaining why this ratio is so large.

5. According to Fact Two, what would your answer to question 4c have been if you calculated it two thousand years ago?

6. What are the factors of production? Name them and briefly describe them in plain English.

7. Using data from the Penn World Tables, calculate the annual growth rate of real GDP per person for China for the years in the table. The Penn World Tables, available free online, are a reliable source of international economic data, and they are very popular among economists.

Year	Real GDP per capita (in 1996 U.S. dollars)	Annual Growth Rate
2000	4,001	
2001	4,389	____
2002	4,847	____
2003	5,321	____
2004	5,771	____

8. Practice with the rule of 70: If you inherit $10,000 this year and you invest your money so that it grows 7 percent per year, how many years will it take for your investment to be worth

$20,000? $40,000? $160,000? (Note: Investments in stocks have grown at an average inflation-adjusted rate of 7 percent per year since the U.S. Civil War. We'll practice this some more in Chapter 7.)

Value today: $10,000. Growth Rate: 7 percent

Number of years until money doubles: ____

Number of years until money quadruples:

____

Number of years until your inheritance is 16X larger: ____

9. More practice with the rule of 70: Suppose that instead, you put your money into a savings account that grows at an inflation-adjusted return of 2 percent per year. How many years will it take to be worth $20,000? $40,000? $160,000? (Note: Bank deposits have grown at roughly this rate over the last 50 years in the United States.)

Value today: $10,000.   Growth Rate: 2 percent

Number of years until money doubles: ____

Number of years until money quadruples:

____

Number of years until your inheritance is 16X larger: ____

10. India and China come up a lot in this chapter. You might wonder why so much time is spent talking about just two countries out of over 180 on the planet. But what fraction of humans live in India and China together?

11. Let's convert Figure 6.5 into words.

Institutions create ____, which in turn affect the amount of ____, ____, and ____ in a country, which, combined with the right kind of ____ generates a level of ____ per person.

THINKING AND PROBLEM SOLVING

1. The average person in Argentina today is about as rich (in inflation-adjusted terms) as his or her parents. How can this be called a "growth disaster?"

2. Before the rise of affordable automobiles and subways, many people used trolleys—small trains on rails that ran along ordinary streets—to get around in urban areas. On trolleys, there is a literal "free rider problem": since the trains were right next to sidewalks, and since trolleys were wide open and never had doors, people could hop on and off very easily. How much money will a trolley lose if it is easy to ride for free? If "free riders" are a big problem, what will happen to the supply of trolley rides? What are a few things the trolley industry could do to solve the problem of free riders?

The trolley: a literal "free-rider" problem.

3. During the Great Leap Forward, millions of Chinese starved to death because not enough food was produced by farmers. Why didn't farmers grow food? In particular, was it because there wasn't enough human capital or physical capital?

The text on the Great Leap Forward era flag reads, in part, "Long live the People's Commune!" Unfortunately, this patriotic appeal didn't work as well as good economic incentives and millions lost their lives. *(Source: Wikipedia, "Great Leap Forward")*

4. Laws that encourage businesses to stay small are often very popular. The laws governing Indian shirt tailors discussed in this chapter are just one example. What are some *noneconomic* (e.g., social, moral, ethical) reasons why voters might want businesses to stay small? What are some *economic* reasons they might want businesses to grow large?

5. Economists use the term "human capital" to refer to education and job skills. How is education like a piece of capital?

6. Many people say that natural resources like oil and minerals are the way to prosperity. Indeed, in an old cartoon by Matt Groening, creator of *The Simpsons*, a professor taught his students, "The nation that controls magnesium controls the universe!" But natural resources have been left out of this chapter completely. Is this a big mistake? (Source: Sala-i-Martin, X., G. Doppelhofer, and R. Miller, "Determinants of Long-Term Economic Growth," *American Economic Review,* September 2004.)

   a. Here are the ten countries in the world that have the highest amount of hydrocarbons (oil, natural gas, etc.) per person, in rank order:

      1. Kuwait
      2. United Arab Emirates (UAE)
      3. Saudi Arabia
      4. Iraq
      5. Norway
      6. Venezuela
      7. Oman
      8. Iran
      9. Trinidad & Tobago
      10. Gabon

   Use the *CIA World Factbook*, a convenient online source of information, to see if most of these countries are prosperous. How many of these 10 countries have a GDP per person that is at least half of the U.S. level? How many are less than 10 percent of the U.S. level? Are any actually higher than the U.S. level?

   b. Now, let's look at the reverse: Let's see if the 10 richest countries in GDP per capita have a lot of hydrocarbon wealth:

      1. Luxembourg
      2. United States
      3. Singapore
      4. Hong Kong
      5. Norway
      6. Australia
      7. Sweden
      8. Canada
      9. Denmark
      10. Japan

The one country on both lists also makes another list in this chapter. Which one is it?

7. Economists often refer to the "natural resource curse," by which they mean that large amounts of natural resources tend to create bad politics because as long as the oil keeps flowing or the diamonds remain plentiful, political leaders don't need to care much about what goes on in the rest of the country.

   a. Which one of the three factors of production do you think matters most to a leader of a resource-rich country? Why? (Note: Does this help explain what you see happening in many resource-rich countries?)

   b. Which one of the five key institutions do you think matters most to a leader of a resource-rich republic? Why? (Note: Does this help explain what you see happening in many resource-rich countries?)

8. Let's figure out how long it will take for the average Indian to be as wealthy as the average Western European is today. Note that all numbers are *adjusted for inflation*, so we're measuring output in "piles of stuff," not "piles of money." India's GDP per capita is $3,000, and (somewhat optimistically) let's say that real output per person there grows at 5 percent per year. Using the rule of 70, how many years will it take for India to reach Italy's current level of GDP per capita, about $24,000 per year?

9. In the Soviet Union, especially in the early decades under Lenin and Stalin, the official doctrine was communism, and the use of incentives was considered a form of treason. One important exception was the military equipment sector, where bonuses were common for engineers who designed and manufactured jets, nuclear missiles, tanks, and rifles. Why was this an exception?

10. Free rider problems are everywhere. For example, some restaurants let every food server keep their own tips. Other restaurants require all of the food servers to put their tips into a tip pool, which then gets divided up equally among all of the servers. It's easy to adjust the tip pool so that people who work more hours or serve more tables get their "fair share," so that's not the issue we're concerned about here. Instead, let's think about how the tip pool changes the server's incentive to be nice to the customer.

   a. To keep it simple, let's assume that a server can be "nice" and earn $100 in tips per shift, or be "mean" and earn $40 in tips per shift. If an individual server goes from being "mean" to being "nice," how much more will he earn in a non-tip-pooling world? (Yes this is an easy question.)

   b. Now let's look at incentives in a tip pool. If all the servers are mean, how much will the average server earn? If all the servers are nice, how much will the average server earn? What's the change in tips per server if *all* of them switch from being mean to being nice?

   c. But in the real world, of course, each server makes her own decision to be mean or nice. Suppose that some servers are being nice and others are being mean, and you're trying to decide whether to be nice or mean. What's the payoff *to you* if you switch your behavior? Does your answer depend on how many other servers are being nice?

   d. So when are you most likely to be nice: When you're in a tip pool or when you keep your own tips? If the restaurant cares a lot about keeping its customers happy, which policy will it follow?

11. If "everyone used to be poor," then how could some ancient civilizations afford to create massive buildings like the pyramids of Egypt and the Buddhist statues of Afghanistan (sadly, the latter were recently destroyed by the Taliban)?

CHALLENGES

1. One way to learn about what makes some countries richer is to run statistical tests to see which factors are good at predicting a nation's level of productivity. Sometimes it turns out that a relationship is just a coincidence (like the fact that people in rich countries eat more ice cream), while other statistical tests really can tell you about the ultimate causes of productivity. A statistical test can't tell you everything, but it might help point you in the right direction. In courses on econometrics and statistics, you can learn about how to run sensible tests.

   Let's look at one well-known set of tests, to see if what you learned in this chapter matches the statistical evidence. Here are 17 variables that turned out to be very strong predictors of a nation's long-run economic performance in literally millions of statistical tests (Source: Sala-i-Martin, X., G. Doppelhofer, and R. Miller, "Determinants of Long-Term Economic Growth," *American Economic Review*, September 2004).

They are in rank order, and a "+" means more of that value was good for long-run productivity:

1. Whether a country is in East Asia (+)
2. Level of K-6 schooling (+)
3. Price of capital goods (−)
4. Fraction of land close to the coast (+)
5. Fraction of population close to the coast (+)
6. Malaria prevalence (−)
7. Life expectancy (+)
8. Fraction of population Confucian (+)
9. Whether a country is in Africa (−)
10. Whether a country is in Latin America (−)
11. Fraction of GDP in mining industries (+)
12. Whether a country was a Spanish colony (−)
13. Years open to relatively free trade (+)
14. Fraction of population Muslim (+)
15. Fraction of population Buddhist (+)
16. Number of languages widely spoken (−)
17. Fraction of GDP spent on government purchases (−)

    a. Which of these factors sound like the "three factors of production?" Which ones do they sound like?
    b. Which of these factors sound like the "five key institutions?" Which ones do they sound like?
    c. Which of these factors sound like geography?

    d. The western United States was a Spanish colony until 1849. On average, former Spanish colonies have had poor economic performance. Does the western United States fit that pattern? Why or why not?

2. What do *you* think creates the good institutions that exist in rich countries? Why don't these institutions—property rights, markets, a society where you can usually trust strangers—exist everywhere on the planet?

3. Why do you think expensive red tape is hard to get rid of in many poor countries? Yes, this is a miniature version of the previous question.

4. Communists thought that their system would be much more efficient than capitalism: They thought that competition between companies was wasteful. Why build three separate headquarters for carmakers (General Motors, Chrysler, and Ford), when you can just build one? Why have three advertising budgets? Why pay for three CEOs? Why not put all the factories together, so that the same engineers can fix problems at all of the plants? Doesn't one large firm maximize economies of scale? These are all good questions. So why do you think communism turned out to be such a disaster, when it sounded like it would be so efficient?

5. The chapter lists five key institutions of economic growth. But isn't there really just one: Good government? Support your argument with facts from this chapter.

CHAPTER APPENDIX

The Magic of Compound Growth Using a Spreadsheet

The rule of 70 gives us a quick way to compute doubling times given a growth rate. We can also use a Microsoft Excel spreadsheet to easily answer more difficult questions. We know, for example, that if GDP per capita starts at $40,000 and if the growth rate is 2 percent then GDP per capita after one year will be $40,800 and after just 35 years it will double to $79,996. We showed this in the chapter using a simple spreadsheet as in Figure A6.1.

FIGURE A6.1

C2	▼	f_x =B2*0.02	
	A	B	C	D
	Year	Beginning GDP (per capita)	Increase in GDP	GDP at end of Year
1				
2	1	$40,000	$800	$40,800
3	2	$40,800	$816	$41,616
4	3	$41,616	$832	$42,448
36	35	$78,427	$1,569	$79,996
37				

Compound Growth in a Spreadsheet: The Long Method

Once we understand the principles, however, we don't need to write each year on a separate line. Instead, we can simplify by using a little bit of mathematical notation.

If our Starting Value for GDP per capita is $40,000 and the growth rate is r percent, for example, 2 percent, and we grow for one year, then our Ending Value will be $40,000 \times (1 + r/100)$. If we grow for two years our Ending Value will be $40,000 \times (1 + r/100) \times (1 + r/100)$, which is the same thing as $40,000 \times \left(1 + \dfrac{r}{100}\right)^2$. More generally, if the growth rate is r percent and we grow for n years then:

$$\text{Ending Value} = \text{Starting Value} \times \left(1 + \frac{r}{100}\right)^n \qquad \textbf{(A1)}$$

We can use this formula to simplify our spreadsheet as in Figure A6.2.

FIGURE A6.2

| B6 | ▼ | f_x | =A6*(1+B1/100)^B2 |

	A	B	C
1	Growth Rate	2	
2	Years	1	
3			
4			
5	Starting Value	Ending Value	
6	40000	40800	
7			

Compound Growth in a Spreadsheet: The Shortcut

Notice that we put the starting level of GDP per capita, or whatever quantity we are interested in (this could also be the amount of money in a bank account, for example), in cell A6, the growth rate is in cell B1, the number of years we want to grow is in cell B2, and thus the formula in cell B6, "=A6*(1+B1/100)^B2", is exactly as in equation A1.

By adjusting the Starting Value, the Growth Rate, and the Number of Years, we can find out how much any amount will grow to given any interest rate over any number of years.

We can also use Excel's Goal Seek ability to work backward to find, say, the number of years it will take growing at 2 percent to reach a certain level of GDP per capita. Remember, for example, that we said in the chapter that starting at a GDP per capita of about $46,000 and growing at a growth rate of 2 percent a year GDP per capita will be $1,000,000 per year in just 155 years. Here's how you can easily find numbers like this. Go to the Tools menu and click Goal Seek (in Excel 2007 go to the Data menu and under the submenu What-If Analysis click on Goal Seek). A box will pop up asking you for three inputs: Set cell ___, To value ___, By changing cell ___. In our case we want to Set cell **B6**, the Ending Value, To value **1,000,000**, by Changing cell **B2**, the number of years. Figure A6.3 shows you what you should see and input. Notice that we also changed the Starting Value to $46,000.

FIGURE A6.3

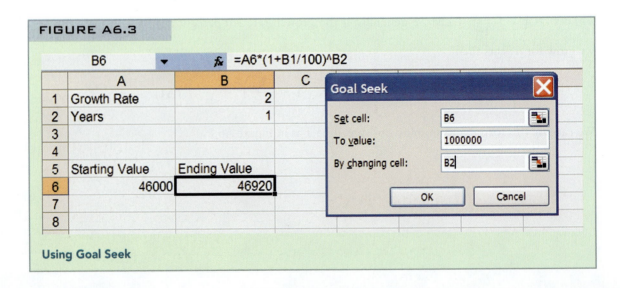

| B6 | ▼ | f_x | =A6*(1+B1/100)^B2 |

	A	B	C
1	Growth Rate	2	
2	Years	1	
3			
4			
5	Starting Value	Ending Value	
6	46000	46920	
7			
8			

Goal Seek

Set cell: B6
To value: 1000000
By changing cell: B2

OK   Cancel

Using Goal Seek

Clicking OK produces what you see in Figure A6.4.

FIGURE A6.4

| | B6 | ▼ | *fx* =A6*(1+B1/100)^B2 | | |

	A	B	C	Goal Seek Status	✕
1	Growth Rate	2		Goal Seeking with Cell B6	OK
2	Years	155.4901699		found a solution.	
3					Cancel
4				Target value: 1000000	
5	Starting Value	Ending Value		Current value: 1000000	Step
6	46000	1000000			
7					Pause
8					
9					

Goal Seek Solves the Problem

Goal Seek has solved the problem! If we start at a value of GDP per capita of $46,000 and we grow at 2 percent a year, then in 155.49 years we will reach a value of GDP per capita of $1,000,000.

By using Goal Seek and varying the inputs, you can find the answer to all kinds of questions. Can you find, for example, how high the growth rate would have to be to reach a level of GDP per capita of $1,000,000 in say 50 years?

CHAPTER APPENDIX QUESTIONS

Use Excel's Goal Seek ability to calculate the following:

1. If a country starts off as rich as the United States, with a GDP per capita of $46,000, and if GDP per capita grows 3 percent per year, then how many years will it take before GDP per capita is $1,000,000 per year?

2. If a country with a GDP per capita of $4,000 at its start grows at 8 percent per year how many years will it take before GDP per capita is $46,000?

3. If you wanted to double $1,000 in 10 years time, what average rate of return would you require on your investment?

7

Growth, Capital Accumulation, and the Economics of Ideas: Catching Up vs. the Cutting Edge

The Chinese economy has been growing at an astonishing rate. In 2006, GDP per capita in China grew by 10 percent. In the same year, GDP per capita in the United States grew by just 2.3 percent. In its entire history, the U.S. economy has never grown as fast as the Chinese economy is growing today. If these rates continue, China will be richer than the United States in less than 25 years. How can this make sense? Is there something wrong with the U.S. economy? Do the Chinese have a magical potion for economic growth?

Remember, in the last chapter we explained that among the key institutions promoting economic growth were property rights, honest government, political stability, a dependable legal system, and competitive and open markets. But for each and every one of these institutions, the United States ranks higher than China, despite China's having made remarkable improvements in recent decades. So why is China growing so much more rapidly than the United States?

To answer this question, we must distinguish between two types of growth, catching up and cutting edge. Countries that are catching up have some enormous advantages. To become rich, a poor country does not have to invent new ideas, technologies, or methods of management. All it has to do is adopt the ideas already developed in the rich countries. As we will see, catch-up countries like China grow primarily through capital accumulation and the adoption of some simple ideas that massively improve productivity.

The United States is the world's leading economy—it is on the cutting edge. Growth on the cutting edge is primarily about developing new ideas. But developing new ideas is more difficult than adopting ideas already in existence. Calculus isn't easy but it doesn't take a genius to understand calculus; it does take a genius to invent calculus. Countries on the cutting edge grow primarily through idea generation.

115

In this chapter, we will do two things. First, we will develop a model of economic growth based on capital accumulation. The model will help us understand some puzzles such as why China is growing so much faster right now than the United States and why the countries that lost World War II, Germany and Japan, grew much faster in the postwar decades than did the winner, the United States. We will also discuss how poor and rich countries can converge in income over time.

Our model of economic growth based on capital accumulation does a good job of explaining catch-up growth but it doesn't help much to explain growth on the cutting edge. If we think about growth in the United States, for example, we probably do not think first about more tractors, buildings, and factories—the sorts of things that characterize growth in China. Instead, we think about iPhones, the Internet, and genetic engineering, that is, new products, new processes, and new ideas. Thus, in the second half of the chapter we turn to cutting-edge growth and the economics of ideas. The economics of ideas explains why growth in the United States is slower than in China, but also why growth in China will slow down. It also suggests, however, that U.S. and worldwide economic growth may become faster in the decades ahead than it has been in the past. To put it bluntly (but regretfully for us), many of you will see more progress in your lifetimes than we will have seen in ours.

The Solow Model and Catch-Up Growth

Let's begin with a model of the wealth of nations and economic growth called the Solow model (after Nobel Prize–winning economist Robert Solow). The Solow model begins with a production function. A production function expresses a relationship between output and the factors of production, namely the exact way in which more inputs will produce more outputs. For simplicity, we assume that there is only one output, Y, which we can think of as GDP, and the three factors of production that we discussed in the last chapter: physical capital written K; human capital, which we write as eL, and can understand as education, e, times Labor; and ideas that increase the productivity of capital and labor, which we write as A. Thus, we can write that output, Y, is a function, F, of the inputs A, K, and eL:

$$Y = F(A, K, eL) \tag{1}$$

That looks abstract but it represents a simple economic truth. If we look at a typical production process, say an automobile factory, output depends on capital (the machines, K), labor (the workers, L, adjusted for their level of skill, so eL), and the whole factory is based on ideas (A), namely the invention of the auto and all the machines that help make it.

We also can think of the entire economy as relying on capital, labor, and ideas on a larger scale. We will focus on the Solow production function as a description of an entire economy because we are looking at the causes and consequences of overall economic growth.

For our first look at the Solow model, we will temporarily ignore changes in ideas, education, and labor. If we assume that A, e, and L are constant, then we can simplify our expression for output as $Y = F(K)$. Notice that because L is constant an increase in K always implies an increase in the amount of capital per worker, K/L, and an increase in Y is also always an increase in output per worker, Y/L.

Capital, Production and Diminishing Returns

Let's make a quick sketch of what our production function, $F(K)$, should look like. More K should produce more Y but at a diminishing rate. On a farm, for example, the first tractor is very productive. The second tractor is still useful, but not as much as the first tractor. The third tractor is driven only when one of the other tractors breaks down (remember that the amount of labor is constant). What this means is that increases in capital, K, produce less output, Y, the more K you already have—so we should have a production function where output increases with more K but at a decreasing rate. Following this logic, Figure 7.1 graphs output, Y, on the vertical axis against capital, K, on the horizontal axis, holding L and the other inputs constant.

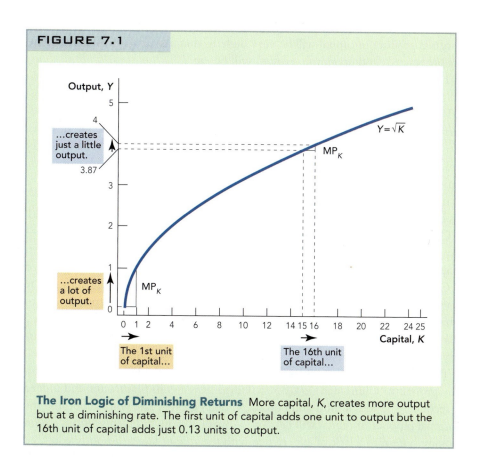

FIGURE 7.1

The Iron Logic of Diminishing Returns More capital, K, creates more output but at a diminishing rate. The first unit of capital adds one unit to output but the 16th unit of capital adds just 0.13 units to output.

Notice from Figure 7.1 that the first unit of capital increases output by one unit, but as more and more capital is added output increases by less and less—this is the "iron logic" of diminishing returns and it plays a key role in the Solow model. Economists call the increase in output when capital increases by one unit the **marginal product of capital**. The graph shows that the marginal product of capital is diminishing.

It can sometimes help to look at a specific production function. In Figure 7.1, we used the production function $Y = F(K) = \sqrt{K}$, which means that output is the square root of the capital input. To see how this works in more detail, plug in some numbers. If $K = 4$, then $Y = \sqrt{4} = 2$. If K increases to 16, then $Y = \sqrt{16} = 4$ and so forth.

The **marginal product of capital** is the increase in output caused by the addition of one more unit of capital. The marginal product of capital diminishes as more and more capital is added.

As we said, the reason the marginal product of capital diminishes is that the first unit of capital (the first tractor) is applied where it is most productive, the second unit is applied to slightly less productive tasks because the first unit is already performing the most productive tasks, the third unit is applied to even less productive tasks, and so on.

Growth in China and the United States   The iron logic of diminishing returns explains quite a bit about why China is now growing so much more rapidly than the United States. Imagine, for example, that a country labors under poor institutions—like a lack of competitive and open markets—so that the incentives to invest in capital are low. Now suppose that new institutions are put into place, perhaps new leaders with better ideas replace the old guard. The new institutions increase the incentives to invest and the capital stock grows. But in a country without a lot of capital but good (or much improved) institutions, the marginal product of capital will be very high. In that case, even small investments pay big rewards and economic growth will be rapid.

This process describes what has happened in China. For most of the twentieth century, China labored under very poor economic institutions. China in the 1950s and 1960s was a growth disaster with mass starvation as a common occurrence. Since the death of Chairman Mao in 1976 and the subsequent move away from communism and toward markets, China has been growing very rapidly. Chinese growth has been rapid because China began with very little capital, so the marginal product of capital was very high, and with the new reforms the investment rate increased dramatically. In addition, of course, China has benefited by opening up to trade and investment with the developed world.

China also grew rapidly because improved productivity in agriculture—brought about primarily by better institutions, as we discussed in the last chapter—meant that several hundred million Chinese rural peasants migrated to Chinese cities. Almost overnight these people went from being subsistence farmers, producing perhaps a few hundred dollars worth of output a year, to urban workers, producing perhaps a few thousand dollars worth of output a year in a factory. This is one of the largest economic migrations in human history and for the most part it has been a resounding success.

The iron logic explains why China is catching up to the United States but also why growth in China will slow down. China now has its first tractor and indeed its second. As it adds a third and beyond, China's growth rate will fall because the marginal product of capital will fall. Also, China has many problems—from a poor banking system to a lack of experience with the rule of law to a poorly educated population. At the moment, these problems are being swamped by the high productivity of capital. But as capital accumulates and the productivity of capital declines, China's problems will become more of a drag on Chinese growth.

Why Bombing a Country Can Raise Its Growth Rate   The iron logic also explains why bombing a country can increase its growth rate. Following World War II, for example, Germany and Japan both grew faster than the United States. It may seem odd at first that the losers of a war should grow faster than the winners, but the iron logic of diminishing returns predicts exactly this result. During World War II the capital stock of Germany and Japan—the factories, the roads, and the buildings—was nearly obliterated by Allied bombing. With so little capital remaining, any new capital was highly productive and meant that Germany and Japan had a strong incentive to put new capital into place. In other words, they grew rapidly as they were rebuilding their economies. It's also the case that Germany and Japan had reasonably good postwar institutions.

But don't make the mistake of envying Germany and Japan their high growth rates. Germany and Japan grew rapidly because they were catching up. Children who have been malnourished often grow rapidly when they are put on a proper diet but it's not good to be malnourished. Similarly, countries whose capital stock has been destroyed will grow rapidly, all else being equal, as they catch up but it is not good to have your capital stock destroyed. Note also that growth in Germany and Japan slowed down as their capital stocks grew and approached U.S. levels; by the 1980s they were growing at close to the U.S. rate. The growth rate in Germany and Japan fell not because they did anything wrong but, again, because the marginal product of capital declines the more capital a country has.

Figure 7.1 explains that more capital means more output, albeit at a diminishing rate. But where does capital come from and where does it go? Capital is output that is saved and invested, but capital depreciates over time. In the next section, we show how these two aspects of capital—investment and depreciation—fit together. Understanding investment and depreciation will prove important for isolating the ultimate sources of economic growth.

	Average Annual Growth Rate of GDP per Capita for Germany, Japan, and the United States	
	1950–1960	1980–1990
Germany	6.6%	1.9%
Japan	6.8%	3.4%
United States	1.2%	2.3%

Capital Growth Equals Investment Minus Depreciation

Capital is output that is saved and invested rather than consumed. Imagine, for example, that 10 units of output are produced. Of the 10 units of output, 7 units might be consumed and 3 units invested in new capital. We write the fraction of output that is invested in new capital as gamma (γ), and in the example just given, $\gamma = \frac{3}{10} = 0.3$.

Figure 7.2 shows how output is divided between consumption and investment when $\gamma = 0.3$. Notice that when $K = 100$, 10 units of output are

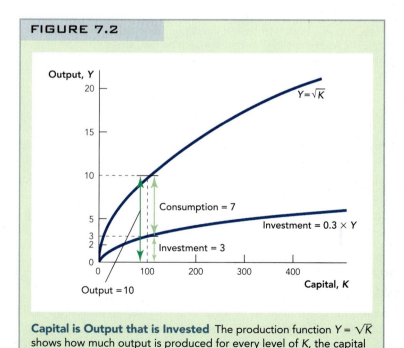

FIGURE 7.2

Capital is Output that is Invested The production function $Y = \sqrt{K}$ shows how much output is produced for every level of K, the capital stock. When $K = 100$, 10 units of output are produced. The investment rate is 0.3 so $0.3 \times 10 = 3$ units of output are devoted to investment. The remaining 7 units of output are consumed.

Rome did not replenish its capital stock.

produced and of these 10 units, 7 units are consumed and 3 units are invested in new capital.

Capital also depreciates—roads wear out, harbors become silted, and machines break down. Thus, if there are 100 units of capital in this period, for example, then 2 units might depreciate, leaving just 98 for use in the next period.

We write the fraction of capital that wears out or depreciates as delta (δ); in the example just given, $\delta = \frac{2}{100} = 0.02$. Figure 7.3 shows how much capital depreciates as a function of the capital stock. When the capital stock is 100, for example, then 2 units of capital will depreciate and when the capital stock is 200, 4 units will depreciate, and so on.

FIGURE 7.3

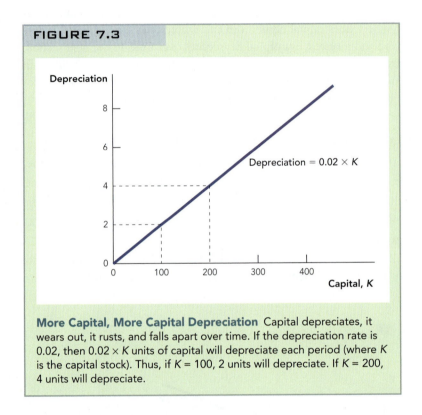

More Capital, More Capital Depreciation Capital depreciates, it wears out, it rusts, and falls apart over time. If the depreciation rate is 0.02, then 0.02 × K units of capital will depreciate each period (where K is the capital stock). Thus, if K = 100, 2 units will depreciate. If K = 200, 4 units will depreciate.

The greater the capital stock, the greater the depreciation, so a country with a lot of roads, harbors, and machines needs to devote a lot of resources to filling potholes, removing silt, and repairing and replacing. In other words, a successful economy must continually replenish its capital stock just to keep going. An economy that does not replenish its capital stock will quickly fall into ruin.

Again, Figure 7.3 shows that capital depreciation increases the greater the capital stock—this will turn out to place another constraint on economic growth.

Why Capital Alone Cannot Be the Key to Economic Growth

We now have everything we need to develop a second important insight from the Solow model. Capital depreciation increases, the greater the capital stock so at some point so much capital will be depreciating every period that *every* unit of investment will be needed just to keep the capital stock constant. When investment just covers capital depreciation, the capital stock stops growing, and when the capital stock stops growing, output stops growing as well. Thus, the iron logic of diminishing returns tells us that capital alone cannot be the key to economic growth. Let's explain this in more detail.

Figure 7.4 focuses attention on the two key functions, the investment function from Figure 7.2 and the depreciation function from Figure 7.3.

FIGURE 7.4

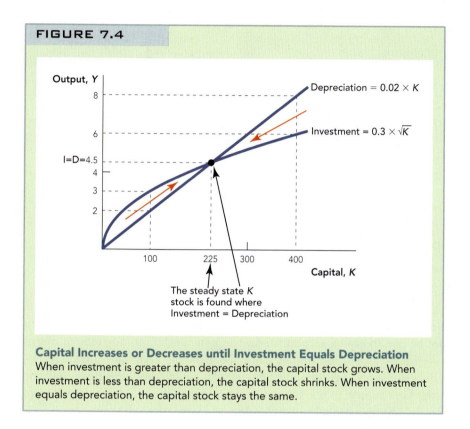

Capital Increases or Decreases until Investment Equals Depreciation
When investment is greater than depreciation, the capital stock grows. When investment is less than depreciation, the capital stock shrinks. When investment equals depreciation, the capital stock stays the same.

Consider first a case where the capital stock grows larger. For instance, when $K = 100$, 3 units of output are invested in new capital and 2 units of capital depreciate. Investment exceeds depreciation so in the next period both the capital stock and output will be larger. Thus, when investment is greater than depreciation (*Investment > Depreciation*) we have economic growth.

Investment increases as the capital stock gets larger, but because of the iron logic, investment increases at a diminishing rate. Depreciation, however, increases with the capital stock at a linear (constant) rate. Thus, at some point investment equals depreciation (*Investment = Depreciation*). At this point, every unit of investment is being used to replace depreciated capital, so the amount of net or new investment (investment after depreciation) is zero. We call this the **steady state** level of capital. At the steady state level of capital, there is no new (net) investment and economic growth stops. We can summarize as follows:

Investment > Depreciation—the capital stock grows and output next period
is bigger
Investment < Depreciation—the capital stock shrinks and output next period
is smaller
Investment = Depreciation—the capital stock and output are constant
(the steady state)

Check the Math
When K = 100, $Y = \sqrt{100} = 10$, of these 10 units 0.3 × 10 = 3 units are invested in new capital. Depreciation is 0.02 × 100 = 2 units so *Investment* (3) > *Depreciation* (2) and the capital stock and output grow.

At the **steady state** the capital stock is neither increasing nor decreasing.

Check the Math
As Figure 7.4 is drawn the steady state occurs when $K = 225$ because:
Investment $= 0.3 \times \sqrt{225} = 4.5$
Depreciation $= 0.02 \times 225 = 4.5$
thus when $K = 225$
Investment = Depreciation

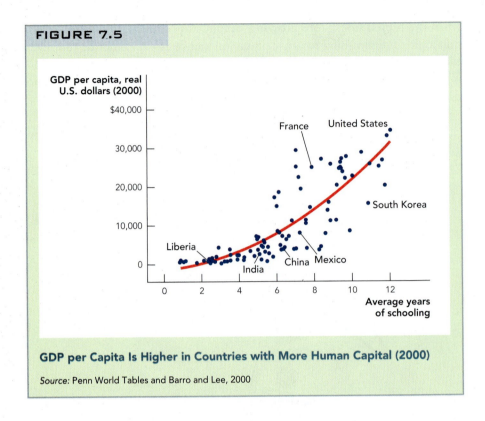

FIGURE 7.5

GDP per Capita Is Higher in Countries with More Human Capital (2000)

Source: Penn World Tables and Barro and Lee, 2000

We learn from our "capital only" model that long-run economic growth cannot be due to capital accumulation. The logic of diminishing returns means that eventually capital and output will cease growing. Economic growth, however, does not seem to be slowing. So what else could drive long-run economic growth? Let's return to the other factors of production that we discussed in Chapter 6—human capital and technological knowledge.

Can increases in human capital drive long-run economic growth? Human capital is an important contributor to the wealth of nations. Figure 7.5 shows that GDP per capita is higher in countries with more human capital, as measured by average years of schooling.

But human capital is just like physical capital in that it has diminishing returns and it depreciates. In other words, an economic principles class is probably the most important economics class that you will take and all the human capital in the world today will be gone in a hundred years. (Why will all the human capital in the world today be gone in a hundred years? Hint: Where will your human capital be in a hundred years?) Thus, within the Solow model, the logic of diminishing returns applies to human capital just as much as to physical capital and neither can drive long-run economic growth.

Better Ideas Drive Long-Run Economic Growth

Can better ideas maintain long-run economic growth? Better ideas let us produce more output from the same inputs of physical and human capital. A personal computer today has about the same amount of silicon and labor input as a computer produced 20 years ago but today's computer is much better—the difference is ideas. Recall our simple production function:

$$Y = \sqrt{K}$$

We can think of better ideas as a way of getting more output from the same input. So remembering that we let A stand for ideas that increase productivity, let's now write our production function as:

$$Y = A\sqrt{K}$$

Notice that an increase in better ideas or technological knowledge—as represented by A—increases output even while holding K constant, that is, an increase in A represents an increase in productivity. Figure 7.6 graphs two production functions. The first is when $A = 1$, the production function that we have been working with all along. The second is when $A = 2$. Notice that when $K = 16$, output is 4 when $A = 1$, but it's 8 when $A = 2$. Technological knowledge means that we can get more output from the same input.

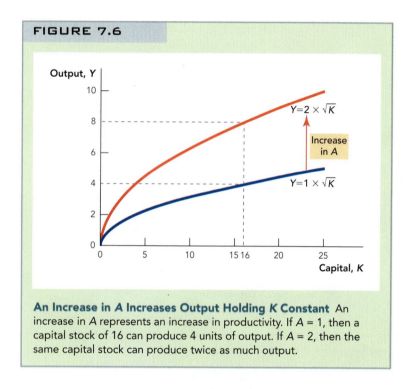

FIGURE 7.6

An Increase in A Increases Output Holding K Constant An increase in A represents an increase in productivity. If $A = 1$, then a capital stock of 16 can produce 4 units of output. If $A = 2$, then the same capital stock can produce twice as much output.

So long as we can develop better ideas that shift the production function upwards then economic growth will continue. In a way, it should be obvious that better ideas are the key to long-run economic growth. How much economic growth would there have been without the discovery of electricity or DNA or the development of the internal combustion engine, the computer chip, or the polymerase chain reaction? It's just not enough to throw more effort at a problem; we have to actually know what we are doing and that boils down to ideas.

Solow himself tried to estimate how much of U.S. economic prosperity was due to capital and labor and how much was due to ideas. He came up with the figure that better ideas are responsible for about three-fourths of the U.S. standard of living. Many economists have subsequently debated the exact number, but no one contests the central importance of ideas and technological progress for human well-being.

So to understand economic growth we must move from capital accumulation to take a closer look at the economics of ideas. To do that head to the section below titled "Growing on the Cutting Edge: The Economics of Ideas." Alternatively, more lessons can be learned from a closer inspection of the Solow model. We delve into these further lessons in the next (optional) section.

The Solow Model—Details and Further Lessons (Optional Section)

Let's return to Figure 7.4, which we also reprint here as Figure 7.7.

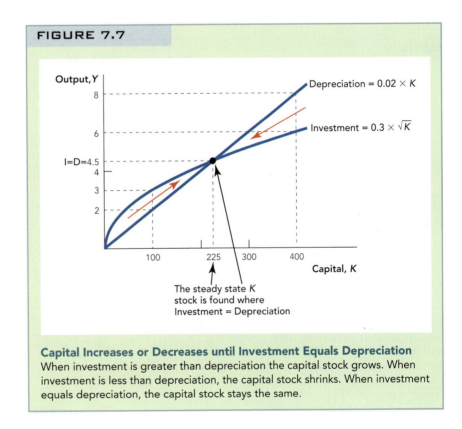

FIGURE 7.7

The steady state K stock is found where Investment = Depreciation

Capital Increases or Decreases until Investment Equals Depreciation
When investment is greater than depreciation the capital stock grows. When investment is less than depreciation, the capital stock shrinks. When investment equals depreciation, the capital stock stays the same.

We know that if *Investment* > *Depreciation* the capital stock increases and if *Investment* = *Depreciation* we are at the *steady state* level of capital, the level of capital such that the capital stock neither increases nor decreases. It's also true that if *Investment* < *Depreciation* then the capital stock and output shrink.

Remember that $Y = \sqrt{K}$, so if we know K we know Y. And if K is growing, then Y is growing. We can see this relationship a little better in Figure 7.8, which plots investment, depreciation, and output in the same graph.

That figure may look complicated, but don't get thrown off the basic idea, which is simply that the capital stock drives output, Y. For example, if K is at the steady state level ($K = 225$, in this case), then Y will also be at a steady state level of output, in this case 15. We take the 225 off the horizontal axis and bounce it off the $Y = \sqrt{K}$ curve to get to GDP = 15 on the vertical axis. Similarly, since K drives Y, whenever K is growing then so is Y. Thus, Figure 7.8

FIGURE 7.8

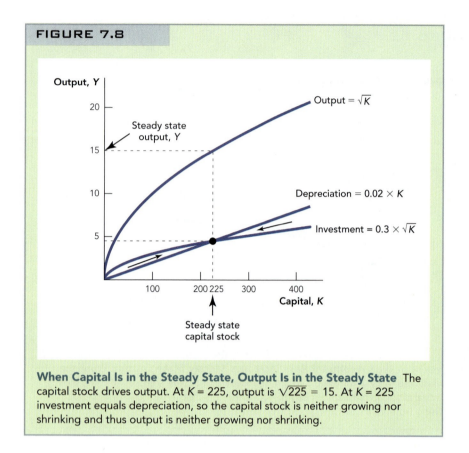

When Capital Is in the Steady State, Output Is in the Steady State The capital stock drives output. At $K = 225$, output is $\sqrt{225} = 15$. At $K = 225$ investment equals depreciation, so the capital stock is neither growing nor shrinking and thus output is neither growing nor shrinking.

demonstrates in a little more detail than we had before that our theory of capital growth is also a theory of economic growth.

The Solow Model and an Increase in the Investment Rate

What happens in the Solow model if γ, the fraction of output that is saved and invested, increases? It is simple: a greater investment rate means more capital, which means more output. An increase in the investment rate therefore increases a country's steady state level of GDP. The result just shows that investment increases the number of "tractors" per worker which raises GDP per worker.

In Figure 7.9 on the next page, we show this intuition in the graph by plotting two investment functions: *Investment* $= 0.3\sqrt{K}$, which means that 3 units of every 10 units of output are saved and invested ($\gamma = 0.3$, as it was in Figure 7.8), and also *Investment* $= 0.4\sqrt{K}$, which means that 4 units of every 10 units of output are saved and invested ($\gamma = 0.4$). Notice that when $\gamma = 0.4$, the new steady state capital stock increases to $K = 400$ and output increases to 20.

Thus, the Solow model predicts that countries with higher rates of investment will be wealthier. Is this prediction of the Solow model consistent with the evidence? Yes. Figure 7.10, also on the next page, shows that GDP per capita is higher in countries that have higher investment rates.

This makes intuitive sense. More savings mean that more capital goods can be produced and consumers can enjoy a higher standard of living. How wealthy would a country be if it spent all of its resources on partying?

The Solow model says that an increase in the investment rate will increase steady state output. But in the Solow model, the iron logic of diminishing returns cannot be forever avoided. When the investment rate increases we have

CHECK YOURSELF

In Figure 7.8
> What happens when the capital stock is 400?
> What is investment?
> What is depreciation?
> What happens to output?

FIGURE 7.9

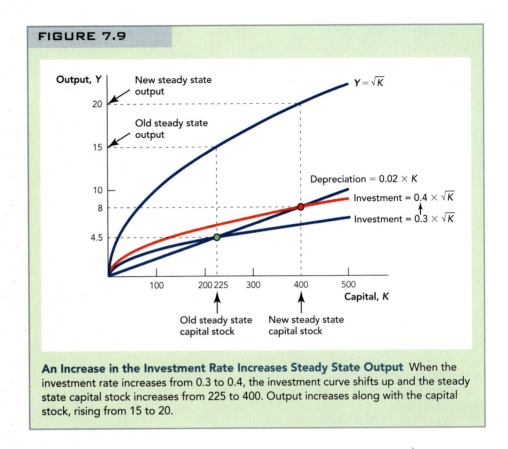

An Increase in the Investment Rate Increases Steady State Output When the investment rate increases from 0.3 to 0.4, the investment curve shifts up and the steady state capital stock increases from 225 to 400. Output increases along with the capital stock, rising from 15 to 20.

FIGURE 7.10

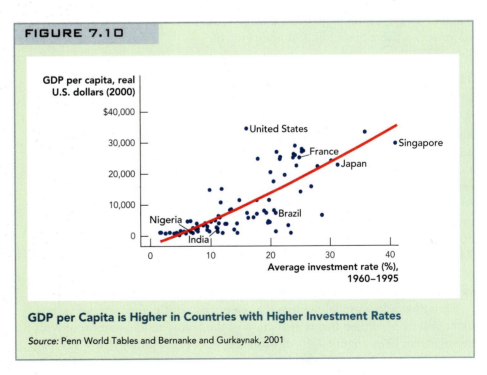

GDP per Capita is Higher in Countries with Higher Investment Rates

Source: Penn World Tables and Bernanke and Gurkaynak, 2001

Investment > *Depreciation* so the capital stock increases and the economy grows. But as more capital accumulates, the iron logic sets in and the economy eventually slows until at the new steady state it stops growing once again. So the level of the capital stock determines the output level but not its growth rate, at least not in the very long run.

For further confirmation of this idea, recall the growth miracle of South Korea from the last chapter. In 1950, South Korea was poorer than Nigeria, while today it is richer than some European nations. The evidence on South Korea's growth is consistent with the Solow model. In the 1950s, the investment rate in South Korea was less than 10 percent of GDP, but the rate more than doubled in the 1970s and increased to over 35 percent by the 1990s. Higher investment rates helped to increase South Korea's GDP, as the country opened many factories and exported cars and electronics to the rest of the world. As South Korea has caught up to western levels of GDP, however, its growth rate has slowed.

Of course, we should remember that investment rates are themselves caused by other factors such as incentives and institutions. No one wants to invest in an economy, for example, where their investments may be expropriated. One of the reasons the investment rate in South Korea increased is that capitalists believed that their investments would be protected.

In this chapter, we have referred to γ as the rate of savings *and* investment, implicitly assuming that savings equals investment. But savings must be efficiently collected and then transformed into investment. The Soviet Union had a high rate of saving but its savings were not invested well, and thus its effective investment rate was very low. In other words, a country that invests its savings poorly is like a country that doesn't invest much at all. A country could also have a low rate of saving but a high rate of investment if it imported savings from other countries. The next chapter will discuss in more detail how financial intermediaries efficiently collect savings, often from around the world, and then transform those savings into productive investments.

The Solow Model and Conditional Convergence

The Solow model also predicts that a country will grow more rapidly the farther its capital stock is below its steady state value. To understand this result, remember that when the capital stock is below its steady state value, investment will exceed depreciation. In other words, the capital stock will grow. Now look again at Figure 7.1—when the capital stock is low, it has a very high marginal product. Thus, when a country's capital stock is below its steady state value, the country will grow rapidly as it invests in capital that has a high marginal product. That's just restating our tractor parable. The tractor is most valuable on the farm that doesn't already have a tractor, as opposed to the farm that is already working with 13 tractors. (A more detailed explanation of this point can be found in the appendix to this chapter.)

We already used this result to explain why China is growing rapidly and why Germany and Japan grew rapidly after World War II. More generally, the Solow model predicts that if two countries have the same steady state level of output, the country that is poorer today will catch up because it will grow faster. We don't know for certain which countries have the same steady state level of output but we might guess, for example, that countries with similar institutions and history have similar steady states. Figure 7.11 on the next page tests this prediction using data from 18 of the 20 founding members of the OECD (Organisation for Economic Co-operation and Development).[1] The average annual growth rate between 1960 and 2000 is on the vertical axis, and real per capita GDP in 1960 is on the horizontal axis. The data clearly show that among the OECD countries the poorer countries grew faster. You can see that lower income in 1960 is associated with higher growth between 1960 and 2000.

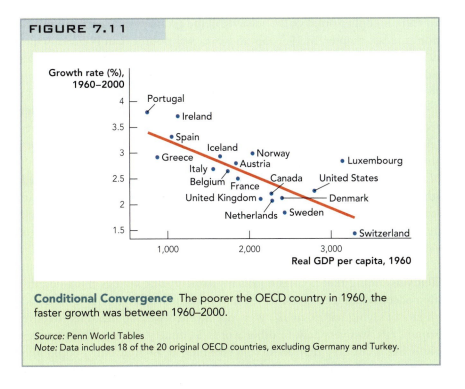

FIGURE 7.11

Growth rate (%), 1960–2000

Conditional Convergence The poorer the OECD country in 1960, the faster growth was between 1960–2000.

Source: Penn World Tables
Note: Data includes 18 of the 20 original OECD countries, excluding Germany and Turkey.

Conditional convergence is the tendency—among countries with similar steady state levels of output—for poorer countries to grow faster than richer countries and thus for poor and rich countries to converge in income.

Since the poorer countries grow faster, they eventually catch up to the richer countries. Thus, over time the OECD countries have converged to a similar level of GDP per capita. We say that the model and the data exhibit **conditional convergence** because we only see convergence among countries that plausibly have similar steady state levels of output. As we know from Chapter 6, we do not observe convergence among all countries—the existence of growth disasters such as Nigeria means that some countries are diverging from the rest of the world rather than catching up.

From Catching Up to Cutting Edge

Several predictions of the simple Solow model are consistent with the evidence—countries with higher investment rates have higher GDP per capita, and countries grow faster the farther their capital stock is from its steady state level. One prediction of the simplest form of the Solow model, however, is inconsistent with the evidence. The simplest form of the Solow model predicts zero economic growth in the long run. Remember, in the long run, the capital stock stops growing because *Investment = Depreciation* and if the capital stock isn't growing then neither is output. The United States, however, has been growing for over two hundred years, so we will need to look at a better developed version of the Solow model. In particular, is there any way to escape the iron logic? Yes, better ideas can keep the economy growing even in the long run.

Solow and the Economics of Ideas in One Diagram

Let's revisit the Solow model one last time and show how better ideas fit within that model. It's simple: better ideas let us produce more output from the same inputs of capital. But when we produce more output, it makes sense to increase consumption and *investment*. So better ideas also increase capital accumulation.

Figure 7.12 shows the process in a diagram. Okay, the diagram is not so simple. Let's take it in steps. Remember that A denotes ideas and a bigger A means that we are working with better ideas that increase output for the same level as capital. So imagine that we begin with A = ideas = 1. The economy is in the steady state and output = 15 (at point a'). Now suppose that A increases to A = 1.5. Better ideas produce more output from the same capital stock, so output immediately increases from 15 at point a' to 22.5 at point b'. But with greater output, investment also increases, moving from point a to point b. Since investment is now greater than depreciation, capital begins to accumulate. Capital accumulates and the economy grows until investment is once again equal to depreciation at point c at which point output is now 33.75 (at point c').

FIGURE 7.12

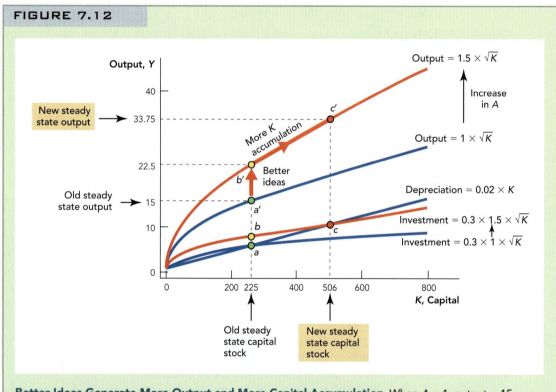

Better Ideas Generate More Output and More Capital Accumulation When A = 1, output = 15 (at point a'). Having better ideas (A = 1.5) means that more output is produced from the same capital stock so output immediately increases from a' to b'. Since investment = 0.3 × Output, more output also means more investment so investment increases from a to b. Since investment is now greater than depreciation, the economy begins to accumulate more capital and thus to grow. The economy grows until a new steady state is reached at point c with capital stock of 506 and output = 33.75 at point c'. Notice that better ideas increase output directly because of higher productivity and indirectly due to more capital accumulation.

Thus, Figure 7.12 shows how the Solow model and the economics of ideas fit together. Better ideas increase output directly and by so doing they increase capital accumulation indirectly. Of course, before we ever reach the new level of output, ideas may have gotten even better! And, thus, the process

CHECK YOURSELF

> What happens to investment and depreciation at the steady state level of capital?

> In Figure 7.9, how much is *consumed* in the old steady state? How much is *consumed* in the new steady state?

> Do countries grow faster if they are far below their steady state or if they are close?

> Do countries with higher investment rates have lower or higher GDP per capita?

of economic growth is a continuous two-step process of better ideas and more capital accumulation.

Growing on the Cutting Edge: The Economics of Ideas

We have learned from the Solow model that better ideas are the key to economic growth in the long run. Capital accumulation alone will not create much growth in the United States or the other developed economies such as Japan and Western Europe because these economies already have so much capital that investment is subject to a lot of depreciation. Instead, these countries are on the cutting edge; they must develop new ideas to increase the productivity of capital and labor. Thus, to better understand economic growth on the cutting edge we must turn to the economics of ideas.

We will emphasize the following:

1. Ideas for increasing output are primarily researched, developed, and implemented by profit-seeking firms.

2. Spillovers mean that ideas are underprovided.

3. Government has a role in improving the production of ideas.

4. The larger the market, the greater the incentive to research and develop new ideas.

Research and Development Is Investment for Profit

In Chapter 6, we emphasized that economic growth was not automatic, and we said that the factors of production do not fall from the sky like manna from heaven. In order to increase output, the factors of production must be produced and organized efficiently. All of this applies to ideas or technological knowledge just as much as to physical and human capital. Once again, incentives are the key. Economic growth requires institutions that encourage investment in physical capital, human capital, and *technological knowledge* (ideas).

In the United States, there are about 1.3 million scientists who research and develop new products, more than in any other country in the world, and most of these scientists and engineers, about 70 percent, work for private firms. (The ratios are broadly similar in other developed countries.)

Private firms invest in research and development when they expect to profit from their endeavors. Thus, the institutions we discussed in the last chapter—property rights, honest government, political stability, a dependable legal system, and competitive and open markets—also drive the generation of technological knowledge. When it comes to knowledge, other institutions are especially important. These institutions include a commercial setting that helps innovators to connect with capitalists, intellectual property rights such as copyright and patents, and a high-quality educational system (we will turn to these issues shortly).

It's not just the number of scientists and engineers that matters for economic growth, as many other people come up with new ideas on their jobs, at school, or at home in their garages. Mark Zuckerberg, for example, wrote the software for Facebook as a Harvard student. Just as important, the business culture and institutions of the United States are good at connecting innovators with business people and venture capitalists looking to fund or otherwise take a chance

on new ideas. Ideas without backers are sterile. In the United States, potential innovators know that if they come up with a good idea, that idea has a good chance of making it to the market. The incentive to discover new ideas is correspondingly strong.

American culture also supports entrepreneurs. People like Apple CEO Steve Jobs, for example, are lauded in the popular media. Historically, however, entrepreneurs were often attacked as job destroyers, as the sidebar on eighteenth-century British entrepreneur John Kay illustrates.

Compared to most other countries, the United States has a very good cultural and commercial infrastructure for supporting new ideas and their conversion into usable commercial products.

Artistic innovation also requires many individuals with a diversity of viewpoints, many sources of support and employment, and businesspeople looking to profit from and support innovations. It's not surprising, therefore, that the United States is also a leader in artistic innovation. American movies, popular music, and dance have spread around the world. But the United States is not just good at popular culture: It is also a leader in abstract art, contemporary classical composition, avant-garde fiction and poetry, and modern dance, to name just a few fields. The lesson is that artistic, economic, and scientific innovations spring from similar sources.

A further significant part of the infrastructure for creativity is property rights. We now turn to one form of intellectual property rights, patents.

Patents Many ideas have peculiar properties that can make it difficult for private firms to recoup their investments in those ideas. In particular, new processes, products, and methods can be copied by competitors. The world's first MP3 player was the Eiger Labs' MPMan introduced in 1998. Ever heard of it? Probably not. Other firms quickly copied the idea and Eiger Labs lost out in the race to innovate. Imitators get the benefit of new ideas without having to pay the costs of development. Imitators, therefore, have lower costs so they tend to drive innovators out of the market unless some barrier prevents quick imitation.

Imitation often takes time and this does give innovators a chance to recoup their investments. The Apple iPhone design, for example, is already being copied by other firms, but until that happens, Apple can exploit monopoly power to sell millions of iPhones for high profits. That is what makes Apple willing to invest in research and development in the first place and that is why the iPhone exists. Firms often compete not by offering the same product at a lower price but by offering substantially new and better products.

Apple also relies on patents to protect its innovations. A patent is a government grant of temporary monopoly rights, typically 20 years from the date of filing. Patents delay imitation, thus allowing innovative firms a greater period of monopoly power. Apple, for example, has patented one of the most distinctive features of the iPhone, the multipoint touchscreen. Apple's patent, filed in 2004, gives Apple the right to prevent other firms from copying its technology until 2024. Still, we may well see other similar devices in the near future if Apple licenses its technology to other firms. Furthermore, competitors are finding ways to produce the same effect using different methods—a majority of patented innovations are imitated within five years.

Nevertheless, Apple's patent gives it some monopoly power, and as you know if you studied micro first, firms with monopoly power raise prices above competitive levels. Thus, patents increase the incentive to research and develop new

John Kay (1704–1780) invented the "flying shuttle" used in cotton weaving, the single most important invention launching the Industrial Revolution. Kay, however, was not rewarded for his efforts. His house was destroyed by "machine breakers," who were afraid that his invention would put them out of a job. Kay was forced to flee to France where he died a poor man.

"The patent system . . . added the fuel of interest to the fire of genius." **Abraham Lincoln (1859).** Lincoln is the only U.S. president to have been granted a patent.

▶▶THE SEARCH ENGINE
You can find Apple's patent on the iPhone's multipoint touchscreen (20,060,097,991) by searching at the U.S. Patent and Trademark Office.

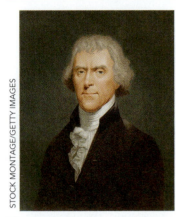

Thomas Jefferson on the Economics of Ideas *"He who receives an idea from me, receives instruction himself without lessening mine; as he who lights his taper at mine, receives light without darkening me. That ideas should freely spread from one to another over the globe . . . seems to have been peculiarly and benevolently designed by nature, when she made them . . . incapable of confinement or exclusive appropriation."*

A good is **non-rivalrous** if two or more people can consume it at the same time. Ideas are non-rivalrous goods.

products, but also increase monopoly power once the products are created. The trade-off between creating incentives to research and develop new products while avoiding too much monopoly power is one of the trickiest in economic policy.[2]

Spillovers, and Why There Aren't Enough Good Ideas

Even when a firm has a patent on its technological innovation and other firms cannot imitate in a direct way, ideas tend to spill over and benefit other firms and consumers. A new pharmaceutical will be patented, for example, but the mechanism of action—how the pharmaceutical works—can be examined and broadly copied by other firms to develop their own pharmaceuticals.

Spillovers have good and bad aspects. The good aspect of imitation or spillovers is that ideas are **non-rivalrous**. If you consume an apple, then I cannot consume the same apple. When it comes to eating an apple, it's either you or me—we can't share what we each consume so economists say that apples are rivalrous. But ideas can be shared. You can use the Pythagorean theorem and I can use the very same theorem at the very same time. The Pythagorean theorem can be shared by all of humanity, which is why economists say that ideas are non-rivalrous.

Since many ideas can be shared at low cost, they *should* be shared—that's the way to maximize the benefit from an idea. The spillover or diffusion of ideas throughout the world is thus a good thing. For instance, the idea of breeding and growing corn originated in ancient Mexico but now people grow corn all over the world. Spillovers, however, mean that the originator of an idea doesn't get all the benefits. And if the originator doesn't get enough of the benefits, ideas will be underprovided. For this reason, while economists know that idea spillovers are good, they also know that spillovers mean that too few good ideas are produced in the first place.

To understand why spillovers mean that ideas will be underprovided, think about why firms explore for oil. Answer: to make money. So what would happen to the amount of exploration if whenever a firm struck oil, other firms jumped in and drilled wells right next door? Clearly, the incentive to explore would decline if firms didn't have property rights to oil *fields*. Firms explore for ideas just like they explore for oil and if other firms can set up right next door to exploit the same *field of ideas,* the incentive to explore will decline.

Figure 7.13 illustrates the argument in a diagram. A profit-maximizing firm invests in research and development (R&D) so long as the private marginal benefit is larger than the marginal cost. As a result private investment occurs until point *a* in Figure 7.13. Spillovers, however, mean that the social benefit of R&D exceeds the private benefit so the optimal social investment is found where the marginal social benefit just equals the marginal cost at point *b*. Since the private benefit to R&D is less than the social benefit, private investment in R&D is less than ideal.

Government's Role in the Production of New Ideas

Can anything be done to increase the production of new ideas? We have already mentioned one important government policy that affects the production of new ideas, namely patents. Patents reduce spillovers and thus increase the incentive to produce new ideas, but they can also slow down the spread of new ideas.

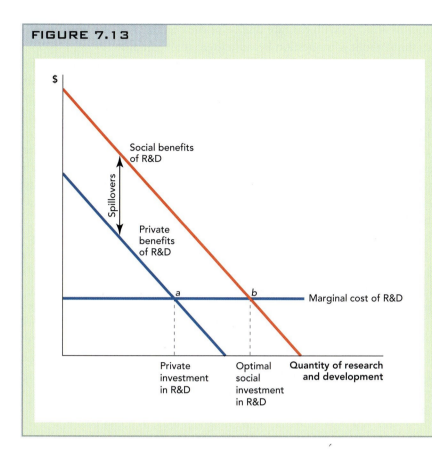

FIGURE 7.13

Spillovers Mean There Is Too Little Investment in R&D The profit-maximizing private investment in R&D is found where the private marginal benefits just equal the (private) marginal costs (point a). Some of the benefits of R&D spill over to people other than the producer. The social benefits of R&D are higher than the private benefits by the amount of the spillover. The optimal social investment in R&D is found where the social marginal benefits just equal the marginal cost (point b). Thus, when the private benefits of R&D are less than the social benefits, private investment in R&D will be less than the optimal social investment in R&D.

The government could also subsidize the production of new ideas. Returning to Figure 7.13, a subsidy or tax break to R&D expenditures, for example, will shift the (private) marginal cost of R&D curve down, thus increasing private investment.

The argument for government subsidies is strongest when the spillovers are largest. The modern world is founded on mathematics, physics, and molecular biology—basic ideas in these fields have many applications so spillovers can be large. But even if the social benefits to basic science are large, the private returns can be small. It's probably easier to make a million dollars producing pizza than it is to make a million dollars producing mathematical theorems. In fact, Thomas S. Monaghan made a billion dollars producing pizza (he's the founder of Domino's) while mathematicians Ron Rivest, Adi Shamir, and Leonard Adleman didn't make nearly so much on their RSA algorithm even though their algorithm is used to encrypt data sent over the Internet and thus forms the backbone for all Internet commerce.

The large spillovers to basic science suggest a role for government subsidies to universities, especially the parts of universities that produce innovations and the basic science behind innovations. Perhaps most importantly universities produce *scientists*. Most of the 1.3 million scientists who research and develop new products in the United States were trained in government-subsidized universities. Thus, subsidies to the hard sciences support the private development of new ideas and those initial subsidies are likely to pay for themselves many times over.

Market Size and Research and Development

Imagine that there are two diseases that if left untreated are equally deadly. One of the diseases is rare, the other one is common. If you had to choose, would you rather be afflicted with the rare disease or the common disease? Take a moment to think about this question because there is a right answer.

If you don't want to die, it's much better to have the common disease. The reason? The costs of developing drugs for rare and common diseases are about the same, but the revenues are greater, the more common the disease. Pharmaceutical companies concentrate on drugs for common diseases because larger markets mean more profits.

As a result, there are more drugs to treat common diseases than to treat rare diseases, and more drugs means greater life expectancy. Patients diagnosed with rare diseases—those ranked at the bottom quarter in terms of how frequently they are diagnosed—are 45 percent more likely to die before age 55 than are patients diagnosed with more common diseases.[3]

Larger markets mean increased incentives to invest in research and development, more new drugs, and greater life expectancy. So imagine this, if China and India were as wealthy as the United States, the market for cancer drugs would be eight times larger than it is today.

China and India are not yet wealthy countries but what this thought experiment tells us is that *people in the United States benefit tremendously when other countries grow rich.*

Like pharmaceuticals, new computer chips, software, and chemicals also require large R&D expenditures. As India, China, and other countries including the United States become wealthier, companies will increase their worldwide R&D investments.

CHECK YOURSELF

> What would happen to the incentive to produce new ideas if all countries imposed high tax rates on imports?

> What are spillovers and how do they affect the production of ideas?

> Some economists have proposed that the government offer large cash prizes for the discovery of cures for diseases like malaria that affect people in developing countries. What economic reasons might there be to support a prize for malaria research rather than, say, cancer research?

The Future of Economic Growth

Over the last 10,000 years, growth in per capita world GDP has been increasing. Growth in per capita GDP was approximately zero from the dawn of civilization to about 1500, increased to 0.08 percent a year between 1500 and 1760, doubled during the next hundred years, and increased even further during the nineteenth and twentieth centuries. Today, worldwide per capita GDP is growing at around 2.2 percent a year.

Could economic growth become even faster? Yes. Let's take a look again at our measure of technological progress, A. We can summarize what we have said about the factors causing A to increase in a simple equation:

$$A(\text{ideas}) = \text{Population} \times \text{Incentives} \times \text{Ideas per Hour}$$

In words, the number of new ideas is a function of the number of people, the incentives to innovate, and the number of ideas per hour that each person has. Of course, this equation is not meant to be exact—it's just a way of thinking about some of the key factors driving technological growth. So let's go through each of the factors and think about what they imply for the future of economic growth.

The number of people is increasing, which is good for idea generation. More important, the number of people whose job it is to produce new ideas is increasing. In all the world today, there are perhaps 6 million scientists and engineers of which 1.3 million come from the United States. These 1.3 million represent about one-half of one percent of the U.S. population, a surprisingly small percentage. Yet for the world as a whole, the ratio of scientists and engineers to population is much lower.

Today, because much of the world is poor, thousands of potentially great scientists will spend most of their lives doing backbreaking work on a farm. If the world as a whole were as wealthy as the United States and could devote the same share of population to research and development as does the U.S. today, there would be more than five times as many scientists and engineers. Thus, as the world gets richer more people will be producing ideas and because of spillovers, these ideas will benefit everyone.

The incentives to innovate also appear to be increasing. Consumers are richer and the world is becoming one giant integrated market due to trade; each of these factors boosts the incentives to innovate.

The incentives to innovate also increase when innovators can profit from their investments without fear of expropriation. The worldwide improvement in institutions—that is the movement toward property rights, honest government, political stability, and a dependable legal system—has been very positive for both innovation and economic growth.

It could be that someday we will run out of new ideas, or new ideas will experience diminishing returns so the number of ideas per hour falls. When the law of diminishing returns applies to ideas as well as to capital, then economic growth will end. There are at least two reasons, however, for thinking that this day of reckoning lies far in the future.

First, many ideas make creating other ideas easier. Sadly, the authors of this book can remember the day when answering even simple questions like who won the 1969 World Series could not be answered without going to a library, consulting a card catalog (don't ask), looking for the appropriate book in the stacks, and then (if the book hadn't been checked out) finding the answer. Today, you can probably find the answer using Google on your cell phone faster than you can read this paragraph. (By the way, it was the New York Mets in one of the greatest upsets of baseball history.) Since we still have many new ideas about creating even more ideas, it does not seem that ideas production has come close to diminishing returns.

The second reason to think that the number of ideas per hour is not yet strongly diminishing comes from one of the pioneers of the economics of ideas, Paul Romer. (Romer is not only a distinguished theorist of ideas, he is a first-class idea entrepreneur; he started Aplia, the online economics test bank and tutorial system that many of you use and which is a good example of an idea that makes learning new ideas easier.) Romer points out that ideas for production are like recipes and the number of potential recipes in the universe is unimaginably vast.

> The periodic table contains about a hundred different types of atoms, which means that the number of combinations made up of four different elements is about $100 \times 99 \times 98 \times 97 = 94,000,000$. A list of numbers like 6, 2, 1, 7 can represent the proportions for using the four elements in a recipe. To keep things simple, assume that the numbers in the list must lie between 1 and 10, that no fractions are allowed, and that the smallest number must always be 1. Then there are about 3,500 different sets of proportions for each choice of four elements, and $3,500 \times 94,000,000$ (or 330 billion) different recipes in total. If laboratories around the world evaluated 1,000 recipes each day, it would take nearly a million years to go through them all.[4]

True, many of the recipes are going to be like chicken liver ice cream (not that good), but the field of ideas that we can explore is so large that diminishing returns may not set in for a very long time.

Putting all this together, economic growth might be even faster in the future than it has been in the past. There are more scientists and engineers in the world today than ever before and their numbers are increasing both in absolute terms and as a percentage of the population. The incentives to invest in R&D are also increasing because markets are getting larger due to globalization and increased wealth in developing countries such as China and India. Better institutions and more secure property rights are spreading throughout the world.

UNDERSTAND YOUR world

We have reason to be optimistic about the future of economic growth but, of course, nothing is guaranteed. In the twentieth century, two world wars diverted the energy of two generations from production to destruction. When the wars ended, an iron curtain isolated billions of people from the rest of the world, reducing trade in goods and ideas—to everyone's detriment. World poverty meant that the United States and a few other countries shouldered the burden of advancing knowledge nearly alone. We must hope that this does not happen again.

□ Takeaway

The Solow model is governed by the iron logic of diminishing returns. When the capital stock is low, the marginal product of capital is high and capital accumulates, leading to economic growth. But as capital accumulates, its marginal product declines until per period investment is just equal to depreciation, and growth stops.

Despite the simplicity of the Solow model, it tells us three important things about economic growth. First, countries that devote a larger share of output to investment will be wealthier. The Solow model doesn't tell us *why* some countries might devote a larger share of output to investment, but we know from Chapter 6 that wealthy countries have institutions that promote investment in physical capital, human capital, and technological knowledge. We will also say more about how financial intermediaries channel saving into investment in Chapter 8.

Second, growth will be faster the farther away a country's capital stock is from its steady state value. This explains why the German and Japanese economies were able to catch up to other advanced economies after World War II, why countries that reform their institutions often grow very rapidly (growth miracles), and why poor countries grow faster than rich countries with similar levels of steady state output.

Third, the Solow model tells us that capital accumulation cannot explain long-run economic growth. Holding other things constant, the marginal product of physical and human capital will eventually diminish, thereby leaving the economy in a zero-growth steady state. If we want to explain long-run economic growth, we must explain why other things are not held constant.

New ideas are the driving force behind long-run economic growth. Ideas, however, aren't like other goods: ideas can be easily copied and ideas are non-rivalrous. The fact that ideas can be easily copied means that the originator of a new idea won't receive all the benefits of that idea so the incentive to produce ideas will be too low. Governments can play a role in supporting the production of new ideas by protecting intellectual property and subsidizing the production of new ideas when spillovers are most likely to be present.

The non-rivalry of ideas, however, means that once an idea is created we want it to be shared, which is a nice way of saying copied, as much as possible. There is thus a trade-off between providing appropriate incentives to produce new ideas and providing appropriate incentives to share new ideas.

An important lesson from the economics of ideas is that the larger the market, whether in terms of people or wealth, the greater the incentive to invest in research and development. Similarly, having more people and wealthier countries increases the number of people devoted to the production of new ideas. Thus, the increased wealth of many developing nations, the move to freer trade in global markets, and the spread of better institutions throughout the world are all encouraging for the future of economic growth.

◻ CHAPTER REVIEW

KEY CONCEPTS

Marginal product of capital, p. 117

Steady state, p. 121

Conditional convergence, p. 128

Non-rivalrous, p. 132

FACTS AND TOOLS

1. Which countries are likely to grow faster: Countries doing "cutting-edge" growth or those doing "catch-up" growth?

2. When will people work harder to invent new ideas: When they can sell them to a market of 10,000 people or when they can sell them to a market of 1 billion? Does your answer tell us anything about whether it's good or bad from the U.S. point of view for China and India to become rich countries?

3. Many people say that if people save too much, the economy will be hurt. They often refer to the fact that consumer spending is two-thirds of GDP to make this point. This is sometimes called the "paradox of thrift."

   a. In the Solow model, is there a paradox of thrift? In other words, is a high savings rate good or bad for a country's long-run economic performance?

   b. What about in the real world? According to the data in Figure 7.10, is there a paradox of thrift?

4. Many people say that "the rich grow richer and the poor grow poorer." Is this what Figure 7.11 says about the countries in that graph? Did the rich countries grow faster or slower than the poor countries?

5. Compared to its fast growth today, is China's economy likely to grow faster or slower in the future?

6. What is more important for explaining the standard of living in the rich countries: Capital or ideas?

7. According to Thomas Jefferson, how are ideas like flames?

8. What is a patent?

9. When will people work harder to invent new ideas: When they can patent those ideas for one year or when they can patent them for 10 years?

10. Which three countries on the list are good examples of "conditional convergence?"

    China

    Ireland

    Argentina

    North Korea

    Greece

11. Let's keep track of a nation's capital stock for five years. Mordor starts off with 1,000 machines, and every year, 5 percent of the machines depreciate or wear out. Fortunately, the people in this land produce 75 machines per year,

every year. The key equation for keeping track of capital is quite simple:

Next year's capital = This year's capital + Investment − Depreciation

Fill in the table.

Year	Capital	Depreciation	Investment
1	1,000	0.05 × 1,000	75
2	1,025		75
3			75
4			75
5			75

THINKING AND PROBLEM SOLVING

1. Consider the following three countries that produce GDP this way:

$$Y = 5\sqrt{K}$$

Ilia: $K = 100$ machines
Caplania: $K = 10,000$ machines
Hansonia: $K = 1,000,000$ machines

What will GDP (Y) be in these three countries? Hansonia has 10,000 times more machines than Ilia, so why isn't it 10,000 times more productive?

2. Consider the data in the previous question: If 10 percent of all machines become worthless every year (they depreciate, in other words), then how many machines will become worthless in these three countries this year? Are there any countries where the amount of depreciation is actually greater than GDP? (This question reminds you that "More machines mean more machines wearing out.")

3. Of course, no country makes *only* investment goods like machines, equipment, and computers. They also make consumer goods. Let's consider a case where the countries in question 1 devote 25 percent of GDP to making investment goods (so γ, gamma, = 0.25). What is the amount of savings in these three countries? In which countries is *Investment < Depreciation*? When is *Investment > Depreciation*?

4. A drug company has $1 billion to spend on research and development. It has to decide on one of two projects:

   a. Spend the money on a project to fight deadly forms of influenza including bird flu.

   b. Spend the money on a project to fight a condition of red, itchy skin known as eczema.

   The company expects both projects to be equally profitable, all things considered: Yes, project A is riskier (since the rare flu may never come along), but if the disease hits, there will be a worldwide market willing to pay a lot of money to cure the flu.

   Then one day, before deciding between A and B, the drug company's CEO reads in the newspaper that the European Union and the United States will not honor patents in the event of a major flu outbreak. Instead, these governments will "break the patent" and just make the drug available everywhere for $1 per pill. The company will only get $1 per pill instead of the $100 or $200 per pill they had expected.

   Given this new information about the possibility that governments will "break the patent," which project is the company likely to spend its research and development money on? (Note: In the wake of the deadly anthrax attacks of 2001, the U.S. government threatened to do just this with the patent for Cipro, the one antibiotic proven to cure the symptoms of anthrax infection.)

5. After World War II, a lot of France's capital stock was destroyed, but it had educated workers and a market-oriented economy. Do you think the war's destruction increased or decreased the marginal product of capital?

6. In the Solow model, you've seen that as the total stock of capital equipment gets larger, the number of machines wearing out grows as well. Often, most investment ends up just replacing worn-out machines. This is actually true in the United States and other rich countries. According to the U.S. National Income and Product Accounts (the official U.S. GDP measures), about 12 percent of total GDP just goes toward replacing worn-out machines and computers and construction equipment.

   a. In the Solow model, if the depreciation rate increases, what happens to the steady state capital level and output level? Answer in words and by using a diagram such as Figure 7.4. (Bonus: if the depreciation rate increases from 0.02 to 0.03 what is the new steady state level of capital and output?)

b. If the Solow model explains an important part of the real world, should countries hope for high depreciation rates or low depreciation rates? How does this square with the observation that when machines wear out, that "creates jobs" in the manufacturing industries?

7. The Solow model isn't useful for only thinking about entire countries: As long as the production function runs into diminishing returns and your total stock of inputs constantly wears out, then the Solow model applies. Consider a professor's knowledge of economics. The more she learns about economics, the more she will forget (depreciation), but the more she knows, the more knowledge she can create (production). So eventually in steady state, she will know only a fixed amount about economics, but what she knows might change over time; some decades she might know a lot about the Federal Reserve while other decades she might know a lot about the electricity market. In any case, knowledge fades away.

a. Apply the Solow model to a chef's skill at cooking.

b. Apply the Solow model to the size of a navy's fleet of ships.

c. Apply the Solow model to the speed of a cheetah, where the input is calories.

8. Many inventors decide that patents are a bad way to protect their intellectual property. Instead, they keep their ideas a secret. Trade secrets are actually quite common: The formula for Coca-Cola is a trade secret, as is Colonel Sander's secret recipe. What is one major strength of keeping a trade secret rather than applying for a patent? What is a major weakness inherent in going down the trade secret route?

9. Since ideas can sometimes be copied quite easily, many people think that we should put more effort into creating new ideas. Let's see if there are trade-offs to having more people creating new ideas. To keep things simple, let's assume that the growth rate of the economy depends on how many people search for ideas, whether in laboratories, or huddled over laptops in coffee shops, or while listening to "Stairway to Heaven" at three in the morning. People either produce stuff or produce ideas. Here's how this economy works:

$$Y_t = (1 - R) \times A_t L \text{ (GDP production function)}$$

$$A_{t+1} = (1 + R) \times A_t \text{ (Technology production function)}$$

There are a total of L people in the society, a fraction $(1 - R)$ of them work in factories and offices making stuff (remember, people working in offices help create output too!), while the remaining fraction R try to come up with good ideas all day long. To keep the story simple, there are no diminishing returns.

a. What's the trade-off here? If 100 percent of the people work to make new ideas ($R = 1$), won't that create a prosperous world?

b. In this society, if people are willing to wait a long time for a reward, should they choose a large R or a small R?

c. Plot out GDP in this society for 5 years if A starts off at 100, L starts off at 100, and R is 10 percent.

Year	A	Y	Y/L
1	100	9,000	90
2	110		
3			
4			
5			

d. Plot out GDP in this society if the society instead chose $R = 20$ percent.

10. In Facts and Tools question 2, we saw that big markets create a big *demand* for inventions. This is an example of what Adam Smith meant when he said that "the division of labor is limited by the extent of the market." Now let's look at how big markets impact the *supply* side of inventions. The big idea is quite simple: *More people means more ideas.*

a. In order to create new ideas, you need to have people trying to come up with new ideas. In 1800, there were approximately 300 million humans on the planet—roughly equal to today's U.S. population. If good ideas are "one in a million," that is, if one person per year out of a million comes up with a world-shaking idea like contact lenses or James Brown's song "The Payback" or the video game Grand Theft Auto, how many great new ideas will occur in the world of 1800? How many will occur in a world of 6 billion people?

b. More realistically, people in the rich countries are most likely to invent earth-shaking ideas and share them with others. There's nothing special about people in rich countries but they have the education and the laboratories and the Internet connections that will make it practical to invent and spread ideas. If only the top 20 percent of the earth's population is really in the running to create new ideas, how many new big ideas will come along each year in 1800 and today?

c. If half of the population of India and China become rich enough to create new ideas (to simplify assume populations of 1 billion each), and start coming up with big ideas at the same rate as the top 20 percent, how many big ideas will India and China alone create for the planet every year?

d. Many people think there are too many people on the planet. (As P. J. O'Rourke once wrote, many people's attitude toward global population is "Just enough of me, way too much of you.") Look at your answer from part b. If the world's population now gets cut in half from the current 6 billion, how many big ideas will come along each year?

11. According to economists Robert Barro and Xavier Sala-i-Martin, convergence isn't just for entire nations: It's also true for states and regions as well. They looked at state-level GDP per capita in the United States in 1880, and then calculated how fast each state grew over the next 120 years. They found that convergence held almost exactly.

a. With this in mind, draw arrows to connect the GDP per capita data on the left with the long-term growth rates on the right.

GDP per capita in 1880	Annual growth rate, 1880–2000
West: $8,500	1.6%
East: $6,300	1.7%
Midwest: $4,700	2.2%
South: $2,800	1.2%

b. Graph the data from part a in the figure below. Does this look like Figure 7.11's story about the OECD countries, or is it quite different?

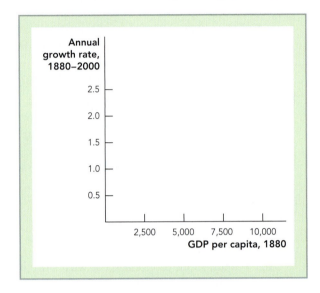

Note: Barro and Sala-i-Martin also found that convergence also held almost exactly for regions of Japan: The areas that were poorest in 1930 grew fastest over the next 70 years. Thus, it is difficult to find major evidence in favor of the commonsense idea that "the poor areas grow poorer."

12. Are we running out of ideas? Economist Paul Romer thinks not. To make things concrete, he notes that if we keep trying out different molecules to search for interesting compounds like new drugs, new plastics, etc., the universe may end from heat death before we finish our search. For example, if we try out 100 different atoms out of the 117+ (and rising!) elements in the periodic table, and only look at the 6-atom molecules, this is 100^6 different molecules. And, of course, many common molecules in our bodies consist of hundreds of atoms, so this only scratches the surface of interesting compounds.

a. If it takes a machine 1 minute to test out and fully analyze a new 6-atom molecule, how many years will it take for this one machine to test out all 100^6 molecules? (Note: Modern biochemists create computer simulations of molecules to analyze whether potential drugs are likely to work in the molecules that make up the human body, but this is only one narrow form of analysis.)

b. How many machines would it take to test out all of these molecules within 100 years?

c. What about all 10-atom molecules: How many years would it take for one machine to test all of these compounds at one per minute? If your computer can handle it, what about all 100-atom molecules, molecules vastly simpler than many proteins in your body?

CHALLENGES

1. Which country would you expect to have a higher rate of investment: A catch-up country or a cutting-edge country?

2. If the government of a poor catch-up country is trying to decide whether to encourage investment or encourage research and development, which of the two should it favor? (Note: in a world of trade-offs, you can't just say "Both are important!")

3. The Solow model makes it quite easy to figure out how rich a country will be in its steady state. We already know that you're in a steady state when investment equals depreciation. In math, that's:

$$\gamma Y = \delta K$$

Since $Y = \sqrt{K}$ in our simplest model, that means that $K = Y^2$:

$$\gamma Y = \delta Y^2$$

There are a lot of ways to solve this for Y— the easiest might just be to divide both sides by Y, and then put everything else on the other side. When you do this, you can learn how steady state GDP depends on the savings rate γ and the depreciation rate δ. Here are a few questions:

a. Many people say that if people save more, that's bad for the economy: They say that spending money on consumer goods keeps the money moving through the economy. Does this model say that?

b. Many people say that when machines and equipment get destroyed by bad weather or war, that makes the economy better off by encouraging businesses and families to spend money on new capital goods. Does this model say that?

4. Let's think about two countries, Frugal and Smart. In Frugal, people devote 50 percent of GDP to making new investment goods, so $\gamma = 0.5$, and their production function is $Y = \sqrt{K}$. In Smart, people devote 25 percent of GDP to making new investment goods, so $\gamma = 0.25$, and their production function is $Y = 2\sqrt{K}$. Both countries start off with $K = 100$.

a. What is the amount of investment in each country this year?

b. What is the amount of consumption (GDP – Investment, or $Y - I$) in each country this year?

c. Where would you rather be a citizen: Frugal or Smart?

5. Which of the following goods are non-rivalrous?

Sunshine

An apple

A national park

A Mozart symphony

The idea of penicillin

A dose of penicillin

6. According to economist Michael Kremer, as human populations have grown over the last million years, so has the human population growth *rate*. This was true until the 1800s. How does Thinking and Problem Solving question 10 help explain why human populations grew faster despite the fact that there were more mouths to feed?

CHAPTER **APPENDIX**

Excellent Growth

Using a spreadsheet, you can easily explore the Solow model and duplicate all the graphs in this chapter. First, label column A, "Capital, K" and put a 1 in cell A2. Second, you can create an increasing series by inputting the formula "=A2+1" in cell A3 and copying and pasting that formula into cells A4 to say A500. Your spreadsheet should look like Figure A7.1.

FIGURE A7.1

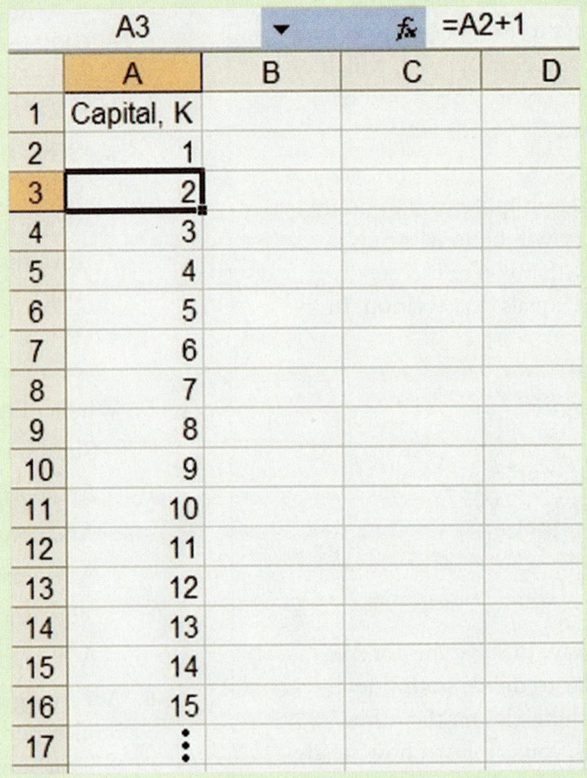

	A3	▾	f_x =A2+1	
	A	**B**	**C**	**D**
1	Capital, K			
2	1			
3	2			
4	3			
5	4			
6	5			
7	6			
8	7			
9	8			
10	9			
11	10			
12	11			
13	12			
14	13			
15	14			
16	15			
17	⋮			

In column B, create a series for Output. Remember that $Y = \sqrt{K}$, so in cell B2 input the formula "=SQRT(A2)" and then copy and paste that formula into B3 to B500, as in Figure A7.2.

Now create the headings Investment, Depreciation, Investment Share, and Depreciation Rate in columns C to F—like in Figure A7.3.

In cell E2, put the investment share, 0.3, used in the text and in cell F2 put the rate of depreciation that we used, 0.02.

In cell C2, which is highlighted, we want to input the formula for investment, which is γY, where γ is the investment share. We could input "=0.3*B2" into C2 but we would like to be able to easily adjust the investment share and see what happens, so we will input "=$E$2*B2". The $E$2 says take the investment share from cell E2 and when we copy and paste this formula it *always* uses cell E2 (not E3, E4, etc.). Copy and paste cell C2 into C3 to C500.

FIGURE A7.2

	B2	▼		f_x =SQRT(A2)	
	A	B	C	D	
1	Capital, K	Output			
2	1	1.00			
3	2	1.41			
4	3	1.73			
5	4	2.00			
6	5	2.24			
7	6	2.45			
8	7	2.65			
9	8	2.83			
10	9	3.00			
11	10	3.16			
12	11	3.32			
13	12	3.46			
14	13	3.61			
15	14	3.74			
16	15	3.87			
17	⋮	⋮			

FIGURE A7.3

	C2	▼		f_x =$E$2*B2		
	A	B	C	D	E	F
1	Capital, K	Output	Investment	Depreciation	Investment Share, γ	Depreciation Rate, δ
2	1	1.00	0.30	0.02	0.3	0.02
3	2	1.41	0.42	0.04		
4	3	1.73	0.52	0.06		
5	4	2.00	0.60	0.08		
6	5	2.24	0.67	0.10		
7	6	2.45	0.73	0.12		
8	7	2.65	0.79	0.14		
9	8	2.83	0.85	0.16		
10	9	3.00	0.90	0.18		
11	10	3.16	0.95	0.20		
12	11	3.32	0.99	0.22		
13	12	3.46	1.04	0.24		
14	13	3.61	1.08	0.26		
15	14	3.74	1.12	0.28		
16	15	3.87	1.16	0.30		
17	⋮	⋮	⋮	⋮		

Depreciation is just δK, where δ is the depreciation rate. As with investment, we might want to alter this parameter so into cell D2 we will input "=$F$2*A2".

That's it! To duplicate the graph in Figure 7.4, for example, just highlight columns A, B, C, and D, click the Chart icon (you can also click Chart in the Insert menu), choose XY (Scatter) and the highlighted sub-type, and then click on finish. (In Excel 2007 click Insert and then Scatter in the Chart submenu to do the same thing.) See Figure A7.4.

FIGURE A7.4

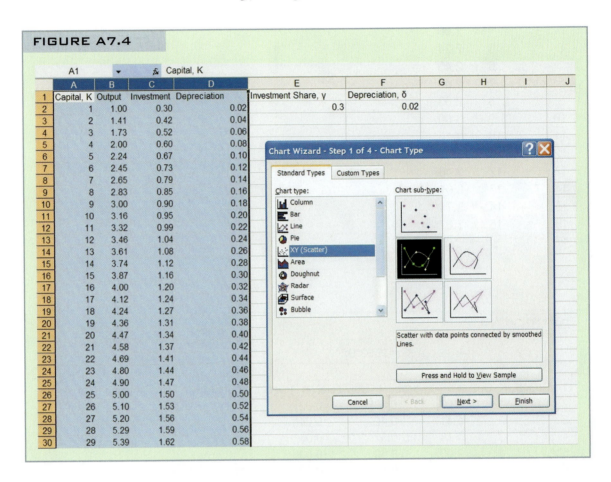

The result is as in Figure A7.5.

If you want to see what happens if the investment share increases to 0.4, as in Figure 7.9 in the chapter, just change cell E2 to 0.4 and the graph will change automatically. You can make other adjustments as well. One thing to watch for is that with parameters too different than the ones we have given, the equilibrium capital stock may be greater than 500. So if you want to see the full picture, you will need to extend the rows even further.

FIGURE A7.5

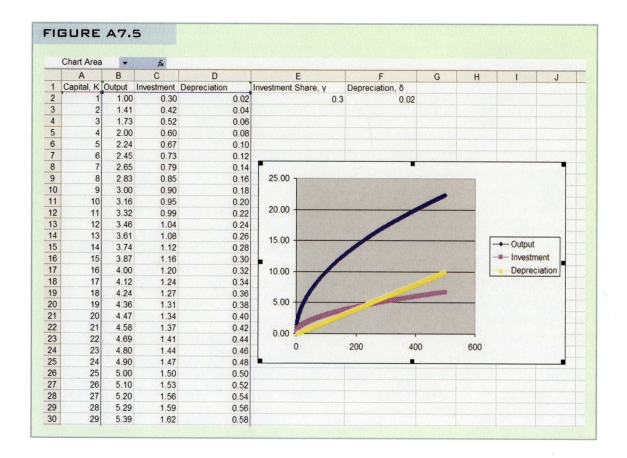

	A	B	C	D	E	F	G	H	I	J
1	Capital, K	Output	Investment	Depreciation	Investment Share, γ	Depreciation, δ				
2	1	1.00	0.30	0.02	0.3	0.02				
3	2	1.41	0.42	0.04						
4	3	1.73	0.52	0.06						
5	4	2.00	0.60	0.08						
6	5	2.24	0.67	0.10						
7	6	2.45	0.73	0.12						
8	7	2.65	0.79	0.14						
9	8	2.83	0.85	0.16						
10	9	3.00	0.90	0.18						
11	10	3.16	0.95	0.20						
12	11	3.32	0.99	0.22						
13	12	3.46	1.04	0.24						
14	13	3.61	1.08	0.26						
15	14	3.74	1.12	0.28						
16	15	3.87	1.16	0.30						
17	16	4.00	1.20	0.32						
18	17	4.12	1.24	0.34						
19	18	4.24	1.27	0.36						
20	19	4.36	1.31	0.38						
21	20	4.47	1.34	0.40						
22	21	4.58	1.37	0.42						
23	22	4.69	1.41	0.44						
24	23	4.80	1.44	0.46						
25	24	4.90	1.47	0.48						
26	25	5.00	1.50	0.50						
27	26	5.10	1.53	0.52						
28	27	5.20	1.56	0.54						
29	28	5.29	1.59	0.56						
30	29	5.39	1.62	0.58						

CHAPTER EXCEL APPENDIX QUESTION

1. Use the instructions in the appendix to set up the Solow model in Excel with the Investment Share, γ, equal to 0.3 and with the Depreciation Rate, δ, equal to 0.02. Both numbers are just what we used in the chapter. Now increase the Investment Share to 0.36.

   a. What is the new level of steady state capital? (Remember, the level of steady state capital is where Investment = Depreciation.)

   b. At the new steady level of capital what is the level of output, Y?

   Now change the Investment Share back to 0.3 and this time increase the Depreciation Rate to 0.025.

   c. What is the new level of steady state capital?

   d. At the steady state level of capital what is the level of output, Y?

   e. Fill in the blanks with your conclusions:

   An increase in the investment share _____ the steady state level of capital and output.

   An increase in the depreciation rate _____ the steady state level of capital and output.

8

Saving, Investment, and the Financial System

On a typical day in 2005, Chinese savers bought $600 million of American bonds, stocks and other financial assets. Americans used those funds to buy homes, to build factories, and to support government programs like Medicare and even the Department of Defense. Chairman Mao would be spinning in his grave because "communist" China is now a key participant in the worldwide market for capital, the very market that gives capitalism its name.

The global market for capital links Chinese savers and American borrowers and it makes both better off. Chinese savers earn a higher rate of return when they can lend to anyone in the world and not just to borrowers in their own village, city, or even country. Access to world capital markets also allows the Chinese to diversify their holdings and so the Chinese have been major investors in Africa as well as the United States.

Americans also benefit from global capital markets. Americans can borrow at lower interest rates, and therefore invest more, when they have access to savings from around the world. The movement of financial capital within a country and around the world is part of the broader process of creating value by moving resources to their most highly valued uses.

This chapter is about savers and borrowers and the institutions—banks, bond markets, and stock exchanges—that bridge the gap between savers and borrowers. These specialized institutions have evolved to lower the costs of connecting savers with borrowers. Figure 8.1 on the next page illustrates.

Recall from Chapters 6 and 7 that savings are necessary for capital accumulation and the more capital an economy has the greater its GDP per capita. So reducing the costs of connecting savers and borrowers is important: connecting savers and borrowers increases the gains from trade and smooths the process of economic growth.

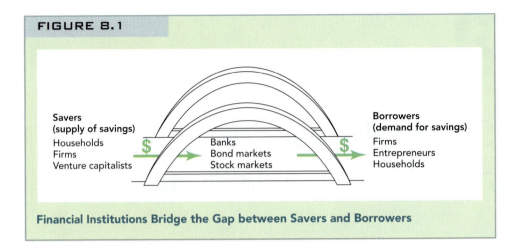

FIGURE 8.1

Savers
(supply of savings)

Households
Firms
Venture capitalists

$ →

Banks
Bond markets
Stock markets

$ →

Borrowers
(demand for savings)

Firms
Entrepreneurs
Households

Financial Institutions Bridge the Gap between Savers and Borrowers

Saving is income that is not spent on consumption goods.

Investment is the purchase of new capital goods.

Before proceeding, let's make it clear what we mean by the words **saving** and **investment**. Saving is income that is not spent on consumption goods. Investment is the purchase of new capital, things like tools, machinery, and factories. It's important to see that the way economists define investment is not the same as the way a stockbroker defines investment. If Starbucks buys new espresso machines for its stores, that's investment. If John buys stock in Starbucks, that is not investment in the economic sense but merely a transfer of ownership rights of already existing capital (see the next chapter for a treatment of how individuals should allocate their funds for their personal "investments"). Most of the trading on stock exchanges is thus not investment in the economic sense because it simply transfers ownership of a stock from one person to another. From an economic point of view, investment requires a net increase in the economy's ability to produce goods and services.

Okay, let's see how savings are mobilized and transformed into investment. We will be using the economist's tools in trade—supply and demand—and we'll start with the supply of savings.

The Supply of Savings

We begin with the left side of Figure 8.1, the supply of savings. Economists have a good but imperfect understanding of what determines the supply of savings. Here are four of the major factors: smoothing consumption, impatience, marketing and psychological factors, and interest rates.

Individuals Want to Smooth Consumption

If you consumed what you earned every year, your consumption over time might look like Path A in Figure 8.2. Along Path A, consumption is equal to income. Consumption is high during your working years, but after retirement consumption drops precipitously—as a result, once you retire and your income falls, you must sell the nice car and give up the fancy lifestyle just to scrape by. Most people would prefer consumption Path B. Along Path B consumption is less than income during the working years because you save for retirement. But when retirement comes, consumption is greater than income as you spend your savings or "dissave."

FIGURE 8.2

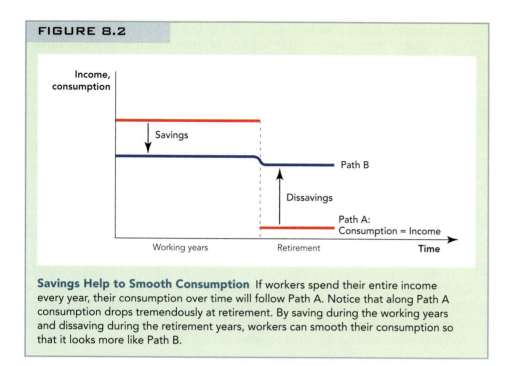

Savings Help to Smooth Consumption If workers spend their entire income every year, their consumption over time will follow Path A. Notice that along Path A consumption drops tremendously at retirement. By saving during the working years and dissaving during the retirement years, workers can smooth their consumption so that it looks more like Path B.

Economists say that Path B is "smoother" than Path A. The desire to smooth consumption over time is a reason to save and, as we will discuss shortly, also a reason to borrow.

The consumption-smoothing theory of saving can tell us something important about AIDS, Africa, and economic growth. Remember from previous chapters that savings are necessary to finance the capital accumulation that generates high standards of living. If there are no savings, investment dries up, economic growth declines, and the standard of living falls.

Now consider that AIDS has dramatically reduced life expectancy in Africa. What is your prediction about savings rates? Imagine that you expected to die in a few years—would you save much? Probably not. Similarly, many poorer Africans don't save much because, sadly, they expect to die young.[1] This gives rise to a vicious cycle. The decline in life expectancy caused by AIDS reduces saving rates, which in turn reduces economic growth and the standard of living and that makes it more difficult to combat diseases like AIDS.

Fluctuations in income are another reason why people save. Some workers, such as salespeople, writers, and home builders have incomes that fluctuate from year to year. Most workers could have unexpected health problems or they could find themselves unemployed and so they also fear that their income might fluctuate. By saving in the good years, workers can build a cushion of wealth to draw from in the bad years, thereby smoothing their consumption across all years.

Individuals Are Impatient

Another reason why people save, or fail to save, is their level of impatience. Most individuals prefer to consume now rather than later so saving is not always easy. Some people, however, are very impatient, others less so. This is what economists call **time preference.** Time preference reflects the fact that today feels more real than tomorrow. The more impatient a person, the more likely that person's savings rate will be low.

Time preference is the desire to have goods and services sooner rather than later (all else being equal).

Impatience is reflected not just in savings but in any economic situation where people must compare costs and benefits over time. The cost of a college degree, for example, comes well before the benefit. To get a college degree, you must pay for tuition and books and, most important, you must give up the income that you could earn from a job, all right now. The benefits of a college degree are large—in 1998 the average worker with a college degree earned almost $20,000 more per year than a worker with just a high school diploma—but all the benefits are in the future. An impatient person will weigh the upfront costs highly and discount the future benefits. Impatient people are unlikely to go to college.

Crime is another economic activity with immediate benefits and future costs so it's not surprising that criminals tend to be impatient people. Similarly, heroin addicts, alcoholics, and smokers all tend to discount the future more heavily than nonaddicts.

Impatience depends in part on circumstances and in part on the person. In one fascinating study, four-year-old children were asked whether they wanted one cookie now or two cookies in 20 minutes. Many years later, the children were evaluated again—the children who had waited were less impulsive and had higher grades than the children who had not waited.[2]

Marketing and Psychological Factors

Marketing matters, even for savings. Often individuals save more if saving is presented as the natural or default alternative. In one study, economists studied retirement savings plans. Some employers automatically enrolled all new employees in a retirement savings plan, leaving the employees the choice to opt out, whereas others required employees to request such an account, in effect asking them to opt in. In the businesses that used automatic enrollment, the savings plan participation rate was 25 percent higher than in the businesses where employees needed to request a retirement account.

The default also mattered for how much was saved. In one firm, the default savings rate was 3 percent of salary. More than a quarter of the workers chose that as their savings rate, despite an employer guarantee of a dollar-for-dollar match on contributions of up to 6 percent of salary. Later, the company switched to a 6 percent default savings rate; in that setting hardly any new workers chose the 3 percent savings contribution rate even though they could have switched with just a phone call.[3]

It's quite surprising how some simple psychological changes, combined with effective marketing and promotion, can change how much people save for their retirement. Behavioral economics, a new and growing field within economics, combines economics, psychology, and neurology to study how people make decisions and how they can be helped to overcome biases in decision making.

The Interest Rate

The quantity of savings also depends on the interest rate, namely how much savers are paid to save. If the interest rate is 5 percent per year, then $100 saved today returns $105 a year from now. If the interest rate is 10 percent per year, then $100 saved today returns $110 a year from now. All else being equal, higher interest rates usually call forth more savings.* Figure 8.3 shows the supply curve for savings. The vertical axis of Figure 8.3 measures the interest rate. The horizontal axis measures savings in dollars. In this example, an interest rate of 5 percent generates total savings of $200 billion and an interest rate of 10 percent generates total savings of $280 billion.

You might wonder why the supply curve for savings has the interest rate on the vertical axis while other supply curves have had price on the vertical axis. In fact, interest rates are just a convenient way of expressing the price of savings. An interest rate of 5 percent, for example, means that the saver will be paid $5 (in one year) for every $100 saved. Thus, we could say that when the price of lending is $5 per $100 saved, the quantity of savings is $200 billion. It's a bit easier, however, to think in terms of interest rates.

The bottom line is that the interest rate is a market price and it has the same properties of market prices that we discussed in the introductory chapters of this book.

The Demand to Borrow

Why do people borrow? People borrow to smooth their consumption path and especially to finance large investments. Let's look at each of these reasons for borrowing.

Individuals Want to Smooth Consumption

Just as people save in order to smooth consumption, one reason people borrow is to smooth consumption. Many young people, for example, borrow so that they can invest in their education. If they had to pay their tuition expenses all at once, many students would have to sell their car or eat nothing but beans and oatmeal for a year. But if tuition payments can be made over many years, as borrowing makes possible, the sacrifices are spread out and become less painful. A student who can borrow can move some of the sacrifices into future periods when the (now former) student has a job and a regular income. Student borrowing is thus another example of how credit markets let people smooth their consumption over time.

The "lifecycle" theory of savings, pioneered by Nobel Laureate Franco Modigliani, puts the demand to borrow and save together. The lifecycle theory

FIGURE 8.3

Interest rate (vertical axis), Savings (in billions of dollars) (horizontal axis). Supply curve upward sloping. At 5% corresponds to $200, at 10% corresponds to $280.

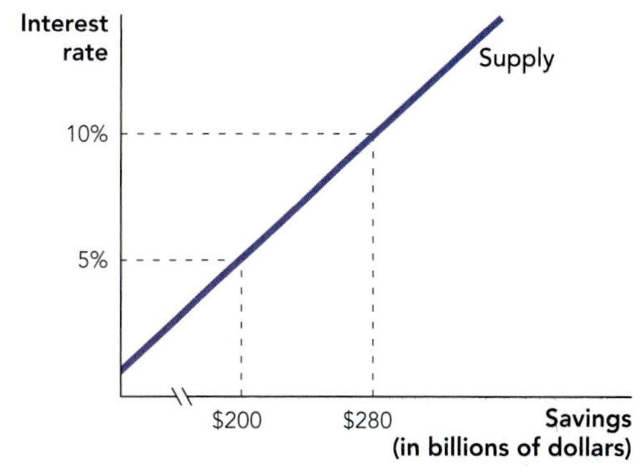

The Higher the Interest Rate the Greater the Quantity Saved At an interest rate of 5 percent, $200 billion is saved. At an interest rate of 10 percent, $280 billion is saved.

CHECK YOURSELF

> Examining Figure 8.1, what is the crucial function that financial institutions perform?

> Financial advisors have warned that increased life expectancy means that many people have not saved enough for their retirement. If true, what will the consumption path of these people look like as they reach their retirement years? Will this consumption path be smooth?

> Can you think of other factors that might generate a demand to save? Hint: Other than retirement what other factors could cause income to be volatile?

---

* In principle, it is possible for the supply curve for savings to be negatively sloped. For instance, if an individual wanted exactly $100 in one year's time, then at an interest rate of 10 percent he or she would need to save $90.91, but at an interest rate of 20 percent he or she would need to save only $83.33. Thus, an increase in the interest rate could reduce savings. The evidence, however, indicates that individual savings rates typically respond positively to higher interest rates. In addition, higher U.S. interest rates also encourage lenders in other countries to move some of their savings to U.S. markets. Both forces mean that the supply curve for savings is upwardly sloped in most circumstances.

is illustrated in Figure 8.4. Income starts out low during the college years and in the early work years. To finance college and to buy a first home, people borrow so their consumption is higher than their income. As workers enter their prime earning years, they save to pay off their college debt and mortgage and they prepare for retirement—during this time period consumption is less than income. As people get older and retire, consumption is once again above income as dissaving (that is, using up savings) occurs. Overall, borrowing, saving, and dissaving help people to smooth out their consumption path over time—although few people would have a consumption path as smooth as the one we have drawn here!

FIGURE 8.4

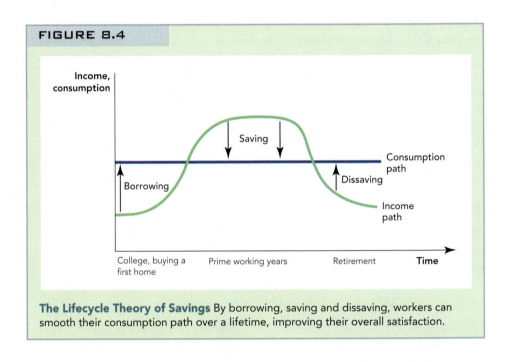

The Lifecycle Theory of Savings By borrowing, saving and dissaving, workers can smooth their consumption path over a lifetime, improving their overall satisfaction.

Governments also borrow for reasons much like consumers. Governments may borrow, for example, to finance unusually large expenditures such as are required to pay for a war, or to pay for large investments such as the interstate highway system. We discuss government taxes, spending, and borrowing at greater length inChapter 16.

Borrowing Is Necessary to Finance Large Investments

Businesses also borrow extensively. Many new businesses can't get underway at all without borrowing. Often the people with the best business ideas are not the people with the most savings, so people with good ideas must borrow funds to start their careers as entrepreneurs.

Fred Smith, the legendary entrepreneur, first laid out the idea for FedEx in an undergraduate paper he had to write for an economics class. Smith's idea, overnight delivery of packages using a hub and spoke system, was great but the problem was that he couldn't start small. To be successful, Smith needed to cover a good part of the country from day one and he didn't have enough of his own money to build an entire network. Smith began FedEx with 16 planes covering 25 cities using money he borrowed and also by selling part ownership of FedEx to venture capitalists, investors willing to accept risk in return for a stake in future profits. FedEx, of course, has been a huge success—it changed the way America does business and made Smith a very wealthy man. By the way, Smith's grade on his paper: C!

More generally, businesses borrow to finance large projects. The costs of developing an apartment building are all upfront; the revenues don't start flowing until the building is completed and the tenants have moved in. In fact, it may take many years before the revenues fully cover all the upfront costs. If a developer like Donald Trump had to wait until he personally had enough funds to pay the upfront costs, he might be able to develop just one or two buildings in his lifetime. By borrowing, developers are able to invest now and develop many more buildings.

The examples of borrowing that we have given share a common theme. A student who can't borrow may not be able to get an education even though the education would be a good investment. A government that can't borrow may not be able to invest in an interstate highway system even though the highway system would pay for itself many times over. A builder who can't borrow may not be able to build an apartment building even though it would be a profitable investment. Thus borrowing plays an important role in the economy—the ability to borrow greatly increases the ability to invest and, as we showed in Chapters 6 and 7, higher investment increases the standard of living and the rate of economic growth.

In Shakespeare's *Hamlet*, Polonius advises "Neither a borrower nor a lender be." But people forget, Polonius was a fool.

The Interest Rate

Of course, the quantity of funds that people want to borrow also depends on the cost of the loan, or the interest rate. Businesses, for example, borrow when they expect that the return on their investment will be greater than the cost of the loan. Thus, if the interest rate is 10 percent, businesses will only borrow if they expect that their investment will return *greater* than 10 percent. If the interest rate is 5 percent, then businesses will only borrow if they expect that their investment will return *greater* than 5 percent. Since more investments will return greater than 5 percent than will return greater than 10 percent, the demand to borrow follows the law of demand: the lower the interest rate, the greater the quantity of funds demanded for investment as well as for other purposes.

In Figure 8.5, $190 billion is demanded when the interest rate is 10 percent and $300 billion is demanded when the interest rate is 5 percent.

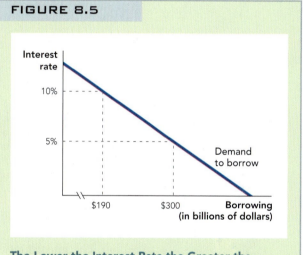

FIGURE 8.5

The Lower the Interest Rate the Greater the Quantity of Funds Demanded At an interest rate of 10 percent borrowers would like to borrow $190 billion. At an interest rate of 5 percent, borrowers would like to borrow more, $300 billion.

CHECK YOURSELF

> Under the lifecycle theory, when is an individual's savings likely to be at its peak?

> If interest rates fall from 7 percent to 5 percent (and all else is the same), what happens to the number of people buying homes? Starting businesses?

Equilibrium in the Market for Loanable Funds

Now that we have covered the supply of savings and the demand to borrow, we can put them together to find an equilibrium in what economists call the **market for loanable funds**. In Figure 8.6 on the next page, the equilibrium interest rate is 8 percent and the equilibrium quantity of savings is $250 billion. Notice that in equilibrium, the quantity of funds supplied equals the quantity of funds demanded.

The **market for loanable funds** is where suppliers of loanable funds (savers) trade with demanders of loanable funds (borrowers). Trading in the market for loanable funds determines the equilibrium interest rate.

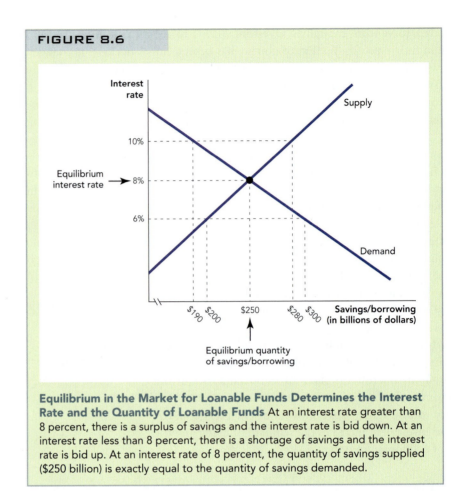

FIGURE 8.6

Equilibrium in the Market for Loanable Funds Determines the Interest Rate and the Quantity of Loanable Funds At an interest rate greater than 8 percent, there is a surplus of savings and the interest rate is bid down. At an interest rate less than 8 percent, there is a shortage of savings and the interest rate is bid up. At an interest rate of 8 percent, the quantity of savings supplied ($250 billion) is exactly equal to the quantity of savings demanded.

The interest rate adjusts to equalize savings and borrowing in the same way and for the same reasons that the price of oil adjusts to balance the supply and demand for oil. If the interest rate were higher than 8 percent, the quantity of savings supplied would exceed the quantity of savings demanded creating a surplus of savings. With a surplus of savings, suppliers will bid the interest rate down as they compete to lend. If the interest rate were lower than 8 percent, the quantity of savings demanded would exceed the quantity of savings supplied, a shortage. With a shortage of savings, demanders would bid the interest rate up as they compete to borrow. (See Chapter 3 for a review.)

Shifts in Supply and Demand

Changes in economic conditions will shift the supply or demand curve and change the equilibrium interest rate and quantity of savings. Consider an economy in which the citizens become less impatient, and more willing to save for the future. These shifts occurred in South Korea in the 1960s and 1970s, once many Korean citizens realized they could copy some aspects of the Japanese economic miracle. Across East Asia more generally, growing life spans and fewer children to support (and fewer children to be supported by, in old age) led to a regional savings boom. An increase in the supply of savings is shown by shifting the supply curve to the right and down (indicating more savings at any interest rate or equivalently a willingness to save any given amount in return for a lower interest rate).

In Figure 8.7, an increase in the supply of savings causes the equilibrium interest rate to fall from 8 percent to 6 percent and the quantity of savings to increase from $250 billion to $300 billion.

FIGURE 8.7

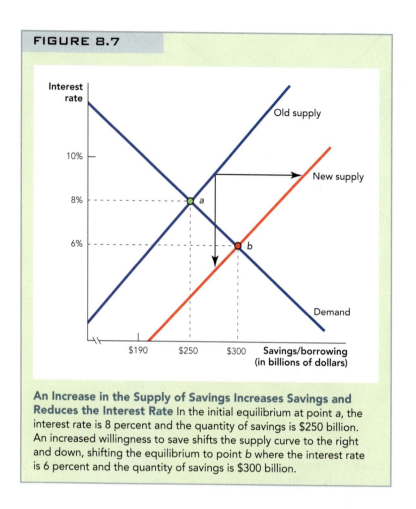

An Increase in the Supply of Savings Increases Savings and Reduces the Interest Rate In the initial equilibrium at point *a*, the interest rate is 8 percent and the quantity of savings is $250 billion. An increased willingness to save shifts the supply curve to the right and down, shifting the equilibrium to point *b* where the interest rate is 6 percent and the quantity of savings is $300 billion.

What did this shift in savings means for South Korea? In 1960, Korea was among the poorest countries in the world but today it is a fully developed nation. South Korea's increased savings were plowed into investment and as we know from our discussion of the Solow model in Chapter 7, one of the key drivers of economic growth is a high rate of investment and capital accumulation.

Of course, a decrease in the supply of savings is shown in the opposite manner, by shifting the supply curve to the left and up.

Sometimes investors become less optimistic, which decreases the demand to invest and borrow. For instance, during a recession many entrepreneurs get scared about the future and they are reluctant to invest. Projects that looked good to investors when the economy is booming may look unprofitable when the economy is in the doldrums. The decrease in investment demand can itself help to spread and prolong the recession, as we discuss at greater length in Chapter 13. In Figure 8.8 on the next page, a decrease in investment demand reduces the interest rate from 8 percent to 6 percent and the quantity of savings from $250 billion to $190 billion.

Sometimes, to counteract the decrease in investment demand during a recession, a government offers a temporary investment tax credit. An investment tax credit gives firms that invest in plants and equipment a tax break. The tax credit

FIGURE 8.8

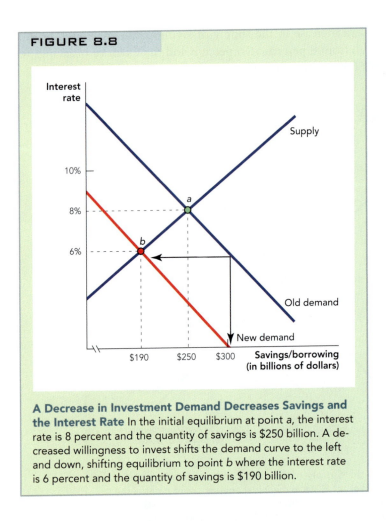

A Decrease in Investment Demand Decreases Savings and the Interest Rate In the initial equilibrium at point *a*, the interest rate is 8 percent and the quantity of savings is $250 billion. A decreased willingness to invest shifts the demand curve to the left and down, shifting equilibrium to point *b* where the interest rate is 6 percent and the quantity of savings is $190 billion.

is usually temporary to encourage firms to invest quickly, when the recession is still in full force. The tax credit means that projects that were unprofitable without the credit are profitable with the credit, so at any given interest rate firms are willing to invest more when a tax credit is available. In other words, the demand to borrow funds shifts to the right (and up) as shown in Figure 8.9.

The Role of Intermediaries: Banks, Bonds, and Stock Markets

Equilibrium in the market for loanable funds does not come about automatically. Savers move their capital, sometimes around the world, to find the highest returns. Entrepreneurs invest time and energy to find the right investments and the right loans. Equilibrium is brought about with the assistance of **financial institutions** such as banks, bond markets, and stock markets.

We will discuss banks, bond markets, and stock markets, but keep in mind the underlying common thread in the discussion. All of these institutions reduce the costs of moving savings from savers to borrowers and help mobilize savings toward productive uses. All of these institutions are middlemen, and they help to coordinate markets. At its core, a bank or a bond market is an institution that helps bring about the equilibrium in Figure 8.6 and helps bring resources to more highly valued uses.

CHECK YOURSELF

> How will greater patience shift the supply of savings and change the interest rate and quantity of savings?

> How will an increase in investment demand change the equilibrium interest rate and quantity of savings?

Financial institutions such as banks, bond markets, and stock markets reduce the costs of moving savings from savers to borrowers and investors.

FIGURE 8.9

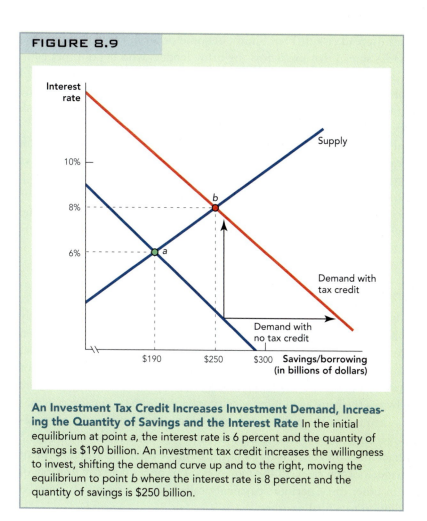

An Investment Tax Credit Increases Investment Demand, Increasing the Quantity of Savings and the Interest Rate In the initial equilibrium at point *a*, the interest rate is 6 percent and the quantity of savings is $190 billion. An investment tax credit increases the willingness to invest, shifting the demand curve up and to the right, moving the equilibrium to point *b* where the interest rate is 8 percent and the quantity of savings is $250 billion.

Banks

In their role as financial intermediary, banks receive savings from many individuals, pay them interest, and then loan these funds to borrowers or investors, charging them interest. Banks seek to earn profit by charging more for their loans than they pay for the savings. To earn this money, they must provide useful "middleman" services by evaluating investments and spreading risk.

Imagine that you, as a bank depositor, had to decide which companies were worth lending money to. Is this guy Fred Smith with his FedEx idea a genius or a kook? Banks don't always get it right, but by specializing in loan evaluation they have a better idea than most of us of which business ideas make sense. When banks specialize, individual savers don't have to evaluate which factories ought to be built or which businesses deserve to be supported.

Even if individuals could evaluate business ideas, it would be wasteful if every saver spent time evaluating the same business. Imagine that a business needs a million dollar loan. One thousand savers are each willing to lend the business $1,000. If each saver spent a day evaluating the quality of the business that would be 999 wasted days of effort. It makes more sense for the lenders to appoint a single person to evaluate the business on behalf of all of them. That's exactly what a bank does. Banks coordinate lenders and minimize information costs. Banks are thus an important example of the benefits of specialization and the division of labor.

Banks also spread risk. If Fred Smith, or some other borrower, defaults on his loan, banks spread that loss across the many lenders who deposit money in the bank. This avoids the risk that you have lent Fred Smith $50,000 and suddenly are out the entire sum. It's less risky and no less profitable to lend, one thousand firms $1 each than to lend one firm $1,000, so the spreading of risk encourages greater lending and investment.

Banks also play a role in the payments system. Money deposited in a bank can be drawn on with a check or debit card or via the ATM. We discuss banks and the payment system at greater length in Chapter 14.

Overall, banks make our lives simpler. We open our accounts, deposit our money, receive our interest payments, and write our checks; at the same time we are participating in the process of economic growth because the bank oversees a process by which our savings are turned into productive investments.

The Bond Market

Instead of borrowing from a bank, well-known corporations can borrow directly from the public. Your local pizza restaurant borrows from a bank, or perhaps even from relatives, because restaurants are a risky business and the finances of that company are hard for outside investors to evaluate. But when it comes to IBM or Toyota, investors can more easily find information about the firm and so they are willing to bypass the bank as an intermediary and lend to the company directly.

When a member of the public lends money to a corporation, the corporation acknowledges its debt by issuing a **bond**. *A bond is a corporate IOU.* The bond contract lists how much is owed to the bond's owner and when payment must be made. In some cases, all the money is owed on a single day (the day of maturity); in other cases, periodic payments, called coupon payments, must be made in addition to a final payment.

The New York Central and Hudson River Railroad Company borrowed money in 1897 for which they issued bonds, one of which is pictured on the left. The bond is an IOU that promises that the Central will pay the owner $1,000 in 1997. In addition, every six months until 1997, the Central promised to pay the owner $17.50. You can see from the picture why the periodic payments are called coupon payments: the coupons are on the right of the bond and can be clipped and sent to the issuer of the bond to receive payment.

Central's bond illustrates one of the advantages of bond finance—large sums of money can be raised now and invested in long-lived assets such as railroad track. The money can then be paid back over a long period of time, in the case of the Central over a 100-year period.

All bonds involve a risk that when the payments come due the borrower will not be able to pay; this is called default risk. The Central, for example, eventually defaulted when it went bankrupt, but it did pay its coupons until 1970. Major bond issues are graded by agencies like Moody's and Standard and Poor's. AAA, for example, is the highest grade issued by Standard and Poor's; that grade indicates, according to the rating agencies, that the bond is very likely to be paid. Grades range all the way from AAA to D when a firm is in default. Bonds rated less than BBB– are sometimes called "junk bonds." It's important to remember that risk can never be perfectly quantified and the rating agencies can be wrong—a point we will return to when we discuss the 2007–2008 financial crisis (see later in this chapter).

If a risky company wishes to borrow money, it has to promise a higher rate of interest because lenders will demand to be compensated for a greater risk of

A **bond** is a sophisticated IOU that documents who owes how much and when payment must be made.

COURTESY OF THE AUTHOR

A 100-year bond issued by the New York Central and Hudson River Railroad Company in 1897. The bond is an IOU that promised the owner $1,000 in 1997 and $17.50 every six months until that time.

default. Why lend to a risky firm unless you have some prospect of earning higher returns?

Thus, the marketplace grades the risks of major investments and charges interest rates accordingly. As of 2007, Berkshire Hathaway, the firm managed by famed investor Warren Buffett, was evaluated by ratings agencies at AAA, the safest possible rating. Berkshire Hathaway was borrowing money at 4.48 percent while Ford Motor Company, which lost $12.6 billion in 2006, was rated only B and was having to pay 5.76 percent. At the time, mortgage rates were not much higher than 5.76 percent so the market was saying that in 2007 lending to the great Ford Motor Company involved about as much risk as lending to the average home buyer. Home loans are as cheap as they are, in part, because if the borrower defaults, the lender can seize the home and resell it; this is harder to do with a series of Ford automobile plants.

Similarly, can you think of one reason why interest rates on home loans are almost always lower than interest rates on vacation loans? The bank can repossess the house but not the vacation! The house is a form of **collateral,** something of value that by agreement becomes the property of the lender if the borrower defaults on the loan. Thus, the market for loanable funds is really a broad spectrum of markets; the interest rates differ depending on the borrower, repayment time, amount of the loan, type of collateral, and many other features of the loan.

> **Collateral** is something of value that by agreement becomes the property of the lender if the borrower defaults.

Greater risk can reduce the supply of funds to the market as a whole. If lenders expect a recession, for example, they may become concerned that many firms will go bankrupt and default on their debt. A lender who was willing to lend at 8 percent when he or she thought the risk was low will demand a higher return if the lender believes the risk of default has increased significantly.

Governments borrow money as well. In 2007 the U.S. government owed about $5 trillion dollars to private borrowers (individuals, firms, and governments other than the U.S. federal government). When the government borrows a lot of money, private consumption and investment can be **crowded out**. Imagine, for example, that the government borrows $100 billion to cover a budget deficit. In Figure 8.10 on the next page, the demand curve for loanable funds shifts to the right by $100 billion increasing the interest rate from 7 percent to 9 percent. The higher interest rate has two effects. First, it draws an additional $50 billion of savings into the market so total savings increase from $200 billion to $250 billion. Since greater savings mean less consumption, we can also say that consumption is reduced by $50 billion. Second, the higher interest rate means that some investments and other projects are no longer profitable so at a higher interest rate private borrowing falls. In Figure 8.10, we show private borrowing falling by $50 billion. Thus, the $100 billion necessary to cover the government's budget deficit comes from a combination of reduced consumption and reduced private investment and other private borrowing.

> **Crowding out** is the decrease in private consumption and investment that occurs when government borrows more.

We will return to the issues of crowding out, government debt, and deficits in Chapters 16 and 17.

When the U.S. government borrows, it issues a variety of different bonds. U.S. Treasury bonds or T-bonds are 30-year bonds that pay interest every 6 months. T-notes are bonds with maturities ranging from 2 to 10 years that also pay interest every 6 months. T-bills are bonds with maturities of a few days to 26 weeks that pay only at maturity. A bond that pays only at maturity is also called a zero-coupon bond or a discount bond since these bonds sell at a discount to their face value.

Treasury securities are desirable for many investors because they are easy to buy and sell and the U.S. government is unlikely to default on its payments. In

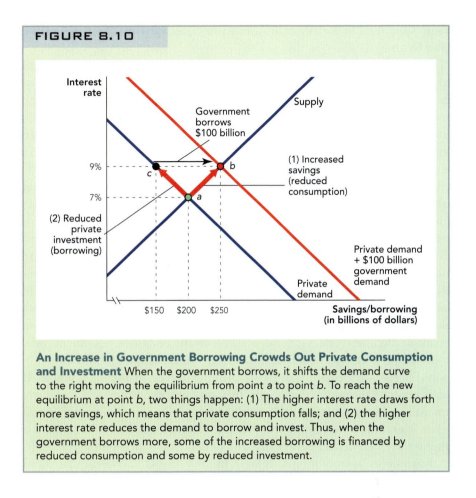

FIGURE 8.10

An Increase in Government Borrowing Crowds Out Private Consumption and Investment When the government borrows, it shifts the demand curve to the right moving the equilibrium from point *a* to point *b*. To reach the new equilibrium at point *b*, two things happen: (1) The higher interest rate draws forth more savings, which means that private consumption falls; and (2) the higher interest rate reduces the demand to borrow and invest. Thus, when the government borrows more, some of the increased borrowing is financed by reduced consumption and some by reduced investment.

general, short-term U.S. government securities tend to be the safest assets, and very short-term bonds, called commercial paper, issued by very large corporations tend to be safe as well. In addition, Treasury securities, especially T-bills, are important in monetary policy; the Federal Reserve buys and sells Treasury securities on a daily basis to influence the money supply (more on this in Chapter 15).

Bond Prices and Interest Rates It's often convenient to express the price of a bond in terms of an interest rate; this is easiest to do with a zero-coupon bond. Suppose, for example, that a bond with very little risk exists that will pay $1,000 in one year's time and that this bond is currently selling for $950. If you were to buy this bond today and hold it until maturity, you would earn $50, ($1,000 − $950), or a rate of return of $5.26\% = \dfrac{\$1000 - \$950}{\$950} \times 100$. Thus, every zero-coupon bond has an implied rate of return that can be calculated by subtracting the price from the value at maturity, often called the face value or FV, and then dividing by the price.

$$\text{Rate of return for a zero-coupon bond} = \frac{FV - \text{Price}}{\text{Price}} \times 100$$

Sellers of bonds must compete to attract lenders, who compare the implied rate of return on bonds with the rate of return on other assets. Imagine, for example, that the interest rate on say a savings account at a bank increases to 10 percent. Would you buy a bond that pays 5.26 percent? Would anyone?

Of course not. So if the interest rate rise to 10 percent, what must happen to the price of this bond? The price must fall. In fact, if the interest rate rises to 10 percent, the price of the bond must fall to $909. Why? Because at a price of $909, the rate of return on the bond is $10\% = \dfrac{\$1000 - \$909}{\$909} \times 100$. Thus, at a price of $909, sellers of bonds will be able to compete with banks, who are paying 10 percent on savings accounts, to attract funds, but at a higher price they won't find any buyers.

Our simple bond pricing example tells us two things of importance. First, equally risky assets must have the same rate of return. If they didn't, no one would buy the asset with the lower rate of return and the price of that asset would fall until the rate of return was competitive with other investments. This is called an **arbitrage** principle and we discuss it at greater length in the appendix to this chapter.

Arbitrage, the buying and selling of equally risky assets, ensures that equally risky assets earn equal returns.

The second important lesson is that interest rates and bond prices move in opposite directions. When interest rates go up, bond prices fall. When interest rates go down, bond prices rise. We will be referring to this principle several times throughout the textbook so do study the principle and make a note of it:

> **Interest rates and bond prices move in opposite directions.**

The inverse relationship between bond prices and interest rates tells us that in addition to default risk, people who buy bonds also face interest rate risk. For instance, perhaps a bond was issued in 2003 at an interest rate of 7 percent. If interest rates for comparable investments later rise to 9 percent, having bought a bond yielding 7 percent was in retrospect a mistake. If, instead, comparable interest rates were to fall to 3 percent, the bond purchase worked out for the better. The buyer locked in a 7 percent return when other rates of return were falling to 3 percent. In other words, bond buyers are making bets that interest rates will fall (bond prices will rise), or at least they are hoping that interest rates will fall. And similarly bond sellers are betting or hoping that interest rates will rise, which means bond prices will . . . do you remember? . . . fall. Again, for more on the relationship between bond prices and interest rates, see the chapter appendix.

The Stock Market

Just as businesses fund their activities by taking out bank loans and selling bonds, they also issue shares of stock. **Stocks** are shares of ownership in a corporation. Owners have a claim to the firm's profits, but remember that profit is revenue minus costs. In other words, profit is what is left over *after* everyone else—creditors, bond holders, suppliers, and employees—have been paid. If profits are high, shareholders benefit. They benefit directly if the firm pays out its profits in dividends or indirectly if the firm reinvests its profits in a way that increases the value of the stock. But if profits are low or negative, shareholders suffer losses.

A **stock** or a share is a certificate of ownership in a corporation.

Stocks are traded on organized markets called stock exchanges. The New York Stock Exchange (NYSE) is the largest in the world. When new stocks are issued, that is called an **initial public offering** or an IPO. An IPO is the first time a stock is sold to the public.

An **initial public offering (IPO)** is the first time a corporation sells stock to the public in order to raise capital.

You'll recall from the beginning of this chapter that simply buying and selling existing shares of stock does *not* increase net investment in the economy.

But when a firm sells *new* shares to the public, it typically uses the proceeds to fund investment, that is, to buy new capital goods. In addition, the possibility of offering equity or ownership in a firm opens the door to many business ventures that might never get off the ground, or might not be able to expand rapidly.

Consider Google. Google is today a household word but when the company began in September 1998 it was headquartered in a garage. Yet in August 2004, Google founders Sergei Brin and Larry Page sold $1.67 billion worth of stock in an IPO. The money helped Google to fund new investments and pay for research and development. In addition, Google's IPO turned the founders and the early investors into millionaires and billionaires. This big payoff was a reward for creating the company and making the early and risky investments that were necessary to get Google off the ground. Stock markets help people with great ideas become rich and that encourages innovation. It is no accident that the United States—one of the most innovative countries in the world—also has the best-developed stock and capital markets.

Selling part of Google to the public also let the founders diversify. If someday another search service bests Google, Brin and Page will not become paupers. This added safety also encourages innovation. People who come up with new ideas know that their wealth will not be locked into one firm.

We'll have a lot more to say about stock markets in Chapter 9, but for now what you need to know is that stock markets encourage investment and growth.

What Happens When Intermediation Fails?

Economic growth cannot occur without savings and those savings must be processed and intermediated through banks, bond markets, stock markets, and so on. Countries without these institutions have smaller markets for loans, use their savings less effectively, and make fewer good investments.[4] But why do some countries have poorly developed banking and financial systems?

The bridge between savers and borrowers can be broken in many ways, including insecure property rights, inflation and controls on interest rates, politicized lending, and massive bank failures and panics. These problems can break the bridge by (1) reducing the supply of savings, (2) raising the cost of intermediation, and (3) reducing the effectiveness of lending. Figure 8.11 illustrates the main ideas.

Insecure Property Rights

Consider, for example, the supply of savings. The expected return on savings depends on more than just the posted rate of interest at the bank. Some governments do not offer secure property rights to savers. That is, saved funds are not immune from later confiscation, freezes, or other restrictions.

During the financial crisis beginning in December 2001, for example, the Argentine government partially froze bank accounts for a year. Many of the banks subsequently went under, which meant that Argentine citizens lost their bank-based savings. This event was not a complete surprise. The Argentine government had a history of freezing bank accounts, such as during 1982 and 1989. Other countries in the region, such as Brazil in 1990, had also frozen bank accounts. Obviously this repeated pattern means that Argentines and Brazilians save less than they otherwise might wish to. Why save when those funds are simply being put up for grabs? Ana, a 40-year-old teacher from Argentina, kept her

UNDERSTAND YOUR world

FIGURE 8.11

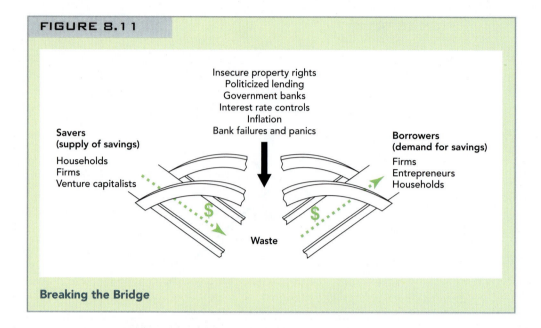

Insecure property rights
Politicized lending
Government banks
Interest rate controls
Inflation
Bank failures and panics

**Savers
(supply of savings)**

Households
Firms
Venture capitalists

**Borrowers
(demand for savings)**

Firms
Entrepreneurs
Households

$

$

Waste

Breaking the Bridge

savings in dollars in her house and then exchanged them for pesos to pay her bills. She said "You just can't put your money in banks here."[5] Ana is right, but unlike money in the bank, which can be lent out to fund investment, money under a mattress does not contribute to economic growth.

If individuals expect that contracts will be broken, they will be reluctant to invest in stock markets as well. For instance, the Russian government often does not respect the rights of minority shareholders and at times it has confiscated or restricted the value of their shareholdings, as in the case of the private energy company Yukos. The result is that many foreign investors are unwilling to put money into Russian ventures. They simply do not trust the Russian government, nor do they believe that Russian courts will enforce contracts impartially.

Law is one side of the equation, but custom and informal trust is another. In a healthy economy, shareholders expect that managers are interested in building their long-run reputations, rather than ripping off the company at every possible opportunity. When managers look only to short-run gains, it is hard to run a business enterprise, as investors will not entrust managers with the control of resources. Systems of monitoring and accounting, no matter how well developed, cannot overcome high levels of mistrust. This is a common problem in developing countries around the world but the Enron, WorldCom, and Madoff scandals demonstrate that the United States is also not immune to these problems. Trust is an important asset throughout the world.

Controls on Interest Rates and Inflation

Price controls on interest rates also cause the loanable funds market to malfunction. Consider a maximum ceiling on the interest rate that can be charged on a loan. Sometimes economists call these ceilings "usury laws"; usury laws date back to medieval times and earlier. Today most American states have usury laws, although often they have loopholes (they don't stop most credit card borrowing, for instance) or they are set at levels too high to influence most loan markets. Nonetheless, a binding and enforceable ceiling on interest rates would look like Figure 8.12 on the next page.

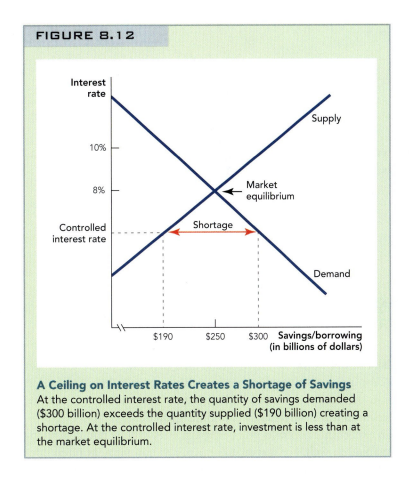

FIGURE 8.12

A Ceiling on Interest Rates Creates a Shortage of Savings
At the controlled interest rate, the quantity of savings demanded ($300 billion) exceeds the quantity supplied ($190 billion) creating a shortage. At the controlled interest rate, investment is less than at the market equilibrium.

The equilibrium is just like our analysis of price controls in Chapter 4. At the artificially low price, there is a shortage of credit, and many people who wish to borrow at the controlled interest rate cannot do so. Moreover, the control on interest rates reduces savings. In Figure 8.12 savings falls from $250 billion at the market equilibrium to just $190 billion at the controlled interest rate. Similarly, just as with price controls on oil, an interest rate control will cause a misallocation of savings and a loss of potential gains from exchange. Perhaps most important, investment, which is determined by the supply of savings, will fall below what it would be at the market equilibrium.

Inflation and controls on interest rates have often combined to destroy the incentive to save and thus to shrink the banking system. Imagine that interest rates are controlled at a nominal rate of 10 percent. Nominal just means the named rate, the rate on paper. At a nominal rate of 10 percent, $100 invested in the bank will return $110 in one year's time. Suppose, however, that inflation is running at 30 percent, which means that a basket of goods that cost $100 at the beginning of the year will cost $130 at the end of the year. Thus, a lender who lends $100 at the beginning of the year needs $130 at the end of the year just to keep even. If the lender only receives $110 at the end of the year, that's just like losing $20. Economists define the real rate of return as the nominal rate minus the inflation rate.

Real interest rate = Nominal interest rate − Inflation rate

In this case, the real interest rate is −20 percent (10 − 30 = −20). Thus, someone who lends at a nominal interest rate of 10 percent when the inflation rate is 30 percent is losing 20 percent per year. Inflation and interest rate

controls turn savings accounts into wasting accounts. This is sometimes called "financial repression," and it is an extreme example of the situation illustrated in Figure 8.12.

When real interest rates turn negative, people take their money out of the banking system, using the cash to invest abroad (if they can), or to buy a real asset like land that is appreciating in value alongside inflation, or to simply consume more. In any of these cases, when many people pull their money out of the banking system, the supply of savings declines and financial intermediation becomes less efficient. Table 8.1 shows a number of examples of severely negative real interest rates. In every case, economic growth was also negative. Countries with negative real interest rates usually have many problems so we can't blame all of the poor economic growth on inefficient financial intermediation. Nonetheless, studies show that even after controlling for other factors, negative real interest rates reduce financial intermediation and economic growth.

TABLE 8.1 Negative Interest Rates and Economic Growth

Country	Years	Real Interest Rate (percent)	Per Capita Growth (percent)
Argentina	1975–1976	–69	–2.2
Bolivia	1982–1984	–75	–5.2
Chile	1972–1974	–61	–3.6
Ghana	1976–1983	–35	–2.9
Peru	1976–1984	–19	–1.4
Poland	1981–1982	–33	–8.6
Sierra Leone	1984–1987	–44	–1.9
Turkey	1979–1980	–35	–3.1
Venezuela	1987–1989	–24	–2.7
Zaire	1976–1979	–34	–6.0
Zambia	1985–1988	–24	–1.9

Source: Easterly, W. 2002. *The Elusive Quest for Growth. Economists' Adventures and Misadventures in the Tropics.* MIT Press, Cambridge MA.

Politicized Lending and Government-Owned Banks

Japanese history from about 1990 to 2005 also illustrates the importance of banks in using a nation's savings effectively. During this period, the Japanese continued to save, but Japanese economic growth was zero or negative for most of these years. How can this have been? Many Japanese banks were bankrupt or propped up by the government. They were not allocating funds efficiently. Other banks were pressured to lend money to well-connected political allies, rather than to the most efficient new businesses. During this period, Japanese banks acted as storehouses for wealth, but they were not effective financial intermediaries. Japanese business innovation, and the Japanese standard of living, suffered accordingly.

In Japan, as in the United States, banks are privately owned so politicized lending, even when it occurs, is limited. But in many other countries most large banks are owned by the government. Government-owned banks are useful to authoritarian regimes that use the banks to direct capital to political supporters. While it might be politically wise for the ruler to support his uncle's firm, that uncle is probably not a superior entrepreneur. One important study by economists Rafael La Porta, Florencio Lopez-de-Silanes, and Andrei Shleifer finds that the larger the fraction of government-owned banks a country had in 1970, the slower was growth in per capita GDP and productivity over the next several decades.[6]

Bank Failures and Panics

Systematic problems in the banking system usually lead to large-scale economic crises. In the onset of America's Great Depression between 1929 and 1933, 11,000 banks—almost half of all U.S. banks—failed. The ripple effects were

grim. Many people lost their life savings; they also had to curtail their spending, which meant that many businesses lost their customers and thus revenue. Many businesses were unable to get loans or daily working capital. Thus, bank failures were followed by a rash of small business failures. It took many years before the American banking system, and the American economy, recovered.

In their seminal work, *A Monetary History of the United States, 1867–1960*, Milton Friedman and Anna Schwartz argued that the Great Depression was brought about in part because the Federal Reserve—the U.S. central bank that is charged with overseeing the general health of the banking industry—failed in its job to prevent widespread bank failures.[7] (See Chapter 12 for further discussion of the Great Depression and Chapter 14 for more on the Federal Reserve.) Economist Ben Bernanke later showed that one of the reasons why bank failures were so crucial in the onset of the Great Depression was because banks provide loans to a particular class of borrowers and lenders.[8] According to Bernanke:

> As the real costs of intermediation increased, some borrowers (especially households, farmers, and small firms) found credit to be expensive and difficult to obtain. The effects of this credit squeeze . . . helped convert the severe but not unprecedented downturn of 1929–30 into a protracted depression.

By the way, if you recognize Bernanke's name, it is with good reason: he is now the chairman of the Federal Reserve. This study of American banking was one of Bernanke's most famous papers as an academic and helped give him the recognition to later be named head of the Federal Reserve.

Bernanke, as chairman of the Federal Reserve, had to face his own intermediation crisis during 2007 and 2008. Sometimes bank loans are "securitized," or bundled together and sold on the market as financial assets. Before the 2007–2008 financial crisis, many mortgage loans were bundled and sold as if they had very low risk. In reality, many of these securitized mortgages turned out to have much higher risk than had been advertised. In part some of the securitized bundles were sold on false terms, in part the credit rating agencies performed poorly, and in part people simply estimated risk incorrectly by assuming that house prices would continue rising more or less indefinitely.

When housing prices started to fall in 2006, many people defaulted on their mortgages and the U.S. economy suddenly ended up in a situation where many banks and other financial intermediaries were holding loans of questionable value. Yet because the mortgages had been bundled and sold many times over in different combinations and permutations, no one knew exactly whose loans were rotten or by how much. Investors suspected that some firms were going under (indeed Bear Stearns, the investment bank did crash, among others) but most investors had little advance notice on where the biggest problems would fall. As a result, no one wanted to lend or invest in banks and other intermediaries that might have significant quantities of mortgage assets on their books. Why lend or invest in a bank when the bank might be gone tomorrow? Investors also became wary of any institution that lent money to potentially troubled banks, even if that institution did not itself hold mortgage-backed assets. But when financial intermediaries can't get new funds, the bridge between savers and borrowers collapses. Indeed, credit markets froze up in parts of 2008 for precisely this reason. Bernanke, fearing a financial panic similar to that

which gripped the Great Depression, responded with some very aggressive and dramatic ways of getting credit markets back on their feet. We'll consider those remedies in more detail in Chapters 14 and 15.

□ Takeaway

Individuals save to prepare for their retirement, to help fund large purchases, and to cushion swings in their income—most generally, savings help individuals, firms, and governments to smooth their consumption over time. Similarly, individuals, firms, and governments borrow to finance large purchases like a home, to invest in new capital, or in the case of governments to finance large expenditures such as are necessary for a war. Once again, borrowing helps agents to smooth their consumption streams. Financial institutions bridge the gap between savers and borrowers.

Financial institutions also collect savings, evaluate investments, and diversify risk. Banks, bonds, and stock markets help finance new and innovative ideas, such as Google and Federal Express. Financial intermediation is a central part of healthy economic growth.

Capital markets are becoming increasingly global, but globalization does not differ in kind from how markets work within a single country or region. Entrepreneurs seek out profitable trading opportunities to bring resources, including investment, to more highly valued economic uses. This happens both within borders and across borders.

Without effective financial intermediation, an economy will end up adrift. Insecure property rights, inflation, politicized lending, and bank failures all contribute to the breakdown of financial intermediation. Whenever possible, government policy should seek to avoid these outcomes.

CHECK YOURSELF

> How do usury laws (controls on interest rates) cause savings to decline?

> Besides decreasing the number of banks, how do bank failures hinder financial intermediation?

> How does awarding bank loans by political criteria or by cronyism (to your pals) affect the efficiency of the economy?

□ CHAPTER REVIEW

KEY CONCEPTS

Saving, p. 148

Investment, p. 148

Time preference, p. 149

Market for loanable funds, p. 153

Financial institutions, p. 156

Bond, p. 158

Collateral, p. 159

Crowding out, p. 159

Arbitrage, p. 161

Stock, p. 161

Initial public offering (IPO), p. 161

FACTS AND TOOLS

1. If people want to smooth their consumption over time, what will they tend to do when they win the lottery: Spend most of it within a year or save most of it for later?

2. A large number of economic and psychological studies demonstrate that people who are impatient in one area of their life tend to be impatient in other areas as well. This isn't true in every single case, but of course that doesn't matter if we're trying to understand the "typical person." Based on your general knowledge and educated guessing:

   a. Who is more likely to smoke: A criminal or a law-abiding citizen?

b. Who is more likely to shoot heroin: A person who saves 20 percent of their income or a person who can't ever find a way to save?

c. Who is more likely to have a lot of credit card debt: A smoker or a nonsmoker?

3. The typical savings supply curve has a positive slope. If a nation's saving supply curve had a perfectly vertical slope, what would that mean?

a. People in this country save the same amount no matter what the interest rate is.

b. People in this country are extremely sensitive to interest rates when deciding how much to save.

4. Consider three countries: Jovenia (average age: 25), Mittelaltistan (average age: 45), and Decrepetia (average age: 75). Based on the lifecycle theory, which of these countries will probably have:

a. High savings rates?

b. High rates of borrowing?

c. High rates of dissaving? (That's spending your past savings.)

Note: The way for entire countries to save is to build up the stock of productive capital either at home (through high investment rates) or abroad (by exporting more than importing, that is, running a trade surplus, and using the proceeds to buy foreign investment goods and assets).

5. Sometimes, in supply and demand models, it's not clear who "supplies" and who "demands." For instance, in the labor market, it's individual workers (not firms) who supply labor. In the loanable funds market, who is usually the supplier and who is usually the demander? Choose the correct answer.

a. Entrepreneurs supply loanable funds and savers demand loanable funds.

b. Entrepreneurs supply loanable funds and savers also supply loanable funds.

c. Entrepreneurs demand loanable funds and savers demand loanable funds.

d. Entrepreneurs demand loanable funds and savers supply loanable funds.

6. In each of the following, answer either "bank account," "bonds," or "stocks."

a. Which investment is typically the riskiest?

b. Which is a corporate IOU?

c. Which one gives you an ownership "share" in a company?

d. Which one usually lets you "withdraw" part of your investment at any time, for any reason?

e. Which form of investment usually spreads your money over the largest number of investment projects?

f. Which is usually rated by private companies like Moody's or Standard and Poor's?

g. Which one is offered by the U.S. government as well as by private corporations?

7. If savers don't feel safe putting their money in banks or buying bonds, what's the best way to sum up what's happening in the market for loanable funds?

a. Supply of savings falls and the interest rate falls.

b. Supply of savings falls and the interest rate rises.

c. Demand for savings falls and the interest rate falls.

d. Demand for savings falls and the interest rate rises.

8. When governments outlaw high interest rates and the ceiling is binding, what probably happens to the total amount of money borrowed?

a. It rises because borrowers are protected from high interest rates.

b. It falls because savers aren't willing to lend as much money at this low interest rate.

c. Both a and b are usually true.

9. Calculate the real interest rate in the following five cases:

a. Nominal interest rate = 4 percent, inflation rate = 2 percent

b. Nominal interest rate = 6 percent, inflation rate = 3 percent

c. Nominal interest rate = 10 percent, inflation rate = 15 percent

d. Nominal interest rate = 0 percent, inflation rate = −2 percent (An example of the Friedman rule: see Challenge question 2 below on this case for further information)

e. Nominal interest rate = 1,000 percent, inflation rate = 1,100 percent (Not uncommon during hyperinflations, as we'll see later)

10. If financial intermediation breaks down, what category of GDP will probably fall the most: consumption, investment, government purchases, or net exports?

11. a. In a competitive banking system, what tends to happen to banks that make low-interest rate loans to the banker's friends: Do they tend to be more successful or less successful than other, more ruthless banks?

  b. Given your answer to the previous question, how do you suspect that politicized government-owned banks stay in business?

THINKING AND PROBLEM SOLVING

1. Let's work out a simple example where a person smoothes her consumption over time. Gwen is a real estate agent, and she knows that she will have some good years and some bad years. She figures that half the time she'll earn $90,000 per year, and half the time she'll earn $20,000 per year. These numbers are after taxes and after saving for retirement. These numbers are all she has to worry about.

  a. If we ignore interest costs just to keep things simple, how much should Gwen consume in the average year?

  b. How many dollars will she save during the good years?

  c. How many dollars will she borrow during the bad years? (Note: "Borrowing," in this context, is basically the same as "pulling money out of savings.")

2. Let's think about how the supply of savings might shift in two different cases.

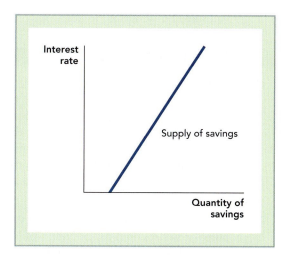

  a. Under current U.S. law, businesses are allowed to automatically enroll you in a savings plan that puts 5 percent of your salary in a retirement fund. Suppose Congress *abolishes*

this law: draw the appropriate shift in the supply curve, and label it "a."

  b. If Americans all go to see the classic Robin Williams/Ethan Hawke film *Dead Poets Society* and decide to *carpe diem,* or if they read the quotes of a famous Mediterranean preacher who said, "Take therefore no thought for the morrow," or if they watch the appalling 1970s sitcom *One Day at a Time,* what direction is the supply of savings likely to shift? Denote this with a new supply curve labeled "b."

3. In this chapter, we focus on three big functions that banks perform:

  I. They evaluate business ideas to see who's worth lending to.

  II. They spread an investment's risk among many different projects.

  III. They make it easier for people to make payments through checks, ATMs, and wire transfers.

  None of these functions are unique to banks. In the following anecdotes, is the person doing function I, function II, or function III?

  a. Emmanuel donates a little money to five different charities, in the hopes that at least one of them will do some good in the world.

  b. In Lorien's family, she's the one who specializes in deciding which bank everyone else in the family will use.

  c. Popeye always has a little cash on hand, so he is always able to lend a little money to Wimpy and Olive Oyl at lunchtime.

  d. George spends his time at the Carlyle Group deciding which companies are worth his investment partners' dollars.

  e. Scooter wants a good education, so he takes a variety of different classes: some history, some economics, some physics.

  f. Frances subscribes to *Consumer Reports* to decide which washing machine to buy.

4. In many poor countries, the banking system just isn't advanced enough to lend money for many large investments. Based on this single fact, where would you expect to see more entrepreneurs coming from rich families rather than poor families: In the rich countries or the poor countries? Why?

5. a. The financial analysts at Lexmark have evaluated five major projects. Each project, if it actually goes forward, will be financed by going to a bank to borrow the money. They've calculated a "break even interest rate": If they can borrow cash to pay for the project at less than that rate, the project will likely be a success; if the rate is higher, then it's not worth it.

	Cost	Break even interest rate
Project A	$100 million	8 percent
Project B	$50 million	12 percent
Project C	$200 million	50 percent
Project D	$25 million	4 percent
Project E	$150 million	10 percent

a. If the interest rate is 11 percent, which projects will Lexmark take on? If the market interest rate is 6 percent, which projects will it take on?

b. Let's turn the above information into a demand curve for loanable funds.

Organize this data to convert it into Lexmark's "loanable funds demand" curve. Note: It will look just like an ordinary demand curve, only with more breaks.

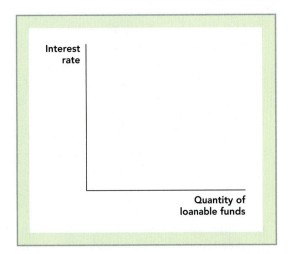

6. In each of the three cases, which bond will usually pay a higher interest rate?

a. A bond rated AAA, or a bond rated BBB?

b. A U.S. government bond, or a General Motors bond?

c. A Citibank bond that gets repaid in 30 years or a Citibank bond that gets repaid in 1 year?

7. Consider your answers to the previous question. When one bond pays a higher interest rate than another bond, is that mostly because savers are less willing to *supply* loanable funds to the higher-rate bond, or because businesses are more interested in *demanding* loanable funds for the higher-rate bond? Why is this so?

8. Consider Figure 8.10. Would a rise in government borrowing make it harder or easier for a new business to sell new stocks in an initial public offering (IPO)? In other words, are government bonds and corporate stocks substitutes for each other or complements to each other?

9. "If the government keeps real interest rates low (either by raising inflation or by decreeing low interest rates), then this encourages extra borrowing by businesses, which leads to more investment purchases, a larger stock of capital equipment, and higher productivity. Therefore, an interest rate ceiling is a good idea." What's wrong with this argument?

10. a. If a zero-coupon bond with a face value of $1,000 payable in 1 year sells for $925, what is the interest rate?

b. If another bond with the same face value and maturity sells for $900, what is the interest rate on this bond?

c. Which bond, that discussed in question a or question b, would you rather invest in? Are you sure? Think again!

CHALLENGES

1. The United States borrows a lot of money from other countries, as we noted at the start of this chapter. If you wanted to use the lifecycle theory to explain this, would you say that the United States is acting like a "young" country, an "old" country, or a "middle-aged" country? There's more than one correct way to answer this question.

2. a. It sure would be nice if the money in your purse or wallet could pay interest, wouldn't it? Nobel laureate Milton Friedman once pointed out that it's actually quite easy for money to pay interest—"real" interest, that is. Money in your wallet or purse (or most checking accounts) pays 0 percent nominal interest. But if the price level is falling, then the buying power of your money is constantly increasing, minute by minute. Let's see how this works.

Calculate the real rate in the following cases:

Real Rate	Nominal Rate	Inflation Rate
	0 percent	–1 percent
	0 percent	–2 percent
	0 percent	–3 percent

b. Using the rule of 70, how many years would it take for the buying power of $1 to double in each of the above three cases?

c. Friedman argued that since, in the United States, the real rate on safe assets tends to be about 2 percent, then the U.S. government should push for an inflation rate of –2 percent (a 2 percent deflation). At this rate of –2 percent, would people want to hold more money in their purses and checking accounts than they do now, less money than now, or would there be no change?

3. Lenders are more willing to lend if the borrower can put up collateral for the loan. Remember that collateral is something of value that by agreement becomes the property of the lender if the borrower defaults. In the United States, many small business owners borrow money for their business by using their houses or business assets as collateral. But in many developing countries, people don't have secure property rights or *title* to the land or house in which they live. In Bangalore, India, for example, it's nearly impossible to say who owns a piece of land and about 85 percent of the people in that city live on a piece of land for which they have no title. How difficult do you think it would be for a small business person in Bangalore to get a modest-sized loan?

CHAPTER **APPENDIX**

Bond Pricing and Arbitrage

Bond pricing may seem complicated but it can be understood with a few simple principles. Let's start with something more familiar than bonds. Suppose that you invest $100 in a savings account that pays a 10 percent rate of interest. How much money will you have in one year? That's easy; every dollar invested at 10 percent turns into $1.10 in one year so $100 invested at 10 percent turns into $110, which we can write as $100 × (1.10) = $110.

More generally, let's call the money that you invest the present value (PV), let's call the interest rate, r, and let's call the money that you will withdraw from the bank in one year the future value (FV). Then, the relationship between PV, r, and FV is simply:

$$PV \times (1 + r) = FV \qquad (1)$$

For example, if you invested $100 in present value at an interest rate of 5 percent, how much money would you have in a year (FV)? Substituting in equation (1) we have $100 × (1.05) = $105.

Okay, now let's ask a slightly more difficult question. Suppose that the interest rate is 10 percent and that in one year you would like to have the future value of $100. How much do you need to put in the bank today? In other words, if the interest rate is 10 percent and you want a future value of $100, what present value do you need to put in the bank? Let's fill in what we know:

$$PV \times (1.10) = \$100$$

To solve for PV divide both sides by 1.10.

$$PV = \frac{\$100}{1.10} = \$90.91$$

Thus, if the interest rate is 10 percent and we want $100 in the bank in one year, we need to invest $90.91 today. More generally, we can rewrite equation (1) in any of the following three ways depending on whether we want to solve for FV, PV, or r:

$$PV \times (1 + r) = FV \qquad (1)$$

$$PV = \frac{FV}{(1 + r)} \qquad (2)$$

$$(1 + r) = \frac{FV}{PV} \qquad (3)$$

We now have everything we need to explain bond pricing. Imagine that the interest rate is 10 percent and suppose that a bond exists that promises to pay $100 in one year's time. Thus, the future value of the bond—conveniently this is also called the face value—is $100, the interest rate, r, is 10 percent, and we want to know PV. We can use version (2) of our equation:

$$PV = \frac{\$100}{1.10} = \$90.91$$

In other words, when the interest rate is 10 percent, a bond promising to pay $100 in one year will sell for $90.91.

Students are often confused by the fact that interest rates and bond prices move in *opposite* directions: that is, when the interest rate rises, bond prices fall and when the interest rate falls, bond prices rise. But now we can explain this result easily. We know that at an interest rate of 10 percent a bond that has a future value of $100 will have a price or present value of $90.91. So what happens to the present value of the same bond when the interest rate falls to 5 percent?

$$PV = \frac{FV}{1 + r}$$

Substituting what we know, we have:

$$PV = \frac{\$100}{1.05} = \$95.24$$

Thus, when the interest rate falls from 10 percent to 5 percent, the price of the bond rises from $90.91 to $95.23.

We can see from version (2) of our formula that the price of a bond rises when the interest rate falls (and vice versa), but what is the economics behind this result? To understand the economics, we will use version (3) of our equation.

Let's suppose that the interest rate falls from 10 percent to 5 percent—in other words, the most that investors can earn on their loanable funds is a 5 percent rate of return. But imagine that instead of rising to $95.24 that the price of a bond paying $100 in one year's time stayed at $90.91. How much could investors earn by investing in this bond? The present value of the bond is $90.91, the future value is $100, so the return *on this bond* is:

$$(1 + r) = \frac{FV}{PV} = \frac{\$100}{\$90.91} = 1.10$$

Now what would you do if every other investment in the economy is earning a 5 percent rate of return but an equally safe bond exists that earns 10 percent? Correct, you would buy the bond paying 10 percent. And what happens when you—and everyone else—starts buying this extraordinary bond? Correct, the bond increases in price and as it increases in price, the return on the bond falls. In fact, the bond will increase in price and its rate of return will fall until it earns a rate of return roughly equal to that on similarly risky investments elsewhere in the economy.

Our last result can be stated more generally: *buying and selling will equalize the rate of return on equally risky assets.* The buying and selling of equally risky assets is called arbitrage. Arbitrage is a very important idea with many more implications than we can address here, but if you continue on in economics or finance you will study arbitrage in more detail.

We have shown how the simplest types of bonds are priced. Many bonds mature in more than one year and many bonds include coupon payments: periodic payments in addition to the final payment at maturity. The formula for determining the present value of a bond that matures in more than one year and that has coupon payments is more complicated than formula 2 but the ideas are exactly the same. We will give one quick example to illustrate.

Let's begin, once again, with a $100 investment in a savings account that pays a 10 percent rate of interest. But this time, let's suppose that we invest the money for two years—what is the future value of this investment? We can break our two-year investment into two one-year investments. We first invest $100 at 10 percent giving us $110 at the end of the first year. We then invest $110 at 10 percent for another year, which gives us $121 at the end of two years. In general terms we can write:

$$[PV \times (1 + r_1)] \times (1 + r_2) = FV \tag{A1}$$

The term in the square brackets is how much we will have after the first year of investment; we then multiply this amount by $(1 + r_2)$, the rate of interest in year two, to give us the amount that we will have at the end of two years.

As we did before, we can divide both sides of equation A1 by $(1 + r_1)(1 + r_2)$ in order to rewrite A1 as:

$$PV = \frac{FV}{(1 + r_1)(1 + r_2)} \tag{A2}$$

Let's use formula A2 to figure out the present value or selling price of a bond that pays $100 in two years when the interest rate in year one and year two is 10 percent. Substituting what we know, we have:

$$PV = \frac{\$100}{(1.10) \times (1.10)} = \$82.64$$

Thus, if the interest rate in year one and year two is 10 percent then a bond that pays $100 two years from now has a present value or selling price of $82.64.

Now here is the big payoff. What is the price of a bond that pays $100 at the end of year one and another $100 at the end of year two? We can easily price this bond because this bond is just a combination of two bonds, one of which pays $100 at the end of year one and one of which pays $100 at the end of year two. But we just calculated the value of these bonds! And, because of arbitrage, the combination bond must sell for the same price as the sum of the two bonds that we calculated earlier or $173.55 = $90.91 + $82.64.

We can also calculate the value of the combination bond directly. When the interest rate is 10 percent, the PV of a bond that pays $100 in one year and another $100 in two years is:

$$PV = \frac{\$100}{1.10} + \frac{\$100}{(1.10) \times (1.10)} = \$173.55$$

Following through on the same logic, we can now calculate the price of very complicated bonds. The present value of a bond that makes potentially different payments every year for n years is:

$$PV = \frac{Payment_1}{(1 + r)} + \frac{Payment_2}{(1 + r)^2} + \frac{Payment_3}{(1 + r)^3} + \ldots \frac{FinalPayment_n}{(1 + r)^n}$$

Bond Pricing with a Spreadsheet

We can calculate the price of bonds like this using a spreadsheet. Figure A8.1 shows a bond that pays $100 in each of the first nine years and then in the tenth year it pays $1,000. The present value of each payment is calculated in Column C. Note that the formula in cell C2=B2/(1+$D$2)^A2 is equivalent to $\frac{Payment_1}{(1 + r)}$. Copying this formula for the nine other payments gives us a column of present values, which we sum up in cell C14 to find the price of the bond, $1,324.70.

FIGURE A8.1

C2			f_x =B2/(1+$D$2)^A2	
	A	B	C	D
1	Year	Payment	Present Value	Interest Rate
2	1	$100	$95.24	0.05
3	2	$100	$90.70	
4	3	$100	$86.38	
5	4	$100	$82.27	
6	5	$100	$78.35	
7	6	$100	$74.62	
8	7	$100	$71.07	
9	8	$100	$67.68	
10	9	$100	$64.46	
11	10	$1,000	$613.91	
12				
13		Sum PV		
14		or Price->	$1,324.70	

You can easily vary the interest rate to see what happens to the price of the bond. If the interest rate rises to 10 percent, for example, we have the result in Figure A8.2 on the next page.

FIGURE A8.2

			C14		f_x =SUM(C2:C11)	
		A	B	C	D
	1	Year	Payment	Present Value	Interest Rate
	2	1	$100	$90.91	0.1
	3	2	$100	$82.64	
	4	3	$100	$75.13	
	5	4	$100	$68.30	
	6	5	$100	$62.09	
	7	6	$100	$56.45	
	8	7	$100	$51.32	
	9	8	$100	$46.65	
	10	9	$100	$42.41	
	11	10	$1,000	$385.54	
	12				
	13		Sum PV		
	14		or Price->	$961.45	
	15				

And thus the price of the bond falls to $961.45. Note once again that a higher interest rate means a lower price for the bond. It's also interesting to see that a higher interest rate has a small effect on payments that come soon (compare the *PV* of the first payment in Figure A8.1 and Figure A8.2), but a very large effect on payments far into the future (compare the *PV* of the final payment in the two scenarios).

One final point of importance. Bond pricing might seem to be far away from your interests but the techniques in this appendix can be used to price and understand any kind of asset that has a payment stream over time. A mortgage, for example, is very similar to a bond except instead of receiving bond payments, you will typically be sending mortgage payments. If you want to compare two different mortgages, for example, a 20-year mortgage and a 30-year mortgage where the mortgages have different interest rates, you will want to compute the present value of each mortgage to find the one with the lowest *PV*. Online mortgage calculators help you to do this. What those calculators do is compute present values using the same types of techniques as found in this appendix.

9

Stock Markets and Personal Finance

In 1992, television reporter John Stossel decided to challenge the experts of Wall Street. As a student, Stossel had taken classes from economist Burton Malkiel whose book, *A Random Walk Down Wall Street,* claimed that the money and fame that went to stock-picking gurus was a sham and a waste. According to Malkiel: "a blindfolded monkey throwing darts at a newspaper's financial pages could select a portfolio that would do just as well as one carefully selected by experts."[1]

Instead of using a monkey, Stossel himself threw darts at a giant wall-sized version of the stock pages of the *Wall Street Journal.* Stossel followed his portfolio for nearly a year and compared the return to the portfolios picked by major Wall Street experts. Stossel's portfolio beat 90 percent of the experts! Not surprisingly, none of the experts would speak to him on camera about their humiliating loss. The lesson, according to Stossel, is that if you are paying an expert a lot of money to pick your stocks, it is probably you who are the monkey.

In this chapter, we explain why Stossel's amusing experiment is backed up by economic theory and by many careful empirical studies. We will also be giving you some investment advice in this chapter. No, we can't promise you the secret to getting rich. Most of the get rich quick schemes sold in books, investment seminars, and newsletters are scams. Economics, however, does provide some important lessons for investing wisely. We won't tell you how to get rich quick, but we can perhaps help you to get richer slowly.

Throughout this chapter, we emphasize a core principle of economics: there's no such thing as a free lunch. That's just another way of saying that you shouldn't expect something for nothing, or trade-offs are everywhere. Let's see how the principle applies to personal finance.

Passive vs. Active Investing

Many people invest in the stock market through a mutual fund. A mutual fund pools money from many customers and invests the money in many firms, in

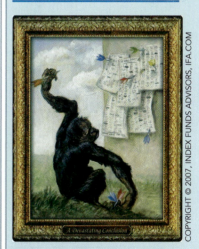

Better than the experts?

UNDERSTAND YOUR **world**

return, of course, for a management fee. Some of these mutual funds, called "active funds," are run by managers who try to pick stocks—these mutual funds often charge higher than average fees. Other mutual funds are called "passive funds" because they simply attempt to mimic a broad stock market index such as Standard and Poor's 500 (S&P 500), a basket of 500 large firms broadly representative of the U.S. economy.

Figure 9.1 shows that in a typical year passive investing in the S&P 500 Index beats about 60 percent of all mutual funds. In any given year, some mutual funds beat the index, but what is telling is that the funds that beat the index are different nearly every year! In other words, the funds that beat the index in one year probably just got lucky that year. One study that looked over 10 years found that passive investing beat 97.6 percent of all mutual funds![1] Overall, it is clear that very few mutual fund managers can consistently beat the market averages.

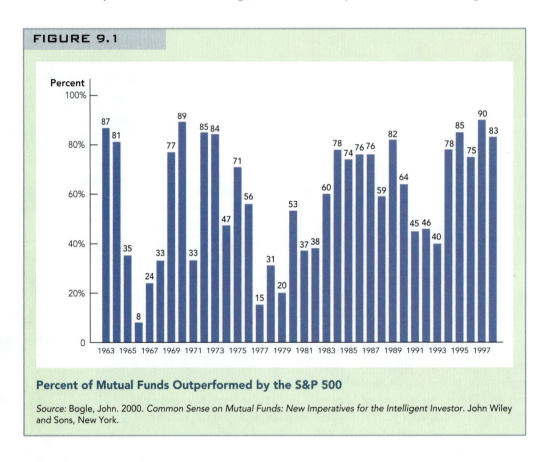

FIGURE 9.1

Percent of Mutual Funds Outperformed by the S&P 500

Source: Bogle, John. 2000. *Common Sense on Mutual Funds: New Imperatives for the Intelligent Investor.* John Wiley and Sons, New York.

It is possible that a very small number of experts can systematically beat the stock market. Sometimes Warren Buffett, who promotes long-term investing for value, is cited as an example of a person who sees farther than the rest of the market. He started out as a paperboy and worked his way up to $52 billion by purchasing undervalued stocks.

Some economists even think that Buffett, and a few others like him, just got lucky. If enough people are out there trying to pick stocks, you're going to have a few who get lucky many times in a row. Take a look at Figure 9.2. At the top of the figure, we start out with one thousand experts, each of whom flips a coin to predict whether the market will go up in the following year or down. After one year, 500 of the experts will turn out to be right. After two years, 250 experts

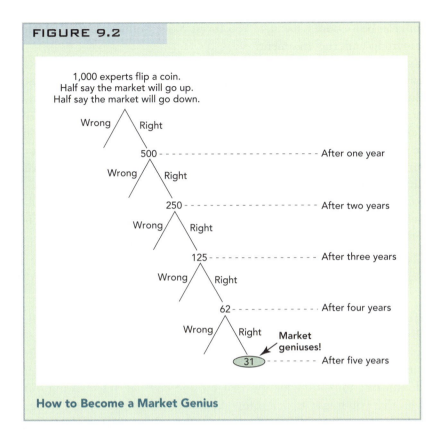

FIGURE 9.2

1,000 experts flip a coin.
Half say the market will go up.
Half say the market will go down.

How to Become a Market Genius

will have been right two years in a row. At the end of 5 years, just 31 out of 1,000 experts will have been right five years in a row. The experts who get it correct every time will be lauded as geniuses on CNBC and their advice will be eagerly sought. But the reality is that they just got lucky.

Is Buffett skilled or lucky? We're not so sure, but we do know this: Right now there is a small industry of people following the moves of Warren Buffett, trying to guess what he will say and do next. It is harder and harder for Buffett to get a big jump on the rest of the stock market. Even if Buffett could beat the market at first, it is not so clear he can beat the market any longer.

Warren Buffett: Genius investor or lucky as a monkey?

Why Is It Hard to Beat the Market?

These results aren't just an accident. Nor is it a statement about the stupidity of mutual fund managers. We know a few of these managers and most of them are pretty smart. Rather, the difficulty of beating the stock market is a tribute to the power of markets and the ability of market prices to reflect information.

Think about it this way: for every buyer of a stock there is a seller. The buyer thinks the price is going up, the seller thinks the price is going down. There is a disagreement. On average, who do you think is more likely to be correct, the buyer or the seller? Of course, the answer is neither. But if on average buyers and sellers have about the same amount of information, stock picking can't work very well.

Consider the following bit of pseudo-investment advice. The number of senior citizens will double by 2020. So the way to make money is to invest in companies that produce goods and services that senior citizens want, things like assisted living facilities, medical care for the elderly, and retirement homes. The baby boom can be a boom for you, If You Invest Now! Sounds plausible right? So, what's wrong with this argument?

All the premises in the argument are true: the baby boomers are retiring and the demand for goods and services that senior citizens want will increase in the future. But investing in firms that produce goods and services for senior citizens is not a sure road to riches. Why not? If it were, why would anyone sell their stock in these firms? Remember, for every buyer there is a seller. If you think the stock is a good buy, why is the seller selling? It's not a secret that the baby boomers are retiring so the stock price of firms that are likely to do well in the future *already* reflects this information.

The **efficient markets hypothesis** says that the prices of traded assets reflect all publicly available information.

Since for every buyer there is a seller, you can't get rich by buying and selling on *public information*. This idea is the foundation of what is called the **efficient markets hypothesis.** The best-known form of this hypothesis states:

> The prices of traded assets, such as stocks and bonds, reflects all publicly available information. Unless an investor is trading on inside information, he or she will not systematically outperform the market as a whole over time.

Let's be clear on what this means. It doesn't mean that market prices are always right, that markets are all powerful, or that traders are calm, cool, and rational people. It just means it is hard for ordinary investors (that probably means you too!) to systematically outperform the market, again unless a trader has inside information—information that no one else has. It's restating our above point that you might as well throw darts at the stock pages as try to figure out which companies will beat the market. The efficient markets hypothesis is just another way of saying there is no such thing as a free lunch.

So what happens if you do have some information that no one else has, then can you make money in the stock market? Yes, but you have to act very quickly. Within *minutes* of the news that the Russian nuclear power plant at Chernobyl had melted down, shares in U.S. nuclear power plant companies tumbled, the price of oil jumped as did the price of potatoes. Why potatoes? Clever traders on Wall Street figured out that the disaster at Chernobyl meant that the Ukrainian potato crop would be contaminated so they bought American potato futures to profit from the coming rise in prices. The traders who acted quickly made a lot of money, but as they bought and sold, prices changed and signaled to other people that something was up. Quite quickly the inside information became public information and the opportunities for profit evaporated.

The only way you can take advantage of information that other people don't have is to start buying or selling large numbers of shares. But once you start the buying or selling, the rest of the market knows something is up. That is why secrets do not last very long in the stock market and that is another reason why it is so hard to beat the market as a whole.

Some people believe that they have found exceptions to the efficient markets hypothesis. For instance, it is commonly believed that you can make more money by buying stocks when prices are low, or by buying right after prices have fallen. That sounds good, doesn't it? Buying at lower prices. It feels like what you do when you go to Wal-Mart. But a stock isn't like buying a lawn chair or a banana. The value of a stock is simply what its price will be in future periods of time. The banana, in contrast, you can simply eat for pleasure, no matter what the future price of bananas. Often lower prices mean that prices are going to stay low or fall even more and that means lower returns on owning stocks. Some studies find that you can do slightly better with your investments by buying right after prices have fallen. But do you know what? If you adjust those higher returns to account for the broker commissions that you have to pay for the extra trading, the higher returns pretty much go away.

A field of study known as "technical analysis" looks for much deeper patterns in stock and asset prices. Maybe you've heard on the financial news that stocks have "broken through a key support point," or "moved into a new trading range." If you dig deeper, you will find a claim that stock prices exhibit predictable mathematical patterns. For instance, if a stock hovers in the range of $100 a share but does not exceed that level, and one day goes over $100, it might be claimed that the stock is now expected to skyrocket to a much higher level. Hardly. One nice thing about studying the stock market is that there is a lot of very good data. One team of economists studied 7,846 different strategies of technical analysis. Their conclusion was that none of them systematically beat the market over time.[2]

For most investors, the efficient markets hypothesis looks like a pretty good description of reality.

CHECK YOURSELF

> Is it better to invest in a mutual fund that has performed well for five years in a row or one that has performed poorly for five years in a row? Use the efficient markets hypothesis to justify your answer.

How to Really Pick Stocks, Seriously

Okay, you probably can't beat the market without a lot of luck on your side. But we do still have four pieces of important advice. *Very* important advice. If you apply this advice over the course of your life, you will probably save thousands of dollars and if you become rich, you may save millions of dollars. (Suddenly this textbook seems like a real bargain!) No, we don't have a get rich quick formula for you, but there are a few simple mistakes you can avoid to your benefit and at no real cost, other than a bit of time and attention. Let's go through each piece of advice in turn.

Diversify

The first secret to picking stocks is to pick lots of them! Since picking stocks doesn't work well, the "secret" to wise investing is to invest in a large basket of stocks—to diversify. Diversification lowers the risk of your portfolio, how much your portfolio fluctuates in value over time.

By picking a lot of stocks, you limit your overall exposure to things going wrong in any particular company. When the energy company Enron went bankrupt in 2001, many Enron employees had put most of their life's wealth in . . . can you guess . . . Enron stock. That's a huge mistake, whether you work at the company or not. If you put all your eggs in one basket, it is a disaster if the handle on that basket breaks. Instead, you should buy many different stocks, in many different sectors of the economy, and, yes, in many countries too. You'll end up with some Enrons, but you'll also have some big winners, such as Google and Microsoft. And if Google and Microsoft have become Enrons and gone under since this book was published, well, that is just further reason why you should diversify!

Modern financial markets have made diversification easy. Mutual funds let you invest in hundreds of stocks with just one purchase. And since stock picking doesn't work well, diversification has no downside—it reduces risk without reducing your expected return.

We are focusing on diversification across stocks but there are all kinds of risks in the world and you should diversify across as many as possible. U.S.

stocks, for example, tend to fluctuate in value along with the growth rate of the U.S. economy. You can reduce this source of risk by including a large number of international firms in your portfolio. Bonds, art, housing, and human capital (your knowledge and skills) all have associated returns and risks and for a given amount of return, you minimize your risk by diversifying across many assets.

If you accept the efficient markets hypothesis, and you accept the value of diversification, your best trading strategy can be summed up very simply. It is called **buy and hold**. That's right, buy a large bundle of stocks and just hold them. You don't have to do anything more. You will be diversified, you will not be trying to beat the market, and you can live a peaceful, quiet life.

Buy and hold: buy stocks and then hold them for the long run, regardless of what prices do in the short run.

Some of the simplest ways to buy and hold mean that you replicate the well-known stock indexes. Just for your knowledge, here are a few of those indexes:

The Dow Jones Industrial Average (or the Dow for short) is the most famous stock price index. The Dow is composed of 30 leading American stocks, each of these counted equally, whether the company is large or small. The Dow is not a very diversified index.

The Standard and Poor's 500 (S&P 500) is a much broader index of stock prices than the Dow; as the name indicates it consists of the prices of five hundred different stocks. Unlike in the Dow, the larger companies receive greater weight in the index than the smaller companies. The S&P 500 is a better indicator of the market as a whole than is the Dow.

The NASDAQ Composite Index averages the prices of all the companies traded on NASDAQ, or National Association of Securities Dealers Automated Quotations. This usually amounts to a few thousand securities, as of 2009 2,916, but of course the number changes all the time. The NASDAQ index gives especially high weight to small stocks and high-tech stocks, at least relative to the Dow or the S&P 500.

Notice that diversification changes our understanding of what makes a stock risky, or not risky. You might at first think that a risky stock is one whose price moves up and down a lot. Not exactly. If investors are diversified, and indeed most of them are, their risk depends on how much their portfolio moves up and down, not how much a single stock moves up and down. A single stock might move up and down all the time but still an overall diversified portfolio won't change in value much if some of your stocks are moving up while others are moving down.

According to finance economists, the riskiest stocks are those that move up and down in harmony with the market. For instance, many real estate stocks are risky because they are highly cyclical. They move up a lot when times are good (and the rest of the market is high) and they move down a lot when times are bad. When a recession comes, a lot of people just can't afford to buy a new house. In contrast, for an example of a relatively safe stock, consider Wal-Mart, the discount outlet. When bad times come, yes, Wal-Mart loses some business. But Wal-Mart also gains some business because people who used to shop at Nordstrom now have less money and some of them will now shop at Wal-Mart. In this regard, Wal-Mart is partly protected from business downturns.[3] Many health care stocks are safe in a similar way. Even if times are bad, you're probably not going to postpone that triple bypass operation; if you do, you won't be around to see when times are good again. In other words, if you care about the risk of a stock, don't just look at how the price of that stock moves. Look at how the price varies with the rest of the market. In the language of finance economists or statisticians, the riskiest stocks are those with the highest *covariance* with the market as a whole.

The lesson here is that if you are worried about risk, think about your portfolio as a whole, rather than obsessing over any single stock. Or let's be more specific: if you are going to become an aerospace engineer, don't buy a lot of stock in aerospace companies. The value of your human capital—which is worth a lot—is already tied up in that industry. Don't make your overall portfolio riskier by putting more eggs in that basket. If anything, buy stocks that do well when aerospace does poorly. More generally, finance theorists say that the least risky assets *for you* are assets that are *negatively correlated* with *your portfolio*. What this means is that you should try to buy assets that rise in value when the rest of your portfolio is falling in value. Are you afraid that high energy prices will cripple the prospects for your career? Buy stock in a company that builds roads in Saudi Arabia. If oil prices stay high, the gains of that road-building company will partially offset your other losses. The lesson applies to more than stocks. If you become a dentist, you run the risk that a new technology will eliminate cavities. So try to limit your risk by diversifying your portfolio: marry an optician or an engineer, not another dentist!

Avoid High Fees

We have some other advice for picking stocks. Avoid investments and mutual funds that have high fees or "loads," as they are sometimes called. It simply isn't worth it.

Let's say for instance that you wish to invest in the S&P 500. Some funds charge management and administrative fees of 0.09 percent of your investment but other funds can charge up to 2.5 percent per year for what is really the same thing! Table 9.1 shows some of the different options for investing in the S&P 500 and their expense ratios, the yearly percentage of your investment that you must pay in fees to the fund's managers.

TABLE 9.1 Don't Pay Higher Fees for the Same Service	
S&P Index Fund	Expense Ratio
Vanguard 500 Index Mutual Fund Admiral Shares (VFIAX)	0.09%
Fidelity Spartan 500 Index Mutual Fund (FSMKX)	0.10%
State Street Global Advisors S&P 500 Index Fund (SVSPX)	0.16%
United Association S&P 500 Index Fund II (UAIIX)	0.16%
USAA S&P 500 Index Mutual Fund Member Shares (USSPX)	0.18%
Schwab S&P 500 Index Fund—Select Shares (SWPPX)	0.19%
Vantagepoint 500 Stock Index Mutual Fund Class II Shares (VPSKX)	0.25%
T. Rowe Price Equity Index 500 Mutual Fund (PREIX)	0.35%
California Investment S&P 500 Index Mutual Fund (SPFIX)	0.36%
MassMutual Select Indexed Equity A (MIEAX)	0.67%
MassMutual Select Indexed Equity N (MMINX)	0.97%
ProFunds Bull Svc, Inv (BLPSX)	2.50%

The funds with the higher fees don't give you much of value in return. The lesson is simple: don't pay the higher fees!

Often when your broker calls you up to make a stock purchase, that purchase involves a relatively high fee (have you ever wondered why the broker is making the call?). Before buying or selling a stock in these circumstances, you should ask what the fee is to make the transaction. Understand the incentives of the person you are dealing with and that means understand that the broker usually earns more, the greater the number of transactions he or she can get you to make. Might that explain why he or she is telling you to buy or sell? Or maybe this really is a "once in a lifetime opportunity."

Even small fees can add up to large differences in returns over time. Let's say you are investing $10,000 over 30 years. If you invest with a firm that charges 0.10 percent a year in fees and the stock market gives a real return of 7 percent a year, then in 30 years you will have earned $74,016. If you invest in a firm that charges 1 percent a year, then in 30 years you will have about $57,434. The higher fees cost you $16,582 and, as we showed above, you probably got nothing for your extra fees. When we looked at economic growth, we saw that small differences in growth or loss rates, when compounded over time, make for a big difference. The same is true for your portfolio.

That brings us to a corollary principle, to which we now turn.

Compound Returns Build Wealth

If one investment earns a higher rate of return each year than another investment, in the long run that makes a big difference. To make this more concrete, if you have a long time horizon you probably should invest in (diversified) stocks rather than bonds.

In the long run, stocks offer higher returns than bonds. Since 1802, for example, stocks have had an average real rate of return of about 7 percent per year while bonds have paid closer to 2 percent per year.[4] Using our now familiar rule of 70, we know that money that grows at 7 percent a year will double in 10 years, but money that grows at 2 percent a year won't double for 35 years. Alternatively, growing at 7 percent a year, $10,000 will return $76,122 in 30 years but if it grows at 2 percent a year, the return will be only $18,113.

Stocks, however, have the potential for greater losses than do bonds because bond holders and other creditors are always paid before shareholders. You are unlikely to lose much money if you buy high grade corporate or government bonds, but the stock market is highly volatile and it does periodically crash. Nonetheless, in American history stocks almost always outperform bonds over any 20-year time period you care to examine, including the period of the Great Depression and World War II. Stocks are simply the better long-term investment.

Of course, that doesn't mean that everyone should invest so heavily in stocks. In any particular year, or even over the course of a month, week, or day, stocks can go down in value quite a bit. If you are 80 years old and managing your retirement income, you probably shouldn't invest much in stocks. If you have to send your twins to college in two years' time, you might want some safer investments as well. Nor does the past necessarily predict the future—just because stocks outperformed bonds in the past doesn't mean that will continue to happen. Remember to diversify!

The No Free Lunch Principle or No Return Without Risk

The differences between stocks and bonds, as investment vehicles, reflect a more general principle. There is a systematic **trade-off between return and risk**. Figure 9.3, for example, shows the trade-off between return and risk on four asset classes. U.S. T-bills are safe but have low returns. You can get a higher return by buying stock in a group of large firms such as in the S&P 500, but the value of those firms fluctuates a lot more than the value of T-bills so to get the higher return you need to bear higher risk.*

The **risk-return trade-off** means higher returns come at the price of higher risk.

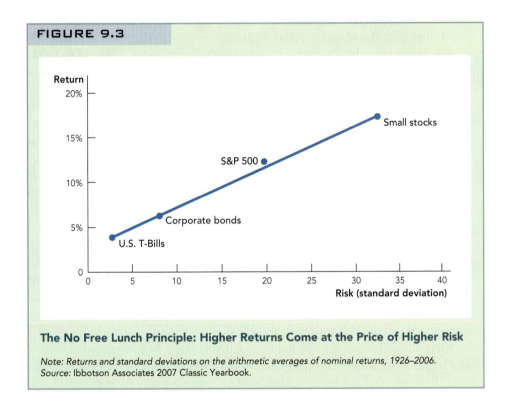

FIGURE 9.3

The No Free Lunch Principle: Higher Returns Come at the Price of Higher Risk

Note: Returns and standard deviations on the arithmetic averages of nominal returns, 1926–2006.
Source: Ibbotson Associates 2007 Classic Yearbook.

If you want even more risk than an investment in the stock market, numerous schemes give you a chance of making a killing. The simplest of such strategies is to take all your money, fly to Las Vegas, and bet on "black" for a spin of the roulette wheel. Yes, there is a 47.37 percent chance that you double your wealth. That's a high return, sort of. Sadly, there is also a 52.63 percent chance that you will lose everything you have, including your credit rating and the trust of your spouse and children. That's what we call high risk.

Remember this story when you hear about a high-flying "hedge fund" or other fancy investment device. It's easy to generate high returns for a few years by getting lucky and doubling down (betting all your winnings again). Take a look again at Figure 9.2. But higher returns come at the expense of higher risk.

---

* We measure risk using the standard deviation of the portfolio return. The standard deviation is a measure of how much the return tends to fluctuate from its average level: thus, the larger the standard deviation, the greater the risk. A rule of thumb is that there is a 68 percent probability of being within ±1 standard deviation of the mean return. For the S&P 500, for example, the mean return is about 12 percent and the standard deviation is about 20 percent so in any given year there is a 68 percent probability that the return will be between −8 percent and 32 percent. Of course, something else could happen with probability 32 percent! But beware! The rule of thumb is only an approximation. Risk in the real world can rarely be modeled with perfect mathematical accuracy.

This no free lunch principle can help you evaluate some other investments as well. Let's say you come into a tidy sum of money and you start wondering whether or not you should invest in art. Overall, should you expect art to be a better or inferior financial investment, compared to the market as a whole?

A lot of people—probably most people—buy art because they want to look at it. They enjoy hanging it on their walls. In the language of economics, art yields "a nonmonetary return," which is just our way of saying it is fun to look at. Now suppose that investments in art earned just as high a return as investments in stocks. In that case, art would be fun to have on the wall and would be an excellent investment. But wait, that sounds like a free lunch doesn't it? So what does the no free lunch principle predict?

We know that the expected returns on different assets, adjusted for risk, should be equal—this is the arbitrage principle we discussed in Chapter 8. So if some asset yields a higher "fun" return those assets should, on average, yield a lower financial return. And that is exactly what we find with art. On average, art underperforms the stock market by a few percentage points a year. You can think of the lower returns as the price of having some beautiful art on your wall. Again, it's the no free lunch principle in action.

This kind of analysis applies not just to art but also to real estate. Let's say you want to buy a home. Can you expect superior or inferior financial returns over time? This question is a little trickier than the art question because two different and opposing forces operate. Let's look at each in turn.

First, a home tends to be a risky asset for most purchasers. Let's say you buy a $300,000 home by putting down $200,000 and borrowing the remainder. That home is probably a pretty big chunk of your overall wealth and it puts you in a relatively nondiversified position. That's risk, people don't usually like risk, and as we saw above riskier assets earn, all other things equal, higher expected returns (the risk-return trade-off).

Second, and probably more important, if you buy a house you get to live in it. The house, like the painting, provides you with personal services and in this case those services are pretty valuable. Many people enjoy their backyard and the feeling of owning a home and being able to paint the walls any color they want. These nonmonetary returns mean that houses can be expected to pay a relatively low financial return.

Indeed, if we look at the financial returns on real estate over a long time horizon, it turns out they are pretty low. In fact, for pretty long periods of time the average financial rate of return on real estate is not much different than zero. One lesson is that houses must be lots of fun!

If you want to see that the downside of real estate investments is not just a recent phenomenon, take a look at Figure 9.4.

In the 50 years from 1947 to 1997, real housing prices hardly changed at all with some blips upward in the late 1970s and late 1980s. Beginning in 1997, a housing boom pushed prices well above any before seen in U.S. history. As you probably know, however, since 2006 prices have tumbled and may be even lower by the time you read this book.

The lesson is that most of the time a house is a good place to live but not a good place to invest. When prices started to rise in 1997 and kept rising year after year, many people thought that real estate was the investment of the century—"they ain't making any more," people said. But the no free lunch principle tells us that precisely because houses are a good place to live, we should not also expect them to be a good investment. All other things equal, fun activities yield lower financial returns than non-fun activities.

FIGURE 9.4

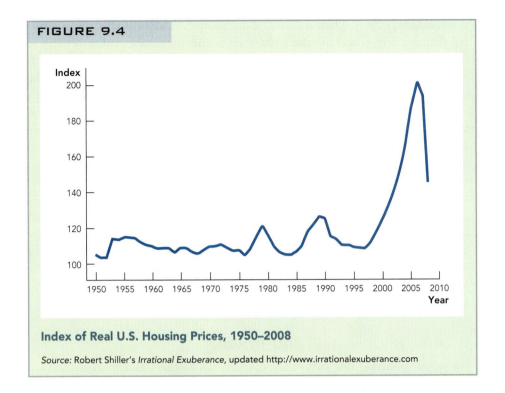

Index of Real U.S. Housing Prices, 1950–2008

Source: Robert Shiller's *Irrational Exuberance*, updated http://www.irrationalexuberance.com

When prices rose, some people got lucky and made a killing, but other people tried to do the same and ended up bankrupt. So don't expect to make a killing in the real estate market and remember to diversify! One more point. Are you one of these people who doesn't like to mow the lawn? Do you dread the notion of choosing homeowner's insurance or worrying about when your roof will fall in? The lesson is simple: don't buy a house, you won't have fun and the financial returns won't make it worth your while.

Other Benefits and Costs of Stock Markets

Throughout this chapter we've recommended against gambling with all or most of your money. We've recommended buy and hold, based on a diversified portfolio. But hey, maybe some of you are into gambling. You know what? If you want to take risk for the sake of risk alone, the U.S. stock market offers the best odds in the world, better than Las Vegas and better than your local bookie. In the U.S. stock market, people on average make money and that is because the productive capacity of the U.S. economy is expanding through economic growth. There is more profit to go around and that means you have a good chance of making some really lucrative investments.

Stocks markets have uses beyond investment. First, as explained in Chapter 8, new stock and bond issues are an important means of raising capital for new investment (investment now in the economic sense of increasing the capital stock). Stock markets also reward successful entrepreneurs and thus encourage people to start companies and look around for new ideas. The founders of Google are now very rich and selling company shares to the stock market helped make them so. A well-functioning stock market helps companies such as Google get going or expand.

Second, the stock market gives us a better idea of how well firms are run. The stock price is a signal about the value of the firm. When the stock price is

UNDERSTAND YOUR **world**

CHECK YOURSELF

> How does investing in stocks of other countries help to diversify your investments?

> Many people dream of owning a football or baseball team. Would you expect the return on these assets to be relatively high or low?

increasing, especially when it is increasing relative to other stocks, this is a signal that the firm is making the right investments for future profits. When the stock is declining, especially when it is declining relative to other stocks, this is a signal that something has gone wrong and perhaps management needs to be replaced. Some critics allege that Google has dominated search but failed with its maps, blog search services, and email accounts. It is not necessarily clear whether these endeavors are making money for the company. Will Google make YouTube into a profitable venture? Are the charges true that "Google has lost it"? It's hard to say in the abstract. But we can look at Google's share price and see if it is going up or down. Market prices give the public a daily report on whether the managers of a company are succeeding or failing.

Third, stock markets are a way of transferring company control from less competent people to more competent people. If a group of people think they know the right way to run a company, they can buy it and put their money where their mouth is, so to speak. Maybe a company should be merged, broken up, or simply look for a new direction. The stock market is the ultimate venue where people bid for the right to make these decisions.

Bubble, Bubble, Toil, and Trouble

It's worth pointing out that stock markets (and other asset markets) have a downside, namely that they can encourage speculative bubbles. A speculative bubble arises when stock prices rise far higher, and more rapidly, than can be accounted for by the fundamental prospects of the companies at hand. Bubbles are based in human psychology and often they are hard to understand, but it seems that at times investors simply get carried away by the prospects for gain and they are not sufficiently sensitive toward the prospects for loss. For instance, many of the new Internet or dot.com stocks had very high prices, circa 2000, even though many of these companies had never earned a dime of profit or for that matter any revenue. Many of the tech stocks were listed on the NASDAQ stock exchange. As you can see in Figure 9.5, in the space of five years the NASDAQ Composite Index more than tripled from a monthly average of about 1,200 to over 4,000 before falling back down again. Many people made a lot of money on the ride up and many people—maybe the same people, maybe others—lost a lot of money on the ride down.

If you can spot speculative bubbles on a consistent basis, yes, you can become very wealthy. But, of course, a speculative bubble is usually easier to detect with hindsight than at the time. Microsoft and Google might have looked like speculative bubbles too; the only problem is that they never burst. Betting too soon that high prices will end is also one way to go bankrupt.

Speculative bubbles are especially hard to spot, in advance, for durable assets such as homes and stocks. We already saw in Chapter 8 that relatively small changes in real interest rates can have big changes in the value of a bond; the same logic is true for stocks and homes as well. If we are discounting the future at a lower rate, assets that pay off in the future can be worth much more. So let's suppose that we see a big run-up in the price of homes or stocks. Is that a bubble? Or is it the market deciding that future values should be discounted at a lower rate? It's not always so easy to tell.

Speculative bubbles, and their bursting, can hurt an economy. During the rise of the bubble, capital is invested in areas where it is not actually very valuable. This was the case with many dot.com firms circa 2000 and also the case

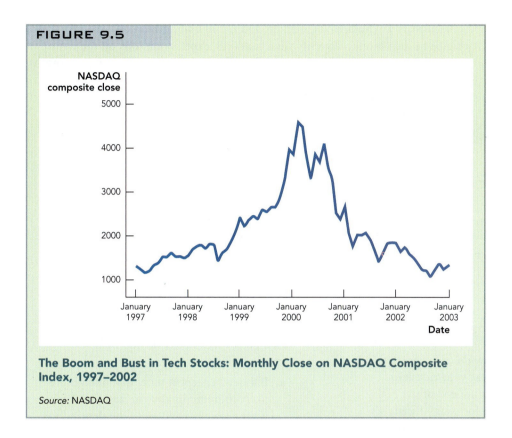

FIGURE 9.5

The Boom and Bust in Tech Stocks: Monthly Close on NASDAQ Composite Index, 1997–2002

Source: NASDAQ

with real estate in the years leading up to the crash of the real estate bubble in 2007–2008. That bubble, by the way, had less to do with stocks but a lot to do with financial assets that were backed by portfolios of mortgages. The analysis of these "asset-backed securities" is similar to that for stocks.

A second wave of problems comes when the bubble crashes. Lower stock prices (or lower home prices) mean that people feel poorer and so they will spend less. This is a negative shock to aggregate demand, a concept we will be explaining at greater length in Chapter 12 (see also Chapter 15 on monetary policy and Chapter 17 on fiscal policy). The collapse of the bubble also means that workers must move from one sector to another, such as from high tech to retailing, or from real estate to export industries. Shifting labor from one sector of an economy to another creates labor adjustment costs, a concept we discuss at greater length in Chapter 13.

Yes, bubbles can be a problem, but few people doubt that we are better off with active trading in stock and asset markets. One partial solution is to have greater transparency in assessing the value of companies and assets. But at least for now there is no surefire solution for getting rid of asset bubbles.

CHECK YOURSELF

> The Federal Reserve has been criticized for not stepping in and bursting the housing bubble, which would have prevented the housing collapse. Do you think this criticism is valid, based on what you read in this section?

□ Takeaway

We have stressed some simple and practical points. It is hard for an investor to consistently beat the market over long periods. You are well advised to diversify your investments. Avoid fees and try to generate a high compound return over time. Understand that the promise of higher returns is often accompanied by higher risk.

Viewed as a whole, stock markets and other trading markets give investors a chance to earn money, diversify their holdings, express opinions on the course of the market, and hedge risks. Stock markets also play a role in financing innovative new firms. Stock markets appear to be subject to speculative bubbles, but active stock markets are an important part of a healthy growing economy.

□ CHAPTER REVIEW

KEY CONCEPTS

Efficient markets hypothesis, p. 180

Buy and hold, p. 182

Risk-return trade-off, p. 185

FACTS AND TOOLS

1. Before we plunge into the world of finance, let's review the rule of 70. Suppose your rich aunt hands you a $3,000 check at the end of the school year. She tells you it's for your education. But what should you *really* do with that extra money? Let's see how much it would be worth if you saved it for a while.

    a. If you put it in a bank account earning 2 percent real annual return on average, how many years would it take before it was worth $6,000? Until it was worth $12,000?

    b. If you put it in a Standard and Poor's 500 (S&P 500) mutual fund earning an average 7 percent real return every year, how many years would it take before it was worth $6,000? Until it was worth $12,000? (Note: $3,000 is the minimum investment for many low-fee mutual funds.)

    c. Suppose you invest a little less than half your money in the bank and a little more than half in a mutual fund, just to play it somewhat safe, so that you can expect a 5 percent real return on average. How many years now until you reach $6,000 and $12,000? (Yes, ignore the fact that you won't have enough money to make the $3,000 minimum investment in the mutual fund.)

2. Let's do something boring just to drive home a point: Count up the number of years in Figure 9.1 where more than half of the mutual funds

managed to beat the S&P 500 index. (Recall that the Standard and Poor's 500 is just a list of 500 large U.S. corporations—it's a list that overlaps a lot with the Fortune 500). What percentage of the time did the experts actually beat the S&P 500?

3. Consider the supply and demand for oranges. Orange crops can be destroyed by below-freezing temperatures.

    a. If a weather report states that oranges are likely to freeze in a storm later this week, what probably happens to the demand for oranges *today*, before the storm comes?

    b. According to a simple supply-and-demand model, what happens to the price of oranges today given your answer to part a.

    c. How does this illustrate the idea that stock prices *today* "bake in" information about *future* events? In other words, how is a share of Microsoft like an orange? (Note: Wall Street people often use the expression "That news is already baked into the price" when they talk about the efficient markets hypothesis.)

4. In the United States, high-level corporate officials have to publicly state when they buy or sell a large number of shares in their own company. They have to make these statements a few days after their purchase or sale. What do you think probably happens (choose a, b, c or d below) when newspapers report these true "insider trades?" (Note: The right answer according to theory is actually true in practice.)

    a. When insiders sell, prices rise, since investors increase their demand for the company's shares.

    b. When insiders sell, prices fall, since investors increase their demand for the company's shares.

c. When insiders sell, prices fall, since investors decrease their demand for the company's shares.

d. When insiders sell, prices rise, since investors decrease their demand for the company's shares.

5. Let's see how fees can hurt your investment strategy. Let's assume that your mutual fund grows at an average rate of 7 percent per year—before subtracting off the fees. Using the rule of 70:

a. How many years will it take for your money to double if fees are 0.5 percent per year?

b. How many years will it take for your money to double if fees are 1.5 percent per year (not uncommon in the mutual fund industry)?

c. How many years to double if fees are 2.5 percent per year?

6. a. If you talk to a broker selling the high-fee mutual fund, what will he or she probably tell you when you ask them, "Am I getting my money's worth when I pay your high fees?"

b. According to Figure 9.1, is your broker's answer likely to be right most of the time?

THINKING AND PROBLEM SOLVING

1. Your brother calls you on the phone telling you that Google's share price has fallen by about 25 percent over the past few days. Now you can own one small slice of Google for only $430 a share (the price on the day this question was written). Your brother says he is pretty sure the stock is going to head back up to $600 very soon and you should buy.

Should you believe your brother? Hint: Remember someone is selling shares whenever someone else is buying.

2. In most of your financial decisions early in life, you'll be a buyer, but let's think about the incentives of people who sell stocks, bonds, bank accounts, and other financial products.

a. Walking in the shopping mall one day, you see a new store: The Dollar Store. Of course, you've seen plenty of dollar stores before, but none like this one: The sign in the window says "Dollars for sale: Fifty cents each." Why will this store be out of business soon?

b. If business owners are self-interested and fairly rational people, will they ever open up this "Dollar Store" in the first place? Why or why not?

c. This "Dollar Store" is similar to stories people tell about "cheap stocks" that you might hear about on the news. Fill in the blank with any prices that make sense: "If the shares of this company were really worth _____, no one would really sell it for _____."

3. How is "stock market diversification" like putting money in a bank account? (Hint: See the previous chapter, which lists the functions that banks actually perform.)

4. Warren Buffett often says that he doesn't want a lot of diversification in his portfolio. He says that diversification means buying stocks that go up along with stocks that go down; but he only wants to buy the stocks that go up! From the point of view of the typical investor, what is wrong with this reasoning?

5. You own shares in a pharmaceutical company, PillCo. Reading the Yahoo! Finance website, you see that PillCo was sued this morning by users of PillCo's new heart drug, Amphlistatin. PillCo's stock has already been trading for a few hours today.

a. When the bad news about the lawsuits came out, what probably happened to the price of PillCo shares within just a few minutes?

b. According to the efficient markets hypothesis, should you sell your shares in PillCo now, a few hours after the bad news came out?

c. In many statistical studies of the stock market, the best strategy turns out to be "buy and hold." This means just what it sounds like: You buy a bunch of shares in different companies and hold them through good times and bad. People often have a tough time with the "bad" part of "holding through good times and bad." What does your answer to part b tell you about this idea?

CHALLENGES

1. Ultimately, a firm is worth what it pays out to its shareholders in dividends. Imagine that beginning next year, a firm pays out the same dividend every year forever. Then, the present value of this stream of dividend payments is:

$$PV = \frac{Dividend}{1 + r} + \frac{Dividend}{(1 + r)^2} +$$

$$\frac{Dividend}{(1 + r)^3} + \cdots \frac{Dividend}{(1 + r)^n} + \cdots$$

where r is the interest rate that we use to discount future payments. (We derived a similar expression in our explanation of bond pricing in the appendix to Chapter 8.) Since no one will want to buy the share for more than its present value, this is also the price of a share of the firm's stock. Infinite series like the above can often be simplified and in this case the present value simplifies to the following:

$$PV = \frac{Dividend}{r}$$

Thus, if the firm is expected to pay a dividend of $10 forever and the interest rate is 7 percent or 0.07, then the value of a share in the firm is $\frac{\$10}{.07} = \$142.86$. Firms aren't expected to last forever, of course, but in many cases that assumption has a surprisingly small effect on the results. A firm expected to pay the same $10 dividend for 30 years, for example, will have a present value of $122.77, almost as high as if it were expected to pay out forever! A slightly more extensive model, called the Gordon growth model, allows for the possibility that dividends might be expected to grow at a constant rate, in which case the infinite series simplifies to the following:

$$PV = \frac{Dividend}{r - g}$$

where g is the expected growth rate of dividends. Now here is the question. Use a calculator or spreadsheet to experiment with different levels of r and g. What happens to the value of the firm when $r > g$ but g gets close to r? When g gets close to r, how do small changes in g affect the stock price? Use this experiment to comment on the difficulty of defining bubbles.

2. What is so bad about bubbles? If the price of Internet stocks or housing rises and then falls, is that such a big problem? After all, some people say, most of the gains going up are "paper gains" and most of the losses going down are "paper losses." Comment on this view.

10

Unemployment and Labor Force Participation

Thirty-six thousand travel agents lost their jobs on November 10, 1999. Actually, it didn't happen quite that fast, but when Expedia.com went public there were 124,000 travel agents in the United States but by 2006 there were less than 88,000. Even though tourism is increasing, travel agents are disappearing as more people book their travel online.

The disappearance of the travel agent represents a recurring story in American history. Many jobs have disappeared—blacksmiths, chimney sweeps, and darkroom technicians, for example, are no longer in demand. Employment in other fields has greatly declined. For example, in 1910 there were 11.5 million farm workers in the United States; today there are less than a million. New jobs, however, have replaced old jobs. Typewriter repairmen are no longer in demand but the Geek Squad, an "elite tactical unit of highly trained Agents that focus solely on computer and other technology support," is hiring. Jobs are growing rapidly in high-tech areas like software engineering and the biosciences, but a wealthier society also means more and better-paying jobs in professions that have been around for a long time. Today, for example, there are over 212,000 professional athletes in the United States—more than in any other country or any other time in history.

A growing economy is a changing economy and *some* unemployment is a necessary consequence of economic growth. The unemployment rate in France, however, has hovered around 10 percent for several decades. High and long-lasting unemployment is unlikely to be caused by economic growth. Thus, there are different types of unemployment with different causes.

Figure 10.1 on the next page illustrates the organization of this chapter. We are going to start at the top with the issue that is most prominent in the economics and business news, namely whether or not workers are employed. We explain

Typewriter repairmen are gone but the Geek Squad has hired thousands of Geeks in the last several years.

LOGO COURTESY OF GEEK SQUAD

FIGURE 10.1

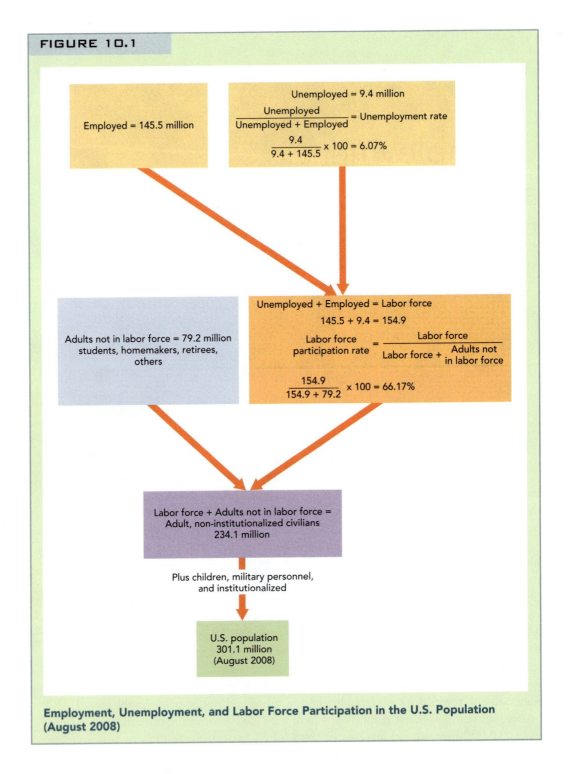

Employment, Unemployment, and Labor Force Participation in the U.S. Population (August 2008)

how unemployment is defined and then the different types of unemployment and their causes.

Don't forget, however, that many individuals neither have a job nor are looking for work—these individuals are not part of the labor force. As we move down the tree we will ask: Why do some people choose to be in the labor force while others do not? Why is it, for example, that most women are in the (paid) labor force today even though this was uncommon in the 1950s? And why is labor force participation for some workers much higher in some countries than in others? The topic of labor force participation makes up the second half of the chapter. And what about total population, at the very bottom of this structure? For that you must take a demography course, but you'll even find a brief discussion of birth control at the close of the chapter.

Defining Unemployment

Is a 6-year-old without a job unemployed? Is someone in prison unemployed? What about a retired 60-year-old? In all cases the answer is no. We want to count someone as **unemployed** only if they are *willing and able to work but cannot find a job.* In practice, this means to be counted as unemployed, a person must be an adult (16 years or older), not institutionalized (e.g., not in prison), a civilian, and, most important, they must be *looking for work.* Similarly, to be counted as employed, a person must be an adult, noninstitutionalized civilian with a job.

In August 2008, there were 9.4 million unemployed persons in the United States and 145.5 million employed persons. Together, the unemployed and the employed make up the **labor force** of 154.9 million (9.4 + 145.5).

The **unemployment rate** is the percentage of the labor force without a job.

$$\text{Unemployment rate} = \frac{\text{Unemployed}}{\text{Unemployed} + \text{Employed}} \times 100$$

$$= \frac{\text{Unemployed}}{\text{Labor force}} \times 100$$

Thus, in August 2008, the unemployment rate was 6.07 percent:

$$\frac{9.4 \text{ million}}{9.4 \text{ million} + 145.5 \text{ million}} \times 100 = \frac{9.4}{154.9} \times 100 = 6.07\%$$

Once we have examined the issue of unemployment, we will investigate some of the determinants of the **labor force participation rate,** the percentage of the adult, civilian, noninstitutionalized population (adults for short) in the labor force.

Figure 10.1 summarizes our discussion by showing how the U.S. population is divided among the employed, the unemployed, and those not in the labor force.

How Good an Indicator Is the Unemployment Rate?

We are interested in the unemployment rate because unemployment, especially long-term unemployment, can be financially and psychologically devastating to the unemployed individuals and their families. Unemployment also means that the economy is underperforming—labor that could be used to produce valuable goods and services is being wasted. The unemployment rate is the single best indicator of how well the labor market is working in both of these senses, but it is an incomplete indicator.

Individuals without a job are not counted as unemployed if they are not actively looking for work. But some people who are unemployed for a long period of time may get discouraged and stop looking for work even though they want a job. It's difficult to know exactly how many **discouraged workers** there

Unemployed workers are adults who do not have a job but who are looking for work.

The **labor force** is all workers, employed plus unemployed.

The **unemployment rate** is the percentage of the labor force without a job.

The **labor force participation rate** is the percentage of adults in the labor force.

Discouraged workers are workers who have given up looking for work but who would still like a job.

>> **SEARCH ENGINE**

Statistics on unemployment and alternative measures of labor underutilization can be found at the Bureau of Labor Statistics.

are because the concept is not well defined. Many people who are happily retired would take a job if the wage were high enough, but should every retired person count as a discouraged worker? The Bureau of Labor Statistics (BLS) keeps statistics on one definition of discouraged workers, which it defines as workers who have not looked for a job in the past four weeks but who are available for work and who have looked for work in the past 12 months. Using this definition, the number of discouraged workers in the United States is small (approximately 0.3 percent of the labor force in 2008).

The unemployment rate also doesn't measure the quality of the jobs people take or how well workers are matched to their jobs. A taxi driver with a PhD in chemistry, for example, is counted as fully employed by the BLS. Similarly, a worker who has a part-time job but who wants a full-time job is counted as fully employed. If we counted these workers as partially unemployed, the unemployment rate would be higher, but defining and measuring partial employment isn't easy. If a taxi driver has a BA in English, should that be counted as almost fully employed? Nearly everyone wants a better job in some dimension (more hours, fewer hours, closer to home, higher wages, better benefits, etc.) so is everyone less than fully employed?

Given these imperfections, economists also look at other measures of labor underutilization and indicators of how well the labor market is performing, such as the labor force participation rate, the number of full-time jobs, and average wages. Fortunately, most of these other indicators (and probably many other job aspects that are more difficult to measure) correlate well with the official unemployment rate. (See Thinking and Problem Solving question #11 for more on this.) When the unemployment rate goes down, for example, wages and benefits usually go up.

Frictional Unemployment

Economists distinguish three types of unemployment: frictional, structural, and cyclical. We start with frictional.

What is the fastest way to sell a house? Lower the price! At a low enough price, any house will sell quickly. So selling houses is easy: It's finding a price that the seller is willing to accept and the buyer is willing to pay that is difficult. In the same way, it's always easy to find a job if you are willing to work for peanuts. Finding a job that you want at a wage that you will accept and the employer will pay, however, takes time and effort. The difficulty of matching employees to employers creates friction in the labor market, and the resulting temporary unemployment is called frictional unemployment. Thus, **frictional unemployment** is short-term unemployment caused by the ordinary difficulties of matching employee to employer.

Scarcity of information is one of the causes of frictional unemployment. Workers do not know all of the job opportunities available to them and employers do not know all the available candidates and their respective qualifications. The Internet has probably lowered the underlying rate of frictional unemployment by making it easier for workers to search for jobs and for firms to search for workers.

Frictional unemployment usually doesn't last very long. If the economy is not in a recession, it might take a few weeks to find a new job, or for specialized workers perhaps a few months but not much longer. Figure 10.2 shows the typical duration of unemployment in the United States. In 2005, a non-recession

CHECK **YOURSELF**

> Other than not working, what other factors are part of the definition of unemployment?
> Define the labor force.
> Is the labor force participation rate close to 100 percent? How is it defined?

Frictional unemployment is short-term unemployment caused by the ordinary difficulties of matching employee to employer.

ZDOROV KIRILL VLADIMIROVICH/SHUTTERSTOCK

year, 35.1 percent of the unemployed were jobless for less than five weeks. Another 30.4 percent were jobless for only 5 weeks to 14 weeks. The remaining one-third were jobless for more than 14 weeks with 11.7 percent jobless for more than a year. In the United States in a non-recession year, a significant fraction of unemployment is frictional.

Later, we will discuss long-term unemployment, especially in Germany, France, Italy, and Spain, and how it differs from unemployment in the United States. In these countries, a much larger fraction of the unemployed are unemployed for more than one year.

Frictional unemployment is a large share of total unemployment because the U.S. economy is so dynamic. Innovation and the relentless pressure of competition drive progress. Progress, however, is not simply creating new jobs and adding them to the old. Rather it's about creating new jobs and destroying old jobs. Webmasters are in; travel agents are out. We can see this process in more detail by looking at statistics on job creation and destruction.

In a typical month in 2005, for example, 230,000 jobs were added to the economy. The figure is impressive but it hides an underlying reality that is even more impressive. In 2005, there were an average of 4.77 million new hires *every month,* but there were also approximately 4.54 million new job separations (quits and layoffs) *every month.* The difference between the hires and the separations is the net number of new jobs (4.77 − 4.54 = 0.23 million or 230,000 new jobs per month). Thus, even in a year when net employment does not change, millions of jobs are created and millions of jobs are destroyed. "Creative destruction," a term coined by economist Joseph Schumpeter, describes this process well.

Creative destruction occurs at the level of the firm and the industry. Even in an industry with constant or increasing employment, the location of employment changes as uncompetitive firms disappear or shrink and new firms grow. K-Mart filed for bankruptcy in 2002 and laid off 34,000 workers, but in that same year its more productive rival, Wal-Mart, hired 139,000 workers.[1]

Creative destruction also occurs at the level of the industry. During the 1970s, for example, the real price of oil increased from about $10 a barrel to nearly $80 a barrel (see Chapter 3, Figure 3.9). The oil shocks required a fundamental reallocation of labor from industries that were heavily dependent on oil to industries less dependent on oil. But it takes more time (and thus more unemployment) for workers to move from one industry to another industry than to move from one firm to another firm in the same industry—this brings us to the topic of structural unemployment.

Structural Unemployment

Structural unemployment is persistent, long-term unemployment. Isn't it redundant to say that unemployment is persistent *and* long-term? Not quite. In France, Germany, Italy, and Spain, for example, approximately 40 to 50 percent of the unemployed have been unemployed for more than one year and this has been true for about 20 years.[2] Very few individuals, however, have been

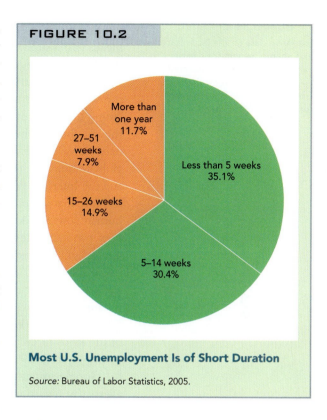

FIGURE 10.2

More than one year 11.7%

27–51 weeks 7.9%

15–26 weeks 14.9%

Less than 5 weeks 35.1%

5–14 weeks 30.4%

Most U.S. Unemployment Is of Short Duration

Source: Bureau of Labor Statistics, 2005.

Structural unemployment is persistent, long-term unemployment caused by long-lasting shocks or permanent features of an economy that make it more difficult for some workers to find jobs.

CHECK YOURSELF

> What is a key cause of frictional unemployment?

> To minimize frictional unemployment, unemployed workers would have to accept the first job they were offered no matter what the wage. Is frictional unemployment always a bad thing?

unemployed for 20 years. The phrase "persistent, long-term unemployment" means that a substantial fraction of the unemployed have been unemployed for more than one year and that this problem has lasted for a long time.

What causes structural unemployment? One cause is large, economy-wide shocks that occur relatively quickly. Adjusting to these shocks can create long-lasting unemployment as the economy takes time to restructure. In addition to the oil shocks, the U.S. economy has had to restructure in recent decades because of the shift from a manufacturing to a service economy, because of globalization and because of new information technologies such as the computer and the Internet.

Note that structural unemployment, if it lasts long enough, brings significant human costs in addition to the loss of economic output. Not only is the economy producing less but the unemployed suffer higher levels of stress, higher rates of suicide, and lower rates of measured happiness. Wanting a job—and not being able to find a good one—is a recipe for misery and social decay.

At some point unemployment can become chronic. It can be harder for an unemployed worker to find a job than for an employed worker to switch jobs. Unemployed workers face two problems. First, the longer a worker remains out of the labor force the more his or her skills atrophy. An administrative assistant unemployed in 1998, for example, would probably have no idea what it meant to "Google something," a critical skill for a job in 2002. Second, hiring managers may regard unemployment as a sign of laziness or other problems. Who would you rather hire: a worker who is looking to switch jobs or a worker who has been unemployed for five years? Unemployment can become a trap and is another reason why unemployment rates in Western Europe are taking so long to return to normal.

Labor Regulations and Structural Unemployment

The late 1970s oil shock (as well as the other shocks listed above) hit the United States as hard as Europe, but in the United States unemployment tends to increase with a shock and then decrease, while in Europe (especially in the big four continental economies: France, Germany, Italy, and Spain), unemployment has increased with shocks and then remained at high levels. Table 10.1 shows that unemployment in the big four European countries has hovered around 10 percent or higher for 20 years and a large fraction of this unemployment has

TABLE 10.1 Unemployment Rates in Europe Versus the United States, 1980–2004

Country	1980–1984	1985–1989	1990–1994	1995–1999	2000–2004	Fraction Unemployed for More Than One Year (2004)
France	7.3%	9.3%	9.6%	10.8%	8.4%	41.6%
Germany	5.9%	6.4%	6.7%	9.8%	8.8%	51.8%
Italy	8.8%	11.6%	10.9%	11.8%	9.3%	49.7%
Spain	15.9%	19.9%	19.6%	20.0%	11.7%	37.7%
United States	8.3%	6.2%	6.6%	4.9%	5.2%	12.7%

Source: OECD Statistics and OECD Employment Outlook, 2005.

been long term. Why have unemployment rates in the United States and Europe behaved so differently?

Structural unemployment has been a more serious problem in Europe than in the United States because of labor regulations. More specifically, unemployment benefits, minimum wages, unions, and employment protection laws benefit some workers, but these regulations can also increase unemployment rates. All of these regulations are more generous and wide-ranging in Europe than in the United States, and that helps explain why structural unemployment is a more serious problem in Europe than in the United States. Let's go through each labor market intervention in turn.

Unemployment Benefits   Unemployment benefits are the most obvious labor regulation that can increase unemployment rates. Unemployment benefits include unemployment insurance, but also other benefits such as housing assistance that may be available in some countries. Table 10.2 shows how much of a worker's take-home pay was replaced by unemployment benefits in France, Germany, Spain, and the United States in 1994.[3] (We focus on 1994 because this is about midway through Europe's long spell of unemployment—there have been only modest changes since then.)

In the first year of unemployment in France, the unemployment benefit system replaced 80 percent of a worker's income. A worker who lost his or her job in France, in

TABLE 10.2 Unemployment Benefit Replacement Rates in Europe Versus the United States, 1994			
	First Year	Second and Third Year	Fourth and Fifth Year
France	80%	62%	60%
Germany	74%	72%	72%
Spain	70%	55%	39%
United States	38%	14%	14%

Note: The data cover a worker with a dependent spouse and are net rates after taking into account taxes and other benefits.

Source: Ljungqvist L., Sargent T. 1998. "The European Unemployment Dilemma." *Journal of Political Economy.* 106(3): 514–550.

Martin, John P. 1996. "Measures of Replacement Rates for the Purpose of International Comparisons: A Note." *OECD Economic Studies.* no. 26: 99–115.

other words, faced only a 20 percent cut in pay. In fact, if we look only at income, and not at the satisfaction that comes from having a job, a French worker who lost his or her job was probably better off—after all an unemployed worker had 80 percent of the income of an employed worker and much more leisure time ("unemployed workers" may also work for pay in the black market). In comparison, the unemployment benefit system in the United States replaced only 38 percent of a worker's pay so a worker who lost his or her job faced a 62 percent cut in pay.

Unemployment benefits also last much longer in Europe than in the United States. In the United States, for example, unemployment benefits fall by more than half after just one year. But in France, Germany, and Spain, unemployment benefits never decrease by so wide a margin.

Given these figures, it shouldn't be surprising that long-term unemployment is much more common in Europe than in the United States (see the last column in Table 10.1). In Europe, the price of unemployment is low, so more unemployment (leisure) is demanded. Or, if you like, workers in Europe can afford to remain unemployed for longer periods than workers in the United States.

In summary, unemployment benefits reduce the incentive for workers to search for and take new jobs. Now switching to look at the demand side of the

labor market, minimum wage, unions, and employment protection laws reduce the incentive of firms to create and offer new jobs.

Minimum Wages and Unions   In the left panel of Figure 10.3, we analyze the minimum wage (see Chapter 4 for a more extensive discussion). The minimum wage raises the price of labor from the market wage to the minimum wage and as labor becomes more expensive firms reduce employment from market employment to minimum wage employment Q_d. At the minimum wage the number of workers looking for work, Q_s, exceeds the number of jobs, Q_d—thus, the minimum wage creates unemployment in the amount $Q_s - Q_d$.

FIGURE 10.3

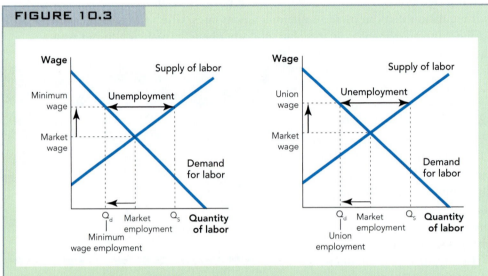

The Minimum Wage and Unions Increase Unemployment In the left panel, the minimum wage raises the wage, thus decreasing the quantity of labor demanded. In the right panel, the union threatens to strike unless the firm pays the union wage. The increase in the wage decreases the quantity of labor demanded.

The **median wage** is the wage such that one-half of all workers earn wages below the median and one-half of all workers earn wages above the median.

In Western Europe, minimum wages have been higher than in the United States. Between 2000 and 2007, for example, the minimum wage in France was about 40 percent higher than in the United States. Minimum wages in Western Europe have also been higher relative to the **median wage** than in the United States. (The median wage is defined so that half of all workers earn less than the median and half more.) In France, the minimum wage has been about 61 percent as large as the median wage. In the United States, the minimum wage has only been about 32 percent as large as the median wage.[4] What this means is that the minimum wage will affect more workers and create more unemployment in France than in the United States. As we discussed in Chapter 7, the minimum wage is more likely to create unemployment among young workers, who tend to be less productive, than among older workers. Thus, in both France and the United States, unemployment rates are higher among the young than the old but in France 23 percent of workers under the age of 25 are unemployed while in the United States 10 percent of these workers are unemployed.[5] The U.S. minimum wage, however, has been rising rapidly in recent years from $5.15 at the beginning of 2007 to $7.25 in 2009.

A **union** is an association of workers that bargains collectively with employers over wages, benefits, and working conditions.

Unions are also more powerful in Europe than in the United States. A union is an association of workers that bargains collectively with employers over wages, benefits, and working conditions. In the United States, most (87 percent) workers are not governed by a union contract; instead, they have an individual contract (written or unwritten) with employers. In many European countries, however, 80 percent of workers or more are governed by a union contract.

Unions can provide value for workers and employers alike, but excessively strong unions have a very similar effect to minimum wages. Unions demand higher wages by using their power to strike and to prevent the firm from hiring substitute labor. In the right panel of Figure 10.3, the union raises the price of labor from the market wage to the union wage. As labor becomes more expensive, firms reduce employment from market employment to union employment Q_d. At the union wage, the number of workers looking for work, Q_s, exceeds the number of jobs, Q_d—thus, unions increase unemployment by the amount $Q_s - Q_d$.

Employment Protection Laws   In the United States, an employee may quit and an employer may fire at any time and for any reason. This is called the **employment at-will doctrine**. There are many exceptions to the at-will doctrine, the most important being that the doctrine can be changed by contract. Many workers, for example, have contractually guaranteed severance packages and tenured university professors cannot be fired at will. Employees can also be restricted by contract. Employees in some industries with a lot of trade secrets are often asked to sign a noncompete agreement when they are hired. If an employee who signs a noncompete agreement quits, he or she may be forbidden, for example, from working for a competitor for a set period. Public law also imposes certain restrictions; employers, for example, are forbidden from hiring or firing on the basis of race, religion, sex, sexual orientation, national origin, age, or handicap status. Despite many exceptions, the at-will doctrine can be thought of as the most basic U.S. labor law.

In most of Europe, labor law is quite different. Portugal's constitution, for example, forbids at-will employment and requires employers to notify the government whenever a worker is dismissed. Moreover, if a Portuguese firm needs to lay off a group of workers, it must get the government's permission. Nor can the firm choose which workers to lay off; instead, it must follow strict guidelines determining which workers will be laid off first (generally the most junior workers are fired first). In addition, laid-off workers must be given 60 days notice, severance pay, and other benefits. Throughout Western Europe, public law and collective bargaining, not contracts, govern things like the length of the workweek, overtime pay, paid leave, temporary employment, notice periods, severance pay, and more.

Hiring and firing costs make labor markets less flexible and dynamic. A European firm with an unexpected increase in orders, for example, will not simply hire more workers. If the firm hired more workers and orders then declined, it would be stuck with workers who it could not lay off without incurring great expense. Thus, hiring and firing costs make firms more cautious and slower to act.

Greater job security is valuable to workers with full-time jobs but the more expensive it is to hire and fire workers, the more difficult it will be for new workers and unemployed workers to find jobs. Imagine, for example, how difficult it would be to get a date if every date required marriage! In the same way, it's more difficult to find a job when every job requires a long-term commitment from the employer.

The World Bank calculates a "rigidity of employment index," which summarizes hiring and firing costs as well as how easy it is for firms to adjust hours

> The **employment at-will doctrine** says an employee may quit and an employer may fire an employee at any time and for any reason. There are many exceptions to the at-will doctrine but it is the most basic U.S. employment law.

of work (e.g., whether there are restrictions on night or weekend hours). A higher index number means that it is more expensive to hire and fire workers and more difficult to adjust hours. Figure 10.4 plots the rigidity index against the percentage of unemployment that is long-term (lasting more than one year). The red line shows the trend in the data; greater rigidity in labor markets is clearly associated with greater long-term unemployment. Notice especially that France, Germany, Italy, and Spain all have high rigidity and high long-term unemployment while the United States has the least rigid labor markets and one of the lowest rates of long-term unemployment.

FIGURE 10.4

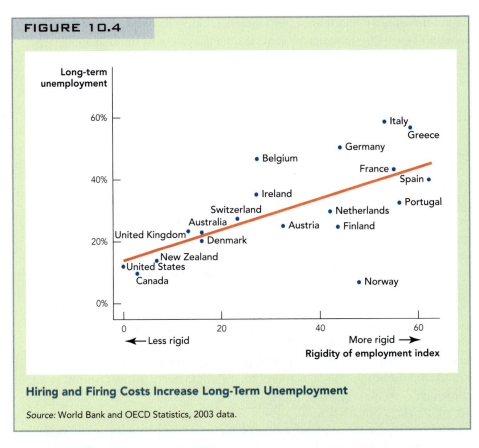

Hiring and Firing Costs Increase Long-Term Unemployment

Source: World Bank and OECD Statistics, 2003 data.

A Tale of Two Riots   The tale of two riots illustrates another effect of employment protection laws. Paris, the city of lights, was lit up by hundreds of burning vehicles in November 2005 as angry, predominantly immigrant youth rioted in the streets. The riots were triggered by accusations of police brutality, but poverty and unemployment were the larger underlying frustrations. Unemployment rates among the rioting youth were over 30 percent.

French firms were reluctant to hire young, minority workers—perhaps, in some instances, because of discrimination, but also because the more expensive it is to hire and fire, the more reluctant firms will be to hire workers without experience and workers for which there is any perceived uncertainty about quality. Once again, if every date required marriage, would you go on a blind date? A blind date might be worth some risk if you can dump a loser, but who will go on a blind date if a date means forever? Returning to firms, young workers are riskier than older workers. Workers without a job are riskier than workers with a job (recall our discussion of the unemployment trap).

And minority workers or workers who in some way differ from the "norm" may be regarded as more risky than typical workers by some employers. Thus, employment protection laws tend to have the most negative effects for young, already unemployed, and minority workers.

The French government was aware of these problems and in response to the riots it proposed to change labor law so that for workers under the age of 26 employment would be at-will for the first two years. The idea was to reassure firms that hiring a young, immigrant worker could be more like a blind date and less like marriage. Of course, this at-will employment is the norm in the United States. For elite French youth, however, the idea that they could be fired at will was upsetting and an infringement of what they considered to be their rights. Several hundred students barricaded themselves in the Sorbonne, the famous Paris university, and called on students everywhere to protest.

Now it was time for the insiders, the young elite, to riot and they proved every bit as adept at burning cars as had the impoverished youth of the year before. Not surprisingly, the elite riots were effective—the French government quickly backed down from the at-will employment doctrine. Unemployment in France, especially among young, immigrant workers remains high.

Summarizing, employment protection laws have the following effects. They:

> Create valuable insurance for workers with a full-time job.

> Make labor markets less flexible and dynamic.

> Increase the duration of unemployment.

> Increase unemployment rates among young, minority, or otherwise "riskier" workers.

Labor Regulations to Reduce Structural Unemployment

In recent years, Europe has begun to change some of its labor regulations to try to reduce long-term unemployment. In Denmark, for example, unemployment benefits were limited to four years and after one year workers who wish to continue receiving benefits must either enroll in job search or job training programs or take public employment. Denmark also subsidizes employers who are willing to train unemployed workers. Denmark and other countries now also have work tests—requirements that unemployed workers who want benefits must prove that they are actively seeking work.[6] These types of laws are called **active labor market policies.**

The United States has been a leader in testing active labor market programs. One of the most successful programs is the simplest—pay workers to get a job! In several large-scale experiments, randomly chosen unemployed workers were told that they would be paid a bonus if they found work early. The workers who were told about the bonus got jobs significantly sooner than those not promised bonuses.

Europe has also been slowly moving toward more flexible labor markets by allowing some exceptions to collective bargaining agreements for certain categories of workers such as young workers, temporary workers, and part-time workers. Remember, however, the tale of the two riots. "Insiders" have been very reluctant to give up their benefits for the sake of the unemployed "outsiders."

CORENTIN FOHLEN/MAXPPP/LANDOV

Outsider riot
Paris suburbs, 2005

DENIS/REA/REDUX

Insider riot
Central Paris, 2006

Active labor market policies like work tests, job search assistance and job retraining programs focus on getting unemployed workers back to work.

Factors That Affect Structural Unemployment

Let's summarize the factors that can increase structural unemployment. These are:

> Large, long-lasting shocks that require the economy to restructure. For example:
>> Oil shocks
>> Shift from manufacturing to services
>> Globalization and global competition
>> Fundamental technology (computers and the Internet)

> Labor regulations:
>> Unemployment benefits
>> Minimum wages
>> Powerful unions
>> Employment protection laws

We also discussed some policies that can reduce structural unemployment. These are:

> Active labor market policies:
>> Job retraining
>> Job-search assistance
>> Work tests
>> Early employment bonuses

CHECK YOURSELF

> Define structural unemployment.
> Why does the term "employment at-will" accurately describe the United States but not Western European countries?

Cyclical unemployment is unemployment correlated with the business cycle.

Cyclical Unemployment

The final category of unemployment is **cyclical unemployment,** or unemployment correlated with the ups and downs of the business cycle. Figure 10.5 graphs the U.S. unemployment rate since 1948. The shaded areas are recessions. Notice that during every recession, unemployment increases dramatically.

Lower growth is usually accompanied with higher unemployment for two reasons. First, and most obviously, when GDP is falling, firms often lay off workers, which increases unemployment. The second reason is more subtle. Higher unemployment means that fewer workers are producing goods and services. When workers are sitting idle, it's likely that related capital is also sitting idle (e.g., factories are boarded up). An economy with idle labor and idle capital cannot be maximizing growth, and that will hurt the ability of that economy to create more jobs.

Figure 10.6 emphasizes the flip side of the idea that lower growth is correlated with increases in unemployment—faster growth is correlated with decreases in unemployment. Figure 10.6 plots changes in the U.S. unemployment rate on the y-axis against growth on the x-axis. As you can see, faster growth in real GDP decreases unemployment. In fact, unemployment tends to fall when growth is above average and it tends to rise when growth is below average. Consider 1982 when the economy was in a deep recession and the unemployment rate increased by 2.1 percent. On the other hand, just two years later, real GDP was growing rapidly at 7.2 percent a year, unemployment was falling, and, partly as a consequence, Ronald Reagan was reelected in a landslide.

FIGURE 10.5

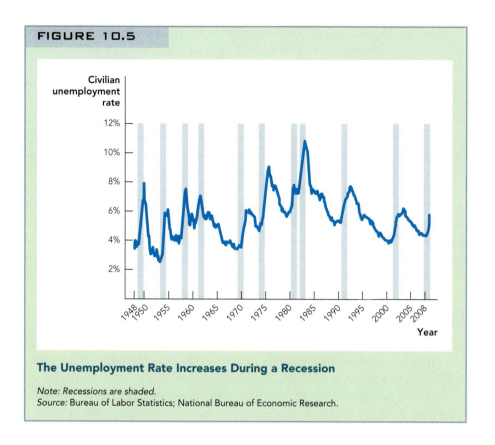

The Unemployment Rate Increases During a Recession

Note: Recessions are shaded.
Source: Bureau of Labor Statistics; National Bureau of Economic Research.

FIGURE 10.6

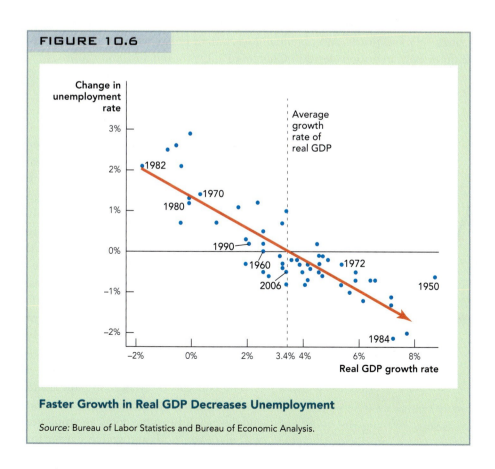

Faster Growth in Real GDP Decreases Unemployment

Source: Bureau of Labor Statistics and Bureau of Economic Analysis.

Although we define cyclical unemployment as unemployment correlated with the business cycle, the cause of cyclical unemployment is a subject of debate among economists, largely because the cause of business cycles is a subject of debate. Some economists think that business cycles are mostly a response to real shocks that require a reallocation of labor across industries. For these economists, a business cycle is nothing more than the economic growth process in action—growth is volatile not smooth. Thus, for these economists, cyclical unemployment is just another example of frictional and structural unemployment.

Other economists, typically of the "Keynesian" persuasion, think that cyclical unemployment is caused by deficiencies in aggregate demand. This concept will be explained in later chapters, but for the time being we can think of this notion of cyclical unemployment as caused by a mismatch between the aggregate level of wages in an economy and the level of prices. The wages demanded by workers are out of synch with the level of prices, so workers are too expensive to hire from the point of view of firms.

To give a simple example, whether a firm wants to hire another worker depends not only on the wage of that worker but on that wage relative to the price of the firm's product (and of course relative to other prices more generally). If Apple can sell an iPod for $200, it is more likely to step up production and hire more workers, than if Apple can sell an iPod for $100. Yet when potential workers make wage demands, they are not always fully aware of the prices and thus the profits available to their employers. Wage demands can be too high, relative to what the firm finds profitable, and this mismatch gives rise to cyclical unemployment. Yet if aggregate demand for goods and services were somehow higher, the higher wage demands perhaps could be justified and the workers could be hired.

We will return to the concepts of real shocks, mismatches between aggregate wages and prices, and potential government policy to reduce cyclical unemployment in greater detail in Chapters 12, 13, 15, and 17.

The **natural unemployment rate** is the rate of structural plus frictional unemployment.

The Natural Unemployment Rate

The **natural unemployment rate** is defined as the rate of structural plus frictional unemployment. Economists typically think of the underlying rates of frictional and structural unemployment as changing only slowly through time as major, long-lasting features of the economy change. Cyclical employment, however, can increase or decrease dramatically over a matter of months. Figure 10.7 plots one estimate of the natural rate against the actual unemployment rate. The natural rate changes only slowly through time and the actual rate of unemployment varies around the natural rate.

The concepts of cyclical, structural, and frictional unemployment are not always clear and distinct. If times are good, an employer will place more ads and search harder for

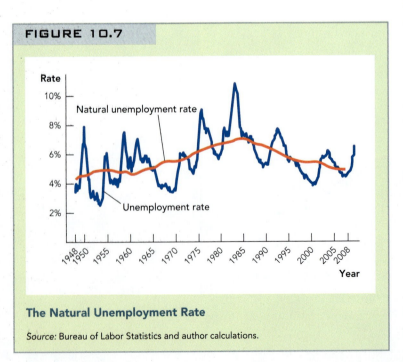

FIGURE 10.7

The Natural Unemployment Rate

Source: Bureau of Labor Statistics and author calculations.

workers. We might say that the frictional rate of unemployment has fallen, but we also might say that the cyclical rate of unemployment has fallen. Both descriptions of the improvement are true. Similarly, how well an economy absorbs, say, displaced auto workers (structural unemployment) will depend on the overall strength of economic conditions. One type of unemployment can even turn into another. Cyclical unemployment, for example, can turn into structural unemployment if workers remain on unemployment benefits for too long, thereby leading to a decline in skills and employment prospects.

Most economists view observed unemployment as a mix of structural, frictional, and cyclical characteristics. The three categories nonetheless give us some useful ideas for organizing the sources of unemployment.

CHECK YOURSELF

> What happens to cyclical unemployment during the business cycle?

> How are economic growth and unemployment related?

Labor Force Participation

So far we've focused on whether people can get a job if they want one, but it is also important to ask whether people *want* a job. We therefore turn from the unemployment rate to the labor force participation rate. Recall that the labor force participation rate is the percentage of the adult, noninstitutionalized, civilian population (adults for short) who are working or actively looking for work. In other words, the labor force participation rate is the percentage of adults who are in the labor force.

$$\text{Labor force participation rate} = \frac{\text{Unemployed} + \text{Employed}}{\text{Adult population}} \times 100$$

$$= \frac{\text{Labor force}}{\text{Adult population}} \times 100$$

In the United States, there are 154.9 million members of the labor force and 234.1 million adult, noninstitutionalized civilians, so the labor force participation rate is:

$$\frac{154.9 \text{ million}}{234.1 \text{ million}} \times 100 = 66.17\%.$$

What determines the labor force participation rate? We will discuss two factors.

1. Lifecycle effects and demographics
2. Incentives

Lifecycle Effects and Demographics

Table 10.3 shows how labor force participation rates vary with age. Only 44 percent of the population aged 16 to 19 are in the labor force. Not surprisingly, most people this age are full-time students not workers. Labor force participation peaks in the prime working years, ages 25–54, when 83 percent of adults are in the labor force. After age 65, most people retire and only 15 percent remain in the labor force.

TABLE 10.3 The Labor Force Participation Rate at Different Ages

Age Range (years)	Labor Force Participation Rate
16–19	44%
25–54	83%
65+	15%

Source: Bureau of Labor Statistics, 2006.

Baby boomers are the people born during the high-birth rate years, 1946–1964.

Lifecycle effects can interact with demographics to change national labor force participation rates. For example, as the **baby boomers** begin to retire in 2008, an increasingly large share of the population will become 65 years of age or older. In 2000, 12.4 percent of the population was 65 years or older, but by 2030 nearly 20 percent of the population will be 65 years or older. In fact, by 2030 it's estimated that 18.2 million people in the United States will be 85 years or older.[7] Since older people are less likely to participate in the labor force, the aging of the U.S. population will lower the labor force participation rate.

Many economists are concerned because falling labor force participation means lower tax receipts. Of greater concern, tax receipts will be falling just as the demands on Social Security and Medicare rise. The head of the U.S. Government Accountability Office, whose job it is to analyze the long-term financial health of the U.S. government, has said in this regard, "when those boomers start retiring en masse, then that will be a tsunami of spending that could swamp our ship of state if we don't get serious."[8] We take up these important issues at greater length in Chapter 16.

A natural response to rising life expectancies and better health at older ages is later retirement. The "normal" retirement age is partly a matter of culture and convention but it is also partly determined by economic incentives, especially taxes—a subject to which we now turn.

Incentives

Why do people join the labor force? A few artists (and some professors!) love to work, but most people work because work pays more than leisure. More specifically, the choice to work depends on the difference between what work pays and what leisure pays. The choice to work, therefore, can be influenced by taxes on workers and benefits paid to nonworkers. Taxes discourage work and benefits encourage nonwork. We can see both of these effects in action by looking at how retirement systems in different countries change the incentives that older people have to work.

Taxes and Benefits Figure 10.8 shows labor participation rates for men ages 55–64 in different countries in 1998. In Belgium, only one-third of men in this age range were working, while in the United States only one-third of men of this age range were retired! Why are there such large differences in labor force participation rates? It's not just cultural differences concerning the right age for retirement.

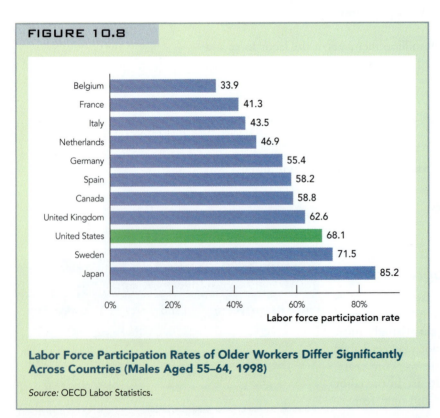

FIGURE 10.8

Labor Force Participation Rates of Older Workers Differ Significantly Across Countries (Males Aged 55–64, 1998)

Source: OECD Labor Statistics.

Country	Labor force participation rate
Belgium	33.9
France	41.3
Italy	43.5
Netherlands	46.9
Germany	55.4
Spain	58.2
Canada	58.8
United Kingdom	62.6
United States	68.1
Sweden	71.5
Japan	85.2

In the United States, a worker of retirement age who continues working is not penalized.* But many countries penalize workers who work past the normal or early retirement age because many countries do not allow a worker to work *and* receive the same government pension. For example, in the Netherlands in the 1990s, a worker who worked past the age of 60 lost one year of benefits. The lost benefits can be thought of as a tax on working. Workers who kept working also had to pay payroll taxes on their wages. The net result was that a worker who worked past the age of 60 in the Netherlands earned less money than a worker who retired! In other words, a worker who did not retire at age 60 had to pay to work. If you had to pay to work, how much work would you do?

Figure 10.9 graphs the labor force participation rate of older men against a measure of the penalty, the implicit tax, on working. Countries with a high implicit tax have a low labor force participation rate.

Early retirement is beneficial for workers if they want to retire early, but taxing older workers at significantly higher rates than younger workers (sometimes at rates above 100 percent!) does not benefit the older workers. Pushing older workers into retirement also imposes significant costs on younger workers who must pay higher taxes because older workers are not contributing to GDP.

Men aged 55–64 are a large share of the population, about 17 percent in most Western European countries, so the tax on working means that millions of men retire early and draw on their pensions instead of continuing to work and produce wealth. The graying of the population that we mentioned earlier is even more serious in Europe than in the United States—in part because the incentives created by European retirement programs greatly decrease the labor force participation rates of older workers.

FIGURE 10.9

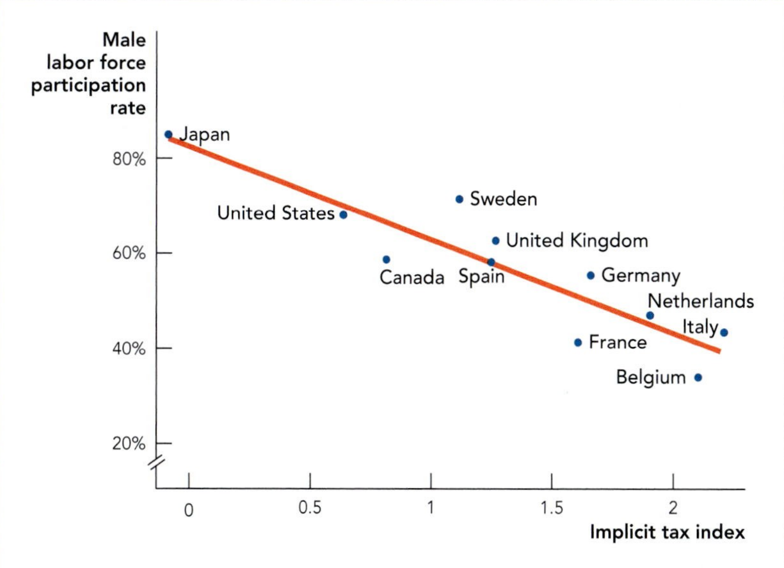

Male Labor Force Participation Declines the Higher Are Implicit Taxes (Males aged 55–64)

Source: OECD Labor Force Statistics, 2005.
Gruber, Jonathan and David A. Wise. 1999. "Introduction and Summary," In J. Gruber and D.A. Wise, (eds.), *Social Security Programs and Retirement Around the World,* University of Chicago Press, Chicago.

Incentives and the Increase in Female Labor Force Participation
Incentives have also played a role in the dramatic increase in the labor force participation rates of women. In 1948, only 35 percent of women aged 25–54 were in

---

* After age 65, Social Security payments are not reduced at all by earnings. Between the ages of 62 and 65, a worker's Social Security payment is reduced when the worker continues to work but payments beginning at age 65 are increased in rough proportion—thus, there is very little penalty to continuing work even at age 62. See Gruber, J. and P. Orszag. 2003. "Does the Social Security Earnings Test Affect Labor Supply and Benefits Receipt?", *National Tax Journal.* 56(4): 755–773.

the (paid) labor force. In 2008, 75 percent of these women are in the labor force. Figure 10.10 plots U.S. labor force participation rates for women since 1948. Notice that the 1970s brought especially large increases in labor force participation rates.

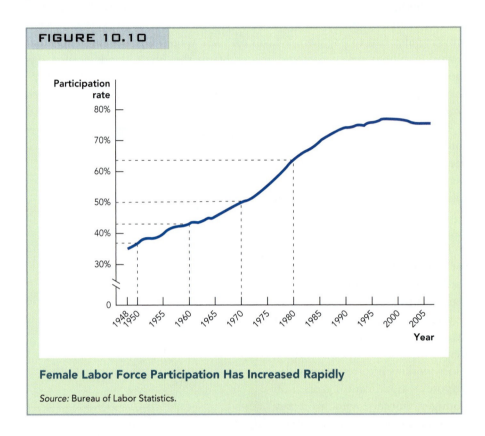

FIGURE 10.10

Female Labor Force Participation Has Increased Rapidly

Source: Bureau of Labor Statistics.

Cultural factors such as the rise of feminism and the growing acceptance of equality for women certainly played a role in rising female labor force participation. But cultural changes do not happen in a vacuum. Changes in the economy such as the move from a manufacturing to a service economy also brought more women to work. Even today, for example, there are almost three times as many male semiskilled factory and machine operators as female operators, but there are more female professionals (lawyers, professors, accountants, etc.) than there are male professionals.[9] As the manufacturing sector declined and the service sector rose, there was less demand for machine operators and more demand for professionals. This raised wages in sectors where females had a comparative advantage, thereby drawing more females into the labor force. In turn, the phenomenon of women in the workplace fueled the rise of feminism.

The growth in women working was especially dramatic in the professions. Figure 10.11 shows the percentage of the first-year students who were female in medical school, dentistry, law, and business programs from 1955 to 2005. From 1955 to about 1970, fewer than 10 percent of first-year students in the professions were females. Beginning around 1970, however, female participation shot up—more than doubling in all professions in just 10 years and continuing to increase until between 40 to 50 percent of all students in professional programs are female.

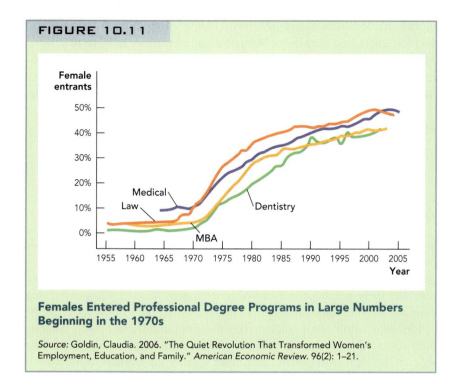

FIGURE 10.11

Females Entered Professional Degree Programs in Large Numbers Beginning in the 1970s

Source: Goldin, Claudia. 2006. "The Quiet Revolution That Transformed Women's Employment, Education, and Family." *American Economic Review.* 96(2): 1–21.

Why did females start entering professional schools in increasing numbers beginning around 1970? Economists Claudia Goldin and Lawrence Katz have an intriguing and controversial answer—the pill.[10]

How the Pill Increased Female Labor Force Participation The pill has been called the greatest technological advance of the twentieth century. For the first time in history, the pill gave women a low-cost, reliable, and convenient method of controlling fertility. Condoms can also prevent unwanted pregnancy, but the pill is easier to use, less prone to error, and more reliable. Among typical users, the pill is seven times more reliable than condoms, and among those who always use the pill according to directions it is 60 times more reliable.

Economists Goldin and Katz argue that the pill lowered the costs of earning a professional degree by giving women greater certainty about the consequences of sex. It takes years of effort to earn a professional degree, and earning a degree while bearing or taking care of a baby is very difficult. Thus, women who wanted a professional degree before the advent of the pill had either to bear the costs of abstinence or risk pregnancy. The pill lowered these costs and increased the incentive of women to invest in a long-term education.

The availability of the pill and the increase in women entering college and professional degree programs do coincide. Although the pill was first sold for contraceptive use in 1960, at that time 30 states banned advertisements for birth control devices and some even banned the sale of contraceptives. It wasn't until 1965 in the landmark case *Griswold v. Connecticut* that the U.S. Supreme Court said states could not ban the sale of contraceptives to *married couples*. Single women could still be prohibited from buying contraceptives until 1972. As laws banning the sale of contraceptives fell, more women bought contraceptives and according to Goldin and Katz more women began to plan for long-term careers.

Goldin and Katz make a plausible argument for their hypothesis (and they provide more evidence than we discuss here); nevertheless, it would be interesting to know if similar effects happened in other countries as the pill became available. Questions like these are on the cutting edge of economics—perhaps some of you will help to answer them.

□ Takeaway

Perhaps the most important lesson of this chapter is that even in the best of times unemployment will exist and fluctuate. The economy is always changing and only through change is there growth. It is important to help workers who are buffeted by change, but there is a difference between helping workers to adjust and trying to prevent adjustment—ultimately, we can do the former but not the latter. As we discussed in this chapter, some labor market policies intended to protect workers have increased structural unemployment in Western Europe compared to the United States. Labor market policies that make it easier for workers to retrain and move to employment have had greater success in keeping long-term unemployment low.

After reading this chapter you should know how unemployment, the unemployment rate, and the labor force participation rate are defined. You should also be able to apply these definitions to data. For example, there are 10 people; 6 have jobs, 1 is looking for work, 1 is a child, 1 is in prison, and the last is retired. What is the labor force? What is the unemployment rate? What is the labor force participation rate?[11] You should also know something about frictional, structural, and cyclical unemployment, which includes defining each and giving examples of their causes.

Finally, it's important to know something about the factors that increase or decrease the labor force participation rate. Changing demographics such as aging baby boomers, technology like the pill, cultural attitudes toward women and work, and government policy such as taxes and pension benefits can all change the labor force participation rate. At the most basic and important level, the labor force participation rate responds to the incentive to work.

Changes in the labor force participation rate can have a large impact on an economy. In much of the world today, women have fewer opportunities to be educated and to fully participate in the paid workforce than men—this failure to fully utilize the talents of women is an enormous loss to these women and to the economy. The labor force participation rates of older workers will become a subject of increasing concern as more workers retire and place increasing demands on pension and health systems not just in the United States but around the developed world.

CHECK YOURSELF

> The marginal tax rate (the tax on additional income) for married couples was reduced significantly during the 1980s. How would this affect the female labor force participation rate?

> Some politicians want to raise the age at which people can collect Social Security benefits, likely postponing retirement for many. How will this change affect the labor force participation rate?

□ CHAPTER REVIEW

KEY CONCEPTS

Unemployed, p. 195

Labor force, p. 195

Unemployment rate, p. 195

Labor force participation rate, p. 195

Discouraged workers, p. 195

Frictional unemployment, p. 196

Structural unemployment, p. 197

Median wage, p. 200

Union, p. 200

Employment at-will doctrine, p. 201

Active labor market policies, p. 203

Cyclical unemployment, p. 204

Natural unemployment rate, p. 206

Baby boomers, p. 208

FACTS AND TOOLS

1. Which of the following people are counted as unemployed?

   A person out of work and actively searching for work

   A person in prison

   A person who wants to work but stopped searching six months ago

   A person who works part time but who wants full-time work

2. According to Figure 10.1, what percent of all Americans are employed? (This number is the "employment–population ratio.") What percent of the labor force is employed?

3. If we count "discouraged workers" as unemployed when calculating the unemployment rate, does the rate more than double, less than double, or remain unchanged?

4. Decide whether each of the following are frictional, structural, or cyclical unemployment.

   a. The economy gets worse, so General Motors shuts down a factory for four months, laying off workers.

   b. General Motors lays off 5,000 workers and replaces them with robots. The workers start looking for jobs outside the auto industry.

   c. About 10 workers per month at a General Motors plant quit their jobs because they

want to live in another town. They start searching for work in the new town.

5. Let's connect the minimum wage model back to the supply and demand model of Chapter 7. Is a minimum wage a price ceiling or a price floor? Does it create a surplus or a shortage in the labor market?

6. Who is more likely to ask politicians for stronger labor unions and laws making it harder to fire workers: insiders who have jobs or outsiders who don't have jobs?

7. Let's look at how the unemployment rate changes during and after a typical recession. In Figure 10.5, does the unemployment rate tend to reach its peak *during* the recession, or does it usually reach its peak *after* the recession?

8. According to Figure 10.7, during which decade was the natural unemployment rate the highest?

9. Take a look at Figure 10.9. About how big is the difference in labor force participation rates between countries with the highest implicit tax rate on older men compared to countries with the lowest implicit tax rate? Round to the nearest 10 percent.

10. Based on the ideas in this chapter, name three labor market policy changes that would be likely to decrease the rate of structural unemployment. There are many more than three possible answers.

THINKING AND PROBLEM SOLVING

1. When the following events happen, does that cause the unemployment rate to rise, fall, or stay the same?

   a. Workers are laid off and start looking for work

   b. People without jobs who are looking for work find work

   c. People without jobs and looking for work give up and stop looking

   d. People without jobs and not looking for work become encouraged and decide to start looking for work

   e. People without jobs and not looking for work take a job immediately

2. Let's see how many jobs have to be destroyed for one *net* job to be created. As noted in the text, millions of jobs are created and destroyed every month. Suppose that 5 millions jobs are destroyed every month and about 5.25 million jobs are created. What is total job destruction divided by net job creation? So how many total jobs are destroyed for every net job created?

3. Take a look at Table 10.2. If you have to pick a country to lose your job in, and you know you're going to be out of work for one year, which country offers the highest one-year average replacement rate? Which offers the highest two-year average replacement rate? If you're going to be out of work for three years, which country offers the highest average rate of wage replacement?

4. When a government raises the minimum wage by $2.00 per hour, where would we expect more jobs to be lost: in the fast food industry or in city government? Why?

5. Let's see how GDP per person can be affected by changes in the fraction of citizens who work. This fraction is better known as the employment–population ratio. To keep things simple, let's assume that every employed worker produces $50,000 worth of output. If the employment–population ratio rises from 50 percent to 55 percent, what happens to GDP per *person*?

6. Calculate the unemployment rate and the labor force participation rate in the following cases:

   a. Employed: 100 million. Population: 200 million. In labor force: 110 million.

   b. Unemployed: 10 million. Population: 200 million. Employed: 90 million.

   c. In labor force: 30 million. Population: 80 million. Unemployed: 3 million.

7. Goldin and Katz looked for the link between birth control and women's labor force participation by looking at the difference between states that acted early to make birth control legal and states that waited until later. Which states do you think had the biggest jump in women joining the labor force: states that legalized birth control earlier or those that legalized it later? (Note: Goldin and Katz provide evidence for the right answer in their paper.)

8. Here's a story economists tell each other: A Nobel prize-winning economist flew in to New York City for a conference. He got into a cab, and started talking with the cab driver. The cab driver said, "Oh, you're an economist? Let me tell you, this economy is terrible. I'm an unemployed architect." The economist immediately replied, "No you're not, you're an employed cab driver." According to the way the U.S. government measures unemployment, who is right?

9. Between 1984 and 2001, the U.S. government made it much easier to get disability payments and the number of disabled people more than doubled from 3.8 million to 7.7 million. Most of the people who try to qualify for disability payments have a tough time finding jobs, and spend a lot of time "out of work and actively searching for work." Once people start receiving disability payments, however, they rarely work again and continue to get the disability payments for decades: These citizens then count as "out of the labor force." What effect did reducing the requirements to get disability payments have on the unemployment rate?

10. It's been said that "once you reach the top of the ladder of opportunity, the first thing to do is pull up the ladder behind you." Let's consider the implications of this adage for labor market outcomes.

    a. When doctors, schoolteachers, and barbers encourage the government to make it harder for people to enter their industries, does this tend to lower or raise the supply of these professionals?

    b. If government requires higher educational and training standards for doctors, schoolteachers, and barbers, does this tend to raise or lower the demand for the services of these professionals?

    c. In equilibrium, taking into account your answers to parts a and b, what is the total effect of this lobbying on the wages of these professionals: Do wages rise, fall, or is the total effect ambiguous? Does the total number of people employed in these professions rise, fall, or is the total effect ambiguous?

11. "The unemployment rate also fails to capture all of the people who have given up looking for work," reports the *New York Times*. This is one of many complaints about how the U.S. government measures the unemployment rate.

But as hinted at in the chapter, the U.S. government actually *does* count these "discouraged workers," and it includes them in the "U-4" and "U-5" definitions of unemployment. The government also has a few other measures of the labor market: It just so happens that the media and economists typically ignore these measures. Let's look at these measures in 2007 and 2008 as the U.S. economy slowed and the official "unemployment rate" rose to see if we get a different story.

	September 2007	September 2008
Official unemployment rate	4.7%	6.1%
U-4 (includes discouraged workers)	4.9%	6.4%
U-5 (also counts a few part-time workers as unemployed)	5.5%	7.1%
U-6 (counts many part-time workers as unemployed)	8.4%	11.0%
Employment as percentage of population	62.9%	62.0%

(*Source:* Bureau of Labor Statistics, Table A-12. "Alternative measures of labor underutilization," http://www.bls.gov.)

Answer the following questions.

a. For each of the five measures calculate the rise in the unemployment rate (or, in one case, the fall in the employment rate.)

b. Do any of these alternate measures indicate that the rise in the unemployment rate was larger than the official measure would indicate? Which ones?

c. Do any of these alternate measures indicate that the rise in the unemployment rate was *twice as big* as the official measure? (That might serve as a rough measure of whether our official measure is off by a lot.) Which ones?

d. Which of these alternate measures indicate at first glance that the labor market is actually a little better than the official measure? What is it about the denominator of this value that makes this change smaller than the rest?

(*Source:* Patrick McGeehan, City's Unemployment Rate Falls to Its Lowest Level in 30 Years, *New York Times*, November 17, 2006.)

CHALLENGES

1. Long-term, structural unemployment is higher in Europe than in the United States, but some European countries have it worse than others. Take a look at Table 10.1. Spain has a lower fraction of long-term unemployment than the other European countries, but a higher rate of unemployment than the other European countries in that table. What can we conclude about the kind of unemployment taking place in Spain?

2. a. If European governments set rules for marriage the same way they set rules for employment—with tough, preset rules that make it hard to end the relationship—would you expect rates of divorce to rise, fall, or can't you tell with the information given?

b. Would the length of marriages rise, fall, or can't you tell with the information given?

c. Would married couples probably be happier (more productive) or less happy (less productive) than under more flexible marriage rules? The last of these three questions might have more than one right answer.

3. When are workers more likely to get a job: six weeks before their unemployment benefits run out, or a week before their unemployment benefits run out? (Note: The correct answer to this question is solidly backed up by U.S. job data.)

4. Take a look at Figure 10.3. In that figure, we're holding "job quality" or "working conditions" constant, and looking at how changes in *wages* impact the quantity of labor supplied and demanded. In many union negotiations, the union and its workers don't push for higher wages. Instead, they push for better working conditions: safer machines, better insurance coverage, or cleaner restrooms.

So now let's model this: Let's hold *wages* constant, and look at how changes in *working conditions* impact the quantity supplied and quantity demanded of labor. Thus, set it up just like a real-life labor negotiation. Draw a conventional supply-and-demand chart, but on the vertical axis, just put "job quality—high or low" instead of "wage." Then, show what happens to the amount of unemployment created when a union successfully negotiates a higher-than-equilibrium job quality.

5. Even though most Americans who become unemployed are only unemployed for a short period of time, when you look at who is unemployed *at a given moment in time*, you'll find that most of the unemployed have been without a job for quite a while. Let's imagine a simple economy to see how to resolve this paradox. In this economy, there are two types of workers, type A workers take one month to find a new job and type B workers take 10 months to find a new job.

Each month, let's assume that *one* type A and *one* type B worker lose their jobs. Notice that *we're assuming that half of all people who lose their jobs today will find new jobs in a month*. But, as we shall see, this implies that most of the unemployed will have been unemployed for a long period of time.

a. In the long-run (or "steady state"), there will be 11 workers out of work in this simple society at any given point in time. Show that this is true by keeping track of the "pool" of unemployed workers in this society for two years. You can start off assuming that the pool is empty at time zero—that no one is unemployed—but you'd get the same steady-state answer regardless of your starting point. You can prove that 11 will be out of work just with pencil and paper or much more quickly with Excel. To help you out, here's an example of what the pool of unemployed will look like in month 7. Keep going with this calculation until you see that the number of workers in the pool no longer changes month to month–this is called the "steady state."

The Unemployment Pool: Month 7	
Shallow End (Type A's)	Deep End (Type B's)
1 Type A worker enters pool (loses job)	1 Type B worker enters pool
1 Type A worker exits pool (find works)	6 Type B workers are already in the pool
	0 Type B workers exit the pool
Total: 1 Type A worker is in the pool (unemployed).	Total: 7 Type B workers are in the pool (unemployed).

b. In the steady state—that is when your pool starts having the same numbers every month—how many of the 11 workers in the unemployment pool have been unemployed for "one month"? How many of the 11 workers in the unemployment pool have been unemployed for more than one month?

c. If you see an economy where most *currently* unemployed workers have been out of work for a long time, does this mean that most *people* who have been unemployed in the last few years were unemployed for a long time? How does this example illustrate your answer?

11

Inflation and the Quantity Theory of Money

Robert Mugabe had a problem. The dictatorial president of Zimbabwe needed money. Unfortunately, Mugabe's policy of seizing commercial farms had driven productive farmers and entrepreneurs out of the country, frightened off foreign investors, and pushed Zimbabwe, once called the breadbasket of Africa, to the verge of mass starvation. Zimbabwe had almost nothing left to tax, but Mugabe still needed money to bribe his enemies and reward his supporters, especially the still loyal Zimbabwean army. Mugabe thus turned to the last refuge of needy governments, the printing press.

Governments and counterfeiters alone can pay their bills by printing money. Beginning in 2001, when inflation was already running at 50 percent per year, Mugabe pushed the printing presses to breakneck speed. Whenever a bill came due or soldiers needed paying it was no problem—just print more money. In May 2006, for example, the government announced plans to print 60 *trillion* Zimbabwean dollars to finance a 300 percent increase in pay for soldiers. Ironically, the payment was delayed because Zimbabwe didn't have enough U.S. dollars to buy ink and paper.[1]

When the ink and paper arrived, the government flooded the economy with more money. The economy, however, could not produce more goods. When more money chases the same goods, the consequences are easy to see: inflation. In Zimbabwe, the inflation rate quickly increased from 50 percent a year to 50 percent a month to more than 50 percent a day! The Zimbabwean economy was disintegrating.

In this chapter, we explain how inflation is defined and measured, the causes of inflation, the costs and benefits of inflation, and why governments sometimes resort to inflation.

Defining and Measuring Inflation

Inflation is an increase in the average level of prices.

The **inflation rate** is the percentage change in the average level of prices (as measured by a price index) over a period of time.

Inflation rate $= \dfrac{P_2 - P_1}{P_1}$

Inflation is an increase in the average level of prices. We measure the average level of prices with an index, the average price from a large and representative basket of goods and services. Thus, inflation is measured by changes in a price index and the **inflation rate** is the percentage change in a price index from one year to the next:

$$\text{Inflation rate } = \frac{P_2 - P_1}{P_1}$$

where P_2 is the index value in year 2 and P_1 is the index value in year 1. A 10 percent inflation rate means, quite simply, that goods and services are priced (on average) 10 percent higher than they were a year ago.

Shifts in supply and demand push prices up and down all the time, but inflation is an increase in the average level of prices. We can think of inflation as an elevator lifting all prices over time. In Figure 11.1, some prices in year 1 are going up and some are going down, but overall the average level of prices is 100. Inflation tends to lift all prices so by year 10 the average level of prices is 200.

FIGURE 11.1

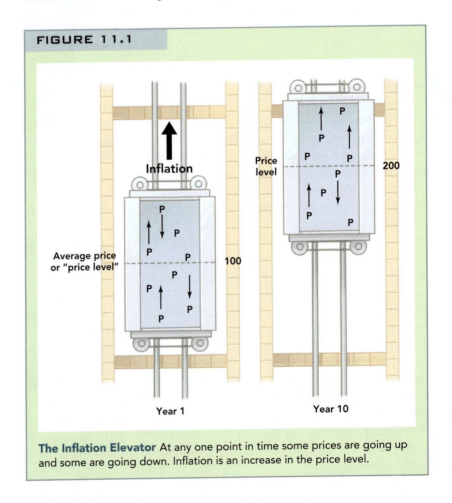

The Inflation Elevator At any one point in time some prices are going up and some are going down. Inflation is an increase in the price level.

Price Indexes

Economists measure inflation using several different price indexes that are based on different bundles of goods:

1. **Consumer price index (CPI):** Measures the average price for a basket of goods bought by a typical American consumer. The index covers some 80,000 goods and is weighted so that an increase in the price of a major item such as housing counts for more than an increase in the price of a minor item like kitty litter.

2. **GDP deflator:** Similar to the CPI, includes all final goods and services, that is, the goods that make up GDP, not just goods bought by consumers. The GDP deflator is used to compute real GDP from nominal GDP.

3. **Producer price indexes (PPI):** Measure the average price received by producers. Unlike the CPI and GDP deflator, producer price indexes measure prices of intermediate as well as final goods. PPI for different industries are often used to calculate changes in the cost of inputs.

For most Americans, the CPI is the measure of inflation that corresponds most directly to their daily economic activity; for businesses and government, the other indexes take on greater relevance. We focus on the CPI unless otherwise indicated.

Inflation in the United States and Around the World

Figure 11.2 shows the annual inflation rate in the United States since 1950. The average inflation rate over this period was 3.9 percent, but in many periods, especially in the 1970s, inflation was significantly higher. Over the past 10 years (1997–2007), inflation in the United States has averaged about 2.6 percent.

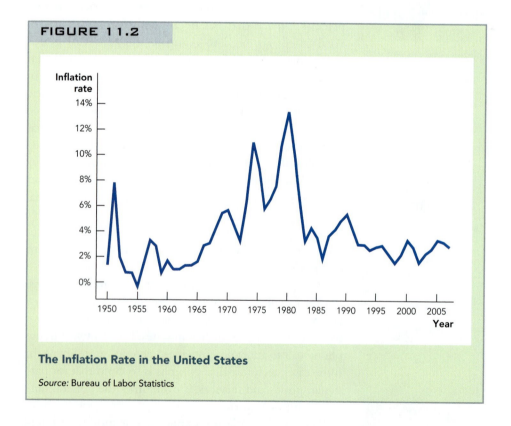

FIGURE 11.2

The Inflation Rate in the United States

Source: Bureau of Labor Statistics

Figure 11.3 on the next page illustrates the cumulative effect of inflation on a large basket of goods. A basket that cost about $10 in 1913 would have cost $36.70 in 1969, $100 in 1982, and $207 in 2007. The height of the line represents the level of the CPI during each year.

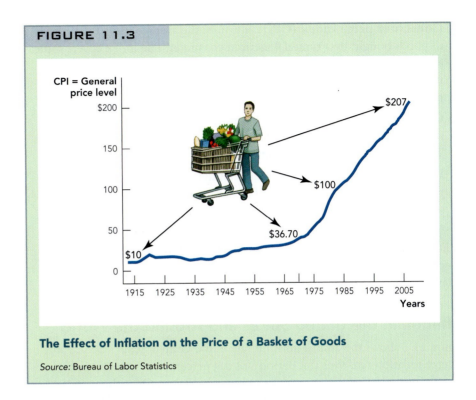

FIGURE 11.3

CPI = General price level

$207

$100

$36.70

$10

1915 1925 1935 1945 1955 1965 1975 1985 1995 2005

Years

The Effect of Inflation on the Price of a Basket of Goods

Source: Bureau of Labor Statistics

A **real price** is a price that has been corrected for inflation. Real prices are used to compare the prices of goods over time.

TABLE 11.1 Average Annual Inflation Rates in Selected Countries (2002–2007)

Country	Inflation Rate (%)
Zimbabwe	735.6
Angola	33.8
Guinea	20.0
Myanmar	19.9
Eritrea	19.7
Russia	11.0
United States	3.0
China	2.1
United Kingdom	1.9
Brunei	0.8
Saudi Arabia	0.7
Hong Kong	0.5
Kiribati	0.4
Japan	0.03

Source: International Monetary Fund, World Economic Outlook Database.

Some 2007 figures estimated.

The CPI is often used to calculate "real prices." A **real price** is a price that has been corrected for inflation. Real prices are used to compare the prices of goods over time. Suppose, for example, that you are told that the average price of a gallon of gasoline was $1.25 in 1982 but double that, $2.50, in 2006. These prices are correct but should we conclude that gasoline was twice as expensive in 2006 than in 1982? No. The CPI was 100 in 1982 and 202 in 2006 so the price of most products doubled during this time period; wages rose as well. Thus, the price of gasoline did not increase over this time period relative to other goods so the real price of gasoline was about the same in 1982 as 2006. In the appendix to this chapter, "Get Real," we show in more detail how you can use data on the Internet to compute real prices over time.

Most prices go up over time, but there are exceptions. Pocket calculators now cost a few dollars; in 1972 they cost $395. In 1927, two-way radio phone service, America to London, cost $75 for five minutes. Today a five-minute phone call to England costs mere pennies with Skype. In some cases, technological progress is so rapid that for particular goods and services, it overcomes the general tendency of prices to rise.

Recent U.S. inflation experience is moderate compared to international inflation rates and the historical record. Table 11.1 displays selected international inflation

rates over the five years from 2002 to 2007. Between 2002 and 2007 Zimbabwe had the highest inflation rate in the world at 735 percent a year. At that rate, prices were doubling about every five weeks but Zimbabwe was just beginning its inflation and in 2008 prices started to increase faster and faster and faster so that by the end of 2008 prices were increasing at a rate of 79,600,000,000 percent per month! On the other end of the spectrum, the countries with the lowest inflation rates had rates of less than 1 percent. Using the rule of 70, we can see that if Japan continues to have an average inflation rate of 0.03 percent the price level in Japan will double in about 2,333 years. From five weeks to 2,333 years, that is quite a difference.

The inflation rate in Zimbabwe is now approaching the worst case on record for an inflation. Table 11.2 presents some figures for major "hyperinflations." The numbers in Table 11.2 are so high they are hard to believe but they are true. In Germany, for example, what cost 1 reichsmark in 1919 cost half a trillion reichsmarks in 1923.

TABLE 11.2 Selected Episodes of Hyperinflation

Nation	Period	Cumulative Inflation Rate (%)	Maximum Inflation Rate on a Monthly Basis (%)
America	1777–1780	2,702	1,342
Bolivia	1984–1985	97,282	196
Peru	1987–1992	17,991,287	1,031
Yugoslavia	1993–1994	1.6×10^9	5×10^{15}
Nicaragua	1986–1991	1.2×10^{10}	261
Greece	1941–1944	1.60×10^{11}	8.5×10^9
Germany	1919–1923	0.5×10^{12}	3,250,000
Zimbabwe	2001–2008	8.53×10^{23}	7.96×10^{10}
Hungary	1945–1946	1.3×10^{24}	4.19×10^{16}

Source: Fisher, Stanley & Ratna Sahay & Carlos A. Vegh. 2002. "Modern Hyper- and High Inflations," *Journal of Economic Literature, American Economic Association,* vol. 40(3): 837–880.

Anderson, Robert B; William A. Bomberger; Gail E. Makinen. 1988. "The Demand for Money, the "Reform Effect," and the Money Supply Process in Hyperinflation: the Evidence from Greece and Hungary Reexamined." *Journal of Money, Credit and Banking,* Vol. 20: 653–672.

http://en.wikipedia.org/wiki/Hyperinflation, http://www.sjsu.edu/faculty/watkins/hyper.htm, http://www.cato.org/zimbabwe

A 500,000,000,000 dinar bank note from a world hyperinflation leader, Yugoslavia circa 1993. At the time 500 billion dinars could buy about $5 worth of goods. Photo courtesy of National Bank of Serbia.

NATIONAL BANK OF SERBIA

Hungary's postwar hyperinflation is the largest on record. The numbers are so high, they are difficult to describe. What cost 1 Hungarian pengo in 1945 cost 1.3 septillion pengos at the end of 1946. Seeing numbers like this, the physicist

CHECK YOURSELF

> If the CPI was 120 this time last year and is 125 right now, what is the inflation rate?

> If the inflation rate goes from 1 percent to 4 percent to 7 percent over two years, what will happen to the prices of the great majority of goods: will they go up, stay the same, go down, or do you not have enough information to say?

> Why do we use real prices to compare the price of goods across time?

Richard Feynman said that really big numbers should not be called "astronomical" but "economical."

The Quantity Theory of Money

We already have a good idea about the causes of inflation from the opening discussion of Zimbabwe. We can now examine the inflationary mechanism in more detail by explaining the **quantity theory of money**. The quantity theory of money does two things: first, it sets out the general relationship between inflation, money, real output, and prices; second, it presents the critical role of the money supply in regulating the level of prices.

Imagine that every month you are paid $4,000 and you spend $4,000. In a year, you spend $4,000 12 times so your total yearly spending is $4,000 × 12 = $48,000. Another way of figuring out your total yearly spending is to add up all the goods that you buy and multiply by their prices. We can write this identity (an equation that must hold true by definition) as:

$$M \times v = P \times Y_R$$

v, velocity of money, is the average number of times a dollar is spent on final goods and services in a year.

where M is the money you are paid, v is the number of times in a year that you spend M (we call v the "**velocity of money**," hence the v), P is prices, and Y_R is a measure of the real goods and services that you buy. A similar identity holds for the nation as a whole, where we interpret M as the supply of money, v as the average number of times in a year that a dollar is spent on final goods and services, P as the price level, and Y_R as real GDP.

Thus, for the nation as a whole we can write:

$$Mv = PY_R$$

$$M = \text{Money supply} \qquad P = \text{Price level}$$
$$v = \text{Velocity of money} \qquad Y_R = \text{Real GDP}$$

With some additional assumptions, the simple identity, $Mv = PY_R$, helps us think through how money affects output and prices. We proceed with two further assumptions, namely that both real GDP (Y_R) and velocity (v) are stable compared to the money supply (M).

Let's discuss why these assumptions are usually reasonable. Over the period we are interested in, real GDP is fixed by the real factors of production—capital, labor, and technology—exactly as we discussed in Chapters 6 and 7 on growth. We know that inflation can be 10 percent, 500 percent, 5,000 percent a year, or much higher. Real GDP, in contrast, never grows by more than say 10 percent a year (and that is extraordinary performance), so changes in real GDP don't seem like a plausible candidate for explaining large changes in prices.

Let's also assume that v, the velocity of money, is stable. The velocity of money is the average number of times a dollar is used to purchase final goods and services within a year. In the example above, v was 12 because you were paid monthly and you spent your entire monthly income of $4,000 12 times in a year. In the U.S. economy today, v is about 8 and it is determined by the same kind of factors that might determine your personal v, factors such as whether workers are paid monthly or biweekly, by how long it takes to clear a check, and how easy it is to find and use an ATM. These factors change over time but only slowly. Other

The **Quantity Theory of Money** in a Nutshell

When v and Y are fixed, (indicated by a top bar) increases in M must cause increases in P.

$$\uparrow \qquad \uparrow$$
$$M\bar{v} = P\bar{Y}_R$$

factors that we will discuss at greater length in the chapters on business fluctuations can change v more quickly but not by enough to account for large and sustained increases in prices. For these reasons, changes in v also do not seem like a plausible candidate for explaining large and sustained increases in prices.

The Cause of Inflation

If Y_R is fixed by the real factors of production and v is stable, then it follows immediately that the only thing that can cause increases in P are increases in M, the supply of money. In other words, inflation is caused by an increase in the supply of money.

How well does this theory hold up? The left panel of Figure 11.4 plots the price level (P) and the supply of money (M) in Peru during its hyperinflation. A product with a price of 1 Peruvian Intis in 1980 would have cost more than *10 million* Intis by 1995. (To reduce the number of zeroes, the Peruvian government changed the name of the currency twice during this period first from Intis to Soles de Oro and then to the Nuevo Sol.) As you can see, the supply of money also increased about 10 million times in lockstep with the increase in prices.

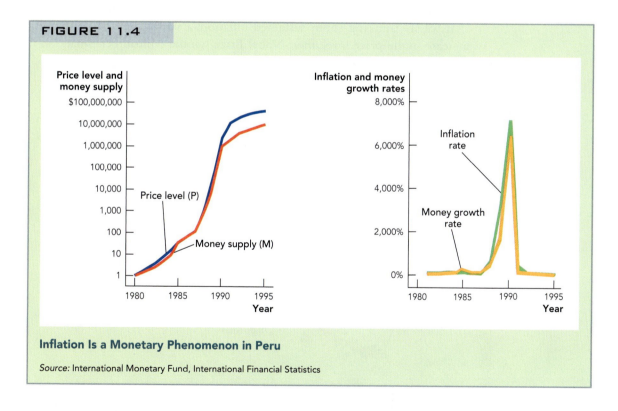

FIGURE 11.4

Inflation Is a Monetary Phenomenon in Peru

Source: International Monetary Fund, International Financial Statistics

The quantity theory of money can also be written in terms of growth rates. We denote the growth rate of any variable with a little arrow over the variable, so $\vec{M}$ is the growth rate of the money supply, $\vec{P}$ is the growth rate of prices, and so forth. If $Mv = PY_R$ then it is also true that[*]:

$$\vec{M} + \vec{v} \equiv \vec{P} + \vec{Y}_R$$

---

[*] To derive this equation, we have used a convenient mathematical fact that if $Y = A \times B$, then the growth rate of Y is approximately equal to the growth rate of A plus the growth rate of B.

We have a special word for the growth rate of prices, $\vec{P}$: inflation! If we assume that velocity isn't changing much, as we did above, then the growth rate of velocity, $\vec{v}$, will be zero or very low. We also know that the growth rate of real GDP, $\vec{Y}_R$, is relatively low, say between 2 percent and at most 10 percent. Thus, if we ignore these two factors, we see immediately that $\vec{M} \approx$ *Inflation Rate*, where $\approx$ means approximately equal. In other words, the quantity theory of money says that the growth rate of the money supply will be approximately equal to the inflation rate.

The right panel of Figure 11.4 shows that during Peru's hyperinflation this was true: as the supply of money grew faster so did the inflation rate, peaking in 1990 at a rate of 7,500 percent per year.

What about other times and places? Figure 11.5 plots inflation rates on the vertical axis versus money growth rates on the horizontal axis for 110 nations between 1960 and 1990. Nations with rapidly growing money supplies had high inflation rates. Nations with slowly growing money supplies had low inflation rates. In fact, as the red line indicates, on average the relationship is almost perfectly linear with a 10 percentage point increase in the money growth rate leading to a 10 percentage point increase in the inflation rate.

If we are thinking about sustained inflation, a significant and continuing increase in the price level, then Nobel Prize winner Milton Friedman has it exactly right: "Inflation is always and everywhere a monetary phenomenon." This is one of the most important truths of macroeconomics.

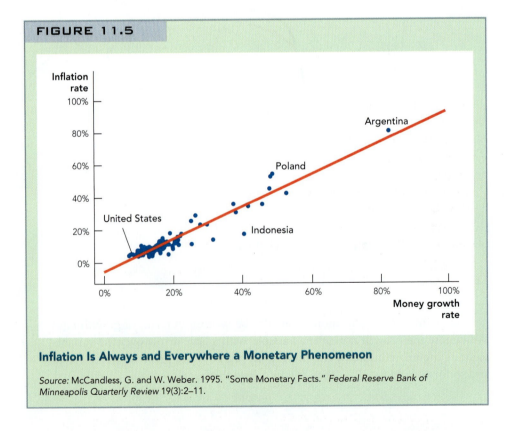

FIGURE 11.5

Inflation Is Always and Everywhere a Monetary Phenomenon

Source: McCandless, G. and W. Weber. 1995. "Some Monetary Facts." *Federal Reserve Bank of Minneapolis Quarterly Review* 19(3):2–11.

Even though large and sustained increases in prices stem from increases in the money supply, changes in v and Y_R can have modest influences on inflation rates. Suppose, for example, that M and v are fixed, then increases in Y_R (real

GDP) must lower prices. In the past, many countries have used a commodity such as gold or silver as money. The dollar, for example, was defined as 1/20th of an ounce of gold between 1834 and 1933. Since the supply of gold or silver usually increases slowly under commodity-money standards, prices typically decrease a bit every year as Y_R increases faster than M.

Finally, even taking the influence of M into account, changes in the velocity of money will affect prices. For instance, increases in the velocity of money can accelerate an already-existing inflation. At the height of the German hyperinflation in 1923, prices were increasing by the minute. Velocity increased in response to this extreme condition. Instead of being paid weekly, for example, workers would be paid as often as three times a day and they would hand off their earnings to their wives, who would rush to the stores to buy food, soap, clothes, *anything* before prices rose even further. Inflation itself caused an increase in velocity, which further fueled inflation.

The velocity of money can also decrease. In an economic panic, individuals may simply hold their money and be afraid to spend it. People might believe that keeping money under the mattress could be less risky than putting money in a bank. During the Great Depression, many people in the United States behaved in precisely this way and the decrease in monetary velocity helped to fuel a **deflation**, a decrease in prices, that worsened the depression. (We discuss the Great Depression at greater length in Chapter 12.) More moderate decreases in velocity or in the growth rate of the money supply would reduce the inflation rate, a **disinflation** rather than a deflation.

Deflation is a decrease in the average level of prices.

A **disinflation** is a reduction in the inflation rate.

The quantity theory also assumes that changes in M cannot change Y_R. In the long run, this makes sense because we know that real GDP is determined by capital, labor, and technology and changes in M won't change any of these factors. Thus, in the long run money is neutral. Imagine, for example, that we doubled the money supply. In the long run, the quantity theory says that prices will double and nothing else will change. We will return to the long-run neutrality of money again and again so let's make a special note of this principle.

In the long run, money is neutral.

Although money is neutral in the long run, it's possible that changes in M can change Y_R in the short run. In particular, under some circumstances increases in M can *temporarily increase* real GDP and decreases in M can *temporarily decrease* real GDP. To see how changes in M could cause changes in real GDP in the short run, let's look at an inflation parable that illustrates how new money works its way through an economy.

An Inflation Parable

Consider a mini-economy consisting of a baker, tailor, and carpenter who buy and sell products among themselves. Now consider what happens when a government like that in Zimbabwe starts paying its soldiers with newly printed money. At first, the baker is delighted when soldiers walk through his door with cash for bread. To satisfy his new customers, the baker works extra hours, bakes more bread, and is able to raise prices. "How wonderful," he thinks, "with the increase in the demand for bread I will be able to buy more clothes and cabinets." Meanwhile, the tailor and carpenter are thinking much the same thing as soldiers are also buying goods from them.

When the baker arrives at the tailor to buy shirts, however, he finds that he has been fooled. The soldiers have bought shirts for themselves and the price of shirts has now gone up. Similarly, the tailor and carpenter discover that the prices of the goods that they want to buy have also increased. Although they earned more dollars, their real wages, the amount of goods that the baker, tailor, and carpenter can buy with their dollars, have decreased.

When the government next wants to buy goods, it faces higher prices and must print even more money to buy just as many goods as before. Moreover, as the new money enters the economy the baker, for example, will now *race* to the tailor and carpenter to try to spend the money before prices rise. Unfortunately, the tailor and carpenter are likely to have had the same idea and the result is that prices increase even more quickly than the time before.

Eventually as the government continues to print money and buy goods, the baker, tailor, and carpenter will come to expect and prepare for inflation. Instead of working extra hours, the baker, tailor, and carpenter will realize that by the time they get to spend their new money, the prices of the goods that they want to buy will have risen in price. Knowing this, the baker, tailor, and carpenter will no longer be so happy to see the soldiers enter their shop waving fistfuls of dollars and they will no longer work extra hours baking more bread, sewing more clothes, or building more cabinets.

The inflation parable tells us that an unexpected increase in the money supply can boost the economy in the short run but as firms and workers come to expect and adjust to the new influx of money, output will not grow any faster than normal. The inflation parable serves us well for now, but the short-run relationship between unexpected inflation and output is a key idea in economics and one we will return to in much greater detail in Chapter 12.

CHECK YOURSELF

> In the long run, what causes inflation?
> What is the equation that represents the quantity theory of money?

The Costs of Inflation

To the person in the street, the costs of inflation are obvious—prices are going up, what could be worse? But most people rarely consider that inflation also raises their wages. (No doubt, we all have a tendency to think that bad events, like price increases, are the fault of others but good events, like higher wages, are due to our own virtues.) If all prices including wages are going up, then what is the problem with inflation?

If everyone knew whether the rate of inflation was 2 percent or 8 percent then everyone could prepare and the exact inflation rate would not matter very much. But instead of everyone knowing the rate it's more often the case that no one knows the rate of inflation! Take a look again at the right panel of Figure 11.4. Inflation in Peru went from 77 percent in 1986 to 7,500 percent in 1990 and then back down to 73 percent in 1992. Who can predict such changes? Even when inflation is more moderate, it can be difficult to predict. In the United States, inflation was 1.3 percent in 1964; the rate more than quadrupled to 5.7 percent in 1970 and increased to 11 percent per year by 1974. Inflation caught most people by surprise. And when inflation decreased from 13 percent in 1980 to 3 percent in 1983, most people were surprised again.

High rates of inflation do create some problems, as we discuss below, but volatile or uncertain inflation is even more costly. We now cover some specific problems or costs introduced by high and volatile inflation. Keep in mind the picture of inflation as a kind of insidious, slow-moving cancer. Inflation destroys the ability of market prices to send signals about the value of resources and opportunities.

Price Confusion and Money Illusion

Prices are signals and inflation makes price signals more difficult to interpret. In our inflation parable, for example, the baker initially thought that the increase in the demand for bread signaled that the real demand for bread had increased. In fact, since all prices were rising, the real demand for bread had not increased. Confusing a nominal signal with a real signal has real consequences. The baker thought that prices were telling him to work harder and produce more bread. When he later discovered that all prices had risen, he knew that he had made a costly mistake.

Now imagine that one day the real demand for bread *does increase,* only now the baker is so used to inflation he ignores the signal. Instead of working harder the baker continues to bake the same number of loaves of bread as before. Opportunities are missed because signals have become obscured.

In a modern economy, it might seem easy enough to figure out whether an increase in demand for bread reflects a real increase in demand or just an increase in the money supply. Just pick up the *Wall Street Journal* and read the articles about monetary policy. But it's not actually so easy. Sometimes the money supply is increasing and the real demand for bread is going up, both at the same time. It is difficult to sort out the relative strength of both influences. Or perhaps the baker never had principles of economics, or, unlike you (!), never had a really good economics textbook.

Human beings are not always perfectly rational, which makes reading signals even more difficult. Even when we should know better, we sometimes treat the higher wages and prices that result from inflation as higher wages and prices in real terms. If the price of a movie goes up 10 percent and other prices including wages go up by about the same amount, we ought to conclude that the real terms of trade have stayed more or less the same. But many people conclude, mistakenly, that movies have become "more expensive." They treat this as a change in relative price: they may see fewer movies or make other decisions based on this new price. Economists call this "money illusion." **Money illusion** is when people mistake changes in nominal prices for changes in real prices.

In short, inflation usually confuses consumers, workers, firms, and entrepreneurs. When price signals are difficult to interpret, the market economy doesn't work as well—resources are wasted in activities that appear profitable but in fact are not, entrepreneurs are less quick to respond to real opportunities, and resources flow more slowly to profitable uses.

Money illusion is when people mistake changes in nominal prices for changes in real prices.

Inflation Redistributes Wealth

In our inflation parable, the government bought bread, shirts, and woodwork simply by printing paper. Where did these real goods come from? They came from the baker, tailor, and carpenter. Inflation transfers real resources from citizens to the government. Thus, *inflation is a type of tax.*

The inflation tax does not require tax collectors, a tax bureaucracy, or extensive record keeping. You can hide from most taxes by keeping your transactions secret and saving your money under the bed. But you can't hide from the inflation tax! Money under the bed is precisely what inflation does tax because as prices rise, the value of the dollars under the bed falls. It's not surprising, therefore, that money-strapped governments in danger of collapsing typically use massive inflation. Almost all the hyperinflations in Table 11.2 involved governments with massive debts or spending that could not be paid for with regular taxes.

Inflation does more than transfer wealth to the government—it also redistributes wealth among the public, especially between lenders and borrowers. To see why, suppose that a lender lends money at an interest rate of 10 percent but that over the course of the year the inflation rate is also 10 percent. On paper, the lender has earned a return of 10 percent—we call this the nominal return. But what is the lender's actual rate of return? The lender is paid 10 percent interest but she is paid in dollars that have become 10 percent less valuable. Thus, the lender's actual rate of return is 0 percent.

Thus, inflation can reduce the real return that lenders receive on their loans, in effect transferring wealth from lenders to borrowers. In the 1970s, for example, high inflation rates meant the real value of 30-year fixed-rate mortgages that were taken out in the 1960s declined tremendously, redistributing billions of dollars from lenders to borrowers. Borrowers benefited but many lenders went bankrupt.

In the late 1970s, however, many people began to expect that 10 percent inflation was here to stay so home buyers were willing to take out long-term mortgages with interest rates of 15 percent or higher. When inflation fell unexpectedly in the early 1980s, these borrowers found that their real payments were much higher than they had anticipated. Wealth was redistributed from borrowers to lenders.

We can explain the relationship between inflation and wealth redistribution more precisely by writing the relationship between the lender's actual rate of return, the nominal rate of return, and the inflation rate as follows:

$$r_{actual} = i - \pi \qquad (1)$$

$$r_{actual} = \text{Actual rate of return, } i = \text{Nominal interest rate}$$
$$\pi = \text{Inflation rate}$$

In words, the actual rate of return is equal to the nominal rate of return minus the inflation rate.

Lenders, of course, will not lend money at a loss. Thus, when lenders *expect* inflation to increase, they will demand a higher nominal interest rate. For example, if lenders expect that the inflation rate will be 7 percent and the equilibrium real rate (determined in the market for loanable funds—see Chapter 8) is 5 percent, then lenders will ask for a nominal interest rate of approximately 12 percent (7 percent to break even given the expected rate of inflation plus the 5 percent equilibrium rate). If lenders expect that the inflation rate will be 10 percent, lenders will demand a nominal interest rate of approximately 15 percent (10 percent to break even given the expected rate of inflation plus the 5 percent equilibrium rate).

The tendency of nominal interest rates to increase with expected inflation rates is called the **Fisher effect** (after economist Irving Fisher,1867–1947). As an approximation,* we can write the Fisher effect as:

$$i = E\pi + r_{equilibrium} \qquad (2)$$

$$i = \text{Nominal interest rate}, \ E\pi = \text{Expected inflation rate}$$
$$r_{equilibrium} = \text{Equilibrium real rate of return}$$

The Fisher effect says that the nominal interest rate is equal to the expected inflation rate plus the equilibrium real interest rate. Most important, the Fisher effect says that the nominal rate will rise with expected inflation. We can see the Fisher effect in Figure 11.6, which graphs the inflation rate and short-term nominal interest rates in the United States from 1955 to 2007.

The **Fisher effect** is the tendency of nominal interest rates to rise with expected inflation rates.

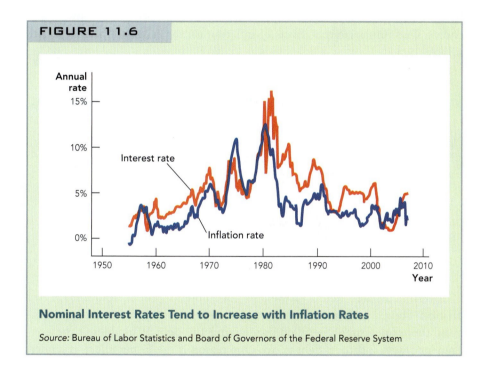

FIGURE 11.6

Nominal Interest Rates Tend to Increase with Inflation Rates

Source: Bureau of Labor Statistics and Board of Governors of the Federal Reserve System

Thus repeating equations (1) and (2) from above we have:

$$r_{actual} = i - \pi \qquad (1)$$

and

$$i = E\pi + r_{equilibrium} \qquad (2)$$

---

* The Fisher effect equation in the text is only approximate. The exact Fisher effect equation is $(1 + i) = (1 + r)(1 + \pi)$. If a lender wants a real rate of return of 5 percent ($r = 0.05$) and the inflation rate is 10 percent ($\pi = 0.1$), then the lender must charge a nominal rate of 1.155 (1.10×1.05) or 15.5%. When inflation rates are low, the approximation works well but not during hyperinflations.

If we substitute i from equation (2) into equation (1), we see that the actual rate of return will be determined in large part by the difference between expected inflation and actual inflation.

$$r_{actual} = (E\pi - \pi) + r_{equilibrium}$$

If $(E\pi < \pi)$, that is, if expected inflation is less than actual inflation, then the actual rate of return will be less than the equilibrium rate and will quite possibly be negative. Wealth will be redistributed from lenders to borrowers.

If $(E\pi > \pi)$, that is, if expected inflation is greater than actual inflation or equivalently if there is an unexpected "disinflation," then the actual rate of return will be higher than the equilibrium rate. Wealth will be redistributed from borrowers to lenders.

Only when $(E\pi = \pi)$, that is, when expected inflation is equal to actual inflation, will the actual return be equal to the equilibrium return. In this case, there will be no unexpected redistribution of wealth between borrowers and lenders. We summarize the effects of inflation on the redistribution of wealth in Table 11.3.

TABLE 11.3 The Redistribution of Wealth Caused by Inflation

Unexpected inflation $(E\pi < \pi)$	Unexpected disinflation $(E\pi > \pi)$	Expected inflation = Actual inflation $(E\pi = \pi)$
Actual rate less than equilibrium rate	Actual rate greater than equilibrium rate	Actual rate equal to equilibrium rate
Harms lenders Benefits borrowers	Benefits lenders Harms borrowers	No redistribution of wealth

Monetizing the debt is when the government pays off its debts by printing money.

Governments are often borrowers so governments benefit from unexpected inflation. Thus, a government with massive debts has a special incentive to increase the money supply—called **monetizing the debt**. Why doesn't the government always inflate its debt away? One reason is the Fisher effect. If lenders expect that the government will inflate its debt away, they will only lend at high nominal rates of interest. To avoid this outcome, the government may try to make a credible promise to keep the inflation rate low.

Another reason the government doesn't always inflate its debt away is that people who buy government bonds are typically voters who would be upset if their real returns were shrunk to zero or less. But what do you think would happen to inflation rates if a nation's debt was owed to foreigners? A government would probably have a stronger incentive to inflate away debt owed to foreigners than debt owed to voters. The U.S. debt is increasingly owed to foreigners, which makes some economists predict a return of inflation in the United States, especially if a future U.S. government finds it difficult to cover its debt with other taxes (see Chapter 16 on fiscal problems in the United States).

It's not only lenders and borrowers that need to forecast future inflation rates. Any contract involving future payments will be affected by inflation. Workers and firms, for example, often make wage agreements several years in advance, especially when unions or other forms of collective bargaining are in place. If the rate of inflation is high and volatile, they are more likely to set wages at the wrong level. Either wages will be too high, and the firm will be reluctant to use more overtime or hire more workers, or wages will be too low, in which case workers are underpaid, they will slack off, and some will quit the job altogether.

Hyperinflation and the Breakdown of Financial Intermediation

If inflation is moderate and stable, lenders and borrowers can probably forecast reasonably well and loans can be signed with rough certainty regarding the real value of the future payments. But when inflation is volatile and unpredictable, long-term loans become riskier and they may not be signed at all. Thus, the real problem of unexpected inflation is not simply that it redistributes wealth, but—even worse—that few long-term contracts will be signed when borrowers and lenders both fear that unexpected inflation or deflation *could* redistribute their wealth.

High and volatile inflation rates have decimated many developing nations. When Peru experienced hyperinflation between 1987 and 1992, private loans virtually disappeared. When firms cannot get loans, they cannot build for future expansion and growth. The price level in Peru is approximately 10 million times higher today than it was in 1997. Who could have predicted these rates of increase or built them into a contract?

The virtual elimination of inflation in Mexico shows how much capital markets can flourish in a stable environment. In the 1980s, the rate of Mexican inflation at times exceeded 100 percent. Long-term loans were very hard to come by. In the United States, it's relatively easy to borrow money for 10, 20, or 30 years or even longer. But as recently as 2002, 90 percent of the local currency debt in Mexico matured within one year.

In the 1990s, the inflation rate in Mexico came down to about 10 percent and more recently it has been 3 percent to 4 percent, close to the rate in the United States. Mexican capital markets have grown rapidly as inflation has been stabilized. In 2006, the Mexican government was able to introduce a 30-year bond, denominated in Mexican pesos; this would have been unheard of as recently as the mid-1990s.

The greater ease and predictability of long-term borrowing also has caused the Mexican mortgage market to take off. It is now relatively easy to obtain a long-term mortgage in Mexico—due largely to lower and less volatile inflation—and many more middle-class Mexicans have been able to afford homes.

Unexpected inflation redistributes wealth throughout society in arbitrary ways. When the inflation rate is high and volatile, unexpected inflation is difficult to avoid and society suffers as long-term contracting grinds to a halt.

Inflation Interacts with Other Taxes

Most tax systems define incomes, profits, and capital gains in nominal terms. In these systems, inflation, even expected inflation, will produce some tax burdens and tax liabilities that do not make economic sense.

To make this concrete, let's say you bought a stock share for $100, and over several years inflation alone pushed its price to $150. The U.S. tax system requires that you pay profits on the $50 gain even though the gain is illusory. Yes, you have more money in nominal terms but that money is worth less in terms of its ability to purchase real goods and services. In real terms, the share hasn't increased in price at all yet you must still pay tax on the phantom gain.

In this case, inflation leads to people paying capital gain taxes when they should not. The overall tax burden rises. The long-run effect is to discourage investment in the first place.

Depending on the details of particular tax systems, inflation can also push people into higher tax brackets or make corporations pay taxes on phantom business profits. In short, inflation increases the costs associated with tax systems.

Inflation Is Painful to Stop

Once inflation starts it's painful to stop—this is one of the biggest costs of inflation. Imagine that the inflation rate has been 10 percent in an economy for some time so that loans, wage agreements, and all kinds of business contracts are based on the expectation that inflation will continue at 10 percent. The government can reduce inflation by reducing the growth in the money supply but what will happen to the economy? When workers, firms, and consumers expect 10 percent inflation, a lower rate is a shock. At first, firms may interpret the lower rate as a reduction in real demand and thus they may reduce output and employment. Furthermore, contracts signed on the expectation of 10 percent inflation are now out of whack with actual inflation. Wage bargains that promised raises of 12 percent per year were modest when inflation was 10 percent, but are huge increases in real wages when the inflation rate is 3 percent. Workers may be thrown out of work as the unexpected increase in their real wage makes them unaffordable. Only in the long run, as expectations adjust, does the economy move to a point where both inflation and unemployment are low.

In the United States, for example, Ronald Reagan was elected to the presidency in 1980 after inflation in the United States hit 13.5 percent a year. By 1983, tough monetary policy had reduced the inflation rate to 3 percent, but the consequence was the worst recession since the Great Depression and an unemployment rate of just over 10 percent. Only in 1988 did unemployment return to near 5.5 percent.

Just Say No

Inflation has been likened to a drug addiction. At first the highs (a booming economy) are good. But soon bigger and bigger doses are needed to generate the same high as before (unexpected inflation turns to expected inflation). Eventually all that is left is the fear of withdrawal (disinflation).

CHECK YOURSELF

> Consider unexpected inflation and unexpected disinflation. How is wealth redistributed between borrowers and lenders under each case?

> What happens to nominal interest rates when expected inflation increases? What do we call this effect?

> What does unexpected inflation do to price signals?

☐ Takeaway

Inflation is an increase in the average level of prices as measured by a price index such as the consumer price index (CPI). A price index can be used to convert a nominal price into a real price, a price corrected for inflation.

Sustained inflation is always and everywhere a monetary phenomenon. In the long run, real GDP is determined by the real factors of production—capital, labor, and technology—so changes in the money supply cannot permanently increase real GDP. Thus, the quantity theory of money is a good guide to how prices respond to changes in the money supply in the long run. Although money is neutral in the long run, changes in the money supply can influence real GDP in the short run for a variety of reasons.

Inflation makes price signals more difficult to interpret, especially when people may suffer from money illusion. Inflation is a type of tax. Governments with few other sources of tax revenue often turn to inflation because the inflation tax is difficult to avoid.

Workers and firms will adjust to a predictable inflation by incorporating inflation rates into wage contracts and loan agreements. The tendency of the nominal interest rate to increase with expected inflation is called the Fisher effect. But inflation is often difficult to predict. When inflation is greater than expected, wealth is redistributed from lenders to borrowers. When inflation is less than expected, wealth is redistributed from borrowers to lenders. The possibility of arbitrary redistributions of wealth in either direction makes lending and borrowing more risky and thus breaks down financial intermediation.

Anything above a mild sustained rate of inflation is generally bad for an economy. Economists disagree, however, as to whether and how much small amounts of well-timed inflation can benefit an economy. In Chapters 12 and 15, we discuss at greater length how policymakers might use the short-run trade-off between inflation and output to smooth recessions and booms. This remains one of the most important and controversial "fault lines" in modern macroeconomics.

◻ CHAPTER REVIEW

KEY CONCEPTS

Inflation, p. 218

Inflation rate, p. 218

Real price, p. 220

v, velocity of money, p. 222

Quantity theory of money, p. 222

Deflation, p. 225

Disinflation, p. 225

Money illusion, p. 227

Fisher effect, p. 229

Monetizing the debt, p. 230

FACTS AND TOOLS

1. What is a "price level"? If the "price level" is higher in one country than another, what does that tell us, if anything, about the standard of living in that country?

2. What are some forces that could cause shocks to v, the velocity of money?

3. When is the inflation rate more likely to have a big change either up *or* down: when inflation is high or when it is low?

4. Who gets helped by a surprise inflation: people who owe money or people who lend money?

5. Who is more likely to lobby the government for fast money growth: people who have mortgages or people who own banks that lent money for those mortgages?

6. Consider the interaction between inflation and the tax system. Does high inflation encourage people to save more or discourage saving? If a government wants to raise more tax revenue in the short run, should it push for higher or lower inflation?

7. Which tells me more about how many more goods and services I can buy next year if I save my money today: the nominal interest rate or the real interest rate? Which interest rate gets talked about more in the media?

8. According to the Fisher effect, if everyone expects inflation to rise by 10 percent over the next few years, where will the biggest effect be: on nominal interest rates or on real interest rates?

THINKING AND PROBLEM SOLVING

1. Calculate inflation in the following cases:

Price Level Last Year	Price Level This Year	Inflation Rate
100	110	
250	300	
4,000	4,040	

2. What does the quantity theory of money predict will happen *in the long run* in these cases? According to the quantity theory, a rise in the money supply can't change v or Y in the long run, so it must affect P. Let's use that fact to see how changes in the money supply affect the price level. Fill in the following table.

M	v	P	Y
100	5		50
150	5		50
50	5		50

3. In the long run according to the quantity theory of money, if the money supply doubles, what happens to the price level? What happens to real GDP? In both cases, state the percentage change in either the price level or real GDP.

4. Much of the economic news we read about can be reinterpreted into our "$Mv = PY$" framework. Turn each of the following news headlines into a precise statement about M, v, P, or Y.

   a. "Deposits in U.S. banks fell in 2015."

   b. "American businesses are spending faster than ever."

   c. "Prices of most consumer goods rose 12 percent last year."

   d. "Workers produced 4 percent more output per hour last year."

   e. "Real GDP increased 32 percent in last decade."

   f. "Interest rates fall: consumers hold more cash."

5. It's time to take control of the Federal Reserve (which controls the U.S. money supply). In this chapter, we're thinking only about the "long run," so Y (real GDP) is out of the Fed's control, as is v. The Fed's only goal is to make sure that the price level is equal to 100 each and every year—that's just known as "price stability," one of the main goals of most governments.

In question 2, you acted like an economic *forecaster*. You knew the values of M, v, and Y and had to guess what the long-run price level would be. In this question, you will act like an economic *policymaker*. You know the values of v and Y, and you know your goal for P. Your job is to set the level of M so that you meet your price-level target.

In some years, there will be long-lasting shocks to v and Y, so your job as a policymaker is to offset those shocks by changing the supply of money in the economy. Some of these changes might not make you popular with the citizens, but they are part of keeping P equal to the price-level target. Fill in the following table.

Year	M	v	=	P	Y
1	25,000	2		100	500
2		4		100	500
3		4		100	400
4		4		100	200
5		2		100	400
6		1		100	600

6. Nobel laureate Milton Friedman often said that "inflation is the cruelest tax." Who is it a tax on? More than one may be correct:

   a. People who hold currency and coins in their wallet, purse, or at home

   b. Businesses that hold currency and coins in their cash registers

   c. People or businesses who keep deposits in a checking account that pays zero interest

   d. People or businesses who keep deposits in a savings account that pays an interest rate higher than the rate of inflation

   e. People or businesses who invest in gold, silver, platinum, or other metals

7. In countries with hyperinflation, the government prints money and uses it to pay government workers. How is this similar to counterfeiting? How is it different?

8. The Fisher effect says that nominal interest rates will equal expected inflation plus the real equilibrium rate of return:

$$i = E\pi + r_{equilibrium} \qquad (2)$$

$$i = \text{Nominal interest rate,}$$
$$E\pi = \text{Expected inflation rate,}$$
$$r_{equilibrium} = \text{Equilibrium real rate of return}$$

Economists and Wall Street experts often use the Fisher effect to learn about economic variables that are hard to measure because when the Fisher effect holds, if we know any two of the three items in the equation we can calculate the third. Sometimes, for example, economists are trying to estimate what investors *expect* inflation is going to be over the next few years, but they only have good estimates of nominal interest rates and the equilibrium real rate. Other times, they have good estimates of expected inflation and today's nominal interest rates, and want to learn about the equilibrium real rate. Let's use the Fisher effect just like the experts do: Use two *known* values to learn about the *unknown* third one.

i	$E\pi$	$r_{equilibrium}$
5%	2%	3%
5%	1%	
5%		8%
	10%	2%
6%		2%
0%	−2%	

Note: The last entry is an example of the "Friedman rule," something that we'll come back to in a later chapter.

CHALLENGES

1. If I get more money, does that typically make me richer? If society gets more money, does it make society richer? What's the contradiction?

2. Why is it so painful to get rid of inflation? Why can't the government just stop printing so much money?

3. Who gets hurt most in the following cases: banks, mortgage holders (i.e., homeowners), or neither?

$E\pi$	π	Who gets hurt?
4%	10%	
10%	4%	
−3%	0%	
3%	6%	
10%	10%	

4. Let's see just how much high expected inflation can hurt incentives to save for the long run. Let's assume the government takes about one-third of every extra dollar of nominal interest you earn (a reasonable approximation for recent college graduates in the United States). You must pay taxes on nominal interest—just like under current U.S. law—but if you're rational you'll care mostly about your real, after-tax interest rate when deciding how much to save.

To make the economic lesson clear, note that in every case, the real rate (before taxes) is an identical 3 percent. In each case, calculate the nominal after-tax rate of return and the real after-tax rate of return. Notice that as inflation rises, your after-tax rate of return plummets.

i	$E\pi = \pi$	$(2/3) \times i$	$(2/3) \times (i - \pi)$
Nominal interest rate	Inflation (no surprises)	Nominal after-tax return	Real after-tax return
15%	12%	10%	−2%
6%	3%		
12%	9%		
90%	87%		
900%	897%		

CHAPTER **APPENDIX**

Get Real! An Excellent Adventure

Suppose that you would like to convert a nominal data series into an inflation-corrected or *real* data series. How do you do it? Let's suppose that you have already imported the nominal data that you want to convert into a spreadsheet. At the U.S. Census Bureau, for example, we found monthly data showing the average price of new houses sold from 1975 to 2006.* We then imported these into a spreadsheet as shown in Figure A11.1. In 2006, the average house price was $304,400, but in 1975 it was only $39,500. Do you think the average new house was really more than seven times as expensive in 2006 as in 1975?

FIGURE A11.1

	A	B	C
1	Year	Month	Avg. House Price
2	2006	8	304400
3	2006	7	314200
4	2006	6	305900
5	2006	5	293900
6	2006	4	310300
7	2006	3	298800
8	2006	2	307900
9	2006	1	301000
10	2005	12	290200
11	2005	11	294400
12	⋮		
13	1975	5	43200
14	1975	4	42000
15	1975	3	42100
16	1975	2	40600
17	1975	1	39500
18			

Inflation has increased all prices, including wages, since 1975 so some of the increase in house prices isn't real. To correct for inflation we need a price index, a measure of how much prices in general have changed. We found several monthly price indexes at the Bureau of Economic Analysis. The most commonly

* http://www.census.gov/const/www/newressalesindex.html

used index is the consumer price index or CPI.* Importing the CPI gives us a spreadsheet like Figure A11.2.

FIGURE A11.2

	A	B	C	D	
1	Year	Month	Avg. House Price	CPI	
2	2006	8	304400	203.7	
3	2006	7	314200	203.2	
4	2006	6	305900	202.3	
5	2006	5	293900	201.9	
6	2006	4	310300	201	
7	2006	3	298800	199.8	
8	2006	2	307900	199.1	
9	2006	1	301000	199	
10	2005	12	290200	197.7	
11	2005	11	294400	197.8	
12	2005	10	293600	199.1	
⋮					
375	1975	7	42300	54	
376	1975	6	42500	53.5	
377	1975	5	43200	53.1	
378	1975	4	42000	53	
379	1975	3	42100	52.8	
380	1975	2	40600	52.6	
381	1975	1	39500	52.3	
382					
383					

The CPI for August 2006 was 203.7 and for January 1975 it was 52.3. Prices in general were about 3.89 times higher (203.7/52.3 = 3.89) in 2006 than in 1975 so a substantial fraction of the increase in house prices wasn't real. We can be more precise by calculating for any year how much a house would have cost in that year if general prices had been at the same level as they were in August 2006. Another way of saying this is that we will convert all prices into "August 2006 dollars."

To convert into August 2006 dollars, we need two more steps. First, we divide every CPI number by the level of the CPI in the 8th month of 2006, 203.7. We call the new series the deflator. Figure A11.3 on the next page gives the picture—note that we copied the formula D2/203.7 into each cell in the Deflator column.

---

* Since housing makes up a large component of the CPI, we should technically use the CPI-Less Shelter, but in practice the two series are nearly identical.

FIGURE A11.3

	E2		▼	*fx* =D2/203.7	
	A	B	C	D	E
1	Year	Month	Avg. House Price	CPI	Deflator
2	2006	8	304400	203.7	1
3	2006	7	314200	203.2	0.9975
4	2006	6	305900	202.3	0.9931
5	2006	5	293900	201.9	0.9912
6	2006	4	310300	201	0.9867
7	2006	3	298800	199.8	0.9809
8	2006	2	307900	199.1	0.9774
9	2006	1	301000	199	0.9769
10	2005	12	290200	197.7	0.9705
11	2005	11	294400	197.8	0.971
12	2005	10	293600	199.1	0.9774
⋮					
375	1975	7	42300	54	0.2651
376	1975	6	42500	53.5	0.2626
377	1975	5	43200	53.1	0.2607
378	1975	4	42000	53	0.2602
379	1975	3	42100	52.8	0.2592
380	1975	2	40600	52.6	0.2582
381	1975	1	39500	52.3	0.2568
382					

Finally, we divide the average house price by the deflator. Note that dividing the average price in August 2006, $304,400, by 1 doesn't change the price—that makes sense because we are converting all prices into August 2006 dollars! Figure A11.4 gives the final picture.

What we have now discovered is that if prices in general were as high in 1975 as they were in 2006, then house prices in 1975 would have been $153,846 instead of the 1975-dollar price of $39,500. Now that we have created a real-price series for housing, we can find the real *increase* in the price of housing. Holding prices constant at 2006 levels, house prices in 2006 were $304,400 and in 1975 they were $153,846, so over this time period houses have about doubled in price ($304,400/$153,846 = 1.98). A doubling is a substantial increase, but it's a lot less than a seven times increase!

FIGURE 11.4

	F2	▼		*fx*	=C2/E2	

	A	B	C	D	E	F
1	Year	Month	Avg. House Price	CPI	Deflator	Avg House Price (Real, $2006)
2	2006	8	304400	203.7	1	304400
3	2006	7	314200	203.2	0.9975	314973
4	2006	6	305900	202.3	0.9931	308017
5	2006	5	293900	201.9	0.9912	296520
6	2006	4	310300	201	0.9867	314468
7	2006	3	298800	199.8	0.9809	304632
8	2006	2	307900	199.1	0.9774	315014
9	2006	1	301000	199	0.9769	308109
10	2005	12	290200	197.7	0.9705	299007
11	2005	11	294400	197.8	0.971	303181
12	2005	10	293600	199.1	0.9774	300383
⋮	⋮					
375	1975	7	42300	54	0.2651	159565
376	1975	6	42500	53.5	0.2626	161818
377	1975	5	43200	53.1	0.2607	165722
378	1975	4	42000	53	0.2602	161423
379	1975	3	42100	52.8	0.2592	162420
380	1975	2	40600	52.6	0.2582	157229
381	1975	1	39500	52.3	0.2568	153846

Can you think of a reason, other than inflation, why houses might be more expensive in 2006 than in 1975? Here's one—the average new house in 1975 was quite a bit smaller than the average new house in 2006. In 1975, for example, 25 percent of houses were less than 1,200 square feet in size! In 2006, only 4 percent of new houses were less than 1,200 feet in size.* So if we wanted to get an even more accurate picture of the true increase in the price of housing, we should calculate the price per square foot of housing. If we were to do that, we would find that the average price of housing has less than doubled. All of this demonstrates that getting real can be quite tricky, but it's worthwhile if we want to correctly understand how the economy has grown and changed over time.

* http://www.census.gov/const/www/charindex.html

12

Business Fluctuations and the Dynamic Aggregate Demand–Aggregate Supply Model

Economic growth is not a smooth process. Real GDP in the United States has grown at an average rate of 3.3 percent per year over the past 50 years. But the economy didn't grow at this rate every day or every month or even every year. The economy advances and recedes, it rises and falls, it booms and busts.

In Chapters 6 and 7, we looked at why some countries are rich and others are poor. In answering that question, we could safely ignore booms and recessions and focus on average rates of growth over periods of many years. We now turn from average growth rates to focus on the deviations from average, namely the booms and the recessions.

Figure 12.1 on the next page illustrates the booms and recessions of the U.S. economy by quarter since 1948. The average rate of growth of real GDP is 3.3 percent per quarter (on an annual basis), as marked by the red line, but the economy rarely grew at an average rate. In a typical recession, the growth rate might drop to −5 percent in some quarters and in a boom the economy can grow at a rate of 7 percent to 8 percent or higher. We call the fluctuations of real GDP around its long-term trend or "normal" growth rate **business fluctuations** or business cycles. **Recessions,** which we defined in Chapter 6 as significant, widespread declines in real income and employment, are shaded.

Recessions are of special concern to policymakers and the public because unemployment increases during a recession. Notice in Figure 12.2 on the next page, for example, how unemployment increases dramatically within each of the shaded regions that are the periods of U.S. recessions.

More generally, a recession is a time when all kinds of resources, not just labor but also capital and land, are not fully employed. During a recession, factories close, stores are boarded up, and farmland is left fallow. We know that some unemployment is a natural or normal consequence of economic growth—in Chapter 10, we called this level of unemployment the natural unemployment

Business fluctuations are fluctuations in the growth rate of real GDP around its trend growth rate.

A **recession** is a significant, widespread decline in real income and employment.

FIGURE 12.1

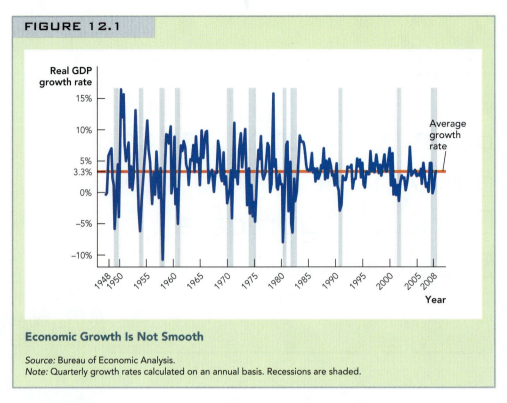

Economic Growth Is Not Smooth

Source: Bureau of Economic Analysis.
Note: Quarterly growth rates calculated on an annual basis. Recessions are shaded.

FIGURE 12.2

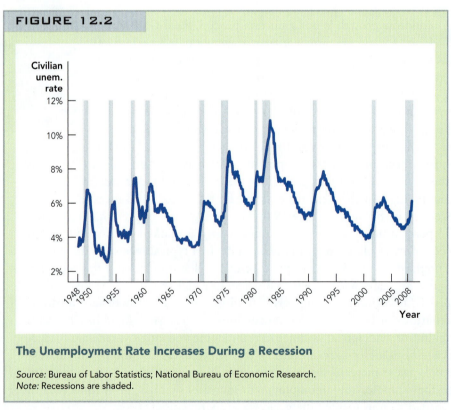

The Unemployment Rate Increases During a Recession

Source: Bureau of Labor Statistics; National Bureau of Economic Research.
Note: Recessions are shaded.

rate—but often unemployment exceeds the natural rate. More generally, when we see a lot of unemployed resources, it is a sign that resources are being wasted and the economy is operating below its potential. One of the goals of economic thinking is to better understand the causes of booms and recessions and perhaps learn how policy might help to smooth out these fluctuations. Recessions are the exception rather than the norm, but still we would all be richer and more secure if we could limit the frequency and severity of recessions.

A Skeleton Model

To understand booms and recessions we are going to develop a dynamic model of aggregate demand and aggregate supply. Our model will show how unexpected economic disturbances or "shocks" can temporarily increase or decrease the economy's rate of growth. We will focus on how an economy responds to two types of shocks, real shocks and aggregate demand shocks.

Models that explain how the economy responds to real shocks are often called Real Business Cycle models while those that focus on aggregate demand shocks are often called New Keynesian models. We think insights from both types of models are important so we will explain real shocks and aggregate demand shocks using the same dynamic AD-AS model.

In this chapter, we only present the model as a skeleton, giving the basics of the curves and how they shift. In the next few chapters, we add flesh to our skeleton by explaining the real-world mechanisms that generate and amplify fluctuations and by showing how monetary policy and fiscal policy might be used to smooth fluctuations.

Ultimately, our dynamic AD-AS model will have three curves: what we call the Solow growth curve, the dynamic aggregate demand curve, and the short-run aggregate supply curve. Let's begin with the Solow growth curve.

The Solow Growth Curve

We learned in Chapters 6 and 7 that economic growth depends on increases in the stocks of labor and capital and on increases in productivity (driven by new and better ideas and better institutions). Thus, the economy has a potential growth rate given by these fundamental or real factors of production. If markets are working well and prices are flexible, then an economy will grow at its potential rate. In other words, when prices are flexible, actual growth will be equal to potential growth. But, we will see later that all prices are not perfectly flexible; in the short run some prices, especially wages, can be "sticky" and because of this an economy need not always be growing at its potential.

We call it the Solow growth curve because Robert Solow, one of the giants of economics, created an important model of an economy's potential growth rate. In Chapter 7, we described Solow's model in more detail, but if you skipped that section don't worry; just think of the **Solow growth rate** as the rate of economic growth given flexible prices and the existing real factors of capital, labor, and ideas.

It's important to understand that the Solow growth rate does not depend on the rate of inflation. As we emphasized in Chapter 11, in the long run money is neutral.* Thus, when we put the inflation rate on the vertical axis of a graph and real growth (the growth rate of real GDP) on the horizontal axis,

The **Solow growth rate** is an economy's potential growth rate, the rate of economic growth that would occur given flexible prices and the existing real factors of production.

---

* Saying that potential growth does not depend on the rate of inflation is a strong form of the money neutrality result that we discussed in Chapter 11. Unexpected and variable inflation can reduce a country's potential growth rate and there are a variety of reasons why even an expected inflation rate might have a small influence on potential growth. Dealing with these issues, however, would complicate our model without leading to a better understanding of our current topic, business fluctuations.

FIGURE 12.3

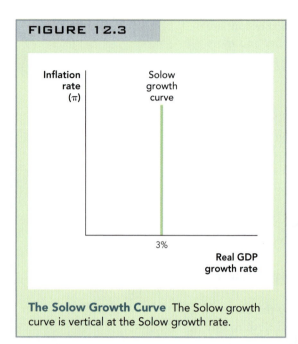

The Solow Growth Curve The Solow growth curve is vertical at the Solow growth rate.

FIGURE 12.4

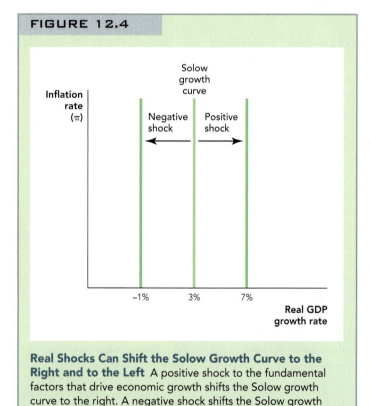

Real Shocks Can Shift the Solow Growth Curve to the Right and to the Left A positive shock to the fundamental factors that drive economic growth shifts the Solow growth curve to the right. A negative shock shifts the Solow growth curve to the left.

A **real shock**, also called a productivity shock, is any shock that increases or decreases the potential growth rate.

the Solow growth curve is very simple—it's a vertical line at the Solow growth rate. Figure 12.3 illustrates the Solow growth curve.

Notice that the Solow growth curve is a vertical line at the Solow growth rate. Once again, the potential growth rate of the economy depends on fundamental factors and not on the rate of inflation.

Shifts in the Solow Growth Curve Take a look again at Figure 12.1, which shows the growth rate of U.S. GDP over time. Although the growth rate has averaged about 3 percent (at an annual rate) per quarter for many years, it has fluctuated around this average. Why?

One reason that the growth rate fluctuates is that economies are continually being hit by shocks, which shift potential growth and thus shift the Solow growth curve. As an example, consider an agricultural economy: Good weather can increase crop production—driving the growth rate up—while bad weather can decrease production, thereby driving the growth rate down.

All economies are subject to shocks not just from the weather but from wars, strikes, new technologies, and sudden changes in the supply of important inputs such as oil. Sometimes the shocks are big, such as a sudden decrease in the oil supply or a major technological advance. But many small shocks impinge on the economy all the time. When many of these small shocks are positive, the economy grows strongly and when many of these shocks are negative the economy slows down.

We call these shocks **real shocks** or productivity shocks because they increase or decrease an economy's fundamental ability to produce goods and services and, thus, they increase or decrease the Solow growth rate. In the next chapter, we say much more about real shocks and how transmission mechanisms spread and amplify shocks. For now, we emphasize that real shocks shift the Solow growth curve. A positive shock, shown in Figure 12.4, shifts the Solow growth curve to the right, increasing real growth. A negative shock shifts the Solow growth curve to the left, decreasing real growth.

The Dynamic Aggregate Demand Curve

Now let's introduce the dynamic aggregate demand curve, or AD curve. The **aggregate demand curve** tells us all the combinations of inflation and real growth that are consistent with a *specified* rate of spending growth. The easiest way to explain a dynamic AD curve is to derive it using the quantity theory of money from Chapter 11. Recall that we can write the quantity theory in dynamic form as:

$$\vec{M} + \vec{v} = \vec{P} + \vec{Y}_R \qquad (1)$$

where $\vec{M}$ is the growth rate of the money supply; $\vec{v}$ is growth in velocity (how quickly money is turning over); $\vec{P}$ is the growth rate of prices, that is, the inflation rate; and $\vec{Y}_R$ is the growth rate of real GDP, which we simplify and call real growth. Thus, we can also write equation 1 as:

$$\vec{M} + \vec{v} = \text{Inflation} + \text{Real growth} \qquad (2)$$

Now imagine that $\vec{M} = 5\%$, $\vec{v} = 0\%$, and real growth is 0%. What is the inflation rate? To answer that question, we substitute what we know into equation 2. Thus, 5% + 0% = Inflation + 0%, so Inflation = 5%. Intuitively, if the money supply is growing by 5 percent a year ($\vec{M} = 5\%$) and velocity is stable ($\vec{v} = 0\%$), then spending is growing by 5 percent a year. But if there are no additional goods to spend the money on, that is, if real growth is 0 percent, then prices must rise by 5 percent. In short, more spending plus the same goods equals higher prices.

An AD curve tells us *all* the combinations of inflation and real growth that are consistent with a specified rate of spending growth. We have just discovered *one* such combination; an inflation rate of 5 percent and a real growth rate of 0 percent are consistent with a spending growth rate of 5 percent. But what other combinations of inflation and real growth are consistent with a spending growth rate of 5 percent?

What would the inflation rate be if, just as before, $\vec{M} = 5\%$ and $\vec{v} = 0\%$ but now real growth = 3%? Once again, we substitute what we know into equation 2. Thus, we have 5% + 0% = Inflation + 3%, so Inflation = 2%. The intuition is quite simple. Inflation is caused when more money chases the same goods. So, if more money is chasing an increased quantity of goods, then, all else being equal, the inflation rate will be less than the increase in money growth.

Thus, we now have *two* combinations of inflation and real growth that are consistent with a spending growth rate of 5 percent. In Figure 12.5 on the next page, point *a* shows an inflation rate of 5 percent and a real growth rate of 0 percent and point *b* shows an inflation rate of 2 percent and a real growth rate of 3 percent. Both of these combinations are consistent with a spending growth rate of 5 percent, *so they belong on the same AD curve.* In fact, from equation 2 we know that all the combinations of inflation and real growth that are consistent with a spending growth rate of 5 percent must satisfy the equation, 5% = Inflation + Real growth. In other words, any combination of inflation and real growth that add up to 5 percent is on the same AD curve. Figure 12.5 shows the AD curve for a spending growth rate of 5 percent. Thus, all the points on this line add up to 5 percent.

Notice also that the AD curve is a straight line with a slope of −1.[*] This means that, given the rate of spending growth, a 1 percentage point increase in real growth reduces inflation by 1 percentage point.

The **aggregate demand curve** shows all the combinations of inflation and real growth that are consistent with a specified rate of spending growth.

Key Equation

$\vec{M} + \vec{v} = \text{Inflation}$
$\qquad + \text{Real Growth}$

Check the Math

If the money supply is growing at 5% per year ($\vec{M} = 5\%$) and velocity is stable ($\vec{v} = 0\%$) then Inflation + Real Growth must equal 5%. If Real growth is 3% then Inflation must be 2%.

---

[*] We can easily show this by rewriting equation 2 in the familiar $Y = b + mX$ format, Inflation = $(\vec{M} + \vec{v}) - 1 \times$ Real growth. Notice that m, the slope of the curve, is −1.

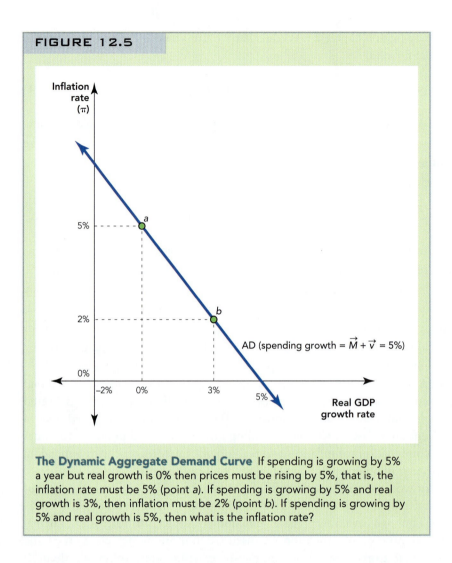

FIGURE 12.5

The Dynamic Aggregate Demand Curve If spending is growing by 5% a year but real growth is 0% then prices must be rising by 5%, that is, the inflation rate must be 5% (point *a*). If spending is growing by 5% and real growth is 3%, then inflation must be 2% (point *b*). If spending is growing by 5% and real growth is 5%, then what is the inflation rate?

Shifts in the Dynamic Aggregate Demand Curve The AD curve for a spending growth rate of 5 percent is all the combinations of inflation and real growth that add up to 5 percent. So, what is the AD curve for a spending growth rate of 7 percent? Right, all the combinations of inflation and real growth that add up to 7 percent. So, now that we know what an AD curve is, we also know how the AD curve shifts. In Figure 12.6, for example, notice that all the combinations of inflation and real growth along the AD curve denoted AD ($\vec{M} + \vec{v} = 5\%$) add up to 5 percent and all the combinations of inflation and real growth along the AD curve denoted AD ($\vec{M} + \vec{v} = 7\%$) add up to 7 percent. Thus, if spending growth increases to 7 percent, either because of an increase in $\vec{M}$ or an increase in $\vec{v}$, then the AD curve shifts up and to the right (outward). The intuition is that increased spending must flow into either a higher inflation rate or into a higher growth rate. Thus, an increase in spending growth shifts the AD curve outward, up and to the right, and, of course, a decrease in spending growth shifts the AD curve inward.

As we have said, an increase in spending growth can be caused by either an increase in $\vec{M}$ or $\vec{v}$. Later on in this chapter and in Chapters 15 and 17 on monetary and fiscal policy respectively, we explain exactly what this means in practice. For now, we just need to remember that increased spending growth shifts the dynamic AD curve outward and decreased spending growth shifts the dynamic AD curve inward.

FIGURE 12.6

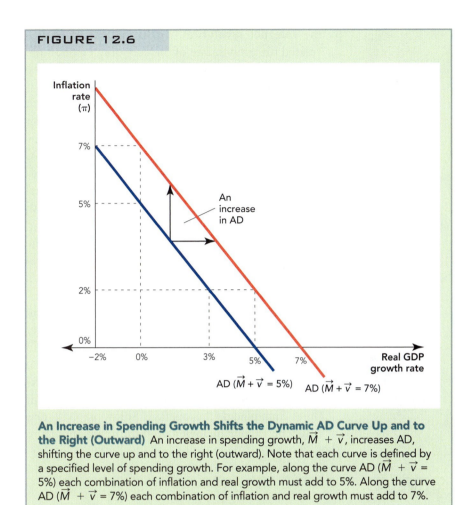

An Increase in Spending Growth Shifts the Dynamic AD Curve Up and to the Right (Outward) An increase in spending growth, $\vec{M} + \vec{v}$, increases AD, shifting the curve up and to the right (outward). Note that each curve is defined by a specified level of spending growth. For example, along the curve AD ($\vec{M} + \vec{v}$ = 5%) each combination of inflation and real growth must add to 5%. Along the curve AD ($\vec{M} + \vec{v}$ = 7%) each combination of inflation and real growth must add to 7%.

Now that we understand the Solow growth curve and the dynamic AD curve, we have enough to introduce the basics of our first model of business fluctuations, the real business cycle model.

The Real Business Cycle Model: Real Shocks and the Solow Growth Curve

Let's put the AD and Solow growth curve together. This will let us explain how business fluctuations can be caused by real shocks, a way of thinking about business fluctuations often called the real business cycle (RBC) model. Figure 12.7 on the next page shows an AD curve in which the growth rate of spending is 10 percent a year and a Solow growth curve that has a growth rate of 3 percent. Since $\vec{M} + \vec{v}$ = Inflation + Real growth, and $\vec{M} + \vec{v}$ = 10%, and Real growth = 3%, we know that inflation is 7% a year. Thus, in this model, the equilibrium inflation rate and growth rate are determined by the intersection of the AD and Solow growth curves.

As we discussed above, the Solow growth rate can increase or decrease when the economy is hit by real shocks. In Figure 12.8 on the next page, we show the effect of a positive and a negative real shock.

A positive real shock shifts the Solow growth curve to the right, increasing real growth. The increase in the supply of goods brought about by a higher real growth rate reduces the inflation rate. During the late 1990s, for example,

CHECK YOURSELF

> If inflation is 2 percent and the Solow growth rate is 5 percent what, if anything, happens to the Solow growth rate when inflation increases to 5 percent?

> If we have a dynamic aggregate demand curve with $\vec{M}$ = 7 percent and $\vec{v}$ = 0 percent, what will inflation plus real growth equal? If we find out that real growth is 0 percent, what is inflation?

> Increased spending growth shifts the dynamic aggregate demand curve which way: inward or outward?

FIGURE 12.7

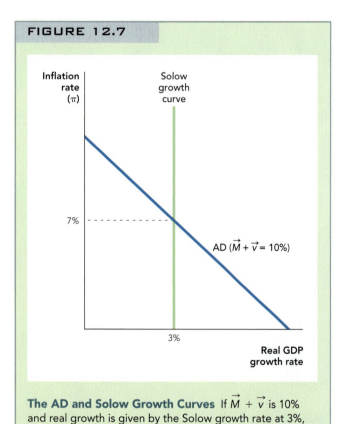

The AD and Solow Growth Curves If $\vec{M}$ + $\vec{v}$ is 10% and real growth is given by the Solow growth rate at 3%, then the inflation rate will be 7%.

the Internet revolution, a positive real shock, increased the growth rate of the economy. Faster, more powerful computers at lower prices helped to keep inflation low.

A negative real shock shifts the Solow growth curve to the left, decreasing real growth. The slower growth rate means fewer new goods to spend money on so the inflation rate increases. In the 1970s, for example, a negative real shock—a sudden, sharp decrease in the relative supply of oil leading to several big jumps in the price of oil—reduced the growth rate and increased inflation.

Shocks to the Solow growth curve will change the growth rate and the inflation rate *temporarily* because the Solow growth curve is always shifting back and forth as new shocks hit the economy. Remember from Figure 12.1 that growth is not smooth. Thus, growth rates fluctuate from quarter to quarter as positive shocks increase growth temporarily and negative shocks reduce growth temporarily. In the United States, growth has fluctuated around approximately 3 percent for about a century. In different times and places, the average Solow growth rate could be higher or lower depending on growth in

FIGURE 12.8

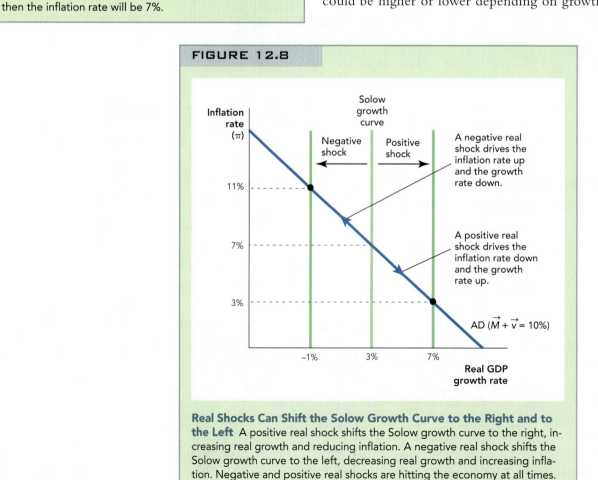

Real Shocks Can Shift the Solow Growth Curve to the Right and to the Left A positive real shock shifts the Solow growth curve to the right, increasing real growth and reducing inflation. A negative real shock shifts the Solow growth curve to the left, decreasing real growth and increasing inflation. Negative and positive real shocks are hitting the economy at all times.

the fundamentals—capital, labor, ideas, and institutions—but every economy will always be subject to real shocks so growth will always fluctuate.

The RBC model is a natural extension of the Solow growth model. In the RBC framework, business fluctuations are simply changes in economic growth in the short run, driven by real shocks, changes in the productive capability of the economy. Let's look at how shocks to the dynamic aggregate demand curve work in the RBC model.

Shocks to Aggregate Demand in the Real Business Cycle Model

A shock to aggregate demand is shown by a shift in the AD curve. Aggregate demand shocks change how much people are willing to spend but since they do not change the potential capacity of an economy to grow, they do not change the Solow growth rate.

Let's work out how a shock to AD, brought about by changes in $\vec{M}$ or $\vec{v}$, influences real growth and inflation in the model that we have developed to this point. Imagine, for example, that $\vec{M}$, the growth rate of money, increases. This means more money in the economy, which increases spending growth, shifting the AD curve outward as we show in Figure 12.9. The outward shift in AD increases the inflation rate but has no effect on real growth. Similarly, a decrease in AD reduces the inflation rate but has no effect on real growth.

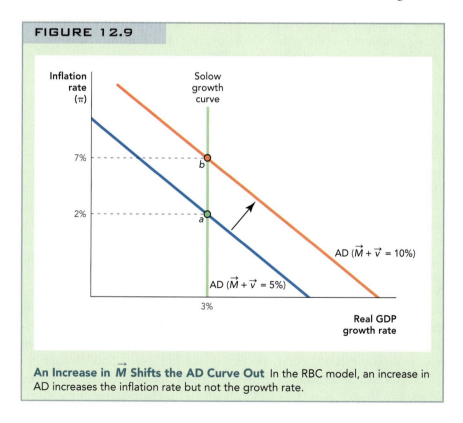

FIGURE 12.9

An Increase in $\vec{M}$ Shifts the AD Curve Out In the RBC model, an increase in AD increases the inflation rate but not the growth rate.

Shifts in AD do not influence real growth in the RBC model because real growth is fixed at the Solow rate by real factors such as the stocks and productivity of labor and capital. Returning again to equation 2, we have it that $\vec{M} + \vec{v} =$ Inflation + Real growth. *If the rate of real growth is fixed by real factors, changes in $\vec{M}$ and $\vec{v}$ can only change the inflation rate.* Notice, for example, that an increase of 5 percentage points in $\vec{M}$ will increase the inflation rate by 5 percentage points. Thus, money is neutral. We know from Chapter 11 that this is a good prediction of what happens in the long run but is money neutral in the short run?

Most economists think that changes in the growth rate of money, especially unexpected changes, will have substantial effects on real growth in the short run. This is one reason why economists and politicians pay close attention to the policies of the Federal Reserve Bank, the institution that controls the supply of money in the American economy. But in the model we have developed so far, a basic RBC model, money is neutral in the short run as well as in the long run. So, if we want our dynamic AD-AS model of business fluctuations to be consistent with how we think the world works, we will need to add to the model.

A key assumption of the model so far, one that leads to the focus on factors like labor, capital, and productivity, is that prices are perfectly flexible. We now turn to what happens when prices are not perfectly flexible. This means adding a new curve to our model.

The New Keynesian Model

Models of the economy with "sticky" (not perfectly flexible) prices are often called New Keynesian models because they are based on ideas first developed by John Maynard Keynes in the 1930s. Since that time, these models have been elaborated by many people, hence the term "New" Keynesian. The key to New Keynesian models is that when some prices are sticky, the economy need not always be growing at its potential. In other words, when prices are sticky, the economy can grow slower or faster than the Solow rate of growth. Since real growth will no longer be determined solely by the Solow rate, we need to develop a new curve to describe the economy during the period in which prices are sticky.

The Short-Run Aggregate Supply Curve

Imagine that the growth rate of the money supply increases and as a result the inflation rate increases from 5 percent to 15 percent. In the long run, we know that wage growth will also increase by 10 percentage points but what would happen to firm profits if wages *do not* grow as fast as prices? If wages do not grow as fast as prices, then production will be very profitable (wages are most firms' biggest cost) and firms will want to hire more workers and expand output. Now, what would happen if inflation falls from 15 percent to 5 percent but wages *do not* fall as quickly? If wages do not fall as quickly as prices, then production will be very unprofitable and firms will want to fire workers and reduce output.

What we have shown in this simple example is that *if* wages are not as flexible as prices, then in the short run inflation and real growth will be positively related—an increase in inflation will increase real growth and a decrease in inflation will decrease real growth. We show such a relationship with a **short-run aggregate supply (SRAS) curve** like that shown in Figure 12.10. We have not yet given you reasons explaining *why* wages might not be as flexible as prices. As we explain these reasons, you will gain a better understanding of the short-run aggregate supply curve.

We will actually give you two reasons why there can be a positive relationship between the inflation rate and the growth rate in the short run. These are:

1. Sticky wages

2. Sticky prices

Let's look at each of these in turn.

CHECK YOURSELF

> In what direction would a technological innovation such as the Internet or cheap fusion power shift the Solow growth curve?

> In the real business cycle model, what effect does a large fall in aggregate demand have on real growth?

In 1936, John Maynard Keynes published a revolutionary book, *The General Theory of Employment, Interest and Money. The General Theory* explained that when prices were not perfectly flexible, deficiencies in aggregate demand could generate recessions.

The **short-run aggregate supply (SRAS) curve** shows the positive relationship between inflation and real growth during the period when prices are sticky.

Sticky Wages When wages do not respond very quickly to changes in economic conditions, economists say that *wages are sticky*. One reason that wages are sticky is that they are not set every day or every month and sometimes wages are not even set every year. Labor contracts with unions, for example, often set wages for two to three years.

Workers and employers understand that inflation will reduce the value of money over time so when wages are set they will be set to grow in accordance with expectations of inflation. But expectations are not always correct. If inflation is greater than expected, then prices will be rising faster than wages so profits will increase and firms will expand output. If inflation is less than expected, then prices will be rising slower than wages so profits will decrease and firms will contract output.

The SRAS curve shows the positive relationship between inflation and real growth in the short run, that is, during the period when wages are sticky. We call it a short run curve because in the long run prices are flexible and thus growth will be at the Solow rate regardless of the inflation rate. Notice that higher inflation *than expected* will increase output and lower inflation *than expected* will decrease output. Thus, every SRAS curve shows the relationship between inflation and output for a given expected inflation rate. The SRAS curve in Figure 12.10, for example, is the SRAS curve given that firms and workers expect an inflation rate of 2 percent. What would happen if workers and producers expected a different rate of inflation?

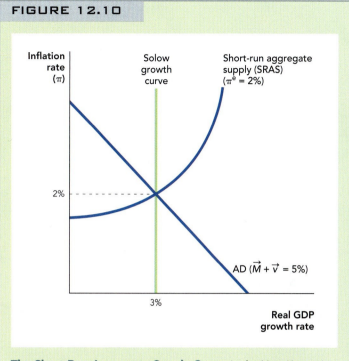

FIGURE 12.10

The Short-Run Aggregate Supply Curve In the New Keynesian model, inflation and real growth are positively related in the short run when prices are sticky. We illustrate this relationship with an upward-sloped, short-run aggregate supply curve.

Shifting the SRAS Curve Figure 12.11 on the next page shows two SRAS curves, one when workers and producers expect an inflation rate of 2 percent, denoted SRAS (π^e = 2%), and the other when workers and producers expect an inflation rate of 4 percent, written SRAS (π^e = 4%). In both cases, the notation π^e means the expected inflation rate. Let's explain why the curves are positioned as they are.

Suppose we begin at point *a* when workers and producers expect inflation of 2 percent and actual inflation is 2 percent. Now imagine that there is an unexpected increase in the inflation rate to 4 percent a year, this moves the economy along SRAS (π^e = 2%) to point *b* where actual inflation is 4 percent and real growth has increased to 7 percent.

What would have happened if workers and producers had *expected* an inflation rate of 4 percent? Remember that *only unexpected inflation increases real growth*. If inflation is expected, it will be built into wages and prices and the growth rate will then be determined solely by real factors. So, if workers and producers expect inflation of 4 percent and actual inflation is 4 percent, then the economy will be at point *c*, a 4 percent rate of inflation and a 3 percent rate of real growth.

If workers and producers expect an inflation rate of 4 percent, then how high must actual inflation be to generate a real growth rate of 7 percent? If workers and producers expect an inflation rate of 4 percent, then actual

The rate of inflation that workers and producers expect is written π^e.

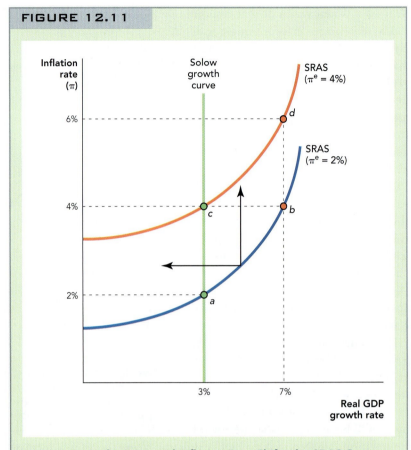

FIGURE 12.11

An Increase in the Expected Inflation Rate Shifts the SRAS Curve Up and to the Left If workers and producers expect an inflation rate of 2% and actual inflation is 2%, then the economy will be at point *a*. If the actual inflation rate increases unexpectedly to 4%, the economy will move along the SRAS (π^e = 2%) curve from point *a* to point *b*.

If workers and producers expect an inflation rate of 4% and actual inflation is 4%, there will be no increase in real growth and the economy will be at point *c*. To increase real growth to 7%, actual inflation needs to be 6% moving the economy along SRAS (π^e = 4%) to point *d*.

Notice that for each level of expected inflation, there is a different SRAS curve. An increase in the expected inflation rate from 2% to 4% moves the economy from SRAS (π^e = 2%) to SRAS (π^e = 4%) or equivalently an increase in the expected inflation rate shifts the SRAS up and to the left.

inflation will have to be higher, in this case 6 percent a year to increase real growth to 7 percent. Thus, an actual inflation rate of 6 percent will move the economy from point *c* along the curve labeled SRAS (π^e = 4 %) to point *d*.

Notice that for every rate of expected inflation, there is a *different* upward sloping SRAS curve. An increase in the expected rate of inflation from 2 percent to 4 percent, for example, moves the economy from SRAS (π^e = 2%) to SRAS (π^e = 4%). Alternatively, we can see from Figure 12.11 that higher rates of expected inflation "shift" the SRAS up and to the left.

The Parable of the Angry Professor We have drawn the SRAS curve to be flatter to the left of the Solow growth curve and steeper to the right of the Solow growth curve. Why?

Remember that one reason why the SRAS has an upward slope is that wages are sticky. And, importantly, wages are *especially* sticky in the downward direction. To see why downward stickiness in wages matters, imagine that expected inflation is 5 percent a year and workers are expecting wage increases of at least 5 percent a year. Now suppose inflation falls unexpectedly to 1 percent. If wage growth also fell to 1 percent, then there would be no problem: Real wages, real growth, and employment would all be constant. But how will workers feel when their salary increase is much less than expected? What will happen to morale and motivation?

One of the reasons that cutting wages or wage growth is so difficult is that everyone knows and understands their nominal wage, their wage in dollars. Every two weeks, most people get a paycheck showing them their nominal wage. Few people, however, know or understand much about their real wage, their nominal wage corrected for inflation or, in other words, the goods and services that their wage is able to purchase. Ultimately, what workers care about is their real wage, but since their nominal wage is so much easier to measure and understand most people pay more attention to their nominal wage, especially in the short run. Focusing on the nominal wage, however, can cause people to behave in peculiar ways. We illustrate this point with the parable of the angry professor.

One year a professor we know—yes, also an economist—received a pay cut. The professor rushed to the office of the department chair screaming bloody murder and threatening to leave or stop preparing for his classes. This professor was very angry. A few years later, the same professor received a pay increase of 3 percent but this was when inflation was running at 6 percent so this professor's real pay fell by 3 percent. Did the professor get angry and run to complain to the department chair? No, he was pretty happy. In real terms, he had received a pay cut but he still felt he got something, some form of recognition, plus it was a little more than what his friends down the hall got. The professor's immediate reaction was driven by the increase in the nominal wage even though a more careful calculation would show that he had received no greater command over goods and services.

Is this professor irrational? Maybe. Is this story for real? For sure. Is he the only person in the world like this? No way. And this guy is an economist who understands how things work. The lesson is that nominal variables can influence real economic choices.

The department chair learned a valuable lesson as well. Sometimes it is harder to cut nominal wages than real wages! The lesson applies to more than the angry professor. People don't like having things taken away from them, even when what is at stake is only symbolic. This is sometimes called an **endowment effect**. Once we possess something or feel we have a right to expect it, we consider it ours and are especially upset to give it up. The economist Truman Bewley interviewed employers and labor leaders, and concluded that the main reason employers don't like to cut wages is that if workers see smaller numbers on their paycheck, their morale declines and they often take their anger out on their employers. In contrast, layoffs get the misery out the door. One study examined pay records of a single large U.S. firm. From over 50,000 observations of wages, wage cuts were found fewer than 200 times, 0.4 percent of the total.

> An **endowment effect** is when people attach special importance to their starting point and have an especially strong dislike for losing that position.

Thus, when inflation slows, growth in nominal wages should also slow but because of downward wage stickiness and confusion between nominal and real wages that process often results in painful declines in employment and real growth.

So why is the SRAS curve steeper above the Solow growth curve? First, wages are less sticky in the upward direction, or in other words not so many people complain when their wages increase! Second, the SRAS curve must turn vertical at some point because there is a limit to how fast the economy can grow. The Solow growth rate can be thought of as the growth rate the economy can sustain in the long run given the growth rates in the fundamental factors of labor, capital, ideas, and institutions. The growth rate can be above the Solow rate if people work overtime and capital is pushed to its limit (e.g., by temporarily running equipment 24 hours a day), but at some point labor and capital are working around the clock and the economy just cannot grow any faster.

Sticky Prices   Wages are not the only prices that can be sticky. When a shock hits an economy, many prices do not move instantaneously to their new equilibrium levels. Why not? First, because it's costly to change prices and, second, because it's often not obvious whether a shock is temporary or permanent or nominal or real. That's a mouthful so let's explain.

Economists call the costs of changing prices **menu costs** because an obvious example is the costs of printing new menus when a restaurant changes its prices. Catalog companies like Lands' End and L.L. Bean face similar costs. Menu costs, however, are more than printing costs. Firms may want to keep prices steady to create trust—if prices are always changing, how do customers know they are getting a fair deal? Firms may also want to keep prices steady because if a firm raises its prices, it gives customers an incentive to search out other firms. Even if other firms are also raising prices, customers who leave may never come back.

Even small menu costs can discourage firms from changing prices when there is uncertainty about whether a shock is temporary or permanent. Imagine that the price of eggs increases. Does the restaurant change the price of an omelet? If the restaurant knew the price change was permanent, then maybe it would. But maybe the price of eggs will go down tomorrow. If the change in the price of eggs is temporary and the firm prints new menus today, it might also have to print new menus again tomorrow. Better to wait and see before printing the new menus. Thus, uncertainty creates incentives for firms to delay a price change until better information comes along.

Small menu costs can also create significant price stickiness when the nature of a shock is uncertain. Imagine that you are a baker—like the baker in Chapter 11's inflation parable—and suddenly you have more customers spending more money in your store than before. That's good news, right? Well, maybe it's not as good as it looks. It could be that more bread is being demanded or it could be that the nation's central bank is printing money at a faster rate and people are spending more on everything. If you knew for certain that people were spending more on bread simply because there were more dollars being printed you would raise prices immediately. But as a businessperson, how do you know whether the increase is a nominal increase or a real increase?

When a baker sees increased spending on bread, there is some chance that she interprets the greater spending as a signal that more people want to eat bread and thus instead of raising prices to completely offset the increased spending, she works longer hours or expands her bakery. Not all entrepreneurs or even most entrepreneurs will expand in this manner but probably some will, and that means that the growth rate increases. Thus, as with sticky wage theory, sticky prices generated by uncertainty over the nature of a shock (real versus

Menu costs are the costs of changing prices.

LWA-SHARIE KENNEDY/CORBIS

nominal) offer another reason why there is a positive relationship between un-expected inflation and real growth in the short run.

Shocks to Aggregate Demand in the New Keynesian Model

In the RBC model, shocks to AD had no effect on real growth but that was because the RBC model assumes prices are fully flexible. Let's now use our New Keynesian model with sticky prices to examine how shocks to aggregate demand can change real growth.

An Increase in $\vec{M}$ in the New Keynesian Model

In Panel A of Figure 12.12, we show an initial equilibrium at point a where in-flation is 2 percent, expected inflation is 2 percent, and the real growth rate is 3 percent.

CHECK YOURSELF

> Contrast wage and price flexibility in the real business cycle and new Keynesian models. Which model assumes significant price and wage stickiness?

> The Solow growth curve is vertical, the short-run aggregate supply curve is not. What explains the difference?

> What happens to the short-run aggregate supply curve when people expect inflation to increase from 2 percent to 3 percent?

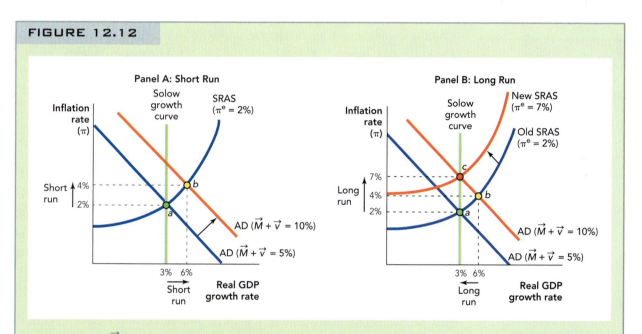

FIGURE 12.12

An Increase in $\vec{M}$ Shifts the AD Curve Out **Panel A:** In the New Keynesian model, an increase in AD increases real growth in the short run. The equilibrium moves from point a to the short-run equilibrium at point b. **Panel B:** In the long run the SRAS curve shifts upward as inflation expectations adjust and wages become unstuck. As a result, real growth will eventually return to the Solow rate and inflation will increase. In the long run, after all transitions are complete, the economy will end up at point c.

Now suppose that the growth rate of the money supply increases unexpect-edly from 5 percent to 10 percent. The injection of more money into the eco-nomic system creates a temporary boom at point b at which point the economy is growing at a 6 percent rate of real growth with inflation of 4 percent. Notice that $\vec{M}$ has increased by 5 percentage points. Some of that increase in spending is reflected in the inflation rate, which increases by 2 percentage points, and because of sticky wages and sticky prices, some of the increase in spending is reflected in real growth, which increases by 3 percentage points.

In Panel B of Figure 12.12, we show what happens in the long run. In the long run, *unexpected inflation always turns into expected inflation* and so the SRAS curve shifts up and to the left. As wages and prices become unstuck and expectations adjust more and more of the increase in $\vec{M}$ is reflected in the inflation rate and less is reflected in the real growth rate. In the long run, after all transitions are complete, all of the increase in $\vec{M}$ is reflected in the inflation rate—$\vec{M}$ increases by 5 percentage points and the inflation rate increases by 5 percentage points and the growth rate returns to the Solow level. Thus, the New Keynesian and RBC models have the same prediction for inflation and growth in the long run (compare Figure 12.9 with Panel B of Figure 12.12). But in the New Keynesian model, an increase in $\vec{M}$ increases real growth in the short run—during the period in which prices and wages are sticky.[*]

Shocks to the Components of Aggregate Demand

Changes in $\vec{v}$ can be broken down into changes in $\vec{C}$, $\vec{I}$, $\vec{G}$, or $\vec{NX}$.

We have already looked at how changes in $\vec{M}$ shift the AD curve so the only other shifter is changes in $\vec{v}$. We can think of changes in $\vec{v}$ as increasing or decreasing the spending rate, holding the money supply constant. To understand why the spending rate might change, it's useful to recall the national spending identity from Chapter 5, $Y = C + I + G + NX$. The national spending identity reminds us that spending is spending on something. For example, if $\vec{v}$ increases that means that the growth rate of C, I, G, or NX must increase—that is, an increase in $\vec{v}$ must be apportioned among an increase in $\vec{C}$, $\vec{I}$, $\vec{G}$, or $\vec{NX}$.

It's often easier to think about changes in $\vec{v}$ working through changes in $\vec{C}$, $\vec{I}$, $\vec{G}$, or $\vec{NX}$ because each of these factors has somewhat different causes and consequences. Let's look at a change in $\vec{C}$. Why might $\vec{C}$ decrease?

A Decrease in $\vec{C}$ in the New Keynesian Model

Fear can cause $\vec{C}$ to decrease. Imagine that consumers suddenly become more pessimistic and fearful about the economy. Workers, for example, might be worried about becoming unemployed, so they build up their cash reserves by slowing down their consumption spending (a reduction in $\vec{v}$ working through a reduction in $\vec{C}$). Thus, fear causes consumers to reduce their spending. What happens?

A decrease in spending growth, a negative AD shock, in the New Keynesian model shifts the AD curve inward, reducing the real growth rate in the short run. Figure 12.13 illustrates. We begin at point *a* with an inflation rate of 7 percent, an expected inflation rate of 7 percent, and a real growth rate of 3 percent. A decrease in spending growth shifts the AD curve inward. With lower spending growth, wage growth should fall to match the reduction in price growth, but because wages are sticky, especially in the downward direction, wage growth remains high so firms are unprofitable, employment falls, and the economy slows.

Thus, in the short run, the economy moves from point *a* to point *b* where the inflation rate is lower and the real growth rate is also lower—in this example at point *b* growth is negative and the economy is in a recession.

[*] For the purpose of making the models simple, we've focused on showing the initial short-run change and then the long-run results, after all the necessary transitions and adjustments have worked their way through the system. But if you're interested in better understanding the transition path to the long run for both real and aggregate demand shocks—and how this relates to some important economic issues about the length and nature of recessions—we cover this in detail in an online appendix to this chapter available at www.SeeTheInvisibleHand.com.

In the long run, fear recedes, wages adjust, and the spending growth rate returns to normal so the economy returns to long-run equilibrium at point *a*. Let's explain the shift back of the AD curve in the long run in greater detail.

Why Changes in $\vec{v}$ Tend to Be Temporary

Changes in $\vec{v}$ (that is, changes in the *growth rate* of C, I, G, or NX) differ from changes in $\vec{M}$ in one respect. $\vec{M}$ can be permanently set at any rate— 5 percent, 17 percent, 103 percent—but changes in $\vec{v}$ tend to be temporary. How do we know this? Recall from Chapter 5 that the shares of GDP devoted to C, I, G, and NX have been quite stable over time. Over the past 50 years, for example, consumption expenditures in the United States have never been less than 60 percent of GDP nor have they ever been more than 71 percent of GDP. Investment expenditures vary more than consumption expenditures on a year-to-year basis, but over time these have also been remarkably stable, never less than 13 percent of GDP nor more than 20 percent of GDP. But if C, I, G, and NX are relatively stable as shares of GDP, it follows that changes in the growth rates of these variables, summarized by $\vec{v}$, must be temporary.

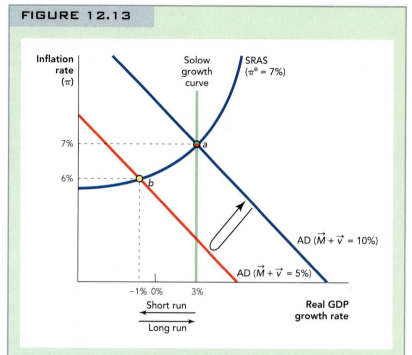

FIGURE 12.13

In the New Keynesian Model, a Temporary Decrease in AD Reduces the Inflation Rate and the Growth Rate in the Short Run At point *a*, spending is growing at a rate of 10% and real growth is 3% so inflation is 7%. If consumers become fearful and reduce their spending, $\vec{v}$ declines so the dynamic AD curve shifts inward. In the short run, wages are sticky so although spending growth declines, wage growth does not. As a result, real growth falls to −1% and the inflation rate falls to 6% at point *b*. In the long run as fear recedes and wages become unstuck, $\vec{v}$ returns to its normal rate, as does real growth.

Imagine what would happen if changes in $\vec{C}$, $\vec{I}$, $\vec{G}$, or $\overrightarrow{NX}$ were not temporary. Suppose, for example, that the government increases the growth rate of government spending, $\vec{G}$, perhaps in an effort to spend an economy out of a recession (this is called fiscal policy, which we study in Chapter 17). The government can do this in the short run, but if $\vec{G}$ were to grow at an unusually high rate year after year, then government purchases would soon dominate the economy. In fact, even if voters did not object, eventually $\vec{G}$ would have to fall because in the long run government spending cannot grow faster than the rate of economic growth (otherwise, government spending would eventually be more than GDP and that is not possible).

Thus, returning to Figure 12.13, we show that a decrease in $\vec{C}$ reduces AD and the rate of inflation in this period. In future periods, however, $\vec{C}$ will return to its normal rate and as it does AD and inflation will return to their previous rates. Notice that because the AD curve shifts back in the long run that *changes in $\vec{C}$, $\vec{I}$, $\vec{G}$, or $\overrightarrow{NX}$ do not change the rate of inflation in the long run.* In other words, sustained inflation requires ongoing increases in the money supply, a truth we've already outlined in Chapter 11.

Other Factors That Shift the AD Curve

We have already said that fear could decrease consumption spending (and, thus, confidence could increase consumption spending). What other factors could change $\vec{C}$, $\vec{I}$, $\vec{G}$, or $\overrightarrow{NX}$?

Fear and confidence play a similar role in investment spending as in consumption spending. If businesspeople fear that the economy is entering a recession, they may want to wait to make large investments. Similarly, confidence about the future will encourage businesspeople to make significant investments.

Wealth shocks can also increase or decrease AD. Imagine, for example, that the stock market or the housing market tumbles. Before the fall in prices consumers might have spent freely expecting that in their retirement years or in an emergency they could sell their stocks or their homes and live on the proceeds. When prices fall consumers suddenly realize that their wealth has fallen so they need to save more, thus they cut back on their spending. In 2008, for example, a simultaneous fall in stocks and housing prices caused a very large decrease in consumption spending. (A positive wealth shock works the opposite way. As the stock market rises, for example, consumers spend more today as their increasing wealth gives them confidence that they will also have plenty in the future.)

Taxes are another important shifter of $\vec{C}$ and $\vec{I}$. An increase in taxes can reduce consumption growth and a decrease in taxes can increase consumption growth. Taxes targeted at investment spending—such as an investment tax credit—can have a similar effect on investment growth. Changes in taxes are also a part of fiscal policy to be studied in Chapter 17.

Big increases in the growth rate of government spending will increase AD, and decreases in the growth rate of government spending will reduce AD. During a war, for example, government spending usually increases at a high rate, thereby shifting the AD curve outward. Government spending can also be timed to try to offset the business cycle (fiscal policy again—see Chapter 17).

The category called net exports consists of exports minus imports. We look at exports and imports more closely in Chapters 18 and 19, but for now the basic idea is simple. If other countries increase their spending on our goods (exports), that increases our AD. If we shift our spending away from domestic goods to foreign goods (imports), that reduces our AD.

Table 12.1 summarizes some of the factors that can shift the dynamic AD curve.

TABLE 12.1 Some Factors That Shift the Dynamic Aggregate Demand Curve

Increase AD (= Higher Growth Rate of Spending) (= Positive AD Shock)	Decrease AD (= Lower Growth Rate of Spending) (= Negative AD Shock)
A faster money growth rate	A slower money growth rate
Confidence	Fear
Increased wealth	Reduced wealth
Lower taxes	Higher taxes
Greater growth of government spending	Lower growth of government spending
Increased export growth	Decreased export growth
Decreased import growth	Increased import growth

Let's now apply the insights from the real business cycle model and the New Keynesian model to understanding the *Great Depression*, a watershed event in U.S. history.

Understanding the Great Depression: Aggregate Demand Shocks and Real Shocks

The Great Depression (1929–1940) was the most catastrophic economic event in the history of the United States; GDP plummeted by 30 percent, unemployment rates exceeded 20 percent, and the stock market fell to less than a third of its original value. Almost overnight America went from confidence to desperation. In fact, the Great Depression was a worldwide event, plaguing almost all the developed nations. In some cases, such as Germany, the economic downturn led to totalitarian regimes followed by war. The 1930s and 1940s were terrible years for the world and bad economic policy was partly at fault.

But the good news is this: We know how to prevent a great depression from happening again. The Great Depression became "great" because policymakers allowed aggregate demand to collapse.

Aggregate Demand Shocks and the Great Depression

The Great Depression occurred in the United States as follows. In 1929, the stock market crashed, creating a mood of pessimism among the American public. In part, this stock market crash had been brought on by tight monetary policy, aimed at limiting a stock market bubble. The fall in stock prices was a wealth shock that made many people feel poorer and so they limited their spending, causing $\vec{C}$ to fall. This, combined with the initial monetary contraction, that is, a reduction in $\vec{M}$, reduced aggregate demand, shifting the AD curve inward to the left.

But that is only the beginning of the story. In 1930, depositors lost confidence in their banks and as they withdrew their money, they created a wave of bank failures. These bank failures meant that people lost their money, again diminishing aggregate demand. Moreover, at the time there was no government deposit insurance so when the first banks failed, people became suspicious of every other bank and rushed to withdraw their money even from banks that were otherwise sound. From 1930 to 1932, there were four waves of banking panics; by 1933, more than 40 percent of all American banks had failed.

The fear and uncertainty created by bank failures, rising unemployment rates, falling consumer confidence, and inconsistent policy making in Washington also reduced investment spending. Between 1929 and 1933, for example, investment spending fell by nearly 75 percent. In many years, spending on new investment was not enough to replace the tools, machines, and buildings that had depreciated due to natural wear and tear. Astoundingly, the U.S. capital stock was lower in 1940 than it had been in 1930.[1]

Furthermore, in 1931, instead of increasing $\vec{M}$, the Federal Reserve allowed the money supply to contract even further. In the early 1930s, the U.S. money supply fell by about a third, *the largest negative shock to aggregate demand in American history*. At that time, the Fed should have been expanding the

CHECK YOURSELF

> What always happens to unexpected inflation in the long run?

> Show what happens to the dynamic aggregate demand curve if consumers fear a recession is coming and cut back on their expenditures.

UNDERSTAND YOUR world

money supply, to drive up output in an emergency situation and also to boost the reserves of failing banks (we analyze monetary policy further in Chapter 15). But, instead, the Fed allowed the money supply to contract and a disaster ensued. Bad decision making caused an additional monetary contraction during 1937–1938, which led to yet another wave of economic distress and it made the Great Depression much longer than it needed to be.

Figure 12.14 shows the story in a diagram. In the late 1920s, the economy was growing at a rate of about 4 percent per year with no inflation. Starting in 1929, a series of brutal shocks to aggregate demand reduced $\vec{C}$, $\vec{I}$, and $\vec{M}$ and by 1932 pushed real growth to a rate of −13 percent and inflation to −10 percent per year. Note that although drawn separately, all these shocks were intertwined as we discussed above.

FIGURE 12.14

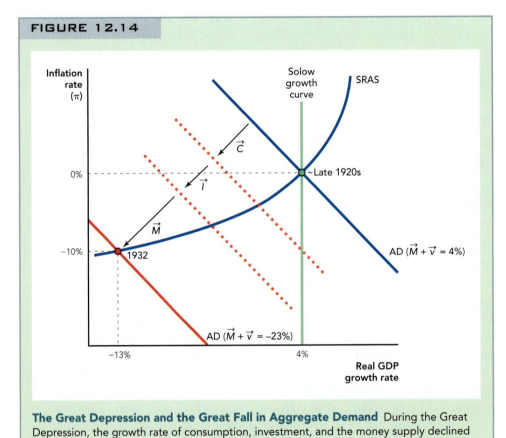

The Great Depression and the Great Fall in Aggregate Demand During the Great Depression, the growth rate of consumption, investment, and the money supply declined dramatically, creating deflation and an unprecedented decline in real growth.

Thus, the Great Depression was due primarily to the *great fall in aggregate demand*. Real shocks, however, also played a role in the Great Depression and in the failure of the economy to recover more quickly from the great fall. Let's take a look at how real factors contributed to the Great Depression.

Real Shocks and the Great Depression

We have already mentioned one real shock—the bank failures—and you can see why bank failures are a real shock by thinking back to Chapter 8 on financial intermediation. Bank failures reduced the money supply and spending (an aggregate demand shock), but they also reduced the efficiency of financial intermediation. As we discussed in Chapter 8, banks play a key role in bridging the gap between savers and investors and as banks failed this bridge collapsed. Some firms could rely on internally generated funds for investment and large firms could turn to the stock and bond markets for new funds. But many small businesses relied on loans from local banks who understood these businesses, and thus many small firms were especially harmed by bank failures.

To sum up the causal chain of events: A fall in $\overrightarrow{M}$ reduced aggregate demand, which led to bank failures, which led to a reduction in the productivity of financial intermediation, a real shock. As you would by now expect, the real shock reduced growth even further. One of the broader lessons of this episode—which is true more generally—is that shocks to AD and shocks to the Solow growth curve are linked in most recessions. In some cases, the shock to AD creates a real shock and in other cases a real shock creates a shock to AD; for instance, the fear and uncertainty created by a real shock can reduce AD by inducing people to cut back on spending and investment.

Some economic policy mistakes during the Great Depression also impeded recovery. As we have already mentioned, the Federal Reserve failed to use its power over the money supply to increase aggregate demand. In addition, there were other policy failures. The Smoot-Hawley Tariff of 1930, for example, raised tariffs (taxes) on tens of thousands of imported goods.[2] In principle a tariff, by taxing foreign goods, can boost demand for domestic goods, thereby increasing AD. (Notice from Table 12.1, our list of factors that can shift AD, that a decrease in imports can increase AD.) But, in reality, retaliations against the Smoot-Hawley Tariff by other countries created a spiraling decline in world trade. When other countries raised their tariffs, U.S. exports fell and remember that a reduction in exports reduces aggregate demand. Unfortunately, the large decline in world trade meant that the net effect of the tariff was to reduce aggregate demand.

A second negative effect of the tariff occurred because *a tariff is a negative productivity shock.* We get the most output from our capital and labor when we specialize in fields in which we have a comparative advantage and then trade for the goods that we produce at a comparative disadvantage (see Chapter 18 for more on comparative advantage). A tariff pushes capital and labor into lower productivity sectors, thereby reducing total output. Another way of seeing this point is to recognize that a tariff has exactly the same effects as an increase in transportation costs. Therefore, a tariff is like a negative productivity shock to the shipping industry, which ripples out to all the other industries dependent on shipping.

As if these shocks were not enough, the United States was beset during the early years of the Great Depression by a natural shock, namely the onset of the so-called Dust Bowl. A severe drought and decades of ecologically unsustainable farming practices turned millions of acres of farmland in Texas, Oklahoma, New Mexico, Colorado, and Kansas to dust. Dust storms blackened the sky, reducing visibility to a matter of feet. Hundreds of thousands of people were forced to leave their homes and millions of acres of farmland became useless.

The Dust Bowl was a real shock.
NOAA George E. Marsh Album

CHECK YOURSELF

> What happened to the U.S. money supply in the early 1930s? Did this primarily or initially affect aggregate demand or the Solow growth curve, and in which direction?

> If, as was said earlier in this chapter, real shocks hit the economy all of the time, should we ignore them in explaining the Great Depression?

In a good year, the real shocks of the Great Depression could have been absorbed without major difficulty, but in a bad year the shocks compounded one another and made a desperate situation even worse.

☐ Takeaway

We've covered a lot in this chapter but the basic point is that we have used the model of dynamic aggregate demand and aggregate supply to analyze business fluctuations. A business fluctuation refers to the fact that the growth rate of GDP is volatile in the short run. A negative rate of growth is known as a recession. A recession is bad because it means that workers are unemployed and economies are not producing as many goods and services as they might.

Using our model we laid out how to analyze two types of shocks, real shocks and aggregate demand shocks. Real shocks are analyzed through shifts in the Solow growth curve. When we focus on real shocks and assume that prices are flexible we call our model of the economy a "real business cycle model." Aggregate demand shocks are analyzed using shifts in the AD curve. Aggregate demand shocks matter most when wages and prices are sticky and thus there is a positive relation between inflation rates and growth rates, which we summarize with a short run aggregate supply curve. When we focus on aggregate demand shocks and sticky wages and prices we call our model of the economy a "New Keynesian model." Some economists tend to emphasize real shocks and flexible prices (the RBC model) while others emphasize aggregate demand shocks and sticky prices (the New Keynesian model), but both types of shocks are important and business fluctuations are best understood when we put these models together.

When you combine the aggregate demand, Solow growth curve, and short-run aggregate supply curves into a single diagram, you can analyze a wide variety of economic scenarios and how they affect the growth rate of the economy. As you will see in future chapters, our model will also help us to explain when government policy can and cannot be used to successfully smooth business fluctuations.

For reasons outlined in the chapter, the aggregate demand curve slopes downward and the short-run aggregate supply curve slopes upward. We also showed how the aggregate demand curve can be broken down into changes in $\vec{M}$ and $\vec{v}$. In addition, changes in $\vec{v}$ can be broken down into changes in $\vec{C}$, $\vec{I}$, $\vec{G}$, or $\overrightarrow{NX}$. You should know and understand how menu costs, uncertainty, and confusion between nominal and real values make wages and prices sticky and how sticky wages and prices create an upward-sloped, short-run aggregate supply curve.

We outlined the history of America's Great Depression from the 1930s using our model. The Great Depression resulted from an unfortunate, concentrated, and interrelated series of aggregate demand and real shocks.

The material in this chapter is central to macroeconomics. If you understand where these curves come from, and how to shift them, you will have a basic toolbox for many macroeconomic questions. You are now ready to tackle many of the core topics of macroeconomics and business cycles.

☐ CHAPTER REVIEW

FACTS AND TOOLS

1. Sort the following shocks into real shocks or aggregate demand shocks. Remember that "shocks" include both good and bad events.

    A fall in the price of oil

    A rise in consumer optimism

    A hurricane that destroys factories in Florida

    Good weather that creates a bumper crop of California oranges

    A rise in sales taxes

    Foreigners watch fewer U.S.-made movies

    Fear

    New inventions occur at a faster pace

    A faster money growth rate

2. Look at Figure 12.2. Let's sum up some basic facts about the link between unemployment rates and recessions. Notice that the shaded bars indicate periods of recession, and wider bars mean longer recessions.

    a. How many recessions have there been since World War II?

    b. Since World War II, how many recessions had unemployment rates of over 10 percent?

    c. Often, the unemployment rate seems to hit its peak after the recession ends: The economy goes back to growing while the unemployment rate rises for a while. As the figure shows, the last two recessions have been clear examples of such "jobless recoveries." Approximately how many times did the

unemployment rate peak after the recession ended?

3. Look at Figure 12.3. When inflation rises, does the Solow growth rate rise, fall, or remain unchanged?

4. Are "real shocks" negative shocks, by definition?

5. When negative real shocks hit, what typically happens to the Solow growth curve: Does it shift left, shift right, or stay in the same place?

6. In the real business cycle model, when negative real shocks hit, what typically happens to the aggregate demand curve? Does it shift left, shift right, or stay in the same place?

7. As Figure 12.1 implies, for the United States, the Solow growth curve has on average been approximately 3 percent real growth per year. If a negative real shock hits, shifting it by 2 percentage points what will happen to real growth: Will it be positive or negative? Would you call the resulting economic conditions a recession?

8. **a.** In the real business cycle model, what does a negative real shock do to inflation: Does it rise, fall, or remain unchanged?

    b. In the real business cycle model, what does a negative real shock do to spending growth: Does it rise, fall, or remain unchanged?

    c. In the real business cycle model, what does a fall in spending growth, that is, a shift inward of the AD curve, do to real growth: Does it rise, fall, or remain unchanged?

9. In the following cases, will real growth rise, fall, or remain unchanged according to the New Keynesian model?

    Expected inflation = 5 percent, Actual inflation = 7 percent

    Expected inflation = 3 percent, Actual inflation = 1 percent

    Expected inflation = 6 percent, Actual inflation = 6 percent

    Expected inflation = 7 percent, Actual inflation = −10 percent

    Expected inflation = −1 percent, Actual inflation = 0 percent

10. Consider the New Keynesian model below. In this relatively unsuccessful economy, the Solow growth rate is 1 percent per year:

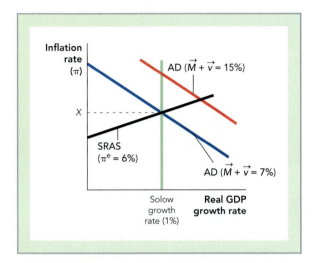

a. Calculate the inflation rate at X in this economy. (Hint: Use the quantity theory.)

b. If spending growth were 15 percent in this economy, what would the inflation rate be in the long run, assuming the Solow growth rate stays fixed?

11. a. The short-run aggregate supply (SRAS) curve is very predictable. When inflation is greater than people expect, SRAS eventually shifts (choose one: up, down) over the next year or so, and when inflation is less than people expect, SRAS eventually shifts (up, down) over the next year or so.

b. Here's another, equally valid way to look at the SRAS curve: When real GDP growth is above the Solow growth rate, SRAS eventually shifts (choose one: right, left) over the next year or so, and when real GDP growth is below the Solow growth rate, SRAS eventually shifts (choose one: right, left) over the next year or so.

c. Explain why the two ways of looking at the SRAS curve are equivalent.

THINKING AND PROBLEM SOLVING

1. Complete the following sentences:

According to the real business cycle model, when real growth is worse than usual, inflation is _____ than usual.

According to the New Keynesian model, when real growth is worse than usual, inflation is _____ than usual.

Since the two models *seem* to make clear-cut predictions about the link between short-term changes in growth and inflation, economists have spent some time trying to find out which of the two models gets more support from the data. In practice, economists find support for both points of view, which is another way of saying that there are real shocks and aggregate demand shocks.

2. a. In the 1970s, the United States had slow growth and high inflation. Which kind of shock and which model better fits these facts?

Real business cycle model: Negative real shock

Real business cycle model: Positive real shock

New Keynesian model: Negative aggregate demand shock

New Keynesian model: Positive aggregate demand shock

b. Using the same categories, explain the late 1990s, when the United States experienced fast growth and falling inflation.

c. Again using the four above categories, explain the early 2000s, when the United States experienced slow growth and falling inflation.

d. Which shock and which model best explains the 1981–1982 recession, when inflation fell quickly and unemployment rose quickly?

3. In the short run, it looks like many workers suffer from an "endowment effect" that makes wages sticky. Let's put this into a familiar supply-and-demand story. To keep things simple, we'll assume that in the long run, workers offer a fixed supply of labor: In other words, while they may be picky about jobs in the short run, in the long run they'll work regardless of the going wage.

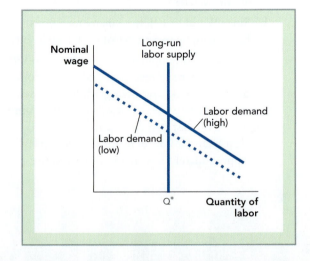

It's the businesses who *demand* labor and workers who *supply* labor. Currently, let's assume the economy starts off at long-run equilibrium, so that the normal number of workers, Q★, are working.

a. Suppose labor demand falls, shifting to the left, as in the figure on the previous page. What does the short-run supply curve for labor look like if workers refuse to take pay cuts even if it means losing their jobs (we can call this the "take this job and shove it" strategy after the famous country and western song). Indicate your answer by drawing a new line on the figure above, labeling it "short-run labor supply." You only need to focus on the area to the left of Q★.

b. Recalling your basic supply-and-demand model, does this fall in labor demand then create a "surplus" of workers or a "shortage" of workers?

c. According to the basic supply-and-demand model, what will happen to the price of labor over time as a result of this fall in labor demand?

4. a. If newspapers and magazines report a lot of good news about the economy, what is likely to happen to velocity?

b. If the Federal Reserve wants to keep aggregate demand (i.e., spending growth) stable, what will it do to the growth rate of the money supply when a lot of good news comes out about the economy: increase it, decrease it, or leave it unchanged? (Hint: In practice, central bankers often call this "leaning against the wind.")

5. In the New Keynesian model, after a monetary shock hits aggregate demand, which curve will shift to bring output growth back to the Solow growth rate: the short-run aggregate supply curve or the aggregate demand curve? (Hint: Which curve is more like a microeconomic story about prices adjusting in order to bring supply and demand into balance?)

6. Let's use the New Keynesian model to think about what happens when bad aggregate demand shocks hit the economy. Consider the following graph.

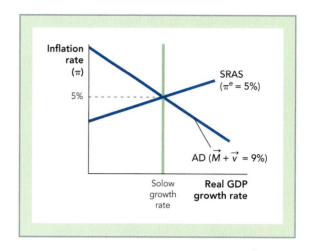

a. Before we get to the bad aggregate demand shock, let's find out what the Solow growth rate is in this economy. Use the quantity theory to find your answer.

b. Because of a fall in the growth of the money supply, spending growth falls to 4 percent per year. Draw the immediate result on aggregate demand in the graph above.

c. This fall in money growth lasts for many years. Eventually, in the long run, workers, business owners, and consumers all adjust their inflation expectations enough so that the economy returns to the Solow growth rate. Draw this new SRAS curve in the figure above.

d. In the long run, after spending growth falls to 4 percent per year, what will the Solow growth rate be? What will inflation be?

7. Real-world economies get hit with lots of shocks to aggregate demand and real shocks. Some shocks clearly fit into the first category, some into the second, and some include a generous mix of both. Let's categorize the following shocks. Only one is a clear case of "both."

Steelworkers go on strike, so less steel is produced

Businesses read about the glories of the Internet, so demand for high-tech investment purchases increase

U.S. senators read about the glories of the Internet, so demand for high-tech government purchases increase

A series of investment banks like Lehman Brothers and Bear Stearns go bankrupt

Around 2000, the glories of the Internet fade a bit so innovations increase at a somewhat slower rate for a few years

The U.S. government launches two costly wars almost simultaneously, so government purchases increase dramatically (referring to World War II, of course)

The U.S. government launches two costly wars almost simultaneously, using the draft to force many men to work much longer hours and supply more labor than they would otherwise

8. Let's have some practice with the dynamic aggregate demand curve. If you want to draw it in your familiar $y = b + mx$ format, you can think of it this way:

Inflation = (Growth in money + Growth in velocity) − Real growth

   a. When you look at a fixed dynamic aggregate demand curve, like in Figure 12.5, what is being held constant? (choose one):

   Spending growth (growth in M + growth in v)

   Real GDP growth (growth in Y)

   Inflation (growth in P)

   b. When you look at a shifting dynamic aggregate demand curve, like in Figure 12.6, what *had* to change to make the curve shift? (choose one):

   Spending growth (growth in M + growth in v)

   Real GDP growth (growth in Y)

   Inflation (growth in P)

   c. According to the quantity theory, which of the following statements *must be* false, and why? More than one may be false.

   "Last year, spending grew at 10 percent, real growth was 4 percent, and inflation was 6 percent."

   "Last year, spending grew at 4 percent, real growth was −2 percent, and inflation was 6 percent."

   "Last year, spending grew at 100 percent, real growth was 0 percent, and inflation was 20 percent."

   "Last year, spending grew at 5 percent, real growth was 5 percent, and inflation was 2 percent."

   "Last year, spending grew at 10 percent, real growth was 5 percent, and inflation was −5 percent."

9. In the New Keynesian model, what is "sticky?" More than one may be true: Wages, Real growth, Prices, Velocity, Money growth, Unemployment

10. During the Great Depression, which of the following were mostly aggregate demand shocks and which were mostly negative real shocks?

   The fall in the growth rate of money

   The fall in farm productivity

   The Smoot-Hawley Tariff Act

CHALLENGES

1. Here is a puzzle. A country with a relatively small positive aggregate demand shock (a shift outward in the AD curve) may have a substantial economic boom, but sometimes countries that have massive increases in the AD curve (hyperinflation countries like Germany before World War II, for example) don't seem to have massive economic booms. Why does a small AD increase sometimes raise GDP much more than a giant AD increase?

2. Some companies raise their workers' pay by giving raises, but others prefer to give one-time bonuses instead.

   a. How might bonuses help solve the problem of the "endowment effect?"

   b. Think about two steel mills facing a big two-year drop in steel demand: In one steel mill, workers have received pay raises every year for five years. In the second mill, most of the pay increases have been through big bonuses at the end of each year. Which steel mill will probably keep more jobs during the two-year downturn? Why?

3. Reconsider your answer to Facts and Tools question 3. If you wanted to draw the Solow growth curve accurately, taking into account the idea that very high rates of inflation are likely to reduce real growth, how would you draw the Solow growth curve?

   a. Would you draw a perfectly vertical curve, a curve with a positive slope, or a curve with a negative slope?

4. **a.** If the New Keynesian model's aggregate demand shocks are the most important drivers of business fluctuations, then should we expect real wages to be procyclical (rising when GDP growth is high) or countercyclical (rising when GDP growth is low)?

   b. If the real business cycle model's real shocks are the most important drivers of business fluctuations, then should we expect real wages to be procyclical or countercyclical?

   c. In Thinking and Problem Solving question 1, we noted that macroeconomists find mixed evidence on the link between business fluctuations and inflation. But there's more agreement on the link between business fluctuations and real wages: The real wage is procyclical, growing quickly during good times and growing slowly or falling during bad times. Which of the two theories is this most consistent with? (We'll revisit this question in the next chapter.)

5. Often, more than one kind of shock hits the economy at once. When this happens, the different shocks *could* push inflation (or real growth) in different directions in the short run, leaving the final short-run result ambiguous. What is most likely to happen to inflation and real output growth in the following cases: Will they rise, fall, or can't you tell with the information given? Note that you will often (maybe always) be able to definitely know the answer for one but not the other.

   a. A nation's scientists invent many new Internet search tools, raising current productivity and making investors optimistic about future inventions as well.

   b. A government raises taxes and its economy has a year of excellent weather for growing crops.

   c. Oil prices skyrocket and the central bank slows the rate of money growth.

13

The Real Business Cycle Model: Shocks and Transmission Mechanisms

I n the last chapter, we introduced the real business cycle model. In this chapter, we look in more detail at shocks and the economic forces, called **transmission mechanisms,** that can amplify the impact of shocks by spreading or transmitting them across time and sectors of the economy.

Let's begin with the idea of shocks. **Shocks** are rapid changes in economic conditions that increase or diminish the productivity of capital and labor, which in turn influences GDP and employment. To understand shocks and to see why they matter, we start with poorer economies, where shocks are easier to see and understand. Later in the chapter, we move to how shocks can create problems for the U.S. and other developed economies.

Transmission mechanisms are economic forces that can amplify shocks by transmitting them across time and sectors of the economy.

Shocks are rapid changes in economic conditions that have large effects on the productivity of capital and labor.

Shocks

There are several billion farmers in the world and for many countries agriculture remains the single-largest contributor to GDP. How much a farm produces depends on the quantity and quality of the inputs of capital and labor, but agricultural output also depends on the weather. When the weather fluctuates, so does output and therefore so does GDP, especially in agricultural economies.

Figure 13.1 on the next page shows how shocks to the weather influence India's agricultural output and GDP. The blue line is the percentage deviation in India's yearly rainfall from the average (1970–1990). Above average rainfall is good for the crops and below average rainfall is bad. In 1975, for example, rainfall was 10.8 percent above average and, in Panel A, we see that agricultural output in that year grew by a bountiful 12.8 percent. In 1979, however, rainfall was 11 percent below average and agricultural output fell by nearly 13 percent, compared to the year before.

FIGURE 13.1

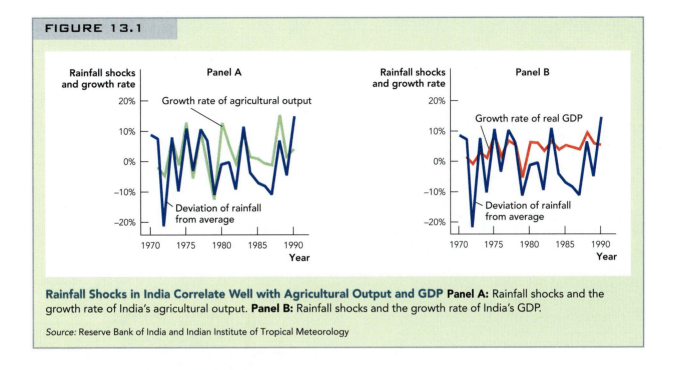

Rainfall Shocks in India Correlate Well with Agricultural Output and GDP **Panel A:** Rainfall shocks and the growth rate of India's agricultural output. **Panel B:** Rainfall shocks and the growth rate of India's GDP.

Source: Reserve Bank of India and Indian Institute of Tropical Meteorology

When India's agricultural output falls, so does India's GDP. It is not just that agriculture contributes to GDP directly but, if farmers struggle, many other sectors of the Indian economy suffer as well. For instance, the demand for tractors will go down and farmers will buy fewer items for their own consumption. Thus, the shock spreads to other sectors of the economy.

Agriculture was the largest contributor to India's GDP, so the shocks to agricultural output caused by the weather have had a big impact on GDP growth. In Panel B of Figure 13.1, the red line shows the growth rate of India's GDP. As expected, GDP boomed in 1975, growing by nearly 10 percent, and busted in 1979 with a decline of 5.2 percent. Note that the booms and busts in GDP are not as strong as the booms and busts in agricultural output because other sectors, less influenced by the weather, also contribute to GDP.

Take a close look at Panel B of Figure 13.1. Does it seem to you that shocks to rainfall are becoming less important to India's GDP since around 1980? Agriculture contributed 40 percent of India's GDP in 1970. Since then, the Indian economy has grown and diversified, and so agriculture contributed only 20 percent of India's GDP in 1990. Therefore, shocks to the weather are becoming less economically important in India over time. In the United States, agriculture contributes around 1 percent to GDP, so yearly variations in the weather don't have much of an effect on GDP. Other shocks, however, can rock the U.S. economy.

Oil Shocks

In an economy with a large manufacturing sector, a reduction in the oil supply is like a reduction in rainfall in an agricultural economy. Oil and machines are complementary, which means they work together, along with labor, to produce output. Thus, when the oil supply is reduced, capital and labor become less productive. Oil greases the wheels of industry, sometimes literally, and with less oil the wheels do not turn as well.

The first oil shock came in late 1973, when many of the oil-producing nations under the guise of OPEC (Organization of Petroleum Exporting

Countries) reduced the global oil supply to protest America's support of Israel in the Middle East. The result was that the price of oil more than tripled in just two years. This became a significant problem for the American economy.

The higher price of oil, for instance, also meant a much higher price for gasoline (oil is one input into gasoline). Higher gas prices reduced the demand for larger cars and increased the demand for smaller cars. The U.S. auto industry was specialized in the production of larger cars and had a difficult time adjusting. Factories cannot simply be switched from the production of one type of car to another—much of the physical capital in an auto factory is specialized. A machine that is used to bend steel is no longer useful when production switches to lightweight, fuel-saving plastic composites. Workers are specialized too in both knowledge and location. Thus, the oil shock meant that many auto plants producing larger cars shut down or were used at less than full capacity. Similarly, autoworkers became unemployed and many had to learn new skills and often they had to move to new jobs.

Not every part of the American economy was harmed. The demand for smaller cars increased, for example, but the U.S. auto industry could not immediately meet that demand. It can take a decade to design and build a new car so it took considerable time for capital and labor to reallocate to the production of smaller American cars. In the meantime, output and employment in the auto industry fell. Similarly, over time, the city of Houston (which services much of the American oil industry) became populated with many former residents of Detroit (which made large American cars) but the transition was costly and disruptive.

Since oil is an important input in many sectors of the economy, high oil prices—or oil shocks—hurt many American industries. Thus, sharp increases in the price of oil can disrupt the economy as a whole. Figure 13.2 shows the price of oil and the last six U.S. recessions. In each case, there was a large increase in the price of oil just prior to or coincident with the onset of recession (oil prices were still very high in the 1981–1982 recession, which was almost a continuation of the

FIGURE 13.2

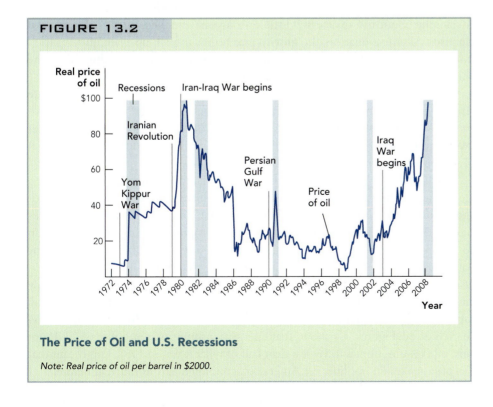

The Price of Oil and U.S. Recessions

Note: *Real price of oil per barrel in $2000.*

1980 recession). The pattern is especially clear with the first three recessions in the graph. In these cases, the onset of a war reduced the oil supply, driving up the price *unexpectedly*. Unexpected shocks are the most costly to deal with.

It's fairly easy to see the impact on the economy of a large increase in the price of oil, but it's harder to eyeball the effect of smaller shocks. Careful statistical analysis, however, can disentangle the effect of oil shocks from the many other shocks that keep on hitting the economy. In Figure 13.3, we show how the economy responds to an unexpected and permanent increase of 10 percent in the oil price.

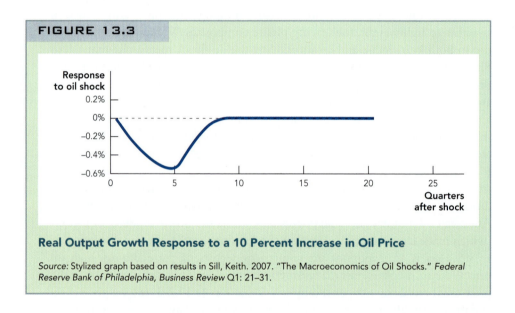

FIGURE 13.3

Real Output Growth Response to a 10 Percent Increase in Oil Price

Source: Stylized graph based on results in Sill, Keith. 2007. "The Macroeconomics of Oil Shocks." *Federal Reserve Bank of Philadelphia, Business Review* Q1: 21–31.

Starting from the normal or trend rate of growth (which is fixed at the 0 point on the vertical axis of the graph), Figure 13.3 shows that a 10 percent increase in the price of oil slows the economy down gradually with the biggest slowdown occurring about five quarters (a little over a year) after the onset of the increase in price. After five quarters, the growth rate begins to pick up again quite quickly and after 10 quarters (two and a half years), the economy has adjusted to the higher price and the growth rate returns to normal.

Thus, a 10 percent increase in the price of oil lowers the GDP growth rate from what it would have been without the price increase for just over two years. The total effect on GDP is a decrease of about 1.4 percent. In other words, if the price of oil had not increased, real GDP would have been about 1.4 percent higher.

Since 2002, the price of oil has increased dramatically and in 2008 peaked at a real price as high as at any time in American history. To be sure, this was not good for the U.S. economy, but the price increase did not cause an immediate recession. Why not? Several answers have been proposed. First, just as the Indian economy has become less dependent on agriculture, so has the American economy become less dependent on oil. Since the price of oil spiked in the 1970s, American producers have learned to protect themselves. The American economy uses energy and oil more efficiently today than it did in the 1970s. In 1970, it took about 1.3 barrels of oil to produce $1,000 of GDP, but in 2004 it took only 0.64 barrels of oil. Figure 13.4 shows that energy consumption per dollar of GDP, not just oil consumption, is today less than half of what it was in 1950. This means that oil price spikes do not hurt the American economy nearly as much as before.

Second, recent increases in the price of oil have been slower and driven by increases in demand due to a growing world economy rather than by sudden cuts in supply. If individuals and firms have time to adjust to a higher price and if the price is driven by a growing economy, it is less likely to cause disruptions.

Third, the U.S. economy may have been lucky because negative oil shocks have been offset in recent years by positive productivity shocks. Remember that shocks can be positive like good weather, as well as negative. In the case of the United States, in the early part of the twenty-first century, productivity grew at especially high rates, mostly because of advances in computers and information technology. Think about how much and how quickly the United States has been transformed by the Internet. Almost all American workplaces during this period became more efficient at processing and storing information. In this case, some positive shocks outweighed the costs of other negative shocks.

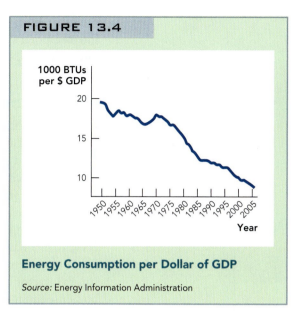

FIGURE 13.4

Energy Consumption per Dollar of GDP

Source: Energy Information Administration

A final reason why oil shocks have been less damaging in recent years may be that the Federal Reserve has responded more appropriately to recent oil shocks than they did in the past. We discuss this explanation, which requires an explanation of aggregate demand and monetary policy, in a later chapter.

Even though oil shocks are less important to the U.S. economy than they used to be, sharp changes in the price of oil are still a major influence on the U.S. economy. A sharp increase in the price of oil, when combined with other shocks, can help to drive the economy into recession. As Figure 13.2 indicates, in late 2007 and early 2008 as the price of oil peaked the U.S. economy did in fact enter into a recession.

Shocks, Shocks, Shocks

Oil and rainfall shocks are only two among many shocks that might hit an economy. Other possible shocks are wars, terrorist attacks, major new regulations, tax rate changes, mass strikes, new technologies such as the Internet, and significant changes in consumer preferences (for example, if consumers suddenly decided they needed to save a larger fraction of their incomes). Most generally, economies are continually hit by many small shocks. Some of the shocks are good, like a productive new technology, and some are bad, like a drought. In a typical year, the good shocks outweigh the bad and the economy grows. People build on previous knowledge and most of the time are able to do better and produce a bit more than in previous years. In a bad year, however, an economy may be hit with a big shock, like an oil shock, or more small shocks are negative than positive and it experiences a recession. It is a bit like playing poker. Every now and then you get a hand of cards that simply cannot be played well, no matter what else you do.

How Transmission Mechanisms Amplify and Spread Shocks

A negative shock reduces output directly—when rainfall is below average the same capital and labor inputs produce less output. But a series of indirect negative effects can amplify shocks and spread them throughout an economy in

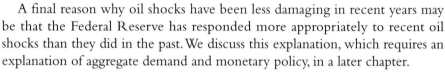

CHECK YOURSELF

> Consider the ubiquity of cell phones throughout the world. How can this ubiquity be considered a positive shock? (Hint: compare with 10 years ago.)

> How would a large and sudden increase in taxes, for example a tax on energy, shift the Solow growth curve?

ways that lower output even further. We focus on five transmission mechanisms: intertemporal substitution, uncertainty and irreversible investments, labor adjustment costs, time bunching, and sticky wages and prices.

Intertemporal Substitution

Let's go back to our farm example. If rainfall is below average, farmers may work less hard and devote less capital to their fields.

Why would farmers choose to use less labor and capital in response to a negative shock? Think about it this way: When the crops are bountiful it makes sense to work from dawn till dusk because each hour of additional work pays a lot—remember the old saying, make hay when the sun shines? But when the crops are poor, the returns to an additional hour of work are low and so farmers may rationally decide to work less. The same is true for applications of capital. When planted crops will blossom, it may be worth paying the fuel costs to run the tractor an extra hour. When planted crops will in any case wither, why bother spending the money on fuel? Just leave the tractor in the shed.

Intertemporal substitution reflects how people choose to allocate consumption of goods, work, and leisure across time to maximize well-being.

Economists call this effect **intertemporal substitution.** That phrase means that a person or a business is most likely to work hard when working hard brings the greatest return. We work hard in some times and rest in others, and of course we pick and choose the spots when we try hardest. We are substituting effort across time and thus the phrase *intertemporal substitution.*

When you study for a test, do you practice intertemporal substitution or do you study an equal amount every day? As a test approaches, you probably study harder, turning down some opportunities for fun. Once the test is over, you study less and have more fun. Intertemporal substitution means that when you study, you study a lot and when you party, well, you know.

Intertemporal substitution, however, is not just about substituting between work and leisure. We pointed out in Chapter 1, for example, that when jobs are plentiful and wages are increasing there is a tendency for fewer people to enter university, but when jobs are scarce and wages are stagnant, more people decide to invest in an education. Students understand that the opportunity cost of getting an education falls when jobs are scarce.

During a boom, people are less likely to retire or take early retirement—why not stay another year or two and bank the high wages? Similarly, stay-at-home parents and other people who might otherwise not work outside the home will choose to enter the workforce during boom periods. During recessions, people are more likely to take early retirement or focus on homemaking. Figure 13.5 shows that when GDP is growing faster than trend, then the employment to population ratio also tends to grow faster than trend. The implication is that the supply of labor increases in a boom and falls during a recession.

Notice that intertemporal substitution magnifies negative economic shocks. When things go a bit bad, the return to work and investing falls and often people work less and invest less, which makes things go just a bit worse. The ripple effects of this process help turn an initial shock into a broader recession. Of course, on the upside, intertemporal substitution can feed an economic boom and make it more intense. If things are going well, many people will be inclined to work harder, which will in turn increase output and make things go even better. Figure 13.6 shows how intertemporal substitution amplifies shocks to the Solow growth curve, which we introduced in Chapter 12. Intertemporal substitution is hardly the only force behind employment decisions (see Chapter 10),

Intertemporal substitution at work during World War II.

FIGURE 13.5

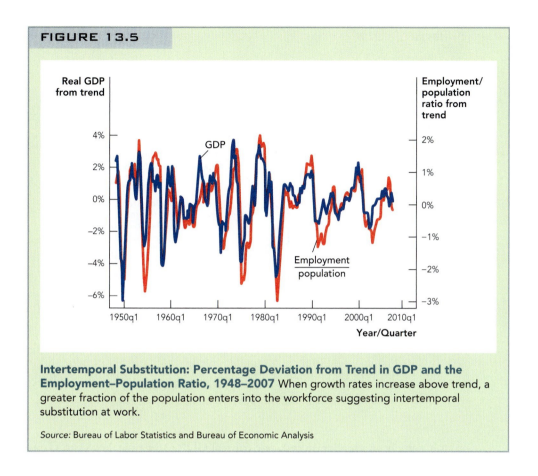

Intertemporal Substitution: Percentage Deviation from Trend in GDP and the Employment–Population Ratio, 1948–2007 When growth rates increase above trend, a greater fraction of the population enters into the workforce suggesting intertemporal substitution at work.

Source: Bureau of Labor Statistics and Bureau of Economic Analysis

but it does play a role in magnifying shocks, both on the upside and the downside.

Once we add intertemporal substitution to the RBC model, real shifts in aggregate demand (AD) can also change the growth rate of the economy. A large increase in government spending, $\vec{G}$, for example, can encourage workers to enter the workforce, temporarily increasing the supply of labor and raising the Solow growth rate. During World War II, for example, government spending increased dramatically and more workers, especially women, were drawn into the labor force. They faced, at least for a while, superior wage opportunities.

In Figure 13.7 on the next page, we show a long-run equilibrium at point *a*. From this starting point, a large increase in $\vec{G}$ shifts the AD curve outward. If intertemporal substitution is *not* important, then the inflation rate increases, but the Solow growth curve does not shift and thus there is no change in the growth rate, as we showed in the last chapter. But if intertemporal substitution is important, then workers respond to the increase in $\vec{G}$ by entering the

FIGURE 13.6

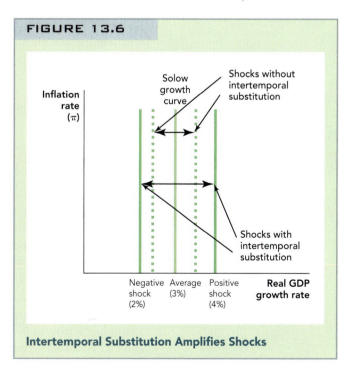

Intertemporal Substitution Amplifies Shocks

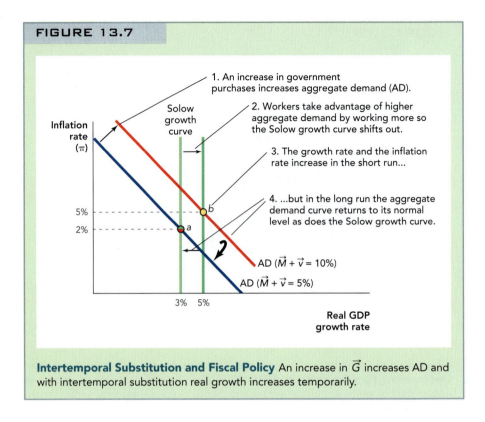

FIGURE 13.7

1. An increase in government purchases increases aggregate demand (AD).

2. Workers take advantage of higher aggregate demand by working more so the Solow growth curve shifts out.

3. The growth rate and the inflation rate increase in the short run...

4. ...but in the long run the aggregate demand curve returns to its normal level as does the Solow growth curve.

Solow growth curve

Inflation rate (π)

5%

2%

b

a

AD ($\vec{M} + \vec{v} = 10\%$)

AD ($\vec{M} + \vec{v} = 5\%$)

3%   5%

Real GDP growth rate

Intertemporal Substitution and Fiscal Policy An increase in $\vec{G}$ increases AD and with intertemporal substitution real growth increases temporarily.

point b, namely at a higher growth rate for real GDP. Over time, however, $\vec{G}$ returns to its normal rate and workers return to their normal effort levels so the economy returns to point a.

Economists disagree on the importance of intertemporal substitution as a way of generating real effects from fiscal policy. For very large shocks such as World War II, the intertemporal substitution story is plausible, but most economists think that the primary reason why an increase in AD has real effects in the short run is the sticky wages, sticky prices story of the New Keynesian model.

Let's turn to another transmission mechanism, uncertainty and irreversible investments.

Uncertainty and Irreversible Investments

Negative shocks also increase uncertainty, which is bad for business investment. Bad news usually also means uncertain news, as the arrival of the bad news causes people to rethink how the world works. For instance, when the 9/11 attacks hit the United States, uncertainty about the future increased. All of a sudden many people started worrying—rightly or wrongly—that subsequent terrorist attacks would be a big problem. The initial response was to hold off on business investment. Until it became clear that such attacks would not become regular occurrences, for instance, many investors were reluctant to fund new construction in New York City. When investors are uncertain, often they prefer to wait and sample more information, before committing themselves.

The key idea here is that many investments are **irreversible investments,** or very costly to reverse. That is, once a new office building has been constructed on Wall Street, it is hard to tear down that building and redeploy the steel and glass to other economic uses. So, before investors build a new skyscraper, they will

Irreversible investments have high value only under specific conditions—they cannot be easily moved, adjusted, or reversed if conditions change.

try to make sure that there will be a demand for the offices. Of course, investors sometime get this wrong, just as commercial real estate overexpanded in the mid- to late 1980s, or too many homes were built in the years preceding the real estate crash of 2007. But prior to expansion, investors want to see many strong signals that market conditions will validate their plans.

The more uncertain the world appears, the harder it is for investors to receive definite signals about where to invest their resources. Investors may see that the demand to watch television programs is shrinking, as it has been for years, but investors do not know which new sectors will be expanding. Will all those extra TV-watching hours be replaced by time spent on Facebook, on Second Life, or by time spent outdoors? When investors wait to see what happens, that means resources are sitting idle rather than being productive. That means lower GDP and it contributes to the economic slowdown.

To see the logic of irreversible investment, just consider the decision to marry. Marriage is a kind of investment and not just in the financial sense. It is making a commitment to the future and it is often for a very long period. Given the seriousness of this commitment, you ought to make (relatively) sure that your marriage is a good idea. If you receive some information causing you to doubt your potential partner (did someone hint he or she is a convicted felon?), maybe you should wait a while and discover the truth before proceeding. Of course, if you wait to decide on marriage, you may also wait to buy a house together, even if buying a house is a good idea. That's just common sense. The point is that the same logic applies to economic investments. Uncertainty usually slows investment and keeps resources in less productive uses.

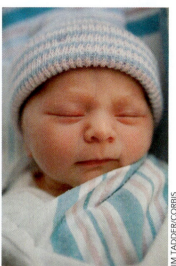

One of the most irreversible investments of them all

Labor Adjustment Costs

Once a negative shock hits the economy, labor must adjust. Workers must look for new jobs, they must move to new areas, and sometimes they must change their wage expectations. Recall from Chapter 10 how search—looking for a new job—is one reason for unemployment. A negative shock to the economy, by remixing opportunities, induces more search and thus causes more search-related unemployment. **Labor adjustment costs** are the costs of shifting workers from declining sectors of the economy to growing sectors.

Labor adjustments to shocks are not always rational in the narrowly economic sense of that term. If an automobile worker is laid off the General Motors assembly line, and he loses his formerly unionized job, he may not be able to find the same wage elsewhere. Currently, the less unionized foreign automakers in the United States pay less than GM does per hour. Some automobile workers without a high school degree may make up to $100,000 per year. It may take a while for that person, if thrown out of work, to admit that he must settle for a lower wage. In the meantime, he is looking for a job and perhaps even rejecting offers that are as good as he will ever find.

The high cost of reversing job decisions can lead to unemployment, just as the costs of reversing investment can cause investors to wait. Again, consider the closure of a Detroit automobile plant and the fate of the former workers. These workers face at least three options: They can wait for the plant to reopen, they can seek another job in Detroit, or they can move to a more prosperous part of the country. Which course of action is best?

It's not always easy to say which choice is best, yet the choice involves a costly-to-reverse decision. Once the house is sold and the belongings are packed and

Labor adjustment costs are the costs of shifting workers from declining sectors of the economy to growing sectors.

moved to Houston, it is costly to go back to Detroit. The unemployed autoworker, rather than moving to Houston, might wait for a while to see what happens, even if he knows the probability of finding a job in Houston is higher than in Detroit. Or if that person opens up a pet shop, it will be hard to shift back into automobile manufacture. So, when faced with these uncertainties, many workers simply will bide their time until the future is clearer. Maybe they'll do some part-time or casual work (or maybe they'll put a new deck on the house), but they probably won't be employed at full productivity. The result is ongoing unemployment, or at least underemployment, and again the initial negative real shock is magnified.

In sum, changes to the world require people to adjust their jobs and their careers. People can't always make those adjustments right away, and in the mean time output and employment will be lower than normal.

Time Bunching

People often bunch their activities at common points in time. Most people work from 9 AM to 5 PM rather than from 10 PM to 6 AM. One reason is that these are daylight hours, but another reason is because everyone else is working during this time. If you and your coworker are in the office at the same time, it is easier to collaborate. Furthermore, it makes working more fun to be there with other people.

We also like to party at the same time and to see movies and concerts with other people. It's not just a question of fun—it is also economics. If you want to cook an elaborate meal, order some fancy bottles of wine, or clean up the house for a party, you want to make sure that enough people attend for those efforts to be worthwhile.

Time bunching is the tendency for economic activities to be coordinated at common points in time.

Most generally, many economic activities **bunch or cluster in time** because it pays to coordinate your economic actions with those of others. That just means that we want to be investing, producing, and selling at the same time that others are investing, producing, or selling.

Bunching occurs across different time frames. There is bunching across the course of a single day; most people don't do their food shopping at 4 AM, even if they live near 24-hour supermarkets. But there is also bunching across weeks, months, and even years. Economic activity tends to cluster together in time just as it clusters together in space. (What do we call a cluster of economic activity in space? A city.)

The clustering of economic activity in time makes buying and selling more efficient, but it also causes shocks to spread through the economy and to spread through time. Let's say that a negative economic shock arrives and the economy slows down in the current period. Many people are less keen to work, and they will save up their working for some point in the future (intertemporal substitution, as we discussed earlier). This effect will induce others to cut back on their work as well. If the Indian farmers mentioned above work less when the weather is bad, then tractor salespeople will probably work less as well. Similarly, if fewer people are showing up at the office, you might be less productive as well. You'll be more likely to stay home and more likely to make your big work effort in some other period, perhaps when you expect the office to be up and running at full speed. So if some people retreat from full-speed work, these decisions spill over onto others and cause them to cut back their effort as well.

The "seasonal business cycle" is one form of economic clustering in time. The fourth quarter of the year—October through December—brings more economic activity than any other time. Production is higher, sales are higher, employment is higher, and GDP grows faster, relative to the other quarters of the year. After Christmas is over, however, the party ends and GDP in the next period is typically lower. Figure 13.8 shows GDP growth rates over recent years. Notice the clear spike downward in GDP in the first quarter of the year (the winter season after Christmas).

FIGURE 13.8

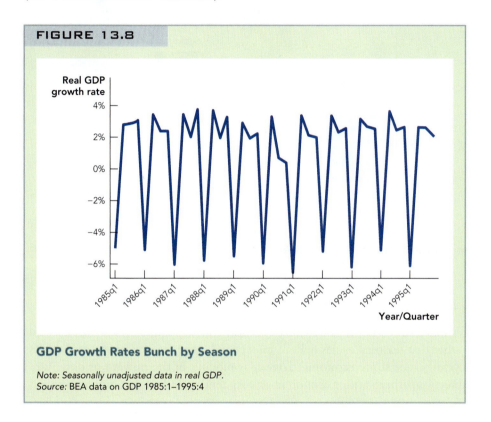

GDP Growth Rates Bunch by Season

Note: Seasonally unadjusted data in real GDP.
Source: BEA data on GDP 1985:1–1995:4

Based on seasonal averages over many more years, Figure 13.9 on the next page shows that GDP typically grows most during the Christmas boom, but slows dramatically in the post-Christmas bust. GDP also grows quickly in the spring season. Growth is positive but not nearly so high in the summer when many people go on vacation.

Most advanced economies have a seasonal business cycle of this nature, usually with the fourth quarter as the boom quarter. Indeed, most economic data is reported on a "seasonally adjusted" basis so if you read that GDP grew in the first quarter by 2 percent, it really means that GDP fell in this quarter less than expected given the season.

Of course, the seasonal cycle booms in the fourth quarter because of Christmas and other gift-giving holidays in December. People are simply spending a lot more money in the fourth quarter. But it is a mistake to think that the entire effect is driven by gift giving. After all, many people simply aren't that generous at Christmas time. But even Scrooge may be more likely to buy things for himself during the Christmas season when there is a superior selection of products and more new products on the shelves. Many people buy in the fourth quarter, due to the economies of clustering, even if they don't care about Christmas for its own sake.

Just as the fourth quarter is the most active, the first quarter—January through March—is the slowest. People just spent large sums of money at Christmas. Yes, many people do look for sales and specials in this period, but overall both production and retail activity simply aren't as intense.

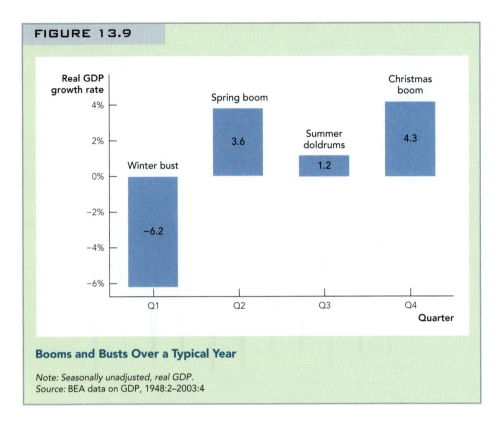

FIGURE 13.9

Booms and Busts Over a Typical Year

Note: Seasonally unadjusted, real GDP.
Source: BEA data on GDP, 1948:2–2003:4

The point is not that we should abolish Christmas or summer vacation, but rather that seasonal cycles help us understand some features of regular business cycles. Once some economic activity is moving in the upward or downward direction, other parts of economic activity tend to follow that momentum.

Sticky Wages and Prices

A final transmission mechanism comes from the New Keynesian theory of business fluctuations that we introduced in Chapter 12. Recall that the emphasis in New Keynesian theory is on how sticky wages and prices mean that shocks to aggregate demand can reduce real growth. It is also the case that sticky wages and prices can amplify real shocks. Let's focus on the sticky wages story and show how sticky wages make a negative real shock even worse.

We begin in Figure 13.10 at point *a* with an inflation rate of 2 percent, expected inflation of 2 percent, and real growth of 3 percent. A negative real shock reduces productivity and shifts the Solow growth curve to the left. If wages were perfectly flexible, then the SRAS curve would simply shift along with the Solow growth curve, placing the economy at point *b*. At point *b*, the economy is in a recession and there will be some increased frictional unemployment as workers adjust to the new situation. But if wages are sticky the situation can get much worse.

Here is the key point: *when the economy grows slowly, wages must grow slowly.* At point *b*, the growth rate of the economy is negative so wages must fall. But suppose that wages are sticky—workers don't like to see a reduction in the growth rate of their wages, let alone an actual fall in wages—thus, for all the reasons we discussed in the last chapter, it will be difficult for firms to lower wages. But if wages aren't falling at point *b*, then firms must cut output and hiring to remain profitable. In addition, to restore profitability, firms will try to raise prices even faster. Notice that the declines in output and hiring and the

FIGURE 13.10

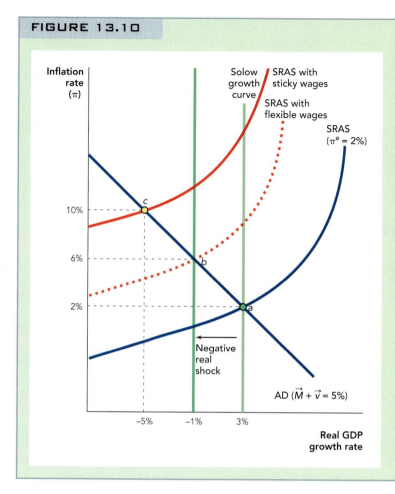

Sticky Wages Can Amplify a Real Shock Beginning at point *a*, a negative real shock shifts the Solow growth curve to the left. If prices and wages were perfectly flexible, the economy would move to a new equilibrium at point *b*. But at point *b* the economy is shrinking, so real wages need to fall. If wages are sticky, wage growth will be too high and firms will be unprofitable. Unprofitable firms reduce employment and thus the SRAS curve shifts even further to the left moving the economy to point *c* with an even lower growth rate and higher inflation rate.

increase in inflation mean that *with sticky wages the SRAS curve shifts farther to the left (and up) than did the Solow growth curve.* As the SRAS shifts to the left and up, the economy moves along the AD curve from point *b* to point *c*, thus the inflation rate increases and the real growth rate falls. At point *c*, the growth rate is −5 percent. Sticky wages have transformed a mild recession into a much more serious recession.

When wages are sticky, a negative productivity shock creates two problems. First, the productivity shocks mean output growth will be lower—that's just the meaning of a negative productivity shock and there's not much that can be done about this effect. The economy's capital is simply less productive. But when wages are sticky, the negative productivity shock also means that wages will be too high and some workers will lose their jobs, or lose hours of employment, thus cutting back aggregate supply even further.

Transmission Mechanisms: Summary

In sum, at least five factors magnify negative economic shocks and help bring business downturns. Those factors are labor supply and intertemporal substitution, uncertainty and irreversible investment, labor adjustment costs, the desire to bunch or cluster economic activity together in time, and sticky wages and prices. The core lesson is this: A medium-sized negative economic shock is capable of causing a disproportionately large downturn in economic production and employment.

We've also worked through these transmission mechanisms to set you up for some of the material to come. As shown in detail in the next few chapters, the government does have some control over aggregate demand through monetary and fiscal policy. Could the government increase AD enough to off-set some of these negative supply shocks and get the economy back to a higher Solow growth rate? Should the government do this and, if so, under what conditions? To answer this and related questions, in the next four chapters we look at the institutions and tools of monetary and fiscal policy. Real business cycles are a very important part of macroeconomic theory, but they are not the whole story.

CHECK YOURSELF

> Immediately after 9/11, most U.S. companies eliminated business travel temporarily. After a few weeks, business travel started to pick up again. Which transmission mechanism came in to play? Go through as many aspects of business travel as you can think of: air travel, transportation to and from airports, hotel stays, meals out and contact with people remaining back in the office. Explain how the unexpected almost-cessation in business travel amplified the original shock.

□ Takeaway

One reason that the economy fluctuates is because of real shocks, namely rapid changes in economic conditions that affect the productivity of capital and labor. Shocks to the weather are clearly evident in the fluctuations of GDP in agricultural economies. In wealthier economies, shocks to major inputs into production processes like oil can generate fluctuations in GDP, such as it has done in the United States and other developed economies. Other possible shocks are wars, terrorist attacks, major new regulations, tax rate changes, mass strikes, new technologies such as the Internet, and significant changes in consumer preferences. Most generally, we get a boom when we have a lucky series of positive shocks and a bust when we have an unlucky series of negative shocks.

Transmission mechanisms magnify shocks. There are five major factors that amplify economic shocks. "Make hay when the sun shines" is a saying that reflects the idea of intertemporal substitution. Work hard when working hard brings the greatest return. Intertemporal substitution means that we respond to negative shocks by working less and positive shocks by working more, thus magnifying the shock.

Shocks, especially negative shocks, often increase uncertainty, and when we are uncertain we, as businesspeople and workers, are less likely to make big decisions. Thus, a negative shock can reduce investment, especially when investments are hard to reverse. Uncertainty can also cause people to delay making big changes such as moving to a better job or selling a house.

Labor adjustment costs can also increase structural unemployment by raising the costs of moving labor from declining sectors of the economy to growing sectors of the economy.

Economic activity does not occur evenly across space or time. Every day there is a boom between 9 AM and 5 PM and a bust between 12 AM and 5 AM. Every year there is a boom around Christmas and a bust after New Year. Time bunching occurs because people work better together and it often makes sense to coordinate production processes. Thus, when one sector of the economy is booming, say because of a positive productivity shock, other sectors tend to follow. The same is true for busts. Thus bunching through time magnifies shocks.

Finally, sticky wages and prices can magnify real shocks. In this case, the growth rate falls because productivity is lower and also because sticky wages create a mismatch between aggregate demand and the Solow growth rate.

The productivity shocks that we have discussed in this chapter play an important role in some business fluctuations. The transmission mechanisms that we have described play an important role in virtually *all* business fluctuations. In the next four chapters, we look more closely at shocks to monetary and fiscal policy and also how monetary and fiscal policy might smooth out some real shocks or in some unfortunate situations possibly make them worse.

◻ CHAPTER REVIEW

FACTS AND TOOLS

1. According to Figure 13.9, the U.S. economy typically grows faster in some quarters than in others.

   a. In which quarter is the gross domestic product actually falling?

   b. What major spending-related holiday occurs just before this big decline in GDP?

2. Take a look at Figure 13.2. In the last few decades, what has usually happened to the price of oil just before or during a recession?

3. When oil price shocks force people to switch jobs, how much GDP are they producing when they are out of work?

4. Do you know anyone who "intertemporally substitutes" their labor? In other words, what are some careers where someone might choose to work more during times when the wage is higher but less when the wage is lower? (Example: Someone with a lawn-mowing business.) Think of three examples of such careers. (Hint: Seasonal jobs provide a lot of easy examples.)

5. When an investment is irreversible, are you likely to make that decision in a hurry or wait until more information comes in?

6. When do you want to study for a test: when your friends are studying for the same test or when they are not? How can this help explain seasonal business fluctuations?

7. If the Solow growth curve increased because of a sudden fall in the price of oil, what would happen to inflation? Assume that spending growth (aggregate demand) does not change—only the growth curve shifts. Draw the shift in the following figure. (Note: In the real world, this happens fairly often. Big declines in the

price of oil happened in 1986 and again in 1998, and the price of oil fell by 50 percent in late 2008.)

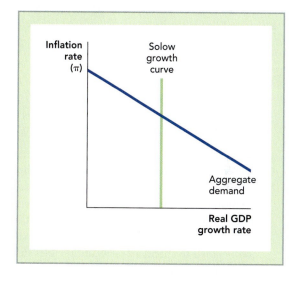

8. Office buildings have a boom-bust cycle every day. At what hours of the weekday do grocery stores have an economic boom? What days of the week do shopping malls have an economic boom?

THINKING AND PROBLEM SOLVING

1. In India, the economy grows faster when there's a lot of rain and grows more slowly when there is a drought. This creates big fluctuations in the economy. If the government wrote laws to smooth out these fluctuations, by paying people to work more in the dry years and by taxing people so that they would work less in the heavy-rain years, would that make the average Indian better off? Why or why not? (Keep your answer in mind during the next recession, when pundits and politicians recommend tax breaks to encourage more hiring.)

2. **a.** According to Figure 13.3, about how long does it take for an oil price shock to have its biggest impact on the economy? How long does it take before the oil shock's effects completely go away?

   b. What might be happening in the labor market that might explain why it takes so long for an oil shock to do its worst?

(Glance through the transmission mechanisms listed in the chapter for some ideas.)

3. When would a restaurant owner prefer to open a new restaurant: one year after an oil shock hits or two years after the oil shock hits?

4. How is marriage like a decision to build a new factory? Which decision is easier to reverse?

5. **a.** Who would you be more likely to hire at your company: someone who has stayed in the same career for years, or someone who tries an entirely new career every time they become unhappy with their job?

   b. How does this help explain why workers are reluctant to quickly move on to a new career when they get laid off?

6. People sometimes use the expression, "Kicking the can down the road." It refers to putting a big decision off until later—it's almost (but not quite!) a synonym for procrastinating, and it's usually used in a negative sense. "Fred graduated and decided to spend a year waiting tables in New York. Grad school? He's kicking the can down the road on that one." What economic idea is equivalent to "kicking the can down the road," and how can it be a good thing?

7. As we note in the chapter, an oil price shock will probably increase the size of an oil-centered city like Houston, Texas. During the time that people are moving to Houston, looking for jobs, and switching jobs to find the best job possible, do you think GDP will be lower than usual or higher than usual? (Try focusing on the *production* part of GDP in answering this question.)

8. In the chapter, we discussed how intertemporal substitution can amplify a boom by causing people to work more and by causing more people to work (while the reverse is true in a recession). Capital is also subject to intertemporal substitution. For example, it's possible to run a factory at close to capacity in one period while putting off maintenance to a later period. How do you think capacity utilization varies across the business cycle? Is capacity utilization procyclical (varies positively with GDP) or countercyclical (varies negatively with GDP)?

9. Can you think of some reasons why the following examples of time bunching and intertemporal substitution might be true? (Yes, you'll notice that there's a blurry line between the two.)

   a. People who work outside work more when the weather is good.

   b. People work when others are also working.

   c. Even nonreligious people who don't give gifts shop more as Christmastime approaches.

   d. Food servers at a restaurant prefer to work the dinner shift.

   What do all of these examples have to do with the business cycle?

CHALLENGES

1. In 1971, Intel invented the first computer microprocessor. In early 1993, the National Center for Supercomputing Applications released the first web browser, Mosaic (which later became Netscape). Both inventions seem like good news, and both inventions created great uncertainty about which business models would succeed in the future: They were game changers. Would these uncertainty-creating inventions encourage businesses to make massive investments quickly, or would they encourage businesses to wait a few years to see how it all pans out?

   Boyan Jovanovic and his coauthors discuss this topic in several papers. For an introduction see Bart Hobijn & Boyan Jovanovic, 2001. The Information-Technology Revolution and the Stock Market: Evidence. *American Economic Review* 91(5): 1203–1220.

2. For the sake of the economy, should the government ban Christmas, and instead encourage people to give gifts throughout the year? Why or why not?

3. How is the previous question similar to this question: Should the government encourage people to move from the East and West coasts to the Midwest and Rocky Mountain states, where the population is less crowded?

4. Part of the real business cycle story is that workers *choose* to work more *because* wages are temporarily high and workers *choose* to work less *because* wages are temporarily low. This is key to the "intertemporal substitution" story of this chapter. The following chart shows how much wages change in the short run: Except in the 1970s, the moves are almost always in a 2 percent range, running from 1 percent higher than average to 1 percent lower than average.

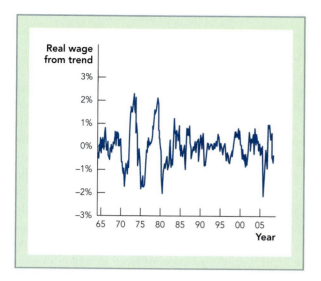

So, when wages move up or down for a year or two, does the number of Americans working move in the same direction at the same time? Let's see. The economic simulation at the bottom of this column is based on actual U.S. data and shows how a 1 percent rise in wages usually impacts the number of Americans employed. Sometimes the effect is bigger than this, and sometimes smaller, but this is the average.

In practice, a 1 percent rise in wages apparently causes a 0.2 percent rise in the number of Americans with jobs. It takes nine months for this to happen.

How much would wages have to rise to raise employment by 1% or 2%, according to these estimates? [Note: This is roughly how much employment rises during a boom.] Is this "wage-channel" effect large enough to explain most of the job fluctuations we see during real-world business cycles?

5. a. The real business cycle model says that Solow growth rate shocks are important, while the aggregate demand curve mostly stays fixed. If this is correct, then should prices be higher than usual or lower than usual during a recession?

b. The following chart has historical U.S. data on the relationship between the price level and real GDP. The chart doesn't fit the RBC model perfectly—no economist would claim that the RBC model explains *all* economic fluctuations, after all. If you take a look at the big swings in the 1970s and early 1980s, especially during recessions, do the facts roughly fit the RBC model, or do they pretty much conflict with the RBC model?

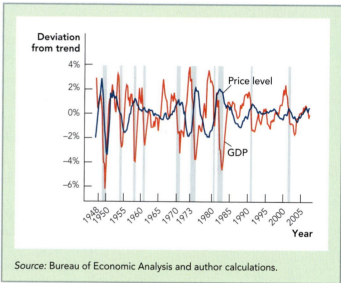

Source: Bureau of Economic Analysis and author calculations.

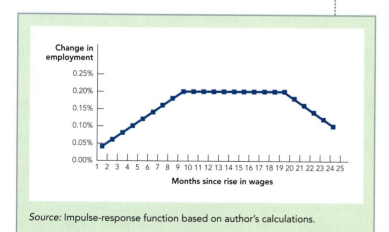

Source: Impulse-response function based on author's calculations.

CHAPTER APPENDIX

Business Fluctuations and the Solow Model

A way of summarizing some of the lessons of this chapter is that at least some business fluctuations are just economic growth in the short run. Economic growth happens in fits and starts rather than smoothly. The economists Finn Kydland and Edward Prescott developed key aspects of the RBC model in the 1980s and were awarded the Nobel prize for their work in 2004. One advantage of thinking about business fluctuations in this way is that they can then be analyzed using a version of the Solow growth model, which is called the real business cycle model. A complete understanding of the real business cycle model requires quite a bit of advanced mathematics, but we can briefly describe the main ideas. Consider the following production function, which is just like that used in Chapter 7 but with the addition of labor as well as capital:

$$Y = A_t \times F(K, L)$$

To recap, output, Y, is a function of the inputs of capital, K, and labor, L. In Chapter 7, we talked about the A factor as an index of ideas. Better ideas mean a larger A, which means that more output can be produced from the same inputs of capital and labor. That is a good interpretation of A in the long run, but we can also think about A as representing *any* factor that influences the productivity of K and L. Thus, if Y is the output of corn then A could be deviations of rainfall from the average. Above average rainfall, say $A = 2$, means that the inputs of K and L produce a lot of corn. Below average rainfall, say $A = \frac{1}{2}$, means that the same inputs of K and L produce less corn.

When we are thinking about long-run economic growth, it doesn't hurt to simplify and think about A as increasing smoothly through time. To analyze business fluctuations, however, we need to recognize that A jumps around. Thus, in the business fluctuation model, A is a productivity shock variable.

The second complication we need to add to the Solow growth model to analyze business fluctuations is to give a more sophisticated account of investment and labor supply. In the Solow growth model investment is a simple function of output, Investment $= \gamma Y$, where the investment rate, γ, is a constant proportion like 0.3. That's not a very realistic assumption. Will savers and investors want to invest the same proportion of output during a recession as during a boom? Probably not, for the reasons we discussed in the chapter (uncertainty, for example). How do savers and investors decide how much and when to invest? This is a complicated decision, requiring savers and investors to forecast future events. Solving this problem is difficult, which is where the complicated mathematics come in, but we know that γ will vary over time.

Similarly, in the growth version of the Solow model, we assumed that L was population and that L was fixed. (It's also easy to think about L as increasing slowly and steadily.) But in the short run, we need to recognize that workers may choose to enter or exit the workforce and choose to take jobs or search for work—intertemporal substitution. As a result, L becomes the labor force and L can change due to changes in the participation rate and the

unemployment rate. How do workers decide how much and when to work? Again, this is a complicated decision problem that requires workers to forecast the future and carefully optimize.

Adding shocks to the Solow model and giving a more sophisticated account of how savers, investors, and workers make decisions creates what is known as the real business cycle model or the standard "neoclassical" model of business cycles. The intuitive account of business fluctuations that we have given in this chapter is based on this model.[*]

Explaining a full RBC model is too advanced for this appendix but we recall that we showed how to simulate the Solow model using Excel in the appendix to Chapter 7. We can easily modify that model to include productivity shocks. Figure A13.1 shows our Excel model with a new column (column B) labeled A. Excel's RAND() formula creates a random number between 0 and 1. If we want a number between X and Y, we can write $= RAND()(Y-X) + X$. We will use our random number as a productivity shock, A_t, so we want a number that can be a little bigger than 1 or a little smaller than 1. Thus, when we get a random number that is greater than 1 that is a positive productivity shock (output increases) and when we get a random number that is less than 1 that is a negative productivity shock (output decreases). Thus, we input into cell B2 = RAND()(1/0.95−0.95) + 0.95 which create a random number between 1/0.95 and 0.95; over many draws this random number is designed so that it will average out to 1. We now modify our output formula in D2 so it reads = B2*C2^(1/2), in other words we multiply the contribution of capital (C2^1/2) by the productivity shock, A_t, which we generated in column B.

FIGURE A13.1

	B2	▼	f_x	=RAND()*(1/0.95-0.95)+0.95						
	A	B	C	D	E	F	G	H	I	J
1	Time	A	Capital, K	Output	Investment	Depreciation	Capital Growth	Y Growth	Investment Share, γ	Depreciation, δ
2	1	0.956905382	200	13.53	4.06	4.00	0.06		0.3	0.02
3	2	0.967909022	200.06	13.69	4.11	4.00	0.11	1.17		
4	3	0.983678593	200.17	13.92	4.18	4.00	0.17	1.66		
5	4	0.952410981	200.34	13.48	4.04	4.01	0.04	-3.14		
6	5	1.018061434	200.37	14.41	4.32	4.01	0.32	6.90		
7	6	1.036326744	200.69	14.68	4.40	4.01	0.39	1.87		
8	7	0.976878889	201.08	13.85	4.16	4.02	0.13	-5.64		
9	8	0.990237834	201.22	14.05	4.21	4.02	0.19	1.40		
10	9	0.963290803	201.41	13.67	4.10	4.03	0.07	-2.68		
11	10	0.994149412	201.48	14.11	4.23	4.03	0.20	3.22		
12	11	1.041301257	201.68	14.79	4.44	4.03	0.40	4.80		
13	12	1.028858954	202.08	14.63	4.39	4.04	0.35	-1.10		
14	13	0.995156067	202.43	14.16	4.25	4.05	0.20	-3.19		
15	14	0.953711687	202.63	13.58	4.07	4.05	0.02	-4.12		
16	15	0.984056799	202.65	14.01	4.20	4.05	0.15	3.19		
	⋮									
377	376	0.997989023	225.44	14.98	4.50	4.51	-0.01	3.46		
378	377	0.973955736	225.42	14.62	4.39	4.51	-0.12	-2.41		
379	378	1.032046001	225.30	15.49	4.65	4.51	0.14	5.94		
380	379	0.961868177	225.44	14.44	4.33	4.51	-0.18	-6.77		
381	380	0.982599886	225.27	14.75	4.42	4.51	-0.08	2.12		

[*] For a more complete but still accessible explanation of this model, see Plosser, Charles I. 1989. Understanding Real Business Cycles. *Journal of Economic Perspectives* 3, No. 3. (Summer, 1989), 51–77.

This model works very much like the Solow model in Chapter 7, but now the random shocks increase or decrease growth around the average Solow growth rate. Figure A13.2, for example, simulates 100 periods of the Solow model around the equilibrium output of 15. Notice how shocks can generate business fluctuations.

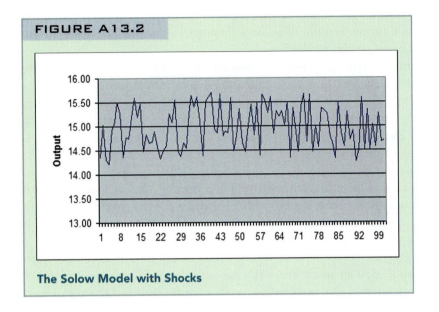

FIGURE A13.2

The Solow Model with Shocks

14

The Federal Reserve System and Open Market Operations

Imagine that you wanted to borrow $2 *trillion*. Whom would you ask? In 2008, the worldwide financial system was in a crisis and banks and other financial institutions wanted to borrow more than $2 trillion—they turned to the only person in the world capable of lending that kind of money, a mild-mannered, former professor of economics named Ben Bernanke. As chairman of the Federal Reserve System (the Fed), Bernanke is sometimes said to be the second most powerful person in the world, after the President of the United States. Bernanke was able to make the loans because he could draw on the awesome power of the Federal Reserve Bank to create money.

What is the Federal Reserve? How does it create money? What does it use its power for?

If you read this chapter, you'll come away with an understanding of the Federal Reserve and its powers. The quick and dirty answer is that through its control of the money supply the Federal Reserve usually has more influence over aggregate demand than any other institution and shifts in aggregate demand can greatly influence the economy in the short run (as we first showed in Chapter 12). So, let's take a look at the Federal Reserve System first, then examine what is meant by the money supply, and finally focus on the tools that the Fed uses to influence the money supply, aggregate demand, and the economy.

What Is the Federal Reserve System?

The Federal Reserve acquires its unique powers through its ability to issue money. Open your wallet or your purse and take a look at some bills. At the top, you will see the words "Federal Reserve Note." In the past, many banks issued their own bank notes, which were used as money. But today the money

we use in the United States is provided by just one bank, the Federal Reserve. Thus, the Federal Reserve has the power to create money—an awesome power that forms the centerpiece of this chapter. The Fed doesn't have to literally print money. It can, as we shall see in more depth later in this chapter, also create money "by computer" by adding reserves to bank accounts held at the Fed. This new money can be given away or lent out in a way that increases aggregate demand.

If the Federal Reserve is a bank, who are its customers? The Fed is both the government's bank and the banker's bank. As the government's bank, the Fed maintains the bank account of the U.S. Treasury. When you write a check to the IRS to pay your taxes, the money ends up in the Treasury's account at the Fed. In addition to receiving money, the U.S. Treasury also borrows a lot of money and the Fed manages this borrowing—that is, the Fed manages the issuing, transferring, and redeeming of U.S. Treasury bonds, bills, and notes. Since the U.S. Treasury is by far the world's largest bank customer—it has more income and it also borrows more than any other bank customer—the Federal Reserve is a large and powerful bank.

In addition, the Fed is also the banker's bank. Large private banks keep their own accounts at the Fed—in part, because some banks are required to hold accounts with the Federal Reserve and in part because other banks and financial institutions want a safe and convenient place to hold their money. The Fed also regulates other banks and it lends money to other banks. Finally, the Fed manages the nation's payment system—the system of accounts that makes it possible to write checks from one bank to another—and it protects financial consumers with disclosure regulations. Many of these and other duties are shared with other state and federal agencies.

Now that we know what the Fed is, let's turn to its most important function: regulating the U.S. money supply. But first we have to understand what the money supply is.

The U.S. Money Supplies

Just about everyone expects to be paid in money. If you show up with money—at least in its appropriate form, hardly anyone will turn you away. In other words, **money** is a widely accepted means of payment.

But money is more than cash. Cash, or currency, is paper bills and coins, which serve as a quick and efficient way of making small transactions. But currency is not so useful for larger transactions, especially between businesses. Often it is easier to pay by check or debit card (which can be thought of as an electronic check) or by credit card (and then pay your bill later by check). For larger purchases, you might transfer money from a savings account to a checking account and then pay by check or debit. All these means of payment are money but they are not currency.

The most important assets that serve as means of payment in the U.S. today are:

1. Currency—paper bills and coins
2. Total reserves held by banks at the Fed
3. Checkable deposits—your checking or debit account
4. Savings deposits, money market mutual funds, and small-time deposits

Money is a widely accepted means of payment.

Figure 14.1 shows the magnitude and proportions of the major means of payment in the United States (there are also some smaller items, such as traveler's checks, that we have omitted):

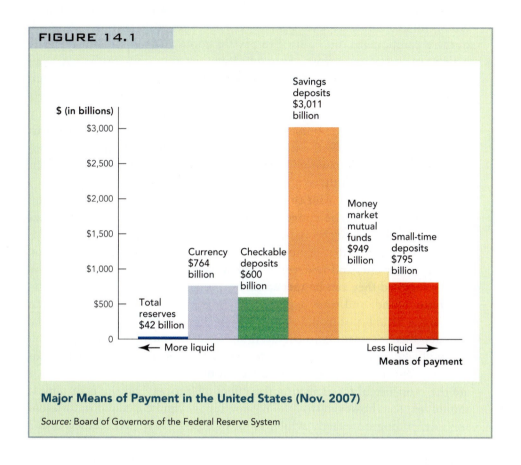

FIGURE 14.1

Major Means of Payment in the United States (Nov. 2007)

Source: Board of Governors of the Federal Reserve System

Let's say a few words about each of these means of payment. "Total reserves" held by banks at the Fed is the means of payment you probably don't have personal experience with, but total reserves play a very important role in the financial system. All major banks have accounts at the Federal Reserve System—accounts that they use for trading with other major banks and for dealings with the Fed itself. It's not currency in these accounts but electronic claims that can be converted into currency if the bank wishes.

If you look at the total for currency (almost $800 billion) and divide it by the American population (about 300 million), that amounts to about $2,500 per person (and even more per adult). Who has this much cash on hand? Of course, some of the money is in ATMs and cash registers and some drug dealers do hold a lot of cash but the real explanation for why so much U.S. cash exists is that quite a bit is used in other countries. Panama, Ecuador, and El Salvador all use the U.S. dollar as their official currency as do some other small nations like the Turks and Caicos Islands. Dollars are also used unofficially in many other unstable countries as a means of preserving and protecting wealth. When Iraqi dictator Saddam Hussein was captured, he had $750,000 in U.S. hundred dollar bills in his hideaway.

Checkable deposits are just like they sound, namely deposits that you can write checks on or can access with a debit card. These are the sorts of deposits we use most often in making daily transactions. Often these are also called demand deposits because you can access this money "on demand."

The largest means of payment are savings accounts, money market mutual funds, and small-time deposits (also called certificates of deposit or CDs). Each of these components can be used to pay for goods and services but typically with a little bit of extra work or trouble. Payments from a savings account can be made, for example, by first transferring the money to a checkable account. A money market mutual fund is a mutual fund invested in relatively safe short-term debt and government securities. Money market mutual funds typically allow you to write some number of checks per year or you can always sell part of your fund and transfer the money to a checkable account. Small-time deposits cannot be withdrawn without penalty before a certain time period has elapsed, usually six months or a year.

A **liquid asset** is an asset that can be used for payments or, quickly and without loss of value, be converted into an asset that can be used for payments.

> A **liquid asset** is an asset that can be used for payments or, quickly and without loss of value, be converted into an asset that can be used for payments. The more liquid the asset, the more it can serve as money. Currency is usually the most liquid asset since currency can be spent almost everywhere. Checkable deposits and reserves are also very liquid, since they can also be spent easily and they can be turned into currency without loss. Money market mutual funds and time deposits are less liquid since sometimes it takes time and a little bit of trouble to turn these assets into currency or checkable deposits. It's possible to use even less liquid assets as means of payment (we will take your house in return for, say, a copy of this textbook), but it is inconvenient. Economists therefore have found that the above components are the most useful for analyzing the effect of "money" on the economy. It should be clear, however, that the money supply can be defined in different ways depending on exactly which kinds of liquid assets are included in the definition.

Economists have created many definitions of the money supply. The three most important are:

> The monetary base (MB): currency and total reserves held at the Fed
> M1: currency plus checkable deposits
> M2: M1 plus savings deposits, money market mutual funds, and small-time deposits

These definitions correspond to an inverted pyramid of ever-expanding size as shown in Figure 14.2.

The Fed has direct control only over the monetary base, the narrowest part of the pyramid. But it's the larger components of the money supply—M1 and M2—that have the most significant effects on aggregate demand; the monetary base simply isn't that big a part of the overall money supply.

The pyramid diagram therefore illustrates one difficulty of central banking. The central bank tries to use its control over MB to influence M1 and M2, but there are many other influences on M1 and M2 so each monetary aggregate can shrink or grow independent of the others. Finally, the Fed ultimately wants to steer aggregate demand, but once again its steering is sometimes wobbly because, although M1 and M2 influence aggregate demand, there are also other influences.

FIGURE 14.2

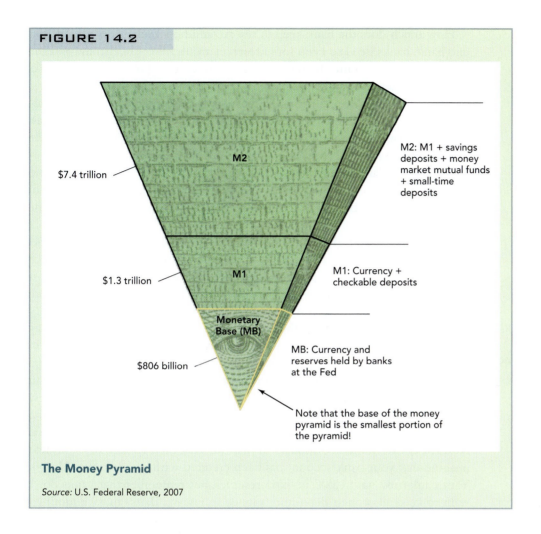

M2: M1 + savings deposits + money market mutual funds + small-time deposits

$7.4 trillion

M2

M1

$1.3 trillion

M1: Currency + checkable deposits

Monetary Base (MB)

$806 billion

MB: Currency and reserves held by banks at the Fed

Note that the base of the money pyramid is the smallest portion of the pyramid!

The Money Pyramid

Source: U.S. Federal Reserve, 2007

To understand how the Fed influences M1 and M2 but also why its influence is sometimes tenuous, we must introduce the concepts of fractional reserve banking, the reserve ratio, and the money multiplier.

Fractional Reserve Banking, the Reserve Ratio, and the Money Multiplier

When you open a bank account, the teller doesn't take your money and put it into a box labeled with your name. Instead the bank holds a *fraction* of your account balance in reserve—hence the term **fractional reserve banking**—and it uses the rest of your money to make loans.

Banks earn profit on these loans. So do you. Competition among banks to attract your funds means that if the bank lends out your money and charges 5 percent interest, the bank must share some of that return with you. The bank will pay you, say, 2 percent for providing the money that they lend. The bank doesn't just pay you interest, it also gives you useful services like check writing and check clearing, which are in part funded from bank profits on loans. Of course, you don't get the full 5 percent return because the bank is bearing risk on the loans, plus paying the costs of making the loans and monitoring the loan borrowers.

CHECK YOURSELF

> Define the monetary base.
> What is the amount of currency in circulation compared to the amount of checkable deposits?

Under **fractional reserve banking**, banks hold only a fraction of deposits in reserve, lending the rest.

The **reserve ratio, RR,** is the ratio of reserves to deposits.

The **money multiplier, MM,** is the amount the money supply expands with each dollar increase in reserves. MM = 1/RR.

How much does the bank keep in reserve and how much does it lend? On one hand, banks need to keep some reserves around. In part, the law and the Federal Reserve require them to keep some reserves. More important, banks need those reserves to meet ordinary depositor demands for currency and payment services. Who would patronize a bank where the ATM machine was always empty? On the other hand, banks don't want to hold too many reserves. Currency sitting in the vault doesn't earn anything for the bank, plus they have to guard it and store it. Thus, there are opportunity costs to holding onto reserves. Banks balance these benefits and costs and thus they decide on the ratio between reserves and deposits. We define the **reserve ratio, RR,** as the ratio of reserves to deposits. If $1 in cash is held in reserve for every $10 of deposits, the reserve ratio is 1/10.

The reserve ratio is determined primarily by how liquid banks wish to be. When banks are worried that depositors might want to withdraw their cash or when loans don't seem so profitable anyway, they want a reserve ratio that is relatively high; when banks aren't worried about depositors demanding cash and when loans are profitable, they want to have a relatively low reserve ratio.

It's also useful to work with the inverse of the reserve ratio, called the **money multiplier, MM.** The money multiplier is the ratio of deposits to reserves, or in this case 10. Why is it called the money multiplier? Imagine that the Federal Reserve creates $1,000 of new money by crediting your bank account with an additional $1,000. Does that sound incredible? In fact, the Fed can create new money at will either by printing it or—the more modern method—by adding numbers to bank accounts held at the Fed. As we shall see below, the Federal Reserve creates billions of dollars in just this way on a regular basis. So let's imagine that your bank account has been credited with an additional $1,000. Your bank now has $1,000 in extra reserves, but remember that banks don't want to keep all of their depositor's money in reserve. Banks make a profit by lending so now that your bank has extra reserves, it will also feel comfortable making more loans. To restore its reserve ratio to 1/10, your bank will want to keep $100 in reserve and make additional loans of $900. So let's say it lends $900 to Sam.

Now here's where it gets tricky. You have an extra $1,000 in your account but in addition Sam now has an extra $900 in his bank account, which for convenience we will assume is held at another bank. Now Sam's bank has an extra $900, but it too doesn't want to hold all of its new money in reserves so it will keep $90 in reserve and make $810 in new loans—thus, the bank's reserve ratio stays at 1/10. The process does not stop there as Sam's bank now lends money to Tom and Tom's bank lends money to Dick and . . . well you get the idea. This process keeps going through a ripple effect as one bank increases its loans, leading to an increase in deposits in another bank, which in turn increases its loans, which leads to an increase in deposits in another bank, which increases its loans . . . and so forth.

What is the end result of the ripple process? There are two ways to see the end result, the long way and the shortcut. We are going to save the long way for the appendix. Here's the shortcut. If banks want a reserve ratio of 1/10, then when the Federal Reserve increases reserves by $1,000, deposits must ultimately increase by $10,000. Now remember that the money multiplier is the inverse of the reserve ratio, or 10. Did you notice that deposits eventually increase by the increase in reserves *multiplied* by the money multiplier? That's why it's called the money multiplier.

Let's summarize: The money multiplier tells us how much deposits expand with each dollar increase in reserves. If the money multiplier is 10, for example, then an increase in reserves of $1,000 will lead to an increase in deposits of $10,000. Since checkable deposits are part of the money supply (M1 and M2), we can also say that an increase in reserves of $1,000 increases the money supply by $10,000. Thus, we have:

$$\text{Change in money supply} = \text{Change in reserves} \times \text{Money multiplier}$$

or

$$\Delta MS = \Delta \text{Reserves} \times MM$$

CHECK YOURSELF

> If the reserve ratio is 1/20, what percent of deposits is kept as reserves?

> If the reserve ratio is 1/20, what is the money multiplier?

> If the Fed increases bank reserves by $10,000 and the banking system has a reserve ratio of 1/20, what is the change in the money supply?

How the Fed Controls the Money Supply

Now that we have seen what the money supply is and why the money multiplier multiplies a change in reserves, let's look at the three major tools the Fed uses to control the money supply. These are:

1. Open market operations—the buying and selling of U.S. government bonds on the open market

2. Discount rate lending and the term auction facility—Federal Reserve lending to banks and other financial institutions

3. Required reserves and payment of interest on reserves—changing the minimum ratio of reserves to deposits, which is legally required of banks and other depository institutions and paying interest on any reserves held by banks at the Fed

Let's look at each in turn.

Open Market Operations

Suppose that the Federal Reserve wants to increase the money supply. How does it do it? As we said earlier, if the Fed wants to create money, it can simply print money or add numbers to bank accounts. But how does the new money find its way into the economy? Imagine, for example, that the Fed added money to its own bank account and bought apples with the new money. At first, the money would flow to apple farmers and then the apple farmers would buy more tractors and television sets and vacations, and the money would flow out to other people who themselves would buy more goods. In this way, the Fed's increase in the money supply would spread throughout the economy. And if the Fed wanted to reduce the money supply, it could sell some of the apples that it had bought earlier.

The Fed, however, doesn't want to buy and sell apples. Apples are difficult to store, expensive to ship, and available in very large quantities during only part of the year. So instead of apples, the Fed buys and sells government bonds, usually short-term bonds called Treasury bills or T-bills (these are also often called Treasury securities or Treasuries). Government bonds can be stored and shipped electronically and the market for government bonds is liquid and deep, which means that the Fed can easily buy and sell billions of dollars worth of government bonds in a matter of minutes.

So, if the Fed wants to change the money supply, it usually does so by buying or selling government bonds. This is called an **open market operation.**

Open market operations occur when the Fed buys and sells government bonds.

To pay for the T-bills, the Fed electronically increases the reserves of the seller, usually a bank or a large dealer in Treasury securities. With more reserves on hand, that bank will respond by increasing its loans beginning the ripple process we described above. That is, banks will make additional loans, the loans will in turn be used to buy goods and pay wages, and people will deposit some of these payments into other banks. The new deposits will increase the reserves of these other banks, which will now also be able to make more loans. Thus, the purchase of bonds by the Federal Reserve leads to a ripple process of increasing deposits, loans, deposits, loans, deposits, more loans, and so forth.

We noted earlier that the change in the money supply is equal to the change in reserves multiplied by the money multiplier, $\Delta MS = \Delta \text{Reserves} \times MM$. It's important to remember, however, that the size of the money multiplier is not fixed. The multiplier is the inverse of the reserve ratio and the reserve ratio is determined by banks. When banks are confident and eager to lend, they will want to keep their reserves relatively low so the money multiplier will be large $(MM = 1/RR)$. In this case, changes at the base of the money pyramid (Figure 14.2) have a relatively large effect on the entire pyramid.

But when banks are fearful and reluctant to lend—that is they wish to hold a high level of reserves, the money multiplier will be low and a change in the monetary base need not change the broader monetary aggregates much at all. In this case, changes at the base of the money pyramid have a relatively small effect on the entire pyramid.

Thus, even though the Fed controls the monetary base, the Fed may not know how much or how quickly changes in the base will change loans and the broader measures of the money supply.

Summarizing, (1) the Federal Reserve can increase or decrease reserves at banks by buying or selling government bonds, (2) the increase in reserves boosts the money supply through a multiplier process, and (3) the size of the multiplier is not fixed but depends on how much of their assets the banks want to hold as reserves.

Open Market Operations and Interest Rates   Conducting monetary policy by buying and selling government bonds rather than, say, apples has another advantage. You may recall from Chapter 8 that bond prices and interest rates are inversely related: When bond prices go up, that is another way of saying interest rates go down, and when bond prices go down, that means interest rates go up. Thus, when the Fed buys or sells bonds, it changes the monetary base and influences interest rates at the same time. Let's go through this in more detail.

When the Fed buys bonds, it increases the demand for bonds, which pushes up the price of bonds, thus lowering the interest rate. So, buying bonds stimulates the economy through two distinct mechanisms, namely higher money supplies and lower interest rates. In a sense, the increase in the money supply increases the supply of loans and the lower interest rates increase the quantity of loans demanded.

When you hear that "the Fed has lowered (or raised) interest rates," do not be confused. The Fed does not "set" interest rates in the same way that a 7-Eleven owner "sets" the price of milk in the store. Instead, interest rates are determined in a broad market through the supply and demand for loans as outlined in Chapter 8. The Fed works through supply and demand, and if the Fed wants short-term interest rates to fall, it has to buy more bonds, thereby influencing market prices.

The Fed Controls a Real Rate Only in the Short Run Lending and borrowing decisions depend on the real interest rate, the interest rate after inflation has been taken into account (see Chapter 11). It's important to understand, therefore, that the Fed has influence on real interest rates only in the short run. Remember from Chapter 11 that money is neutral in the long run—that neutrality includes real interest rates. Similarly, remember from Chapter 12 that an increase in aggregate demand (AD) increases the real growth rate only in the short run. Thus, the long-run neutrality of money, the long-run neutrality of aggregate demand, and the long-run neutrality of Federal Reserve influence over real rates are all different sides of the same "coin."

The Fed has the most influence over a short-term interest rate called the Federal Funds rate. The **Federal Funds rate** is simply the *overnight* rate (that's really short term!) for a loan from one major bank to another. Banks lend not only to entrepreneurs and consumers and home buyers but also to other banks and financial institutions.

> The **Federal Funds rate** is the overnight lending rate from one major bank to another.

Since the Federal Reserve can easily change the reserves of major banks through open market operations, it can exercise especially tight control over the Federal Funds rate. In fact, monetary policy is usually conducted in terms of the Federal Funds rate. For example, instead of deciding to increase the money supply by $50 billion, the Fed might decide to reduce the Federal Funds rate by a quarter of a point—the Fed will then buy bonds until the Federal Funds rate drops by a quarter of a point. Similarly, if the Fed wants to increase the Federal Funds rate, it will sell bonds until the Federal Funds rate increases by the desired amount.

The Fed usually focuses on the Federal Funds rate because it is a convenient signal of monetary policy, it responds very quickly to actions by the Fed, and it can be monitored on a day-to-day basis. In contrast, the broader measures of the money supply, such as M1 and M2, are more difficult to measure and monitor because they require data from many different corners of the banking system. But don't forget that the Fed controls the Federal Funds rate through its control over the monetary base.

Discount Rate Lending and the Term Auction Facility

The second tool in the Fed's toolbox is lending. Remember the more than $2 trillion we discussed in the opening that banks and other financial institutions borrowed in 2008? Now we know why the Fed had the power to make these loans: The Fed can create money at will. Thus, the Fed is often said to be the **lender of last resort.** When all other institutions have run out of funds or fear to lend, banks and other financial institutions may still turn to the Fed. The Fed's ability to quickly lend enormous sums in a crisis is a very powerful tool. Let's see how it works in more detail.

> A **lender of last resort** loans money to banks and other financial institutions when no one else will.

The Fed has several methods of making loans. In normal times, the Fed offers to lend to banks at the **discount rate** and a bank that borrows from the Fed is often said to be borrowing from the discount window. If banks borrow from the Fed that increases the money supply. The Fed lends to banks by simply adding extra (electronic) dollars to their accounts at the Fed. These loans increase the monetary base directly, and indirectly they may encourage banks to lend more money, increasing M1 and M2. Of course, when banks pay back these loans, the monetary base shrinks once again. Discount window borrowing therefore tends to be used for short-run "tide-me-overs" rather than for long-run monetary policy decisions.

> **Discount rate** is the interest rate banks pay when they borrow directly from the Fed.

Market traders read the discount rate as a signal of the Fed's attitude or "stance," namely the Fed's willingness to allow the money supply to increase. When the Fed lowers the discount rate, the market reads this as signaling an expansionary monetary policy. But of course, the lower discount rate doesn't directly affect the monetary base unless banks actually borrow more from the Fed.

Most of the time, most banks are not borrowing from the discount window. It is expected that if a bank is in good health, it will borrow most of its credit needs from other banks or financial institutions, not the Fed. The discount window is intended to help out banks in financial stress when they cannot borrow from the private sector. In fact, if a bank suddenly starts borrowing a lot of money from the discount window, usually it receives a rapid but discreet inquiry from the Fed, asking what exactly is wrong. Banks do not generally want to be in this position.

Nonetheless, all banks know that discount window borrowing is available if they get into financial trouble. For instance, if Citigroup lends money to Wells Fargo, Citigroup knows that Wells Fargo could borrow at the discount window to repay Citigroup, if need be. The very existence of the discount window makes private bank loans work more smoothly, even if the discount window isn't being used.

Note that the possibility of financial troubles at a bank stems from the very nature of fractional reserve banking. Loans are the main asset of fractional reserve banks, so the value of the bank depends on how willing and able borrowers are to repay their loans.

A solvency crisis occurs when banks become insolvent.

An insolvent bank has liabilities that are greater than its assets.

One potential problem—known as a **solvency crisis**—occurs when banks become **insolvent**: The value of a bank's loans falls so far that the bank can no longer pay back its depositors. Banks usually hold "capital" as a cushion against such losses but of course the scope of the losses may exceed the capital of the bank. In this context, the use of the word "capital" refers to a very specifically defined legal term, not just to the word "capital" in the general economic sense. The legal formula for bank capital is complex, but the core intuition is that banks are required to hold some of their assets in relatively safe forms in order to provide a protective cushion to shield depositors against potential losses. A bank with a lot of capital is in little danger of defaulting. Internationally coordinated regulations, supported by the Fed, impose capital requirements on U.S. banks.

In 2008, we saw an extraordinary development: The U.S. Treasury acted to "recapitalize" parts of the U.S. banking system. That is, the Treasury invested additional money into these banks to boost their future prospects, in return for the promise that banks would someday repay this investment. The fear was that many U.S. banks were insolvent, due to bad real estate loans and other investment mistakes. This recapitalization was under the authority of the U.S. Treasury, but it was very much an action in conjunction with the Federal Reserve. The goal of recapitalization is to get banks on their feet again and thus get them lending again. Whether or not this action counts as "monetary policy" in the formal sense of that term, it has many of the same effects as monetary policy, namely that it encourages bank lending and thus money supply growth.

A liquidity crisis occurs when banks are illiquid.

A second potential problem is called a **liquidity crisis**. Maybe the bank assets are good, but there is a potential problem if all the depositors want their money back at the same time. A bank might have a lot of good assets on its books, like long-term loans that are repaid over time, but the income from those loans is not available right away. But how do depositors know whether a bank's assets are good? Often they don't. As a result, fear can turn solvent banks into **illiquid banks** very quickly. During the Great Depression, for example, even a rumor that a bank might go under caused depositors to rush to their bank to get their money out before it was too late—thus, causing even good, solvent banks to go under!

To avoid bank runs such as occurred during the Great Depression, the Federal Deposit Insurance Corporation (FDIC) was created. The FDIC guarantees bank deposits up to $250,000 for each depositor name on an account (in practice, the guarantee is often even larger in value). Since depositors know their deposits are insured, they have less reason to run to the bank to withdraw their deposits even if they do hear rumors. Thus, the mere existence of the FDIC can reduce bank panics even if the FDIC never has to pay out.

If despite the FDIC guarantee many people do want to withdraw their funds, the Federal Reserve System can act as a lender of last resort to help banks meet their obligations. Ideally, the Fed uses the discount window to lend to illiquid (but solvent) institutions and waits for them to regain their liquidity and return to financial health. Of course, in practice, especially during an emergency, it is not always easy to tell which banks are insolvent and which are merely illiquid.

If the Fed knows a bank is insolvent, usually the best thing to do is to pay off depositors and close down that bank before it can incur any further losses. The 2008 Treasury recapitalization of U.S. banks was a break from this traditional practice; the judgment at the time was that too many banks might be insolvent for the economy to survive widespread bank closures, so the Treasury decided to offer aid to banks instead.

The Term Auction Facility During the financial crisis of 2007–2008, sparked initially by problems in the subprime mortgage market (more on this in the next chapter and see also Chapter 8), the Fed went considerably beyond its traditional role in helping out financial institutions.

First, the Fed set up a Term Auction Facility. The Term Auction Facility is best understood in contrast to the discount rate. The discount rate sets an interest rate and then the Fed waits to see how many banks want to borrow. One problem with the discount rate is that banks may not borrow, for fear of admitting to the market that they are in a weak position. The Term Auction Facility had the Fed announce that it wanted to inject a certain quantity of reserves into banks; those funds were then auctioned until the rate was low enough that banks would borrow the money. Furthermore, the Fed loosened collateral requirements for its loans and stressed to banks that there would be no negative stigma from borrowing from the facility. In other words, the Term Auction Facility and related lending activities were designed to give the Fed more control over the money supply, to get around some of the problems discussed above.

The amount of extra lending done by the Fed during the period of the financial crisis was staggering. For instance between December 2007 and May 2008, the Fed lent approximately $475 billion to the U.S. banking system, mostly to restore liquidity to credit markets. Over the course of the year, the Fed lent over $2 trillion in total. To put that latter figure in perspective, it is over $6,000 for every person in the United States. Of course to the extent those banks end up as insolvent, the taxpayer will pick up the resulting losses.

An **illiquid bank** has short-term liabilities that are greater than its short-term assets but overall has assets that are greater than its liabilities.

Required Reserves and Payment of Interest on Reserves

Open market operations and lending are the Fed's most important tool in normal times, but the Fed has several other ways of influencing the money supply and thus aggregate demand. The Fed, for example, can change the ratio of **required reserves.** By force of law, the Fed tells banks that their deposits must be backed by a certain amount of reserves, either currency or reserves held at the Fed. As of spring 2009, the legally mandated reserve ratio is 0 percent for deposit liabilities under $10.3 million, 3 percent for liabilities under $44.4 million, and 10 percent for liabilities more than this sum. This is called the reserve requirement.

If the Fed lowers the required reserve ratio, this may boost the money supply. For instance, if the reserve ratio for some specified set of bank liabilities is cut from 10 percent to 5 percent, a dollar in reserves may lead to more loans.

The reserve requirement, however, is not the most important tool of monetary policy. With or without Fed regulations, banks need to hold reserves anyway, if only to reassure their customers and to conduct regular business, as we mentioned above. Ordinary business demands tend to be a more important determinant of the reserve ratio than the Fed. For instance, the Fed might lower the required reserve ratio but there is no guarantee banks will use that new freedom to make more loans. Not all loans are profitable for a bank, if only because not all potential borrowers are likely to repay.

The Fed may also eliminate required reserves altogether in the not too distant future because as of 2008, the Fed has another instrument at its disposal: It can vary the rate of interest that it pays banks on reserves held at the Fed. In previous times, banks received no interest payments on reserves. Not surprisingly, banks wished to minimize those holdings because they brought no profit. In trying to minimize reserves, however, banks sometimes worked at cross-purposes with the Fed, especially when the Fed wanted to make sure that the banking system had plenty of reserves on hand for payment purposes. But now the Fed is paying interest on those reserves, and the Fed consciously varies that interest rate to help achieve the goals of monetary policy.

The Federal Reserve and Systemic Risk

We have covered the three major tools the Fed has to control the money supply: open market operations, lending, and required reserve regulation and the payment of interest on reserves. In times of crisis, the Fed can and has gone beyond these tools to address problems with the financial system that extend beyond banks.

In times of crisis, for example, the Fed has decided that its lender of last resort function is not restricted to traditional banks alone. In March 2008, the Fed made extensive loan guarantees to JP Morgan, which was in the midst of purchasing the failing company of Bear Stearns, a financial institution but not a bank in the traditional sense. In fact, Bear Stearns, which falls under the legal definition of "investment bank," is regulated by the Securities and Exchange Commission. The Fed's view was that Bear Stearns owed a lot of money to banks (true), so if Bear Stearns failed a lot of banks would fail too, thus causing the money supply to plummet. The Fed therefore thought that it needed to prevent Bear Stearns from shutting down to prevent much bigger problems. The Fed probably had a reasonable worry and they acted promptly to address

Required reserves are the portion of their deposits that banks are required by law to hold as reserves.

CHECK YOURSELF

> Underline the correct answers. The Fed wants to lower interest rates: It does so by (buying/selling) bonds in an open market operation. By doing this, the Fed (adds/subtracts) reserves and through the multiplier process (increases/decreases) the money supply.

that worry. Nonetheless, the market has since been wondering what exactly are the powers and duties of the Fed since it acted outside of its traditional legal mandate. The Fed also has loaned many billions of dollars to the insurance company American International Group (AIG), again under the rationale that AIG owed a lot of money to banks. The financial crisis of 2007–2008 has led to a true blurring of the functions of the Fed and it is widely recognized that a more comprehensive redefinition of the Fed's responsibilities is needed.

The general issue in the Bear Stearns case and also the AIG case is called **systemic risk.** Systemic risk simply means that the failure of one financial institution can bring down other institutions as well, just as if a chain of dominoes were collapsing. Do you know the old joke: "If you owe your banker a million dollars and can't pay, you have a problem. If you owe your banker a billion dollars and can't pay, your banker has a problem." Preventing the spread of systemic risk is one of the most important things the Fed does.

> **Systemic risk** is the risk that the failure of one financial institution can bring down other institutions as well.

There is, however, a problem. Whenever the Fed acts to limit systemic risk, it insulates at least some banks from the financial consequences of their bad decisions. For instance, a bank that lent too much money to Bear Stearns now knows it doesn't have to worry so much the next time around because the Fed will probably step in to bail them out. When individuals or institutions are insured, they tend to take on too much risk—incentives matter—and economists call this the problem of **moral hazard.** A homeowner who is insured, for example, has a reduced incentive to install smoke alarms, which is one reason why insurance companies give discounts to those who do install alarms. In the case of banks, the longer-run consequence of moral hazard is that banks will be less careful about their financial commitments. Limiting systemic risk while checking moral hazard is the fundamental problem the Fed faces as a regulator of bank safety.

> **Moral hazard** occurs when banks and other financial institutions take on too much risk, hoping that the Fed and regulators will later bail them out.

When it comes to the Fed's lender of last resort function, it can be said that we live in interesting times. A great deal has been changing in the last few years and those changes probably are not over. The general tendency has been for the Fed to become much more active and to assume greater powers in the case of emergency and perhaps during normal times as well.

Revisiting Aggregate Demand and Monetary Policy

Now that we have covered the major tools of the Federal Reserve, let's remember that what the Fed ultimately wants to do is to use its tools to influence aggregate demand (AD). Let's imagine, for example, that the Fed wants to increase aggregate demand and it chooses to do so by buying bonds in an open market operation. The bond purchase increases the monetary base and decreases short-term interest rates. The increase in the base increases deposits and loans through the multiplier process, and the decrease in interest rates stimulates investment (and consumption) borrowing. As a result—if all goes well, AD increases. The increase in AD then influences the economy as we discussed in Chapter 12 and is shown in Figure 14.3 on the next page. Beginning at point a, an increase in $\overrightarrow{M}$ shifts the aggregate demand curve outward moving the economy to point b where inflation and the real growth rate are higher. In the long run, after transition the economy will move to point c with a higher inflation rate (money neutrality again) but a growth rate given by the fundamentals at the long-run Solow level.

CHECK YOURSELF

> If a large bank makes some bad lending mistakes, will the Fed always let the bank bear the brunt of its mistakes and go under? If not, what justification will the Fed use?

> Consider the moral hazard that could arise if the Fed bailed out large banks. If you work at a large bank and lose a lot of money betting that oil prices would rise when they in fact fell, what incentive would you have to double your bet the next time?

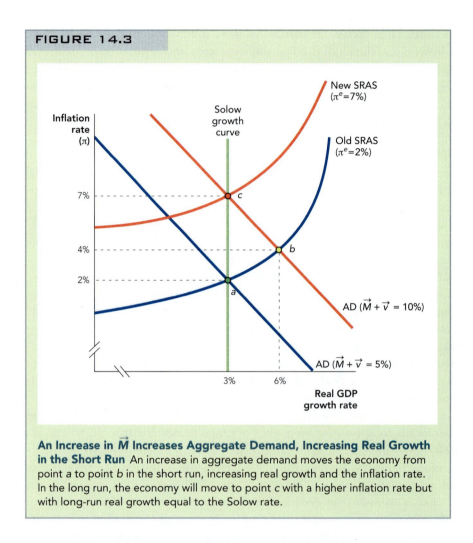

FIGURE 14.3

An Increase in $\vec{M}$ Increases Aggregate Demand, Increasing Real Growth in the Short Run An increase in aggregate demand moves the economy from point a to point b in the short run, increasing real growth and the inflation rate. In the long run, the economy will move to point c with a higher inflation rate but with long-run real growth equal to the Solow rate.

We now know that the process is not quite so simple. The Fed can buy bonds and increase the monetary base, but these actions do not increase aggregate demand by any guaranteed amount, since we don't know exactly how much M1 and M2 will go up in response to the higher monetary base. Nor do we know exactly how much the lower interest rates will stimulate investment spending, especially since the Fed has the most influence over *short-term* rates, while most investment spending will depend on longer-term rates. In addition, all of these processes take time and the lags from action to response are not fixed but may vary. If the Fed acts to reduce interest rates today, for example, it may take 6 to 18 months before aggregate demand and economic growth begin to respond significantly. In the meantime, economic conditions may change.

Thus, to estimate the effect of its actions on aggregate demand, the Fed must try to predict and monitor many variables determining the size and timing of the response to its actions. Some of the things the Fed must try to predict and monitor are:

> Will banks lend out all the new reserves or will they lend out only a portion, holding the rest as excess reserves?

> How quickly will increases in the monetary base translate into new bank loans and thus larger increases in M1 and M2?

> Do businesses want to borrow? How low do short-term interest rates have to go to stimulate more investment borrowing?

> If businesses do borrow, will they promptly hire labor and capital, or will they just hold the money as a precaution against bad times?

The Federal Reserve's power should not be underestimated but increasing or decreasing aggregate demand is not like turning a tap on and off. The Fed has a limited set of tools and it must constantly adapt those tools to new circumstances and conditions. We will be taking up the difficulties and dilemmas of monetary policy in the real world at greater length in the next chapter.

Who Controls the Fed?

The power to create money out of thin air and to lend trillions of dollars is an awesome power. How is this power controlled?

The Fed has a seven-member Board of Governors, who are appointed by the President and confirmed by the Senate. Governors are appointed for 14-year terms and cannot be reappointed—this means a single President will rarely appoint a majority of the board. Once appointed, members of the Board of Governors cannot be easily fired. The chairperson of the Fed is appointed by the President from among the members of Board of Governors and confirmed by the Senate for a term of four years.

Although we say "the Fed," the Fed is not just one bank but 12 Federal Reserve Banks each headquartered in a different region of the country.* The regional structure of the Fed explains another peculiarity: The Fed is a quasi-private, quasi-public institution. Each regional bank is a nonprofit bank with nine directors: six of these directors are elected by commercial banks from the region and three are elected by the Board of Governors. Six of the directors must be nonbankers and these are drawn from business, labor, academia, and other fields. In 2008, for example, the chairman of UPS was a director of the Atlanta Federal Reserve Bank, the president of Yarnell Ice Cream was a director of the St. Louis Federal Reserve Bank, and the head of the New York State AFL-CIO was a director of the New York Federal Reserve Bank. The directors of the regional banks appoint a regional bank president. Finally, the presidents of the regional banks participate, along with the Board of Governors, in the Federal Open Market Committee, the most important committee of the Federal Reserve and the one that controls open market operations.

Confused? Yes, it is confusing and we have spared you many of the details! Perhaps it will help to know that the confusing structure of the Federal Reserve system has a purpose. The Federal Reserve is powerful, so in keeping with the U.S. system of checks and balances, the power of the Fed is dispersed—no single President appoints all the governors of the Fed, the governors do not have complete control over Fed policy, the regional bank presidents come from all over the United States, and they are appointed by directors who are drawn not just from banking but from a wide variety of fields.

The bottom line is that the Federal Reserve is usually one of the most independent agencies in the U.S. government. It is relatively insulated from politics,

CHECK YOURSELF

> If money is neutral in the long run, why would the Fed want to increase the money supply in the short run?

> How will fear about the economy entering a recession affect the disposition of banks to lend? How will this affect the Fed's ability to shift aggregate demand in a recession?

---

* The headquarters of the 12 regional banks are located in Boston, New York, Philadelphia, Cleveland, Richmond, Atlanta, Chicago, St. Louis, Minneapolis, Kansas City, Dallas, and San Francisco.

party, and elections—perhaps only the Supreme Court is more independent. That said, in the financial crisis of 2008, the Fed had to work closely with the Treasury Department (for one thing, Treasury resources were required to re-capitalize banks) and in that sense it was much less independent than usual. In general, the independence of the Federal Reserve worries some people who would prefer that the Fed be more directly accountable to democratically elected politicians. Other people are concerned that if the Federal Reserve could be controlled directly by, say, the President this would give the President the power to order the Federal Reserve to expand the money supply and boost the economy just before an election.

Political pressures have been put on the Federal Reserve and some chairper-sons have been less independent than others. In 1972, President Nixon asked Arthur Burns, the chair of the Fed, to stimulate the economy before the elec-tion. Burns did stimulate the economy and Nixon won in a landslide, but the economic gains were temporary. Not surprisingly, inflation was too high for the rest of the 1970s. This was not a proud moment in the history of the Federal Reserve or the presidency.

Overall, an independent Federal Reserve is defended by most economists as part of the U.S. system of checks and balances.

☐ Takeaway

To return to the opening of this chapter, we now have a sense why the Fed chair-person is (possibly) the second most powerful person in the world. The Federal Reserve is the government bank and the banker's bank and it has the power to cre-ate money. The ability to create money, regulate the money supply, and potentially lend trillions of dollars means that the Fed has significant powers to influence ag-gregate demand in the world's largest economy.

The concept of "the money supply" can refer to several different measures. It is important to know the major definitions of the money supply and how they differ. The Fed controls the money supply by buying and selling government bonds in what are called open market operations.

By buying and selling bonds, the Fed changes bank reserves. A change in re-serves changes the money supply through a multiplier process of rippling loans and deposits. The final result is that $\Delta MS = \Delta\text{Reserves} \times MM$. The money multiplier, however, changes over time, so the Fed's influence over aggregate demand is sub-ject to uncertainty in both impact and timing.

When the government buys securities, the interest rate decreases and that stim-ulates consumption and investment borrowing. When the government sells securi-ties, the interest rate increases, thereby reducing borrowing for either consumption or investment. For day-to-day operations, the Fed focuses its attention on the Federal Funds rate, the interest rate on overnight loans between major banks. The Fed has the most influence over real rates of interest in the short run. The Fed has little influence over long-run real rates of interest.

The Fed serves as a "lender of last resort" for banks and for major financial insti-tutions that find themselves in trouble. Preventing "systemic risk"—or the spread of financial problems from one institution to another—is one of the Fed's most im-portant jobs.

□ CHAPTER REVIEW

KEY CONCEPTS

Money, p. 290

Liquid asset, p. 292

Fractional reserve banking, p. 293

Reserve ratio, RR, p. 294

Money multiplier, MM, p. 294

Open market operations, p. 295

Federal Funds rate, p. 297

Lender of last resort, p. 297

Discount rate, p. 297

Solvency crisis, p. 298

Insolvent bank, p. 298

Liquidity crisis, p. 298

Illiquid bank, p. 299

Required reserves, p. 300

Systemic risk, p. 301

Moral hazard, p. 301

FACTS AND TOOLS

1. Let's find out what counts as money. In this chapter, we used a typical definition of money: "A widely accepted means of payment." Under this definition, are people using "money" in the following transactions? If not, why not?

   a. Lucy sells her Saab to Karen for $1,000 in cash

   b. Lucy sells her Saab to Karen for $1,000 worth of old Bob Dylan records

   c. Lucy sells her Saab to Karen for $1,000 in checking account balances (transferred by writing a check)

   d. Lucy sells her Saab to Karen by Karen promising $1,000 worth of auto-detailing services over the next year

   e. Lucy sells her Saab to Karen for $1,000 worth of Revolutionary War-era continental dollars

2. Define the following

   a. The monetary base, MB

   b. M1

   c. M2

3. a. Suppose that banks have decided they need to keep a reserve ratio of 10 percent—this

guarantees that they'll have enough cash in ATM machines to keep depositors happy, and enough electronic deposits at the Federal Reserve so that they can redeem checks presented by other banks. What is the money multiplier in this case?

   b. If depositors start visiting the ATM a lot more often, will banks want to have a higher reserve ratio or a lower reserve ratio? Will this increase the money multiplier or lower it?

4. If the Federal Reserve wants to lower interest rates via open market operations, should it buy bonds or should it sell bonds?

5. Practice with money multipliers. Think of the "money supply" (MS) as equal to either M1 or M2.

   a. RR = 5%, Change in reserves = $10 billion. MM = ?; Change in MS = ?

   b. RR = ?, Change in reserves = −$1,000, MM = 5; Change in MS = ?

   c. RR = 100%, Change in reserves = $10 billion. MM = ?; Change in MS = ?

6. In the previous question, one example assumed that banks kept a 100 percent reserve ratio. Some economists have recommended that *all* banks be required by law to keep 100 percent of their deposits in the bank vault, at the Federal Reserve, or invested in ultrasafe investments such as short-term U.S. Treasury bills.

   a. If this happened, what would the money multiplier be equal to?

   b. If this happened, would the interest rate on bank deposits probably go up or down?

   c. If this happened, would people be more likely or less likely to invest their savings in bank alternatives, such as bonds, mutual funds, or their cousin's lawn-mowing business?

7. The main interest rate that the Federal Reserve tries to control is the Federal Funds rate, the interest rate that banks charge on short-term (usually overnight) loans to other banks. Let's see how much interest a bank can earn if it lends money at the Federal Funds rate.

   Virginia Community Bank has $2,000,000 of extra cash sitting in its account at the Federal Reserve Bank of Richmond. It gets a call from Bank of America asking to borrow the whole

$2,000,000 for 24 hours. (This is typical: it's usually the smaller banks lending money overnight to the bigger banks.)

a. If the *annual* interest rate on federal funds is 4 percent, what (approximately) is the *one-day* interest rate on federal funds? (Note that interest rates, like GDP growth rates, are usually reported as "per year," just as speeds are reported as miles "per hour.")

b. How many dollars of interest will Virginia Community Bank earn for lending this money for one day?

c. If Virginia Community Bank lent this amount every day at the same rate for an entire year, how much interest would it earn?

8. Let's use the model of the supply and demand for bank reserves to explain how the Federal Reserve can change aggregate demand in the short run. Remember that the Federal Reserve controls the *supply* of bank reserves, but private banks create *demand* for bank reserves.

a. After a meeting, the Federal Reserve's Open Market Committee votes to cut interest rates from 2 percent to 1.5 percent. How will they make this happen: Will they increase the supply of reserves or decrease the supply?

b. As a result of your answer to part a, will banks usually lend more money in response, or will they lend less money? Will this tend to increase the nation's money supply, lower it, or will it have no net effect on the money supply?

c. Will this typically increase aggregate demand or lower it?

9. We mentioned that the central bank can influence a short-run real interest rate—this is because in the short run the inflation rate is relatively constant but the central bank can adjust the nominal rate on short-term loans. Recall that after investing in a T-bill, the real rate that investors receive is:

Real interest rate = Nominal interest rate − Inflation

a. If inflation is 3 percent and the Fed wants the real rate on short-term loans to be 2 percent, what should it set the nominal Fed Funds rate equal to?

b. If inflation is 3 percent, and the Fed wants to encourage borrowing by cutting the real rate on short-term loans to −1 percent, what should it set the nominal Fed Funds rate equal to?

c. If inflation is 6 percent, and the Fed wants to discourage borrowing by raising the real rate on short-term loans to 4 percent, what should it set the nominal Fed Funds rate equal to?

THINKING AND PROBLEM SOLVING

1. Whether an asset is "liquid" often depends on what situation you are in. For each of the pairs of assets below, which is more liquid in the particular setting?

You want to buy a sofa:

A savings account or currency

You want to trade for a bologna sandwich in elementary school:

A peanut butter and jelly sandwich or sushi

You want to buy a house:

Currency or a checking account

You live in a postapocalyptic wasteland:

Rice or currency

You are traveling across Europe during the Middle Ages:

Gold coins or works of art

You are an investment banker buying a corporation:

U.S. Treasury bonds or currency

2. a. Who is more likely to take bigger risks: a trapeze artist with a safety net beneath or a trapeze artist without a safety net?

b. Who is more likely to take bigger risks with his deposits: a bank CEO in a country where there is a lender of last resort or a bank CEO in a country where there is no lender of last resort?

c. Who is more likely to spend more time searching for a well-run, safe bank: a depositor living in a country with government-run deposit insurance or a depositor living in a country without government-run deposit insurance?

d. Do government-run central banks and deposit insurance both increase moral hazard problems, both decrease moral hazard problems, or do they push in different directions when it comes to moral hazard?

3. a. In the short run, if the Fed wants to cut short-term, nominal interest rates, what does it do: Does it increase the growth rate of money or decrease the growth rate of money? Why? Will this tend to lower the real rate or will it tend to lower inflation?

b. In the long run, if the Fed wants to cut short-term, nominal interest rates, what does it do: Does it increase the growth rate of money or decrease the growth rate of money? Why? Will this tend to lower the real rate or will it tend to lower inflation?

4. Let's watch a bank create money. Last Wednesday, the Bank of Numenor opened for business. The first customer, Edith, walked in the door with 100 pieces of silver to deposit in a new checking account. The second customer, Max, walks in the door a few minutes later, asking to borrow 50 pieces of silver for a week. The bank lends Max the silver. Just to keep things simple, assume these are the *only* financial transactions in Numenor. And just to be clear: silver pieces are either "currency" or "reserves": Silver in Max or Edith's hands is "currency," while silver in the bank is "reserves."

a. How much "money" is there in the Numenor economy before Edith walks into the bank?

Monetary base:

M1:

b. How much "money" is there in the Numenor economy after Edith makes her deposit, but before Max walks in for his loan?

Monetary base:

M1:

c. How much "money" is there in the Numenor economy after the Bank makes Max the loan?

Monetary base:

M1:

d. Which action created money: Edith's deposit or Max's loan?

5. You are a bank regulator working for the Federal Reserve. It is your job to see whether banks are solvent or insolvent, liquid or illiquid. Fit each bank below into one of the following four categories:

Liquid and solvent (best)

Illiquid but solvent (probably needs short-term loans from other banks or from the Fed)

Liquid but insolvent (should be shut down immediately: could fool people for a while if not for your good efforts)

Illiquid and insolvent (should be shut down immediately)

a. Bank of DelMarVa

Short-term assets	*Short-term liabilities*
$10 million	$6 million
Total assets	*Total liabilities*
$40 million	$50 million

b. Bank of Escondido

Short-term assets	*Short-term liabilities*
$6 million	$10 million
Total assets	*Total liabilities*
$50 million	$40 million

c. Bank of Previa

Short-term assets	*Short-term liabilities*
$12 million	$10 million
Total assets	*Total liabilities*
$50 million	$40 million

d. Bank of Cambia

Short-term assets	*Short-term liabilities*
$8 million	$10 million
Total assets	*Total liabilities*
$30 million	$40 million

e. Bank of Marshall

Short-term assets	*Short-term liabilities*
$120 million	$100 million
Total assets	*Total liabilities*
$500 million	$400 million

6. We mentioned that banks are reluctant to borrow from the Fed's discount window because it's looked down on by other banks: Other banks think that if a bank needs to use the discount window, it's probably not very healthy. So where you get your loans is a *signal* about what kind of bank you are. Which of the following would seem like bad signs? If you think one or more of the cases are ambiguous, explain.

a. Your friend borrows money from a federal student loan program.

b. Your friend borrows money from a payday loan store.

c. Your friend pays for ordinary living expenses by borrowing with her credit card.

d. Your friend borrows money from her parents.

e. Your friend borrows money from an illegal loan shark.

7. Does the House of Representatives get to vote on who becomes the chairperson of the Federal Reserve Board? If not, who *does* get to vote?

8. In the nation of San Ysidro, the central bank raises the required reserve ratio without changing the amount of reserves. (Note: The U.S. Federal Reserve actually did this in 1937–1938, while the U.S. economy was slowly emerging from the Great Depression.)

a. Will this tend to shift the aggregate demand curve to the left or to the right?

b. In the short run, what will this do to inflation and real growth? (The correct answer to this question is what actually happened to the United States in the 1937–1938 period.)

CHALLENGES

1. We mentioned how difficult it can be for the Federal Reserve to actually control aggregate demand: Its control over the broader money supply (M1 and M2) is weak and indirect, plus it can't control velocity very much at all. Let's translate the following bullet points from the chapter into an expanded aggregate demand equation. You know that increasing AD means increasing spending growth, $\vec{M} + \vec{v}$, but now you know that M (growth in M1 or M2, money measures that include checking accounts) depends on growth in the monetary base (MB) and on the money multiplier (MM). That means that an increase in AD requires an increase in $\vec{MB} + \vec{MM} + \vec{v}$.

Let's apply this fact to the following cases mentioned in the chapter. In all cases, the Federal Reserve is trying to boost AD by raising $\vec{MB}$. But if there's a fall in $\vec{MM}$ or a fall in $\vec{v}$ at the same time, the Fed's actions might do nothing to AD. In each case below, what are we concerned about: A fall in $\vec{MM}$ or a fall in $\vec{v}$?

a. Will banks lend out all the new reserves or will they lend out only a portion, holding the rest as excess reserves?

b. How quickly will increases in the monetary base translate into new bank loans and thus larger increases in M1 and M2?

c. If businesses do borrow will they promptly hire labor and capital, or will they just hold the money as a precaution against bad times?

2. In the past, the Federal Reserve didn't pay interest on reserves kept in Federal Reserve banks: For an ordinary U.S. bank, money kept at the Fed earned zero interest, just like money stored in a vault or in an ATM machine. In 2008, the Fed started paying interest on deposits kept at the Fed.

a. Once the Fed started paying interest, what would you predict would happen to demand for reserves by banks: Would they demand more reserves or fewer reserves from the Fed?

b. If a central bank starts paying interest on reserves, will private banks tend to make more loans or fewer loans, holding all else equal? (Hint: Does the opportunity cost of making a car loan rise or fall when the central bank starts paying interest on reserves?)

c. Let's put parts a and b together, keeping in mind the fact that bank loans create money. That means that your answer to part b also tells you about the money supply, not just about the loan supply. If a central bank starts paying interest on reserves, will the reserve ratio chosen by banks tend to rise or fall? And will the money multiplier tend to rise or fall?

d. Your answer to part c tells us that when the central bank starts paying interest on reserves, there's going to be a shift in M1 and M2, the broad forms of money supply that include money created through loans. But there are a lot of ways to affect the money supply, so if there's one force pushing the money supply in one direction, we can find another tool to push the money supply in the opposite direction. Therefore, if a central bank chooses to start paying interest on reserves, but it wants M2 to remain unchanged, what should the bank do to the supply of reserves: Should it increase the supply of reserves or decrease the supply of reserves?

3. Economist Bennett McCallum says that in order to push interest rates down in the long run, the central bank needs to raise interest rates in the short run. How can this be true?

CHAPTER **APPENDIX**

The Money Multiplier Process in Detail

Just to recap from the chapter, when the Federal Reserve conducts an open market operation, we said that the money supply changes by the change in reserves times the money multiplier, $\Delta MS = \Delta \text{Reserves} \times MM$. If the Fed buys government bonds, for example, this increases bank reserves, which increases the money supply by the increase in reserves times the money multiplier.

We've already mentioned the idea of a ripple effect: As one bank increases its loans, this leads to an increase in deposits in another bank, which in turn increases its loans, which leads to an increase in deposits in another bank, which increases its loans . . . and so forth.

Now it is time to look at this multiplier process in more detail.

It's helpful to examine a simple form of accounting statement called a T-account. On the left side of a T-account, we list the bank's assets, and on the right side, we list the bank's liabilities. An asset is simply something that represents wealth or value to the bank. In our simple T-accounts, the only assets a bank can have are its reserves and its portfolio of loans. A liability refers to a debt or something owed to someone else. In our simple T-accounts, the only liabilities a bank can have will be deposits (the bank owes the depositor the money in his or her account).

Now suppose that the Fed buys a government bond for $1,000 from a dealer in Treasury securities. The dealer has an account at the First National Bank and thus the Federal Reserve adds $1,000 to the dealer's account. As a result, the First National Bank's liabilities (its deposits) increase by $1,000, but the bank now also has an extra $1,000 in reserves. The First National Bank's T-account looks like this:

First National Bank			
Assets		**Liabilities**	
Reserves:	+$1,000	Deposits:	+$1,000
Loans:			

But what will the First National Bank do with its reserves? The bank wants to make a profit so it will take a portion of its reserves and lend them out. Suppose that the bank keeps $100 in reserves and lends out $900. The bank's T-account now looks like this:

First National Bank			
Assets		**Liabilities**	
Reserves:	$100	Deposits:	$1,000
Loans:	+$900		

Notice that the ratio of the bank's reserves to deposits is $100/$1,000 or 0.1; thus, the reserve ratio = 0.1. Now the firm or person that borrowed the $900 did so to purchase goods and services. Let's suppose that the borrower wrote a check for a cruise to Luxury Vacations Inc., which has an account at the Second National Bank. Luxury Vacations Inc. deposits the check into its account at the Second National Bank so the T-account of the Second National Bank now looks like this:

Second National Bank			
Assets		**Liabilities**	
Reserves:	+$900	Deposits:	+$900
Loans:			

Notice that the Second National Bank's reserves have increased by $900. What does the bank want to do with these reserves? Lend them! Suppose that the Second National Bank also wants a reserve ratio of 0.1 so the Second National Bank keeps $90 in reserves and lends out $810. Its T-account now looks like this:

Second National Bank			
Assets		**Liabilities**	
Reserves:	$90	Deposits:	$900
Loans:	+$810		

Are you beginning to see the multiplier in action? Let's do one more. Suppose that the person or firm who borrowed money from the Second National Bank wanted the money to buy a computer. The borrower writes a check to Apple who deposits the money in their account at the Third National Bank. The T-account of the Third National Bank now looks like this:

Third National Bank			
Assets		**Liabilities**	
Reserves:	+$810	Deposits:	+$810
Loans:			

The Third National Bank also wants to make a profit, so it lends out a portion of its reserves, leading to a T-account like this:

Third National Bank			
Assets		**Liabilities**	
Reserves:	$81	Deposits:	$810
Loans:	+$729		

So let's summarize what we have so far:

| | The Banking System Assets | | Liabilities |
	Reserves	Loans	Deposits
First National Bank	+$100	+$900	+$1,000
Second National Bank	+$90	+$810	+$900
Third National Bank	+$81	+$729	+$810
. . .	. . .	. . .	. . .

Notice that the process doesn't stop with the Third National Bank but continues onward. What is the final result of this process of expansion? Let's focus on what is happening to deposits and see if we can get to the answer a little quicker by figuring out the pattern.

At the First National Bank deposits increase by $1,000, at the Second Bank deposits increase by $900, or $0.9 \times \$1,000$, at the Third Bank deposits increase by $810 or $0.9^2 \times \$1,000$. If you guessed that at the Fourth Bank deposits would increase by $729 or $0.9^3 \times \$1,000$ you are correct so the total process looks like this:

$$\$1,000 \times (1 + 0.9 + 0.9^2 + 0.9^3 + \ldots (0.9)^n)$$

This is an example of an infinite geometric series and mathematics can show that $(1 + 0.9 + 0.9^2 + 0.9^3 + \ldots (0.9)^n)$ converges to $\dfrac{1}{1 - 0.9}$ so deposits will increase by:

$$\$1,000 \times \frac{1}{1 - 0.9} = \$1,000 \times \frac{1}{0.1} = \$1,000 \times 10$$

The last expression should look familiar. Remember that we assumed in our derivations that each bank wanted a reserve ratio of 0.1 so the money multiplier, $MM = 1/RR = 10$. Thus, the last statement says that deposits increase by the increase in reserves ($1,000) times the money multiplier, 10. The increase in the money supply can be measured by the increase in deposits. Thus, we have that $\Delta MS = \Delta \text{Reserves} \times MM$ exactly as we said in the chapter. Aren't you glad we saved the details for the appendix!

We can summarize by looking at how the initial increase in reserves created by the Fed open market purchase of bonds affects the entire banking system. A multiplier similar to that for deposits applies to reserves and loans so the final result looks like this:

The Banking System	Assets		Liabilities
	Reserves	Loans	Deposits
First National Bank	+$100	+$900	+$1,000
Second National Bank	+$90	+$810	+$900
Third National Bank	+$81	+$729	+$810
. . .	. . .	. . .	. . .
Total	$1,000	$9,000	$10,000

Note that we can measure the increase in the money supply by either the increase in the banking system's assets, Reserves + Loans, or by the increase in the banking system's liabilities, namely deposits. Thus, either way the money supply increases by the $10,000, or more generally $\Delta MS = \Delta \text{Reserves} \times MM$ as we have said before.

Let's make one qualification. In the multiplier process we went through, we assumed that every borrower wrote a check for every dollar of their loan and kept none of the money in cash. Thus, if a loan was made for $900, then somewhere in the banking system deposits increased by $900. If any of the borrowers keep some of their loan in cash, however, then the multiplier process does not operate on the cash component. For example, if a borrower receives a loan for $900 and writes a check for $800, keeping $100 in cash, then the multiplier process works only on the $800. Thus, the public's demand for cash also influences the multiplier process and complicates the Fed's job because the demand for cash can change over time.

15

Monetary Policy

The Nobel Prize-winning economist Milton Friedman once likened monetary policy to throwing money from a helicopter. Thus, when *Business Week* asked in 2008, "Will 'Helicopter Ben' Ride to the Rescue?" they were asking whether Ben Bernanke, the chairman of the Federal Reserve, would be able to use monetary policy to jolt the economy out of a looming recession.

In reality, the Federal Reserve rarely uses helicopters in its rescue operations. As we discussed in Chapter 14, the Fed uses three primary tools to influence aggregate demand (AD), namely (1) open market operations in which the Fed buys bonds which increases the money supply and reduces interest rates, or the Fed sells bonds which decreases the money supply and increases interest rates; (2) lending to banks and other financial institutions; and (3) changes in reserve requirements and the interest rate paid on reserves. These are the essential methods through which the Fed affects the real economy.

In this chapter, we take for granted *how* the Fed influences AD and turn more directly to three key practical questions: When *should* the Fed try to influence AD, when *will* the Fed be able to influence AD, and when will the influence on AD *result* in higher GDP growth rates?

We start with the best case for monetary policy: where it is clear what the Fed should do in general terms, such as responding to negative monetary shocks, and when the Fed has a good chance of being successful. We then consider some reasons why even in the best case the Fed doesn't always know which detailed course of action is best. We next consider why some of the other cases—such as negative real shocks—are much harder for the Fed to respond to effectively. Finally, we learn that there are some cases, such as positive real shocks, where it's not clear what the best monetary policy is. We end with a look at the financial crisis that started in 2007.

Monetary Policy: The Best Case

Let's start with the most straightforward case, namely a negative shock to aggregate demand. Suppose, for example, that the rate of growth of the money supply or $\vec{M}$ falls. Imagine, for example, that entrepreneurs are suddenly more pessimistic about the future state of the economy. Entrepreneurs will wish to borrow less, banks will wish to lend less, and the growth rates of M1 and M2 will fall, causing a fall in aggregate demand.

In terms of our basic dynamic AD-AS diagram, the AD curve shifts down and to the left, moving the economy from point *a* to point *b* as shown in Figure 15.1. Of course, you're already familiar with that basic result from Chapter 12 on aggregate supply and aggregate demand. As you can see, the negative shock (if not counteracted by the Fed) means that the growth rate of output will decline. If the monetary contraction is severe enough, the rate of output growth can even turn negative, bringing the economy into a recession, just as we have discussed in Chapters 12 and 14.

Eventually, the economy will recover from the negative monetary shock. If the reduction in $\vec{M}$ is permanent, for example, wage growth will decline from 10 percent to 5 percent and the economy will move to point *c*. But as we pointed out in Chapter 12, wages are often sticky, especially in the downward direction,

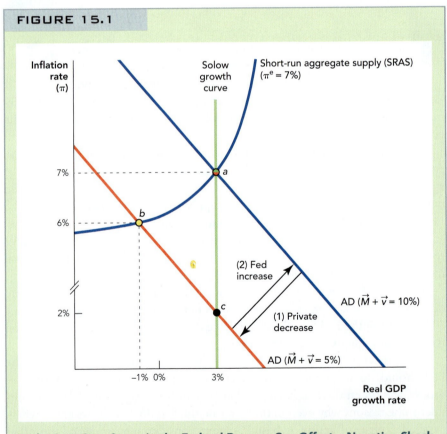

FIGURE 15.1

In the Best Case Scenario the Federal Reserve Can Offset a Negative Shock to AD with an Increase in $\vec{M}$ A decrease in AD (Step 1) shifts the AD curve inward, shifting the equilibrium from point *a* to point *b*. If the Federal Reserve acts quickly, an increase in $\vec{M}$ (Step 2) will move the economy back to point *a* without a prolonged recession.

so it may take time and considerable unemployment before the economy adjusts to the decline in $\vec{M}$.

But if the Fed can increase the rate of growth of the money supply, reducing interest rates and encouraging more bank lending and investor borrowing, then the AD curve shifts back up and to the right. Using the policy tools outlined in Chapter 14, the Federal Reserve is able to push the AD curve back to its original position so the economy will transition from point *a* to *b* thereby reducing the severity and length of the recession. In essence, instead of allowing the economy to adjust to a decrease in AD, which may require lower growth and higher unemployment, the Federal Reserve quickly restores AD to its previous level.

But Figure 15.1 makes monetary policy look too easy—what could be easier than shifting a curve? Two difficulties make it hard for the Fed to get this right all the time:

1. The Federal Reserve must operate in real time when much of the data about the state of the economy is unknown.

More specifically, it takes time for data to be gathered. Data are often released on a monthly or quarterly basis. Sometimes data are amended, after the fact. Then, it takes time for data to be interpreted and for problems to be recognized. Was the dip in employment last month a precursor of a recession or was it an exception? If the price of oil went up last month, does that indicate a longer-term trend or was it the result of some temporary shock? Is a decline in the stock market predicting a future recession or not? In the recent financial crisis, the first major signs of trouble in the subprime market came in August 2007, but most investors—and also the Fed—had no idea that so many banks and financial firms would fail, or be on the brink of failing, over the next year. In fact as late as the spring of 2008, GDP growth figures were still strongly positive and not everyone thought the United States was headed for a recession.

2. The Federal Reserve's control of the money supply is incomplete and subject to uncertain lags.

Recall from Chapter 14 that an increase in the money supply typically affects the economy with a lag that can vary in time from 6 to 18 months. And remember in atypical situations, if banks aren't willing to lend, then although the Fed may increase the monetary base, the larger monetary aggregates and thus aggregate demand won't increase very much in response. Thus, if banks are slow to lend, then the Fed can easily undershoot, generating a smaller shift in AD and a smaller increase in the rate of economic growth than is desirable. But a larger stimulus is not necessarily better because if the economy recovers before the money supply works its magic, the Fed can easily end up overshooting its goal—producing a higher rate of inflation than is desirable.

Figure 15.2 on the next page portrays the more realistic case for monetary policy in which too little stimulation pushes the economy only to point *c* where growth is still sluggish. But "Too much" monetary stimulation pushes the economy to point *d* with a higher than desirable inflation rate at 9 percent (and a growth rate that is high but unsustainable in the long run). Only with the "Just right" or Goldilocks amount of stimulation does the economy quickly return to its long-run balanced growth path at point *a*. We would like it if the Fed hit the Just right or Goldilocks amount of stimulation every time, but don't forget: Goldilocks is a fairy tale.

FIGURE 15.2

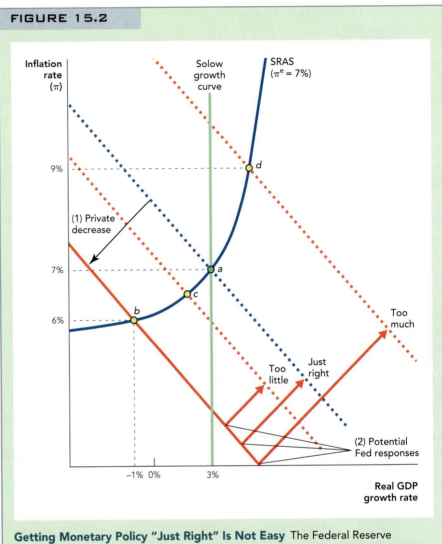

Getting Monetary Policy "Just Right" Is Not Easy The Federal Reserve operates in real time when much of the data about the economy is unknown. In addition, the Fed's control of aggregate demand is of uncertain magnitude and timing. As a result, the Fed may respond to a fall in AD (Step 1) with too little, too much, or just the right amount of stimulus (Step 2).

Rules vs. Discretion

The possibility of the "Too little" and "Too much" responses, or in other words the imperfections of monetary policy, has led to a debate over rules vs. discretion when it comes to monetary policy. Ideally, monetary policy tries to adjust for shocks aggregate demand, but it is often debated whether these adjustments are effective in reducing the volatility of output. If the Fed responds too often in the wrong direction or with the wrong strength, GDP volatility will increase rather than decrease.

Economists who think that the Fed is likely to make a lot of mistakes believe that apart from extreme cases, the Fed is best advised to follow a consistent policy and not try to adjust to every aggregate demand shock. A typical monetary rule would set target ranges for the monetary aggregates like M1 or M2 or for the rate of inflation. Nobel Prize winner Milton Friedman, for example, advocated a strict rule in which the money supply would grow by 3 percent a year every year; since the U.S. economy has a long-run growth rate near 3 percent, he thought this would provide for rough price stability over time. Other rules would allow for some adjustment in Fed policy depending on the state of the economy, but these adjustments would be stated in advance and the Fed would not be allowed to make policy "on the fly."

The advocates of discretion, in contrast, do not wish to tie the hands of the central bank in advance. They admit that central banks make many mistakes but still think that the Fed's adjustments on average push the economy in the right direction and thus lower volatility.

Reversing Course and Engineering a Decrease in AD

Suppose that the Federal Reserve does overstimulate, pushing the aggregate demand curve "Too much" in Figure 15.2. What then? Remember from our discussion in Chapter 11 that inflation makes price signals more difficult to interpret, creates arbitrary redistributions of wealth, and makes long-term planning and contracting more difficult, among other problems. Thus, we don't want inflation to be too high. But, we also know from Chapters 11 and 12 that bringing down the rate of inflation is costly because prices and wages are not fully flexible in the downward direction. That means economies sometimes get stuck between a rock and a hard place—between continuing a costly rate of inflation or reducing it at the risk of a recession.

Many economists think that the Federal Reserve did overstimulate the economy in the 1970s; and, as a result, by 1980, the inflation rate hit 13.5 percent a year. Ronald Reagan was elected to the presidency in part to change economic policies. By 1983, tough monetary policy under Reagan and cigar-chomping Federal Reserve Chairman Paul Volcker had reduced the inflation rate to 3 percent, but the consequence was a very severe recession with an unemployment rate of just over 10 percent.

The **disinflation** experiment was costly, but unlike the **deflation** of the Great Depression, when prices fell, it was a policy chosen on purpose. The 1980s disinflation broke the back of inflation and provided the foundation for the 25 or so years of successful economic growth—and mostly low unemployment—that the American economy enjoyed since that time.

Since World War II there have been six episodes when the Fed deliberately put the brakes on money growth, most prominently the shift beginning with the 1980 presidential election just mentioned. In every case, the tighter monetary policies were followed by declines in output. On average, industrial production, 33 months later, was 12 percent lower than otherwise would have been expected. But again, these contractions aren't always bad. Sometimes a contraction is necessary to bring down the rate of inflation. Of course, economists debate which of these contractions were needed and which were not.

Whether or not a particular contraction is a good idea, economists do agree on one point: A monetary contraction goes best when it is **credible,** namely when market participants expect the central bank to carry through its tough stance. This makes sense if you think through exactly why a disinflation is difficult for an economy. A sufficiently radical disinflation leads to unemployment because wages and prices are sticky, especially in the downward direction (as we explained in Chapter 12). If nominal wage growth is too high, some workers will end up being very expensive and employers will choose to lay them off. So, the key to a less painful disinflation is to increase nominal wage flexibility. Now imagine that a central bank has announced a disinflation but no one really believes it, or people believe it only halfheartedly. Nominal wages probably

AP PHOTO/CHICK HARRITY

Paul Volcker, chairman of the Federal Reserve in 1980, had to choose between high inflation or high unemployment.

A **disinflation** is a significant reduction in the rate of inflation.

A **deflation** is a decrease in prices, that is, a negative inflation rate.

A monetary policy is **credible** when it is expected that a central bank will stick with its policy.

aren't going to grow more slowly and when the disinflation comes, if indeed it does come, the unemployment cost will be high. Alternatively, if the coming disinflation is widely expected, then workers will be prepared for slower wage growth and will quickly adjust to what they know is inevitable. Thus, a credible disinflation reduces the unemployment effects of disinflation. So, the lesson is this: If a central bank wishes to undertake a disinflation, it has to be ready to stay the course and it should announce and explain its policy very publicly. This is called making monetary policy credibile.

The Fed as Manager of Market Confidence

Fear and confidence are some of the most important shifters of aggregate demand. And one of the Federal Reserve's most powerful tools is not its influence over the money supply but its influence over expectations, namely its ability to boost **market confidence**. Recall from Chapter 13 that when investors are uncertain, they often prefer to wait, to delay, and to try to learn more information, before they commit themselves. In addition, remember that one reason we see a lot of time bunching or clustering of investments is that it pays to coordinate your economic actions with those of others—that is, you want to be investing, producing, and selling at the same time that others are investing, producing, or selling. Uncertainty, therefore, can create what economists call a *bandwagon effect* on investment—I am uncertain and so delay my investments, you follow suit not because of uncertainty alone but because your investment is less likely to work well if it doesn't happen at the same time as my investment (time bunching or coordination of investment). Moreover, the fact that you cut back investment verifies that my decision to cut back was a good idea so no one can be accused of behaving irrationally.

> **Market confidence:** One of the Federal Reserve's most powerful tools is its influence over expectations, not its influence over the money supply.

Uncertainty drives people away from investment spending and toward assets like cash. Holding cash isn't very productive but cash and other similar assets are what you want when you are in "wait and see" mode. In terms of our model of aggregate demand, an increase in the demand for cash is indicated by a decrease in $\vec{v}$. At the same time, increased uncertainty will lead to a fall in $\vec{M}$, as both borrowers and lenders will cut back, and M1 and M2 will grow at lower rates. Both the $\vec{v}$ and the $\vec{M}$ changes work to shift the aggregate demand curve inward or to the left as in Figure 15.1 near the beginning of this chapter.

To cite an example, uncertainty increased after the terrorist attacks of September 11, 2001. Although the devastation in Manhattan was extreme, the economic cost of the attack was small relative to the size of the U.S. economy. Nevertheless, if enough people had taken the attack as a signal to reduce investment, the bandwagon effect could have created a severe recession. The Federal Reserve stepped in to try to prevent this from happening by lending billions of dollars to banks. In the week before September 11, for example, the Federal Reserve lent about $34 million to banks, a trivial amount. On September 12, the Federal Reserve lent $45.5 *billion* to banks.

The mere fact that the Federal Reserve sent a countersignal—we are going to massively maintain or increase AD if necessary—helped stabilize expectations, reduce fear, and raise confidence. The Federal Reserve can't always prevent an increase in uncertainty from reducing $\vec{v}$ and $\vec{M}$; sometimes uncertainty really does increase, such as when a war is imminent, and waiting is the appropriate response. But the Fed often can reduce the bandwagon effect and stabilize expectations toward a more positive outcome.

Monetary policy is often about changing expectations and perceptions, rather than just manipulating numbers and equations. That's one reason why central banking can be so difficult and why it is an art as well as a science.

The Negative Real Shock Dilemma

A very difficult case for monetary policy is when the economy is hit by a negative real shock such as a rapid oil price increase. As we saw in Chapters 12 and 13, a negative real shock shifts the Solow growth curve to the left (and the SRAS curve shifts by the same amount in the absence of sticky prices and wages). That means a higher rate of price inflation and a lower growth rate for GDP, again as we previously covered. How should monetary policy respond?

Unfortunately, monetary policy is much less effective at combating a real shock than an aggregate demand shock. In Figure 15.3, the economy is hit by a negative real shock and the Solow growth curve shifts to the left, moving the economy from point a to point b.

As before, the Federal Reserve can increase aggregate demand by increasing the money growth rate, but now the economy is less productive than before,

CHECK YOURSELF

> How do problems with data affect the Fed's ability to set monetary policy that is "just right"?

> Why did Milton Friedman argue for a set rule of 3 percent money growth per year? Why not 2 percent or 0 percent?

FIGURE 15.3

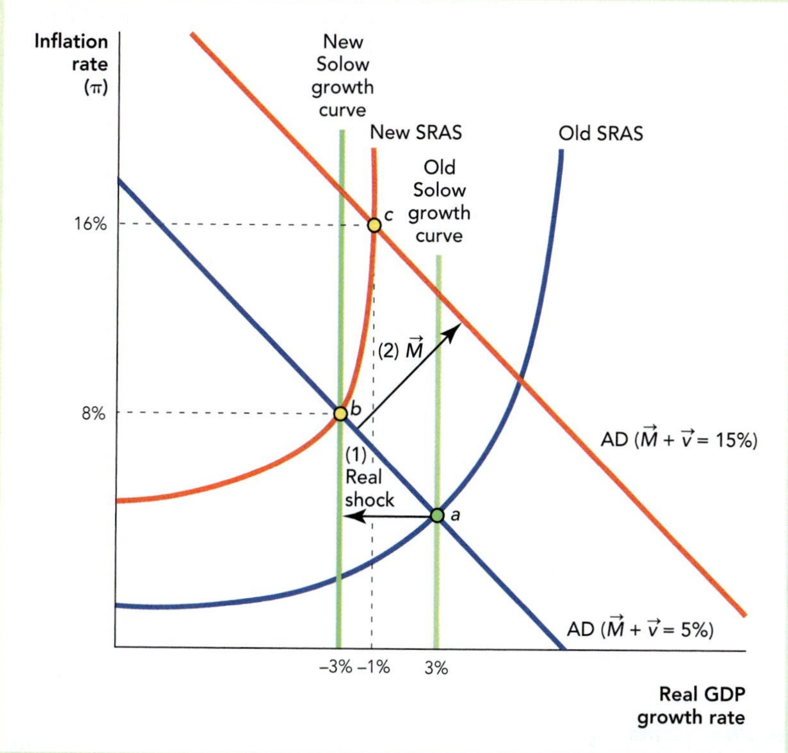

Monetary Policy Is Less Effective at Combating a Real Shock A real shock shifts the Solow growth curve to the left (Step 1), moving the economy from point a to a recession at point b. To combat the recession, the Federal Reserve increases M (Step 2). Due to the real shock the economy is now less productive than before and so the increase in aggregate demand shifts the economy to point c where the growth rate is a little bit higher but the inflation rate is much higher.

due to the real shock. As a result, an increase in $\vec{M}$ will not move the economy back to point *a*. Instead, most of the increase in $\vec{M}$ will show up in inflation rather than in real growth so the economy will shift from point *b* to point *c*, with a much higher inflation rate and a slightly higher growth rate.

Is it worthwhile responding to a real shock with an increase in AD? Maybe not. Although an increase in $\vec{M}$ may increase the growth rate a little, the inflation rate increases by a lot and, as we just saw in our discussion of the Volcker disinflation, higher inflation now can cause serious problems later. In particular, if the inflation rate gets too high, the Fed has to reduce inflation, thereby creating a lot of unemployment. In essence, with a real shock we have little choice but to take our lumps.

Alas, the situation is not quite so simple because real shocks are often accompanied by shocks to short-run aggregate supply and aggregate demand. In Chapter 13, for example, we discussed how sticky wages and prices can amplify a real shock, shifting the SRAS curve back to the left even further than the Solow growth curve. Moreover, we also showed how uncertainty and fear generated by a real shock can reduce consumption and investment, which shift the AD curve inward. The result is illustrated in Figure 15.4.

The real shock shifts the Solow growth curve to the left moving the economy from point *a* to point *b*. If prices were perfectly flexible, this would be the end of the story—real growth would fall but so would wages; and employment would fall only somewhat (due to adjustment factors as outlined in Chapter 13). But if wages are sticky and don't fall when real growth falls, then firms will be unprofitable and employment must decline considerably, driving real growth even lower. As in Chapter 13, we show this process by shifting the SRAS curve to the left (and up) even farther than the Solow growth curve initially shifted; this additional shift moves the economy to point *c*. The fear and uncertainty now reduce investment and consumption growth, which shifts the AD curve inward, therefore moving the economy to point *d*.

Confused? Don't worry, that is exactly how the economists at the Federal Reserve feel. Figure 15.4 looks imposing, but it is really putting together three things you already know well. A negative real shock shifts the Solow growth curve to the left; sticky wages and prices amplify the real shock by shifting the SRAS even more to the left (and up) than the Solow growth curve; and a negative shock to aggregate demand shifts the AD curve to the left and down. You have seen each of these curves shift alone: Figure 15.4 combines the three negative shifts in one diagram.

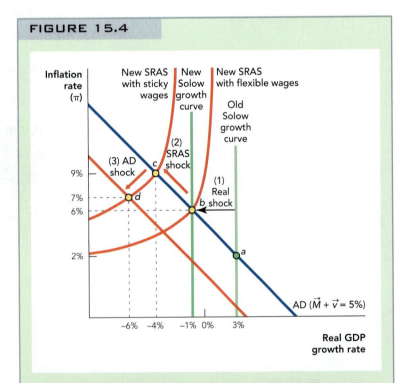

FIGURE 15.4

Real Shocks, SRAS Shocks, and AD Shocks Often Come Together
A real shock shifts the Solow growth curve to the left (Step 1), moving the equilibrium from point *a* to point *b*. If wages or other prices are sticky, the SRAS shifts to the left (Step 2) even further than the Solow growth curve, moving the equilibrium to point *c*. Fear and uncertainty can then reduce AD (Step 3), shifting the equilibrium to point *d*. Note that for clarity, we have suppressed the label for the new AD curve and also the old SRAS curve, which runs through point *a*.

We are also quite serious when we say that a combination of shocks like this can confuse economists at the Federal Reserve! Don't forget that in addition to the problems you face as students, the Federal Reserve is looking at real-time data, which as we have noted are often uncertain and subject to revision.

So what should be done in such a situation? One approach is to focus on the inflation rate, which has jumped from 2 percent to 7 percent. What is the recipe for reducing inflation? Correct—a *decrease* in $\vec{M}$. In the 1970s, for example, the Federal Reserve often responded to supply shocks, such as an oil shock, by decreasing $\vec{M}$ and *reducing* aggregate demand. That means taking the AD curve and shifting it even further back to the left through the use of monetary policy. In Figure 15.5, we show the new equilibrium at point *e*. The reduction in $\vec{M}$ reduces the inflation rate from 7 percent to 6 percent but also reduces economic growth and by more than the supply shock alone would have done.

Some economists have argued that the Federal Reserve's actions in trying to stem inflation were even

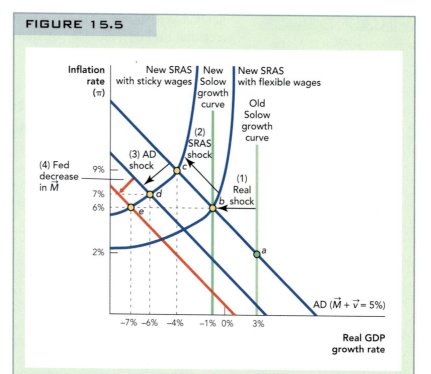

FIGURE 15.5

The Federal Reserve's Dilemma When Responding to a Real Shock
A real shock shifts the Solow growth curve to the left (Step 1), moving the equilibrium from point *a* to point *b*. If wages or other prices are sticky, the SRAS shifts to the left (Step 2) even further than the Solow growth curve, moving the equilibrium to point *c*. Fear and uncertainty can then reduce AD (Step 3), shifting the equilibrium to point *d*. At point *d*, the inflation rate is much higher than at point *a*, but reducing inflation with a cut in $\vec{M}$ (Step 4) reduces real growth even further, pushing the economy to point *e*. Note that for clarity we have suppressed the old SRAS curve which runs through point *a* and also the labels for the two new AD curves.

worse for the economy than the oil shocks. Interestingly, the most prominent critic of the Federal Reserve's actions in the 1970s was Ben Bernanke and consistent with his criticism, when he was Fed chairman and faced with rising oil prices in 2007–2008, he did not contract the growth rate of the money supply.[1]

Today central bankers are more likely to think that a central bank should respond to a negative real shock by holding the growth rate of the money supply steady or perhaps even expanding the growth rate a bit. If the central bank expands $\vec{M}$, it may be able to lessen or even reverse the AD shock so the economy would end up at point *c* in Figure 15.5 (or Figure 15.4).

As you can see, GDP takes less of a hit than in the previous case, but the new equilibrium involves a higher rate of inflation. Again, you may have wondered in the section above on engineering a disinflation, why the rate of inflation might have ended up too high in the first place. Now you know at least one way inflation can end up too high and that also helps us understand why the dilemmas of monetary policy arise so frequently.

The bottom line is that with a real shock the central bank faces a dilemma: It must choose between too low a rate of growth (with a high rate of unemployment) and too high a rate of inflation. The central bank in fact stands a

CHECK YOURSELF

> Looking at Figure 15.4, if the Fed wanted to restore some growth in the economy to deal with high unemployment, what would it do? What would be the problem of acting in this way?

> Suppose that the Fed reacts to a series of negative real shocks by increasing AD every time. What will happen to the inflation rate?

good chance of getting a mix of both problems. The lesson is this: if you are a central banker, hope that you don't face too many negative real shocks in your term!

The Problem with Positive Shocks: The 1997–2006 Housing Boom and Bust

If negative shocks are bad, then surely positive shocks are great! Who could be against fast growth, falling unemployment, and rising incomes? Unfortunately, for a central banker, even positive shocks can be worrisome, especially if they contain the seeds of their own destruction. Let's take a look at the housing boom that ended in 2006.

In 1997, inflation-adjusted house prices were close to their average levels over the previous half-century. Only four years later, the price of the average home nationwide exceeded anything ever seen before in the United States. Prices continued to rise for another five years, peaking in 2006 at nearly twice the average price in 1997. Figure 15.6 shows the extent of the boom in real house prices compared to historical trends.

As the price of real estate rose, so did the economy. High and rising house prices, for example, encouraged new home construction. During the boom, some builders were working 60 or 80 hours a week instead of 40. From 2002 to 2005, 6 million new houses were built. The boom in construction contributed to the boom in other sectors of the economy.

In addition, the boom increased aggregate demand: first, from the new employment and higher wages in the construction sector and, second, previous homeowners felt wealthier as they saw their homes rising in value each year. Homeowners who feel wealthier tend to spend more money and even borrow money on the hope or expectation that rising wealth will let them pay the money back in the future.

FIGURE 15.6

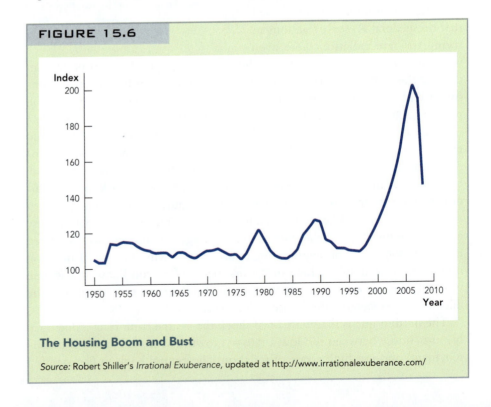

The Housing Boom and Bust

Source: Robert Shiller's *Irrational Exuberance*, updated at http://www.irrationalexuberance.com/

The problem, of course, came when the price of real estate started to fall in 2006. New home construction dropped very quickly. Homeowners felt poorer and started to spend less, reducing $\overrightarrow{C}$. In addition, the real estate crash contributed to a freezing up of financial intermediation as banks and other intermediaries took huge losses on poor investments in mortgage securities (as we discussed in Chapter 9). Since bank lending is a main generator of M1 and M2, this means lower rates of growth for the money supply. As a result, economic growth rates started to decline. By fall 2008, the growth rate was negative, meaning that the American economy was shrinking.

The negative shock of the bust can be analyzed using the dynamic AS-AD model just as we have outlined above. As we've already discussed in Chapter 14, the Fed took many patchwork actions after the bad news became fully evident in 2007. The key question we want to address in this section is this: What if anything could or should the Fed have done in advance of the crash, that is, when housing prices were booming? Or more generally, how should the Fed respond to positive economic shocks?

Many economists argue that the rise of real estate prices during this period was a "bubble," as that concept is defined in Chapter 9. That is, the increase in prices was due to shifts in market psychology and successive waves of irrational exuberance. These people argue that Alan Greenspan (the chairman of the Federal Reserve from 1987 to 2006) should have warned the market or tried to cool down the economy by raising interest rates.

If indeed the cycle was driven by a real estate bubble, the Fed might have been able to smooth out fluctuations in the economy by "popping the bubble" with tight monetary policy before housing prices rose too high. In that scenario, the economy would have had a more moderate boom but also a more moderate downturn; that probably would have been preferable if possible.

But monetary policy is, again, not so simple. First, it is not always easy to identify when a bubble is present, for reasons we discussed in Chapter 9. If everyone knew it was an unsustainable bubble, then everyone should have invested accordingly and bet against the bubble, thereby enriching themselves and also stopping the bubble in the first place. Of course, that isn't what happened and the bursting of the bubble was in large part a surprise to many people, including the Fed. Also, don't make the mistake of thinking that if prices rise a lot and then fall that must mean a bubble was present. Prices can rise and fall for reasons closely related to fundamentals and still cause macroeconomic problems.

Second, monetary policy is a crude means of "popping" a bubble. Monetary policy can influence *aggregate* demand, but monetary policy can't push the demand for housing down and keep the demand for everything else up. Thus, popping a bubble means reducing the growth rate of GDP for the broader economy as a whole. Is it worth the price, especially when we do not always know when we have an unsustainable bubble on our hands?

Note, however, that in addition to monetary policy, the Fed does have the power to regulate banks and it probably could have restrained some of the "subprime," no-questions asked mortgages that were sold during the boom and later went into default. That would have been the best way of limiting the bubble without taking down the broader economy.

Economists have not settled on what to do when asset prices like housing prices or stock prices boom. Booms are great while they last, but when the bust

It seemed so much easier in the textbook.
Federal Reserve Chairman Ben Bernanke.

ALEX WONG/GETTY IMAGES

CHECK YOURSELF

> How can the Fed tell when increases in asset prices reach the bubble stage?

> If the Fed thinks there is a bubble in housing prices and contracts the growth in the money supply to pop it, what collateral damage can it cause?

comes the repercussions can be very costly. The bottom line is this: Monetary policy is difficult in the worst of times and it's not easy in the best of times.

☐ Takeaway

Summarizing, we can point toward a few key lessons:

The Fed has some influence over the growth rate of GDP through its influence over the money supply and thus AD. An increase in $\vec{M}$ increases AD and a decrease in $\vec{M}$ decreases AD.

When faced with a negative shock to AD, the central bank can restore aggregate demand through an expansionary monetary policy. Monetary policy, however, is subject to uncertainties in impact and timing and getting it "Just right" is not guaranteed. Poor monetary policy can decrease the stability of GDP.

If in responding to a series of recessions the Fed increases $\vec{M}$ too much, it may find that it later has to contract $\vec{M}$ when inflation becomes too high. Usually this process—called a disinflation—is painful and it results in a recession. A disinflation goes best when the central bank has some degree of credibility in its attempt to set things right.

A central bank would like low unemployment and low inflation, but it is not always possible to achieve both goals. When a negative real shock comes, the Fed must choose between allowing low rates of growth, excessively high rates of inflation, or some combination of both. There is no easy way out of this dilemma.

Monetary policy is difficult in the worst of times and it's not easy in the best of times. Positive real shocks may generate booms that can become bubbles in asset prices like housing prices or stock prices. How to recognize and respond to asset price booms is not obvious and the economics of asset price booms is unsettled.

Real shocks and aggregate demand shocks are always mixed and not easy to disentangle. The data on which central bankers operate are often slow to arrive and subject to revision. As a result, central banking is as much art as science.

☐ CHAPTER REVIEW

KEY CONCEPTS

Disinflation, p. 317

Deflation, p. 317

Credible, p. 317

Market confidence, p. 318

FACTS AND TOOLS

1. This chapter is concerned mostly with how monetary policy might be able to return an economy *quickly* to the Solow growth rate after a shock. But as we saw in Chapter 11's discussion of the quantity theory of money, a market economy has a correction mechanism to return itself *slowly* to the Solow growth rate after a shock: flexible prices. Let's review the quantity theory, and remember that in the quantity theory, inflation does *all* of the adjusting.

Recall: $\vec{M} + \vec{v}$ = Inflation + Real growth

a. Consider the nation of Kydland. Before the shock to Kydland's economy, $\vec{M}$ = 10 percent, $\vec{v}$ = 3 percent, real growth = 4 percent. What is inflation?

b. In Kydland, $\vec{v}$ falls to 0 percent, but $\vec{M}$ stays the same. In the long run, what will inflation equal? What will real growth equal?

c. Consider the nation of Prescottia. Before the shock to Prescottia's economy, $\vec{M}$ = 2 percent, $\vec{v}$ = 4 percent, real growth = 2 percent. What is inflation?

d. In Prescottia, $\vec{v}$ rises to 8 percent. In the long run, what will inflation equal? What will real growth equal?

e. Consider the nation of Friedmania. Before the shock to Friedmania's economy, $\vec{M}$ = 3 percent, $\vec{v}$ = 0 percent, real growth = 3 percent. What is inflation?

f. In Friedmania, $\vec{M}$ falls to 1 percent. In the long run, what will inflation equal? What will real growth equal?

2. We've just reviewed the quantity theory of money, which is a theory that shows how the economy fixes itself in the long run. But as economist John Maynard Keynes famously said, "In the long run we are all dead." Let's bring SRAS back into the model, and play the role of a central banker reacting to a rise in velocity growth.

a. The diagram below shows the economy growing at the Solow growth rate with 10 percent inflation. Illustrate what happens if consumers and investors become more optimistic. Clearly label the new growth rate on the *x*-axis with the words "high-AD real growth," and label the new inflation rate on the *y*-axis with the words "high-AD inflation."

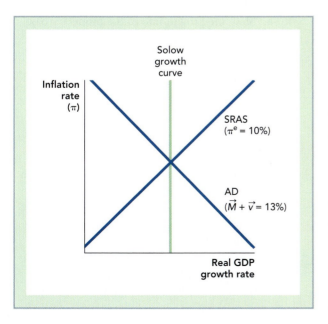

b. Once the central banker sees this rise in AD, she decides to fully reverse it with monetary policy. In the graph above, illustrate what happens if she does her job just right.

c. If she does her job just right, what will the inflation rate be? Provide an exact number.

3. Let's look at the Federal Reserve's dilemma when there's a positive shock to the Solow growth rate. We'll consider the reverse of Figure 15.3.

a. In the figure below, illustrate the effect of this positive Solow growth shock, ignoring the possible effect of sticky wages and prices.

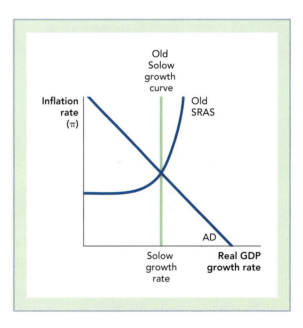

b. If the central bank kept AD fixed, would inflation be higher or lower after this positive real shock? Would real growth be higher or lower after this positive real shock?

c. If the central bank wants to return inflation to its old level, should it raise money growth or lower it?

d. If the central bank wants to return real growth to its old level, should it raise money growth or lower it?

e. Economists say that central bankers face a "cruel trade-off" between inflation and real growth when a Solow growth shock hits. Do your answers to parts c and d fit in with this theory?

4. All of the following are called "rules." Which of the following so-called rules are actually like "rules" and which are more like "discretion"? How can you tell the difference?

   a. Congress passes a law providing automatic cost of living increases to Social Security every year. (Note: This is current U.S. law.)

   b. Congress follows a rule to vote every few years on how much to increase Social Security payments—votes that usually occur just before an election. (This was the law before 1972.)

   c. The Federal Reserve follows the famous "Taylor rule" for setting the federal funds rate:

   Nominal rate = 2 percent + Inflation + 0.5 × (Real growth rate − Solow growth rate)

   d. The Federal Reserve follows a rule of "doing whatever seems right at the time."

   e. The police follow a rule of questioning anyone loitering outside of a bank who looks suspicious.

   f. The police follow a rule of questioning anyone loitering outside of a bank who is dressed in bulky clothing that could conceal a weapon.

5. Let's consider a case that has some similarities to Figure 15.2. We mentioned that it's difficult for the Fed to know what's really happening to the economy in real time. This is similar to the well-known "fog of war," where wartime news accounts often turn out to be exaggerations of the real story. In this question, the Federal Reserve thinks that consumer pessimism has pushed AD down by 10 percent, but in reality, the pessimism has only pushed AD down by 5 percent.

   a. In the following figure, illustrate two AD curves: "AD with false shock" (AD-F to save room) and "AD with true shock" (AD-T).

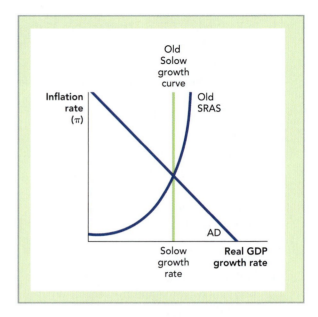

   b. If the central bank wants to use monetary policy to reverse a 10 percent shock to AD, it will have to raise money growth by 10 percent. Now draw two more AD curves on the figure above: "Fed reacts to false shock" (FR-F to keep it short) and "Fed reacts to true shock" (FR-T).

   c. After the central bank overreacts to the exaggerated news reports of economic calamity, what is the final result: Will real growth be higher or lower than before the shock hit? Will inflation be higher or lower than before the shock hit?

6. Which of the following would be methods that the Fed could use to "maintain market confidence" when a negative AD shock hits?

   a. Slow the growth rate of the monetary base.

   b. Raise the interest rate on "discount window" loans.

   c. Promise to increase the growth rate of money if the economy worsens further.

   d. Sell Treasury bills and buy bank reserves through open market operations.

   e. Raise the reserve requirements for banks.

7. When talking about the economy, people often make a distinction between policies that work "only in theory" compared to those that work "in practice." In theory, a fall in money growth slows down the economy in the short run. In the six episodes since World War II when, as we discussed, the Fed deliberately put the brakes on money growth, did this theory work "in

practice" every single time, most of the time but not all of the time, or did this theory fail most of the time?

8. A monetary policy is said to be *credible* if the central bank will have an incentive to do tomorrow what it says today that it will do tomorrow. Other policies may be credible or noncredible. Which of the following policies are credible?

   a. A student promises to study for the final after going to the frat party.

   b. A long-established store offers "Guaranteed satisfaction or your money back."

   c. A government promises never to bail out banks that take on too much risk and go bankrupt.

9. **a.** When a financial bubble collapses, is that more like a fall in aggregate demand or a fall in the Solow growth rate?

   b. When a financial bubble collapses, what is more likely to happen as a result: A fall in inflation or a rise in inflation?

10. Central banks and voters alike usually want higher real growth and lower inflation. What kind of shock makes that happen? (Note: This is similar to the type of shock that causes higher quantity and lower price in a simple supply-and-demand model.)

THINKING AND PROBLEM SOLVING

1. Let's reenact a simplified version of the 1981–1982 Volcker disinflation. Expected inflation and actual inflation are both 10 percent, real growth is 3 percent, and to keep it simple assume that velocity growth is zero. (Historical note: In fact, velocity growth shifted quite a lot during this period, which made Volcker's job harder than in this problem. Otherwise, the numbers are close to the historical facts.) Thus, we have:

   AD: Money growth = Inflation + Real growth

   Let's define a simple SRAS curve:

   SRAS: Inflation = Expected inflation + 1 × (Real growth rate − Solow growth rate)

   Notice that this equation gives a positive relationship between inflation and real growth for a fixed Solow growth rate and expected inflation rate.

   a. First, let's calculate how fast the money supply grew back when inflation was 10 percent in 1980 and real growth was at the Solow rate of 3 percent. How fast did the money supply grow at this point, before Volcker started fighting inflation? (Hint: Use the AD equation.)

   b. Now, let's calculate how fast Volcker will let the money supply grow in the long run, after he pulls inflation down to 4 percent per year. Remember, he'll assume that in the long run, the economy will just grow at the Solow growth rate. (Hint: Use AD again.)

   c. In the short run, when Volcker cuts money growth to the rate you calculated in part b, the economy won't grow at the Solow rate. Instead, real output will grow at whatever rate the SRAS dictates. In terms of algebra, this means you have to combine SRAS and AD: it's a system of two equations and two unknowns (inflation and real growth: You know the values of money growth, expected inflation, and the Solow growth rate already). In the short run, what will real growth and inflation be?

2. Now, let's reenact the Volcker disinflation in an alternate universe where the central bank is more credible. In this world, workers are more likely to believe the Fed when it says it's going to fight inflation. So, when they see Volcker cut money growth in 1981, workers become much more willing to take slower-growing wages. (Notice how a credible Fed creates more flexible wages, as if the workers were "led by an invisible hand.") This will make the SRAS steeper, as we saw in our original discussion of short-run aggregate supply.

   Our model economy is thus as follows:

   SRAS: Inflation = Expected inflation + 2 × (Real growth rate − Solow growth rate)

   AD: Money growth = Inflation + Real growth

   a. Answer part c of the previous question again, now in this world with a more-credible Fed and a steeper SRAS.

   b. Let's see how far this can go: What if workers pay constant attention to the Fed's every move and will slow their wage demands the moment they see Volcker tightening the money supply? Answer the previous question

with "100" in the place of "2" in the SRAS equation. Feel free to round your answers to the nearest percent.

c. If you were a central banker trying to cut inflation, and you want to keep real growth as close as possible to the Solow growth rate, what would you prefer: a steep SRAS (i.e., workers with flexible wages), or a flatter SRAS (i.e., workers with sticky wages)?

3. The Fed plays an important role in maintaining market confidence. As Chairman Greenspan put it in a 1997 address: "In [financial crises] the Federal Reserve *stands ready* to provide liquidity, if necessary. . . . The objectives of the central bank in crisis management are to . . . prevent a contagious loss of confidence." [emphasis added]

By *standing ready* to provide loans to banks in an emergency, the Fed can often prevent emergencies from happening in the first place. In each of the examples below, how does the fact that someone or something *stands ready* to cure the bad outcome help prevent the bad outcome from ever happening in the first place?

a. A security guard stands inside a bank.

b. Federal agents guard Fort Knox, where about one-half of the U.S. government's gold is stored.

c. The Federal Reserve promises to insure almost 100 percent of bank deposits.

d. Police, worried about possible riots during spring break in Palm Springs, California, bring in police from other cities.

4. In the United States, the government's data on real growth improve over time. For instance, we now know that in the early 1970s, the economy was actually growing 4 percent faster than people thought at the time. At the time, the Fed thought the economy was in a deep recession, so it mistakenly boosted money growth. The Fed's overreaction caused inflation. Real-time surveys in the early 1970s depicted an awful economy, but as economic historians have gone back to the data, they found that the economy wasn't as awful as they thought: Someone just put the thermometer in the fridge.

Economists at the Philadelphia Federal Reserve have collected data on how our view of the economy has changed over time. This "real-time data" is summarized by Croushore and Stark in a review article entitled "A Funny Thing Happened On the Way to the Data Bank: A Real-Time Data Set for Macroeconomists."

Let's use their summary of the data and a six-sided die to see just how inaccurate our real-time views of the economy actually are.

a. We're going to reenact the 1970s, and we'll start figuring out how error-filled the government's growth estimates will be. Croushore and Stark report that on average:

I. One-sixth of the time, measured growth is 2 percent better than actual growth.

II. One-third of the time, measured growth is 1 percent better than actual growth.

III. One-third of the time, measured growth is 1.5 percent worse than actual growth.

IV. One-sixth of the time, measured growth is 3 percent worse than actual growth.

Find a six-sided die (or use Excel to simulate same) and record your rolls below. If you've rolled a 1, count that in category I, if you roll a 2 or 3, place that in category II, a four or five goes in category III, and if you roll a six, place that in category IV. Then write down how much measurement error you'll have for that year.

Example: If your first roll was a 4, that places you in category III; so write down "−1.5 percent" as the amount of measurement error for 1971.

(Note: Psychologists and behavioral economists have found that people are pretty bad at generating truly random numbers on their own, so it's best to just roll the die.)

Year	Roll (value)	Category	Measurement Error (percent)
1971			
1972			
1973			
1974			
1975			
1976			
1977			
1978			
1979			
1980			

b. Let's see what values we get when we add together the true real growth rate (which economists will only know years later) with the measurement error in the previous table. For "true real growth," we use the most recent data in the table below—but of course even these estimates could change in the future. The sum is the actual government data that will wind up in the Federal Reserve chair's hands.

Example: If your first roll was a 4, that placed you in category III; so subtract 1.5 percent from the true 1971 growth rate to yield a real-time government report of 1.9 percent annual growth.

Year	True Real Growth	Government Data (percent)
1971	3.4%	
1972	5.3%	
1973	5.8%	
1974	−0.5%	
1975	−0.2%	
1976	5.3%	
1977	4.6%	
1978	5.6%	
1979	3.2%	
1980	−0.2%	

c. In your simulation, how many times was the government data off by 2 percent or more?

d. If the Solow growth rate in the 1970s was actually 3.6 percent (the average growth rate in the 1970s), then in how many years did your government data give values *below* 3.6 percent when true real growth was *above* 3.6 percent? How often did the reverse occur, with your government data *above* the Solow rate while true real growth was *below*?

e. Add together your two values from part d. This is the number of times that even a *very good* central banker would have wanted to push AD in the wrong direction: it's the number of times this weather vane was pointing in entirely the wrong direction.

(Note: You might be wondering whether the U.S. government tends to exaggerate extra-good economic news just before an election. As far as economists can tell, the answer is no, at least when it come to the official GDP number. U.S. GDP estimates contain mistakes before an election just as often as usual, but those mistakes don't tend to favor the political party in power. In Japan, though, GDP reports *do* tend to be extra-optimistic just before an election. For more, see Faust, Rogers, and Wright, "News and Noise in G-7 GDP Announcements," online at the Federal Reserve Board's website.)

5. We discussed how hard it is to keep AD stable or put it back "where it belongs" after a shock. Alan Blinder, a former vice-chairman of the Federal Reserve, noticed that this was a major problem. In his book *Central Banking in Theory and Practice,* he argued that this was a good reason for the Fed to take baby steps whenever it needed to make big shifts in AD. Sometimes you're better off taking two years to slowly and carefully undo an AD shock rather than shift it back quickly and inaccurately in one year.

To illustrate, let's see how things turn out if you, the central banker, take two years rather than one year to react to a negative velocity shock. You have better control over AD if you make small moves than if you make big moves, but big moves can get you back to the Solow growth rate more quickly: As so often in economics, you face a trade-off.

In this question, your ultimate goal is to get AD back to 5 percent per year; the Solow growth rate is 3 percent, and expected inflation is always 2 percent per year.

Starting point:

AD: 1 percent = Inflation + Real growth rate

SRAS: Inflation = Expected inflation + (Real growth rate − Solow growth rate)

a. Slow approach: Add 2 percent per year to AD for two years (through some mix of money growth and higher confidence). What will real growth equal each year?

	Start	End of Year 1	End of Year 2
Real Growth			

b. Fast approach: Assume that you tried to add 4 percent to AD in Year 1, but you mistakenly add 7 percent instead (through some mix of excess bank lending and irrational exuberance). In the second year, you tried to correct by cutting back by 3 percent, but you mistakenly cut back by 4 percent (through some mix of slower bank lending and investors' loss of confidence). What will real growth equal each year?

	Start	End of Year 1	End of Year 2
Real Growth			

c. You can see how the "best approach" is a matter of taste, but which method would you expect a central banker to prefer if Congress has to decide whether to reappoint the central banker to a new four-year term in a few months?

6. Milton Friedman and Anna Schwartz argued in the last chapter of their *Monetary History of the United States* that a shift in money growth will usually cause velocity to shift in the same direction: So higher money growth causes optimism, and slower growth causes pessimism. They believed that velocity had its own shocks, as well.

a. Let's run through some examples of how this might work, in a setting where the Fed wants to keep AD stable at 10 percent. To keep things simple, we'll just assume that the Fed can control money growth perfectly, and we'll assume that a 1 percent change in money growth causes a 0.5 percent shock to velocity growth in the same direction. Fill in the table below.

In each case, AD = Initial velocity shock + Money growth + Velocity shock caused by money growth

Year	Initial Velocity Shock	Money Growth	Velocity Shock Caused by Money Growth
1	4%	4%	4% × 0.5 = 2%
2	3%		
3	16%		
4	8%		
5	4%		
6	0%		

b. If velocity does tend to move in the direction of money growth, how does this change the Fed's response to economic shocks: Should it take bigger moves or smaller moves in money growth when a shock comes along?

7. We saw that real shocks and AD shocks often occur simultaneously. When this happens, unless we know the exact size of each shock, we can't be sure of the effect on both inflation *and* real growth: We'll only know one or the other for sure.

In each case below, we can be *sure* that *one* of the four events will happen:

A fall in inflation

A rise in inflation

A fall in real growth

A rise in real growth

In the cases below, which change can we confidently predict?

a. The banking system becomes less efficient at building bridges between savers and borrowers, and investor confidence declines: A negative real shock and a negative velocity shock occur simultaneously.

b. The banking system becomes less efficient at building bridges between savers and borrowers, and the Federal Reserve increases money growth: A negative real shock and a positive money shock occur simultaneously.

c. Biologists learn how to use computer simulations to rapidly search for molecules that would make promising medicines, and investors become optimistic about future profit opportunities: A positive real shock and a positive velocity shock occur simultaneously.

8. One argument for giving discretion to central bankers is that sometimes emergencies come along that a simple rule can't solve. Suppose there's a massive, permanent negative shock to velocity. Naturally, if the central bank has discretion, it will immediately respond by boosting money growth. But let's look at the alternative:

a. Suppose that the central bank follows a fixed 3 percent annual monetary growth rule, like Milton Friedman sometimes recommended. In the short run, what will the velocity shock do to real growth and to inflation?

b. In the long run, what will this velocity shock do to real growth and to inflation?

c. If voters are concerned only about real growth in the long run, will they favor rules, will they favor discretion, or will they be indifferent between the two?

d. If voters are impatient, and concerned only about real growth in the short run, will they favor rules, will they favor discretion, or will they be indifferent between the two?

e. Which kind of voters favor discretion: those with a long-run horizon or those with a short-run horizon?

CHALLENGES

This chapter has more Challenge questions than usual. Take this as a sign of how difficult monetary policy really is!

1. Practice with the best case: You are the central banker, and you have to decide how fast the money supply should grow. Your economy gets hit by the following AD shocks and your job is simply to neutralize them: just push money growth in the opposite direction of the shock.

   In all of the cases below, assume that there's no change whatsoever to the Solow growth rate, and assume that before the shock, you're at your optimal inflation rate and optimal real growth rate. (Yes, this really is the best case!) These are all shocks, so think of each case study below as preceded by the word, "Suddenly . . . ." Given the shocks to $\vec{v}$, velocity, should the central bank react by raising money growth or by cutting money growth?

   a. Investors become pessimistic about future profit opportunities.

   b. State governments increase spending on schools, prisons, and health care.

   c. The federal government passes a national sales tax.

   d. The federal government increases military spending.

   e. Foreigners buy fewer American-made airplanes and movies.

   f. American consumers start buying fewer domestically made Hondas and more imported Hondas.

   g. Domestically made computers, cars, and furniture all become much more durable and longer lasting.

2. Milton Friedman famously said that changes in money growth affect the economy with "long and variable lags." That means that if the government increases growth in the monetary base this month, the money multiplier takes a few months to turn this into growth in checking and savings deposits, and it takes a few months more before businesses and consumers actually spend this money to purchase goods and services. Let's see how this changes our views of the previous question.

   In each case from the previous question, the Fed predicts how long the velocity shock itself will last: we call this "shock duration" in the table below. After that time, velocity growth will go back to its old level. Additionally, in each case, the Fed's staff of PhD economists estimates how many months it will take for a change in money supply to actually push AD in the desired direction: This is the "monetary lag."

   The question is quite simple: If monetary lags are shorter than the shock duration—if the Fed has "fair warning"—then a shift in AD will be stabilizing. If not, then a shift in AD will be like mailing a birthday card to your mother the day before her birthday: Possibly destabilizing. So, in which cases below should the Federal Reserve change money growth?

Case	Monetary Lag (months)	Shock Duration (months)	Shift in Money Growth: Stabilizing or Destabilizing?
a.	14	8	
b.	18	12	
c.	20	Permanent	
d.	12	24	
e.	16	9	
f.	10	Permanent	
g.	18	Permanent	

3. One of the reasons it's hard to be a monetary policymaker is because it's so hard to tell what's actually going on in the economy. It's a lot like being a doctor in a world before X-rays, MRIs, and inexpensive blood tests: When the patient complains about a stomach ache, you don't know if it's caused by food poisoning or by a tumor the size of a grapefruit.

In each of the cases from the first question, consider the fact that your data are often quite unreliable (Fed Chair Alan Greenspan was famous for holding meetings with 100 staff economists, peppering them with questions about the quality of their data on the economy, and often knowing more than his own staff economists about the strengths and weaknesses of various surveys of the U.S. economy). To make matters more difficult, the Federal Reserve has to forecast the behavior of Congress, which is at least as difficult as predicting the behavior of businesses: Politicians often claim they are going to raise or cut spending or taxes, but then fail to do so.

If in cases a, b, and d above, the Fed chairman decides that the forecasted shocks really aren't very likely to happen, then taking into account your answers to questions 1 and 2, in which cases should the Fed actually do nothing whatsoever in response to news about the economy?

4. We explained how a central bank has an important role in maintaining confidence: "High confidence" keeps velocity growth and the money multiplier from falling. But as we've seen, sometimes one has to be cruel to be kind.

President Franklin Roosevelt followed this "tough love" approach during the Great Depression. Soon after taking office, he closed all banks for a four-day "bank holiday." During this holiday, he gave his first Fireside Chat, a radio address where he explained his policies to the American people in plain language. After the four-day holiday, he still kept one-third of all U.S. banks closed (mostly small farmer banks with one or two branches). Over the next few years, only half of this one-third eventually reopened.

Thus, FDR's bank holiday pushed the broad U.S. money supply (M1 or M2) down. Nevertheless, the economy grew quickly during FDR's first year, 1933. Why? Because FDR promised that the banks that reopened were the safest banks, and he promised that the federal government would keep these safer banks open through generous discount window lending. This boosted confidence and encouraged people to borrow from and lend to the remaining banks.

As Milton Friedman and Anna Schwartz put it in their classic book *A Monetary History of the United States*: "The emergency revival of the banking system contributed to recovery by restoring confidence in the monetary and economic system and thereby inducing the public . . . to raise velocity . . . rather than by producing a growth in the stock of money" (p. 433).

Let's see how an emotional concept like "confidence" shows up mathematically. To keep things simple, we'll look at AD in terms of growth in nominal GDP (growth in dollar sales) rather than growth in real GDP (growth in actual output). We'll compare the "before" and "after," so we'll skip over 1933, the year of the biggest banking crisis and of FDR's solution to the crisis:

Year	M2	v
1932	$35.3 billion	2.16
1934	$33.1 billion	2.36

a. What was the level of nominal GDP in 1932 and 1934?

b. What was the growth of M2 between these two years?

c. What was the growth of velocity between these two years?

d. What was the growth of nominal GDP between these two years?

e. If velocity growth had been zero during this period (perhaps due to low confidence), but money growth stayed the same, what would have happened to nominal GDP growth?

5. Central bankers often believe that their hands are tied by the public. Arthur Burns, the Fed chairman under President Nixon, reportedly said in the November 1970 Federal Reserve board meeting that "he did not believe the country was willing to accept for any long period an unemployment rate in the area of 6 percent." In other words, if AD shocks or Solow growth shocks came along that pushed the unemployment rate up, Burns believed he had to boost AD to help the economy: The voters wouldn't tolerate anything else.

a. In the early 1970s, the economy was hit with some negative Solow growth shocks, the most famous of which were the massive oil price increases caused by the OPEC oil embargo. Inflation started off at 4 percent, and Burns actually behaved according to his

stated philosophy. What did Burns do to AD in the 1970s: Did he raise it or lower it?

b. If Burns had kept AD fixed instead of shifting it as he did, would inflation have been lower or higher than it actually turned out to be?

c. According to our model, did Burns' actions raise, lower, or have no impact on the Solow growth curve?

d. If in the 1970s the United States had been hit by negative AD shocks instead of negative Solow growth shocks, and Burns had followed his same philosophy, would inflation have been higher or lower than it actually turned out to be?

6. Central bankers are reluctant to try to pop alleged bubbles. Which topics covered in this chapter might explain why they are reluctant to do so?

7. We mentioned Milton Friedman's advice that central bankers should follow a "fixed money growth rule," where the broad money supply (M1 or M2) grows the same rate every year. Other economists have instead recommended that central bankers follow "nominal GDP targeting," which is similar to a fixed AD curve. Assume that the central bank really can control money growth and velocity growth within a reasonable period of time if it tries to do so.

a. What is the difference between a fixed money growth rule and nominal GDP targeting from the point of view of the AD equation?

b. If velocity shocks never occur, what's the best policy for keeping AD as stable as possible: fixed money growth, nominal GDP targeting, or are both equivalent?

c. If velocity shocks are common, what's the best policy for keeping AD as stable as possible: fixed money growth, nominal GDP targeting, or are both equivalent?

8. The previous question assumed that the central bank can really control money growth and velocity growth within a reasonable period of time. Instead, let's work with the more realistic assumption that it takes about a year for a change in monetary policy to actually influence money growth: Even though the central bank can increase bank reserves literally within *minutes* through open market operations or the term auction facility, it takes months for banks to find out who they should lend to. And as you know, most money is created through bank loans.

In this question, the central bank *tries* to follow nominal GDP targeting so that AD grows at 7 percent per year. In other words, the central banks tries to set the money growth rate so that velocity growth plus money growth equals 7 percent. Each year, it responds to *that year's* velocity growth, but the response won't actually kick in until next year (think of this as driving a car with loose steering: You steer to the right, but the car only starts moving to the right about two seconds later).

a. Fill in the table below. Notice that in each year, Actual AD = Velocity growth + Money growth. In the first year, the central bank observes velocity growth of 3 percent and thus targets money growth of 4 percent. The next year money grows at 4 percent as targeted, but velocity growth in that year is 1 percent so Actual AD grows at 5 percent. In Year 2, the central bank observes velocity growth of 1 percent and thus targets money growth of 6 percent. Keep going.

Year	Velocity Growth	Target Money Growth	Money Growth	Actual AD
1	3%	4%	n/a	n/a
2	1%	6%	4%	5%
3	9%	–2%	6%	15%
4	6%			
5	2%			
6	5%			
7	0%			
8	4%			
9	6%			
10	5%			

b. Every year, the central bank tries to keep AD = 7 percent, yet it never accomplishes its goal. How do "long lags" explain this failure?

c. How would this table look if you had followed Friedman's 3 percent money growth rule instead? Don't calculate any numbers, just answer verbally: Would the swings tend to be bigger than in the table or smaller?

9. a. Central bankers must manage expectations. Suppose that inflation is running at 10 percent and the central banker would like to lower inflation to 2 percent *without* reducing real growth. What should the central banker tell the public? And at what level should the central banker set money growth? Assume that velocity shocks are zero and that the Solow growth rate is 3 percent.

Draw the new SRAS and AD curves.

b. Suppose that the public does believe the central banker. What temptation might the central banker face? (Hint: Imagine that it is an election year and the central banker would like to see the current administration reelected.)

c. If the central banker is not believed what will happen? Use your answers to parts a and b to discuss the importance of independent central banks.

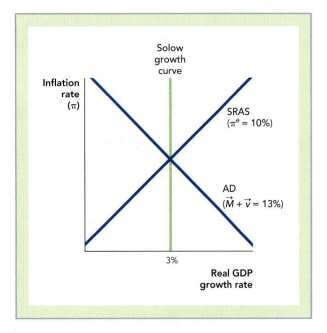

16

The Federal Budget:
Taxes and Spending

Some people do better from the federal government than others. Take Ida May Fuller. In 1940, Ida May received Social Security check #00-000-001, the very first in the program's history. Ida May's working career had almost ended by the time Social Security began, so she had paid just $24.75 in Social Security taxes and she got almost all of that back with her first check, which was for $22.54. Moreover, Ida May lived to be 100, so by the time she died in 1975, she had received a total of $22,888.92 in benefits.

You can see why Ida May is smiling. But will you be smiling from federal taxes and spending? After all, you will pay Social Security taxes throughout your working life, and what about the benefits? You can be pretty sure that unlike Ida May, you won't receive almost a thousand times more than what you put in.

More generally, the federal government spends over 18 percent of GDP and it raises in taxes just under 17 percent of GDP. That's a lot of money, more than $2.5 trillion in spending. Where does all that money come from? Where does it all go? And for how long can the U.S. government keep spending more than it raises in taxes?

Tax Revenues

As of 2007, the federal government was taking in about $2.4 trillion a year, or about $8,000 for every person in the United States. The federal government takes in money in many ways, but three sources—the individual income tax, the Social Security and Medicare taxes, and the corporate income tax—account for more than 90 percent of the revenue. Figure 16.1 on the next page shows the major sources of revenue for the U.S. government.

Ida May Fuller received the very
first Social Security check.

UNDERSTAND YOUR
world

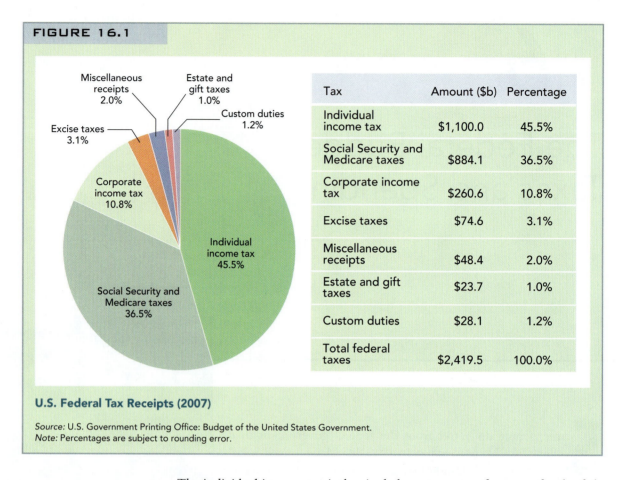

FIGURE 16.1

Tax	Amount ($b)	Percentage
Individual income tax	$1,100.0	45.5%
Social Security and Medicare taxes	$884.1	36.5%
Corporate income tax	$260.6	10.8%
Excise taxes	$74.6	3.1%
Miscellaneous receipts	$48.4	2.0%
Estate and gift taxes	$23.7	1.0%
Custom duties	$28.1	1.2%
Total federal taxes	$2,419.5	100.0%

U.S. Federal Tax Receipts (2007)

Source: U.S. Government Printing Office: Budget of the United States Government.
Note: Percentages are subject to rounding error.

The individual income tax is the single largest source of revenue for the federal government. The second category, Social Security and Medicare taxes (a few other smaller taxes are also included in this category), includes the "FICA tax" you have seen on your paycheck—these taxes are so named because unlike the income tax, the revenue from these taxes is tied to specific programs. Social Security and Medicare taxes have increased in recent decades and now bring in almost as much money as the income tax. Corporate income taxes are a distant third. The other sources are much smaller and they include excise taxes such as taxes on gasoline and alcohol, capital gains taxes, user fees, estate and gift taxes, and custom duties or tariffs. Let's take a closer look at the three largest sources of revenue.

The Individual Income Tax

Most Americans are required to file an income tax return with the federal government. On this form a person reports his income and the tax code determines how much money is due. The current schedule of marginal tax rates for a typical taxpayer, someone who is married filing jointly with their spouse, is shown in Figure 16.2.

The **marginal tax rate** is the tax rate that you must pay on an additional dollar of income. Figure 16.2 tells us that if you earn less than $15,650, then the marginal tax rate, the rate on an additional dollar of income, is 10 percent (some deductions are allowed—see below). If you earn between $15,650 and $63,700, the rate of tax on an additional dollar of income is 15 percent. If you earn between $63,700 and $128,500, you must pay 25 percent of any additional income to the federal government. Marginal tax rates increase in uneven steps

The **marginal tax rate** is the tax rate paid on an additional dollar of income.

FIGURE 16.2

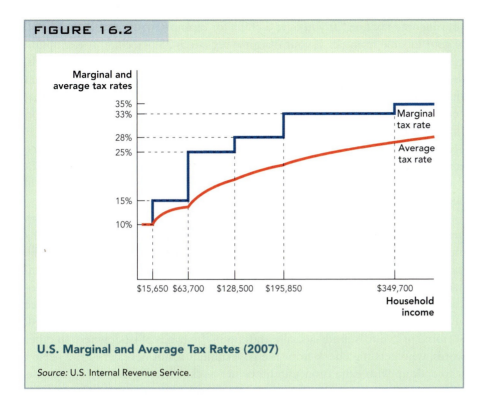

U.S. Marginal and Average Tax Rates (2007)

Source: U.S. Internal Revenue Service.

until the top marginal tax rate of 35 percent is reached on any income earned greater than $349,700.

We care about the marginal tax rate because, as usual in economics, it's the *marginal* rate that matters for determining things like the incentive to work additional hours. If you are considering doing an extra carpentry job for spare cash, you don't care what tax you are paying on the money you've already earned. You care about how much additional tax you will be paying on the extra money that you might earn if you choose to take the job.

Marginal tax rates today are lower and flatter than they have been in the past. In 1960, for example, the lowest marginal tax rate was 20 percent and the highest rate was 91 percent! Of course in the further past, rates were much lower than today. In 1913, when the income tax began, the top marginal rate was just 7 percent and that rate didn't take effect until annual income was over $10 million (in today's dollars).

Your **average tax rate** is simply your total tax payment divided by your total income. If your income is $50,000, for example, then your total income tax under the current system can be calculated as follows. You pay 10 percent on the first $15,650 or $1,565, then you pay 15 percent on the next $34,350 ($50,000 − $15,650) or $5,153, for a total tax of $6,718. Your average tax rate is then

$$\frac{\$6718}{\$50,000} \times 100 = 13.4\%$$

Unfortunately the tax system is not quite as simple as we have presented so far because not every dollar of income is taxed. Tax professionals say that some income is *exempt* from taxation. Each person, for example, generally gets one tax exemption for him or herself, one exemption for a spouse, and one exemption for each child or dependent. In 2006 each exemption let you have $3,300 of

The **average tax rate** is the total tax payment divided by total income.

your income tax free.[1] If you have a child, for example, you can exempt $3,300 of your income from tax. If your marginal tax rate is 25 percent, that exemption means that your taxes fall by about $825 a year (0.25 × $3,300). In other words, the federal government, using the tax system, makes it cheaper to have another child compared to spending your money on say a new car. This also means that people with the same income may pay different tax amounts. The exemption amount is indexed for inflation so it typically increases a bit every year.

The tax system also allows for deductions. Like exemptions, deductions reduce your taxable income, but only if you have specific expenses. The most important deductions are for home mortgage interest, donations to charity, state and local taxes, and very high medical expenses.

For instance, if you buy a house, the interest payments on your mortgage can (usually) be deducted from your taxable income. So, if you are paying $1,000 a month in mortgage interest and you are facing a 25 percent marginal tax rate, the mortgage interest deduction will save you about $250 a month in taxes. Does this make buying a house cheaper? Not by as much as you might think. The tax deduction means that more people want to buy houses and that drives up the price of houses, especially in places like Manhattan where the amount of land is fixed. So, some of "your" subsidy actually ends up in the hands of landowners. In other words, who gets the check from the government is not necessarily the person who ends up with extra money in his or her pocket. More generally, economists understand that who really pays a tax or a subsidy can be quite different from who must send the check to the government or how those taxes and subsidies are described to the public. That point will not be the focus of this chapter—see your microeconomics textbook for more—but do keep it in mind as you think about the different taxes in the American economy.

Taxes on Capital Gains and Interest and Dividends The income tax is a tax on your labor income and also on any income you receive from your investments, namely your interest income, your dividends, and your capital gains. You receive interest income for instance on your savings and checking accounts, and this income usually is taxed as if it were labor income.

If you own shares of stock, you likely receive dividends, which are regular income payments paid out of corporate earnings. You must pay taxes on those dividends, and the current rate of taxation is 15 percent for most people, 5 percent for low-income individuals.

The taxation of capital gains is more complicated. You receive a capital gain, for instance, if you buy stock at $100 a share and later resell it at $200 a share. Your capital gain is the extra $100 you made from the rise in the value of the stock. You pay a tax on those profits and currently the standard capital gains rate is 15 percent if you hold the stock for over one year, with a 5 percent rate for low-income individuals. Capital gains taxes are paid only when the assets are actually sold and not in the mean time while the assets are simply being held.

As is often the case in our tax system, the real rates people pay are not the same as the rates written into the tax code. For instance, capital gains allow for "loss offsets." If you gain $100 selling one stock and lose $100 selling another, usually the two sums cancel each other out in the calculation of your tax liability. If you know how to group your winners and losers together at the right time, the true rate of capital gains taxation you face may be much lower than the published rate of 15 percent.

Republicans and Democrats often disagree about how much investment income should be taxed. Democrats often favor higher taxes on investment income, on the grounds that the rich invest quite a bit and thus taxing investment income means the rich will bear a larger share of the tax burden. Republicans are more likely to argue that lower taxes on investment spur investment and thus economic growth, creating jobs, raising wages, and contributing to general prosperity in the long run.

The Alternative Minimum Tax (AMT)   There is yet another complication to the American tax system, and that is the **alternative minimum tax,** or AMT. The AMT was started in 1969 after a televised congressional hearing revealed that 155 households with income over $200,000 (about $1.2 million in today's dollars) had paid no income tax. These families had done nothing illegal, but they had managed to take advantage of tax laws to avoid income taxes. Thus, the original goal of the AMT was to make sure that it would not be possible to avoid all income tax.

The AMT requires taxpayers to make two computations. First, they must compute what they owe under the standard tax code, then they must compute what they owe under the AMT, which is typically based on a flat rate of either 26 percent or 28 percent, with no deductions allowed. The taxpayer must then pay whichever number is higher.

The AMT was supposed to hit just a few hundred families among the super-rich but it was never adjusted for inflation, so every year more and more people became subject to the AMT. In 2006, around 3.5 million Americans paid the AMT and it's now often the case that families earning $100,000 a year or less are paying the AMT and thus paying more taxes than under the regular tax code. The number of Americans covered by the AMT will likely continue to rise by the millions. The increasing reach of the AMT is in fact the largest tax increase in recent times, although it is rarely explained or presented as such. Both Republicans and Democrats claim they are unhappy about the growing reach of the AMT, but the two parties cannot agree on how to change or replace it, or how to make up for the lost revenue, should the AMT be restricted in its application.

Social Security and Medicare Taxes

Almost all workers in the United States pay the Federal Insurance Contributions Act tax, better known as the FICA tax for the acronym that you will see on your payroll check. The FICA tax is 6.2 percent of your wages on the first $106,800 of income. In addition, your employer also pays a 6.2 percent tax on the same earnings so the total FICA tax is 12.4 percent. The FICA taxes fund Social Security payments.

Many Americans believe "I pay half of this tax, my employer pays the other half," but this isn't quite right. As we've already mentioned, the person who appears to pay a tax isn't always the person who actually pays. In reality, economic research shows that the employer's payment is mostly taken out of the worker's prospective wage; in other words if your employer didn't have to pay the FICA tax your wages would be higher.* Much of the burden of the FICA tax falls on workers, not employers.

> **Alternative minimum tax (AMT)** is a separate income tax code that began in 1969 to prevent the rich from not paying income taxes. It was not indexed to inflation and is now an extra tax burden on many upper middle class families.

Even the simplified tax forms are complex.

---

* In fact, exactly this situation occurred in Chile when it privatized its social security program in 1981. Beginning in 1981, employers no longer had to pay social security taxes for their employees. The fall in employer taxes, however, did not result in extra profits. Instead, wages rose as the payroll tax fell—exactly as predicted by tax incidence theory. Other studies in the United States show that when the government mandates that firms provide benefits to their employees such as health benefits, wages fall. Thus, employees rather than employers pay for mandated benefits. On Chile and for references to other studies, see Gruber, J, 1997. "The Incidence of Payroll Taxation: Evidence from Chile," *Journal of Labor Economics* 15(3), S72–S101.

Medicare is partly financed out of general revenues and partly financed out of special payroll taxes. For most workers, 1.45 percent is withheld from their paychecks in the form of a Medicare premium and the employer pays another 1.45 percent. Again, workers pay much of the employer's premium in the form of lower wages. Self-employed individuals pay the full 2.9 percent themselves.

The Corporate Income Tax

In the United States, the corporate income tax rate is generally 35 percent. This is one of the highest rates in the world. The rate of 35 percent, however, is applied to a legal measure of income, but the tax code is so constructed that a good accountant can often make corporate income come out very low, even for profitable corporations. In fact, some apparently profitable corporations manage to define their income and expenses in such a way that they often don't pay any corporate income tax at all. Maybe you've heard of Boeing, the large and profitable airplane manufacturer; over a recent period of five years the company has paid an average tax rate of 0.7 percent.[2] Other companies aren't so well situated to take advantage of such tax breaks and accounting maneuvers.

Who pays the corporate income tax? Not corporations, which in the final analysis are legal fictions. All taxes are eventually paid by human beings. The corporate income tax is paid initially by shareholders and bondholders of corporations who earn a lower rate of return on their investments. More generally, the rate of return will fall on all forms of capital and in the long run that will also mean somewhat lower wages for workers and higher prices for goods and services.

The Bottom Line on the Distribution of Federal Taxes

Once we add in deductions, exemptions, corporate taxes, payroll taxes, excise taxes, the AMT, and assumptions about tax incidence (who pays the tax), what is the final result? It's not an easy calculation but the best estimate of the distribution of federal taxes by income class is shown in Table 16.1.

TABLE 16.1 Who Pays Federal Taxes?

Income Category	Average Pretax Income	Effective Tax Rate on All Federal Taxes	Share of Total Federal Tax Revenue
Bottom 20 percent	$15,900	4.3%	0.8%
Second 20 percent	$37,400	9.9%	4.1%
Middle 20 percent	$58,500	14.2%	9.3%
Fourth 20 percent	$85,200	17.4%	16.9%
Top 20 percent	$231,300	25.5%	68.7%
Top 10 percent	$339,100	27.4%	54.7%
Top 5 percent	$520,200	28.9%	43.8%
Top 1 percent	$1,558,500	31.2%	27.6%

Source: Congressional Budget Office, 2005

Table 16.1 shows that if we divide households into categories according to how much they earn, then households with income in the bottom 20 percent, those with average incomes of $15,900, pay 4.3 percent of their income to the federal government. As income rises so does the effective tax rate so that households in the top 20 percent of income, with average incomes of $231,300, pay 25.5 percent of their income to the federal government. The effective tax rate continues to rise if we look at the "super-rich," households in the top 10 percent, 5 percent, and 1 percent of earnings. The effective tax rate for households in the top 1 percent of income, with average yearly incomes of $1,558,500, is 31.2 percent, higher than for any other income category.

It is sometimes said that the rich do not pay taxes in the United States. That is false. Whether they pay *enough* taxes depends on your point of view, but despite all the deductions, exemptions, loopholes, and so forth, the U.S. tax system is **progressive**—people with higher income pay a higher percentage of their income in tax to the federal government than people with lower income.

In contrast to a progressive tax is a **flat tax,** which has a constant tax rate applied to income at all levels of earning. If the tax code were radically simplified to eliminate almost all deductions including the deductions for mortgage interest and charitable giving, then by some calculations a flat rate of around 19 percent would raise approximately the same revenue as today.[3] A flat tax has a number of desirable properties. Simplification of the tax code would be appreciated by many taxpayers and elimination of deductions and loopholes would encourage people to make investment, consumption and work decisions for good economic reasons rather than merely to reduce tax payments.

The disadvantage of a flat tax is that moving to a flat tax would require lowering rates on the rich and raising rates on the middle class and poor. If you compare the effective tax rate paid by different income classes under the current tax code—shown in Table 16.1—with a flat rate of 19 percent, you can see that tax rates for the rich and poor could change quite dramatically under a flat tax. Proponents of a flat tax, including Republican Steve Forbes and Democrat Jerry Brown, argue that the efficiency advantages of a flat tax mean that even people who paid a higher tax rate would, with increased economic growth, pay less in total tax.

Even if a flat tax were significantly more efficient than our current tax code, it's hard to see how the United States could ever move to such a system. Do you remember what we said about the effect of the mortgage interest deduction on house prices? The mortgage interest deduction raises house prices, so eliminating the deduction would cause a fall in house prices. Is it any wonder that neither Jerry Brown's nor Steve Forbes's tax plans caught on when they ran for president? Other countries, including Russia, the Czech Republic, and Estonia have moved toward a flat tax recently, however, so it will be interesting to see how they fare.

Returning to the current U.S. tax code, the effective tax rate is higher on the rich and the rich have more money—put these two things together and we can calculate who pays for the federal government. The final column in Table 16.1 shows the share of the $2.4 trillion in federal tax revenues that is paid for by each income category. The finding is that the rich, and especially the very rich, bear by far the largest share of the federal tax liability. The top 10 percent of households by income, for example, pay more than half of federal taxes, and the top 1 percent alone pay over a quarter of all federal taxes.

A **progressive tax** has higher tax rates on people with higher incomes.

A **flat tax** has a constant tax rate.

A **regressive tax** has higher tax rates on people with lower incomes.

CHECK YOURSELF

> In the early 1800s, the young United States received most of its revenue from taxes on trade with other countries (custom duties). Today, what percent of federal revenues come from custom duties?

> Individual income taxes plus Social Security and other payroll taxes represent what percent of federal revenues? (Review Figure 16.1 if necessary.)

> Consider Table 16.1. Let's start with a person in the fourth quintile, earning $80,000 pretax. Using the effective tax rate, what did this person pay in tax? Now consider a person in the top quintile who earns $160,000 pretax. What did this person pay in tax? Compare the amount of tax paid by both. Does this provide evidence that the tax system is progressive?

State and Local Taxes In addition to federal taxes, most people pay state and local taxes, so the federal tax burden is not the end of the story. Overall, state and local taxes are about half the level of federal taxes, just under 10 percent of GDP. Compared to the federal government, states raise more of their revenues, about 20 percent on average, from sales taxes. Since sales tax rates are the same for everyone, regardless of income, state and local taxation as a whole is less progressive than income taxation. Thus, state and local taxes probably make the overall tax system a little bit less progressive than the federal tax system but it does depend on the state.

Spending

Almost two-thirds of the U.S. federal budget is spent on just four programs: Social Security, defense, Medicare, and Medicaid. Combined, these four programs account for 64.3 percent of federal spending in 2007, as we illustrate in Figure 16.3. Interest on the national debt and various unemployment insurance programs and welfare programs are also large. Everything else—spending on roads, education, police, prisons, science and technology, agriculture, the environment, and more—accounts for just 17.2 percent of the budget. Let's take a closer look at the big items to see just where our tax money goes.

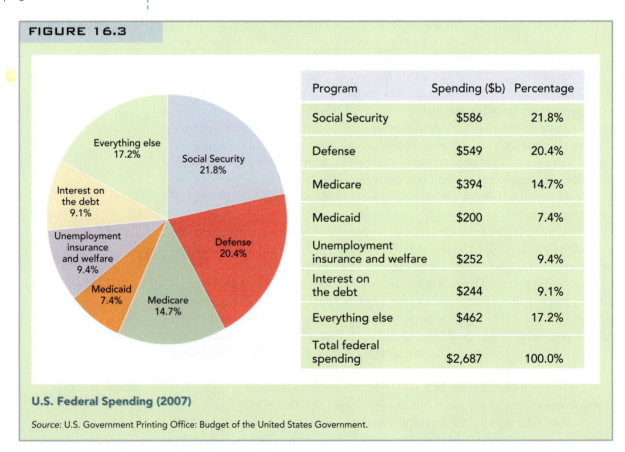

FIGURE 16.3

Program	Spending ($b)	Percentage
Social Security	$586	21.8%
Defense	$549	20.4%
Medicare	$394	14.7%
Medicaid	$200	7.4%
Unemployment insurance and welfare	$252	9.4%
Interest on the debt	$244	9.1%
Everything else	$462	17.2%
Total federal spending	$2,687	100.0%

U.S. Federal Spending (2007)

Source: U.S. Government Printing Office: Budget of the United States Government.

Social Security

If measured in terms of dollars paid out, Social Security is the single largest government program in the world. In 2007, $586 billion of benefits were paid to nearly 50 million beneficiaries.

We've already seen how the Social Security tax works. If you are wondering where that money goes, Social Security is run on a "pay as you go" basis. That means that when the government takes in your dollars, the money does not go into an account or trust with your name on it. The money is shipped out right away to the current elderly, who of course are receiving benefits. When you become old, you'll get your benefits from taxes on the young at that later point in time.

Every year the federal government sends Americans letters telling us how much money is in "our" personal social security accounts. Don't be misled. There is no money in "your account," there isn't a "your account" at all. Those letters are just the government's prediction of how much you'll get back some day. Of course, since you are in the meantime a voter, don't be surprised if those predictions turn out to be a little bit optimistic.

Social Security benefits are set at a basic minimum, but most people's benefits are defined by a complex formula depending on how long they worked, what their average earnings were over their working life, whether or not they are married, what year they retire, and at what age. In recent years, the average retiree has been paid $1,000 a month so one immediate lesson is that you shouldn't count on Social Security alone to support you in your old age.

President Franklin D. Roosevelt signing the Social Security bill.

The age at which workers can claim their full retirement benefits was 65 for many years but, because the Social Security program was getting very expensive, in 1983, the full retirement age was made to slowly increase depending on when the worker was born. You—assuming you were born after 1960—must wait until age 67 to claim your full retirement benefits. Some people advocate increasing the full retirement age again so you may want to keep an eye on the age at which you will be able to claim full benefits. A worker can start claiming some benefits as early as age 62 but people who opt for early retirement get a lower monthly payment. Benefits are indexed to the level of wages in the United States, so over time benefits rise automatically with general increases in prosperity.

Do you recall Ida May Fuller from the introduction? She paid $24.75 in Social Security taxes and received $22,888.92 in payments. Ida May's example is extreme but the basic idea is quite general. Workers who retired in the early years of Social Security received full benefits even though they paid Social Security taxes for only a portion of their working life. In addition, the Social Security tax rate increased over time, rising from 2 percent in 1940 to today's rate of 12.4 percent. The higher tax rate on today's workers funds larger benefits for *yesterday's* workers— even though yesterday's workers paid a lower tax rate on their earnings.

It's not surprising, therefore, that Social Security has become less generous over time. To see how generous Social Security is, we can add up all the taxes an individual can expect to pay into Social Security and then subtract all the benefits an individual can expect to receive from Social Security, being sure to adjust for the fact that taxes must be paid before benefits are received (a present value calculation; note that the concept of present value has been defined in the appendix to Chapter 8). Table 16.2 does just this for a single male worker with different average wages and retiring in different years.

Table 16.2 tells us that a single male with low lifetime earnings who retired in 1975

TABLE 16.2 Net Benefits of Social Security (Single male assuming various retirement years and average wages)			
Average Wages	Retiree Turned 65 in 1975	Retiree Turns 65 in 2010	Retiree Turns 65 in 2030
Low	$46,807	$8,286	$3,062
Medium	$53,999	–$43,255	–$85,945
High	$52,284	–$95,212	–$193,874

Source: Steuerle and Carasso, 2004.
Low, medium, and high earnings are $30,000, $60,000, and $120,000 in inflation adjusted 2004 dollars.

received $46,807 more in Social Security benefits over his prospective lifetime than he paid in taxes. Now consider the same low-wage worker except that now he is scheduled to retire in 2010 instead of 1975—this worker can expect to receive only $8,286 more in benefits than he pays in taxes. If the same worker retires in 2030, he can expect to receive just $3,062 more in benefits than he pays in taxes. Thus, the Social Security program is becoming less generous over time, in large part because the program was very generous to workers who have already retired.

We can also see from Table 16.2 that Social Security redistributes wealth across income classes. A low-wage worker who retires in 2030 will receive $3,062 more in benefits than he pays in taxes, but for medium- and high-wage workers Social Security is a net cost. A medium-wage worker retiring in 2030 will pay $85,945 more in Social Security taxes than he will receive in benefits and a high-wage worker will pay $193,874 more in taxes than he will receive in benefits. Thus, Social Security is not just a retirement system—it's also a welfare system.

As usual, there are complications, only three of which we will mention here. Social Security pays more to married couples than to singles. A married man gets 50 percent more than a single man with the same earnings, even if his spouse has never worked. (The same is true for married females with nonworking spouses.) Thus, Social Security is more beneficial for married people than singles.

Social Security pays more the longer you live, so anyone with greater life expectancy gets a bigger benefit from Social Security (remember Ida May Fuller lived to 100!). Similarly, anyone with lower life expectancy doesn't get as good a deal from Social Security as they would otherwise. If you are 55, for example, and your doctor tells you that you have five years left to live, you don't get to make an early withdrawal from "your" Social Security account.

Because Social Security redistributes toward those with higher life expectancy, it's better for females than for males. In other words, a single woman with the same earnings as a single man will get more from Social Security because on average she will live longer. More generally, different individuals are treated differently by Social Security depending on their wealth, life expectancy, marriage status, and other factors.

Defense

In 2007, the official budget for the Department of Defense plus defense-related activities like nuclear weapons research was $549 billion. Even that figure did not include much of the expenses for the wars in Iraq and Afghanistan, which are funded outside the usual budgetary process and amounted to about $120 billion in 2007. Nor does the defense budget include spending on benefits to veterans, which falls under other spending.

The United States spends much more on its military than does any other country in the world. Table 16.3 presents some data on the top 10 countries by military expenditure. Do we get value for our money? Unfortunately, assessing how much we should spend on the military goes

TABLE 16.3 Top Ten Countries by Military Expenditure (Billions of U.S. Dollars)

Country	Military Expenditure (in billions)
United States	$549
China	$140
Russia	$79
India	$73
United Kingdom	$55
Saudi Arabia	$53
France	$48
Japan	$37
Germany	$33
Italy	$30

Source: Budget of the U.S. Government and Stockholm International Peace Research Institute.
Note: Military expenditures are as of 2007 and converted into 2005 U.S. dollars using purchasing power parity rates.

well beyond standard economics and into issues of foreign policy. That is an important question but it isn't a topic for this book.

Medicare and Medicaid

Medicare reimburses the elderly for much of their medical care spending, covering hospital stays, doctor bills, and prescription drugs. To be eligible for Medicare, an individual should be 65 or older and have worked for at least 10 years in a job paying Medicare premiums. Many of the disabled are covered as well, even if they have not held such jobs.

In fiscal year 2007, Medicare spending amounted to $394 billion. Social Security and Medicare, taken together, comprise 36.5 percent of the U.S. federal budget. Together these programs are by far the largest undertakings of the U.S. government, and both are programs that transfer money to the elderly.

Medicare does not pay all medical bills outright. Instead, beneficiaries are required to pay some percent of the charges, known as a copayment. A beneficiary also has to pay for relatively small charges, which is known as a deductible. Many of the elderly buy private insurance to pay for the gaps in their Medicare coverage.

In addition to Medicare, you may have heard of Medicaid. Whereas Medicare covers the elderly, Medicaid covers the poor and the disabled. Of course, some of the elderly are poor as well and these people are eligible for both programs. The federal government and state governments pay for Medicaid jointly, but the program itself is run through state governments at the state level. As of fiscal 2007, Medicaid expenditures were around $200 billion, which is just a little more than half the expenditures of Medicare.

Unemployment Insurance and Welfare Spending

It is a common myth that most of the money spent by our federal government goes to welfare programs. In reality, federal welfare payments (not including Medicaid) amount to about $252 billion per year or 9 percent of the federal budget.

Remember, other than defense, the largest spending programs are Social Security and Medicare, and these programs primarily transfer wealth to the elderly, not to the poor. Since we will all be elderly sooner or later (at least if we are lucky), these transfers eventually go to virtually all Americans. Of course, some of the people receiving Social Security and Medicare are poor and there is some redistribution to the poor within these programs but on average the elderly are a little bit wealthier than other Americans.

Most welfare payments fall into a few common categories. First, personal welfare payments are made to poor households with children. The largest of these is called Temporary Assistance for Needy Families. Since 1996, an individual cannot receive these benefits for more than five years in a lifetime. Housing vouchers under the Section 8 program give poor households a voucher that subsidizes a portion of their rent. Unemployment insurance makes payments to people who are out of work and is not restricted to the poor.

Especially important is the Earned Income Tax Credit (EITC), which is now the main form that antipoverty policy takes at the federal level. The EITC, quite simply, pays poor people cash through the tax system depending on how much they earn. So, for instance, if you are married, have a child, and earn $20,000 a year, you are below the poverty line and the EITC will supplement your income, giving you over $2,000 for the year. With more than one child, the credit goes up to almost $4,000. In 2007, over $35 billion was spent on the EITC and these federal programs are supplemented by a wide variety of state and local welfare programs for the poor.

Everything Else

Before discussing paying interest on the national debt, let's look at everything else. Everything else accounts for all the other spending programs of the federal government, which includes:

> Farm subsidies

> Spending on roads, bridges, and infrastructure

> The Disaster Relief Fund

> The Small Business Administration

> The Food and Drug Administration

> All federal courts

> Federal prisons

> The FBI

> Foreign aid

> Border security

> NASA

> The National Institutes of Health

> The National Science Foundation

> Financial assistance to students

> The wages of all federal employees

All of these programs add up to a large amount of money, about $462 billion in total, but none of these programs is large compared to Social Security, defense, or Medicare.

A common misconception about the budget involves foreign aid. When polled, 41 percent of Americans said that foreign aid is one of the two largest sources of federal expenditure. In reality, foreign aid is about 1 percent of the overall federal budget; the exact number depends on how that term is defined since sometimes "foreign aid" and "military assistance" are difficult to distinguish.

You may have heard about "earmarks" as one component of discretionary domestic spending. An earmark arises when a congressperson puts a favored expenditure for his or her district into a broader bill. For instance, Rep. James Clyburn earmarked $3 million for a golf program in a defense appropriations act. It is estimated that earmarks in fiscal 2006 amounted to $29 billion.

Many earmarked expenditures are wasteful, but if a politician claims that he or she will pay for new spending programs or tax cuts by cutting "waste"—beware! Our trip through the federal budget shows that cutting waste may sound good, but the reality is that most of the money is being spent in the big programs. And overhead expenses for Social Security and Medicare are quite low, so it is hard to cut spending on those programs without cutting actual benefits. There's no such thing as a free lunch. If we want more spending, taxes must rise. If we want lower taxes, spending must fall.

Is this defense spending?

KEN REDDING/CORBIS

The National Debt, Interest on the National Debt, and Deficits

The final category of spending we will discuss is interest on the national debt. If you Google the "U.S. national debt," you will probably find a number around $11 trillion, but quite a bit of this amount is held by other branches of the federal government. The Social Security Trust Fund, for example, holds billions of dollars in Treasury bonds, which simply represent an IOU on future Social Security payments. It is important to look not just at our current expenses, but also at the expenses we are committed to in the future, such as Social Security payments. Since we are committed to a lot more than Social Security payments, however, we will hold off on looking at our future commitments for a moment.

A better measure of our current debt is the **national debt held by the public,** which is all federal debt held by individuals, corporations, state or local governments, foreign governments, and other entities other than the federal government itself. The national debt held by the public is as of 2009 just over $7 trillion. From now on when we talk about the national debt, the federal debt, or just the debt we mean the national debt held by the public.

> The **national debt held by the public** is all federal debt held outside the United States government.

Seven trillion dollars is a very big number, but it has to be compared with another very big number, GDP, which is about $14 trillion. Thus, the United States has a debt-to-GDP ratio of 50 percent. Is this a big number? Mortgage lenders often require a debt-to-income ratio of less than 36 percent so few people would recommend that *you* carry that much debt. The U.S. government will live for a lot longer than you or we will so for the federal government this debt-to-GDP ratio is not excessive. Figure 16.4 shows the debt-to-GDP ratio since 1940. Today's debt-to-GDP ratio of 50 percent is large but not as large as the ratio has been in the past. More worrying is that in 2007 the debt was only five trillion dollars so the national debt is rising very quickly.

The highest debt-to-GDP ratio in U.S. history occurred in 1946 at 108 percent. As we discussed in Chapter 8, it makes sense for you to borrow to pay for large expenses, thereby smoothing your consumption, and the same thing is true for the U.S. government. The government borrowed heavily to finance emergency expenditures for World War II, but following the war the debt-to-GDP ratio slowly declined until the 1980s. In the 1980s, a combination of tax cuts and increases in defense spending increased the debt-to-GDP ratio. The ratio then fell as the economy expanded and the federal government briefly ran a series of budget surpluses under President Clinton in the 1990s. More recently, the debt-to-GDP ratio increased slightly due to further tax cuts and defense spending under former President George W. Bush and is now increasing sharply due to the recession that began in late 2007 and government spending designed to stimulate the economy under President Obama.

Every year, the government must pay interest to the people who lent it money, namely the bondholders. If your debt is $100 and the interest rate is 5 percent, then you owe the lender $5 a year in interest payments. It works the same way with the national debt. The national debt in 2007 was about $5 trillion and the average interest rate on U.S. debt in 2007 was 5 percent, so in 2007

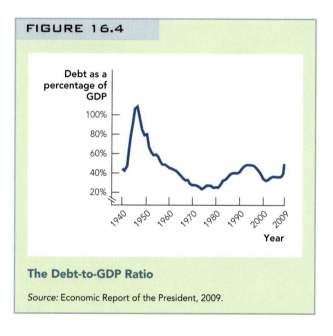

FIGURE 16.4

Debt as a percentage of GDP

The Debt-to-GDP Ratio

Source: Economic Report of the President, 2009.

the federal government had to pay about $250 billion in interest payments to bondholders. (The exact number, which you can see in Figure 16.3, was $244 billion.) Interest on the debt is about 9.1 percent of the federal budget or about 2 percent of GDP and will increase as the debt-to-GDP ratio increases. As we discuss further below, we need to keep an eye on the national debt.

Sometimes television commentators suggest it makes a big difference if the debt of the U.S. government is held by foreigners or Americans. From a purely economic point of view, however, this distinction does not matter. The real decision is made when the money is spent on goods and services and what matters is how the money is spent. If, years later, interest payments go to foreigners, that is because the foreigners have invested in the United States. This is economically beneficial for the United States and the fact that foreigners also may become wealthy is an economic plus not a minus. You can make a moral or ethical judgment that Americans ought to be spending less and saving more (which would mean less borrowing from foreigners), but low savings would be an even greater problem without foreign investors.

> The **deficit** is the annual difference between federal spending and revenues.

We now need to make a distinction between the national debt and the deficit. The debt is the total amount of money owed by the federal government at a point in time. It is a cumulative total of previous obligations. The **deficit** is the difference—this year—between what the government is spending and what the government is collecting in revenues. You can think of the deficit as the annual change in the national debt.

The top half of Figure 16.5 shows federal government spending (green) and revenues (blue) as a percentage of GDP from 1960 to 2009. When spending is greater than revenues, the government must borrow to make up the difference— the difference is the deficit, shown in the bottom half of Figure 16.5 also as a percentage of GDP (and as a negative value). In 1990, for example, the federal government spent almost 22 percent of GDP, but it collected only 18 percent of GDP in tax revenues. Since government spending was greater than revenues,

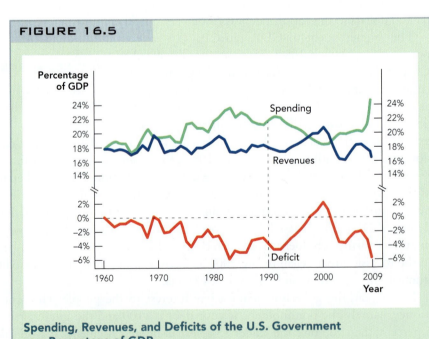

FIGURE 16.5

Spending, Revenues, and Deficits of the U.S. Government as a Percentage of GDP

Source: Economic Report of the President, 2009.

the government had to borrow the difference so in 1990 the deficit was about 4 percent of GDP (22 percent − 18 percent).

Will the U.S. Government Go Bankrupt?

We said earlier that the current debt-to-GDP ratio of 50 percent is large but not unprecedented. Nevertheless, many economists are worried about the future debt-to-GDP ratio. The Congressional Budget Office (CBO), for example, argues that "under any plausible scenario, the federal budget is on an unsustainable path—that is, the federal debt will grow much faster than the economy over the long run."[4] The Congressional Budget Office's projections for the debt-to-GDP ratio are shown in Figure 16.6. (Note that these projections were made in 2007 before the debt jumped by two trillion dollars—so the projections today would be even a little bit worse.) According to the CBO, if taxes and spending trends do not change significantly, the debt-to-GDP ratio will soar to rates well above any seen in U.S. history.

The main forces driving the CBO's projections are not recessions but demographics and increasing health care costs. The U.S. population is getting older. In 2008, about 12 percent of the population was aged 65 or older, but in 2030, 19 percent of the population will be 65 or older. The increase in the number of elderly people means higher Social Security and Medicare payments. As a fraction of GDP, for example, Social Security payments will have to increase by about 41 percent if benefits are to be maintained at promised levels. More elderly people also means we will see increases in Medicare payments, although in this case an even bigger problem than demographics is rising health care costs per person.

In recent decades, health care costs per person have been rising more than twice as fast as GDP per capita. If health care costs continue rising at their current rate, those costs will account for a larger and larger part of the economy. Because of Medicare and Medicaid, health care costs will consume a larger and larger share of the federal budget.

When we add together spending increases that we can expect to occur because of an older population and rising health care costs, the result is Figure 16.7 on the next page.

To understand Figure 16.7, first take a look at the solid red line: this is total spending on programs (i.e., not including interest on the national debt) over approximately the past 50 years and projected into the future. Notice that over the past 50 years spending on programs has fluctuated around 18 percent of GDP. Tax revenues, the solid black line, have been a little bit lower on average, leading to deficits in most years, but not very large deficits in percentage terms.

As we enter the future, however, an increasingly older population and higher health care costs are projected to increase spending far above past totals. The main cause of higher spending is a modest but significant increase in Social Security payments relative to GDP and a large increase in Medicare and Medicaid spending. Notice that the CBO projects all other government spending programs, including defense, shown by the purple line to *decline* as a percentage of GDP—if that scenario proves overly optimistic, spending could rise even more than is shown in these projections.

CHECK YOURSELF

> When you retire, you will receive Social Security benefits and most Americans will also receive Medicare benefits. Right now, what percentage of federal spending is represented by Social Security plus Medicare payments?

> Why is it important to consider the debt-to-GDP ratio rather than just the absolute amount of the national debt? What does this ratio tell us?

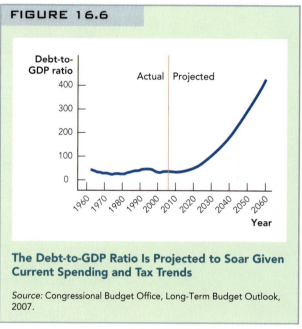

FIGURE 16.6

The Debt-to-GDP Ratio Is Projected to Soar Given Current Spending and Tax Trends

Source: Congressional Budget Office, Long-Term Budget Outlook, 2007.

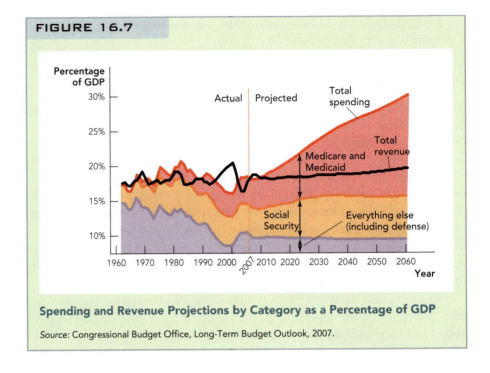

FIGURE 16.7

Spending and Revenue Projections by Category as a Percentage of GDP

Source: Congressional Budget Office, Long-Term Budget Outlook, 2007.

UNDERSTAND YOUR
world

If spending increases rapidly and taxes rise only modestly, the result will be a soaring debt-to-GDP ratio, which is where the CBO's scary projection seen in Figure 16.6 comes from. But the CBO is not really predicting a soaring debt-to-GDP ratio. Instead, they are suggesting that *something else must change*—either government spending must decrease or taxes must increase or perhaps health care costs cannot continue on their current upward spiral.

The Future Is Hard to Predict

So what will happen? Will spending decrease or will taxes increase? No one knows. On the one hand, the United States does have a history of relatively low taxes. Americans fought the Revolutionary War, in part, as a protest against British taxes even though British Americans had one of the smallest tax burdens in the world! The modern income tax didn't begin until 1913 and that required a separate amendment to the Constitution. Even as late as 1916, the federal government accounted for less than 5 percent of GDP.

Taxes and federal spending increased dramatically during 1916–1919 and 1942–1945, corresponding to World War I and World War II, respectively. But since that time federal taxes and spending have been fairly stable—as we noted above, around 18 percent of GDP. When taxes have increased, there have often been backlashes, when Americans elect politicians who promise to cut taxes. So, will Americans accept much higher tax rates in the future than they ever have in the past? Will you?

If taxes and spending in the United States do increase, this would make the United States more like other developed countries. Figure 16.8 shows total government spending by country, including spending by federal, state, and local governments. Government in the United States today spends a smaller fraction of GDP than in most other developed countries. As a result, spending could increase substantially in the United States over the next several decades and the United States would still be spending at levels comparable to Germany, Italy, and the Netherlands today.

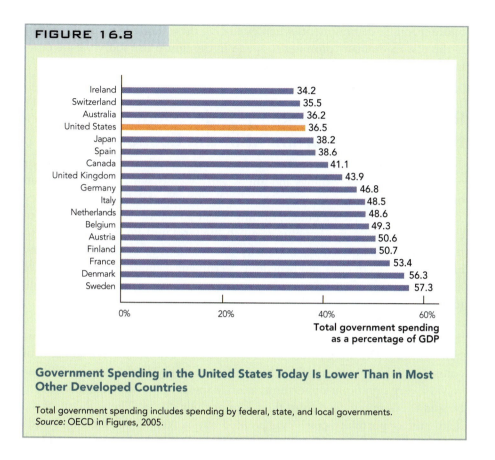

FIGURE 16.8

Country	Total government spending as a percentage of GDP
Ireland	34.2
Switzerland	35.5
Australia	36.2
United States	36.5
Japan	38.2
Spain	38.6
Canada	41.1
United Kingdom	43.9
Germany	46.8
Italy	48.5
Netherlands	48.6
Belgium	49.3
Austria	50.6
Finland	50.7
France	53.4
Denmark	56.3
Sweden	57.3

Government Spending in the United States Today Is Lower Than in Most Other Developed Countries

Total government spending includes spending by federal, state, and local governments.
Source: OECD in Figures, 2005.

Could spending be cut? We have already cut some projected Social Security spending by increasing the age of retirement. Perhaps we can cut spending even more—but don't expect the elderly to take this sitting down! And remember a large part of the growth in spending is due to rising health care costs. Many people talk about slowing the growth of health care costs but it isn't so easy. There is a lot of waste in health care markets, but also there are many wonderful innovations. Drugs known as statins lower our cholesterol and new surgical procedures save many lives; a triple bypass operation is now more or less standard procedure. It's not so easy to sort out the good medical procedures from the bad ones, and so by most accounts health care costs will continue to rise. Other countries do spend a smaller fraction of their GDP on health care costs, but the *growth* in health care costs is pretty similar throughout the developed world.

Don't forget that whatever happens, the news is actually quite good for the most part. Americans are living longer than ever before and many medical advances are paying off. Let's say you thought you would live to be 80 but then you learn you will live to be 100 instead. You might worry about how to finance your now-longer retirement and perhaps you might even despair that it seems impossible. But this is the kind of problem that we can live with!

Another scenario is that GDP will grow faster in the future than it has in the past. We outlined one case for optimism in Chapter 7. Nevertheless, although we hope for the best, it's probably wise to plan if not for the worst then at least for the most likely outcome, and that will require some painful tax increases or spending cuts.

One general lesson is that we cannot judge the fiscal health of the federal government simply by looking at today's budget or today's deficit. New government programs often grow over time and we ought to think about implicit

The federal government has not planned for future expenses. Have you?

future spending commitments when evaluating these new programs. Politicians in the past made many promises to spend in the future and today we are dealing with the legacy of these promises.

Revenues and Spending Undercount the Role of Government in the Economy

This chapter has mostly been about federal revenues and expenditures. But our government does many things and imposes many costs, which do not show up on any formal budgetary accounts. The Environmental Protection Agency (EPA), for instance, has a budget of only about $8 billion yet its real reach, in terms of both costs and benefits, is much higher. The EPA has the power to regulate how business affects the environment and its mandates involve many billions of dollars of costs and benefits. Government spending is one measure of how government affects the economy, but it is not a complete or fully accurate measure.

Governments take many other actions that commandeer resources from the private sector but do not show up as full budgetary expenditures. For instance, until 1973 the United States ran a military draft. Drafted soldiers, of course, are relatively cheap if you just look at their paychecks, but the draft involves a very significant opportunity cost. Many people who were ill suited to be soldiers were removed from their jobs or their studies. The real cost of the draft—the opportunity cost—was pointed out by Milton Friedman, who advocated a move to a volunteer army. The United States had to pay soldiers more, so military costs appeared to go up. In reality, the volunteer army reduced the total cost to society of providing national defense by freeing up more productive labor, even if that efficiency was not reflected in the government's budget statements.

☐ Takeaway

An examination of the current federal budget reveals some key points. First and foremost is the simple point that the federal government takes in and spends a great deal of money. It is hard to imagine revenues and spending of over $2.5 *trillion*.

Next, it is useful to recognize where this money comes from. Contrary to what some people might think, the corporate income tax represents only a little over 10 percent of total tax revenues. The huge majority of tax revenues—over 82 percent—come from individuals in the form of individual income taxes and tax on wages linked to Social Security and Medicare.

For many people, it is surprising to learn what the federal government spends its money on. The obvious category of defense spending represents around 20 percent of spending. Over one-third (36.5 percent) of the federal budget goes for Social Security and Medicare payments. Comprehensive general transfers to the elderly represent far more money than do welfare expenditures per se.

What about the future? The U.S. tax system is very complicated and not always transparent in its effects. Nevertheless, we can estimate future expenditures and revenues as a way of understanding the fiscal strength or weakness of a nation. It is very likely that federal expenditures will rise in the future, most of all because of rising Medicare expenditures. One question is whether and how federal revenues will rise to keep the budget sufficiently close to balance.

□ CHAPTER REVIEW

KEY CONCEPTS

Marginal tax rate, p. 336

Average tax rate, p. 337

Alternative minimum tax (AMT), p. 339

Progressive tax, p. 341

Flat tax, p. 341

Regressive tax, p. 341

National debt held by the public, p. 347

Deficit, p. 348

FACTS AND TOOLS

1. a. Consider Table 16.1. We can use these data to find out what percentage of federal taxes is paid from the "top down" by the top 40 percent, top 60 percent, or top 80 percent of income earners. Likewise, we can count from the "bottom up" by the bottom 40 percent, 60 percent, or 80 percent of income earners. Fill in the table below.

Share of Total Federal Tax Revenue		Share of Total Federal Tax Revenue	
Everyone	100%	Everyone	100%
Bottom 20%		Top 80%	
Bottom 40%	4.9%	Top 60%	
Bottom 60%		Top 40%	85.6%
Bottom 80%		Top 20%	

b. Given these data, which of the following are true?

a) The bottom 60% of taxpayers pay less than 25% of federal taxes.

b) The top 80% of taxpayers pay over 98% of federal taxes.

c) The top 40% of taxpayers pay less than 60% of federal taxes.

2. In 2007, corporate income taxes were about 11 percent of total federal revenue. Use Figure 16.5 to help estimate what fraction of GDP represents corporate income taxes.

3. a. Let's explore the difference between the average income tax rate and the marginal income tax rate. In the simple land of Rabushka, there is only one tax rate, 20 percent, but workers don't have to pay tax on the first $10,000 of their income. For every dollar they earn above $10,000, they pay 20 cents on the dollar to the Lord High Mayor of Rabushka.

The easy way to calculate the tax bill is the same way that America's IRS does: Subtract $10,000 from each person's income and call the remainder "taxable income." Multiply taxable income by 0.20, and the result is "tax due." Fill in the table below.

Income	Taxable Income	Tax Due	Marginal Tax Rate	Average Income Tax Rate
$5,000	$0	0	0%	0%
$10,000	$0	0	0%	0%
$15,000	$5,000	$1,000	20%	6.7%
$20,000				
$50,000				
$100,000				
$1,000,000				

b. Is the marginal tax rate ever lower than the average tax rate?

c. As a worker's income rises and rises past $1,000,000, will the average tax rate ever be greater than 20 percent?

d. Just to make sure you know what these terms mean in plain English: For an accountant making $50,000 per year, what percentage of her income goes to the Lord High Mayor?

Note: This simple tax system is quite similar to the plan that economist Robert Hall and political scientist Alvin Rabushka spell out in their book, *The Flat Tax*, widely available for free online. Hall and Rabushka estimate that a system like this one would raise roughly the same amount of revenue as the current federal income tax.

4. a. Do most federal government transfers of cash go to the elderly or to the poor?

b. Do most federal government purchases of health care go to the elderly or to the poor?

5. a. According to Table 16.2, which generation gets the best deal from Social Security: The one turning 65 in 1975, in 2010, or in 2030?

b. Out of the nine categories in Table 16.2, which kind of worker gets the best deal overall from Social Security?

6. Based on the information in this chapter, let's see who gets a better deal, a greater net-benefit, from Social Security. In each pairing, choose one, or write "unclear."

Women or men?

Married couples or singles?

People born in 1910 or people born in 1965?

High-income earners or low-income earners?

7. There are a lot of ways to slice up the U.S. budget. With this in mind, which of the following statements are true, according to Figure 16.3?

a. Most of the federal budget is spent on welfare and foreign aid.

b. About half of the federal budget goes toward Medicare, Medicaid, and Social Security combined.

c. More than half of the federal budget goes toward Medicare, Medicaid, Social Security, and interest on the debt combined.

d. The federal government spends about $1,830 on the military per person in the United States.

8. Pundits and commentators often state (correctly) that entitlement spending (spending on Medicare, Medicaid, and Social Security) is going to explode in the future. But by lumping all three together, we obscure the source of the explosion. Review Figure 16.7.

a. Which of the three really won't be "exploding" all that much compared to the other two?

b. Which category of federal spending is projected to actually decline in future decades?

THINKING AND PROBLEM SOLVING

1. By U.S. law, your employer pays half of the payroll tax and you, the worker, pay the other half. We mentioned that according to the basics of supply and demand, the part of the tax paid by the employer is likely to cut the worker's take-home pay. Let's see why. We'll start off in a land without any payroll taxes and then see how adding payroll taxes (like FICA and Medicare) affects the worker's take-home pay.

a. Who is it that "supplies labor?" Is it workers or firms? And who demands labor? Workers or firms?

b. The chart below illustrates the pretax equilibrium. Mark the equilibrium wage and quantity of labor in this market. In part c, remember that this "wage" is the amount paid directly to workers.

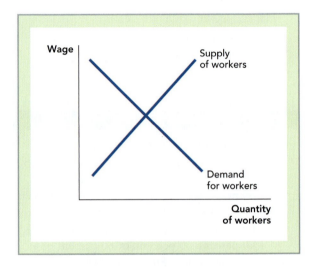

c. Suppose the government enacts a new payroll tax of 10 percent of worker wages, "paid" 100 percent by employers. What will happen to the typical firm's demand for labor? In other words, when firms learn that every time they hire a worker, they have to pay not only that worker's wage but they must also pay 10 percent of that worker's wage to the government, will that increase or decrease their willingness to hire workers? After you answer in words, also illustrate the shift in the graph above.

d. So, in the equilibrium with a new 100 percent-employer-paid payroll tax, will worker's take-home wages be higher or lower than beforehand?

e. Imagine that most workers want full-time jobs to support their families whether the wage is high or low. What does this imply about the shape of the supply curve? Redo the analysis with the new supply curve and discuss the exact effect on wages of the payroll tax.

2. It's easy to confuse the "federal deficit" with the "federal debt." We'll work out an example to make the differences clear. To keep the math simple, we'll falsely assume that in this land of Barrovia, the government can borrow from the public at an interest rate of 0 percent—so there is no interest on the debt. We will also assume that the government is unwilling to print money to finance its budget so the only way to finance a deficit is by borrowing. The debt inherited from 2011 is 4,000 credits (C4,000, in the local notation). Fill in the accompanying table.

Note: The relationship between deficits and debts is similar to the relationship between investment and the capital stock, which we investigated back in Chapters 6 and 7: The first is a "flow" while the second is a "stock"; the first is like a river while the second is like a lake.

Year	Revenue	Spending	Deficit	Debt
2012	C100	C120	C20	C4,020
2013	C80	C130	C50	
2014	C110	C140		
2015	C120	C150		
2016	C120	C160		

3. Social Security is primarily a pay-as-you-go program, which means that the government pays retirees their promised benefits by taxing today's workers. Imagine that Social Security moved to a fully funded program in which today's workers (or the government on their behalf) invested in assets, such as stock and bonds, to pay for their own retirement.

   a. Discuss some of the costs and benefits of a fully funded program.

   b. Discuss some of the difficulties of transitioning to the new system. Hint: If today's workers pay for their own future retirement, who will pay today's retirees?

4. Under current law, homeowners get a big tax break: The details of the tax break really don't matter as much as the mere fact that if you make mortgage payments on a home that you live in, your taxes will be lower than otherwise.

   a. Suppose that Congress eliminated the tax break for homeowners. What will this law do to the demand for homes: Raise, lower, or have no impact?

   b. What will be the net effect of eliminating the break on the price of houses?

   c. Given your answers to parts a and b comment on who gets the benefits of the tax break. Is it

people who buy homes? Sellers? (Be careful, sellers were buyers once!) Why could eliminating the tax break prove difficult?

5. Calculating taxes on capital gains takes a little work, but if you buy and sell stocks, bonds, works of art, or homes, you'll probably have to do this at some point. Let's practice. In a few cases below, the price will fall—just record that as a negative rise (a "capital loss," in tax jargon, and calculate the negative "tax due").

   a. Fill in the table below.

Item	Purchase price 2015	Sale Price 2020	Capital Gain	Tax Due at 15% rate
10 Shares of Microsoft Stock	$1,200	$1,250	$50	$7.50
1 Share of Berkshire Hathaway stock	$8,000	$11,000		
100 Shares of GM stock	$1,000	$500		
1 Picasso napkin sketch	$15,000	$14,000		
1 Mexican Amate folk painting	$2,000	$3,500		

   b. One nice thing about the capital gains tax is that you can choose what year to pay it by choosing what year to sell your investment. If you wanted to sell your single share of Berkshire stock and your Picasso in the same year, how much tax would you pay?

6. How big is the tax break from the $3,300 per child income tax deduction for:

   a. Families in the 10 percent tax bracket?

   b. Families in the 25 percent tax bracket? (Hint: This is worked out in the chapter.)

   c. Families in the 35 percent tax bracket?

7. a. If 1 percent of federal spending goes toward foreign aid, then what percent of U.S. GDP goes toward foreign aid? Figures 16.3 and 16.5 will help.

   b. If 20 percent of federal spending goes toward defense spending, then what percent of U.S. GDP goes toward defense spending?

c. If $30 billion of federal spending goes toward earmarked appropriations, what percent of federal spending goes toward earmarks?

8. Some people argue that a large national debt will make future generations poorer. One way to test this is to see what happened after the last time the United States had a large national debt: after World War II. As Figure 16.4 shows, the debt-to-GDP ratio was over 100 percent, more than double today's ratio. Let's compare this to Figure 5.3 and Figure 10.5, which shows the growth rate of GDP and the unemployment rate, respectively.

a. During the 1950s, was the growth rate lower than average? How about during the 1960s?

b. During the 1950s, was the unemployment rate higher than average? How about during the 1960s?

c. Overall, is it fair to say that the two decades after the massive World War II debt were worse than average?

Note that this single case doesn't count as conclusive proof: Perhaps the United States just got lucky, or the federal government did an unusually good job spending its World War II expenditures to build up its capital stock (a point emphasized in the excellent Francis Ford Coppola film *Tucker: The Man and His Dream*), or perhaps a massive short-term debt doesn't cause much economic trouble. You can learn more about these possible explanations in other economics courses.

9. Which of the following actual government programs show up as costs in the federal budget?

The Department of Labor mandates the minimum wage for workers.

The Environmental Protection Agency mandates that cars have equipment to keep pollution levels low.

The National Oceanic and Atmospheric Administration forecasts the weather.

The Coast Guard rescues sailors from a sinking yacht off the coast of Cape Cod.

The Border Patrol requires that all vehicles driving on highways out of San Diego be stopped to be inspected for the presence of illegal aliens.

CHALLENGES

1. In 1989, Senator Bob Packwood asked Congress's Joint Committee on Taxation how much extra revenue the government would raise if it just started taxing 100 percent of all income over $200,000 per year. The Joint Committee crunched some numbers and reported an answer: $204 billion per year.

a. What is wrong with this answer?

b. Under Packwood's proposal, what would the marginal tax rate be at $250,000 per year? At $500,000 per year?

Note: Packwood asked the Joint Committee this question not because he wanted to raise taxes that high, but to make a point. The tale of his efforts—and the efforts of Ronald Reagan, Dan Rostenkowski, Bill Bradley, and many others—to improve the U.S. tax code in the 1980s is compellingly told in Birnbaum and Murray's book *Showdown at Gucci Gulch: Lawmakers, Lobbyists, and the Unlikely Triumph of Tax Reform.*

2. Today, many government transfer programs are run through the tax code. The Earned Income Tax Credit (EITC), which we discussed in this chapter, is one important example. The federal government also has a variety of other "refundable tax credits," that is, spending programs run through the tax code. These blur the line between "tax breaks" and "government spending." This may explain their popularity: voters and politicians who like tax breaks can claim that these programs are tax breaks, while voters and politicians who like higher government spending can claim that these programs are government spending.

a. Your income is $20,000 per year. You pay your initial tax bill of $5,000 but the government sends you a $1,000 tax refund because you have a young child. What is your after-tax income, including the value of the government check?

b. Your income is $20,000 per year. You pay your initial tax bill of $5,000 and the government sends you a $1,000 check because you have a young child. What is your after-tax income, including the value of the government check?

c. Your income is $20,000 per year. You pay your initial tax bill of $500 but the government sends you a $1,000 tax refund because you have a young child. What is your after-tax income, including the value of the government check?

d. Your income is $20,000 per year. You pay your tax bill of $500 and the government sends you a $1,000 check because you have a young child. What is your after-tax income, including the value of the government check?

 e. In which of these cases does the government check seem like "government spending" to you, and why? You may find more than one case applicable—this question borders on the philosophical.

3. a. If the debt-to-GDP ratio rose to 100 percent and the interest rate on the debt were 5 percent per year, what fraction of GDP would go toward paying interest on the debt?

 b. If this happened, would interest on the debt be a bigger share of GDP than Social Security is today?

 c. In your opinion, do you think that Americans would tolerate spending this much of the national income on interest payments for past spending? More important, do you think Americans would want their politicians to stop making the interest payments and just default on some or all of the federal debt? Why or why not?

4. Currently, the U.S. government offers "food stamps" to poor Americans. These "stamps" are pieces of paper that look like Monopoly money and can be spent just like money at many grocery stores. The government has a complex formula that determines how much each poor person gets each month in food stamps (or more often these days, government-provided debit cards).

 Let's suppose that instead, the government decides to pay 95 percent of every poor person's food bill, as long as it is purchased at a typical grocery store: The poor person would make a "copayment" of 5 percent of the total bill, and the federal government would reimburse the grocery store for the remaining 95 percent. Just to keep things simple, let's assume that the government has a good way to make sure that poor people can't resell this food to others.

 a. Which method would probably lead to more spending on food: the current method or the 5 percent copayment method? Why?

 b. If food companies like Kellogg's and Quaker Oats start inventing new, more delicious dishes at a rapid rate, under which method will the federal government's food spending grow fastest: the current method or the 5 percent copayment method?

 c. Which method is more like how most people pay for health care including the elderly and the poor under the federal government's Medicare and Medicaid programs: the current method or the 5 percent copayment method?

 d. Recall that health care is a field of rapid innovation. How can your answer to parts b and c explain the rapid growth of medical spending?

5. When discussing the statements sent to you by the federal government that predict your future Social Security payments, we said, "don't be surprised if those predictions turn out to be a little bit optimistic." Consider why this might be *wrong*: Why might these predictions be too *pessimistic*, precisely because Social Security recipients are also voters? Hint: Senior citizens are more likely to vote than younger citizens.

17

Fiscal Policy

The U.S. economy was falling toward a severe recession. The S&P 500 stock index was plummeting. And in the third quarter of 2008 consumer spending dropped by 3.7 percent, the largest fall in 28 years. Consumer spending is about 70 percent of GDP (as you will recall from Chapter 5) so the sudden drop in spending pushed down the growth rate of GDP. To encourage more spending, President George W. Bush had authorized the Treasury to send checks to millions of U.S. taxpayers. Could the new money jump-start the economy? Not this time. Consumer confidence was ebbing. Even with a few extra bucks in their pocket, consumers weren't ready to spend. The economy continued to worsen and in 2009 President Barack Obama tried a different approach: hundreds of billions in new government spending on roads, bridges, education and other infrastructure. If the American consumer wouldn't spend, then the American government would.

Fighting a recession with tax cuts and fighting a recession with increased government spending are two forms of fiscal policy. **Fiscal policy** is federal government policy on taxes, spending, and borrowing that is designed to influence business fluctuations.

In this chapter, we use the dynamic aggregate demand and aggregate supply curves familiar to you from Chapter 12 to understand fiscal policy. We start with the situations in which fiscal policy is most effective, move to the cases where fiscal policy doesn't matter much at all for macroeconomic performance, and close by considering when an activist fiscal policy is downright harmful.

As we said, there are two general categories of fiscal policy used to fight a recession:

1. The government spends more money.
2. The government cuts taxes, giving people more money to spend.

Fiscal policy is federal government policy on taxes, spending, and borrowing that is designed to influence business fluctuations.

In both cases, the goal is more spending, although in the first case the new spending comes from government and in the second it comes from the private sector. We will start by focusing on expansionary fiscal policy done through increases in government spending because that is the most straightforward case of fiscal policy and the underlying issues are easiest to identify.

Fiscal Policy: The Best Case

An economic recession is underway and fear is in the air. Worried about their future, consumers cut back on consumption growth; that is, $\vec{C}$ falls. Consumers are spending less in order to build up their cash reserves so we can also say equivalently that $\vec{v}$ falls. Figure 17.1 shows the result: The fall in $\vec{C}$ shifts the AD curve to the left and down, moving the economy from a long-run equilibrium at point a to a short-run equilibrium at point b. At point b, the growth rate is negative and the economy is in a recession.

The problem at point b is that consumers want to hold more money and this means that the rate of inflation must decrease. Wages and prices, however, are sticky (see Chapter 12) so when spending growth declines, instead of just

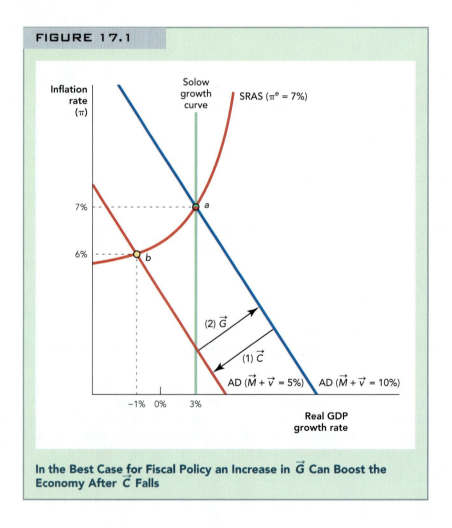

FIGURE 17.1

In the Best Case for Fiscal Policy an Increase in $\vec{G}$ Can Boost the Economy After $\vec{C}$ Falls

a decrease in inflation, we get a decrease in real growth as well. In terms of our dynamic AD curve, we have $\vec{M} + \vec{v} =$ Inflation $+$ Real growth. $\vec{M}$, by assumption, isn't changing and in the short run the decrease in $\vec{v}$ is split between a decrease in inflation and a decrease in real growth.

In the long run, prices and wages will become "unstuck," fear will pass, and $\vec{C}$ will return to its normal growth rate so the economy will transition until it returns to point a. But in John Maynard Keynes's famous phrase "in the long run, we are all dead." Can government do anything to make recovery a reality now? Quite possibly so.

Remember that the components of aggregate demand are $\vec{C}$, $\vec{I}$, $\vec{G}$, and $\vec{NX}$. The government has (some) control over $\vec{G}$ so if $\vec{C}$ falls, why not increase $\vec{G}$ to compensate? In Figure 17.1, we show how an increase in $\vec{G}$ can shift the AD curve to the right and up, thereby putting the economy on a transition path back to point a, reversing the decline in $\vec{C}$ and ending the recession.

An increase in $\vec{G}$ means the government is spending more money—and thus commanding more real resources—so where does the money come from? That's a very good question. The money must come from taxes or increased borrowing and, as we will see shortly, that will mean reduced aggregate demand from some quarters, thereby making the increase in $\vec{G}$ less effective. But, in the best case scenario, the increase in $\vec{G}$ is still effective because more spending creates more growth which supports the increased spending.

Can an economy really pull itself up by its bootstraps? Yes. Since John Maynard Keynes's *The General Theory of Employment, Interest and Money* (1936), economists have understood that in some situations spending can increase growth, or as economists like to say *demand can create its own supply*. More generally, the reason this is possible is that at point b the economy is operating *inefficiently*. Remember that the economy has the capital, the labor, and the technology to grow at the rate given by the Solow growth curve, so when the economy is operating at point b, it is growing at less than potential; it is growing more slowly than is possible given the fundamental factors of production. The increase in $\vec{G}$ puts the economy back on track and, if everything goes well, the increase more than pays for itself.

The Multiplier

To understand how an increase in government spending can generate growth, let's look a little more closely at what economists call the multiplier. In the best case scenario, the increase in $\vec{G}$ doesn't even have to be as large as the fall in $\vec{C}$ in order to restore the economy because as $\vec{G}$ increases so does $\vec{C}$. Let's explain how this can happen.

Imagine that Joe becomes worried about unemployment so he cuts back on his daily consumption of mocha Frappuccinos in an effort to hold more cash in reserve. But remember that Joe's spending is the coffee shop owner's income (as we discussed in Chapter 5). Thus, when Joe cuts back on his spending, the coffee shop owner may cut back on her spending by, for example, hiring fewer employees or not investing in that fancy new Clover coffee machine. Thus, the decrease in Joe's spending is added to the decrease in the coffee shop owner's spending, which is added to the decrease in the spending

FIGURE 17.2

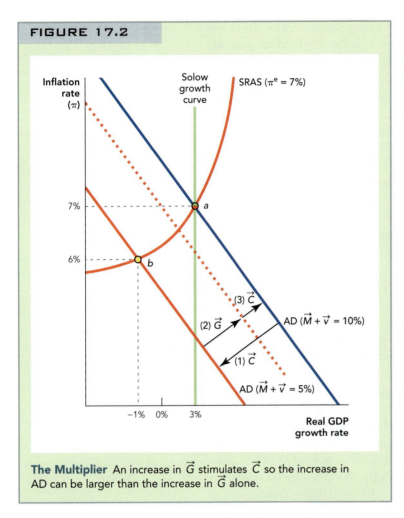

The Multiplier An increase in $\vec{G}$ stimulates $\vec{C}$ so the increase in AD can be larger than the increase in $\vec{G}$ alone.

The **multiplier effect** is the additional increase in AD caused when expansionary fiscal policy increases income and thus consumer spending.

CHECK YOURSELF

> What are the two types of expansionary fiscal policy?

of her employees and so forth. Now on an ordinary day, Joe is worried about unemployment, but Jennifer gets a new job so Joe's reduction in consumption is matched by Jennifer's increase and the net effect, even taking into account all the multiplier effects, is zero.

Trouble starts when a lot of people fear unemployment and reduce their spending at the same time. When many people reduce their spending, this reduces other people's income and these people then reduce their spending and so forth in a multiplier process. But now who will act as Jennifer to restore the economy to growth? In this situation, the government may take the place of Jennifer. By spending more to build a dam, for example, the government not only increases aggregate demand directly, it also increases the income of dam workers who spend more on haircuts, which increases the income of barbers, who spend more on restaurant meals and so forth. In Figure 17.2, we show that the increase in $\vec{G}$ stimulates an increase in income and thus an increase in $\vec{C}$ (we have drawn the figure so the net increase in AD is exactly the same as in Figure 17.1). Since the increase in $\vec{C}$ multiplies the effect of expansionary fiscal policy on AD, this effect is called the **multiplier effect**.

All of this sounds great. The government can offset decreases in AD with increases in $\vec{G}$ and because of the multiplier effect, it doesn't even have to spend that much. As you probably expected, however, the real world isn't quite so simple.

The Limits to Fiscal Policy

There are four major limits to fiscal policy. Three of these limits have to do with the difficulty of using fiscal policy to shift aggregate demand (AD).

1. **Crowding out:** If government spending crowds out or leads to less private spending, then the increase in AD is reduced or neutralized on net.

2. **A drop in the bucket:** The economy is so large that government can rarely increase spending enough to have a large impact.

3. **A matter of timing:** It can be difficult to time fiscal policy so that the AD curve shifts at just the right moments.

The fourth limit is that even if fiscal policy shifts AD that may not solve the problem. The best case for fiscal policy is when a recession is caused by a decrease in aggregate demand. But sometimes the problem isn't that people aren't spending enough, the problem is that people don't have enough to spend. In other words, some recessions are caused by real shocks of the type we analyzed in Chapter 13. As we will see, fiscal policy doesn't work well at combating real shocks. Thus, in addition to the difficulty of shifting AD we also have:

4. Real shocks: Shifting AD doesn't help much to combat real shocks.

Let's look at each of these limits in turn, noting that we are sticking with our basic scenario of an increase in government spending before we turn to the second type of expansionary fiscal policy, a decrease in taxes.

Crowding Out

When increased government spending comes at the expense of reduced private spending, we have the phenomenon of **crowding out.** Crowding out means that the initial shift in AD is less than the amount of the new government spending.

To consider an example, if the federal government builds a new interstate highway, that highway must be paid for. That means either higher taxes or more government borrowing (i.e., selling government bonds to the private sector). Both the taxes and the sale of bonds decrease aggregate demand, although perhaps with different timing. Let's now consider those two financing scenarios in more detail, namely raising taxes and borrowing by selling more government bonds.

> **Crowding out** is the decrease in private spending that occurs when government increases spending.

Raising Taxes to Finance Fiscal Policy   The simplest case for understanding crowding out is when the new government spending is financed by an increase in taxes. That means the government spends more money but of course higher taxes mean that private individuals have less money to spend.

More concretely, let's say that government increases taxes by $300 million, all of which it spends building a new highway. What would the private sector have done with that $300 million? Let's assume that the private sector would have spent $270 million of the $300 million and simply held on to the other $30 million. Because the $270 million would have been spent by the private sector anyway, in this case the initial increase in short-run aggregate demand is only $30 million, or one-tenth of what was spent in gross terms on the new highway. So, if the private sector is spending, say, 90 percent of real income, fiscal policy won't be very effective for stimulating aggregate demand. If government spends an extra dollar, 90 cents of that dollar would have been spent anyway. Only 10 percent of a given government expenditure will represent a net boost to aggregate demand.

At lower rates of private spending, more government spending does usually boost short-run aggregate demand. The government spends more money, whereas the private sector probably was not keen to have spent that entire amount right away. So fiscal policy will be most effective when people are otherwise afraid to spend their money. The latter scenario fits the story of the Great Depression that we discussed in Chapter 12 and also corresponds most closely to Figure 17.1 when the decrease in AD was caused by a decrease in $\overrightarrow{C}$.

Selling More Bonds to Finance Fiscal Policy   Rather than raising taxes today, the government often pays its bills with borrowed money. It's like using a credit card: You don't have to pay the bill today, but you do have to pay the bill sooner or later. Let's look at what happens when the government borrows from the private sector to fund a spending increase.

Imagine that the government prints a bond and sells that bond to investors. The bond is an IOU, a promise to pay the investors in the future. The government sells the bond today and pockets the cash. With more cash in hand, the government can increase spending without increasing taxes. (Alternatively the government could keep its own spending the same but cut taxes—we analyze this case further below.)

If government and consumers are spending more and taxes are the same, is there no crowding out? Not so fast. Remember that someone bought the bonds that the government sold. Where did the money to buy bonds come from?

In the simplest case, people bought more bonds instead of buying other financial assets. So, people buy more government bonds but fewer private bonds. If the private bonds were used to finance factories, then growth in investment, $\vec{I}$, declines. This is another form of crowding out, and of course if crowding out is 100 percent of the initial change in fiscal policy, aggregate demand won't shift out at all. The economy is simply substituting one form of spending for another form of spending.

Remember also what happens to interest rates when the government sells bonds. Selling bonds pushes bond prices down, which pushes interest rates up. In other words, to sell more bonds, the government must offer a higher interest rate. A higher interest rate will encourage people to save more—you might think that is good but "saving more" is another way of saying "spending less." Thus, when the government sells bonds and uses the proceeds to increase spending, some of the money comes from reduced private spending. So, there are two sources of crowding out in this case: Selling more bonds reduces private investment and also reduces private consumption, as we first showed in Chapter 8.

Given the possibilities for crowding out, bond-financed expansionary fiscal policy is most likely to be effective when the private sector is, for some reason, reluctant to spend or invest. This is often the case in a depression or in times of great uncertainty or when people, for whatever reason, are simply holding onto their cash. In this case, the government investments do not displace comparable private investments, as the private investments would not have been forthcoming in any case.

This point introduces a recurring theme of this chapter: *The case for fiscal policy is strongest when the economy is in a recession because aggregate demand is too low.*

Now let's turn away from an increase in government spending and consider tax rebates and tax cuts, which are also designed to boost the flow of spending in the economy.

Tax Rebates and Tax Cuts as a Tool of Fiscal Policy   Instead of government spending increases, tax rebates and tax cuts are another form of expansionary fiscal policy. In early 2008, for example, the economy was weakening due to, among other factors, a slump in housing prices. The Bush administration tried to increase consumer spending by sending many taxpayers a check, called a tax rebate, for $300–$600 or about $78 billion in total.

If taxpayers spend the extra money from a rebate, aggregate demand shifts up and to the right, just as with increases in government spending. But taxpayers might also use their rebate to pay down debt. But if the government borrows money to fund a rebate and taxpayers turn around and use the same money to reduce their debt, there is no increase in spending at all!

In fact, something like this happened in 2008. Taxpayers used most of their rebate, about $62 billion of the $78 billion in total, to reduce their debt rather than to increase their spending. As a result, the net fiscal stimulus was not very large.

It makes sense for consumers to use tax rebates to pay off debt. Do you remember the idea of consumption smoothing from Chapter 8? As a rule, consumers want to avoid big ups and downs in consumption so when consumers are hit with a temporary negative shock like unemployment, they take on debt. When they are hit with a temporary positive shock, like an unexpected check from the government, they often pay down debt. As a result of consumption smoothing, a temporary tax rebate tends to create a small increase in spending over many years rather than a big increase in spending now; the latter, of course, is what the government wants to boost the economy.

If a temporary tax rebate doesn't increase spending very much, what if politicians promise to make the rebate permanent? Yes, if consumers believe the rebate is permanent, they will spend more of it. But will consumers believe that a rebate is permanent when they can see that the government is borrowing a lot of money? The debt must be paid sometime, right? If consumers know that the government has a lot of debt and the government reduces taxes today, what do you think consumers will expect to happen to taxes tomorrow? We will return to this important question below when we introduce the idea of Ricardian equivalence.

A tax rebate is different from a cut in marginal tax *rates*. A rebate means that taxpayers are handed a check—it's just as if your Uncle Sam gives you some cash for your birthday. A rebate does not increase the incentive to invest or work. To increase the incentive to invest or work, the government must cut marginal tax *rates,* the additional tax that must be paid on additional earned income (see Chapter 16 for more on marginal tax rates). Cuts in tax rates as opposed to rebates have *two* expansionary effects, the spending effect and an additional incentive effect from the increased incentive to invest and work.

Consider a temporary investment tax credit. An investment tax credit gives businesses a tax cut or payment if they make an investment in, say, plant or machinery. The tax credit increases the incentive to invest but more importantly it increases the incentive to invest *now,* when times are tough. In other words, a temporary tax credit can accelerate investments that would have happened anyway (intertemporal substitution as we discussed in Chapter 13). In a similar way, a temporary reduction in the payroll tax or in the sales tax can encourage employers to hire more workers and consumers to spend more now—before the tax rises again—in this way increasing aggregate demand. If times are tough, this may be worthwhile.

A Special Case of Crowding Out: Ricardian Equivalence A tax cut opens the possibility of a special type of crowding out. If we hold government spending constant through time, then a tax cut today must be matched by a tax increase in the future. But if people recognize and understand that lower taxes today are *equivalent* to higher taxes tomorrow, then lower taxes today won't increase aggregate demand.

Imagine that people are patient and very forward-looking. When the government cuts taxes today, these people realize that this means higher taxes in the future. These far-sighted people will plan accordingly and save more today. Basically, they are saving more so that the future tax payments don't cause them to give up familiar habits or move into old-age poverty; this "consumption smoothing" was explained in Chapter 8.

Ricardian equivalence occurs when people see that lower taxes today means higher taxes in the future, so instead of spending their tax cut they save it to pay future taxes. When Ricardian equivalence holds, a tax cut doesn't increase aggregate demand even in the short run.

Is the Ricardian equivalence realistic?

"I got a tax cut this year, son. But that means that your taxes will be going up in the future so I'm going to save more."

If people save their tax cut instead of spending it, the aggregate demand curve does not shift to the right and there are no systematic macroeconomic effects. This scenario is sometimes called **Ricardian equivalence,** after the nineteenth-century British economist David Ricardo.

Most economists think it is unrealistic to stipulate that people understand their future tax burden and save accordingly to offset future tax burdens. Tyler *knows* that *he* doesn't behave this way (and he's a trained economist), but he does see some signs of this behavior from Alex. So Ricardian equivalence probably describes some people but not most people. In any case, to the extent that Ricardian equivalence reflects how people plan, bond-financed tax cuts are less effective in the short run than otherwise.

We've run through a few different cases. It is convenient to sum them up in the form of a diagram in Figure 17.3.

FIGURE 17.3

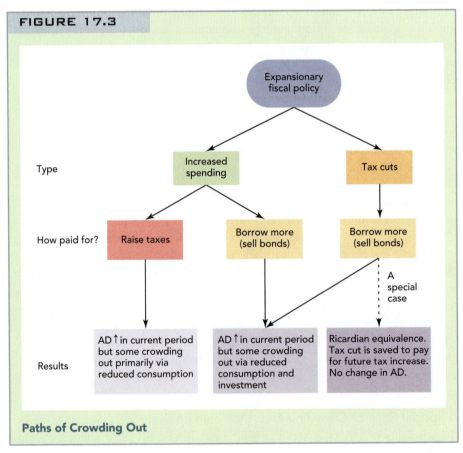

Paths of Crowding Out

Figure 17.3 reminds us that expansionary fiscal policy can consist of either increased spending or tax cuts and this policy can be paid for with either higher taxes or borrowing. Higher taxes reduce private spending, which means that some of the increased government spending has crowded out private spending. If the government borrows the money, some crowding out will still occur as private investment and private consumption fall. If Ricardian equivalence holds, then increased government borrowing to finance a tax cut will be matched by increased private saving and crowding out will be 100 percent.

A Drop in the Bucket: Can Government Spend Enough to Stimulate Aggregate Demand?

Surprisingly, one of the biggest problems with government spending as a boost to aggregate demand is simply that most changes in government spending are not very large in the short run. If changes to government spending are not large in the short run, the boost to aggregate demand won't be very large either.

In the contemporary United States, changes in fiscal policy, in percentage terms, simply aren't that large in a typical year. Most of the federal budget is determined well in advance and is remarkably stable. As we have seen in the previous chapter, among the largest budget categories are national defense, Social Security, Medicare, and interest on the debt. Those categories alone account for more than 60 percent of spending in a typical year and these programs are more or less on automatic pilot, with their yearly levels of spending set by automatic formulas or by previous agreements or commitments. Non-security federal discretionary spending is less than 20 percent of the federal budget and most of this is not seriously up for grabs in any given year. Government spending, in today's world, simply does not change very much in percentage terms on a year-to-year basis.

The fiscal stimulus plan passed under President Obama in 2009 is the largest fiscal stimulus since military spending rose tremendously during World War II. Even this $800–$900 billion dollar stimulus, however, is spread over 3–4 years so at its peak the stimulus is about 2% of annual GDP. Depending on the balance of the multiplier and crowding out effects, the net increase in spending could be somewhat larger or smaller than 2%. These are large numbers relative to previous stimulus plans but, although significant, they are still modest compared to the total size of the economy. As noted, typical post-World War II stimulus plans are much smaller than 2% of GDP so economists will be carefully evaluating the effects of this historic stimulus.

A Matter of Timing

Bad timing provides another reason why fiscal policy is often not very effective, even in the short run. The United States Constitution stipulates that both Congress and the president must approve all expenditures. There are two houses of Congress, and of course legislation must pass through various committees. Sometimes an emergency stimulus occurs quickly, as in the 2008 case discussed above, which Congress passed a mere two weeks after President Bush requested it. But often the proposed fiscal projects are complicated and the budget cycle takes place over many months or sometimes even years; it can take a long time for new bills to be conceived, written, debated, and passed. Specific expenditures often must be coordinated with state and local governments, or the projects must produce environmental impact statements, or they must survive legal challenges. Even once the money is in place, it takes time to spend it; for instance you can't build a large airport or dam all at once and it doesn't make sense to pay every contractor in advance.

In short, even a single government expenditure can take years to move from dream to reality. Yet fiscal policy is often intended to correct short-term problems in the business cycle. By the time the fiscal policy is in place, macroeconomic conditions often have changed entirely.

The list of relevant lags includes the following:

1. Recognition lag—The problem must be recognized.

2. Legislative lag—Congress must propose and pass a plan.

3. Implementation lag—Bureaucracies must implement the plan.

4. Effectiveness lag—The plan takes time to work.

5. Evaluation and adjustment lag—Did the plan work? Have conditions changed? (Return to lag 1!)

Tax cuts, the other major form of fiscal policy, also involve lags and uncertainties, at least with respect to their role in stimulating aggregate demand.

John F. Kennedy promoted some of the most famous tax cuts in American history, lowering tax rates from 91 percent to 70 percent at the top of the income distribution and from 20 percent to 14 percent at the bottom, with similar cuts applied to the rates in between. Most economists think these changes were a good idea for long-run economic growth, but it is not so clear that they served as effective fiscal policy. These were among the largest tax cuts in the post–World War II era, but even so they were only 1.9 percent of national income, and of course not all of that was spent.

This action was seen as highly decisive at the time, but the lags were significant. The Kennedy tax cuts were discussed in 1961, proposed in 1962, enacted in 1964, and probably had little effect on the economy until 1965–1967. That doesn't imply those tax cuts were a bad idea, but it does show just how slow fiscal policy can be.

President George W. Bush cut marginal tax rates in 2001, 2002, and 2003. The latter tax cuts came quite quickly after a recession loomed following 9/11 (in part because the tax cuts were mostly planned in advance for other reasons). But these tax cuts were not very effective as fiscal policy either. Each cut was less than 1 percent of national income, the economy was already recovering, plus most of the tax cuts went to relatively high-income groups, who tend to save their surplus funds. If we are thinking in terms of fiscal policy alone, tax cuts to the poor would probably result in more spending, except of course, that the poor don't pay that much in taxes.

Unemployment insurance benefits are often extended during a recession. This may be a good idea to help people through tough times, but we should not count on these measures to revive the economy because the total increase in spending relative to the size of the economy is just too small.

Monetary policy is also subject to lags, but these are generally shorter than for fiscal policy. Once the Federal Reserve recognizes a problem, it can act very quickly to implement changes to monetary policy. After 9/11, for example, the Federal Reserve stepped in the next *day* with massive infusions of cash to the banking system. The Federal Reserve can also evaluate and adjust their plan quickly as the economy responds or fails to respond. Fiscal policy, in contrast, is rarely adjusted in response to changes in economic conditions. The only place where fiscal policy might have an advantage over monetary policy is through the effectiveness lag. As we discussed in Chapters 14 and 15, the effectiveness of changes in monetary policy depends on matters like how willing banks are to lend and businesses are to borrow. A spending program, in contrast, typically has a direct impact on economic conditions, at least once the money is put into the economy.

Automatic Stabilizers   Some kinds of fiscal policy are built right into the tax and transfer system, and they do take effect without significant lags; these are called **automatic stabilizers.** Virtually all economists recognize the virtue of automatic stabilizers in keeping aggregate demand on a steady and regular course.

Fiscal policy automatically changes to keep private spending higher during bad economic times. For instance, when the economy is doing poorly, income, capital gains, and corporate profits are all down. As a result, most people and businesses will pay lower taxes and, given that the American tax system is progressive (see Chapter 16), possibly a lower tax rate as well. The lower tax burden makes aggregate demand more robust than it otherwise would be. The lower taxes don't offset the curse of hard times (lowering your taxes by lowering your income is not the preferred way to go) but they soften the blow. Pretax incomes are perhaps falling, but post-tax incomes are not falling by as much.

Welfare and transfer programs also provide automatic stabilizers. When the economy is declining, increasing numbers of people apply for welfare, food stamps, unemployment insurance, and other programs designed to help low-income groups. These groups receive more income, and because of their precarious economic situation, they tend to spend that money pretty quickly. That also helps maintain aggregate demand.

Of course, it is not just fiscal policy that provides automatic stabilizers. When people save during good times and use their savings to tide them over in bad times (consumption smoothing, as we discussed in Chapter 8), it's an automatic stabilizer. Private market innovations, most of all credit, have also contributed to stabilization. Even though the 2008 credit crisis pared back some kinds of borrowing, it is still easier today to take out a second mortgage on one's home than it was 30 years ago. If you need to send your kid to college, you can borrow more rather than cutting your spending ruthlessly. That way you can pay back the money over time, for a smoother adjustment. Credit cards, durable assets, and the increased availability of used goods (eBay), and discount outlets, all allow the economy to weather hard times more easily than before.

> **Automatic stabilizers** are changes in fiscal policy that stimulate AD in a recession without the need for explicit action by policymakers.

Government Spending versus Tax Cuts as Expansionary Fiscal Policy

Before turning to the last limit on fiscal policy, the fact that fiscal policy does not work well with real shocks, let's briefly examine the differences between the two types of fiscal policy we have discussed, namely government spending and tax cuts. The differences between these types of fiscal policy are political and also economic. Let's discuss the political differences first.

A tax cut or tax rebate puts more spending in the hands of the private sector while an increase in government spending puts more spending in the hands of the government. People who are skeptical about government spending typically prefer fiscal policy to work through tax rebates and tax cuts rather than through changes in government spending.

Consider the infamous "Bridge to Nowhere," a proposed bridge in Alaska that was to connect the town of Ketchikan (population 8,900) with its airport on the Island of Gravina (population 50) at a cost to federal taxpayers of $320 million. At present, a ferry service runs to the island, but some people in the

Fiscal policy that we don't want.

town complain that it costs too much ($6 per car). If the town's residents had to pay the $320 million cost of the bridge themselves—that's $35,754 each!—do you think they would want the bridge? Of course not, so if the bridge is ever built, it may raise measured GDP but the costs will still exceed the benefits. That is a type of fiscal policy that we don't want.

On the other hand, people who think that the U.S. government is not spending enough will tend to prefer that fiscal policy work through spending increases. The U.S. highway system is generally regarded as a highly productive investment of capital. If we can find equally productive public investments such as improvements to schools, science funding, and infrastructure ("bridges to somewhere"), then the case for public investment is strong and if we can time these spending increases to help offset a recession so much the better.

Do you recall our opening example? It's a useful illustration of the political differences over fiscal policy. George Bush and Barack Obama both used expansionary fiscal policy to fight a recession but Bush, a Republican, focused on tax cuts while Obama, a Democrat, focused on government spending.

What about the economic differences? A disadvantage of tax cuts that we have already mentioned is that tax cuts don't necessarily lead to new spending if consumers save their new money. In contrast, government spending is spending by definition and thus has a more certain influence. Tax cuts, however, can usually happen more quickly than new government spending since with a tax cut the government doesn't have to decide what to spend the money on. Government spending can sometimes also happen quickly, but when it happens too quickly, we have to worry that it may not be well spent.

Fiscal Policy Does Not Work Well to Combat Real Shocks

We have assumed so far that the problem fiscal policy needs to address is a deficiency in aggregate demand. But imagine, for example, that the recession is caused not by a fall in $\vec{C}$, but by a real shock that reduces the productivity of capital and labor, shifting the Solow growth curve to the left. In Figure 17.4, for example, a real shock shifts the Solow growth curve to the left, moving the economy from point a to point b.

As before, the economy is in a recession at point b. Now suppose that government responds by increasing $\vec{G}$. As usual, the aggregate demand curve shifts out, but now the economy is less productive than before, due to the real shock. As a result, an increase in $\vec{G}$ will not move the economy back to point a. Instead, most of the increase in $\vec{G}$ will show up in inflation rather than in real growth so the economy will shift from point b to point c with a much higher inflation rate and a slightly higher growth rate. As you may recall, the analysis is very similar to the analysis of monetary policy when facing a real shock.

In fact, the situation for fiscal policy is worse than Figure 17.4 indicates because when the problem an economy faces is a real shock, there is no inefficiency. Thus, unlike in Figure 17.1, the increase in $\vec{G}$ is unlikely to create much new growth and most of (perhaps even all of) $\vec{G}$ will *crowd out* other spending. (Another way of seeing this is to remember that the Solow growth curve shows the real rate of growth when the economy is operating at its full potential and neither fiscal nor monetary policy can increase the growth rate above the Solow

FIGURE 17.4

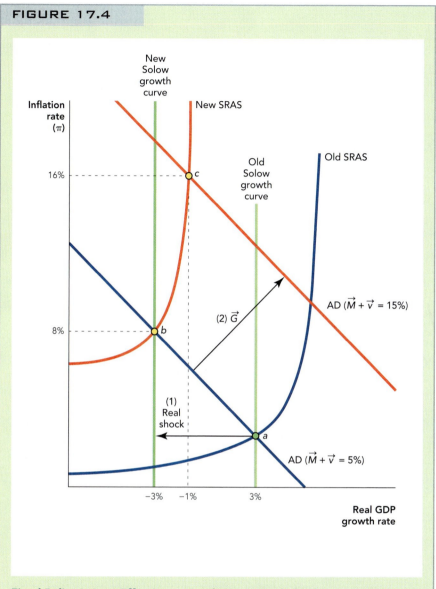

Fiscal Policy Is Less Effective at Combating a Real Shock A real shock shifts the Solow growth curve to the left (Step 1), moving the economy from point *a* to a recession at point *b*. To combat the recession, the government increases $\vec{G}$ (Step 2) but due to the real shock the economy is now less productive than before, and so the increase in aggregate demand shifts the economy to point *c* where the growth rate is a little bit higher but the inflation rate is much higher.

rate for very long.) As a result of crowding out, the situation is more likely to be like that in Figure 17.5 on the next page where an increase in $\vec{G}$ at best moves the economy from point *b* to point *d*, where the growth rate is only slightly higher than it would have been without fiscal policy.

The economy is subject to both aggregate demand shocks and real shocks. John Maynard Keynes, the economist who first hammered home the importance of fiscal policy in response to an aggregate demand shock, called his theory and book, *The General Theory*. Keynes was a brilliant, path-breaking economist, one of the greatest of all time, but after many decades of debate

FIGURE 17.5

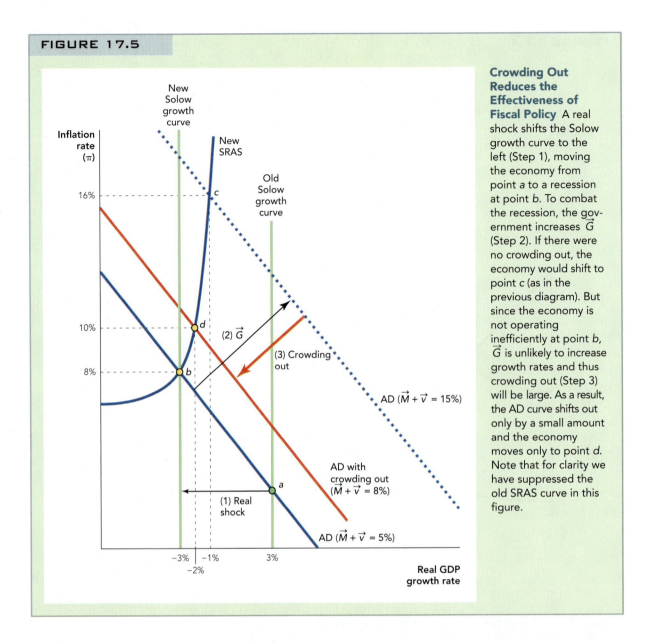

Crowding Out Reduces the Effectiveness of Fiscal Policy A real shock shifts the Solow growth curve to the left (Step 1), moving the economy from point *a* to a recession at point *b*. To combat the recession, the government increases $\vec{G}$ (Step 2). If there were no crowding out, the economy would shift to point *c* (as in the previous diagram). But since the economy is not operating inefficiently at point *b*, $\vec{G}$ is unlikely to increase growth rates and thus crowding out (Step 3) will be large. As a result, the AD curve shifts out only by a small amount and the economy moves only to point *d*. Note that for clarity we have suppressed the old SRAS curve in this figure.

most economists today think a better title for his book would have been *The Special Theory*. Since some recessions are driven by real shocks, fiscal policy will not always be an effective method of combating a recession.

When Fiscal Policy Might Make Matters Worse

If expansionary fiscal policy is paid for by borrowing, taxes will rise in the future. When taxes rise, people will have less money to spend and aggregate demand will fall. Ideal fiscal policy will increase AD in bad times and pay off the bill in good times. Unfortunately, governments often find it easier to increase spending in bad times than they do to increase taxes in good times. As a result, there are deficits in most years and the total debt grows larger, as we discussed in Chapter 16. When the debt is large, governments must spend a large fraction of their budget on interest payments alone. This usually means there is less room for expansionary fiscal policy when it is needed.

CHECK YOURSELF

> What happened to make the 2008 Bush tax rebate less powerful than anticipated?

> Explain why a permanent cut in income tax rates can create a larger fiscal stimulus than a temporary cut.

> Keeping your answer to the previous question in mind, why does a permanent investment tax credit create a *smaller* fiscal stimulus than a temporary investment tax credit?

In extreme situations, debt can be such a problem that *expansionary fiscal policy can reduce real growth*. Some countries are so heavily in debt that any more government borrowing runs the risk of total economic collapse. Take for instance Argentina, which had a major financial crisis in the 1999–2002 period; in those years, Argentine GDP fell by rates of −3.4 percent, −0.8 percent, −4.4 percent, and −10.9 percent, respectively.[1] That's not a good record. In the years leading up to this collapse, the Argentine government spent more and more, and did not pay off its bills. By 2002, Argentine government debt was 150 percent of GDP, a very high level. (For purposes of contrast, the U.S. federal government has net debt of about 50 percent of GDP although that level is rising.) The Argentine government could not pay off these debts and the final result was the largest default by a government in the history of the world.

In the years leading up to the collapse, many investors feared that the Argentine currency would lose most of its value and that the economy would fall apart. More government spending led to more anxiety, rather than economic stimulation.

So, in this setting, if the government increases spending, aggregate demand does not go up. Instead private spending and production fall by so much that real GDP falls (i.e., more than 100 percent crowding out!). Aggregate demand falls because in times of great uncertainty, people save or hoard their money in anticipation of hard times ahead. In the case of Argentina, people put their wealth into bank accounts in Miami or Switzerland, rather than investing it at home or spending it in the shops of Buenos Aires. Of course, that flight of capital only hastened the economic collapse.

We've mentioned Argentina, but similar scenarios (the details differ) have occurred in many other lesser developed nations, including Thailand, Indonesia, and Mexico. The lesson is this: Too high of a debt can drive a nation to ruin by undercutting the credibility of everything a government does and whether that government can meet its commitments. The United States isn't in that position at this time, but if you wish to understand global events, you need to realize that fiscal policy has an immediate negative effect in many economic situations, especially when the credibility of the government is low.

So When Is Fiscal Policy a Good Idea?

The macroeconomic case for government spending is strongest when the government faces some immediate emergency, such as a war, a worsening depression, or a natural disaster. Government spending is best for the macroeconomy when it is worth incurring some long-run costs to get a short-run economic boost.

It is also the case—as with monetary policy—that fiscal policy is most effective when the relevant shock is to aggregate demand and there are many unemployed resources. For these reasons, most economists look back on the Great Depression of the 1930s and see expansionary fiscal policy as a good idea in that setting. As we saw in Chapter 12, the Great Depression was primarily caused by a reduction in aggregate demand rather than by a productivity shock, so increasing aggregate demand was the right type of solution.

Furthermore, at the time, rates of unemployment were sometimes as high as 25 percent, which meant that the degree of crowding out was probably not very large. Let's say that the federal government hires some workers to build a dam. If the government is simply pulling already-employed workers from other

When unemployment is at 25% there is less private spending to crowd out.

jobs, we shouldn't expect this to help the economy much. But if those people otherwise would have been out of work, we should expect a greater economic stimulus in the short term. In other words, when it comes to these workers, the government investment is not crowding out alternative private investments. The government investment is creating economic activity in addition to private investments.

In addition, the increase in government spending during the Great Depression was relatively rapid and quite dramatic in percentage terms. Roosevelt, the architect of the New Deal, won the election in 1932. By 1936, federal government spending was more than twice what it had been in 1932.

Notice that today rates of unemployment range more often between 4 percent and 8 percent so increased government spending is likely to draw people from one job to another job rather than from unemployment to work. It would also be more difficult for the federal government to increase spending by as large a percentage as it did in the 1930s. So for these reasons, fiscal policy is less likely to be successful today than it was in the 1930s, and crowding out is more likely to happen.[2]

In spite of short-term gains, the aggregate demand effects of more government spending do not boost the long-term growth rate. Expansionary fiscal policy is best thought of as a way to deliver a short-term boost to an ailing economy.

So let's sum up when fiscal policy is most likely to matter:

1. When the economy needs a short-run boost, even at the expense of the long run.

2. When the problem is a deficiency in aggregate demand rather than a real shock.

3. When many resources are unemployed.

□ Takeaway

Fiscal policy is most effective in times of emergency, when there are unemployed resources due to a fall in aggregate demand, and when the economy needs an immediate short-term boost. In contrast, fiscal policy is not usually a good means of boosting long-term growth.

Even for macroeconomic purposes, fiscal policy sometimes doesn't work. "Crowding out"—the replacement of private spending by government spending—sometimes means that fiscal policy isn't very effective. Furthermore, if people worry a great deal about their future tax burdens, fiscal policy driven by tax cuts will not be very effective. Most important, most changes in government spending aren't big enough, or quick enough, to have significant and positive macroeconomic impact.

Other forms of fiscal policy are less visible. Automatic stabilizers, built into the tax and transfer systems, help to stabilize aggregate demand.

Some countries, especially some of the world's poorer countries, take fiscal policy too far. They accumulate very large levels of debt. The finances, currencies, and sometimes even the governments of those countries become unstable. Even if good fiscal policy doesn't always do a lot of good, bad fiscal policy can do a great deal of harm.

□ CHAPTER REVIEW

KEY CONCEPTS

Fiscal policy, p. 359

Multiplier effect, p. 362

Crowding out, p. 363

Ricardian equivalence, p. 366

Automatic stabilizers, p. 369

FACTS AND TOOLS

1. What shifts AD to the left: a rise in taxes or a cut in taxes? Does this push $\overrightarrow{v}$ up or push it down?

2. Let's see what the "three difficulties with using fiscal policy" look like in real life. Categorize each of the three stories below as either 1) Crowding out, 2) A drop in the bucket or 3) A matter of timing.

   a. During a recession, the State of New York hires 1,000 new trash collectors. The state legislature in Albany takes six months to pass a law to hire the new trash collectors, and because of government rules and paperwork, the government actually hires the workers 18 months after the recession has begun.

   b. During a recession, the State of New York hires 1,000 new trash collectors. Five hundred of the new trash collectors, however, were just people who quit their jobs as restaurant employees in order to take the better-paying trash collector jobs.

   c. During a recession, the State of New York hires 1,000 new trash collectors. However, during the course of the recession, 300,000 additional people in New York lose their jobs.

3. When people "buy government bonds," are they borrowing money or saving money?

4. Imagine you live in the land of Ricardia, where every citizen is a Ricardian and thus "Ricardian equivalence" is 100 percent true. Government spending never changes in Ricardia: It's a fixed amount every year. Thus, when the Ricardian government cuts taxes, it has to pay for the government spending by borrowing more money and raising future taxes to repay the debt.

   a. When Ricardian income taxes are cut, what will Ricardian citizens do with the extra money in their paycheck: Will they spend all of it, save all of it, or spend some and save the rest?

   b. Suppose that instead of a tax cut, the Ricardian government just sends citizens "rebate" checks. What will Ricardian citizens do with the extra money from these rebate checks: Will they spend all of it, save all of it, or spend some and save the rest?

5. It's often very difficult to get the timing of fiscal policy right. In this chapter, we listed five relevant lags.

   a. If each of the lags lasts three months, is the total lag longer or shorter than the typical recession since World War II? Data on the length of recessions is here: http://www.nber.org/cycles.html. Look at the bottom of the column titled "Contraction."

   b. Of the five lags, the last one only involves watching how things turned out. If there are only four important lags, and they last three months each, will the average recession last longer than the average fiscal policy lag?

6. You're flipping through the newspaper, reading about shocks that have hit the U.S. economy and reading what Congress is planning to do about the shocks. (Remember that "shocks" can be either good or bad.) Is Congress even getting the direction of its response right? And if it is getting the basic direction correct, is it fighting against a Solow growth shock, where a fiscal response may not be very effective? While these policy choices will each have effects on long-run growth and on income distribution, in this chapter you should only focus on the effect on aggregate demand. Fit each of the following cases into one of three categories:

   1. Wrong direction

   2. Correct direction for an AD shock

   3. Correct direction for a Solow growth shock, but expect a big change in inflation

   a. Many banks have failed, and the money supply has fallen. In response, Congress decides to raise income taxes to pay down the federal debt. (Historical note: This policy response was similar to FDR's campaign platform when he ran for president in 1932.)

b. Many banks have failed, and the money supply has fallen. In response, Congress decides to cut back on government purchases to save money.

c. A wave of investor euphoria ("irrational exuberance") about the Internet has increased spending growth. Congress raises income taxes on the richest Americans in response.

d. Oil prices double over the course of a year, from $2 per gallon to $4 per gallon. In response, Congress sends $300 checks to every American family so that people can better afford to pay for gas.

e. Oil prices double over the course of a year, from $2 per gallon to $4 per gallon. In response, Congress raises taxes on companies that refine and deliver petroleum products.

f. The Federal Reserve has followed a slow-money-growth policy, despite the wishes of Congress. In response, Congress cuts taxes and increases government purchases.

7. Which of the following is an "automatic stabilizer" in the U.S. economy? There may be more than one:

a. Consumers usually spend some of their savings and eat food from the pantry during recessions.

b. Business owners usually purchase more capital equipment whenever profits fall.

c. Governments automatically transfer cash to the unemployed when the economy is weak.

d. When Americans have less demand for U.S-manufactured products, foreigners might pick up some of the slack, buying these unsold U.S.-made goods.

8. Why was the Great Depression an especially appropriate time to use fiscal policy rather than just monetary policy alone?

9. U.S. net government debt is about 50 percent of GDP. If it rose to 100 percent of GDP, and the interest rate on the debt were 5 percent (not far from the truth at present), then what fraction of U.S. GDP would go toward paying interest on the debt? (Note: After World War II, U.S. debt was greater than 100 percent of GDP.)

10. Which kind of aggregate demand shift has fewer lags: changes in monetary policy or changes in fiscal policy?

THINKING AND PROBLEM SOLVING

1. a. In the chapter, we wrote that Tyler does not save and plan according to the theory of Ricardian equivalence but Alex is more of a "Ricardian." In light of this, who probably cuts back their spending the most when their taxes temporarily rise: someone like Tyler who is not "Ricardian" or someone like Alex who is?

b. If the U.S. government wants to use fiscal policy to shift AD around easily, which one would the U.S. government prefer to make more copies of: Tyler or Alex?

2. Using the figure below, suppose that a change in fiscal policy shifts AD from AD(1) to AD(2). Which response below would be most likely to cause that shift? Choose one of a, b, c, or d.

a. A rise in taxes OR a rise in government spending

b. A rise in taxes OR a fall in government spending

c. A fall in taxes OR a rise in government spending

d. A fall in taxes OR a fall in government spending

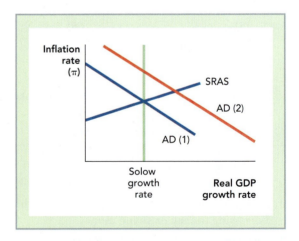

3. Consider the figure below. Suppose that there's a rise in $\vec{v}$ due to business optimism—what Keynes called the "animal spirits" of investors. This pushes us to AD(2). If the government's goal is to keep output close to the Solow growth rate, and if fiscal policy is the tool that the government wants to use, what should it do? Choose one of a, b, c, or d.

a. A rise in taxes OR a rise in government spending

b. A rise in taxes OR a fall in government spending

c. A fall in taxes OR a rise in government spending

d. A fall in taxes OR a fall in government spending

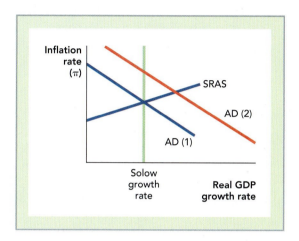

4. Consider the following imaginary newspaper quote, the type that you often read when Congress passes a tax rebate during a recession:

   "Many Americans report that they will put the tax rebate straight into their savings accounts or use it to pay off credit cards that they maxed out during the recent economic boom."

   If Congress is trying to shift AD to the right, are these kinds of quotes good news or bad news from Congress's point of view?

5. Which of the following government policies are "automatic stabilizers" for the economy?

   Unemployment insurance

   Temporary tax cuts that Congress passes when bad economic news hits

   Temporary spending increases that Congress passes when bad economic news hits

6. **a.** Which policy is likely to shift aggregate demand more? In which direction will it shift?

   A tax increase that occurs in the same year as a spending increase

   A tax increase that occurs without a spending increase

   b. Why is this so?

7. Ricardian equivalence is the idea that people might just use the extra money from their tax cuts to buy the very government bonds that pay for the tax cut. Let's think about the opposite situation: If Ricardian equivalence is true, and the government *raises* taxes (holding spending constant), how does the average person's behavior change? In other words, how do they react to a tax increase?

8. Again, think about the extreme case of crowding out known as Ricardian equivalence. In real life, few citizens buy or sell government bonds directly; instead, normal people put their money in a bank (or invest it in a mutual fund), and then their bank (or mutual fund) uses that money to buy government bonds.

   a. So does a tax cut mean banks will get more deposits, fewer deposits, or can't you tell with the information given?

   b. How will the average bank's behavior change as a result of this tax cut, taking your response to part a into account?

9. We discussed three situations where fiscal policy is most likely to matter (though fiscal policy is best when *all* three are true):

   1. When the economy needs a short-run boost.

   2. When the problem is low AD, not low Solow growth.

   3. When many machines and workers are unemployed.

   Let's fit each of the following news stories into one (or more) of the above categories.

   a. World War II ends, and millions of U.S. soldiers return home. (Note: As a matter of history, returning WWII soldiers were overwhelmingly employed by the private sector.)

   b. Consumption spending declines dramatically as people fear a recession.

   c. Foreigners decide they are unwilling to buy U.S.-made airplanes because of rumors they read on the Internet.

10. Fiscal policy cannot cure all ills. Sometimes:

    X. The economy needs a long-run boost.

    Y. The problem isn't low AD, but low Solow growth.

    Z. Almost all machines and workers are employed; they're just not very productive.

Sort the following cases into either "fiscal solution possible" or "productivity problem."

a. American wages have grown slowly for many years.

b. Peasants in the Middle Ages are using primitive tools to produce food.

c. Peasants in the Middle Ages suffer from a drought that hurts the season's crops.

d. American workers get laid off by the hundreds of thousands because of a rapid collapse in investment purchases.

e. Schools are doing a bad job teaching students, so students become ineffective employees.

f. High taxes on investment discourage people from saving and building up the capital stock for future workers to use.

g. High taxes on investment discourage businesses from purchasing investment goods.

CHALLENGES

1. When we discussed unemployment in Chapter 10, we noted that people will search a long time to find a good job. So it might only take you two weeks to find a minimum wage job, but it might take you six months to find a job paying five times the minimum wage. Let's investigate how this simple fact might cause expansionary fiscal policy to *increase* the unemployment rate, at least temporarily.

In the United States, federal contracts to build roads, bridges, or buildings must pay higher-than-average wages. The law requiring this is known as the Davis-Bacon Act, or the "prevailing wage law."

a. If the unemployment rate is 6 percent before a rise in government purchases, and if a rise in government purchases induces the typical unemployed person to search 10 percent longer in the hopes of finding a high-paying government job, what will the value of the unemployment rate be after the rise in government purchases? Only consider the impact of this waiting-for-a-good-job effect.

b. If the government wanted to get the good aggregate-demand stimulating effects of fiscal policy, but wanted to eliminate this extra waiting-for-a-good-job unemployment, how could it change current law to do so?

2. Nobel Laureate Amartya Sen has pointed out that one way to prevent starvation during droughts in the poorest countries is to just pay peasants to build roads, sewer lines, and other public goods during these droughts. In the poorest countries, these peasants have no savings accounts, and almost no way to borrow money. In rich countries by contrast, most people have savings accounts and credit cards.

a. Is the poor-country "multiplier" probably bigger or smaller than the rich-country multiplier, based on these facts?

b. All countries get hit by shocks, but not all countries have the same automatic stabilizers. Based on these facts, which countries probably have smoother GDP growth: Poor countries or rich countries? (Note: The answer that is true in theory is also true in practice, a point emphasized in a 1995 paper in the *American Economic Review* by Garey and Valerie Ramey, "Cross-Country Evidence on the Link between Volatility and Growth.")

3. If the U.S. government wanted to, it could just say that everyone who gets an unemployment insurance check is "employed in searching for a job," and the government could claim that these government employees are producing "job search services." Recall that in the official definition of GDP, government *purchases (G),* do not include *transfer payments* like unemployment checks and Social Security.

a. Would this change in the definition of GDP increase GDP? Would it improve well-being?

b. If the government permanently defined unemployed people as "employed in job search," then over the course of a few decades as the economy fluctuated, would GDP look more volatile or less volatile than it does under the regular definition? (Hint: You might find it easier to answer if you consider GDP from the "factor income" perspective.)

4. We usually think about crowding out as a decrease in private consumption or investment in response to an increase in government purchases. But the idea works in reverse as well, an idea we might call "crowding in." Consider the economy below.

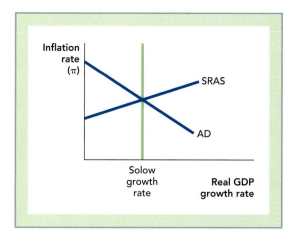

a. Starting from this initial position, the economy is hit by one shock: A large *decrease* in government purchases, perhaps caused by the end of a war. Holding the growth of C, I, and NX constant for a moment, illustrate this shock above, labeling the change "Fall in growth of G."

b. Now consider a possible side effect of the fall in the growth of G: the reversal of crowding out or crowding in. If there is 100 percent crowding in what happens to the AD shift you described in part a?

c. If there were 100 percent crowding out/in and no multiplier effect, what can we say about the effect of a change in the growth of G on aggregate demand?

d. Consider all of the laid-off government workers in this question: If there were 100 percent crowding out/in and no multiplier effect, where do these laid-off workers end up?

5. According to recent estimates by Susan Woodward and Robert Hall, an extra dollar of government purchases raises GDP by one dollar—so there is little evidence for a "multiplier effect" in the short run, but also little evidence for "crowding out" in the short run. (Perhaps both effects are at work, but they just happen to balance out in practice.) Let's use these estimates as a rule of thumb to solve the following economic puzzles:

a. U.S. GDP is about $14 trillion. In a typical recession, GDP is about 2 percent below the Solow growth rate. If Congress wants to return GDP to the Solow growth rate by increasing government purchases, how big a rise in government purchases should it enact? Give your answer in dollars.

b. Canadian GDP is about $1.2 trillion (U.S. dollars). If Canadian GDP is 3 percent above its Solow growth rate, and the Canadian Parliament wants to change government purchases to return to the Solow growth rate, what change in government purchases should it enact, measured in U.S. dollars?

c. How do your answers to parts a and b change if there's stronger crowding out, and the multiplier falls to 0.5? (In other words, a rise in G of $1 raises GDP by only $0.50.) Answer in U.S. dollars.

d. How do your answers to parts a and b change if there's a bigger multiplier effect on consumer spending, and the multiplier rises to 2? (In other words, a rise in G of $1 raises GDP by $2.) Answer in U.S. dollars.

18

International Trade

Economics textbooks should never have chapters on "International Trade." The word "international" suggests that international trade is a special type of trade requiring new principles and arguments. But when Joe and Frank trade, Joe and Frank are made better off. When Joe and Francisco trade, Joe and Francisco are made better off. The politics are different but the economics doesn't change much if Frank lives in El Paso and Francisco lives in Ciudad Juarez. International trade is trade. Thus, the real subject of this chapter is the economics of trade and the politics of international trade. We begin by asking "why trade?" We then explain how trade can be analyzed using the tools you already know, namely demand and supply. We close by evaluating some of the arguments, both economic and political, against international trade.

Why Trade?

We will focus on three benefits of trade:

> The division of knowledge

> Economies of scale and creating competition

> Comparative advantage

The Division of Knowledge

Without trade, civilization would collapse and billions of people would starve. How long could you survive if you had to grow your own food? Yet most of us can make enough money in a day to buy more food than we could grow in a year. *Specialization* followed by trade vastly increases productivity. Why? Farmers have two immense advantages in producing food compared to economics

Contra Episode 61, even Spock's brain could not come close to running a modern economy. For this reason, some economists consider "Spock's Brain" to be the worst *Star Trek* episode *ever*.

Reducing trade barriers, Berlin 1989

professors or students: they know more about farming and they can afford to buy large-scale farming machines. Both of these advantages flow from specialization and trade.

The human brain is limited and there is much to know. Thus, it makes sense to divide knowledge across many brains and then trade. In a primitive agricultural economy in which each person or household farms for themselves, each person has about the same knowledge as the person next door. In this case, the combined knowledge of a society of one million people barely exceeds that of a single person.[1] A society run with the knowledge of one brain is a poor and miserable society.

In a modern economy, many millions of times more knowledge is used than could exist in a single brain. In the United States, for example, we don't just have doctors—we have neurologists, cardiologists, gastroenterologists, gynecologists, and urologists, to name just a few of the many specializations in medicine. Knowledge increases productivity so specialization increases total output. All of this knowledge is productive, however, only because each person can specialize in the production of one good and then trade for all other desired goods. Without trade, specialization is impossible.

The extent of specialization in a modern economy explains why no one knows the full details of how even the simplest product is produced. A Valentine's Day rose may have been grown in Kenya, flown to Amsterdam on refrigerated airplanes, and trucked to Topeka by drivers staying awake with Colombian coffee. Each person in this process knows only a small part of the whole but with trade and market coordination, they each do their part and the rose is delivered without anyone needing to understand the whole process.

The extent of specialization in modern society is remarkable. We have already mentioned the many specializations in medicine. We also have dog walkers, closet organizers, and manicurists. It's common to dismiss the latter jobs as frivolous, but trade connects all markets. It's the dog walkers, closet organizers, and manicurists who give the otolaryngologists—specialists in the nose, ear, and throat—the time they need to perfect their skills.

The division of knowledge increases with the extent of the market. Economic growth in the modern era is primarily due to the creation of new knowledge. Thus, one of the most momentous turning points in the division of knowledge happens when trade is extensive enough to support large numbers of scientists, engineers, and entrepreneurs, all of whom specialize in producing new knowledge.

Consider the many ideas and innovations that make life better, from antibiotics, to high-yield, disease-resistant wheat, to the semiconductor. Insofar as those goods have originated in one place and then been spread around the world, improving the lives of millions or billions, it is because of trade.

Every increase in world trade is an opportunity to increase the division of knowledge and extend the power of the human mind. During the communist era, for example, China was like an island cut off from the world economy: one billion people who neither traded many goods nor many ideas with the rest of the world. The fall of the Berlin Wall and the opening to the world economy of China, Russia, Eastern Europe, and other nations greatly adds to the productive stock of scientists and engineers and is one of the most promising signs for the future of the world. Billions of minds have been added to the division of knowledge and cooperation has been extended further around the world than ever before.

Economies of Scale and Creating Competition

One way that specialization and trade increase total production is by increasing knowledge. Specialization and trade also make it profitable to use specialized machines. A person who must grow his own wheat and bake his own bread cannot afford a combine thresher or ovens that bake bread in assembly line fashion. A combine thresher that speeds the separation of grain from husk by 20 percent, for example, isn't worth the expense when you have just 10 acres to thresh, but at 1,000 acres, the savings can be significant. Similarly, the cost per loaf of bread is lower when 25,000 loaves of bread are produced an hour, as is true in a modern bakery, than when 100 loaves of bread are produced in a day. By specializing and trading, people can take advantage of the cost savings associated with large-scale production. Economists call those cost savings **economies of scale.**

Taking advantage of economies of scale is one reason why many European countries have joined the European Union (EU), an agreement to remove many trade barriers between member nations by creating a single market. The EU was inspired by the creation of a single market called the "United States" by the original American states and it has many of the same benefits. It makes no more sense for every country to have its own automobile or aircraft manufacturer than it does for every U.S. state to have its own auto and aircraft manufacturer. Instead, by forming a single market, countries in the EU can specialize and every country can benefit from the cost savings that occur when automobiles and aircraft are produced with specialized, large-scale production techniques.

Economies of scale are closely related to another advantage of international trade, creating competition. If an industry enjoys large economies of scale but trade barriers prevent competition from foreign producers, there will be only a few domestic firms. Without foreign competition, these firms will have the ability to raise prices and reduce output.

In the 1980s, for example, so-called voluntary export restraints reduced imports of Japanese automobiles into the United States. As a result, U.S. consumers had to pay more for Japanese automobiles, about $1,300 extra. But it wasn't only buyers of Japanese automobiles who faced higher prices. Buyers of domestic automobiles also had to pay more, about $660 more per car. Prices of domestic cars increased because GM, Ford, and Chrysler knew that with less pressure from international competition, they could increase prices. The profits of the big three went up during this period and consumers bore the costs.

International trade keeps domestic firms competitive and on their toes. Interestingly, so long as domestic firms know that foreign firms stand ready to compete, domestic firms cannot raise their prices by much. Thus, consumers can benefit from a free trade policy even if no trade actually occurs!

Comparative Advantage

A third reason to trade is to take advantage of differences. Brazil, for example, has a climate ideally suited to growing sugar cane, China has an abundance of low-skilled workers, and the United States has one of the best-educated workforces in the world. Taking advantage of these differences suggests that world production can be maximized when Brazil produces sugar, China assembles iPods, and the United States devotes its efforts to designing the next generation of electronic devices.

> **Economies of scale** mean that costs per unit fall with increases in production.

Absolute advantage is the ability to produce the same good using fewer inputs than another producer.

Comparative advantage: It's a good thing

Martha Stewart may be the world's best ironer but she doesn't do her own ironing. Every hour Martha spends ironing is an hour less she has to run her billion-dollar business. The cost of ironing is too high for Martha Stewart, even if she is the world's best.

Martha can be most productive if she does what she does *most* best.

Taking advantage of differences is even more powerful than it looks. We say that a country has an **absolute advantage** in production if it can produce the same good using fewer inputs than another country. But to benefit from trade, a country need not have an absolute advantage in production. For example, even if the United States did have the world's best climate for growing sugar, it might still make sense for Brazil to grow sugar and for the United States to design iPods, if the U.S. had a bigger advantage in designing iPods than it did in growing sugar.

Here's another example of what economists call comparative advantage. Martha Stewart doesn't do her own ironing. Why not? Martha Stewart may in fact be the world's best ironer but she is also good at running her business. If Martha spent more time ironing and less time running her business, her blouses might be pressed more precisely but that would be a small gain compared to the loss from having someone else run her business. It's better for Martha if she specializes in running her business and then trades some of her income for other goods, such as ironing services, and of course many other goods and services as well.

The idea of comparative advantage is subtle but important. In order to give a precise definition, let's explore comparative advantage using a simple model. Suppose that there are just two goods, computers and shirts, and one input, labor. Assume that in Mexico, it takes 12 units of labor to make one computer and 2 units of labor to produce one shirt, and in the United States it takes 1 unit of labor to produce either good. Notice that the United States can produce both computers and shirts using less labor than in Mexico. Thus, in this example, the United States has an absolute advantage in both computers and shirts. Table 18.1 summarizes.

Since the United States can produce computers and shirts using less labor than Mexico, it's natural to wonder whether the United States has anything to gain from trade with its less productive neighbor. Mexicans may similarly wonder whether they have everything to lose from trading with their more productive neighbor. Both of these fears are unfounded. Mexico and the United States can each benefit from trade. Let's see how.

First, let's use the information in Table 18.1 to calculate the cost of shirts and computers. But remember from Chapter 2 that the real cost of producing a good is not the money cost but the *opportunity cost,* the best alternative that society must give up to get the good. Thus, we will calculate the opportunity cost of shirts and computers. We begin with shirts in the United States because that case is easy and requires only some easy-to-use ratios. The United States can produce one additional shirt by producing one less computer so the opportunity cost of a shirt in the United States is one computer.

What about Mexico? Mexico can produce an additional shirt by producing one-sixth less of a computer. In other words, by moving 2 units of labor—which could produce one-sixth of a computer—from computer production to shirt production, Mexico can produce one additional shirt.

Now here is the key. The (opportunity) cost of a shirt in the United States is one computer but the (opportunity) cost of a shirt in Mexico is just one-sixth of a computer. Thus, even though Mexico is less productive than the United States, Mexico has a lower cost of producing shirts! Since Mexico has the lowest opportunity cost of producing shirts, we say that Mexico has a **comparative advantage** in producing shirts.

TABLE 18.1 Labor Units Required to Produce Computers and Shirts in Mexico and the United States

	1 Computer	1 Shirt
Mexico	12	2
United States	1	1

A country has a **comparative advantage** in producing goods for which it has the lowest opportunity cost.

Now let's look at the opportunity cost of producing computers. Again, the trade-off for the United States is easy to see: It can produce one additional computer by giving up one shirt so the cost of one computer is one shirt. But to produce one additional computer in Mexico requires giving up six shirts! Thus, the United States has the lowest cost of producing computers or, economists say, it has a comparative advantage in producing computers. Table 18.2 summarizes.

We now know that the United States has a high cost of producing shirts and a low cost of producing computers. In Mexico, it's the reverse: Mexico has a low cost of producing shirts and a high cost of producing computers.

The theory of comparative advantage says that to increase its wealth a country should produce the goods it can make at low cost and buy what it can make only at high cost. Thus, the theory says the United States should make computers and buy shirts. Similarly, the theory says that Mexico should make shirts and buy computers. Let's use some numbers to see whether the theory holds up in our example.

Suppose that both Mexico and the United States have 24 units of labor and they each devote 12 units to producing computers and 12 units to producing shirts. Using the figures from Table 18.1, we can see that Mexico will produce one computer and six shirts and the United States will produce 12 computers and 12 shirts. At first, there is no trade so production in each country is equal to consumption. Table 18.3 summarizes.

Notice that total production is 13 computers and 18 shirts. Now, can Mexico and the United States make themselves better off through trade? Yes.

Imagine that Mexico moves 12 units of its labor out of computer production and into shirt production. Thus, Mexico specializes completely by allocating all 24 units of its labor to shirt production, thereby producing 12 shirts. Similarly, suppose that the United States moves 2 units of its labor out of shirt production and into computers—thus producing 14 computers and 10 shirts. The situation is now as in Table 18.4.

Now compare total production in Table 18.3 with total production in Table 18.4. Total production has increased with specialization! By specializing as comparative advantage would dictate, the two countries can increase total production by one computer and four shirts.

So to finish the story, can you now see a way in which both Mexico and the United States can be made better off? Sure! Imagine that the United States trades one computer to Mexico in return for three shirts. Mexico is now able to consume one computer and nine shirts (three more shirts than before trade; compare with Table 18.3), while the United States is able to consume 13 computers (one more than before

TABLE 18.2 Opportunity Costs

	Opportunity Cost of 1 Computer	Opportunity Cost of 1 Shirt
Mexico	6 Shirts	1/6 of a Computer
United States	1 Shirt	1 Computer

Mexico is the low cost producer of shirts.

The United States is the low cost producer of computers.

TABLE 18.3 Production = Consumption in Mexico and the United States (No Trade)

Country labor allocation (computers, shirts)	Computers	Shirts
Mexico (12, 12)	1	6
United States (12, 12)	12	12
Total Production	13	18

TABLE 18.4 Production in Mexico and the United States (Specialization)

Country labor allocation (computers, shirts)	Computers	Shirts
Mexico (0, 24)	0	12
United States (14, 10)	14	10
Total Production	14	22

trade) and 13 shirts (one more than before trade). Both Mexico and the United States are better off, as Table 18.5 illustrates.

TABLE 18.5 Consumption in Mexico and the United States (Specialization and Trade)

Country	Computers	Shirts
Mexico	1	9 (+3)
United States	13 (+1)	13 (+1)
Total Consumption	14	22

Thus, when each country produces according to its comparative advantage and then trades, total production and consumption increase. Importantly, both Mexico and the United States gain from trade even though the United States is more productive than Mexico at producing *both* computers and shirts.

The theory of comparative advantage not only explains trade patterns but it also tells us something remarkable: a country (or a person) will *always* be the low-cost seller of some good. The reason is clear: the greater the advantage a country has in producing A, the greater the cost to it of producing B. If you are a great pianist, the cost to you of doing anything else is very high. Thus, the greater your advantages in being a pianist, the greater the incentive you have to trade with other people for other goods. It's the same way for countries. The more productive the United States is at producing computers, the greater its demand will be to trade for shirts. Thus, countries with high productivity can always benefit by trading with lower productivity countries, and countries with lower productivity need never fear that higher productivity countries will outcompete them in all goods.

When people fear that a country can be outcompeted in everything, they are making a common mistake, namely confusing absolute advantage with comparative advantage. A producer has an absolute advantage over another producer if it can produce more output from the same input. But what makes trade profitable is differences in comparative advantage, and a country will always have some comparative advantage.

Thus, everyone can benefit from trade. From the world's greatest genius down to the person of below average ability, no person or country is so productive or so unproductive that they cannot benefit by inclusion in the worldwide division of labor. The theory of comparative advantage tells us something vital about world trade and about world peace. Trade unites humanity.

see the invisible hand

Comparative Advantage and Wages Comparative advantage is a difficult story to grasp. Most of the world hasn't got it yet so don't be too surprised if it takes you some time as well. You may at first be bothered by the fact that we did not explicitly discuss wages. Won't a country like the United States be uncompetitive in trade with low-wage countries like Mexico?

In fact, wages are in our model, we just need to bring them to the surface. Doing so will provide another perspective on comparative advantage.

In our model, there is only one type of labor that can be used to produce either computers or shirts. In a free market, all workers of the same type will earn the same wage.* So, in this model there is just one wage in Mexico and one wage in the United States. We can calculate the wage in Mexico by summing up the total value of *consumption* in Mexico and dividing by the number of workers.† We can perform a similar calculation for the United States. To do

---

* In a free market, the same good will tend to sell for the same price everywhere. Imagine that the wages in computer manufacturing exceed the wages in shirt manufacturing. Everyone wants a higher wage so workers in the shirt industry will try to move to the computer industry. As the supply of workers in computer manufacturing increases, however, wages in the computer sector will fall. And, as the supply of workers in shirt manufacturing decreases, wages in that sector will increase. Only when workers of the same type are paid the same wage is there no incentive for workers to move.
† We calculate the value of consumption because at the end of the day workers care about what they consume, not what they produce.

this, we need only a price for computers and a price for shirts. Let's suppose that computers sell for $300 and shirts for $100 (this is consistent with trading one computer for three shirts as we did earlier). Let's look first at the situation with no trade (see Table 18.3). The value of Mexican consumption is $1 \times \$300$ plus $6 \times \$100$ for a total of $900. Since there are 24 workers, the average wage is $37.50. The value of U.S. consumption is $12 \times \$300 + 12 \times \$100 = \$4,800$ so the U.S. wage is $200.

Now consider the situation with trade (see Table 18.5). The value of Mexican consumption is now $1 \times \$300 + 9 \times \$100 = \$1,200$ for a wage of $50 while the U.S. wage is now $216.67 (check it!). Wages in both countries have gone up, just as expected.

But notice that the wage in Mexico is lower than the wage in the United States, both before and after trade. The reason is that the productivity of labor is lower in Mexico. Ultimately, it's the productivity of labor that determines the wage rate. Specialization and trade lets workers make the most of what they have—it raises wages as high as possible given productivity—but trade does not directly increase productivity.* Trade makes both Einstein and his less clever accountant better off, but it doesn't make the accountant a skilled scientist like Einstein.

In summary, workers in the United States often fear trade because they think that they cannot compete with low-wage workers in other countries. Meanwhile, workers in low-wage countries fear trade because they think that they cannot compete with high productivity countries like the United States! But differences in wages reflect differences in productivity. High productivity countries have high wages, low productivity countries have low wages. Trade means that workers in both countries can raise their wages to the highest levels allowed for by their productivities.

Adam Smith (1723–1790) author of the *Wealth of Nations* and one of the greatest economists of all time. When Smith could not finish teaching one semester, he told his students he would refund their tuition. When the students refused the refund saying they had learned so much already, Smith wept. We, however, will not refund the purchase price of this book even if you only read half of it. We are not as good economists as was Adam Smith.

Adam Smith on Trade

As promised, we have so far talked about trade without distinguishing it much from "international trade." Adam Smith had an elegant summary connecting the argument for trade to that for international trade:

> It is the maxim of every prudent master of a family never to attempt to make at home what it will cost him more to make than to buy. The tailor does not attempt to make his own shoes, but buys them of the shoemaker. The shoemaker does not attempt to make his own clothes, but employs a tailor. What is prudence in the conduct of every private family can scarce be folly in that of a great kingdom. If a foreign country can supply us with a commodity cheaper than we ourselves can make it, better buy it of them with some part of the produce of our own industry employed in a way in which we have some advantage.[2]

Analyzing Trade with Supply and Demand

Now that we have discussed some of the fundamental reasons for trade, let's look at trade—and trade restrictions—using tools that you are already familiar with: demand and supply.

---

* Trade can increase productivity by allowing for exploitation of economies of scale, improving the division of knowledge, and diffusing information about advanced production techniques. These advantages of trade are important but the logic of comparative advantage does not require an increase in productivity.

Figure 18.1 shows a domestic demand curve and a domestic supply curve for semiconductors. If there were no international trade the equilibrium would be, as usual, at $P^{no\ trade}$, $Q^{no\ trade}$. Suppose, however, that this good can also be bought in the world market at the world price. To simplify, we will assume that the U.S. market is small relative to the world market, so U.S. demanders can buy as many semiconductors as they want without pushing up the world price. In terms of our diagram, the world supply curve is flat (perfectly elastic) at the world price.

FIGURE 18.1

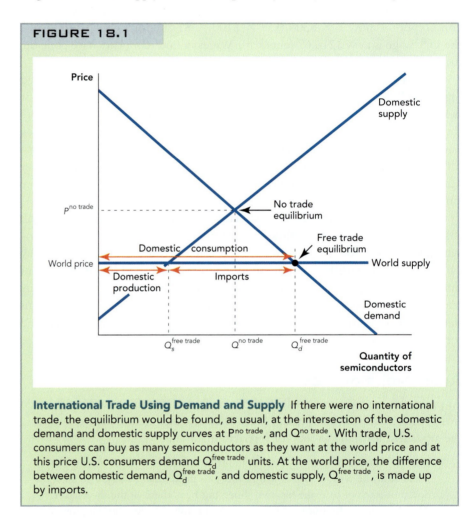

International Trade Using Demand and Supply If there were no international trade, the equilibrium would be found, as usual, at the intersection of the domestic demand and domestic supply curves at $P^{no\ trade}$, and $Q^{no\ trade}$. With trade, U.S. consumers can buy as many semiconductors as they want at the world price and at this price U.S. consumers demand $Q_d^{free\ trade}$ units. At the world price, the difference between domestic demand, $Q_d^{free\ trade}$, and domestic supply, $Q_s^{free\ trade}$, is made up by imports.

Given that U.S. consumers can buy as many semiconductors as they want at the world price, how many will they buy? As usual, we read the quantity demanded off the domestic demand curve so at the world price, U.S. consumers will demand $Q_d^{free\ trade}$ semiconductors. How many semiconductors will be supplied by *domestic* suppliers? As usual, we read the quantity supplied off the domestic supply curve so domestic suppliers will supply $Q_s^{free\ trade}$ units. Notice that $Q_d^{free\ trade} > Q_s^{free\ trade}$, so where does the difference come from? From imports. In other words, with international trade, domestic consumption is $Q_d^{free\ trade}$ units; $Q_s^{free\ trade}$ of these units are produced domestically and the remainder, $Q_d^{free\ trade} - Q_s^{free\ trade}$, are imported.

Analyzing Tariffs with Demand and Supply

Many countries, including the United States, restrict international trade with tariffs, quotas, or other regulations that burden foreign producers but not domestic producers—this is called **protectionism**. A **tariff** is simply a tax on imports.

Protectionism is the economic policy of restraining trade through quotas, tariffs, or other regulations that burden foreign producers but not domestic producers.

A **tariff** is a tax on imports.

A **trade quota** is a restriction on the quantity of foreign goods that can be imported: Imports greater than the quota amount are forbidden or heavily taxed.

Figure 18.2 shows how to analyze a tariff. The figure looks imposing but it's really the same as Figure 18.1 except that now we analyze domestic consumption, production, and imports before and after the tariff. Before the tariff, the situation is exactly as in Figure 18.1, $Q_d^{\text{free trade}}$ units are demanded, $Q_s^{\text{free trade}}$ units are supplied by domestic producers, and imports are $Q_d^{\text{free trade}} - Q_s^{\text{free trade}}$.

A **trade quota** is a restriction on the quantity of goods that can be imported: Imports greater than the quota amount are forbidden or heavily taxed.

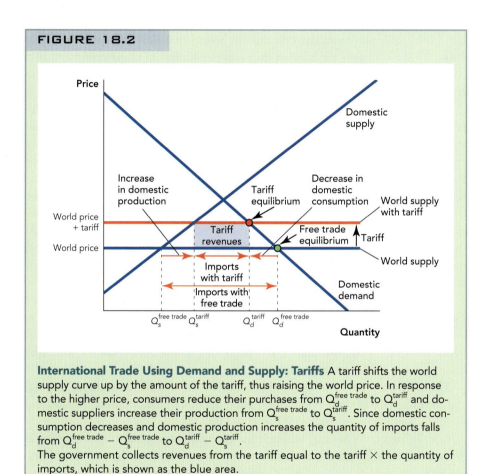

FIGURE 18.2

International Trade Using Demand and Supply: Tariffs A tariff shifts the world supply curve up by the amount of the tariff, thus raising the world price. In response to the higher price, consumers reduce their purchases from $Q_d^{\text{free trade}}$ to Q_d^{tariff} and domestic suppliers increase their production from $Q_s^{\text{free trade}}$ to Q_s^{tariff}. Since domestic consumption decreases and domestic production increases the quantity of imports falls from $Q_d^{\text{free trade}} - Q_s^{\text{free trade}}$ to $Q_d^{\text{tariff}} - Q_s^{\text{tariff}}$.
The government collects revenues from the tariff equal to the tariff × the quantity of imports, which is shown as the blue area.

The tariff is a tax on imports so—just as you learned in Chapter 2—the tariff (tax) shifts the world supply curve up by the amount of the tariff. For example, if the world price of semiconductors is $2 per unit and a new tariff of $1 per semiconductor is imposed, then the world supply curve shifts up to $3 per unit.

At the new, higher price of semiconductors, two things happen. First, there is an increase in the domestic production of semiconductors as domestic suppliers respond to the higher price by increasing production. In the diagram, domestic production increases from $Q_s^{\text{free trade}}$ to Q_s^{tariff}. Second, there is a decrease in domestic consumption from $Q_d^{\text{free trade}}$ to Q_d^{tariff} as domestic consumers respond to the higher price by buying fewer semiconductors. Since the quantity produced by domestic suppliers rises and the quantity demanded by domestic consumers falls, the quantity of imports falls. Specifically, imports fall from $Q_d^{\text{free trade}} - Q_s^{\text{free trade}}$ to the smaller amount $Q_d^{\text{tariff}} - Q_s^{\text{tariff}}$.

Figure 18.2 illustrates one more important idea. A tariff is a tax on imports so tariffs raise tax revenue for the government. The revenue raised by a tariff is the tariff amount times the quantity of imports (the quantity taxed). Thus, in Figure 18.2 the tariff revenue is given by the blue area.

The Costs of Protectionism

Now that we know that a tariff on an imported good will increase domestic production and decrease domestic consumption, we can analyze in more detail the costs of protectionism. The U.S. government, for example, greatly restricts the amount of sugar that can be imported into the United States. As a result, U.S. consumers pay more than double the world price for sugar—in the early 2000s, U.S. consumers paid about 20 cents per pound of sugar compared to a world price of around 9 cents per pound. So, let's look in more detail at the costs of sugar protectionism.

To simplify our analysis, we make two assumptions. First, we assume that the tariff is so high that it completely eliminates all sugar imports. Although a small amount of sugar is allowed into the United States at a low tariff rate, anything above this small amount is taxed so heavily that no further imports occur. Our assumption that the tariff eliminates all sugar imports is not a bad approximation to what actually happens. Second, we assume that if we had complete free trade, all sugar would be imported. This is also a reasonable assumption because, as we will explain shortly, sugar can be produced elsewhere at much lower cost than in the United States. Making these two assumptions will focus attention on the key ideas. See Challenge Question 1 in the end of chapter questions for a more detailed analysis.

In Figure 18.3, we show the market for sugar. If there were complete free trade in sugar, U.S. consumers would be able to buy at the world price of 9 cents per pound and they would purchase 24 billion pounds. U.S. producers cannot compete with foreign producers at a price of 9 cents per pound so with free trade all sugar would be imported.

The tariff on sugar imports is so high that with the tariff there are no imports and the U.S. price of sugar—found at the intersection of the domestic demand and domestic supply curve—rises to 20 cents per pound.

Recall that a tariff has two effects: it increases domestic production and reduces domestic consumption. Each of these effects has a cost. First, the increase in domestic production may sound good—and it is good for domestic producers as we shall see below—but domestic producers have higher costs of production than foreign producers. Thus, the tariff means that sugar is no longer supplied by the lowest-cost sellers and resources that could have been used to produce other goods and services are instead wasted producing sugar. Second, due to higher costs the price of sugar rises and fewer people buy sugar, reducing the gains from trade. Let's look at each of these costs in more detail.

Sugar costs more to grow in the United States than in say Brazil, the world's largest producer of sugar, because the climate in the U.S. mainland is not ideal for sugar growing and because land and labor in Florida, where a lot of U.S. sugar is grown, have many alternative uses that are high in value. Sugar farmers in Florida, for example, have to douse their land with expensive fertilizers to increase production—in the process creating environmental damage in the Florida Everglades.[3] The excess resources—the fertilizer, land, and labor—that go into producing U.S. sugar could have been used to produce other goods like oranges and theme parks for which the United States and Florida are better suited.

Recall from Chapter 2 that the supply curve tells us the cost of production so at the equilibrium price the cost of producing an additional pound of sugar

▶▶ SEARCH ENGINE

Information on sugar and the U.S. sugar tariff can be found from the *USDA Economic Research Service, Sugar Briefing Room.*

FIGURE 18.3

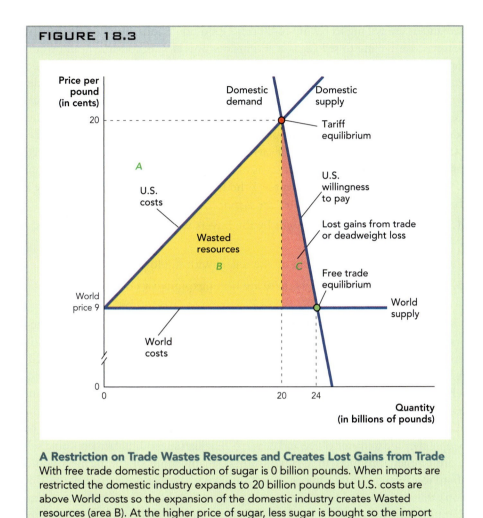

A Restriction on Trade Wastes Resources and Creates Lost Gains from Trade
With free trade domestic production of sugar is 0 billion pounds. When imports are restricted the domestic industry expands to 20 billion pounds but U.S. costs are above World costs so the expansion of the domestic industry creates Wasted resources (area B). At the higher price of sugar, less sugar is bought so the import restriction also creates Lost gains from trade (area C).

How to smuggle sugar

The high price of U.S. sugar has encouraged smuggling and attempts to circumvent the tariff. In the 1980s when the U.S. price was four times the world price, Canadian entrepreneurs created super-high-sugar iced tea. The "tea" was shipped into the United States and then sifted for the sugar, which was resold.

To combat this entrepreneurship, the U.S. government created even more tariffs for sugar-containing products like iced tea, cake mixes, and cocoa.

Source: Economic Report of the President 1986, Chapter 4.

in the United States is exactly 20 cents. In other words, in the United States it takes 20 cents worth of resources like land and labor to produce one additional pound of sugar. That same pound of sugar could be bought in the world market for just 9 cents so the tariff causes 11 cents worth of resources to be wasted in producing that last pound of sugar.

The total value of wasted resources is shown in Figure 18.3 by the yellow area labeled Wasted resources; that area represents the difference between what it costs to produce 20 billion pounds of sugar in the United States and what it would cost to buy the same amount from abroad. We can calculate the total value of wasted resources using our formula for the area of a triangle.

The height of the yellow triangle is 20 − 9 or 11 cents per pound, the base is 20 billion pounds, so the area is 110 billion cents, or $1.1 billion. The sugar tariff wastes $1.1 billion worth of resources.

Notice that if the sugar tariff were eliminated, the price of sugar in the United States would fall to the world price of 9 cents per pound and U.S. production would drop from 20 billion pounds to 0 pounds. It's important to see that the reduction in U.S. production is a *benefit* of eliminating the tariff because it frees up resources that can be used to produce other goods and services.

There is another cost to the tariff. Remember from Chapter 2 that the demand curve tells us the value of goods to the demanders, so at the equilibrium price

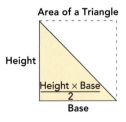

Area of a Triangle

Height

$\frac{\text{Height} \times \text{Base}}{2}$

Base

demanders are willing to pay up to 20 cents for a pound of sugar. World suppliers, however, are willing to sell sugar at 9 cents per pound. U.S. consumers and world suppliers could make mutually profitable gains from trade, but they are prevented from doing so by the threat of punishment. The value of the lost gains from trade, which economists also call a deadweight loss, is given by the pink area. Again, we can calculate this area using our formula for the area of a triangle ((20 − 9) cents per pound × 4 billion pounds divided by 2) = 22 billion cents or $0.22 billion.

Thus, the total cost of the sugar tariff to U.S. citizens is $1.1 billion of wasted resources plus $0.22 billion of lost gains from trade for a total loss of $1.32 billion.

Do you remember from Chapter 3 the three conditions that explain why a free market is efficient? Here they are again:

1. The supply of goods is bought by the buyers with the highest willingness to pay.

2. The supply of goods is sold by the sellers with the lowest costs.

3. Between buyers and sellers there are no unexploited gains from trade nor any wasteful trades.

A tariff or quota that restricts consumers from trading with foreign producers means that the market is not free, so we should expect some of the conditions in our list to be violated. In this case, conditions 2 and 3 are violated. A tariff reduces efficiency because the supply of goods is no longer sold by the sellers with the lowest costs and with a tariff there are unexploited gains from trade between buyers and sellers.

Some of these benefits of trade may sound pretty abstract, but for a lot of people they are a matter of life and death. If Brazilian sugar cane farmers could sell more of their products to U.S. consumers, many more of the farmers could afford to eat better or to improve their housing with proper water and sewage. But don't think the United States is the only party at fault here. The Brazilian government places a lot of tariffs on foodstuffs from the United States and for many Brazilians, including the very poor, this makes food more expensive. The end result is that U.S. consumers pay a high price for sugar and poor Brazilians have less to eat and less money to spend when they need to take their kids to the doctor.

Winners and Losers from Trade

We can arrive at this same total loss in another revealing way. The sugar tariff raises the price of sugar to U.S. consumers, which reduces consumer surplus. Recall from Chapter 2 that consumer surplus is the area underneath the demand curve and above the price. Thus, consumer surplus with the tariff is the area above the price of 20 cents and below the demand curve (not all of which is shown in by Figure 18.3). As the price falls from 20 cents to 9 cents, consumer surplus increases the area A + B + C, which has a value (check it!) of $2.42 billion. Or, put differently, the tariff costs consumers $2.42 billion in lost consumer surplus.

The tariff increases price which increases producer surplus, the area above the supply curve and below the price. Thus, the tariff increases U.S. producer surplus by area A, which has a value of $1.10 billion.

Notice that U.S. consumers lose more than twice as much from the tariff as U.S. producers gain. The loss to U.S. citizens in total is $2.42 billion of consumer loss minus $1.10 billion of U.S. producer gain, for a total loss of $1.32 billion a year, *exactly as we found before*.

Our two methods of analyzing the cost of the sugar tariff are equivalent, but they emphasize different things. The first method calculates social loss directly

and emphasizes where the loss comes from: wasted resources and lost gains from trade. The second method focuses on *who* gains and *who* loses. Domestic producers gain but U.S. consumers lose even more.

Why does the government support the U.S. sugar tariff when U.S. consumers lose much more than U.S. producers gain? One clue is that the costs of the sugar tariff are spread over millions of consumers so the costs per consumer are small. The benefits of the tariff, however, flow to a small number of producers, each of whom benefits by millions of dollars. As a result, the producers support and lobby for the tariff much more actively than consumers oppose the tariff.

The costs of all this lobbying point our attention to yet another cost of protectionism. When a country erects a lot of tariffs against foreign competition, the producers in that country will spend a lot of their time, energy, and money lobbying the government for protection. Those same resources should be spent on production and innovation, not lobbying. Protectionism tends to create a society that pits one interest group against the other and seeds social discord. Free trade, in contrast, creates incentives for people to cooperate toward common and profitable ends.

CHECK YOURSELF

> Who benefits from a tariff? Who loses?

> Why does trade protectionism lead to wasted resources?

> If there are winners and losers from trade restrictions, why do we hear more often from the people who gain from trade restrictions than from the people who lose?

Arguments against International Trade

It would take several books to analyze all the arguments against international trade. We will take a closer look at some of the most common arguments:

> Trade reduces the number of jobs in the United States.

> It's wrong to trade with countries that use child labor.

> We need to keep certain industries at home for reasons of national security.

> We need to keep certain "key" industries at home because of beneficial spillovers onto other sectors of the economy.

> We can increase U.S. well-being with strategic trade protectionism.

Trade and Jobs

When the United States reduces tariffs and imports more shirts from Mexico, the U.S. shirt industry will contract. As a result, many people associate free trade deals with lost jobs. As economists, however, we want to trace the impact of lower tariffs beyond the most immediate and visible effects. So let's trace what happens when a tariff is lowered, paying particular attention to the effect on jobs.

When the price of shirts falls, U.S. consumers have more money in their pockets that they can use to buy other goods. The increased consumer spending on Scotch tape, bean bag chairs, X-ray tests, and thousands of other goods leads to increased jobs in these industries. These jobs gains may be more difficult to see than the job losses in the U.S. shirt industry but they are no less real. But what about the money that is now going to Mexican shirt producers instead of to U.S. shirt producers? Isn't it better to "Buy American" and keep this money at home?

When Mexican producers sell shirts in the United States they are paid in dollars. But what do Mexicans want dollars for? Ultimately, everyone sells in order to buy. Mexican producers might use their dollars to buy U.S. goods. In this case, the increased U.S. spending on imports of Mexican shirts leads directly to increased Mexican spending on U.S. goods (i.e., U.S. exports).

But what happens if the Mexican shirt producers want to buy Mexican goods or European goods rather than U.S. goods? In order to buy Mexican or European goods, the Mexican shirt producers will need pesos or euros. Fortunately, they can trade their dollars for pesos or euros on the foreign exchange market. Suppose the Mexicans trade their dollars to someone in Germany who in return gives them euros. Why would a German want to trade euros for dollars? Remember that people sell in order to buy. Thus, Germans want dollars so that they can buy U.S. goods (or U.S. assets, a topic we take up at further length in Chapter 19). So once again, the increased spending on Mexican shirt imports leads to an increase in U.S. exports (in this case to Germany) and thus an increase in jobs in U.S. exporting industries.

Our thought experiment reveals an important truth: *We pay for our imports with exports.* Think about it this way: Why would anyone sell us goods if not to get goods in return? Thus, trade does not eliminate jobs—it moves jobs from import-competing industries to export industries.

When a tariff on shirts is reduced, it's easy to see the jobs lost at local shirt factory. It's more difficult to see the jobs gained in export industries such as computer production, but the increase in jobs is no less real. And remember although trade does not change the number of jobs it does raise wages, as we demonstrated in the section on comparative advantage.

Of course, it's traumatic to lose a job and not all workers can easily transfer from shirt making to computer production. But in a dynamic and growing economy, job loss and job gain are two sides of the same coin. Thomas Edison ended the whale oil industry with his invention of the electric lightbulb in 1879. This was bad for whalers but good for people who like to read at night (and very good for the whales). The phonograph destroyed jobs in the piano industry (darn that Edison, again!), CDs destroyed jobs in the record industry, and today MP3s are destroying jobs in the CD industry. And, yet somehow with all these jobs being destroyed, employment and the standard of living keep trending upward.

Job destruction is ultimately a healthy part of any growing economy, but that doesn't mean we have to ignore the costs of transitioning from one job to another. Unemployment insurance, savings, and a strong education system can help workers respond to shocks. Trade restrictions, however, are not a good way to respond to shocks. Trade restrictions save *visible* jobs, but they destroy jobs that are just as real but harder to see.

Thomas Edison, destroyer of jobs or benefactor of humanity? Yes.

The Pin Factory
Lewis Hine photograph of bowling alley boys in New Haven, Conn. Circa 1910.

Child Labor

Is child labor a reason to restrict trade? In part, this is a question of ethics on which reasonable people can disagree but our belief, for which we will give reasons, is that the answer is no.

In 1992, labor activists discovered that Wal-Mart was selling clothing that had been made in Bangladesh by subcontractors who had employed some child workers. Senator Tom Harkin angrily introduced a bill in Congress to prohibit firms from importing any products made by children under the age of 15. Harkin's bill didn't pass, but in a panic the garment industry in Bangladesh dismissed 30 to 50 thousand child workers. A success? Before we decide, we need to think about what happened to the children who were thrown out of work. Where did these children go? To the playground? To

school? To a better job? No. Thrown out of the garment factories, the children went to work elsewhere, many at jobs like prostitution with worse conditions and lower pay.[4]

In 2009, about 18 percent of all children aged 5–14 around the world work for a significant number of hours. The vast majority of these children work in agriculture, often alongside their parents, and not in export industries. Restrictions on trade, therefore, cannot directly reduce the number of child workers and by making a poor country poorer, trade restrictions may increase the number of child workers. In fact, studies have shown that more openness to trade increases income and reduces child labor.[5]

Child labor is more common in poor countries and it was common in nineteenth century Great Britain and the United States when people were much poorer than today. Child labor declined in the developed world as people got richer.

The forces that reduced child labor in the developed world are also at work in the developing world. The vertical axis of Figure 18.4 shows the percentage of children ages 10–14 who are laboring in 132 countries across the world. Real GDP per capita is shown on the horizontal axis. The size of the circles is proportionate to the total number of child laborers so although the percentage of child laborers is much higher in Burundi (48.5 percent) than in India (12 percent), there are many more child laborers in India. The lesson of Figure 18.4 is that economic growth reduces child labor.

FIGURE 18.4

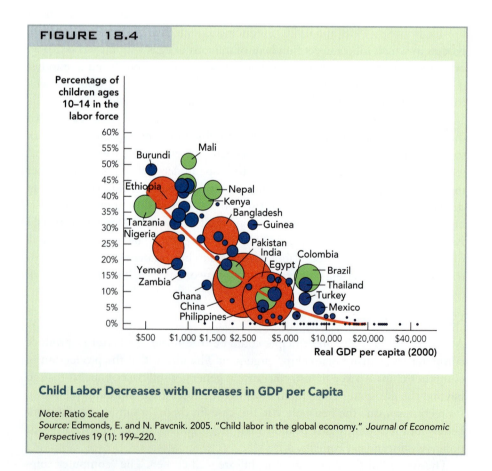

Child Labor Decreases with Increases in GDP per Capita

Note: Ratio Scale
Source: Edmonds, E. and N. Pavcnik. 2005. "Child labor in the global economy." *Journal of Economic Perspectives* 19 (1): 199–220.

The real cause of child labor is poverty, not trade. Thus, to reduce child labor, we should focus on reducing poverty rather than on reducing trade; putting up trade barriers is likely to be ineffective or even counterproductive.

Governments and nonprofits from the developed world can help developing countries reduce child labor by helping them to improve the quality of schooling and to lower the opportunity cost of education. In Bangladesh, at about the same time that child workers were being thrown out of work by the Harkin bill, the government introduced the Food for Education program. The program provides a free monthly stipend of rice or wheat to poor families who have at least one child attending school that month. The program has been very successful at encouraging school attendance. Even more important, increased education of children today means richer parents tomorrow—parents who will no longer feel crushed by the forces of poverty, or in other words parents who will have enough wealth to feed their children *and* send them to school.[6]

Trade and National Security

If a good is vital for national security but domestic producers have higher costs than foreign producers, it can make sense for the government to tax imports or subsidize the production of the domestic industry. It may make sense, for example, to support a domestic vaccine industry. In 1918, more than a quarter of the U.S. population got sick with the flu and more than 500,000 died, sometimes within hours of being infected. The young were especially hard hit and as a result life expectancy in the United States dropped by 10 years. No place in the world was safe, as between 2.5 percent to 5 percent of the entire world population died from the flu between 1918 and 1920. Producing flu vaccine requires an elaborate process in which robots inject hundreds of millions of eggs with flu viruses. In an ordinary year there are few problems with buying vaccine produced in another country, but if something like the 1918 flu swept the world again it would be wise to have significant vaccine production capacity in the United States.[7]

Don't be surprised, however, if every domestic producer in trouble claims that their product is vital for national security. Everything from beeswax to mohair, not to mention steel and computer chips, has been protected in the name of national security. It's common for protectionists to lobby under the guise of some other motive. Many people are legitimately concerned about working conditions in developing countries but does it surprise you that U.S. labor unions are often the biggest lobbyists for bills to restrict trade on behalf of "oppressed foreign workers"? As Youssef Boutros-Ghali, Egypt's minister for trade put it, "The question is why all of a sudden, when third world labor has proved to be competitive, why do industrial countries start feeling concerned about our workers? . . . . It is suspicious."[8]

Key Industries

Another argument that in principle could be true is the "it's better to produce computer chips than potato chips" argument. The idea is that the production of computer chips is a key industry because it generates spillovers, benefits that go beyond the computer chips themselves (see Chapter 7 for more on spillovers). Protectionism isn't the best policy in this case (in theory, a subsidy would work better), but if a subsidy isn't possible then protectionism might be a second best policy with some net benefits.

The words "in principle," and "might" are well chosen. The "computer chips are better than potato chips" argument can't be faulted on logic alone, but it's

NORM EGGERT

Vital for National Security?
In 1954 the U.S. government declared that mohair, the fleece of the Angora goat, was vital for national security (it can be used to make military uniforms). For nearly forty years mohair producers received millions of dollars in annual payments. Finally, after much ridicule, the program was eliminated in 1993 . . . only to be reestablished in 2002. Hard to believe? Yes, but we aren't kidding around.

not very compelling. To address this particular example, most computer chips today are cheap, mass-manufactured commodities. The United States rightly doesn't specialize in this type of manufacturing and is better off for it, even though this used to be a common argument for protectionism against foreign computer chips.

Second, no one knows which industries are the ones with the really important spillovers. In the late 1980s, many pundits argued that HDTV would be a technology driver for many related industries. Japan and the European Union subsidized their producers to the tune of billions of dollars. The United States lagged behind. In the end, however, Japan and the EU chose an analog technology that is now considered obsolete and HDTV has yet to produce significant benefits for the broader economy, even if it does give you a really nice picture at home.

Strategic Trade Protectionism

In some cases, it's possible for a country to use tariffs and quotas to grab up a larger share of the gains from trade than would be possible with pure free trade policy. The idea is for the government to help domestic firms to act like a cartel when they sell to international buyers. Oddly, the way to do this is to limit or tax exports. A tax or limit on exports reduces exports but can drive up the price enough so that net revenues increase. Of course, this can only work if international buyers have few substitutes for the domestic good. Could this work in practice? Yes, in many ways OPEC is a possible example. OPEC limits exports and because the demand for oil is inelastic this increases oil revenues.

Oil is a special good, however, because it is found in large quantities in just a few places in the world. The United States would have a much harder time using strategic trade protectionism because there are more substitutes for U.S. produced goods. The U.S. economy, or any advanced economy, would also have another problem. Oil is Saudi Arabia's only significant export so when they raise the price of oil, the rest of the world can't threaten to retaliate by putting tariffs on Saudi Arabia's other exports. But if the United States were to try to grab up a larger share of the gains from trade, in say computers, other countries could respond with tariffs on our grain exports. A trade war could easily make both countries worse off. Trying to divide the pie in your favor usually makes the pie smaller.

Trade and Globalization

Having trouble understanding the theory of international trade? GrowingStars.com offers online tutors who are available 24 hours a day, 7 days a week to help you understand difficult topics in economics.* GrowingStars tutors ought to understand international trade: The tutors live in India.[10]

Declines in transportation costs, integration of world markets, and increased speed of communication have made the world a smaller place. But globalization is not new; rather it has been a theme in human history since at least the Roman Empire, which knit together different parts of the world in a common economic and political area. When these trade networks later fell apart, the subsequent era was named "The Dark Ages."

Later, the European Renaissance arose from revitalized trade routes, the rebirth of commercially based cities, and also the spread of science from China,

COURTESY WAL-MART STORES, INC.

Wal-Mart: SuperProductivity
Surprisingly, the biggest factor in the productivity boom of the 1990s was not a Silicon Valley high-tech firm but improvements in the retail and wholesale sector. Wal-Mart alone was responsible for one-eighth of these productivity gains and Wal-Mart innovations in warehouse logistics, wireless bar code scanning, and database integration spread throughout the retail industry. Computer chips may be better than potato chips, but apparently *selling* potato chips is best of all.[9]

CHECK YOURSELF

> Over the past 30 years, most U.S. garment manufacturing has moved overseas, to places such as India and China, where wages are lower. The result of this shift has been a sizeable drop in the number of garment workers in the United States. While bad for these workers, why has this trend been a net benefit for the United States?

> What would happen if the U.S. government decided that computer chip manufacturing was a strategic national industry and provided monetary grants to Silicon Valley companies? Trace the effects of this policy on Silicon Valley companies, foreign competitors, and the cost and benefit to U.S. taxpayers and consumers.

---

* We are using GrowingStars as an example of globalization. We have not evaluated the services of GrowingStars or any online tutors and make no recommendation for or against any such service.

India, and the Middle East. Periods of increased trade, and the spread of ideas, have been among the best for human progress. As economist Donald Boudreaux puts it "globalization is the advance of human cooperation across national boundaries."[11]

□ Takeaway

Specialization and trade create enormous increases in productivity. Without trade, the knowledge used by an entire economy is approximately equal to the knowledge used by one brain. With specialization and trade, the total sum of knowledge used in an economy increases tremendously and far exceeds that of any one brain. Specialization and trade also let us take advantage of economies of scale.

International trade is trade across political borders. The theory of comparative advantage explains how a country, just like a person, can increase its standard of living by specializing in what it can make at low (opportunity) cost and trading for what it can make only at high cost. When we apply the logic of opportunity cost to trade, we discover that everyone has a comparative advantage in something so everyone can benefit from inclusion in the worldwide market.

Restrictions on trade waste resources by transferring production from low-cost foreign producers to high-cost domestic producers. Restrictions on trade also prevent domestic consumers from exploiting gains from trade with foreign producers. Domestic producers can benefit from trade restrictions, but domestic consumers lose more than the producers gain. Trade restrictions sometimes persist because the benefits from restrictions are often concentrated on small groups who lobby for protection, while the costs of restrictions are spread over millions of consumers and can be small for each individual.

High productivity countries have high wages, low productivity countries have low wages. Trade means that workers in both countries can raise their wages to the highest levels allowed for by their productivities. International trade does not raise productivity directly but can help poor countries raise their productivity indirectly by diffusing knowledge and capital.

We have set out various common arguments for restricting trade. Some of these arguments are valid but they are usually of limited applicability.

Globalization is not new but an important theme in history and one connected with human progress.

□ CHAPTER REVIEW

KEY CONCEPTS

Economies of scale, p. 383

Absolute advantage, p. 384

Comparative advantage, p. 384

Protectionism, p. 388

Tariff, p. 388

Trade quota, p. 389

FACTS AND TOOLS

1. Use the idea of the "division of knowledge" to answer the following questions.

   a. Which country has more knowledge: Utopia, where in the words of Karl Marx, each person knows just enough about hunting, fishing, and cattle raising to "hunt in the morning, fish in the afternoon, [and]

rear cattle in the evening," or Drudgia, where one-third of the population learns only about hunting, one-third only about fishing, and one-third only about cattle raising?

b. Which planet has more knowledge: Xeroxia, each of whose one million inhabitants knows the same list of one million facts, or Differentia, whose one million inhabitants each know a different set of one million facts? How many facts are known in Xeroxia? How many facts are known in Differentia?

2. In the *Wealth of Nations*, Adam Smith said that one reason specialization makes someone more productive is because "a man commonly saunters a little in turning his hand from one sort of employment to another." How can you use this observation to improve your pattern of studying for your four or five college courses this semester?

3. "Opportunity cost" is one of the tougher ideas in economics. Let's make it easier by starting with some simple examples. In the examples below, find the opportunity cost: Your answer should be a *rate*, as in "1.5 widgets per year" or "6 lectures per month." Ignoring Adam Smith's insight from the previous question, assume that these relationships are simple linear ones, so that if you put in twice the time you get twice the output, and half the time yields half the output.

a. Erin has a choice between two activities: She can repair one transmission per hour or she can repair two fuel injectors per hour. What is the opportunity cost of repairing one transmission?

b. Katie works at a customer service center and every hour she has a choice between two activities: Answering 200 telephone calls per hour or responding to 400 emails per hour. What is the opportunity cost of responding to 400 phone calls?

c. Deirdre has a choice between writing one more book this year or five more articles this year. What is the opportunity cost of writing half of a book this year, in terms of articles?

4. a. American workers are typically paid much more than Chinese workers. *True or false:* This is largely because American workers are typically more productive than Chinese workers.

b. Julia Child, an American chef (and World War II spy) who reintroduced French cooking to Americans in the 1960s, was paid much more than most American chefs. *True or false:* This was largely because Julia Child was much more productive than most American chefs.

5. The Japanese people currently pay about four times the world price for rice. If Japan removed its trade barriers so that Japanese consumers could buy rice at the world price, who would be better off and who would be worse off: Japanese consumers or Japanese rice farmers? If we added all the gains and losses to the Japanese, would there be a net gain or net loss? Who would make a greater effort lobbying, for or against, this reduction in trade barriers: Japanese consumers or Japanese rice farmers?

6. The supply curve for rice in Japan slopes upward, just like any normal supply curve. If Japan eliminated its trade barriers to rice, what would happen to the number of workers employed in the rice-producing industry in Japan: Would it rise or fall? What would these workers probably do over the next year or so? Will they ever work again?

7. In Figure 18.3, consider triangles B and C. One of these could be labeled "Workers and machines who could be better used in another sector of the economy," while the other could be labeled "Consumers who have to pay more than necessary for their product." Which is which?

8. In his book *The Choice,* economist Russ Roberts asks how voters would feel about a machine that could convert wheat into automobiles.

a. Do you think that voters would complain that this machine should be banned, since it would destroy jobs in the auto industry?

b. Would this machine *in fact* destroy jobs in the auto industry? If so, would roughly the same number of jobs eventually be created in other industries?

c. Here is Roberts's punch line: If voters were told that the wonder machine was in fact just a cargo ship that exported wheat and imported autos from a foreign country, how would voters' attitudes toward this machine change?

9. According to the *Wall Street Journal* (August 30, 2007, "In the Balance"), it takes about 30 hours to assemble a vehicle in the United States. Let's use that fact plus a few invented numbers to sum up the global division of labor in auto manufacturing. In international economics, "North" is shorthand for the high-tech developed countries of East Asia, North America, and Western Europe, while "South" is shorthand for the rest of the world. Let's use that shorthand here.

a. Consider the productivity table below: Which region has an absolute advantage at making high-quality cars? And low quality cars?

	Number of Hours to Make One High-Quality car	Number of Hours to Make One Low-Quality Car
North	30	20
South	60	30

b. Using the information in the productivity table above, estimate the opportunity cost of making high- or low-quality cars in the North and in the South. Which region has a comparative advantage (i.e., lowest opportunity cost) for manufacturing high-quality cars? For low-quality cars?

	Opportunity Cost of Making One High-Quality car	Opportunity Cost of Making One Low-Quality Car
North	_____ low-quality cars	_____ high-quality cars
South	_____ low-quality cars	_____ high-quality cars

c. There are one million hours of labor available for making cars in the North, and another one million hours of labor available for making cars in the South. In a no-trade world, let's assume that two-thirds of the auto industry labor in each region is used to make high-quality cars and one-third is used to make low-quality cars. Solve for how many of each kind of car will be produced in North and South, and add up to determine total global output of each type of car. (Why will both kinds of cars be made? Because the low-quality cars will be less expensive.)

	Output of High-Quality Cars	Output of Low-Quality Cars
North		
South		
Global output		

d. Now, allow specialization. If each region completely specializes in the type of car in which they hold the comparative advantage, what will global output of high-quality cars be? Of low-quality cars? In the table below, report your answers. Is global output in each kind of car higher than before? (We'll solve a problem with the final step of trade in the Thinking and Problem Solving section.)

	Output of High-Quality Cars	Output of Low-Quality Cars
North		
South		
Global output		

THINKING AND PROBLEM SOLVING

1. Fit each of the following examples into one of the three reasons for trade:

I. Division of knowledge

II. Economies of scale/creating competition

III. Comparative advantage

a. It is the 1950s. The American auto industry makes mediocre cars at high prices. The main reason they can do this is because they face little pressure to improve. Once the Japanese start making mediocre cars at low prices in the 1970s, American firms feel a pressure to improve their products.

b. Two recently abandoned cats, Bingo and Tuppy, need to quickly learn how to catch mice in order to survive. If they also remain well groomed, they stand a better chance of surviving: Good grooming reduces the risk of disease and parasites. Each cat could go it alone, focusing almost exclusively on learning to catch mice. The alternative would be for Bingo to specialize in learning how to groom well and for Tuppy to specialize in learning how to catch mice well.

c. Former President Bill Clinton, a graduate of Yale Law School, hires attorneys who are less skilled than himself to do routine legal work.

2. Let's see how important "economies of scale" can be. Assume that it costs $1 billion to build a new computer chip facility. (The true cost would be more like $3 billion, as an Internet news search for "computer chip factory cost" will demonstrate.) Once the factory is open, it costs only $1 to produce an additional chip.

a. What is the total cost of producing one chip? (Be sure to include the cost of building the factory.)

b. What is the total cost of producing 100,000 chips? What is the average cost per chip? (Average cost equals total cost divided by number of chips.)

c. What is the average cost per chip of producing 1 million chips? The average cost per chip if the company makes one billion chips? (Notice how this is similar to Chapter 7's discussion of the positive relationship between market size and research activity. Such "scale effects" are common in economics.)

d. Just to make a profit, the price of a computer chip must be more than the average cost of making that chip ($P > AC$, as they say in microeconomics). Canada's population is 34 million: If Canada had to

make its own computer chips in a billion-dollar factory, and it needed to make one chip per person, could computer chips sell for less than $10 each? Could they sell for less than $100 each?

3. Nobel Laureate Paul Samuelson said that comparative advantage is one of the few ideas in economics that is both "true and not obvious." Since it's not obvious, we should practice with it a bit. In each of the cases below, who has the absolute advantage at each task, and who has the comparative advantage?

a. In 30 minutes, Kana can either make miso soup or she can clean the kitchen. In 15 minutes, Mitchell can make miso soup; it takes Mitchell an hour to clean the kitchen.

b. In one hour, Ethan can bake 20 cookies or lay the drywall for two rooms. In one hour, Sienna can bake 100 cookies or lay the drywall for three rooms.

c. Kara can build two glass sculptures per day or she can design two full-page newspaper advertisements per day. Sara can build one glass sculpture per day or design four full-page newspaper ads per day.

d. Data can write 12 excellent poems per day or solve 100 difficult physics problems per day. Riker can write one excellent poem per day or solve 0.5 difficult physics problems per day.

4. a. Just to review: Back in Chapter 4 on price ceilings and floors, we illustrated price ceilings with a horizontal line below the equilibrium price. Did price ceilings create surpluses or shortages?

b. The horizontal line in Figure 18.1 doesn't represent a surplus or a shortage. What does it represent?

c. Figure 18.1 considers the case of a country that can buy as many semiconductors as it wants at the same world price. Why do people in this country only buy $Q_d^{\text{Free Trade}}$ units? Why don't they buy more of this inexpensive product?

5. Figure 18.1 looks at a case where the world price is below the domestic no-trade price. Let's look at the case where the world price is *above* the domestic no-trade price. We'll work with the market for airplanes shown in the figure below.

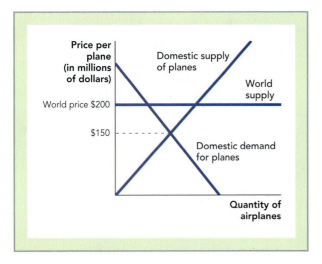

a. In the above figure, use the Quantity axis to label $Q_S^{\text{free trade}}$ and $Q_D^{\text{free trade}}$. This is somewhat similar to Figure 18.1.

b. What would you call the gap between $Q_S^{\text{free trade}}$ and $Q_D^{\text{free trade}}$?

c. Also following Figure 18.1, label "domestic consumption" and "domestic production."

d. Will domestic airplane buyers—airlines and delivery companies like FedEx—have to pay a higher or a lower price under free trade compared to the no-trade alternative? Will domestic airplane buyers purchase a higher or a lower quantity of planes if there's free trade in planes?

e. Based on your answer to part d, would you expect domestic airplane demanders to support free trade in planes or oppose it?

6. The federal education reform law known as No Child Left Behind requires every state to create standardized tests that measure whether students have mastered key subjects. Since the same test is given to all students in the same grade in the state, this encourages all schools within a state to cover the same material. According to the division of knowledge model, what are the costs of this approach?

7. In the text, we discuss sugar farmers in Florida who use unusually large amounts of fertilizer to produce their crops; they do so because their land isn't all that great for sugar production. If we translate this into the language of the supply curve, would these Florida sugar farms be those

on the lower-left part of a supply curve, or those along the upper-right of the supply curve? Why?

8. In this chapter, we've often emphasized how specialization and exchange can create more *output*. But sometimes the output from voluntary exchange is difficult to measure and doesn't show up in GDP statistics. In each of the following cases, explain how the two parties involved might be able to make themselves *both* better off just by making a voluntary exchange.

a. Alan received two copies of *Gears of War* as birthday gifts. Burton received two copies of *Halo* as birthday gifts.

b. Jeb has a free subscription to *Field and Stream* but isn't interested in hunting. George has a free subscription to the *Miami Herald* but isn't all that interested in Florida news.

c. Pat has a lot of love to give, but it is worthless unless received by another. Terry is in the same sad situation.

9. According to Chinese government statistics, China imported 140,000 sedans in 2007. Let's see what would happen to consumer and producer surplus if China were to ban sedan imports. To keep things simple, let's assume that if sedan imports were banned, the equilibrium price of sedans (holding quality constant!) would rise by $5,000.

a. In the figure below, shade the area that represents the total gains when sedan imports are allowed into China.

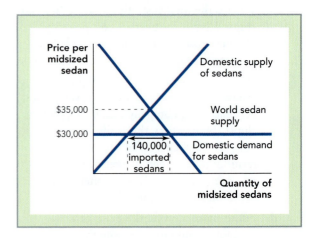

b. Once China bans the import of sedans, what is the dollar value of the lost gains from trade? (Hint: The chapter provides the formula.)

c. If sedan imports are banned, Chinese sedan producers will be better off and Chinese sedan consumers will be worse off. A polygon in the figure above shows the surplus that will shift from consumers to producers. Write the word "transfer" in this polygon. (Hint: It's not the area you calculated in part b.)

10. Here's another specialization and exchange problem. This problem is wholly made-up, so that you won't be able to use your intuition about the names of countries or the products to figure out the answer.

a. Consider the productivity table below: Which country has an absolute advantage at making rotids? At making taurons?

	Number of Hours to Make One Rotid	Number of Hours to Make One Tauron
Mandovia	50	100
Ducennia	150	200

b. Using the information in the productivity table above, estimate the opportunity cost of making rotids and taurons in Mandovia and Ducennia. Which country has a comparative advantage at manufacturing rotids? At making taurons?

	Opportunity Cost of Making One Rotid	Opportunity Cost of Making One Tauron
Mandovia	____taurons	____rotids
Ducennia	____taurons	____rotids

c. There are one billion hours of labor available for making products in Mandovia, and two billion hours of labor available for making products in Ducennia. In a no-trade world, let's assume that half the labor in each country gets used to make each product. (In a semester-long international trade course, you'd build a bigger model that would determine just how the workers get divided up according to the forces of supply and demand.) Fill in the table.

	Output of Rotids	Output of Taurons
Mandovia		
Ducennia		
Total output		

d. Now, allow specialization. If each country completely specializes in the product in which they hold the comparative advantage, what will total output of rotids be? Of taurons? Is total output of each product higher than before?

	Output of Rotids	Output of Taurons
Mandovia		
Ducennia		
Total output		

e. Finally, let's open up trade. Trade has to make both sides better off (or at least no worse off), and in this problem as in most negotiations, there's more than one price that can do so (just think about haggling over the price of a car or a house). Let's pick out a case that makes one side better off, and leaves the other side just as well off as in a no-trade world. The price both sides agree to is three rotids for two taurons. Ship 5 million taurons in one direction, and 7.5 million rotids in the other direction (You'll have to figure out on your own which way the trade flows). In the table below calculate the amount that each country gets to consume. Which country is better off under this set of prices? Which one is exactly as well off as before?

	Consumption of Rotids	Consumption of Taurons
Mandovia		
Ducennia		
Total consumption		

f. This time, the trade negotiations turn out differently: It's two rotids for one tauron. Have the correct country ship 10 million rotids, have the other send 5 million taurons, and fill out the table below. One way to make sure you haven't made a mistake is to make sure that "total consumption" is equal to "total output" from part d: We can't create rotids and taurons out of thin air! Are both countries better off than if there were no trade? Which country likes this trade deal better than the deal from part e?

	Consumption of Rotids	Consumption of Taurons
Mandovia		
Ducennia		
Total consumption		

CHALLENGES

1. In the chapter, we focused on a sugar tariff that eliminated all imports. Let's now take a look at the case where the sugar tariff eliminates some but not all imports. We will also examine the closely related case of a quota on sugar imports. The figure below shows a tariff on sugar that raises the U.S. price to 20 cents per pound but at that price some sugar is imported even after the tariff.

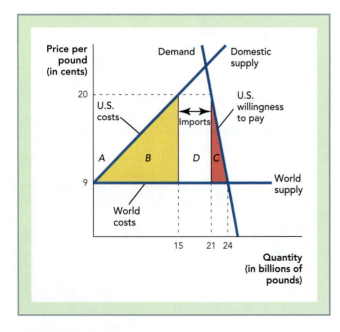

a. Label the free trade equilibrium, the tariff equilibrium, wasted resources, lost gains from trade, and tariff revenues.

b. Now imagine that instead of a tariff, the U.S. government uses a quota that forbids imports of sugar greater than 6 billion pounds. (Equivalently imagine a tariff that is zero on the first 6 billion pounds of imports but then jumps to a prohibitive level after that quantity of imports—this is closer to how the system works in practice.) Under the quota system what does area D represent? Would importers of sugar prefer a tariff or a quota?

c. The sugar quota is allocated to importing countries based on imports from these countries between 1975 and 1981 (with some subsequent adjustments). For example, in 2008 Australia was given the right to export 87 thousand metric tons of sugar to the United States at a very low tariff rate while Belize was given the right to export 11.5 thousand metric tons of sugar to the United States at a very low tariff rate. How do you think these rights are allocated to firms within the sugar-exporting countries?

d. Discuss how the quota and the way it is allocated could create a misallocation of resources that would further reduce efficiency relative to a tariff that resulted in the same quantity of imports.

2. In a 2005 *Washington Post* article ("The Road to Riches Is Called K Street"), Jeffrey Birnbaum noted that there were 35,000 registered lobbyists in Washington, D.C., people whose primary job is asking the federal government for something. A lobbyist who comes with long experience as an aide to a powerful politician will earn at least $200,000 per year. Many lobbyists (not all) are attempting to restrict trade in order to turn consumer surplus into producer surplus.

a. Let's focus just on the lobbyists who are restricting trade. If the United States were to amend the Constitution to permanently ban all tariffs and trade restrictions, these lobbyists would lose their jobs, and they'd have to leave Washington to get "real jobs." Would this job change raise U.S. productivity or lower it?

b. Would most of these lobbyists likely earn more after the amendment was enacted or less?

c. How can you reconcile your answers to parts a and b?

3. Let's think a little more about Thinking and Problem Solving question 9. If quality *weren't* held constant, what would you expect to happen to the additional Chinese sedans produced after the import ban? Would they be as good as the ones that used to be imported? (Hint: Which types of sedans do you think that China imports? Low quality or high quality? Why?)

4. In Facts and Tools question 9, we didn't do the final step: trade. There's more than one price at which both sides would agree to an exchange. What is the *complete* price range (number of low-quality cars per high-quality car) that would make both sides better off?

19

International Finance

"Why are we spending our dollars in China and Japan rather than in Ohio and Michigan?"

"Why does America have such a large trade deficit?"

"We need to keep our money at home, not send it abroad!"

So run some common questions and complaints about globalization and international finance. The more connected the world economy becomes, the more these kinds of questions arise and increase in importance.

In the last chapter, we discussed how specialization and trade let us take advantage of the division of knowledge, economies of scale, and comparative advantage and thus raise the standard of living. Gains from trade occur when individuals within a nation trade and people in different countries trade.

It's important to keep these deep principles in mind when we discuss trade, but we also want to understand more about the kind of international financial events discussed on a daily basis on the financial blogs and in the newspapers. What does it mean when we are told that the dollar is "strong" or "weak"? What is a trade deficit and is it worse than a trade surplus? And why are the students in the picture protesting against the World Bank and the International Monetary Fund? What are these strange institutions?

As we will see, some knowledge of international finance is extremely practical. If you wish to do international business, make international investments, or understand how an exchange rate crisis can wreck an economy, you need to know some basic truths about international finance. Understanding international finance will also help you to pick the best place to take a good vacation. And you will even learn why many James Bond movies have a scene set in Switzerland.

Protesters clash with police in Washington, D.C., at the annual meeting of the IMF and World Bank, April 2000.

REUTERS/CORBIS

407

On the surface, international finance is one of the most intimidating fields of economics because the presence of different currencies can be confusing. So let's begin with some of the key principles behind this chapter:

1. Gains from trade occur when people trade across different countries with different currencies, just as gains from trade occur within a single nation with a single currency.

2. The rate of savings is a key variable in understanding international trade and finance.

3. Market equilibrium means that, at the margin, the gains from holding or spending one currency are equal to the gains from holding or spending some other currency. That sounds simple but we'll see that this principle will be a building block for understanding the market value of one currency relative to another.

The U.S. Trade Deficit and Your Trade Deficit

Let's start by looking at the trade deficit in more detail. In 2006, Americans exported (sold) to China $55.2 billion worth of goods and they imported (bought) from China $287.7 billion in goods. The difference between what Americans exported to China and what they imported from China, −$232.5 billion, is called the U.S. **trade deficit** with China.

> A **trade deficit** occurs when the value of a country's imports exceeds the value of its exports.

The U.S. trade deficit with China is controversial. In response to the trade deficit, some politicians, like America's first female Speaker of the House, Nancy Pelosi, called for a tariff on all imports of Chinese goods. To understand this debate, it will be useful to begin with some trade deficits closer to home, namely your trade deficit with your local supermarket.

Do you shop at Giant, Safeway, or the Piggly Wiggly? If you do, you run a trade deficit with those stores. That is, you buy more goods from them than they buy from you (unless of course you work at one of these stores or sell them goods from your farm). We too, the authors of this book, run a trade deficit with supermarkets. In fact, we have been running a trade deficit with Whole Foods for many years. Is our Whole Foods deficit a problem?

> A **trade surplus** occurs when the value of a country's exports exceeds the value of its imports.

Our deficit with Whole Foods isn't a problem because it's balanced with a **trade surplus** with someone else. Who? You, the students, whether we teach you or whether you have bought our book. You buy more goods from us than we buy from you. We export education to you, but we do not import your goods and services. In short, we run a trade deficit with Whole Foods but a trade surplus with our students. In fact, it is only because we run a trade surplus with you that we can run a trade deficit with Whole Foods. Thanks!

The lesson is simple. Trade deficits and surpluses are to be found everywhere.

The fact that the United States has a trade deficit with one country is not, taken alone, special cause for worry. Trade across countries is very much like trade across individuals. Not every person or every country can run a trade surplus all the time. Suddenly a trade deficit does not seem so troublesome, even though the word "deficit" makes it sound like a problem or an economic shortcoming.

What if the United States runs a trade deficit not just with China or Japan or Mexico but with the world as a whole, as indeed it does? Is that a bad thing?

This will require some deeper investigation. So far we have only looked at the flow of goods from the grocery store to you or from China to the United States, but for every flow of goods there is a corresponding and opposite flow of money or financial claims. When China sells us goods, we pay for those goods in dollars. At the present time, China (and other countries) is not using all of those dollars to buy U.S. goods and thus the United States is running a trade deficit on net. What is China doing with the dollars and is this cause for concern? We need some more tools and a few more terms to answer these questions.

The Balance of Payments

Let's start with the international balance of payments. The **balance of payments** is a yearly summary of all the economic transactions between residents of one country and residents of the rest of the world. The balance of payments records sales of goods and services and also transfers of financial claims including stocks, bonds, loans, and ownership rights. We can also speak of the balance of payments with a specific country such as the balance of payments with China.

That sounds a little forbidding, but let's go back to your trade deficit with the local supermarket. You spend money at the supermarket but earn money through your job. In the simplest case, when there is no borrowing or lending, a person's trade deficits must be matched with other trade surpluses. In other words, if you want to spend you must earn so your balance of payments does in fact balance (nets out to zero).

Now let's make this more realistic by adding borrowing and lending. Suppose you take out a student loan to pay for books, supplies, and housing. You have to pay back the loan someday, but in the mean time you are running a trade deficit. You are spending but you are not earning or "exporting" equivalent goods and services. In this case, your trade deficit is balanced with a loan, which we call a capital inflow or **capital surplus.** When we add up your trade deficit and the capital surplus, the balance of payments once again nets out to zero.

In the long run, unless you default on the loan, your trade deficit must disappear, and indeed it must turn into a trade surplus. That is, someday you will get a job and use your surplus earnings to pay back the bank loan. Paying back the loan limits your future consumption, that is, your ability to buy goods and services, but all things considered your earlier borrowing was still a good idea, at least if you invested the money well.

We have seen that you can finance a trade deficit with a job or a loan. How else could you finance a trade deficit? If you had assets from previous transactions, you could sell the assets and spend the proceeds. If you owned some land, for example, you could sell the land creating a capital surplus, which would offset your current deficit. Similarly, if you had reserves of cash from previous periods you could draw on your reserves to finance a deficit. The more assets or cash that you had from previous transactions, the longer you could live the partying lifestyle by spending more than you were earning in the current period. Notice that when we add up the trade deficit, the capital inflow, and the changes in reserves, the balance of payments still balances.

We can write down these relationships as an identity, an equality that is always true:

$$\text{Earning} - \text{Spending} = \text{Changes in debt} + \text{Changes in ownership of assets} + \text{Changes in your cash reserves}$$

If earnings are less than spending, then you are running a trade deficit. A trade deficit must be balanced by increases in debt (written as a negative number),

The **balance of payments** is a yearly summary of all the economic transactions between residents of one country and residents of the rest of the world.

A country runs a **capital surplus** when the inflow of foreign capital is greater than the outflow of domestic capital to other nations.

sales of assets, or reductions in cash reserves. The reverse holds as well: If earnings are greater than spending, then a trade surplus must be balanced by reductions in debt, purchases of assets, or increases in cash reserves.

If you can understand that equation—and indeed you live it every day—you can understand the basic categories of international finance. The terms simply become a little more complicated once we move to the bigger level of a nation.

The international balance of payments presents a comparable expression:

$$\text{Current account} = (-)\text{Capital account} + \text{Change in official reserves}$$

Now let's go through each term in detail.

The Current Account

The **current account** is the sum of the balance of trade, net income on capital held abroad, and net transfer payments.

The **current account** is the sum of three items:

1. The balance of trade (exports minus imports of goods and services)

2. Net income on capital held abroad, including interest and dividends

3. Net transfer payments, such as foreign aid

What unites the items in the current account is that they all measure transactions that are fully completed or closed out in a *current* period; they do not require any further transfer of funds in the future. To relate these categories back to the example of a single individual, category (1) is like earnings minus spending; category (2) is like earning money on a savings bond that your grandmother gave you when you were 10 ("interest income from abroad"); and category (3) is like getting money from relatives ("foreign aid").

Now let's apply these concepts to the United States. The U.S. current account will be higher and positive to the extent that, for instance, (1) America exports a lot of tractors, (2) American-owned beer factories in Canada pay high dividends to Americans, and (3) America receives foreign aid (this latter example is not usually the case). To consider the alternative, the current account balance will be lower and negative to the extent that, for instance, (1) America buys imported grapes from Chile, (2) German investments in Florida pay high dividends to Germans, and (3) America sends foreign aid to Afghanistan.

Categories (2) and (3) in a country's current account tend to be stable over time. We can simplify by speaking as if the current account was just the balance of trade, exports minus imports. But keep in the back of your mind that terms (2) and (3) can be important for some countries. Foreign aid, for example, is important for smaller and poorer nations, when it can account for 10 percent or more of GDP. But when it comes to the United States, the balance of trade and the capital account are where we find most of the action.

The Capital Account, Sometimes Called the Financial Account

The **capital account** measures changes in foreign ownership of domestic assets including financial assets likes stocks and bonds as well as physical assets.

The **capital account** measures changes in foreign ownership of domestic assets including financial assets likes stocks and bonds as well as physical assets. When the Chinese government buys American government bonds or when Japanese investors buy assets like Rockefeller Center in Manhattan, the capital account of the United States increases. More generally, when there is more investment going into a country than out, that country is running a capital account surplus. When investment is leaving a country that is called a capital account deficit; an example is when Zimbabwe residents send their money abroad rather than investing under their corrupt dictatorship. Less dramatically, many banks in New Zealand are owned by Australian companies and that represents a shift of capital from Australia to New Zealand.

Notice how the capital account differs from "net income held on foreign assets abroad," component (2) of the current account, mentioned above. When a Belgian buys a U.S. stock, the U.S. *capital account* increases (money flows into the United States). Three months later, when that same Belgian receives a dividend from the company, the U.S. *current account* decreases as "net income held on foreign assets abroad" suddenly is higher for Belgium. The capital account measures transactions like buying a stock that may result in future financial flows. The current account measures current financial flows.

The investments in the capital account are divided into the following categories:

Foreign direct investment (FDI)—When foreigners construct new business plants or set up other specific and tangible operations in the United States.

Portfolio investment—When foreigners buy U.S. stocks, bonds, and other asset claims. Unlike FDI, this switches the ownership of already existing investments and it does not immediately create new investment on net.

Other investment—This usually consists of movements of bank deposits. For instance, a wealthy French citizen might shift his or her bank account from Paris to New York.

The Official Reserves Account

This third category measures reserves or currency held by the government. This can include foreign currencies, gold reserves, and also International Monetary Fund (see below) claims known as special drawing rights (SDRs), but for simplicity we will focus on foreign currencies. Sometimes governments stockpile U.S. dollars or other currencies such as the euro. Right now the Chinese government and central bank have stockpiled more than $1 trillion worth of U.S. dollars and dollar-denominated assets.

How the Pieces Fit Together

To understand the balance of payments in its totality, consider more concretely how this accounting identity stays in balance. Say that Wal-Mart decides to buy more toys from China. Spending money on the toys increases the current account deficit of the United States. Toy makers in China receive the money and must do something with it. If they take the money and use it to buy American tractors, the current account is back in balance. If they take the money and invest it back in the United States, say by buying stocks, the American capital account surplus goes up by an equivalent amount. If they take the money and send it to a bank in New York, the capital account surplus goes up (this time in the "other investment" category). If they keep the money in a Chinese bank, there has been a change in reserves. No matter what they do with the money, the balance of payments will balance.

Two Sides, One Coin

Usually the major changes in the balance of payments come through the current account and the capital account, rather than through changes in official reserves. So, a country that is running a current account deficit, such as the United States, balances its payments by running a capital account surplus. Similarly, a country, such as China, that is running a current account surplus, is usually also running a capital account deficit.

Figure 19.1 shows the U.S. balance of payments from 1980 to 2005. Notice that the two accounts are close to mirror images—when the current account is in deficit (negative), the capital account is in surplus (positive), and vice versa.

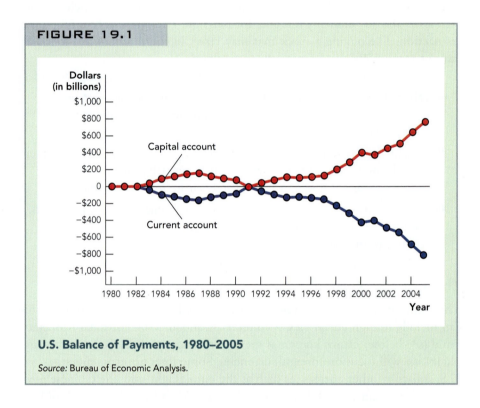

FIGURE 19.1

U.S. Balance of Payments, 1980–2005

Source: Bureau of Economic Analysis.

UNDERSTAND YOUR **world**

The current and capital account are two sides of the same coin. The media and politicians typically focus on the trade deficit, but it's equally correct to look at the other side of the coin, the capital account surplus.

Now that we know that a trade deficit is typically balanced by a capital account surplus, let's go back to our opening question and ask whether our trade deficit is a problem. First, note that this is the same thing as asking whether our capital account surplus is a problem. A surplus sounds better than a deficit so it is not surprising that many economists who think that trade deficits are not a problem focus on the flip side, the capital account surplus. We call the most optimistic view of those who focus on the capital account the "Great Place to Invest" view. We call the less optimistic view the "Foolishly Saving Too Little" view. Let's start with optimism.

"The United States Is a Great Place to Invest." In this view, the trade deficit is driven by the fact that foreigners want to invest in the United States, the world's wealthiest country and largest single, unified market. Instead of using dollars to buy U.S. cars, foreigners are using dollars to buy bonds and stocks and this inflow of investment is great for the United States. A capital account surplus will necessitate a current account deficit, but this is no problem. The investments in America will create more wealth and allow the United States to pay off future obligations without major problems. The fact that America is borrowing or selling assets is from this perspective like borrowing money or selling assets to pay for medical school—it isn't a problem because the investment will pay off with a high-wage job. Advocates of this view sometimes speak of the rest of the world as having a "savings glut," namely a lot of savings but no good place to put them, other than in the United States that is.

Not all economists who focus on the capital account are optimists, however. It's also possible to look at the inflow of capital and ask why are American savings so low? We'll call this the "Foolishly Saving Too Little" view.

"Americans Are Foolishly Saving Too Little." In this view, the reason that capital is flowing into the United States is that Americans are consuming too much and not saving enough. Proponents of this view often tie the trade deficit with the government's budget deficit. The U.S. government is spending more than it is taxing and the difference is being made up by borrowing from foreigners, creating a capital account surplus. In this view, a day of reckoning will come. Foreign investments in America represent a claim on American assets and someday the U.S. government will have to pay off those investment claims. This will lower American living standards and bring higher taxes, as well as the pain of significant economic adjustments. American borrowing from this perspective is like borrowing to buy a closet full of Manolo Blahnik shoes—fun while it lasts but not necessarily wise.

Happy feet for $3,145 a pair, but what happens when the bill comes due?

DUSKO DESPOTOVIC/CORBIS

The Bottom Line on the Trade Deficit

The bottom line is this: Most economists think that the trade deficit per se is not a problem. As we discussed in Chapter 18, trade is beneficial for the United States and as we showed above there is nothing peculiar about running a trade deficit—we all run trade deficits in some areas (e.g., with Whole Foods) and for some periods of time (e.g., when we finance education with a student loan). Countries, in this respect, are no different than individuals.

The trade deficit, however, might indicate or *signal* a problem of low savings. If the United States has a problem with low savings, however, then it's better to address the savings problem directly—in which case the balance of trade will take care of itself—rather than blaming the Chinese or obsessing over the balance of trade numbers. Quotas, tariffs, and trade wars, for example, are unlikely to solve a savings problem. Indeed, if the United States is saving too little, then Americans are at least fortunate that they can borrow in international markets so that investment remains high even when U.S. savings rates are low.

To the extent that Americans are saving too little, there is a stronger case for reducing the government's budget deficit by a combination of tax hikes and spending cuts. In the "Foolishly Saving Too Little" view, the United States is spending too much and the government could do its share to limit this problem by saving more, which means moving closer to a balanced budget or perhaps even running a surplus. We discussed the government budget deficit at greater length in Chapter 16.

Let us now turn to exchange rates. Working with the concepts in the balance of payments identity, we can see how supplies and demands will determine the relative values of different currencies.

What Are Exchange Rates?

The most common means of payment in most (but not all!) foreign countries is a foreign currency and not the U.S. dollar. So, if you travel to a foreign country and you want to buy goods and services in that country, you will usually

An **exchange rate** is the price of one currency in another currency.

▶▶ SEARCH ENGINE

For current information on exchange rates search for the "Yahoo currency converter."

have to buy foreign currency with U.S. dollars. An **exchange rate** is the price of one currency in terms of another currency.

Yahoo! finance prints a table like Table 19.1 every day. Table 19.1 gives exchange rates that held on February 28, 2007.

TABLE 19.1 Major Currency Exchange Rates						
Currency	U.S. $	¥en	Euro	Can $	U.K. £	Swiss Franc
1 U.S. $	1	118.225	0.7571	1.1718	0.5103	1.2218
1 ¥en	0.008458	1	0.006404	0.009912	0.004317	0.010335
1 Euro	1.3208	156.1516	1	1.5477	0.674	1.6138
1 Can $	0.8534	100.8918	0.6461	1	0.4355	1.0427
1 U.K. £	1.9596	231.6679	1.4836	2.2962	1	2.3942
1 Swiss Franc	0.8185	96.763	0.6197	0.9591	0.4177	1

We can read this table in either the vertical or horizontal direction. Read vertically it tells us that the price of one yen is 0.008458 dollars, the price of one euro is 1.3208 dollars, the price of one Canadian dollar is 0.8534 U.S. dollars, and so forth. Read horizontally it tells us that the price of one dollar is 118.225 yen, 0.7571 euro, 1.1718 Canadian dollars, and so forth. Notice that there are always two ways of writing the price of a currency. We can say that one yen trades for 0.008458 dollars or that one dollar trades for 118.225 yen—this sometimes causes confusion so always make sure you know which rate is being quoted!

Exchange Rate Determination in the Short Run

Exchange rates, like other market prices, are determined by supply and demand. For each currency, there is a price in every other currency. At any given moment, the exchange rate for a currency is determined by the intersection of the supply and demand for that currency. Figure 19.2, for example, shows the supply and demand for yen and the exchange rate in dollars per yen.

Notice that we have written "Dollars per yen" ("$/yen" in many books) on the vertical axis. This is the price of one yen in dollars. If this price goes up—that is we move up along the vertical axis—it means that the Japanese yen is stronger, namely it takes more dollars to buy one yen. If this price goes down, the Japanese yen is weaker.

In this chapter when we are analyzing the supply and demand for yen we will always put

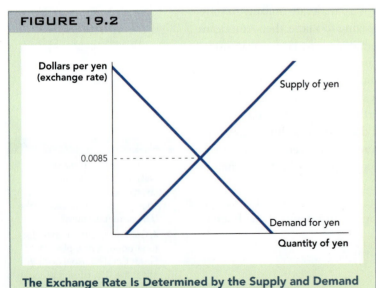

FIGURE 19.2

The Exchange Rate Is Determined by the Supply and Demand for Currencies The exchange rate, the number of dollars it takes to buy one yen, is determined by the supply and demand for yen. In this case, the equilibrium exchange rate is 0.0085 dollars for one yen.

the price of yen, "Dollars per yen," on the vertical axis. But if we analyze the supply and demand for dollars, we will put the *price of dollars* in, say, euros per dollar on the vertical axis.*

Let's now look at some factors that can shift the demand and supply curves.

Changes in Demand for a Currency   The first principle is simple:

1. An increase (decrease) in the demand for a country's exports tends to increase (decrease) the value of its currency.

When Japanese cars become popular around the world, this strengthens the value of the yen. For instance, when U.S. car dealerships order more Toyotas from Japan, they must (ultimately) pay for the cars in yen. An increase in the demand for Japanese goods, therefore, shifts the demand curve for yen up and to the right, illustrated in Figure 19.3.

As usual, an increase in demand increases the price. In this case, the price of one yen increases from 0.0085 dollars to 0.0090 dollars. An increase in the price of a currency is also called an **appreciation**.

Increasing exports are not the only way a currency can change in value. We also have a second principle:

2. The more desirable (undesirable) a country is for foreign investment, the higher (lower) the value of that nation's currency.

Ever since the signing of NAFTA (North American Free Trade Agreement) and the evolution of real democracy in Mexico, American investors have been keener to invest in that country. To invest in Mexico, an American business must convert dollars into pesos, thereby shifting the demand curve for pesos to the right and raising the value of the peso. In this context, note that a "stronger peso" means a "weaker dollar," or whatever other currency we are considering.

An **appreciation** is an increase in the price of one currency in terms of another currency.

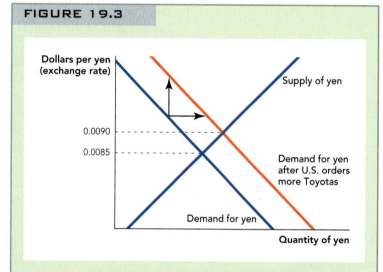

FIGURE 19.3

Dollars per yen (exchange rate)

Supply of yen

0.0090

0.0085

Demand for yen after U.S. orders more Toyotas

Demand for yen

Quantity of yen

An Increase in the Demand for Yen Increases the Price of Yen
An increase in the demand for Toyotas increases the demand for yen, which shifts the demand curve for yen outward (up and to the right). The increase in the demand for yen increases the exchange rate from 0.0085 dollars per yen to 0.0090 dollars per yen.

Alternatively, many governments of sub-Saharan Africa have failed to secure the property rights of foreign investors. The demand to invest is correspondingly weak, shifting the demand curve for these countries' currencies to the left and lowering the value of these currencies.

High interest rates, all other factors held equal, is another factor that attracts investment, increasing the demand for and thus the value of a currency. For instance, if New Zealand "Kiwi bonds" are yielding 9 percent, and U.S. Treasury securities of comparable maturity are yielding 4 percent, this favors the strength of the New Zealand currency. (The New Zealand currency is also called the dollar; investors sometimes say "the Kiwi dollar" to avoid confusion with the U.S. dollar.) Investors will be more inclined to hold New Zealand securities, and

---

* Other textbooks or sources, however, might put "yen per dollar" (or yen/$) instead of "dollars per yen" on the price axis. Either way is correct so long as you remember which one you are working with.

of course to do so they must use the New Zealand currency, thereby shifting out demand.

There is yet another cause of stronger demand for a currency:

3. An increase in the demand to hold dollar reserves boosts the value of the dollar on international markets.

Many governments and central banks hold dollars as a "reserve currency." This means simply that dollars are a preferred means of saving and enjoying liquidity. Of all the currencies held in the world for these official reserves purposes, American dollars comprise two-thirds of the total.

The U.S. dollar is truly a global currency. If a Brazilian company buys a turbine engine from Turkey, they are probably billed in dollars and probably pay in dollars, not the currency of either Turkey or Brazil. If Colombian drug dealers bury some money in their backyard, it is probably dollars. When these demands for dollars rise, the dollar becomes more valuable. Again, the demand curve for dollars will shift to the right. However, if the Colombian government ever succeeds in stopping the drug trade, the demand for U.S. dollars would fall and the demand curve for dollars would shift back to the left.

The Swiss franc, by the way, is another global reserve currency. Even though Switzerland is a small country, it has a long tradition of peace and stability, and to some extent bank secrecy. The Swiss franc is viewed as a "safe haven" currency, even when the rest of the world is experiencing trouble. This is one reason why the Swiss franc tends to be relatively strong. Furthermore, the proverbial "bad guys" used to have secret Swiss bank accounts (since 9/11 and the growth of financial investigations, they're not so secret any more) and to invest some of their money in Swiss francs; that is one reason why so many James Bond movies have scenes there, and of course because the Alps are pretty on the big screen.

A **depreciation** is a decrease in the price of a currency in terms of another currency.

Changes in the Supply of a Currency   An increase in the supply of a currency causes the currency to lose some of its value, that is, fall in price. A fall in the price of a currency is also called a **depreciation**. Figure 19.4 shows the effects of an increase in supply, a shift of the supply curve down and to the right.

If the Federal Reserve increases the supply of U.S. money, this will reduce the value of the dollar relative to other currencies. The not-so-surprising result, as shown in Figure 19.4, is a lower value for the U.S. dollar on world markets.

You may recall from Chapter 11 that the government in Zimbabwe has been printing trillions of Zimbabwe dollars, causing a large increase in the Zimbabwean inflation rate. At the beginning of 2002, for example, one Zimbabwe dollar was worth about 0.018 of a U.S. dollar or just under 2 cents. With the massive increase in the supply of Zimbabwean dollars, the value of the Zimbabwean dollar fell, so that by 2006 one Zimbabwe dollar was worth less than 0.00001 of a U.S. dollar or about one thousandth of a U.S. penny.

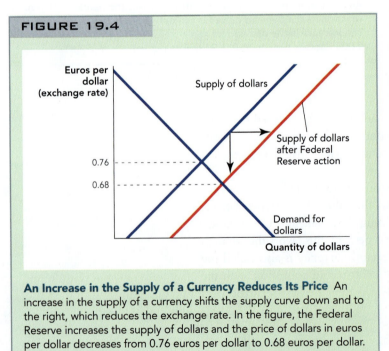

FIGURE 19.4

An Increase in the Supply of a Currency Reduces Its Price   An increase in the supply of a currency shifts the supply curve down and to the right, which reduces the exchange rate. In the figure, the Federal Reserve increases the supply of dollars and the price of dollars in euros per dollar decreases from 0.76 euros per dollar to 0.68 euros per dollar.

A tighter monetary policy, which means a decrease (or slower increase) in the supply of a currency, would shift the supply curve up and to the left and raise the value of the dollar as we show in Figure 19.5.

Exchange Rate Determination in the Long Run

These changes play themselves out in foreign exchange markets every day. But a full explanation outlines why the supply and demand curves lie where they do in the first place, and not just what happens when they shift.

To see the broader picture, consider that the value of a currency is derived, ultimately, from the value of what it can purchase. Money buys or is a potential claim on goods, services, and investments. Given this fact, equilibrium requires that the return to spending a dollar in Chicago, Berlin, or Paris—whether on goods, services, or investments—all yield the same expected return.

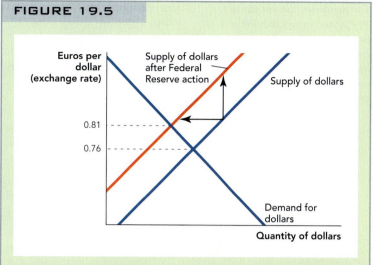

FIGURE 19.5

A Decrease in the Supply of a Currency Increases Its Price A decrease in the supply of a currency shifts the supply curve up and to the left. In the figure, the Federal Reserve decreases the supply of dollars and the price of dollars in euros increases from 0.76 euros per dollar to 0.81 euros per dollar.

Before we can explain this point fully and use it to give a more exact account of exchange rates, we must first outline the difference between real and nominal exchange rates.

We are already familiar with the distinction between real and nominal variables from earlier chapters. To recap, in a domestic setting how much a dollar is worth depends on the level of prices for goods and services. We now extend this same comparison to Cairo, Amsterdam, and Rio de Janeiro. How much a dollar is worth in Cairo depends on two things: the exchange rate between the dollar and the Egyptian pound, and the level of prices for goods and services in Egypt, measured in Egyptian pounds.

If you look at the financial news, you will see that one dollar buys more than one hundred Japanese yen, as of February 19, 2007, when the rate was 119.63 yen per dollar. At first glance, it might appear that the Japanese yen is a very weak currency. Why should it take so many yen to buy a dollar, if not for the weakness of the yen? But it is wrong to think that the stated rate of exchange reflects the relative weakness of the yen.

If one dollar buys 120 yen, we know only the **nominal exchange rate,** which is simply the rate at which you can exchange one currency for another; this is the rate you find quoted in the newspaper or on Yahoo! as we described above.

The **real exchange rate** is the rate at which you can exchange the goods and services of one country for the goods and services of another. To calculate the real exchange rate between the U.S. and Japan, for example, you need to know the nominal exchange rate plus the price of a similar basket of goods in both the United States and Japan. Notice that an exchange rate of one dollar to 120 yen means very different things, depending whether an order of sushi costs one yen, one million yen, or about 240 yen (the true price, roughly). If an order of sushi costs two dollars in the United States and 240 yen in Japan then the real exchange rate is about 1:1.

The **nominal exchange rate** is the rate at which you can exchange one currency for another.

The **real exchange rate** is the rate at which you can exchange the goods and services of one country for the goods and services of another.

The **purchasing power parity (PPP) theorem** says that the real purchasing power of a money should be the same, whether it is spent at home or converted into another currency and spent abroad.

The Purchasing Power Parity Theorem The purchasing power parity (PPP) theorem is the following:

> **The real purchasing power of a money should be about the same, whether it is spent at home or converted into another currency and spent abroad.**

Put in other words, the quantity of goods and services that can be obtained for a given currency should be about the same everywhere, adjusting for the costs of trading those goods and services. The core idea is that spending your dollars in Chicago, or converting them into yen and spending them in Osaka (which might include buying Japanese goods and shipping them back home for resale), should yield about the same benefits.

More concretely, the PPP theorem makes two predictions. First, Toyotas in Japan should cost about as much as Toyotas in California; the same should be true for other individual goods. Second, the cost of a general bundle of goods and services should be about the same everywhere.

The **law of one price** says that if trade were free, then identical goods should sell for about the same price throughout the world.

Purchasing power parity is an application of the **law of one price,** the principle that if trade were free then identical goods should sell for about the same price throughout the world. If Toyotas were cheaper in Tokyo, it would make sense to buy Toyotas in Japan and ship them to the United States. Conversely, if Toyotas are cheaper in the United States, they will be shipped to Japan. Of course, shipping cars from one country to another is not the only way to gain from a difference across prices. Toyota might set up a new auto plant in Tennessee rather than in Osaka, thereby shifting supply into the North American market.

That example is only for cars but the principle can be extended to a broader set of possible transactions. The return to spending a dollar (or yen, or euro, etc.) at home or abroad must be roughly equal, and exchange rates and prices will adjust to equalize those returns. Those adjustments will determine the real exchange rate between any two currencies.

Recall from Chapter 11 that in the long run, money is neutral. We used that principle to explain why in the long run the money supply does not influence real GDP, real interest rates, or real prices. Exactly the same principle applies here, except that now we apply the principle to two monies! Since money is neutral in the United States and money is neutral in Japan, neither the supply of dollars nor the supply of yen can change the real exchange rate in the long run. In other words, governments or central banks set nominal exchange rates, but market forces set the real exchange rate. As usual, however, this applies only in the long run. In the short run, as we discuss further below, the government can influence the real exchange rate and this will be important for macroeconomic policy.

The Purchasing Power Parity Theorem Is only Approximately True Purchasing power parity is limited by the costs of trading, transacting, and shuffling resources. That is one reason why purchasing power parity holds only approximately. At least three constraints on trade prevent prices from being fully equalized across borders:

1. **Transportation costs.** The price of cement might be much higher in Japan than California, but it still will not be profitable to put cement on a boat and ship it from California to Japan. Cement is very heavy and the shipping would cost a great deal. Purchasing power parity applies only to the extent that goods can be transported easily. Notice also that many

personal services—haircuts are the classic example—cannot easily be shipped, although sometimes the labor behind those services can migrate from one country to another. Thus, purchasing power parity is more likely to hold for goods that are cheap to ship, like oranges, than for cement or haircuts.

2. **Some goods cannot be shipped at all.** Sipping a coffee in Paris is different than going to a Starbucks in suburban Ohio, even if the coffee is the same. The coffee can be transported cheaply but Paris cannot be shipped.

Similarly, an apartment in London, Canada, costs less than a similar-sized apartment in London, England. Canada cannot easily cut off its land and ship it to England so prices of apartments will not equalize. More generally, the price of land and any good that uses a lot of land in its production will not equalize across countries.

3. **Tariffs and quotas.** To the extent that governments tax or otherwise restrict trade, prices will not equalize across countries. Tariffs or quotas will hinder market exchange and thus the arbitrage of differing prices.

These restrictions show that purchasing power parity will hold approximately—rather than strictly—for a broad basket of goods and services. In other words, living in London, England, will remain more expensive than living in London, Canada.

Deviations from purchasing power parity are often large and long lasting for services. Goods are easy to transport and so tend to equalize in price more than services, which are difficult to transport. Services, therefore, are cheaper in poorer countries because immigration laws limit the extent to which labor can move from poor countries to rich countries. Wages on the American side of the border are much higher than wages on the Mexican side of the border. The result is that a haircut is much cheaper in Mexico than in the United States. One of the thriftier authors of this textbook often gets his hair cut during trips to Mexico for this reason! Servants are also much cheaper in poorer countries. Even a middle class family in Mexico, India, or Thailand will often employ many servants. The services of a physician, even a high-quality Western trained physician, are also cheaper in poorer countries; that explains why many people are going to India for plastic surgery or hip replacements—plus you can see the Taj Mahal after your surgery is over. Computers, iPods, automobiles, and other goods that can be easily shipped are not systematically cheaper in poorer countries.

How close the real world fits purchasing power parity depends on the nations involved and their ease of trading. As trading costs fall, purchasing power parity is more likely to hold closely. As trading costs rise, the bounds become looser. Purchasing power parity holds more exactly true between the United States and Canada—similar and adjacent countries—than between Japan and Mexico. Note that the concept of "tradeable" is a matter of degree, not an absolute, so how much purchasing power parity holds is a matter of degree as well.

Purchasing power parity also holds more tightly in the long run than in the short run. In the short run, trading costs might hinder entrepreneurs from erasing differences in prices. In the long run, it is more likely that entrepreneurs will find a way to bring prices closer together across international borders.

When it comes to the short run, and within the boundaries set by purchasing power parity, economists still debate the causes of daily exchange rate movements. About $1.9 *trillion* in foreign exchange transactions take place in a typical day. Most of those trades are speculative, done to earn a profit by trying

Paris, Las Vegas. There is no parity here.

to outguess the market. The short-run froth of daily price movements is set largely by psychology and expectations. Traders are guessing at the long run of where the market is headed, as shaped by supply and demand, but some of the short-run trading is just guessing at the short-run behavior of other traders. Sometimes the small, short-run movements in exchange rates are called "noise," which is the economist's polite way of saying we don't understand what causes them or what they mean.

How Monetary and Fiscal Policy Affect Exchange Rates and How Exchange Rates Affect Aggregate Demand

Monetary and fiscal policy will alter the exchange rate and trade balance (exports minus imports) of a country. To understand how, keep in mind that an approximate version of purchasing power parity (for tradable goods) holds in the long run, but that deviations from parity are possible in the short run.

Monetary Policy

Imagine that the Federal Reserve increases $\vec{M}$ through open market operations, a concept discussed in our chapters on the Federal Reserve and monetary policy. The increase in $\vec{M}$ shifts the supply curve for dollars down and to the right, which will result in a lower exchange rate (a depreciation). In the short run, dollar prices are sticky so as far as the rest of the world is concerned it's as if U.S. goods went on sale! Let's look at this in more detail.

Imagine that Caterpillar tractors sell for $50,000 and the exchange rate starts out at one euro per dollar so in Europe a Caterpillar tractor costs €50,000. Now suppose that as a result of Fed actions the exchange rate depreciates so that a European needs only 0.8 euros to buy a dollar. The dollar price is still $50,000 but because of the change in the exchange rate the price in euros has fallen from €50,000 to €40,000, which is in essence a 20 percent discount. Thus, a depreciation will increase U.S. exports. Recall from Chapter 12 that an increase in exports increases AD, which boosts the economy in the short run.

Figure 19.6 shows the process in a diagram. Keep in mind that this is exactly the same analysis of an increase in aggregate demand that we discussed in Chapter 12 and also in the chapters on monetary and fiscal policy. The only difference is that the *source* of the shift in AD is now a depreciation in the exchange rate; the mechanics are exactly as before.

The economy begins at point *a* in long run equilibrium. The increase in $\vec{M}$ causes a depreciation in the exchange rate, which in turn reduces the price of U.S. exports. As a result, exports increase, AD increases, and the growth rate of the economy increases, moving the economy in the short run to point *b*. But what about the long run?

In the long run, money is neutral, which means that domestic prices will rise to match the increase in $\vec{M}$. As a result, the nominal exchange rate will be lower but the real exchange rate—in the long run—won't have changed much, if at all. So, in the long run the real depreciation (the sale on U.S. exports) proves to be temporary and so the boost in exports is temporary as well. But if the increase in $\vec{M}$ is not reversed, the U.S. inflation rate increases. Thus, in the long run, the

FIGURE 19.6

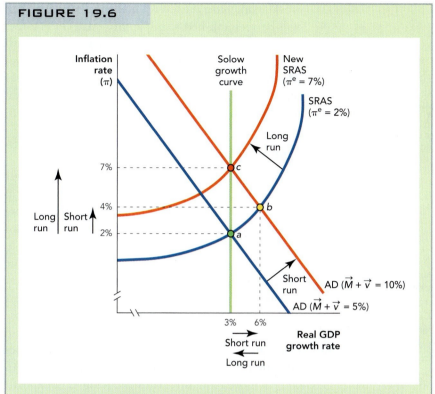

A Depreciation Increases AD in the Short Run An increase in the growth rate of the money supply pushes the exchange rate down (a depreciation). As a result, exports increase, AD increases and the growth rate increases, moving the economy from point *a* to point *b*. In the long run, the domestic inflation rate increases enough to restore the real exchange rate so there is no longer a boost to exports and the economy moves to a new long-run equilibrium at point *c*.

economy moves from point *b* to point *c* and the boost to real output growth is not permanent.

We can, however, see one additional reason why politicians and central banks sometimes favor increases in the growth rate of money, $\vec{M}$. An increase in $\vec{M}$ usually will boost a nation's exports and thus employment. It will appear the economy is doing better, at least for a little while but, as usual, the boost to the economy is temporary and it raises the possibility of higher inflation rates.

Furthermore, although the depreciation makes exports cheaper, it makes imports more expensive. The diminished ability of the nation to invest abroad at good prices or buy imports at good prices—because of the lower real exchange rate—is a less visible but real cost of the lower real exchange rate. The lower real exchange rate nonetheless represents a political temptation, if only because the economy at least appears stronger when exports increase in the short run.

That's it for aggregate output. When it comes to the real exchange rate itself, the path of the market to equilibrium looks like the one portrayed in Figure 19.7 on the next page. Once a Fed action is announced, the dollar moves on international currency markets within seconds. Prices for most goods and services, even if they are relatively flexible, do not respond with this speed. So, at first the dollar has lower international value in real terms.

For a decrease in $\vec{M}$, the process is the reverse. In the short run, the real exchange rate will appreciate, causing U.S. exports to be more expensive on

FIGURE 19.7

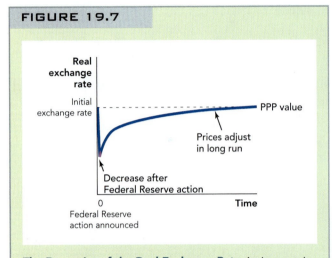

The Dynamics of the Real Exchange Rate An increase in $\vec{M}$ increases the supply of dollars, thus causing a depreciation in the nominal exchange rate. Domestic prices are sticky so at first the nominal depreciation is also a real depreciation. Over time, however, domestic prices rise, so in the long run the real exchange rate returns to its fundamental value as determined by approximate purchasing power parity.

CHECK YOURSELF

> In the short run, what will happen to exports if the Fed increases the money supply? What will happen in the long run?

> Which tends to be more effective in an open economy: monetary policy or fiscal policy?

A **floating exchange rate** is one determined primarily by market forces.

A **fixed or pegged exchange rate** means that a government or central bank has promised to convert its currency into another currency at a fixed rate.

Dollarization occurs when a foreign country uses the U.S. dollar as its currency.

world markets. In the long run, the real exchange rate will be reestablished at the approximate PPP value. Notice that we can see once again why nations with a high rate of inflation—nations that ought to lower $\vec{M}$—may be reluctant to do so. In the short run, a reduction in $\vec{M}$ reduces exports, reducing AD and reducing the real growth rate in the short run.

Fiscal Policy

Expansionary fiscal policy, or an increase in the budget deficit, will raise domestic interest rates. As explained in Chapters 8 and 17, when government borrows more money, the demand for loanable funds shifts outward and interest rates go up.

As a result, the higher interest rates will cause the nation—let's say the United States—to run a greater surplus on its capital account. That is, more foreigners will want to invest in the United States to enjoy those high interest rates. The greater demand to invest will cause an appreciation of the U.S. dollar. What does an appreciation of the dollar do to U.S. exports? An appreciation makes U.S. exports more expensive, thus reducing U.S. exports. Thus, a budget deficit can cause a trade deficit. These are sometimes called "the twin deficits."

We now see one more limitation of fiscal policy. The boost to domestic aggregate demand, resulting from the new government spending, will to some extent be offset by the greater difficulty of exporting at the new and higher real exchange rate. Total aggregate demand—domestic plus foreign—might not go up at all. In other words, the New Keynesian argument for fiscal policy that we discussed in Chapter 17 is less justified the more open the economy. This is yet another reason why monetary policy has typically become more important than fiscal policy as a tool of macroeconomic management.

Fixed vs. Floating Exchange Rates

So far we have treated the case of **floating exchange rates** with currency prices determined in open world markets. This is by far the most common scenario in the world today and indeed throughout history.

Still, in other cases the world has seen **fixed or pegged exchange rates**, where currencies do not fluctuate against one another on a daily basis. Fixed exchange rate systems can take three forms:

1. Simply adopting the money of another country

Panama, Ecuador, and El Salvador all use U.S. dollars as their currency; this is called **dollarization**. The central banks of these nations have no active role in managing their money supplies.

The disadvantage of this approach is that Ecuador must buy and save enough dollars to use that currency. The advantage is that, once in place, Ecuador receives the monetary policy of the United States. Once the transition is made, the common currency runs on automatic pilot. Overall, it is plausible that the U.S. Fed does a better job than would an Ecuadorian central bank. Indeed, at the time of dollarization in 2000, the rate of inflation in Ecuador was above 50 percent. Today, the rate of inflation in Ecuador roughly tracks that of the United States and of course this is much lower.

2. Setting up a currency union

Many European countries gave up their currencies and created the euro, a common currency under the supervision of the European Union and (as of early 2009) shared by 16 different EU countries. The wealthier European countries, such as Germany and France, saw the euro as a way to unify Europe economically. Some of the poorer countries, such as Greece, saw the euro as a way to obtain a more stable currency. In any case, all of these countries allow the European Central Bank to control their common monetary policy; the euro does not belong to any single country. The euro, however, is unique and no other comparable arrangement exists today.

3. Backing a currency with high levels of reserves and promising convertibility at a certain rate

A country could promise to convert its currency into U.S. dollars, or some other currency, at a specified rate. Holding sufficient reserves of the foreign currency to ensure conversion would make this promise more credible. Since 1983, Hong Kong has pledged that 7.80 Hong Kong dollars are equal to one U.S. dollar and required Hong Kong banks to have full American backing for any note issued. For many years, Austria pegged its currency to the value of the German mark, prior to adopting the euro.

Option 3 is, of course, a matter of degree. Economists refer to a "peg" to describe a relatively rigid commitment to a specified conversion rate. A **dirty or managed float** refers to a relatively loose commitment to a floating exchange rate. Under a dirty float, a currency will vary in value daily, although the central bank or treasury will intervene if that currency moves too far outside of a band of intended or pre-announced values.

The Problem with Pegs

The pegging option has become less popular over time. Many nations have attempted currency pegs, but usually they have failed. For instance, Thailand, Indonesia, Brazil, and Argentina, among others, all tried to peg their currencies to the U.S. dollar or to a weighted basket of currencies. In each case, the peg was broken by speculators, largely because these countries did not and could not match the monetary and fiscal policies of the United States. Why hold one Argentine peso—supposedly equal in value to a dollar throughout the late 1990s—when you can hold a U.S. dollar instead?

When Argentina pegged its currency to the U.S. dollar in 1991, it promised that one Argentine peso was equal in value to one U.S. dollar. For a while, markets believed this promise. The Argentine economy was doing well, foreign investment was flowing in, and the Argentine government instituted many desirable economic reforms.

But over time people began to doubt whether this peg could be maintained. Eventually the weaknesses of the Argentine economy became revealed more clearly. The government was unable to bring about true fiscal balance. Many foreign investors began to believe that the Argentine peg would break and that the one-to-one rate would go away. This would mean that one peso would become worth less than one U.S. dollar. Many people who had invested in pesos withdrew their money from the country or tried to convert their

Due to Hong Kong's currency peg, these 10 Hong Kong dollars could be exchanged for $1.29 U.S.

TOM GRILL/CORBIS

A **dirty or managed float** is a currency whose value is not pegged but governments will intervene extensively in the market to keep the value within a certain range.

peso holdings into dollars before the one-to-one rate disappeared. Argentine citizens panicked as well, and many of them also sought to convert their pesos into U.S. dollars.

The resulting rush to convert pesos into dollars put great strain on the peso. The Argentine government did not have enough U.S. dollars to keep up the value of the peg. The result was that the peso fell from being worth a dollar (January 6, 2002) to being worth about 26 cents (June 28, 2002), across the course of only five and a one-half months. In other words, the Argentine government had to officially announce a new peg with a much lower value for the Argentine currency.

The rapid reduction in the official exchange rate ruined the economic reputation of the country and the withdrawal of money from the country led to a collapse of the banking system. This is sometimes called capital flight. Argentina probably would have been better off had it never pegged its currency in the first place.

Overall, the lesson is simple. Most countries should not attempt exchange rate pegs. An effective peg requires a very serious commitment to a high level of monetary and fiscal stability. If a country doesn't have as sound an economy as the United States, in the long run it cannot peg to the U.S. dollar.

CHECK YOURSELF

> When the value of a country's currency is determined by the forces of supply and demand, is this a floating exchange rate or a fixed exchange rate?

> Who controls the monetary policy of the European Union?

What Are the IMF and the World Bank?

To close this chapter let us look at two very controversial global institutions, the International Monetary Fund and the International Bank for Reconstruction and Development, more commonly known as the World Bank. These institutions have occasioned protests, the throwing of bricks, conspiracy theories, and political T-shirts. What is up? Are they noxious carriers of evil global forces, benevolent do-gooders, or something else altogether?

For the most part, these agencies are bureaucracies. They do some good, some bad, but they are not as important—for better or worse—as many people think.

International Monetary Fund

Today the International Monetary Fund (IMF) serves as an international lender of last resort. That is, when countries experience financial troubles, the IMF steps in to organize a rescue package, lend money, and monitor the economic situation. Often the loans are tied to a country's willingness to take the IMF's economic advice.

The IMF, created after the end of World War II, is located in Washington, D.C., but it is a "multilateral" institution. It is set up by the world's governments and is independent of any single government. It receives a monetary allocation from each government and also may earn income from its loans. Historically, the director of the IMF is a European. The director reports to a board, and board membership is roughly proportional to how much money a country puts into the institution. The United States, Western Europe, and Japan exercise a dominant influence in this regard, but the staff is drawn from around the world.

The IMF was very active in the Asian currency crises of the 1990s—in Indonesia, Thailand, and South Korea—and in the Argentine financial crisis starting in 2001. Critics of the IMF, such as Nobel Laureate Joseph Stiglitz, charge that it forces borrowing governments to cut government spending, tighten monetary policy, and raise interest rates. In other words, the claim is that the IMF has encouraged contractionary macroeconomic policies when (perhaps) expansionary policies were called for. Defenders of the IMF have argued that the advice is more subtle than is often portrayed, tough fiscal reforms are sometimes needed, or that borrowing countries do not in fact follow the advice, regardless of whether or not it is good advice.

The World Bank

The World Bank also dates from the immediate aftermath of World War II. It was designed to facilitate the flow of capital to poor countries, especially those parts of the world not being served by private capital markets. The full-time staff of about 10,000 employees is headquartered in Washington, D.C., right next to the IMF. The Bank is ruled by a board, whose members are drawn from supporting nations, and a president who has historically been an American.

Mostly the World Bank lends money for specific projects in developing countries. This includes loans for water projects, roads, dams, health care, and environmental projects, among other activities. World Bank loans are tied to the use of Bank expertise and the understanding that the borrowing country will work cooperatively with the Bank.

In 2006, the World Bank lent $21 billion to developing nation governments, and collected about $15 billion in loan repayments. Currently the Bank's largest borrower, by far, is China. Other top borrowers are India, Brazil, Mexico, and Turkey. This has led to debate over the Bank's proper mission. China receives at least $70 billion in foreign investment per year, while it is sitting on over $1 trillion in foreign currency reserves. So why is the World Bank lending to China? Private capital markets are today much more active than in the early days of the Bank, so it is no longer clear that the World Bank is filling a gap in a useful way. Defenders of the Bank note that much of China remains poor, and the Chinese loans turn a profit and help the Bank carry out its mission in poorer places like Africa.

The World Bank also gives away money, lends it out at very low rates of interest, or makes loans that it does not expect will be repaid. This is the aid side of the Bank, which is separate from the Bank's loans. To an increasing extent, the Bank's aid is flowing to sub-Saharan Africa.

Critics claim that the Bank does not pay enough attention to results. The commercial incentive is for the Bank to make many loans. The lent funds first go to governments and then they often are used to purchase goods and services from Western companies. For instance, a World Bank loan to Senegal might help finance a contract with a French company for the supply of urban water. This benefits commercial interests in the countries that control the Bank. Accountability is often low, since each year another round of loans will be made in any case. The World Bank makes money off its loans, so perhaps not enough attention is paid to whether those projects deliver their promised benefits. Defenders note that the Bank has responded to criticism in the past, improved its environmental record, and avoided many previous mistakes. Foreign aid is a difficult business to succeed at, and many people believe that the World Bank is overall a force for good.

The IMF and the World Bank attract so much attention because they are seen as icons of global capitalism. Furthermore, both groups hire many technocrats, and neither is subject to direct accountability through democratic rule. They seem to stand above national borders and make decisions, while reporting to no one. They encourage poor countries to borrow money and those debts cannot always be repaid. Such are the charges, but the reality is more prosaic. Both agencies are highly constrained in what they can accomplish, if only because their resources are limited and they deal frequently with contrary governments. At the margin, they make a difference, but they are not the driving forces behind global capitalism.

□ Takeaway

International currencies are a tricky business, but basic economic principles hold internationally as well as nationally. Contrary to the statements of many politicians, trade deficits are not necessarily a problem, unless a country is investing foolishly or not saving enough. In either case, the trade deficit is not the root of the relevant problem. Instead of complaining about America's current trade deficit with China, it is better to consider how the United States might save more. The trade balance is simply one side of the coin, with the capital account serving as the other side. If a lot of capital is flowing into a country, that country also will be running a trade deficit.

Exchange rates are set in active markets, changing by the second every day, and following the laws of supply and demand. Monetary policy can affect real exchange rates in the short run, but not in the long run. In the long run, exchanges rates are set according to purchasing power parity, so that profits cannot be made buying goods in one country and shipping them to another.

Both monetary and fiscal policies will affect a country's real exchange rate in the short run and these exchange rate effects will influence aggregate demand by affecting some mix of exports, imports, and the flow of capital from one country to another.

Most countries today have floating exchange rates with values determined in international currency markets. Fixed or pegged exchange rates are possible but in most circumstances they are difficult to maintain over the longer run. Thus, a combination of currency unions and floating exchange rates has increasingly become the global norm.

□ CHAPTER REVIEW

KEY CONCEPTS

Trade deficit, p. 408

Trade surplus, p. 408

Balance of payments, p. 409

Capital surplus, p. 409

Current account, p. 410

Capital account, p. 410

Exchange rate, p. 414

Appreciation, p. 415

Depreciation, p. 416

Nominal exchange rate, p. 417

Real exchange rate, p. 417

Purchasing power parity (PPP) theorem, p. 418

Law of one price, p. 418

Floating exchange rate, p. 422

Fixed or pegged exchange rate, p. 422

Dollarization, p. 422

Dirty or managed float, p. 423

FACTS AND TOOLS

1. Start with the facts about the trade deficit (also known as the "balance of trade"), the most widely discussed part of the balance of payments. Head to the database run by the Federal Reserve Bank of St. Louis, http://research.stlouisfed.org/fred2. In the search box, look for data on two series, "EXPGSCA" (real annual exports in year 2000 dollars) and IMPGSCA (real annual imports in year 2000 dollars). Below each graph, you should see the raw annual data for the last five years.

   a. What was the level of exports for each of the last five years? Did exports rise every year?

   b. What was the level of imports for each of the last five years? Did imports rise every year? If not, did exports and imports fall at the same time?

   c. How big was the trade deficit (or surplus) each year?

   d. Divide each year's number by real GDP for each year (GDPCA): What was the trade deficit (or surplus) as a percentage of GDP each year? In years where GDP fell from the previous year, did the trade deficit rise or fall?

2. Practice with the balance of payments:

   Current account + Capital account = Change in official reserves

   a. Current account = −$10, Capital account = +$15. What is the change in reserves?

   b. Current account = −$10, Change in reserves = −$3. What is the capital account?

   c. Your college expenses = $12,000, Income from your barista job = $4,000. What is your current account? If you haven't changed your reserves (i.e., cash savings) at all, what is the capital account (i.e., borrowing from parents or bank)?

3. a. Consider two headlines: "Money is pouring into the U.S. faster than ever" versus "Record U.S. trade deficit." How can both be true simultaneously?

   b. Consider two headlines: "Money is fleeing the U.S. faster than ever" versus "Record U.S. trade surplus." How can both be true simultaneously?

4. In the chapter, two stories about the deficit are told: "the great place to invest" story and the "foolishly saving too little" story. In the examples below, which is more like the "great place to invest" story and which is more like the "foolishly saving too little" story?

   a. Goofus uses his student loan money to buy a nice flat-screen TV and can't afford most of his textbooks. Gallant uses his student loan money to buy his textbooks and coffee that keeps him awake during study sessions.

   b. Charlie borrows money from his dad, Martin, to attend the right parties, make useful industry connections, and build his career. Emilio borrows money from his dad to attend fun parties, meet fun people, and, well, that's about it.

   c. America 1 borrows money to invest in her future. America 2 borrows money to pay for a spending binge.

5. a. According to Table 19.1, how many Japanese yen could you get for one dollar on February 28, 2007? Use the currency converter on Yahoo! Finance to find out how many yen you could buy for a dollar today.

   b. Given your answer to the previous question, did the buying power of the dollar rise or fall over this period? (Get this one right: It's crucial to understanding exchange rates.)

   c. Repeat parts a and b for one other currency in Table 19.1.

6. According to the purchasing power parity theorem, what must be approximately equal across countries: the nominal exchange rate or the real exchange rate?

7. a. According to purchasing power parity theory, a country with massive inflation should also experience a massive fall in the price of its currency compared to other currencies (a depreciation). Is this what happened in Zimbabwe, or did the opposite occur?

   b. Hyperinflation is defined as a rapid rise in the price of goods and services. According to purchasing power parity theory, does hyperinflation also cause a rapid rise in the price of foreign currencies?

8. Which international financial institution focuses on the long-run health of developing countries: The IMF or the World Bank? Which one

focuses on short-run financial crises in developing countries?

9. Let's translate between newspaper jargon about exchange rates and the economic reality of exchange rates.

   a. Last week, the currency of Frobia was trading one for one with the currency of Bozzum. This week, one unit of Frobian currency buys two units of Bozzumian currency. Which currency "rose?" Which currency became "stronger? "Which currency "appreciated?"

   b. The currency in the nation of Malvolio becomes "weaker." Now that it's weaker, can 10 U.S. dollars buy more of the Malvolian currency than before or less than before?

   c. A college student travels from the United States to Germany. Just before he leaves, he changes $400 into euros. He spends only half the money while in Germany, so on his return to the United States, he exchanges his euros back into dollars. However, while he was admiring Munich's historic Marienplatz, the dollar "weakened" considerably. Is this good news or bad news from the college student's point of view?

10. **a.** When the Japanese government slows the rate of money growth, will that tend to strengthen the yen against the dollar or weaken the yen against the dollar?

   b. When the Japanese government slows the rate of money growth, will the dollar tend to appreciate against the yen or will the dollar tend to depreciate against the yen?

   c. When Americans increase their demand for Japanese-made cars, will that tend to strengthen the yen against the dollar or weaken the yen against the dollar?

   d. When Americans increase their demand for Japanese-made cars, will the dollar tend to appreciate against the yen or will the dollar tend to depreciate against the yen?

THINKING AND PROBLEM SOLVING

1. Practice with the current account: Which of the following tend to raise the value of Country X's current account?

   a. Country X sends cash to aid war victims in Country Y.

   b. Investors living in Country X receive more dividend payments than usual from businesses operating in Country Y.

   c. Investors living in Country Y receive more interest payments than usual from businesses operating in Country X.

   d. Immigrants from Country Y who live and work in Country X send massive amounts of currency back to their families in Country Y.

   e. The government of Country X imports more jet fighters and missiles from Country Y.

2. Practice with the capital account: Which of the three categories of the capital account does each belong in? Which of the following tend to raise the value of Country X's capital account?

   a. A corporation in Country Y pays for a new factory to be built in Country X.

   b. A corporation in Country Y sells all of its stock in a corporation located in Country X to a citizen of Country X.

   c. A citizen of Country Y purchases 20 percent of the shares of a corporation in Country X from a citizen of Country X.

   d. A business owner in Country X pays for a new factory to be built in Country Y.

3. Let's translate "Americans are foolishly saving too little" into a simple GDP story. Recall that GDP = C + I + G + Net exports. GDP is fixed and equal to 100 throughout the story: After all, it's pinned down by the production function of Chapter 7. Thus, the size of the pie is fixed: The only question is how the pie is sliced into C, I, G, and net exports. To keep it simple, assume that I + G = 40 throughout.

   a. The "saving too little" story comes in two parts: In part one (now), the United States has high C and low (really, negative) net exports. If C = 70, what do net exports equal? Is this a trade deficit or a trade surplus?

   b. In part two (later), foreign countries are tired of sending so many goods to the United States, and want to start receiving goods from the United States. Net exports now become positive, rising to +5. What does C equal? If citizens value consumption, which period do they prefer: "now" or "later?"

4. Let's translate "The United States is a great place to invest" into a simple GDP story. Recall that GDP = C + I + G + Net exports. In this story, foreigners build up the U.S. capital stock by pushing investment (I) above its normal level. Thus, GDP equals 100 in the "now" period but equals 110 in the "later" period. To keep it simple, assume that C + G = 80 throughout.

   a. The "great place to invest" story comes in two parts: In part one (now), the United States has high I and low (really, negative) net exports. If I = 35, what do net exports equal? Is this a trade deficit or a trade surplus?

   b. In part two (later), foreign countries are tired of sending so many machines and pieces of equipment to the United States, and want to start receiving goods from the United States. Net exports now become positive, rising to +5. What does I equal?

5. The market for foreign currencies is a lot like the market for apples or cars or fish, so we can use the same intuition—as long as we keep reminding ourselves which way is "up" and which is "down." Consider the market for something called "euros" (maybe it's a new breakfast cereal) and measure the price in dollars. Discuss the following cases:

   a. The people who make "euros" decide to produce many more of them. Is this a shift in supply or in demand, and in which direction? What does this do to the price of euros?

   b. Consumers and businesses decide that they'd like to own a lot more euros than before. Is this a shift in supply or in demand, and in which direction? What does this do to the price of euros?

   c. There's a slowdown in the production of euros, initiated by the executives in charge of euro production. Is this a shift in supply or in demand, and in which direction? What does this do to the price of euros?

   d. Suppose that the price of apples rises. Using the same language as in questions a and b, would you describe this as a strengthening of the dollar or a weakening of the dollar?

6. Now that we've built up some intuition about exchange rates, let's apply the principles more thoroughly. In this question, we discuss the U.S.-China exchange rate. Officially, the Chinese government fixed this exchange rate for years at

a time, but in this question, we treat it as a market rate that can change every day.

   a. In the figure below, shift the appropriate curves to illustrate the effect of the following news story: Chinese factory sells poisonous dog food.

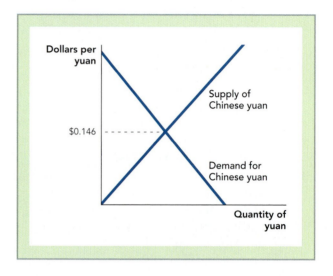

   b. Does this news story raise or lower the price of the yuan? Does this strengthen or weaken the Chinese currency? Does this strengthen or weaken the U.S. dollar?

7. Nobel Laureate Robert Solow once jokingly noted, "I have a chronic [trade] deficit with my barber, who doesn't buy a darned thing from me." Is this a problem? Why or why not? How does this relate to the U.S.-China, U.S.-Mexico, and U.S.-Japan trade deficits?

8. Corey, a young entrepreneur, notices that cigarette lighters sell for only $0.50 each in Utah but they sell for $1.00 each in Nevada.

   a. If Corey wants to make money by buying and selling lighters, where should he buy the lighters and where should he sell them?

   b. If many other people imitate Corey's behavior, what will happen to the supply of lighters in Utah (rise, fall, unchanged)? What will happen to the supply of lighters in Nevada (rise, fall, unchanged)?

   c. What will the behavior in part b do to the price of lighters in Utah? In Nevada?

   d. According to the law of one price, what can we say about the price of cigarette lighters

in Nevada after all of this arbitrage? More than one of the following may be true:

Less than $1.00 each

More than $1.00 each

The same as the Utah price

9. At Christmas, five-year-old Gwen runs a massive trade deficit with her parents: She "exports" only a wrapped candy cane to her parents, but she "imports" a massive number of video games, dolls, and pairs of socks.

   a. Is this trade deficit a good thing for Gwen?

   b. When Gwen turns 25, her parents insist on being repaid for all those years of Christmas presents—that is, they require her to run a "trade surplus." Is this "trade surplus" good news for Gwen? Why or why not?

10. a. Suppose that the price level in the United States doubled, while the price level in the U.K. remained unchanged. According to purchasing power parity theory, would the dollar/pound nominal exchange rate double or would it fall in half?

    b. In practice, PPP tends to hold more true in the long run than in the short run, because many prices are sticky. So if the U.S. money supply increased dramatically—a big enough rise for the price level to double in the long run—would this be good news for British tourists headed to the United States or would it be good news for U.S. tourists headed to Britain? Incidentally, would this be good news or bad news (in the short run) for U.S. tourists staying in the United States?

CHALLENGES

1. In our basic model, a rise in money growth causes currency depreciation: We also know from Chapter 12 and Chapter 15 on monetary policy that a rise in money growth normally raises aggregate demand and boosts short-run real growth. But in the 2001 Argentine crisis and the 1997 Asian financial crisis, a currency depreciation seemed to cause a massive *fall* in short-run output.

   a. What type of shock could cause a currency depreciation to be associated with a fall in short-run output?

   b. In both the Argentine and the Asian crises, these countries' banking sectors were hit especially hard: They had made big promises

to pay their debts in foreign currencies—often dollars—and the depreciation made it impossible for them to keep those promises. What became more "expensive" as a result of the depreciation: foreign currency (dollars, yen, pounds) or domestic currency?

   c. In these crises, depreciation created bankruptcies: These bankruptcies are what causes the shock discussed in part a. To avoid this outcome in the future, Berkeley economist Barry Eichengreen, an expert on exchange rate policy, recommended that businesses in developing countries should encourage foreigners to invest in stock that pays dividends rather than in debt. He believed this would make it easier for countries to endure surprise depreciations. Why would he recommend this?

2. In Panama, a dollarized country, a Big Mac is about 30 percent cheaper than in the United States. Why?

3. A supply-and-demand model can illustrate the difficulty of keeping a fixed exchange rate: It's much the same as any other price floor. Consider the fixed exchange rate below. Sparta uses a currency called the spartonian, Athenians use the aton, and the Spartans have chosen a fixed exchange rate of two atons per spartonian:

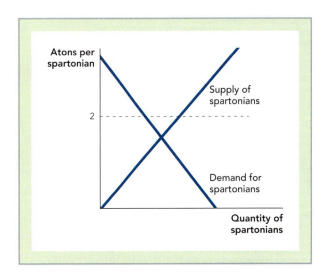

   a. In a typical supply-and-demand model, what would you call the gap that exists between quantity supplied and quantity demanded at this fixed exchange rate: a surplus or a shortage? Of which currency?

b. If the Spartan government wants to keep this exchange rate fixed, what will tend to happen to its official reserve account supply of atons: Will it rise, or will it tend to fall? (Hint: Remember that the suppliers of spartonians want to buy atons. How does this explain why governments of fixed exchange rate countries hold large amount of foreign currencies in their accounts?)

c. If demand for spartonians fell because of a weak Spartan economy, would this make it harder or easier for this government to maintain the exchange rate?

d. If the Spartan government wanted to bring quantity supplied and quantity demanded closer together, would it want to slow money growth or raise money growth? When real world countries have "overvalued" currencies, do you think they should fix it by slowing money growth or by raising money growth?

4. a. Ecuador is currently dollarized: Bank accounts are denominated in U.S. dollars, for example. If Ecuadoreans believe rumors that the country is going to go off the dollar and is going to convert all bank account deposits into a new unit of money called the "Ecuado" (similar to what Argentina actually did in 2001), what will this probably do to the Ecuadorean banking system?

b. "There is no such thing as a fixed exchange rate: Just pegs that haven't been changed . . . yet." Explain how this belief, by itself, can make it hard for a country to maintain a fixed exchange rate. Does this belief have a direct impact on the demand for a currency or on the supply of a currency?

5. We said that "an effective peg requires a very serious commitment to a high level of monetary and fiscal stability." As in our discussion of monetary policy, people's *beliefs* about what government *might* do in the future put limits on what governments should do *today*. Discuss how "commitment" can keep an exchange rate stable. Compare with how commitment can make it easier to keep inflation low. What can a government do in these situations to convince foreign investors and domestic citizens that it will keep its commitments? (Certainly, there is more than one good way to answer this question: The problem of creating commitment is an active area of research across the social sciences.)

Appendix A

Reading Graphs and Making Graphs

Economists use graphs to illustrate both ideas and data. In this appendix, we review commonly used graphs, explain how to read them, and give you a few tips on how you can make graphs using Microsoft Excel or similar software.

Graphs Express Ideas

In economics, graphs are used to express ideas. The most common graphs we use throughout this book plot two variables on a coordinate system. One variable is plotted on the vertical or y-axis, while the other variable is plotted on the horizontal or x-axis.

In Figure A.1, for example, we plot a very generic graph of variable Y against variable X. Starting on the vertical axis at Y = 100, you read across to the point at which you hit the graph and then down to find X = 800. Thus, when Y = 100, X = 800. In this case, you can also see that when X = 800, then Y = 100. Similarly, when Y = 60, you can read from the graph that X = 400, and vice versa. As you may recall, the slope of a straight line is defined as the rise over the run or rise/run. In this case, when Y rises from 60 to 100, a rise of 40, then X runs from 400 to 800, a run of 400, so the slope of the line is 40/400 = 0.1. The slope is positive, indicating that when Y increases so does X.

Let's now apply the idea of a graph to some economic concepts. In Chapter 2, we show how a demand curve can be constructed from hypothetical data on the price and quantity demanded of oil. We show this here as Figure A.2.

The table on the left of the figure shows that at a price of $55 per barrel buyers are willing and able to buy 5 million barrels of oil a day (MBD), or more simply at a price of $55, the quantity demanded is 5 MBD. You can read this information off the graph in the following way. Starting on the vertical axis, locate the price of $55. Then look to the right for the point where the

FIGURE A.1

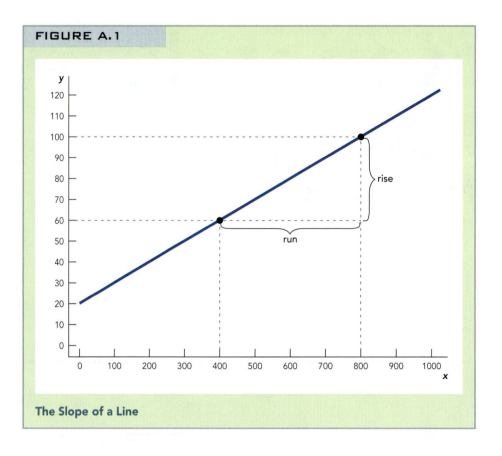

The Slope of a Line

FIGURE A.2

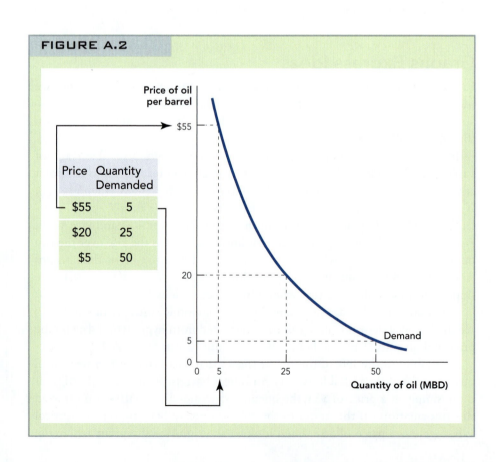

$55 price hits the demand curve: looking down from this point, you see that the quantity demanded is 5 million barrels of oil per day. How about at a lower price of $20 per day? Start at $20 on the vertical axis and read to the right until the price hits the demand curve, then read down. Can you see that the quantity demanded at this price of $20 per barrel is 25 million barrels of oil per day?

We said that graphs express ideas, so what is the idea being expressed here? The most important fact about a demand curve is that it has a negative slope, that is, it slopes downward. This tells us the important but simple idea that as the price of a good falls, the quantity demanded increases. This is key: as the price of a good such as oil falls, people demand more of it.

A demand curve is a description of what *would happen* to the quantity demanded as the price of a good changed *holding fixed all other influences on the quantity of oil demanded*. (In this sense, demand curves are hypothetical and we rarely observe them directly.)

The quantity of oil demanded, for example, depends not just on the price of oil but on many other factors such as income or the price of other goods like automobiles and population, to name just a few of many influences. Today's demand curve for oil, for example, depends on today's income, price of automobiles and population. Imagine, for example, that average income today is $10,000, the price of an average automobile is $25,000 and world population is 7 billion. The blue curve in Figure A.3 shows the demand curve for oil under these conditions. Note that there are also many other influences on the demand for oil that we don't list but that are also being held fixed. Most importantly, if any of these conditions changes then the demand curve for oil will shift.

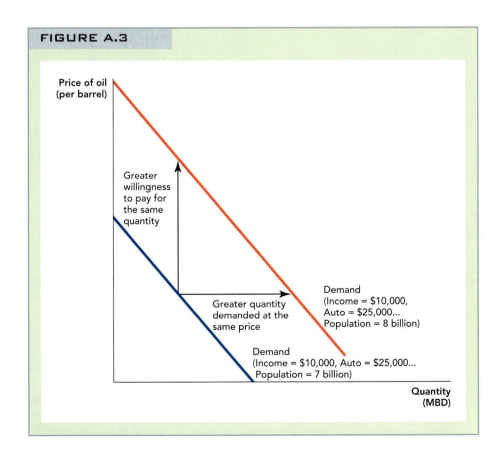

FIGURE A.3

Price of oil (per barrel)

Greater willingness to pay for the same quantity

Greater quantity demanded at the same price

Demand (Income = $10,000, Auto = $25,000... Population = 8 billion)

Demand (Income = $10,000, Auto = $25,000... Population = 7 billion)

Quantity (MBD)

If world population increases to 8 billion, for example, there will be a new demand curve for oil. With a greater population, there will be more barrels of oil demanded at every specific price so the demand curve will shift to the right. Equivalently, as the population increases, there will be a greater willingness to pay for any given quantity of oil so the demand curve will shift up. Thus, we say that an increase in demand is a shift in the curve up and to the right shown by the red curve in Figure A.3. Chapter 2 explains in greater detail how a demand curve shifts in response to changes in factors other than price.

What is important to emphasize here is that a demand curve is drawn holding fixed every influence on the quantity demanded other than price. Changes in any factor that influences the demand for oil other than price will produce a new demand curve.

One more important feature of two variables graphed in a coordinate system is that these figures can be read in two different ways. For example, as we mention in Chapter 2, demand curves can be read both horizontally and vertically. Read "horizontally," you can see from Figure A.4 that at a price of $20 per barrel demanders are willing and able to buy 25 million barrels of oil per day. Read "vertically," you can see that the maximum price that demanders are willing to pay for 25 million barrels of oil a day is $20 per barrel. Thus, demand curves show the quantity demanded at any price or the maximum willingness to pay (per unit) for any quantity.

FIGURE A.4

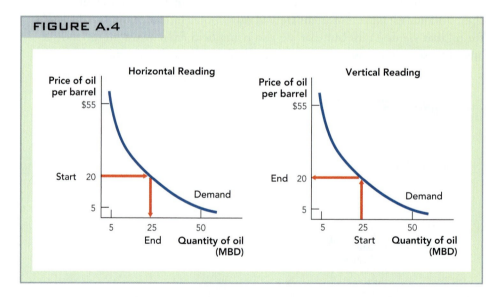

It may seem difficult at first to interpret these graphs, but as you will see, graphs are amazingly useful for thinking about difficult economic problems. It's like learning to drive a car—at first it's not easy and you will make some mistakes but once you learn how to drive your ability to do things and go places increases enormously. The same thing is true with graphs!

Data Graphs

As well as expressing ideas, graphs can also be used to illustrate data. In Chapter 5, for example, we point out that GDP can be broken down according to the national spending identity into these components: Consumption, Investment, Government Purchases, and Net Exports (Exports minus Imports), that is, $GDP = Y = C + I + G + NX$. U.S. GDP for 2007 is shown in Table A.1.

TABLE A.1 U.S. GDP 2007 (in billions of dollars)

Category	GDP
Consumption	9,710.2
Investment	2,130.4
Government	2,674.8
Net Exports	–707.8
GDP (Total)	13,807.6

Source: Bureau of Economic Analysis

If you type the components into Excel, as shown in Figure A.5, you can use the sum function to check that the components do add up to GDP.

Highlighting the data in columns A and B and clicking Insert > Column > Clustered Column and (with a few modifications to add axis titles and to make the graph look pretty), we have the graph on the left side of Figure A.6.

The graph on the right side of Figure A.6 shows exactly the same data only on the right side we chose Stacked Column (and we switched the rows and columns). Sometimes one visualization of the data is more revealing than another so it's a good idea to experiment a little bit with alternative ways of presenting the same data. But please don't get carried away with adding 3D effects or other chart junk. Always keep the focus on the data, not on the special effects.

FIGURE A.5

	A	B	C	D
	B7		f_x =SUM(B2:B5)	
1	Category	GDP		
2	Cons	9710.2		
3	Inv	2130.4		
4	Govt	2674.8		
5	NX	-707.8		
6				
7	GDP (Total)	13807.6		
8				

FIGURE A.6

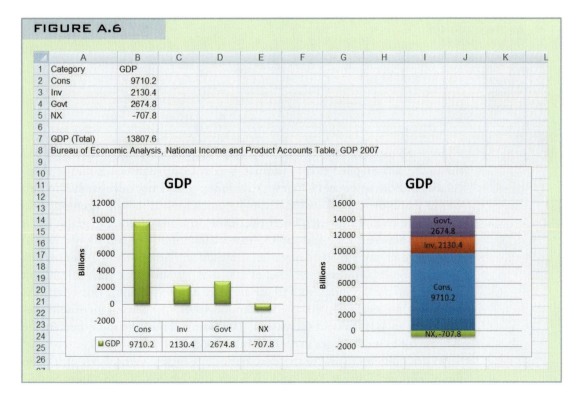

In Chapter 9, we explain the economics of stocks, bonds, and other investments. A lot of financial data is available for free on the web. We used Yahoo! Finance, for example, to download data for the value of the S&P 500 Index on the first trading day of the month from 1950 to the end of 2000. The data is graphed in Figure A.7.

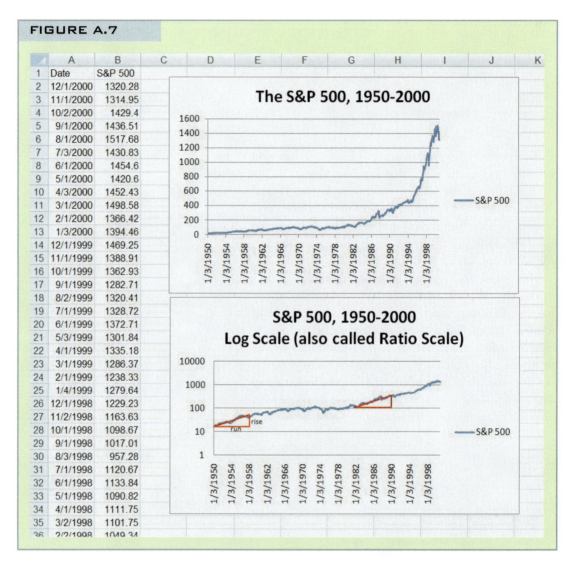

FIGURE A.7

To graph the S&P 500 data, we used a line graph. The top graph in Figure A.7 shows the data graphed in the "normal" way with equal distances on the vertical axis indicating equal changes in the index. That's not necessarily the best way to graph the data, however, because a quick look at the top figure suggests that stock prices were rising faster over time. In other words, the graph looks pretty flat between 1950 and approximately 1980, after which it shoots up. The appearance of faster growth, however, is mostly an illusion. The problem is that when the S&P 500 was at the level of 100, as it was around 1968, a 10 percent increase moves the index to 110, or an increase of 10 points. But when the index is at the level of 1,000, as it was around 1998, a 10 percent increase moves the index to 1,100, or an increase of 100 points. Thus, the same percentage increase looks much larger in 1998 than in 1968.

To get a different view of the data, right-click on the vertical axis of the top figure, choose "Format Axis" and click the box labeled "Logarithmic Scale," which produces the graph in the bottom of Figure A.7 (without the red triangles, which we will explain shortly).

Notice on the bottom figure that equal distances on the vertical axis now indicate equal percentage increases or ratios. The ratio 100/10, for example, is the same as the ratio 1,000/100. You can now see at a glance that if stock prices move the same vertical distance over the same length of time (as measured by the horizontal distance) then the percentage increase was the same. For example, we have superimposed two identical red triangles to show that the percentage increase in stock prices between 1950 and 1958 was about the same as between 1982 and 1990. The red triangles are identical so over the same 8-year period, given by the horizontal length of the triangle, the run, the S&P 500 rose by the same vertical distance, the rise. Recall that the slope of a line is given by the rise/run. Thus, we can also say that on a ratio graph, equal slopes mean equal percentage growth rates.

The log scale or ratio graph reveals more clearly than our earlier graph that stock prices increased from 1950 to the mid-1960s but were then flat throughout the 1970s and did not begin to rise again until after the recession in 1982. We use ratio graphs for a number of figures throughout this book to better identify patterns in the data.

Graphs are also very useful for suggesting possible relationships between two variables. In Chapter 10, for example, we present evidence that labor employment laws in much of Western Europe that make it difficult to fire workers also raise the costs of hiring workers. As a result, the percentage of unemployment that is long term in Europe tends to be very high. To show this relationship, we graphed an index called the "rigidity of employment index," produced by the World Bank. The rigidity of employment index summarizes hiring and firing costs as well as how easy it is for firms to adjust hours of work (e.g., whether there are restrictions on night or weekend hours). A higher index number means that it is more expensive to hire and fire workers and more difficult to adjust hours. We then graphed a country's rigidity of employment index against the share of a country's unemployment rate that is long term (lasting more than a year).

The data for this graph are shown in Figure A.8.

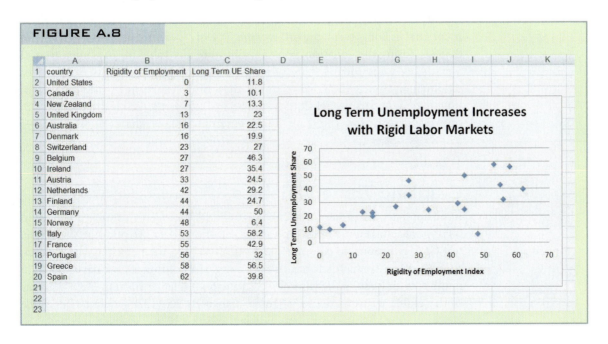

FIGURE A.8

	A	B	C	D	E	F	G	H	I	J	K
1	country	Rigidity of Employment	Long Term UE Share								
2	United States	0	11.8								
3	Canada	3	10.1								
4	New Zealand	7	13.3								
5	United Kingdom	13	23								
6	Australia	16	22.5								
7	Denmark	16	19.9								
8	Switzerland	23	27								
9	Belgium	27	46.3								
10	Ireland	27	35.4								
11	Austria	33	24.5								
12	Netherlands	42	29.2								
13	Finland	44	24.7								
14	Germany	44	50								
15	Norway	48	6.4								
16	Italy	53	58.2								
17	France	55	42.9								
18	Portugal	56	32								
19	Greece	58	56.5								
20	Spain	62	39.8								
21											
22											
23											

Long Term Unemployment Increases with Rigid Labor Markets

We can do something else of interest with this data. If you right-click on any of the data points in the figure, you will get the option to "Add Trendline." Clicking on this and then clicking the two boxes "Linear" and "Display Equation on Chart" produces Figure A.9 (absent the red arrow, which we added for clarity).

FIGURE A.9

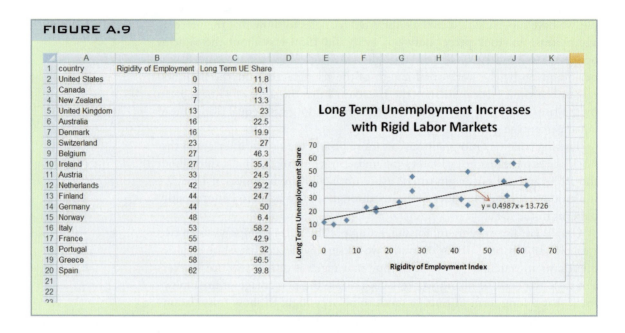

	A	B	C
1	country	Rigidity of Employment	Long Term UE Share
2	United States	0	11.8
3	Canada	3	10.1
4	New Zealand	7	13.3
5	United Kingdom	13	23
6	Australia	16	22.5
7	Denmark	16	19.9
8	Switzerland	23	27
9	Belgium	27	46.3
10	Ireland	27	35.4
11	Austria	33	24.5
12	Netherlands	42	29.2
13	Finland	44	24.7
14	Germany	44	50
15	Norway	48	6.4
16	Italy	53	58.2
17	France	55	42.9
18	Portugal	56	32
19	Greece	58	56.5
20	Spain	62	39.8

The black line is the linear curve that "best fits" the data. (Best fit in this context is defined statistically; we won't go into the details here but if you take a statistics class you will learn about ordinary least squares.) Excel also produces for us the equation for the best-fit line, $Y = 0.4987 \times X + 13.726$. Do you remember from high school the formula for a straight line, $Y = m \times X + b$? In this case m, the slope of the line or the rise/run is 0.4987 and b, the intercept, is 13.726. The slope tells us that a 1 unit increase in the rigidity of employment index (a run of 1) increases the share of unemployment that is long term by, on average, 0.4987 percentage points (a rise of 0.4987). Using the equation, you can substitute any value for the index to find a predicted value for the share of long-term unemployment. If the rigidity of employment index is 15, for example, then our prediction for the long-term unemployment share is $21.2065 = 0.4987 \times 15 + 13.726$. If the index is 55, our prediction for the long-term unemployment share is $41.1545 = 0.4987 \times 55 + 13.726$.

Graphing Three Variables

In Chapter 18, we present evidence that child labor decreases with increases in GDP per capita. Figure A.10 shows a subset of that data. We put our X variable, real GDP per capita, in column B and our Y variable, the percentage of children ages 10–14 in the labor force, in column C. In column D, we have the total number of children in the labor force. In Burundi, a larger fraction (48.5 percent) of the children are in the labor force than in India (12.1 percent), but since

FIGURE A.10

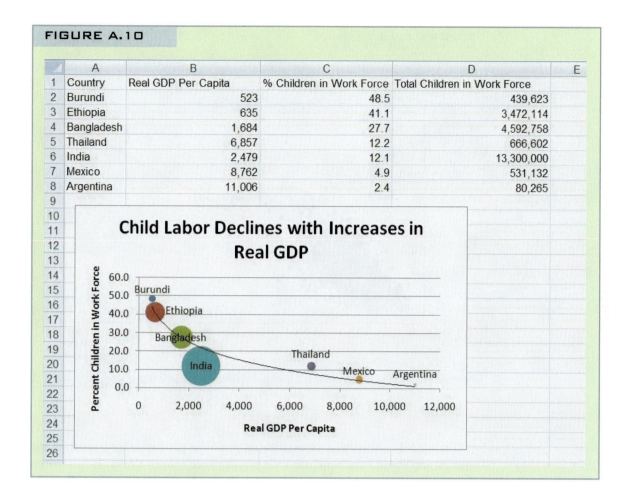

	A	B	C	D	E
1	Country	Real GDP Per Capita	% Children in Work Force	Total Children in Work Force	
2	Burundi	523	48.5	439,623	
3	Ethiopia	635	41.1	3,472,114	
4	Bangladesh	1,684	27.7	4,592,758	
5	Thailand	6,857	12.2	666,602	
6	India	2,479	12.1	13,300,000	
7	Mexico	8,762	4.9	531,132	
8	Argentina	11,006	2.4	80,265	

Burundi is a small country, the total number of children in the labor force is larger in India. To understand the problem of child labor, it's important to understand both types of information so we put both types of information on a graph.

Excel's bubble chart will take data arrayed in three columns and use the third column to set the area of the bubble or data point. In Figure A.10, for example, India has the largest number of children in the labor force and so has the bubble with the largest area. The area of the other bubbles is in relative proportion so Mexico's bubble is 1/25th the size of India's bubble because there are 1/25th as many children in the labor force in Mexico as in India. (Unfortunately, Excel doesn't label the bubbles automatically so we added these by hand.)

Cause and Effect

Do police reduce crime? If so, by how much? That's a key question that economists and criminologists are interested in understanding because local governments (and taxpayers) spend billions of dollars on police every year and would like to know whether they are getting their money's worth. Should they spend less on police or more? Unfortunately, it's surprisingly difficult to answer this question. To illustrate why, Figure A.11 shows the relationship between crime per capita and police per capita from across a large number of U.S. cities.

FIGURE A.11

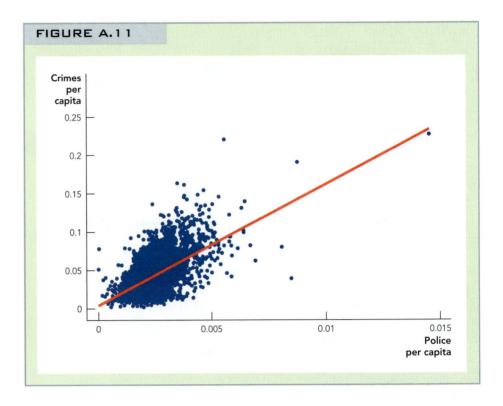

Figure A.11 shows that cities with more police per capita have more crime per capita. Should we conclude that police cause crime? Probably not. More likely is "reverse causality," crime causes police—that is, greater crime rates lead to more hiring of police. We thus have two chains of potential cause and effect, more police reduce crime and more crime increases police. Unfortunately, you can't tell much about either of these two potential cause-and-effect relationships by looking at Figure A.11, which shows the correlation between police and crime but not the causation. But if you want to estimate the value of police, you need to know causation not just correlation. So what should you do?

The best way to estimate how much police reduce crime would be to take say 1,000 roughly similar cities and randomly flip a coin dividing the cities into two groups. In the first group of cities, double the police force and in the second group do nothing. Then compare crime rates over say the next year in cities with and without an increase in police. If the cities with an increase in police have lower rates of crime, then you can safely ascribe this difference to the effect of police on crime. What makes the correlation evidence in Figure A.11 difficult to interpret is that increases in crime sometimes cause increases in police. But if you increase the number of police randomly, you eliminate the possibility of this "reverse causality." Thus, if crime falls in the cities that have *random increases in police,* the cause is most plausibly the increase in police. Similarly, if crime were to increase in cities that have random decreases in police, the cause is most plausibly the decrease in police.

Unfortunately, randomized experiments have at least one big problem—they are very expensive. Occasionally, large randomized experiments are done in criminology and other social sciences but because they are so expensive we must usually look for alternative methods for assessing causality.

If you can't afford a randomized experiment, what else can you do? One possibility is to look for what economists call quasi-experiments or natural experiments. In 1969, for example, police in Montreal, Canada, went on strike and there were 50 times more bank robberies than normal.[1] If you can think of the strike as a random event, not tied in any direct way to increases or decreases in crime, then you can be reasonably certain that the increase in bank robberies was caused by the decrease in police.

The Montreal experiment tells you it's probably not a good idea to eliminate all police, but it doesn't tell you whether governments should increase or decrease police on the street by a more reasonable amount, say 10 percent to 20 percent. Jonathan Klick and Alex Tabarrok use another natural experiment to address this question.[2] Since shortly after 9/11, the United States has had a terror alert system run by the Department of Homeland Security. When the terror alert level rises from "elevated" (yellow) to "high" (orange) due to intelligence reports regarding the current threat posed by terrorist organizations, the Washington, D.C. Metropolitan Police Department reacts by increasing the number of hours each officer must work. Because the change in the terror alert system is not tied to any observed or expected changes in Washington crime patterns, this provides a useful quasi-experiment. In other words, whenever the terror alert system shifts from yellow to orange—a random decision with respect to crime in Washington—the effective police presence in Washington increases. Klick and Tabarrok find that during the high terror alert periods when more police are on the street, the amount of crime falls. Street crime such as stolen automobiles, thefts from automobiles, and burglaries decline especially sharply. Overall, Klick and Tabarrok estimate that a 10 percent increase in police reduces crime by about 3 percent. Using these numbers and figures on the cost of crime and of hiring more police, Klick and Tabarrok argue that more police would be very beneficial.

Economists have developed many techniques for assessing causality from data and we have only just brushed the surface. We can't go into details here. We want you to know, however, that in this textbook when we present data that suggests a causal relationship—such as when we argue in Chapter 18 that higher GDP leads to lower levels of child labor—that a significant amount of statistical research has gone into assessing causality, not just correlation. If you are interested in further details, we have provided you with the references to the original papers.

APPENDIX A QUESTIONS

1. We start with a simple idea from algebra: Which of the graphs at the top of the next page have a positive slope and which have a negative slope?

2. When social scientists talk about social and economic facts, they usually talk about a "positive relationship" or a "negative relationship" instead of "positive slope" or "negative slope." Based on your knowledge, which of the following pairs of variables tend to have a "positive relationship" (a positive slope when graphed), and which have a negative relationship? (Note: "Negative relationship" and "inverse relationship" mean the same thing. Also, in this question, we're only talking about correlation, not causation.)

   a. A professional baseball player's batting average and his annual salary.

   b. A professional golfer's average score and her average salary.

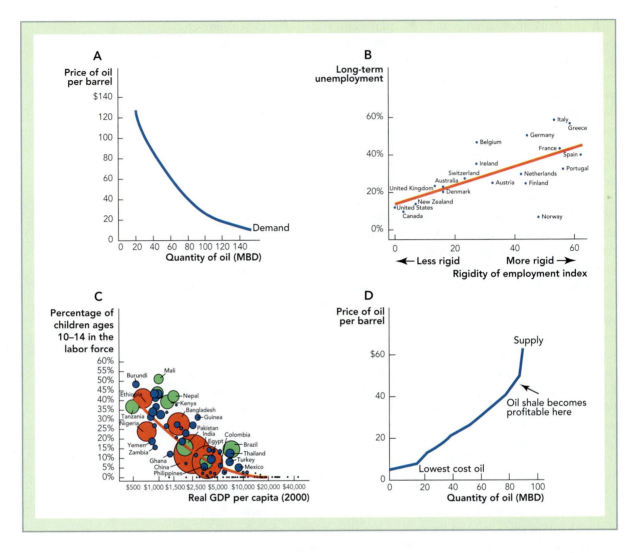

c. The number of cigarettes a person smokes and her life expectancy.

d. The size of the car you drive and your probability of surviving a serious accident.

e. A country's distance from the equator and how rich its citizens tend to be. (For the answer, see Robert Hall and Charles Jones. 1999. Why Do Some Countries Produce so Much More Output per Worker than Others? *Quarterly Journal of Economics.* 114: 83–116.)

3. Let's convert Klick and Tabarrok's research on crime into a simple algebra equation. We reported the result as the effect of a 10 percent increase in police on the crime rate in Washington, D.C. In the equation below, fill in the effect of a 1 percent increase in the police on the crime rate:

The percent change in crime = _____ ✕ The percent change in police officers

4. Let's read the child labor graph [A.10] horizontally and then vertically:

a. According to the trendline, in a typical country with 10 percent of the children in the labor force, what's the real GDP per person?

b. According to the trendline, when a country's GDP per person is $2,000, roughly what percentage of children are in the labor force?

5. Let's take another look at the ratio scale, and compare it to a normal scale.

    a. In Figure A.7, which one is presented in ratio scale and which in normal scale?

    b. In the top graph, every time the S&P 500 crosses a horizontal line, how many points did the S&P rise?

    c. In the bottom graph, every time the S&P 500 crosses a horizontal line, how many *times* higher is the S&P?

6. As a scientist, you have to plot the following data: The number of bacteria you have in a large petri dish, measured every hour over the course of a week. (Note: *E. coli* bacteria populations can double every 20 minutes) Should this data be plotted on a ratio scale and why?

7. Educated people are supposed to point out (correctly) that "correlation isn't proof of causation." This is an important fact—which explains why economists, medical doctors, and other researchers spend a lot of time trying to look for proof of causation. But sometimes, correlation is good enough. In the following examples, take the correlation as a true fact, and explain why the correlation is, all by itself, useful for the task presented in each question.

    a. Your task is to decide what brand of car to buy. You know that Brand H usually gets higher quality ratings than Brand C. You don't know what causes Brand H to get higher ratings—maybe Brand H hires better workers, maybe Brand H buys better raw materials. All you have is the correlation.

    b. Your task is to hire the job applicant who appears to be the smartest. Applicant M has a degree from MIT, and applicant S has a degree from a typical state university. You don't know what causes MIT graduates to be smarter than typical state university graduates—maybe they start off smarter before they get to MIT, maybe their professors teach them a lot, maybe having smart classmates for four years gives them constant brain exercise.

    c. Your task is to decide which city to move to, and you want to move to the city that is probably the safest. For some strange reason, the only fact you have to help you with your decision is the number of police per person.

8. If you haven't practiced in a while, let's calculate some slopes. In each case, we give two points, and you can use the "rise over run" formula to get the right answer.

    a. Point 1: $x = 0, y = 0$. Point 2: $x = 3, y = 6$

    b. Point 1: $x = 6, y = -9$. Point 2: $x = 3, y = 6$

    c. Point 1: $x = 4, y = 8$. Point 2: $x = 1, y = 12$

9. We mentioned that a demand curve is a hypothetical relationship: It answers a "what if" question: "What if today's price of oil rose (or fell), but the average consumer's income, beliefs about future oil prices, and the prices of everything else in the economy stayed the same?" When some of those other features change, then the demand curve isn't fixed any more: It shifts up (and right) or left (and down). In Figure A.3, we showed one shift graphically: Let's make some changes in algebra:

The economy of Perovia has the following demand for oil:

$$\text{Price} = B - M \times \text{Quantity}$$

When will B tend to be a larger number:

a. When population in Perovia is high or when it is low?

b. When the price of autos in Perovia is high or when it is low?

c. When Perovian income is high or when it is low?

10. Using the raw data from this chapter, use Excel to replicate simple versions of any two of our graphs. Figures A.6, A.7, A.9, and A.10 all provide the data you'll need. If you're adventurous, feel free to search out the newest GDP data and S&P 500 data on the Bureau of Economic Analysis (BEA) website and Yahoo! Finance, respectively.

Appendix B

Solutions to Check Yourself Questions

Here are suggested answers to the Check Yourself questions found within the chapters.

Chapter 2

Page 20

1. As the income of Indian workers rises, this will lead to an increase in the demand for automobiles. At first as income rises, workers may demand more charcoal bricks for heating, but charcoal bricks are a dangerous and unpleasant way to heat a home so as income increases beyond a certain level, workers will demand fewer charcoal bricks. Thus, a good can be a normal good over some levels of income and an inferior good over other (usually higher) levels of income.

2. As the price of oil rises, some people will substitute mopeds for automobiles so the demand for mopeds will increase.

Page 27

1. Improvements in chip-making technology have driven down the costs of this input so the supply of computers increases meaning that the supply curve for computers shifts to the right/down.

2. The ethanol subsidy lowers the cost of producing ethanol, therefore increasing the supply of ethanol (the supply curve for ethanol shifts to the right/down).

Chapter 3

Page 35

1. If the demand for large trucks and SUVs falls unexpectedly, auto companies will find that at the current price they have a surplus of trucks and SUVs. The quantity supplied is greater than the quantity demanded so they will lower prices in order to sell already-manufactured trucks and SUVs.

2. Sellers have produced too many clothes if they have them available at outlet malls where price discounts are the norm. Sellers are cutting their prices to reduce the surplus and move the clothes out the door.

Page 38

1. As the price of cars goes up, the least-valued wants will be the first to stop being satisfied. For example, parents may be more reluctant to buy their teenage sons and daughters a new automobile.

2. If telecommunication firms overinvest in fiber-optic cable, for example, they will have to lower the price of using fiber-optic lines. For example, a company such as Verizon will offer fiber-optic Internet and phone connections at discount prices. The ensuing losses from price cutting will dampen future investment in fiber-optic cable. More generally, firms invest in order to make a profit. If firms overinvest, they will take losses, which give them an incentive to invest carefully.

Page 42

1. If flooding destroys some of the corn and soybean crops, these crops will have a decrease in supply. This decrease in supply will lower the equilibrium quantity and increase the equilibrium price.

2. If resveratrol (from Japanese knotweed) increases life expectancy in fish, people might think it will have the same effect in humans, and so more people will demand it, increasing demand. This will increase the price of Japanese knotweed, and will lead to an increase in the quantity grown.

3. The demand for hybrid cars will increase as the price of gas increases, that is, the demand curve shifts to the right/up. We show this in Figure 3.7: think of the New demand as the demand for hybrids when the price of gas is high and the Old demand as the demand for hybrids when the price of gas is low. The price of hybrids will rise with an increase in demand, especially in the short run.

Page 46

1. The price of oil rose in 1991 primarily because of a supply shock, the Persian Gulf War. (It would also be okay to label this as a demand shock because the demand for oil increased when people expected that the war would reduce the supply of oil.) Bonus points if you recognized both possibilities.

2. From 1981 to 1986, the price of oil fell steadily. The higher price in the preceding years encouraged exploration, which several years later led to increased supply especially from non-OPEC sources.

Chapter 4

Page 59

1. If you are moving to rent-controlled New York City, you will find a shortage of apartments. Over time, rent ceilings that are below market prices will lead to shortages.

2. Key money is similar to a bribe. We discussed bribes under wasteful lines and other search costs.

3. In rent-controlled New York over time, rent-controlled buildings will deteriorate. If landlords cannot make a decent return under rent control, they will cut their costs. One way of doing this is to let the upkeep of buildings decline.

Page 64

1. A price flour above the market equilibrium price will encourage an increase in supply, thus leading to a surplus. The European Union faces a butter mountain.

2. The price floor for milk is above the equilibrium price and so has led to a surplus of milk. The government has purchased this surplus and has in effect given it away to elementary schools and high schools. This is why students pay far below market cost for the cartons of milk.

Chapter 5

Page 73

1. The purchase of wheat flour used to make bread is the purchase of an intermediate good. Thus, it is not counted in GDP: only final goods are counted in GDP.

2. Pokemon cards were counted in GDP when they were first produced. Selling used Pokemon cards on eBay does not contribute to GDP.

3. Because the worker from Colombia earns his money in New York, this is considered part of the GDP of the United States, not Colombia. GDP counts what is produced within a country, whether by its citizens or others.

Page 73

1. The growth rate is found by subtracting $5,803 billion from $5,995 billion, and then dividing that number by $5,803 billion:

$$(\$5,995 - \$5,803)/\$5,803 = \$192/\$5,803 = 0.033 \text{ or } 3.3 \text{ percent}$$

Page 76

1. China has a high GDP but a low GDP per capita.

2. Of the top 15 countries by GDP ranked in Table 5.1, Canada, Spain, and South Korea have GDP under $1 trillion but have considerable GDP per capita.

3. We convert nominal variables into real variables to account for price changes so that we can make comparisons over time.

Page 77

1. Business fluctuations are the short-run movements in real GDP around its long-term trend.

2. It is sometimes difficult to determine if an economy is in a recession because of simple data problems: it takes time to collect data, then the conclusions drawn from the data may be revised once additional data become available after additional time has passed.

Page 80

1. Consumption (C) is the largest component of national expenditure, averaging 64.5 percent.

2. Consumption expenditures are more stable than investment expenditures. It's usually easier to delay investment than consumption so consumption normally varies only slightly, but investment expenditure can vary dramatically, especially in an economic downturn, as businesses hold off on investment. For these reasons, the part of consumption that is most volatile is consumption of durable goods such as cars and major appliances because the purchase these goods can usually be easily delayed.

3. The income approach is the flip side of the spending approach: every dollar that someone earns in income is a dollar of income that someone else has spent.

Page 84

1. GDP measures things for which market values can be obtained. It does not measure things such as illegal activities or clean air because it is difficult to determine their market values.

2. Two countries that have the same level of GDP per capita do not necessarily have the same level of inequality. Let's take Country A and Country B, each of which has only two citizens. Country A's citizens earn $999 and $1, respectively, with GDP per capita of $500. Country B's citizens earn $500 and $500, respectively, with GDP per capita of $500 also. Note that the two countries have the same GDP per capita but they have different levels of inequality.

3. Because they do not account for everything, GDP statistics are not perfect. Nevertheless, they are useful in giving a good sense of how the value of what a nation produces changes over time.

Chapter 6

Page 97

1. According to Figure 6.2, approximately 30 percent of the world's population lived in China in 2000.

2. Using the rule of 70, if you make 5 percent on your savings, it will take 70/5 or 12 years for your savings to double. At 8 percent, it will take 70/8 or a little under 9 years to double.

3. According to Figure 6.4, Japan's real GDP per capita crossed the $10,000 barrier around 1970 and the $20,000 barrier around 1990. Using the rule of 70, we know that it took 20 years to double, or

$70/x = 20$. Therefore, the growth rate was approximately 3.5 percent per year over this time span.

Page 99

1. The United States has much more physical capital—tools, machines, equipment—than China, but China has more than Nigeria.

2. Physical capital, human capital, and technological knowledge are the three primary factors of production.

Page 106

1. Five institutions that promote economic growth are property rights, honest government, political stability, a dependable legal system, and competitive and open markets.

2. The Wars of the Roses were a time of civil war. Economic growth tends to decline in such times. During Henry VII's unquestioned reign, economic growth picked up dramatically.

3. Under a system of collective farming where corn production was shared, increased individual effort would bring very little reward to the individual. Because individual incentives were poor, you would expect limited corn production, maybe even starvation.

Chapter 7

Page 124

1. As more capital is added, the marginal product of capital declines.

2. Capital depreciates because machines wear out over time and have to replaced, roads wear out and need to be repaired or replaced, bridges wear out. As the capital stock increases, the total amount of capital depreciation increases.

Page 125

1. In Figure 7.8, when the capital stock is 400, depreciation is higher than investment.

2. When capital is 400, investment is 6 units.

3. When capital is 400, depreciation is 8 units.

4. When depreciation is greater than investment, the capital stock shrinks.

Page 130

1. At the steady state level of capital, investment and depreciation are equal.

2. In Figure 7.9, output is 15 units available to be consumed in the old steady state, and 20 units in the new steady state.

3. The farther they are below their steady state level, the faster countries can grow.

4. Countries with higher investment rates have higher GDP per capita.

Page 134

1. High tax rates on imports would reduce trade and thus lower the incentive to produce new ideas.

2. Spillovers occur when ideas benefit other consumers and firms, besides the creator of the idea. If the creator of an idea cannot get the full benefit of the idea, this will reduce the incentive to generate new ideas.

3. The economic reason to support a prize for malaria research rather than cancer research is that the incentive to produce cancer drugs is already high because of a large and wealthy market. Malaria tends to be located in poorer countries where people have a lower ability to pay for drugs and thus the incentive to develop new drugs is lower.

Chapter 8

Page 151

1. Financial institutions build a bridge between savers and borrowers.

2. If people have saved enough for their retirement, they can have a smooth consumption path over their lives. If greater life expectancy means that not enough has been saved for retirement, then consumption during the retirement years will have to be lower than currently planned. Thus, the consumption path throughout their lifetimes will not be smooth.

3. Other than retirement, numerous potential things can generate a demand to save because these things can cause income to be volatile: loss of a job, chronic illness, or accidents that cause some bodily harm. One saves for a rainy day.

Page 153

1. Under the lifecycle theory, individual savings are likely to be at their peak during an individual's prime earning years.

2. If interest rates fall from 7 percent to 5 percent, all else being equal, this is a fall in the price of borrowed funds. This fall in price will encourage more people to buy homes (they now may be able to afford something they could not afford before) or start businesses.

Page 156

1. Greater patience will shift the supply of savings curve to the right, leading to an increase in the quantity of savings and a decrease in the equilibrium interest rate.

2. An increase in investment demand shifts the demand curve to the right, leading to an increase in the equilibrium interest rate and an increase in the quantity of funds demanded and supplied.

Page 162

1. The primary role of financial intermediaries is to reduce the costs of moving savings from savers to borrowers and investors.

2. Interest rates and bond prices move in opposite directions. If you own a bond paying 6 percent in interest and the interest rate falls to 4 percent, the price of the bond must go up. If interest rates rise to 8 percent, the price of the 6 percent bond must fall.

3. An IPO is a first-time sale of a firm's stock to the market, and so usually increases net investment: the firm can take this new capital and use it to

expand the business. Buying shares of stock from someone else, in contrast, is buying shares already issued and represents a transfer of ownership, not a net increase to investment: the firm does not get the purchase price of the stock.

Page 167

1. Usury laws are price ceilings. Remember from Chapter 4 that price ceilings cause shortages. If savers can get only the ceiling rate rather than the market rate for their savings, they will save less.

2. Bank failures can hinder financial intermediation in a variety of ways. If savers become reluctant to put their money in banks, for example, the supply of credit will decline and the cost of borrowing will rise. This can lead to a credit crisis as credit dries up.

3. Lending money to political cronies or pals lowers the efficiency of the economy because loans do not go to their highest-valued uses.

Chapter 9

Page 181

1. According to the efficient markets hypothesis, one cannot consistently beat the market. Therefore, past performance is not a good guide to future success. On average, mutual funds that have performed well in the past are no more likely to perform well in the future than mutual funds that performed poorly in the past.

Page 187

1. Investing in the stocks of other countries helps to diversify your investments because the economies of other countries do not always rise and fall at the same time as the U.S. economy. If all economies tended to rise and fall together, there would not be any large benefits in diversifying across countries.

2. If many people dream of owning a football or baseball team, it is likely that the rewards to owning one go beyond monetary rewards. Thus, the monetary return on these assets is likely to be relatively low.

Page 189

1. This question is being hotly debated by many economists. It can be said that identifying and bursting bubbles is harder than it looks. How does the Federal Reserve know when there is a bubble? Increases in prices do not necessarily signify a bubble. Even if it can be said to be fairly certain that a bubble is present, how does the Federal Reserve burst the bubble while avoiding widespread collateral damage?

Chapter 10

Page 196

1. To be counted as unemployed in the United States, as well as not working, you have to be an adult (16 years or older), not institutionalized (not in jail), a civilian (not a soldier), and actively looking for work.

2. The labor force is defined as all workers, employed and unemployed.

3. The labor force participation rate varies slightly year to year but is approximately 66 percent (2008). It is defined as the labor force (consisting of employed and unemployed workers) divided by all adult non-institutionalized civilians.

Page 197

1. Frictional unemployment is caused by the ordinary difficulties of matching employee to employer. A reason for the difficulty of matching employer to employee is scarcity of information.

2. Some frictional unemployment is not bad if it means that prospective employers and prospective employees take the time to determine whether they are a good fit. Being forced to take the first job offered is not a good way to establish a good fit.

Page 204

1. Structural unemployment is persistent, long-term unemployment caused by long-lasting shocks or permanent features of an economy that make it more difficult for some workers to find jobs.

2. In the United States, "employment at will" fairly accurately describes the employment situation: employees may quit at any time and employers may fire an employee at any time and for any reason. In contrast, laws in Western European countries hinder the ability of employers to act at will. For example, in Portugal any business must get the government's permission to lay off workers, and even then the business must follow guidelines as to who can be laid off first.

Page 207

1. Cyclical unemployment is determined by the business cycle. It increases during a recession and decreases during a boom.

2. Lower growth is correlated with increasing unemployment; higher growth is correlated with decreasing unemployment.

Page 212

1. Lowering the marginal tax rate for married couples provided an incentive for more women to enter the labor force because they could now keep more of their pay rather than have it taxed away.

2. Raising the age that one can obtain Social Security benefits increases the incentive to stay in the labor force longer, thus increasing the labor force participation rate.

Chapter 11

Page 222

1. Using the formula on page 218, $(125 - 120)/120 = 4.16$ percent.

2. If the inflation rate goes from 1 percent to 4 percent to 7 percent over a period of two years, the prices of a great majority of goods are likely to go up.

3. Use real prices rather than nominal prices to compare the price of goods over time. Real prices subtract out the effect of inflation and thus give a

better measure of whether a particular good is becoming more or less expensive over time compared to most other goods and services.

Page 226

1. In the long run, inflation is always and everywhere a monetary phenomenon: growth in the money supply causes inflation.

2. The quantity theory of money is Mv = PY.

Page 232

1. Under unexpected inflation, wealth is redistributed from lenders to borrowers. Under unexpected disinflation, wealth is redistributed from borrowers to lenders.

2. When the expected inflation rate increases, nominal interest rates rise to compensate. We call this the Fisher effect.

3. Unexpected inflation distorts price signals. They become more difficult to interpret. This leads to waste.

Chapter 12

Page 247

1. If inflation is 2 percent and climbs to 5 percent, this does not affect the Solow growth curve, the economy's fundamental ability to produce goods and services.

2. Because $\vec{M} + \vec{v} = \vec{P} + \vec{Y}_R$ in the dynamic AD/AS model, if $\vec{M}$ equals 7 percent and $\vec{v}$ equals 0 percent, by definition inflation plus real growth will equal 7 percent. If in this situation we find that real growth equal 0 percent, then inflation must be 7 percent.

3. Increased spending growth shifts the dynamic aggregate demand curve outward.

Page 250

1. A technological innovation such as the Internet shifts the Solow growth curve to the right.

2. In the real business cycle model, a large fall in aggregate demand has no effect on real growth.

Page 255

1. The New Keynesian model presumes significant wage and price stickiness. The real business cycle model is based on flexible prices and wages.

2. The Solow growth curve is vertical because price and wage stickiness do not affect the fundamental productive capacity of the economy over the long run. However, price and wage stickiness do affect aggregate supply in the short run, and this accounts for the fact that the SRAS curve is *not* vertical.

3. When people expect inflation to increase from 2 percent to 3 percent, the SRAS shifts up and to the left.

Page 259

1. In the long run, unexpected inflation always becomes expected inflation.

2. If consumers fear a recession and cut back on their expenditures, the dynamic aggregate demand curve will shift inward.

Page 262

1. The U.S. money supply fell in the early 1930s. This initially affected aggregate demand (the AD curve shifted inward—down/left), not the Solow growth curve. The decrease in aggregate demand resulted in bank failures that decreased the productivity of financial intermediation, which was a real shock, and so affected the Solow growth curve, shifting it to the left.

2. In an ordinary year, the real shocks of the 1930s might have been shrugged off but the combination of large shocks to AD and real shocks at the same time made the Great Depression great.

Chapter 13

Page 273

1. Putting down phone lines is very expensive, compared to the cost of putting up cell-phone towers. Cell phones have improved communications in all countries, but the change has been most dramatic in less-developed countries. This has been a positive shock throughout the world.

2. A large and sudden increase in taxes would suppress economic activity especially in the short run as consumers and firms reallocated from more energy intensive sectors of the economy to less energy intensive sectors. The reallocation would decrease the fundamental capacity of the economy to produce goods and services, which is a shift of the Solow growth curve to the left.

Page 282

1. The 9/11 attacks brought a high level of uncertainty into the economy. No one knew if more attacks were planned so no one wanted to be on an airplane. Cutting back on air travel hurt the airlines and all associated businesses: airports, airport services such as food vendors, companies that provide transportation to and from airports. When no one flew on airplanes to take business trips, some local business trips were still undertaken (by train or car), but longer trips (such as cross-country travel) came to a standstill. As travel declined, so did the need for hotel rooms and restaurant meals out. Hotels were hit hard: cutting the price of hotel rooms had little effect when uncertainty dried up business travel. The near-cessation in business travel amplified the economic effects of the attacks nationwide: attacks in New York had nationwide repercussions.

Chapter 14

Page 293

1. The monetary base is defined as currency plus reserves held by banks at the Fed.

2. In November 2007, there was $764 billion of currency in the United States compared to around $600 billion in checkable deposits. Thus, currency accounts for more than checkable deposits.

Page 295

1. If the reserve ratio is 1/20, then 5 percent of deposits are kept as reserves.

2. If the reserve ratio is 1/20, then the money multiplier is 20.

3. If the Fed increases bank reserves by $10,000 and the reserve ratio is 1/20, then the change in the money supply is $200,000.

Page 300

1. The Fed wants to lower interest rates. It does so by *buying* bonds in open market operations. By doing this, the Fed *adds* reserves and through the multiplier process, it *increases* the money supply.

Page 301

1. The Fed might not let a large bank fail if it fears systemic risk, the possibility that the failure will bring down other banks and financial institutions. In this case, the Fed will use its powers as the lender of last resort to support a bank that is "too big to fail."

2. Moral hazard increases my incentives to double my bet to make up for a large loss. If the Fed always bails out large banks, my actions will never lead to the bank's bankruptcy, so why not take the chance?

Page 303

1. Money is neutral in the long run but has a short-run effect on the economy. This explains the Fed's concerns with the money supply in the short run.

2. If banks are afraid of a recession, they will be more reluctant to lend. This will hamper the Fed's ability to shift aggregate demand in a recession. In this case, the Fed is sometimes said to be "pushing on a string."

Chapter 15

Page 319

1. Data problems affect the Fed's ability to set monetary policy that is "just right" because they make it difficult for the Fed to determine just what is going on with the economy. If the Fed does not know exactly what is going on, it cannot prescribe the correct medicine.

2. Milton Friedman argued for a 3 percent money growth rate because the long-run growth rate for the U.S. economy trends around 3 percent. When money growth equals long-run growth in the economy, there will be a tendency for price stability.

Page 322

1. Looking at Figure 15.4, if the Fed wanted to restore some growth to the economy, it could work to increase aggregate demand. The problem is that increasing growth in this case comes at the expense of adding more inflation. This is the policy dilemma.

2. If the Fed increases AD every time in response to a series of negative real shocks, the inflation rate will climb. Eventually, the Fed will have to act to reduce inflation, possibly pushing the economy into a recession.

Page 324

1. The Fed can never be certain when asset prices reach the bubble stage. Bubbles are easier to identify with hindsight but even then identification is a judgment call.

2. Collateral damage to a contraction in the money supply could be reducing the growth rate for GDP for the broader economy as a whole.

Chapter 16

Page 342

1. Customs duties now account for only 1.2 percent of federal revenues.

2. Individual income taxes plus Social Security and other payroll taxes represent 82 percent of federal revenues.

3. A person in the fourth quintile pays an effective federal tax rate of 17.4 percent. On an income of $80,000, this would be $13,920 in tax. A person in the top quintile pays an effective rate of 25.5 percent on income of $160,000, thus a tax of $40,800. Because the person who made twice as much paid more than twice as much in tax, this gives evidence of progressivity in the tax system.

Page 349

1. Social Security and Medicare spending currently account for 36.5 percent of federal spending.

2. GDP gives us an idea of the capacity of the economy to pay debt so the debt–to–GDP ratio tells us what the debt is relative to the capacity to pay the debt.

Page 352

1. In the next 40 years, Social Security and especially Medicare and Medicaid are likely to increase relative to GDP. This means that the level of overall government spending relative to GDP is likely to increase.

2. If the pace of idea generation quickens, this will lead to a positive shift in the Solow growth curve. In other words, the economy will be able to produce more goods and services. This would lead to a decrease in the debt–to–GDP ratio (all other things equal). This would increase the government's ability to pay for increased benefits for retirees.

Chapter 17

Page 362

1. The two types of expansionary fiscal policy are the government spends more money, or the government cuts taxes and thereby gives people more money to spend.

INDEX

Note: Page numbers followed by f indicate figures; those followed by n indicate notes; those followed by t indicate tables.

8. U.S. Comptroller General David Walker speaking on *60 Minutes*, see http://www.cbsnews.com/stories/2007/03/01/60minutes/main2528226.shtml.

9. The U.S. Equal Employment Opportunity Commission collects statistics on job patterns by industry. See *Job Patterns For Minorities and Women in Private Industry* (EEO-1), available online at http://www.eeoc.gov/stats/jobpat/jobpat.html.

10. **Goldin, Claudia and Lawrence F. Katz.** 2002. "The Power of the Pill: Oral Contraceptives and Women's Career and Marriage Decisions." *Journal of Political Economy*, 110(4): 730–770.

11. There are 6 employed workers and 1 unemployed worker so there are 7 people in the labor force. Of the 7, 1 is unemployed so the unemployment rate is 1/7 = 14.3 percent. The adult, civilian, noninstitutional population is 8, of these, 7 are in the labor force, so the labor force participation rate is 87.5 percent.

Chapter 11 Notes

1. See *Zimbabwe Has No Money to Print Currency*, November 3, 2006, http://www.newzimbabwe.com/pages/inflation66.14226.html.

Chapter 12 Notes

1. **Higgs, Robert.** 1997. "Regime Uncertainty: Why the Great Depression Lasted So Long and Why Prosperity Resumed after the War." *The Independent Review*, 1(4): 561–590.

2. For a good overview of the tariff and its effects, see **O'Brien, Anthony.** "Smoot-Hawley Tariff." *EH.Net Encyclopedia*, edited by **Robert Whaples.** August 15, 2001. http://eh.net/encyclopedia/article/obrien.hawley-smoot.tariff

3. Solon, Gary, Barsky, Robert, and Parker, Jonathan A. 1994. "Measuring the Cyclicality of Real Wages: How Important Is Composition Bias?" *Quarterly Journal of Economics,* 109 (February): 1–25.

Chapter 15 Notes

1. **Bernanke, Ben S., Mark Gertler, & Mark Watson.** 1997. "Systematic Monetary Policy and the Effects of Oil Price Shocks." *Brookings Papers on Economic Activity*, 1: 91–157.

Chapter 16 Notes

1. http://www.wwwebtax.com/miscellaneous/exemptions.htm

2. On Boeing, "The Taxman Barely Cometh." *Business Week*, December 3, 2007: 56–58.

3. **Hall, Robert E. & Alvin Rabushka.** 2007. *The Flat Tax—Revised and Expanded.* Stanford, CA: Hoover Institution.

4. Congressional Budget Office. 2007. *The Long Term Budget Outlook, 2007.* Available online at http://www.cbo.gov/ftpdocs/88xx/doc8877/12-13-LTBO.pdf, last accessed Nov. 20, 2008.

Chapter 17 Notes

1. **Hornbeck, J.F.** 2004. "Argentina's Sovereign Debt Restructuring." Congressional Research Service, RL 32637.

2. On New Deal fiscal policy, see **Hansen, Alvin.** 1963. "Was Fiscal Policy in the Thirties a Failure?" *Review of Economics and Statistics*, 45:320–323.

Chapter 18 Notes

1. On this point see **Sowell, Thomas.** 1980. *Knowledge and Decisions.* New York: Basic Books. And see also Chapter 4 of **Reisman, George.** 1996. *Capitalism: A Treatise on Economics.* Ottawa, IL: Jameson.

2. **Smith, Adam.** 2006. *An Inquiry into the Nature and Causes of the Wealth of Nations.* Methuen and Co., Ltd. 1904 [1776]. Ed. Edwin Cannan. Library of Economics and Liberty, Book IV, II. 2.11. 2 August. http://www.econlib.org/library/Smith/smWN13.html.

3. See **Schwabach, Aaron.** 2002. "How protectionism is destroying the Everglades." *National Wetlands Newsletter*, 24(1): 7–14 on the environmental cost of sugar production.

4. See **Bellamy, Carol.** 1997. *The state of the world's children—1997.* Unicef and Oxford University Press, 23. Available from http://www.unicef.org/sowc97/.

5. See **Edmonds, Eric V. & Nina Pavcnik.** 2006. "International trade and child labor: Cross-country evidence." *Journal of International Economics,* January: 115–140.

6. On the Food for Education program, see **Ahmed, A., & C. del Nino**. 2002. *The Food for Education Program in Bangladesh: An Evaluation of Its Impact on Educational Attainment and Food Security, FCND DP No. 138.* International Food Policy Research Institute and Meng, Xin, and Jim Ryan. 2003. *Evaluating the Food for Education Program in Bangladesh.* Working Paper from Australian National University, Australia South Asia Research Centre.

7. On the 1918 flu, see **Barry, John M.** 2005. *The Great Influenza: The Epic Story of the Deadliest Plague in History.* Penguin. New York. On policy for a future pandemic, see **Cowen, Tyler.** 2005. *Avian Flu: What Should Be Done.* Mercatus Center Working Paper. Available at http://www.mercatus.org/repository/docLib/20060726_Avian_Flu.pdf.

8. Quoted in **Norberg, Johan.** 2003. *In Defense of Global Capitalism.* Washington, D.C.: Cato Institute.

9. **Johnson, Bradford.** 2002. "Retail: The Wal-Mart Effect." *McKinsey Quarterly*, (1):40–43.

10. See **Paley, Amit R.** 2006. "Homework help, from a world away: Web joins students, cheap overseas tutors." *Washington Post*. Monday, May 15; A01. Available at http://www.washingtonpost.com/wp-dyn/content/article/2006/05/14/AR2006051401139_pf.html. See also **Bray, Hiawatha.** 2006. "Online tutoring pays off at home, abroad." *The Boston Globe*, March 28.

11. **Boudreaux, Donald J.** 2008. *Globalization.* Westport, CT: Greenwood Press.

Appendix A Notes

1. **Clark, Gerald.** 1969. "What Happens When the Police Go On Strike." *New York Times Magazine*, November 16, sec. 6: 45, 176–185, 187, 194–195.

2. **Klick, Jonathan, & Alexander Tabarrok.** 2005. "Using Terror Alert Levels to Estimate the Effect of Police on Crime." *Journal of Law & Economics*, 48(1): 267–280.

Chapter 5 Notes

1. Data on automobiles are from the Statistical Abstract of the United States. Prices from http://www.nada.org/Content/NavigationMenu/Newsroom/NADADAta/20062/NADA_Data_2006.pdf. Data on computers are from Information Technology Industry Council, http://www.itic.org/statistics.php.

2. Bureau of Economic Analysis website (www.bea.gov), Table 2.3.3.

3. See Federal Reserve Board. 2009. "Flow of Funds Accounts of the United States: Flows and Outstandings, Fourth Quarter 2008." Available online at: http://www.federalreserve.gov/releases/z1/Current/z1.pdf

4. For data on business regulations worldwide see the World Bank's website, http://www.doingbusiness.org/.

5. http://rru.worldbank.org/Discussions/Topics/Topic18.aspx

6. http://www.gapminder.org/

7. See **Dollar, David & Aart Kraay**. 2004. "Trade, Growth, and Poverty." *Economic Journal*, 114(493): F22–F49.

Chapter 6 Notes

1. See United States Department of Agriculture, Economic Research Service. 2007. "Agricultural Productivity in the United States." http://www.ers.usda.gov/Data/AgProductivity/.

2. This account draws upon **McMillan, John**. 2002. *Reinventing the Bazaar*. New York, NY: W.W. Norton and Company, and **Zhou, Kate Xiao**. 1997. *How Farmers Changed China*. Boulder, CO: Westview Press.

3. **Hall, Robert E**. & **Charles I. Jones**. 1999. "Why do some countries produce so much more output per worker than others?" *Quarterly Journal of Economics*: 83–116.

4. **Lewis, William W.** 2004. *The Power of Productivity*. Chicago, IL: University of Chicago Press.

Chapter 7 Notes

1. Germany is excluded for lack of data. Turkey is excluded because its history and institutions were quite different from the other founding members of the OECD.

2. Is there a way to reduce the trade-off between dynamic and static efficiency? Some ideas are suggested by **Tabarrok, Alexander**. 2002. "Patent Theory versus Patent Law." *Contributions to Economic Analysis & Policy*. 1(1), Article 9. http://www.bepress.com/bejeap/contributions/vol1/iss1/art9. And see also **Kremer, Michael**. 1998. "Patent Buyouts: A Mechanism for Encouraging Innovation." *Quarterly Journal of Economics*: 1137–1167.

3. Rare is defined as a disease at the bottom quarter of incidence in the United States in 1998; common is defined as a disease at the top quarter of incidence. See **Lichtenberg, Frank R. & Joel Waldfogel**. "*Does* Misery Love Company? Evidence from Pharmaceutical Markets Before and After the Orphan Drug Act" (June 2003). NBER Working Paper No. W9750. Available at SSRN: http://ssrn.com/abstract=414248.

4. **Romer, Paul**. 2007. "Economic Growth." *The Concise Encyclopedia of Economics*. David R. Henderson, ed. Liberty Fund, Indianapolis.

Chapter 8 Notes

1. **Bloom, David E., David Canning & Bryan S. Graham.** 2002. "Longevity and Life Cycle Savings." NBER Working Paper No. W8808. Available at SSRN: http://ssrn.com/abstract=302569

2. **Shoda, Y., W. Mischel, & P. Peake**. 1988. "Predicting Adolescent Cognitive and Self-Regulatory Competencies from Preschool Delay of Gratification: Identifying Diagnostic Conditions." *Developmental Psychology*, 26: 978–986.

3. **Beshears, John, James Choi, David Laibson, & Brigitte Madrian**. *The Importance of Default Options for Retirement Savings Outcomes: Evidence from the United States*. http://www.nber.org/aginghealth/summer06/w12009.html

4. **Levine, Ross & Zervos, Sara**. 1998. "Stock Markets, Banks, and Economic Growth," *American Economic Review*, vol. 88(3): 537–558.

5. **Blustein, Paul.** 2005. *And the Money Kept Rolling In (and Out): Wall Street, the IMF, and the Bankrupting of Argentina*. New York, NY: Public Affairs Press, 191.

6. See **La Porta, Rafael, Florencio Lopez-De-Silanes, & Andrei Shleifer**. 2002. "Government Ownership of Banks." *Journal of Finance, American Finance Association*, 57(1): 265–301.

7. **Friedman, Milton, & Anna J. Schwartz**. 1963. *A Monetary History of the United States, 1867–1960*. Princeton, NJ: Princeton University Press.

8. **Bernanke, Ben**. 1983. "Nonmonetary Effects of the Financial Crisis in the Propagation of the Great Depression." *The American Economic Review*, 73(3): 257–276.

Chapter 9 Notes

1. For a comprehensive review of efficient markets and the performance of mutual fund managers see **Hebner, Mark T**. 2007. *Index Funds: The 12 Step Program for Active Investors*. Irvine, CA: IFA Publishing.

Chapter 10 Notes

1. On K-Mart see http://en.wikipedia.org/wiki/Kmart; on Wal-Mart see the 2002 Annual Report, http://walmartstores.com/Files/annual_2002/page16.html.

2. Data on unemployment and its duration may be found in various issues of the OECD Employment Outlook and on the Web at http://www.oecd.org/statsportal/0,2639,en_2825_293564_1_1_1_1_1,00.html.

3. The Italian system is more difficult to describe than the systems in the other countries and it has changed considerably over time.

4. See OECD Statistics, http://stats.oecd.org/wbos/default.aspx, for minimum wages relative to median wages. For minimum wages relative to average wages, see **Lothar Funk & Hagen Lesch**. 2005. *Minimum Wages in Europe*. European Foundation for the Improvement of Living and Working Conditions. Available online at http://eurofound.europa.eu/eiro/2005/07/study/tn0507101s.html#contentpage.

5. **Salanie, Bernard & Guy Laroque**. 2002. "Labor Market Institutions and Employment in France." *Journal of Applied Econometrics*: 17, 25, 48. And **Ford, Peter**. 2005. "Deep Roots of Paris Riots." *Christian Science Monitor*. November 4, 2005. And for the United States, Bureau of Labor Statistics.

6. **Martin, John P.** 2000. "What works among active labour market policies: Evidence from OECD Countries' Experiences." *OECD Economic Studies*, No. 30: 79–113.

7. **Kotlikoff, Laurence & Scott Burns**. 2004. *The Coming Generation Storm*. Cambridge, MA: MIT Press.

REFERENCES

Chapter 1 Notes

1. Quoted in **Christopher, Emma.** 2007. "'The Slave Trade is Merciful Compare to [this]': Slave Traders, Convict Transportation and the Abolitionists." In **Christopher, E., C. Pybus, & M. Rediker** (eds.). 2007. *Many Middle Passages.* Chapter 6: 109–128. Berkeley, CA: University of California Press.

2. **Chadwick, Edwin.** 1862. "Opening Address of the British Association for the Advancement of Science." *Journal of the Statistical Society of London*, 25(4): 502–524.

3. **Chadwick** op cit.

4. On the impact of new drugs, see **Lichtenberg, Frank.** 2007. "The Impact of New Drugs on U.S. Longevity and Medical Expenditure, 1990–2003." *American Economic Review*, 97(2): 438–443.

5. **Celis 3rd, William.** 1991. "Study Finds Enrollment is Up at Colleges Despite Recession." *The New York Times*, December 28.

Chapter 2 Notes

1. On changing U.S. demographics and their impact on the economy, see **Kotlikoff, Laurence J. & Scott Burns.** 2004. *The Coming Generational Storm.* Cambridge, MA: MIT Press.

2. *International Herald Tribune*, http://www.iht.com/articles/ap/2007/07/31/business/EU-FIN-MKT-Oil-Prices.php

3. Information Resources Inc. 2005. Times and Trends. September 16.

4. The Paleontological Research Institution, http://www.priweb.org/ed/pgws/history/spindletop/lucas_gusher.html.

5. Energy Information Institute, http://www.eia.doe.gov/emeu/perfpro/btab22.html

6. On the costs of oil production, see OPEC and the High Price of Oil, Joint Economic Committee, United States Congress, http://www.house.gov/jec/publications/109/11–17–05opec.pdf.

Chapter 3 Notes

1. **Smith, Vernon.** 1991. Experimental Economics at Purdue, in *Papers in Experimental Economics*, ed. **Smith, V. L.**, Cambridge, England: Cambridge University Press, originally appeared in *Essays in Contemporary Fields of Economics*, edited by **Horwich, G. & J. P. Quirk**, Purdue University Press, 1981.

2. **Conover, Ted.** 2006. "Capitalist Roaders." *New York Times Magazine*, July 2: 31–37, 50.

Chapter 4 Notes

1. *Business Week* (February 16, 1974, p.122) quoted in Bradley (1996, 1635).

2. Prices were frozen at levels no higher than the May 25, 1970, price or a price at which 10 percent or more of transactions took place in the 30 days prior to August 14, 1971. Some adjustments for seasonal differences were allowed for some products, such as fashion items, but not for oil. See **Bradley, Robert Jr.** 1996. *Oil, Gas and Government: The U.S.*

Experience, Vol. 2. Lanham, MD: Rowman and Littlefield, 1607–1608.

3. See **Hall, Thomas E.** 2003. *The Rotten Fruits of Economic Controls and the Rise from the Ashes, 1965–1989.* New York, NY: University Press of America.

4. **Bradley, Robert Jr.** 1996. *Oil, Gas and Government: The U.S. Experience, Vol. 1.* Lanham, MD: Rowman and Littlefield.

5. See "Summary of Steps Ordered by Nixon to Meet Energy Crisis." 1973. *Washington Post*, November 26: A12.

6. "The Shortage's Losers and Winners." 1973. *Time.* December 10.

7. **Grayson, Jackson C.** 1974. "Let's End Controls – Completely." *The Wall Street Journal,* February 6: 14.

8. Data are from the Bureau of Labor Statistics, "Characteristics of Minimum Wage Workers: 2005," http://www.bls.gov/cps/minwage2005.htm.

9. See "50 Years of Research on the Minimum Wage," U.S. Congress Joint Economic Committee, for a listing and abstract of many studies on the minimum wage. Recent studies include **Neumark, David & William Wascher.** 1992. Employment Effects of Minimum and Subminimum Wages: Panel Date on State Minimum Wage Laws. *Industrial and Labor Relations Review*, 46(1): 55–81, **Deere, Donald, Kevin M. Murphy, & Finis Welch.** 1995. "Employment and the 1990–1991 Minimum-Wage Hike." *American Economic Review*, 85(2): 232–237. Not all studies find a significant reduction in employment. See **Card, David, & Krueger, Alan B.** 1994. "Minimum Wages and Employment: A Case Study of the Fast-Food Industry in New Jersey and Pennsylvania." *American Economic Review*, vol. 84 (September): 772–793 for a well designed study that challenges the conventional wisdom.

10. "Characteristics of Minimum Wage Workers: 2005," http://www.bls.gov/cps/minwage2005.htm.

11. On the minimum wage in Puerto Rico in 1938, see **Rottenberg, Simon.** 1981. "Minimum Wages in Puerto Rico." In **Rottenberg** (ed.) *The Economics of Legal Minimum Wages.* Washington, D.C.: American Enterprise Institute: 327–339, and **Rustici, Thomas.** 1985. "A Public Choice View of the Minimum Wage." *Cato Journal* 5(1):103–131.

Beginning in 1974, the Puerto Rican minimum wage was raised in steps to the U.S. level, creating a repeat of the experiment of 1938. The results were the same. Freeman and Freeman (1991) estimate that the increase in the minimum wage reduced the number of jobs in Puerto Rico by 8 to 10 percent. See **Freeman, Alida Castillo, & Richard B. Freeman**, 1991. "Minimum Wages in Puerto Rico: Textbook Case of a Wage Floor?" National Bureau of Economic Research Working Paper No. 3759 (June).

12. On deregulation, see **Peltzman, Sam.** 1989. "The Economic Theory of Regulation After a Decade of Deregulation." *Brookings Papers on Economic Activity. Microeconomics*, 1–59.

13. On deregulation, see **Morrison, Steven A. & Clifford Winston.** 1986. *The Economic Effects of Airline Deregulation.* Washington, D.C.: Brookings.

tariff a tax on imports

technological knowledge knowledge about how the world works that is used to produce goods and services

time bunching the tendency for economic activities to be coordinated at common points in time

time preference the desire to have goods and services sooner rather than later (all else being equal)

trade deficit the annual difference that results when the value of a country's imports exceeds the value of its exports

trade quota a restriction on the quantity of goods that can be imported: imports greater than the quota amount are forbidden or heavily taxed

trade surplus the annual difference that results when the value of a country's exports exceeds the value of its imports

transmission mechanisms economic forces that can amplify shocks and transmit them across time and sectors of the economy

tying a form of price discrimination in which greater use of one good requires the purchase of a second good from the same firm; HP printers and HP ink are an example

unemployed workers adults who do not have a job but who are looking for work

unemployment rate the percentage of the labor force who are unemployed

union an association of workers that bargains collectively with employers over wages, benefits, and working conditions

velocity of money, v the average number of times a dollar is spent on final goods and services in a year

dollar increase in reserves; MM = 1/RR where RR is the reserve ratio

moral hazard the situation that exists when people who are insulated from risk tend to take on more risk; in macroeconomics, occurs when banks and other financial institutions take on too much risk, expecting that the Fed and regulators will later bail them out

multiplier effect the additional increase in AD caused when expansionary fiscal policy increases income and thus consumption and investment spending

national debt held by the public all federal debt held outside the U.S. government

natural rate of unemployment the rate of structural plus frictional unemployment

net exports the value of exports minus the value of imports

nominal exchange rate the rate at which you can exchange one currency for another

nominal variables variables, such as nominal GDP, that have not been adjusted for changes in prices

non-rivalrous goods goods that can be consumed by two or more people at the same time, such as an idea

normal good a good for which demand increases when income increases

open market operations the buying and selling of government bonds by the Fed

opportunity cost the value of possibilities lost when a choice is made

perfect price discrimination (PPD) the situation that exists when each customer is charged his or her maximum willingness to pay

physical capital the stock of tools including machines, structures, and equipment

price ceiling a maximum price allowed by law

price discrimination the selling of the same product at different prices to different customers

price floor a minimum price allowed by law

producer surplus the producer's gain from exchange, or the difference between the market price and the minimum price at which a producer would be willing to sell a particular quantity

producer surplus (total) an amount measured by the area above the supply curve and below the price

progressive tax a type of tax that imposes higher tax rates on people with higher incomes

protectionism the economic policy of restraining trade through quotas, tariffs, or other regulations that burden foreign producers but not domestic producers

purchasing power parity theorem the principle that the real purchasing power of money should be roughly the same, whether it is spent at home or converted into another currency and spent abroad

quantity demanded the quantity that buyers are willing and able to buy at a particular price

quantity supplied the quantity that sellers are willing and able to sell at a particular price

real exchange rate the rate at which you can exchange the goods and services of one country for the goods and services of another

real price a price that has been corrected for inflation, used to compare the prices of goods over time

real variables variables such as real GDP, that have been adjusted for changes in prices by using the same set of prices in all time periods

recession a significant, widespread decline in real income and employment

regressive tax a type of tax that imposes higher tax rates on people with lower incomes

required reserves the minimum percentage of reserves a bank is required to hold, as dictated by the Fed

reserve ratio (RR) the ratio of reserves to deposits

Ricardian equivalence the theory according to which people understand that, for a given level of government spending, lower taxes today mean higher taxes in the future and therefore save the money from a tax cut to pay future taxes; when Ricardian equivalence holds, a tax cut doesn't increase aggregate demand even in the short run

risk-return trade-off the dynamic whereby higher returns come at the price of higher risk

saving income that is not spent on consumption goods

shocks rapid changes in economic conditions that affect the productivity of capital and labor

shortage a situation in which the quantity demanded is greater than the quantity supplied

solvency crisis a situation that exists when many banks are insolvent; i.e., have liabilities greater in value than assets

steady state in a model of economic growth, a situation in which the capital stock is neither increasing nor decreasing

stock a share of ownership in a corporation

structural unemployment persistent, long-term unemployment caused by long-lasting shocks or permanent features of an economy that make it more difficult for some workers to find jobs

substitutes two goods for which a decrease in the price of one leads to a decrease in demand for the other

supply curve a function that shows the quantity supplied at different prices

surplus a situation in which the quantity supplied is greater than the quantity demanded

systemic risk the risk that the failure of one financial institution can bring down other institutions as well

average cost (cost per unit) as quantity increases

efficient market hypothesis the claim that the prices of traded assets reflect all publicly available information

employment at-will doctrine the policy that an employee may quit and an employer may fire an employee at any time and for any reason; the most basic U.S. employment law despite many exceptions to it

equilibrium price the price at which the quantity demanded is equal to the quantity supplied

equilibrium quantity the quantity at which the quantity demanded is equal to the quantity supplied

exchange rate the price of one currency in terms of another currency

federal funds rate the overnight lending rate from one major bank to another

financial intermediaries institutions such as banks, bond markets, and stock markets that reduce the costs of moving funds from savers to borrowers and investors

fiscal policy federal government policy on taxes, spending, and borrowing that is designed to influence business fluctuations

Fisher effect the tendency of nominal interest rates to rise one to one with expected inflation rates

fixed exchange rate (also known as a **pegged exchange rate**) an exchange rate based on the promise of a government or central bank to convert its currency into another currency at a fixed (set) rate.

flat tax a tax rate that is constant across income levels

floating exchange rate an exchange rate determined primarily by market forces

fractional reserve banking a system in which banks hold only a portion of deposits in reserve, lending the rest

free rider someone who consumes a resource without working or contributing to the resource's upkeep

frictional unemployment short-term unemployment caused by the ordinary difficulties of matching employee to employer

GDP (gross domestic product) per capita GDP divided by population

government purchases spending by all levels of government on final goods and services not including transfers

gross domestic product (GDP) the market value of all final goods and services produced within a country in a year

gross national product the market value of all final goods and services produced by a country's permanent residents, wherever located, in a year

human capital the productive knowledge and skills that workers acquire through education, training, and experience

illiquid bank a bank whose short-term liabilities are greater than its short-term assets but overall has assets that are greater than its liabilities

incentives rewards and penalties that motivate behavior

inferior good a good for which demand decreases when income increases

inflation an increase in the general or average level of prices

inflation rate the percentage increase in the average level of prices (as measured by a price index) over a period of time

initial public offering (IPO) the first instance of a corporation selling stock to the public in order to raise capital

insolvent bank a bank whose liabilities are greater in value than its assets

institutions the "rules of the game" that structure economic incentives

intertemporal substitution the allocation of consumption, work, and leisure across time to maximize well-being

investment expenditures private spending on tools, plant, and equipment

used to produce future output; i.e., the purchase of new capital goods

irreversible investments investments that cannot be easily moved, adjusted, or reversed if conditions change

labor adjustment costs the costs of shifting workers from declining sectors of the economy to growing sectors

labor force all workers, employed plus unemployed

labor force participation rate the percentage of adults in the labor force

law of one price the principle that if trade were free, then identical goods should sell for about the same price throughout the world

lender of last resort a lender that loans money to banks and other financial institutions when no one else will, often a central bank or a country's Treasury or Finance department

liquid asset an asset that can be used for payments or, quickly and without loss of value, be converted into an asset that can be used for payments

liquidity crisis a situation that occurs when banks do not have enough liquid assets to meet their liability demands

marginal tax rate the tax rate paid on an additional dollar of income

market for loanable funds the market where suppliers of loanable funds (savers) trade with demanders of loanable funds (borrowers), thereby determining the equilibrium interest rate

median wage the wage such that one-half of all workers earn wages below that amount and one-half of all workers earn wages above that amount

monetizing the debt the result of government paying off its debts by printing money

money a widely accepted means of payment

money illusion the false perception that occurs when people mistake changes in nominal prices for changes in real prices

money multiplier, MM the amount the money supply expands with each

GLOSSARY

absolute advantage the ability to produce the same good using fewer inputs than another producer

active labor market policies policies that focus on getting unemployed workers back to work, such as job-search assistance, job-retraining programs, and work tests

alternative minimum tax (AMT) a separate income tax code, begun in 1969 to prevent the rich from not paying income taxes; not indexed to inflation and thus now an extra tax burden on many upper middle class families

appreciation an increase in the price of one currency in terms of another currency

arbitrage the practice of taking advantage of price differences for the same good in different markets by buying low in one market and selling high in another market

automatic stabilizers changes in fiscal policy that stimulate AD in a recession without the need for explicit action by policymakers; unemployment insurance is one example of an automatic stabilizer

average tax rate the total tax payment divided by total income

baby boomers people born during the high–birth rate years of 1946–1964

balance of payments a yearly summary of all the economic transactions between residents of one country and residents of the rest of the world

bond a sophisticated IOU that documents who owes how much and when payment must be made

bundling the requirement that products be bought together in a bundle or package

business fluctuations or **business cycles** the short-run movements in real GDP around its long-term trend

buy and hold the practice of buying stocks and holding them for the long run, regardless of what prices do in the short run

capital account in the balance of payments, the account that measures changes in foreign ownership of domestic assets, including financial assets like stocks and bonds as well as physical assets

capital surplus the excess that exists when the inflow of foreign capital into a country is greater than the outflow of domestic capital to other nations

collateral something of value that by agreement becomes the property of the lender if the borrower defaults

comparative advantage the advantage possessed by a country when it produces goods for which it has the lowest opportunity cost

complements two goods for which a decrease in the price of one leads to an increase in the demand for the other

conditional convergence the tendency—among countries with similar steady state levels of output—for poorer countries to grow faster than richer countries and thus for poor and rich countries to converge in income

consumer surplus the consumer's gain from exchange, or the difference between the maximum price a consumer is willing to pay for a certain quantity and the market price

consumer surplus (total) an/amount measured by the area beneath the demand curve and above the price

consumption private spending on final goods and services

credible referring to a monetary policy when it is expected that a central bank will stick with that policy

crowding out the decrease in private consumption and investment that occurs when government borrows more; also, the decrease in private spending that occurs when government increases spending

current account in the balance of payments, the sum of the balance of trade, net income on capital held abroad, and net transfer payments

cyclical unemployment unemployment correlated with the business cycle

deadweight loss the total of lost consumer and producer surplus when not all mutually profitable gains from trade are exploited.

deficit, fiscal the annual difference that results when federal government spending exceeds revenues

deficit, trade see trade deficit

deflation a decrease in the average level of prices; i.e., a negative inflation rate

demand curve a function that shows the quantity demanded at different prices

depreciation a decrease in the price of a currency in terms of another currency

dirty or managed float a currency whose value is not fixed but for which governments will intervene extensively in the market to keep its value within a certain range

discount rate the interest rate banks pay when they borrow directly from the Fed at the discount window

discouraged workers jobless individuals who have given up looking for work but who would still like to find a job

disinflation a reduction in the inflation rate

dollarization a foreign country's use of the U.S. dollar as its currency

economic growth the growth rate of real GDP per capita.

economies of scale the advantages of large-scale production that reduce

Chapter 19

Page 413

1. If an inhabitant of Nebraska buys a German sports car for $30,000, this lowers the U.S. current account balance by $30,000.

2. If a German sports car manufacturer opens a new plant in South Carolina, this investment is a capital account surplus for the United States.

3. The current and capital accounts are two sides of the same coin. When the capital account is in surplus, the current account will tend to mirror that in deficit, and vice versa.

Page 420

1. If the U.S. dollar is a safe haven currency, then in times of risk people will demand dollars, increasing their value.

2. If the Fed increases the money supply, this will reduce the value of the dollar compared to the euro.

3. If purchasing power parity holds and the nominal exchange rate is one pound for two dollars, a Big Mac should cost £2 in London if it costs $4.00 in New York.

4. A tariff will hinder market exchange and thus the arbitrage of differing prices. This limits purchasing power parity.

Page 422

1. In the short run, a Fed increase in the money supply will cause a depreciation in the exchange rate, leading to an increase in U.S. exports. In the long run, the temporary boost to exports will dissipate, and the increase in the money supply will lead to inflation.

2. In an open economy, monetary policy is more effective than fiscal policy. Expansionary monetary policy will tend to reduce interest rates, causing a currency depreciation and increased exports. In contrast, expansionary fiscal policy will tend to increase interest rates, causing an appreciation of the exchange rate and reduced exports.

Page 424

1. A floating exchange rate describes when the value of a country's currency is determined by the forces of supply and demand.

2. The European Central Bank controls the monetary policy of the European Union.

Page 372

1. The 2008 tax rebate was less powerful than expected because many people saved the rebate and paid down debt, rather than spending it.

2. A permanent cut in income tax rates can generate a larger fiscal stimulus than a temporary cut because people likely will save a large portion of a temporary tax cut, to pay for future taxes. But if the tax cut is permanent, they may choose to spend more. Of course, telling people that a tax cut is permanent is quite different from getting people to believe that it is permanent!

3. A permanent investment tax credit produces a smaller fiscal stimulus than a temporary investment tax credit because to get the temporary tax credit firms must spend money on equipment right away but a permanent investment tax credit gives firms the option of waiting to invest.

Chapter 18

Page 387

1. Specialization increases productivity because it increases knowledge and through economies of scale makes it more profitable to employ productive capital.

2. If people can't trade for other goods, they won't specialize in producing just one good. Thus, trade is necessary if people are to benefit from specialization.

3. Alex Rodriguez has a comparative advantage in playing baseball, but Harry has a comparative advantage in mowing Alex's lawn because Harry faces a much lower opportunity cost in mowing lawns than Alex Rodriguez does.

Page 393

1. Domestic producers gain from a tariff and domestic consumers lose.

2. Trade protectionism leads to wasted resources because it shifts production from the lowest cost producers to higher cost producers.

3. You hear more often about people who gain from trade restrictions than people who lose because the gains from trade restrictions are concentrated on a few winners while the losses are diffused over many losers. Even though the total gains are smaller than the total losses the concentrated benefits mean that the winners have a greater incentive to argue for trade restriction than the losers do to argue against.

Page 397

1. The movement of the garment trade overseas has been a net benefit for the United States because clothing is now much cheaper for U.S. consumers and U.S. workers specialize in the fields in which they are most productive.

2. If the U.S. government subsidized the Silicon Valley computer industry, it would encourage more computer chip manufacturing, but at a higher cost (production would not be as efficient). This would be a waste of resources. Foreign competitors would be pushed out of the industry. Consumers of computer chips would benefit from the subsidy but they would benefit by less than the cost to U.S. taxpayers.

MACROECONOMICS ESSENTIALS

Dynamic Aggregate Demand–Aggregate Supply

The **Solow growth rate** is an economy's potential growth rate, the rate of economic growth that would occur given flexible prices and the existing real factors of production. (page 243)

Rearranging the quantity theory we have an equation for the **aggregate demand curve.**

$$\vec{M} + \vec{v} = \text{Inflation} + \text{Real growth}$$

The aggregate demand curve shows all the combinations of inflation and real growth that are consistent with a specified rate of spending growth. (page 245)

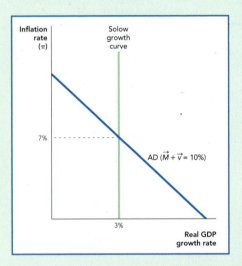

A **positive real shock** increases the potential growth rate of the economy and shifts the Solow growth curve to the right. A **negative real shock** shifts the Solow growth curve to the left. (page 248)

An AD curve and shocks to the Solow growth curve are the essential elements of the **Real Business Cycle model.**

The **short-run aggregate supply (SRAS) curve** shows the positive relationship between inflation and real growth during the period when prices and wages are sticky. (page 250)

An SRAS curve and **aggregate demand shocks** (shifts in the AD curve) are the essence of the **New Keynesian model.**

Transmission mechanisms transmit and amplify shocks. Intertemporal substitution, uncertainty and irreversible investments, labor adjustment costs, time bunching, and sticky wages and prices are all transmission mechanisms. (page 274)

Fiscal or monetary policy can be used to increase aggregate demand, reversing a decline in private demand. (page 314)

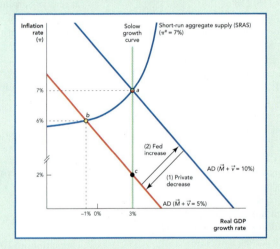

Fiscal and monetary policy are less effective when a recession is caused by a real shock. (page 319)

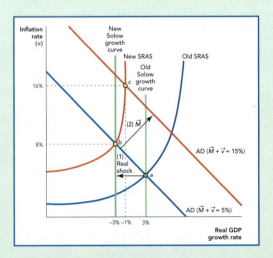